PROVENANCE AND POSSESSION

E. H. Gombrich Lecture Series

Provenance and Possession

ACQUISITIONS FROM THE PORTUGUESE
EMPIRE IN RENAISSANCE ITALY

K.J.P. LOWE

PRINCETON UNIVERSITY PRESS

PRINCETON & OXFORD

This book is published as part of the E. H. Gombrich lecture series, cosponsored by the Warburg Institute and Princeton University Press. The lectures upon which this book is based were delivered in June 2019.

Published by Princeton University Press
41 William Street, Princeton, New Jersey 08540
99 Banbury Road, Oxford OX2 6JX

press.princeton.edu

All Rights Reserved
ISBN: 978-0-691-24684-0
ISBN: (e-book): 978-0-691-24689-5

British Library Cataloging-in-Publication Data is available

Editorial: Ben Tate and Josh Drake
Production: Danielle Amatucci
Publicity: William Pagdatoon and Charlotte Coyne

Jacket image: Alonso Sánchez Coello, *Infanta Isabel Clara Eugenia and Magdalena Ruiz* (detail), 1585–1588. Oil on canvas. Madrid. © Photographic Archive Museo Nacional del Prado.

This book has been composed in Arno Pro

Printed in the United States of America

10 9 8 7 6 5 4 3 2 1

CONTENTS

ILLUSTRATIONS

Figures

Colour Plates

PREFACE

THE TALE of how this book came into being is not one of linear progression, but of serendipity and coincidence. I have always been an archival historian of Renaissance Italy—one of my old teachers used to talk of the split between archival historians and book historians—and all archive rats dream of momentous archival finds. This narrative, however, shows that it is not just a question of finding documents but, in the first place, of choosing an interesting field or topic in which to seek out the documents and, in the second, of being able to decipher and understand their import when they are found. I have been fortunate enough to have made important archival discoveries in the past, and the account journal presented here in chapters 4 and 5 constitutes another. Yet there were twenty years between the first time I ordered Miscellanea medicea 713 in the Archivio di stato in Florence on 14 April 1997—looking for material to compose some introductory paragraphs on the sub-Saharan African population in Renaissance Lisbon—and the second time, in 2017. The first time I saw it, I did not understand why it might be important, and wrote in the margin of my notes, 'Why on earth would there be so many chickens on board this ship?' This was no ordinary trip, and these were no ordinary chickens, but turkeys and guinea fowl—although I failed to recognise either of these realities. Always attracted to any collection of documents labelled 'Miscellanea', which often contain rich pickings, I had ordered Miscellanea medicea 713 because Iberian 'slaves' were mentioned in the catalogue entry.[1] From my cursory glance in 1997, I concluded there was nothing here of interest to me, and I quickly returned the volume. How wrong I was, and how much difference twenty years can make.

---

1. It is now standard to substitute 'enslaved person' for 'slave'. There are arguments both for and against this practice; I have decided to use both terms, but wish to make clear that the word 'slave' in what follows incorporates the meaning 'person who has been enslaved', and that no other interpretation is possible.

xi

Returning from Portugal after the opening of an exhibition at the Museu Nacional de Arte Antiga in Lisbon that I had co-curated entitled *A cidade global: Lisboa no Renascimento*, I went into the Archivio di stato in Florence on 7 March 2017 to continue with my work on sub-Saharan Africans in Renaissance Italy. I had amassed a long list of archival documents I wanted to check; included on it was Miscellanea medicea 713. On a whim, I ordered it, and this time round, one glance was enough for me to realise how extraordinary it was, and how its contents would unsettle, undermine or augment some of the accepted beliefs about the early years of Cosimo de' Medici's collecting practices.

In the intervening years, I had increasingly come to consider the critical role played in Renaissance Europe by Lisbon as a global entrepôt. My interest in Portugal and its trading empire arose too from random circumstances. I wish I could say that it was a result of forethought, but it wasn't. In 1985, when I finished my Ph.D and needed a job, Margaret Thatcher was prime minister in England and the universities had entered a period of budget cuts: there were no academic posts. Instead, one was advertised at the University of Hong Kong: I applied, and started work there in the autumn. As an historian of Renaissance Europe, I thought living in the Far East was a short-term measure and that it would not be sensible to try to learn Cantonese or Mandarin. In any case, learning Mandarin would have required considerably more time each week than I had to spare (I had to prepare a new course of sixty lectures on early modern Europe). Instead, I decided to enrol in the free classes offered by the Portuguese consulate, mainly used by Chinese who had been born in Macau and who were eligible for Portuguese citizenship if they passed a Portuguese exam. As I already knew French and Italian, Portuguese was less daunting. This grounding in Portuguese helped me pay attention to the role played by Lisbon and the Portuguese trading empire in the fifteenth and sixteenth centuries when I returned to Europe.

I arrived in Hong Kong almost entirely ignorant of everything to do with the city, China or the Far East, and was mesmerised by the array of goods on offer. So I have some sympathy for Bastiano Campana, the agent sent to Portugal and Spain on a buying trip for Cosimo de' Medici in 1547–48, whose purchases form the basis of chapters 4 and 5 below. Imagine a Tuscan who had never previously left Tuscany, transplanted in the mid-sixteenth century to Lisbon, the most global city in the world, with a rather bewildering remit to buy for his employer, the ruler of Florence, Cosimo de' Medici, anything non-European, rare and unusual that looked interesting. How should he approach his task? Did he have a budget? Were there items that were too expensive? There were so many objects available to purchase from the worldwide Portuguese trading empire that stretched across Africa, Asia and South America that would have been unfamiliar. Should he choose the most outlandish or the most glittering, a new take on something old, or something altogether new? The answer is that as his first purchase he bought a very rare and desirable wild animal as a pet, succumbing to an eye-catching young golden lion tamarin from Brazil, small enough to hold in his hand, decked out in earrings. The size, colour and appearance of this smallest of monkeys made its allure obvious, not hidden, and no prior knowledge of tamarins was required in order to make the purchase. It cost the sizeable sum of nine gold ducats.

Campana's unpublished account journal in Misc. med. 713 allows a precious glimpse of what an untutored agent on the Iberian peninsula could acquire in terms of global goods for his Medici masters. But it really offers considerably more, revealing, for example, selections of cargoes from the Americas, India and the Far East; the vagaries of global fashion; competition between European rulers; the extensive networks of Italians in Iberia; and the perceived value of enslaved people, foreign goods and non-European animals, by including the prices paid for them. It also illuminates the manner in which many European collections were formed. The account journal permits Campana's personality to shine through, as he articulates an enhanced sense of narrative. Although he is buying on behalf of the Medici, he makes the choices and the purchases his own, and it is his voice we hear recording and explaining them. These new records are gems.

I should perhaps own up that studying Italian Renaissance history at university had not been for me a matter of deep consideration either. An unusual conjunction of circumstances meant that I was given five minutes, rather than the usual few weeks, to decide which second-year optional subject and which third-year special subject I wanted to take. I stared at the lists. Because my father had served in the British army in Italy during the Second World War, and had fallen in love with the country, he had taken his children there on holiday. So, rather than Assyria, Argentina or India (all of which sounded alluring, but which were places I had never been), I plumped for Italy: the second-year course on the Italian Renaissance at the Warburg Institute run by Michael Baxandall and David Chambers (with occasional appearances from Ernst Gombrich) and the third-year course on Renaissance Florence at Westfield College and the Warburg Institute run by Nicolai Rubinstein and David Chambers. I was nineteen, and none of these names meant anything to me.

From listening to Ernst Gombrich in an undergraduate seminar to giving the Gombrich lectures is quite a distance. How astoundingly lucky I was! I have never looked back.

———

More immediately, this book started life in June 2019 as three Gombrich lectures at the Warburg Institute in London. The Warburg focuses on the history of the classical tradition, broadly conceived, and the remit of the Gombrich lectures is to address any part of that history. My own offerings engaged with two of the central elements of that tradition, knowledge and slavery, with classical concepts such as rarity and novelty, and with classical behaviours such as collecting. All elements, concepts and behaviours were transformed or reinvented by the new realities in fifteenth- and sixteenth-century Europe occasioned by the Portuguese voyages around the globe, and all were set within the framework of Renaissance Italy, the heartland of the classical tradition. The interconnectedness between Europe and the other continents was made flesh. Having to turn three lectures into a book, rather than starting to write a book on a fully-fledged 'topic', perhaps makes one search in a more concentrated manner than usual for unifying themes. I followed the documents at the core of the lectures, and in order to understand them, I had to go deep into their contexts—and it was in the knitting together of the contexts that I found the unifying themes.

This study is concerned with explanation and context rather than with theory, although sometimes theories are very useful tools for explanation. This difference in approach is a result of a concomitant difference in methodology. My starting points have been documentation and objects, both more grounded than theories, and both requiring copious contextual explanation. Those more interested in theory start not with documents and objects, but with theories. The two main foci here are provenance and possession, and the book allows a disquisition on what, if anything, was the relationship between them. It lingers over the processes of transformation effected on news, objects, people and animals by their movement across long distances. News can be repackaged as fact, objects repurposed, people labelled 'things' rather than humans, animals turned from wild beasts into fashionable pets. Although provenance matters in order to know where to acquire goods, it is possession, however defined, that enables all of these transformations; in the process, provenance often becomes pushed to one side or 'forgotten'. The power inherent in possession is lasting, whereas knowledge of provenance is very frequently temporary.

The dual-pronged subject of what Renaissance Italy knew of the Portuguese voyages, and what influence the Portuguese overseas expansion exerted on the Italian Renaissance (or indeed on Renaissance Italy)—being both under-studied and vast—could be approached in a number of ways. Although various literary specialists have shown more initiative, the subject is not only under-studied but largely unconsidered by historians or those interested in historical sources. Pioneers in the field—who were the exceptions—include Federigo Melis, Virginia Rau, Marco Spallanzani, Carmen Radulet, Luisa D'Arienzo and Stefania Elena Carnemolla, who took advantage of some of the extraordinarily wide-ranging documentation relating to the Portuguese voyages available in Italian archives, especially in Florence.[2] In historical terms, the best studied aspects have been Italians in Lisbon who participated in the overseas voyages, as financiers, merchants or navigators,[3] and Italian–Portuguese collaboration in Florence in connection with contemporary Portuguese cartographic updating. Reasons for a lack of engagement abound, and cut across scholarly difficulties, national practices and historical traditions. They include the sheer size of the subject; its cross-disciplinary nature; historical specialisation and the perceived gulf between the types of topic—that is, between the maritime physical and technological advances of Portugal as opposed to the landlocked cerebral and artistic advances of Italy, and the types

2. Carmen M. Radulet, *Os descobrimentos portugueses e a Itália: Ensaios filológico-literários e historiográficos* (Lisbon, 1991), esp. pp. 37–57, 'Tipologia e significado da documentação italiana sobre os descobrimentos portugueses'; Carmen M. Radulet, 'Coleccionar e conservar, produzir e divulgar em Itália documentação sobre *Os descobrimentos portugueses* (sécs. XV–XVII)', in *As novidades do mundo: Conhecimento e representação na época moderna; Actas das VIII Jornadas de história ibero-americana e XI Reunião internacional de história da náutica e da hidrografica* (Lisbon, 2003), pp. 225–40 at 230; Stefania Elena Carnemolla, *Fonti italiane dei secoli XV–XVII sull'espansione portoghese* (Pisa, 2000).

3. Already in 1541 Pierfrancesco Giambullari could give a lecture on Dante to the Accademia Fiorentina in which he spoke of the contribution of Florentine merchants to the Portuguese and Spanish 'explorations' of Africa, the East and America. See Pierfrancesco Giambullari, *Lezioni di messer Pierfrancesco Giambullari, aggiuntovi L'origine della lingua fiorentina, altrimenti Il gello* (Milan, 1827), pp. 3–33 at 8; Michel Plaisance, 'Une première affirmation de la politique culturelle de Côme Ier: La transformation de l'Académie des "Humidi" en Académie Florentine (1540–1542)', in André Rochon, ed., *Les Écrivains et le pouvoir en Italie à l'époque de la Renaissance* (Paris, 1973), ser. 1, pp. 361–438 at 427–28; Elizabeth Cropper, 'Vernacular Identities: The Accademia fiorentina and the Poetics of Portraiture', in *The Medici: Portraits and Politics, 1512–1570*, ed. Keith Christiansen and Carlo Falciani, exh. cat., The Metropolitan Museum, New York (New York, 2021), pp. 48–78 at 68.

of historian interested in these two types of topic—even though both topics were driven by innovation and novelty; the national narratives of Portugal and, since the nineteenth century, of Italy that prioritised national achievements at the expense of contributions by foreigners or non-nationals; and the fragmentary way in which the regional and local histories of Italy and Portugal are conceptualised, backed up by inflexible university systems that sometimes prioritised research on the local, and perceived a division between archival, cultural and intellectual history. Some of these barriers have come down in the last twenty years, and a distinctive field of study now visibly and insistently beckons for scholarly engagement, as what was seen in the past as unattractive becomes historically fashionable. The practice of slavery is being re-evaluated and rewritten, especially in the light of the Black Lives Matter movement. The cultural, material and global turns in history reinforce work across and between countries and cultures, champion research involving objects, and anything with global underpinnings. As a consequence, the dual-pronged subject is garnering a raft of new scholarly enterprises.

ACKNOWLEDGEMENTS

THIS BOOK evolved from the Gombrich lectures I gave at the Warburg Institute in June 2019. I should like to thank Mick O'Malley, the director who in 2017 invited me to give them, and Bill Sherman, the current director. The library of the Warburg Institute has been central to every academic and intellectual endeavour I have ever attempted, and this one was no exception. I am grateful to all its librarians, past and present. However, while I was able to benefit from using the library in the preparation of the lectures, I wrote a draft of the core of this book during the Covid lockdown of 2020, when the Warburg was closed—and there is no escaping the fact that it is a 'Covid book', although I have tried hard to minimise the deleterious effects of this.

I am also indebted to all the archivists whose private and public domains I have been permitted to enter, especially those at the Ospedale degli Innocenti di Firenze, the Archivio di stato di Firenze and the Archivio Segreto Vaticano (now renamed the Archivio Apostolico Vaticano), where I spent most time. Working with new, unpublished archival material is slow; it is painstaking and labour-intensive. And in order to make sense of what one finds, one also needs to be able to converse with (pick the brains of?) experts in a wide array of fields. A project like this, that crosses regions, countries, empires, continents and language and ethnic groups, as well as multiple disciplines and approaches, makes one even more dependent than usual on the kindness and accumulated expertise of others. This work would not have been possible in this form without their input.

Unfortunately, some of those who were instrumental in my writing this book are now dead. My decision in 1985 to start learning Portuguese by attending the free Portuguese lessons put on by the Portuguese consulate in Hong Kong has led my research in ways that could never have been foreseen. I should like to acknowledge again my Portuguese teacher there, Rubye Maria de Senna Fernandes Pereira (d. 2018), who captivated my interest in all things Portuguese. Later Vasco Graça Moura (d. 2014) was kind enough to champion a three-day conference I ran at the National Gallery in London in 1995 on 'Links between Portugal and Italy in the Renaissance' that became *Cultural Links between Portugal and Italy in the Renaissance* (Oxford, 2000); his help was invaluable, and some of the foundations of that work also underpin this book. I should also like to acknowledge the influence of Don Weinstein's (d. 2015) early interest in the Italy–Portugal nexus, and the importance of Constance Blackwell's (d. 2018) early support. Several others much more knowledgeable than me, with whom I would have been able to test my arguments, are similarly unavailable. I am especially conscious of the lack of Nicolai Rubinstein (d. 2002), with whom in particular I would very much like to have discussed Lorenzo de' Medici's engagement with the Portuguese voyages of exploration. In Nicolai's absence, Lorenz Böninger has been as generous as ever, and his encyclopaedic knowledge of German cartographers and printers in Florence has been tremendously helpful. I also very much regret that I am not able to talk through the new information about the Kongolese oliphants in the Pitti with Ezio Bassani (d. 2018), whose foundational scholarship on African ivories has influenced every single scholar in the field.

I am an Italianist and I have only been able to get to grips with the Portuguese material to the extent that I have because of the quite extraordinary generosity of Hugo Miguel Crespo, Annemarie Jordan Gschwend and Pedro Pinto. Annemarie's presence has been indispensable. Similarly, Alessio Assonitis has been exceptionally generous, painstakingly tutoring me in matters relating to Cosimo I, and in readings and meanings of abstruse sixteenth-century Italian.

In the course of the last twenty-five years, I have benefited from conversations with myriad specialists. Friends and colleagues who have read chapters or portions of the book include Alessio Assonitis, Zoltán Biedermann, Lorenz Böninger, Georgia Clarke, Lizzy Currie, Trevor Dean, Francesca Fiorani, Annemarie Jordan Gschwend, Paul Kaplan, Hannah Lee, Amanda Lillie, Dennis Romano and Sarah Ross. I am very grateful for all their comments and help. Further friends and colleagues who have contributed greatly (some in the form of a stray aside that has made me reconsider, others with specialist knowledge that I lack, others still with bibliographic or archival references) include Maurizio Arfaiuoli, Michael Backman, Jim Banker, Richard Barker, Federico Botana, Beverly Brown, Melissa Bullard, Lucas Burkart, David Chambers, Valentina Conticelli, Gary Deirmandjian, Gérard Delille, Filippo de Vivo, Simon Ditchfield, Tom Earle, Paulla Ebron, Sarah Falla, Michael Fend (with a particularly pertinent 'so what?' question), Sheila ffolliott, the late Roberto Fiorentino,

Lucia Frattarelli Fischer, Julian Gardner, Simon Goodwin, Ingrid Greenfield, Francesco Guidi Bruscoli, Tamar Herzig, Paul Holberton, Megan Holmes, Liz Horodowich, Philippa Jackson, Kirstin Kennedy, Henrique Leitão, the late Michele Luzzati, Arthur MacGregor, Lia Markey, Giuseppe Marcocci, Marco Masseti, Eugene McLaughlin, James Nelson Novoa, Mick O'Malley, Marianne Pade, Diana Bullen Presciutti, Charles Robertson, Isabel dos Guimarães Sá, Gianfranco Salvatore, Karl Schlebusch, Takuya Shimada, Marco Spallanzani, Joaneath Spicer, Arne Spohr, Carlo Taviani, Anna Teicher, John Thornton, Ellyn Toscano, Maria Antonietta Visceglia, Ningfen Wang, Alison Wright.

Two kindly Latinists, Gastón Javier Basile and David Rundle, have helped with Latin queries, and Maia Herzfeld and Bella Scherer have provided assistance with German.

I should also like to record my debt to all those who in 2016–17 at the Museu Nacional de Arte Antiga in Lisbon taught me so much about Portuguese visual and material culture in the fifteenth and sixteenth centuries, especially Joaquim Oliveira Caetano, José Alberto Seabra Carvalho, Anísio Franco, Ana Kol and António Pimentel. Parts of this book offer postscripts to the 2017 exhibition curated by Annemarie Jordan Gschwend and me entitled *A cidade global: Lisboa no Renascimento/The Global City: Lisbon in the Renaissance* at that museum, which in turn was based on the book by Annemarie and me, *The Global City: On the Streets of Renaissance Lisbon* (London, 2015).

Throughout the vicissitudes of the last five years, Eugene McLaughlin has held steady, but he has also constantly encouraged me to question academic opinions and rethink preconceptions. I am grateful for all of this.

Brought up since youth as a Soderini partisan, it has sometimes felt unsettling to be spending so much time in the company of the Medici; I would like to make clear that my loyalties still lie with the Soderini.

The Leverhulme Trust and I Tatti, The Harvard University Center for Italian Renaissance Studies, provided funding or sustenance while this project was in embryo and then in progress. Remarkably, both of them provided it twice, allowing me the necessary time to carry out some of the archival work on which this book is based. I acknowledge their support with gratitude.

Finally, I should like to thank Princeton University Press's senior editor in the humanities, Ben Tate, for his good humour and unswerving editorial support, Dimitri Karetnikov, illustration manager, for patiently guiding me towards improved illustrations, and Francis Eaves, whose fine-grained copy editing saved me from many errors.

ABBREVIATIONS

AOIF   Archivio dell'Ospedale degli Innocenti, Firenze

ASF   Archivio di stato di Firenze

        MAP   Mediceo avanti il Principato

        MdP   Mediceo del Principato

    Misc. med.   Miscellanea medicea

        NA   Notarile antecosmiano

ASMa   Archivio di stato di Mantova

ASMo   Archivio di stato di Modena

ASV   Archivio Segreto Vaticano, Città del Vaticano

BAV   Biblioteca Apostolica Vaticana, Città del Vaticano

DBI   *Dizionario biografico degli italiani*, 95 vols to date
(Rome and Turin, 1960–)

DGLAB/   Direccão-Geral do Livro, dos Arquivos e das Bibliotecas,
ANTT   Arquivo Nacional Torre do Tombo, Lisbon

        CC   Corpo Cronológico

        NA   Núcleo Antigo

MMA 1   António Brásio, ed., *Monumenta missionaria africana:
África ocidental (1471–1531)* (Lisbon, 1952)

MMA 3   António Brásio, ed., *Monumenta missionaria
africana: África ocidental (1570–1599)* (Lisbon, 1953)

RIS/2   Rerum Italicarum Scriptores, second series
(Città di Castello 1900–1917; Bologna 1917–75)

PROVENANCE AND POSSESSION

1

Provenance and Its Discontents

EVIDENCE, RELEVANCE, LANGUAGE, KNOWLEDGE

Provenance

Two fruitful ways of providing a background framework for this study lie in inserting new documentation into broader flows and circulation of Renaissance people and objects, and in adverting to the global and European connections that made them happen. Provenance is critical to both. The two approaches both allude to the near universally accepted theory of *histoires croisées* that has effectively killed stone dead any nationalistic beliefs that individual countries or areas were immune to outside influence in any period.[1] But the level and extent of sixteenth-century connections still require detailed dissection and exposition. Even if dwelling on comparison has given way to searching for connection, the types and number of these need to be exposed. As Sanjay Subrahmanyam has pointed out, connections occur in multiple spheres—material, ideas, concepts—and are of varying intensity, duration or complexity.[2] An understanding of connection, however, is dependent upon informed knowledge of context, and context collapse or context cancellation in relation to the past is rife in the twenty-first century. This book could perhaps be seen as, against the current, an exercise in context enhancement: in minute focusing on the documents and objects in order to extract as much as possible from them about the

---

1. Michael Werner and Bénédicte Zimmermann, 'Beyond Comparison: *Histoire croisée* and the Challenge of Reflexivity', *History and Theory*, 45.1 (2006), pp. 30–50.

2. Sanjay Subrahmanyam, *Empires between Islam and Christianity, 1500–1800* (Albany, NY, 2019 [Delhi, 2018]), p. 22.

known context in a period-appropriate fashion. Unlike the histories of tobacco and chocolate, which in the right hands allow a retelling of empire from the periphery to the centre,[3] the focus here remains on how Europe reacted to Portuguese overseas expansion, or more precisely, how parts of Italy catalogued and reacted to the arrival in their midst of goods, animals and people from the Portuguese trading empire.

Whenever an observation connected to the debate over the relative importance of a centre and peripheries seems relevant to these narratives, it has been flagged, but often the absence of information about provenance—understood here in the sense of its place of origin—precludes this, except in its most basic sense. Provenance is now held to be an almost inalienable part of any object or possession of any value, a sine qua non, without which not only the authenticity but also the moral worth of the object is called into question. Provenance defines the object, and defines reaction to it. All movement is towards the introduction of new systems and new technologies that provide a novel kind of transparent provenance, wherever possible embedded within the object itself, preempting the possibility of manufacturing fakes or interfering with the record. This is true for everything from cars to digital currencies. A wider understanding of the meaning of provenance would encompass a detailed history of all the places where an artefact had been since its manufacture or creation, a veritable 'object itinerary',[4] and wherever possible and relevant, this wider understanding of the term has been employed. It is here that perhaps the greatest disparity between the importance of provenance in the Renaissance and the importance of provenance in the twenty-first century can be seen. Provenance is a fundamental part of context, and yet in the fifteenth and sixteenth centuries, by itself it appears that it was often considered irrelevant. There is an exception to this— when knowledge of prior ownership, understood as a form of provenance, can be seen, like a pedigree in an animal, to enhance status. In these particular instances, the prestige of prior ownership, by association, raises the quality of the 'possessed' object, making provenance critical.[5]

3. Marcy Norton, *Sacred Gifts, Profane Pleasures: A History of Tobacco and Chocolate in the Atlantic World* (Ithaca, NY, 2008), p. 12.

4. Rosemary A. Joyce, 'From Place to Place: Provenience, Provenance and Archaeology', in Gail Feigenbaum and Inge Reist, eds, *Provenance: An Alternate History of Art* (Los Angeles, 2012), pp. 48–60 at 48, 54, 58.

5. Gail Feigenbaum, 'Manifest Provenance', in Gail Feigenbaum and Inge Reist, eds, *Provenance: An Alternate History of Art* (Los Angeles, 2012), pp. 6–28 at 7 and 22; Elizabeth A. Pergam, 'Provenance as Pedigree: The Marketing of British Portraits in Gilded Age America', in Gail

Three of the most commonly used words in connection with the lure of the consumer revolution of the Renaissance in general and goods from the overseas Portuguese empire in particular are new, rare and exotic. All effectively make implicit reference to provenance at least in a broad sense; all require further interrogation. The three words can be conjoined but can also each stand alone. News and the new were only sometimes linked, and novelty was just one of a range of newsworthy criteria.[6] The attraction of the new was often commented upon,[7] and was clearly a motivating factor in gift-giving[8] and in the formation of collections of extra-European objects. Yet it is not so clear whether rarity was seen as a lesser form of novelty: whether a new object would always be more interesting than a rare object. It is possible to conjecture that a new object made of inexpensive materials would be of interest, but that a piece of rare African gold jewellery, seen before but very infrequently, would elicit greater covetousness. Ingrid Greenfield is right to remind us that new and rare objects and goods were greeted with wonder, but she refutes the use of the category of the exotic, saying that the word *exotica* was not used in Italian until the eighteenth century.[9] But the adjective *esotico/a* was in use in the sixteenth century in its primary meaning, taken straightforwardly from the Latin *exoticus*, which in its turn had been taken from the Greek, to indicate something from outside, something foreign, as signalled by its prefix *exo-*.[10]

Feigenbaum and Inge Reist, eds, *Provenance: An Alternate History of Art* (Los Angeles, 2012), pp. 104–22 at 104.

6. Kate Lowe, 'Africa in the News in Renaissance Italy: News Extracts from Portugal about Western Africa Circulating in Northern and Central Italy in the 1480s and 1490s', *Italian Studies*, 65.3 (2010), pp. 310–28 at 314 and 320.

7. For example, Giovanni Boccaccio, *Decameron*, ed. Vittore Branca, 2 vols (Bologna, 2004), 2, p. 1152.

8. Giovanni da Empoli in Lisbon to Lorenzo de' Medici, 9 January 1515, writes that he is sending 'certe gemtilezze' that he has brought back from Malacha; he thinks Lorenzo will like them 'per eser chosa nuova'. Marco Spallanzani, *Giovanni da Empoli, un mercante fiorentino nell'Asia portoghese* (Florence, 1999), p. 215.

9. Ingrid Greenfield, 'A Moveable Continent: Collecting Africa in Renaissance Italy', Ph.D dissertation, University of Chicago, 2016, pp. 44–45.

10. The first known instance in print seems to have been in Francesco Colonna's *Hypnerotomachia Poliphili* (Venice, 1499), p. 356: 'tra tante celeste et dive persone [io] solo contemptibile et exotico'. Here the usage emphasises the prefix 'exo', stressing his outsider status. Giovanvettorio Soderini in the sixteenth century wrote of 'gl'uccelli exotici' in *Il trattato degli animali domestici*, ed. Alberto Bacchi Della Lega, (Bologna, 1903), p. 263. See Salvatore Battaglia, *Grande dizionario della lingua italiana*, 25 vols (Turin, 1961–2009), 5, p. 366.

This usage clearly had and has relevance.[11] Catarina Santana Simões clarifies that in the early sixteenth-century in Portugal, the country in which many of the so-called exotic objects arrived in Europe, the word was associated with an 'exterior provenance' and could be used as a descriptor of anything that had been 'decontextualised from its place of origin'.[12] This is an interesting extension of the debate on the relevance of provenance, in which the meaning of exotic has been downgraded from 'inherently desirable' to 'having no secure place of origin'. In this sense, perhaps, its trajectory could be compared to that of the word *indiano* (see below), which underwent a similar transformation, from referring to a specific place to indicating a generic extra-European nowhere. But Simões goes further, claiming that as the word exotic does not have symbolic depth, it is essential that it be coupled with the concept of the marvellous, which does, in order to understand why non-European objects have been coveted since antiquity.[13] The argument has turned full circle, to the wonder with which new and rare objects have always been greeted. This significant baggage should be understood to accompany the use of the word exotic whenever it appears, like a tag spelling out contextual collapse and provenance non-knowledge at the same time as desirability. The so-called global turn in history has reinforced rather than diminished the use of the words new, rare and exotic, which frequently take the place of more complicated, less easy evaluation of the route whereby these objects arrived in, and were dispersed around, Europe. Here, care will be exercised whenever these words are chosen.

Evidence

This book's way into the subject is through a renewed focus on evidence, much of it previously unpublished, both documentary and in the form of still extant objects. This means that two different sets of methodologies are in use. Archival documents form the skeleton, sometimes more and sometimes less complete, but usually identifiable, of a body that is fleshed out where possible with objects that have endured and survived. When the documentary evidence

11. But see Bruno A. Martinho, 'Beyond Exotica: The Consumption of Non-European Things through the Case of Juan de Borja (1569–1626)', Ph.D thesis, European University Institute, 2018, e.g., pp. 28–29, who prioritises a theoretical over a linguistic understanding.

12. Catarina Santana Simões, 'The Symbolic Importance of the "Exotic" in the Portuguese Court in the Late Middle Ages', *Anales de Historia del Arte*, 24 (2014), pp. 517–25 at 525.

13. Simões, 'Symbolic Importance', p. 525.

concerns people, animals or objects, further traces of these have been sought, either in additional records or in visual representations. Unlike Venice, whose claim to hegemony over the Americas took the form of a great number of printed books and maps, thus ensuring that place was paramount and that the Americas remained at the forefront of the Venetian imagination,[14] much of the Italian peninsula's engagement with the Portuguese imperial world depended on decontextualised exotic goods and enslaved peoples, dissociated from their places of origin. In Venice, the encounter can be characterised as focused but virtual; elsewhere, it was imprecise but 'real'. With a subject of this scale, coverage over the *longue durée* is not possible, so instead three discreet sets of unpublished documentation, at three particular moments in a timeframe between the 1450s and the 1590s, in two particular cities, Florence and Rome, have been chosen as sites of analysis.

The finding of new and relevant documents has been the driving force behind the choice of years and places, which however can be easily justified and presented as something entirely positive, because the chronological distance separating them has added to the possible axes of analysis, prompting some intriguing, and rather unexpected, comments about change over time. Each set of documentation takes a different form, and each provides different insights: the first consists of short descriptive records in the entry ledger of a civic institution, the second is an account journal of an overseas trading/buying trip, and the third is a large body of private and professional correspondence. If they are united at all (beyond their ability to elucidate the two central questions), it is because they are all in some sense narrative, more so than the majority of documents, which often record only one piece of information at one particular moment, whereas these often allow historical backstories of objects and people to be reconstructed, even if slight or lopsided or partial. In this, they are unusual. It is also the case that the prior lives and afterlives of the human and other protagonists in these sets of documents can often be triangulated, because of the extraordinarily rich record systems in fifteenth- and sixteenth-century Florence and Rome, and the archives in Lisbon still extant after the 1755 earthquake, which provide more context than might have been expected. It is clear too that there is substantial tension between the ends for which the documents were created, and the uses to which historians put them and the information that historians extract from them—and that this tension

14. Elizabeth Horodowich, *The Venetian Discovery of America: Geographic Imagination and Print Culture in the Age of Encounters* (Cambridge, 2018).

or indeed gap also always needs to be articulated and analysed. It is far too simplistic merely to extract whatever snippets appear to be relevant without pausing to consider the genesis, context and *raison d'être* of the documentary material. Documents are created for a reason; without one, they do not just come into being. And the reasons for documents' existence dictate how they are constructed and written, what is included and excluded, and what the parameters of the written material are. The circumstances that led to the creation of the records under consideration require as much concentrated dissection as the documents themselves, prompting an added layer of unwrapping concerning the why and how of production to exhibit more clearly the rationale behind the records. So another way of encapsulating what is being analysed here is to ask, 'In what ways is the Portuguese empire being inscribed into Italian documentation? Was it seen as important?'

It sometimes happens, as in the instance of the Ospedale degli Innocenti records examined in one of the case studies here, that the documents, notwithstanding the straitjackets of their formulae, are sufficiently flexible to incorporate information that subsequently will allow a recreation of aspects of societal change, even if that can never have been part of the bundle of reasons for their existence. But that is quite rare. In the example of the Innocenti records, the unchanging nature of the formulae is itself the reason why it is now possible to map the arrival of change, because its seeds can be traced in minute detail. Much of the time, far from allowing a recreation of the way in which change has been introduced, documents provide some 'facts' or information, but leave a mass of loose ends that remain loose ends for centuries, only being tied up if other records subsequently emerge. Yet it is in the time-consuming perusal and interpretation of these loose ends that much of the best historical speculation lies, with the loose ends—rather than the 'facts'—often being the most useful part of the new material. Interpretation of this sort is only possible when the genesis, context and *raison d'être* of the documentary material are thoroughly understood.

This whole book can be viewed as a reflection on method, or more precisely, on the effect that choices about method have on scholarly outcomes. Here, new material is used first and foremost to prompt reflection: it is not just a question of material revealing new 'facts' but also, just as—if not more—importantly, an issue of the new and diverse material requiring constant, thoughtful interrogation and critical analysis. Nothing is fixed in such a way that it cannot be undone by consideration of new documentation, and this process is constantly repeated as more documentation comes to light, is set alongside the already existing documentation, and is reconsidered in its turn. Everything is tested and retested. While most historians accept that the type of historical record greatly influences what can be ascertained, and that different results emerge from different sorts of records, in many cases historical subjects are still addressed by historians predominantly via one type of source. This reduces the usefulness of the research, because the resultant history will always be only one part of a much greater story, and the greater, more complete story is only accessible through engagement with a plethora of different types of documentation. Each source has its own built-in advantages and disadvantages, the latter of which need to be counterbalanced if at all possible by other types of source, with different foci. Analysis is more likely to be closer to being 'correct' when it involves cocktails of varying kinds of documentation, so working with combinations of archival sources is of paramount importance, and new varieties of source material are particularly welcome. If research findings cannot be dissociated from the type of material investigated, and each type of material reveals only one part of an immensely larger picture, clearly the larger picture can only edge towards an approximation of what the past might have been like if a wide variety of sources is interrogated. Methodology matters.

Documentary evidence is also notable for its chronological and local divergences and shifts in terminology—and the dual-pronged research question here necessitates an awareness of this in two major European languages. Choices of particular words infuse phrases with meanings that have to be unlocked. Occasionally the new information is in itself the main gain, but once again it needs to be stressed that it is often not the 'facts' themselves that are revelatory or that alert the reader to meaning, but the words used to present these 'facts'. As always, it is the patterns and the absences in these documents that are the most illuminating aspects. The ability to notice and interpret patterns is the single most useful archival skill.

The evidence of objects is rather split. In some cases, the objects exist, but lack documentation, whereas in others documents about objects exist, but the objects themselves no longer do so or cannot be identified; in which case a word-echo is all that is left of their material form. In exceptional cases, both objects and documentation exist; and in the most exceptional cases, objects, documentation and contemporary visual representation of them all exist— but this is almost unheard of, even in the happy hunting grounds of Renaissance Italy. Doing object-based research on the basis of the extant object, without any documentary back-up, provides its own rewards, and a great deal can be ascertained from material, technique and style; but documents can provide other focused information of great importance, such as maker's name, date of production, commission, price and sale history, and similarly important background information, such as workshops, and the number of such objects produced.

Some current scholarship on objects has attempted to posit that they possess their own agency.[15] There is scholarly disagreement about whether the agency of things is primary—a form of agency related to their lives and interactions that can have a direct impact or effect on humans, even if as objects they lack conscious human intentionality; or merely secondary—a form of agency given to them by humans.[16] Both these propositions seem to require a redefinition of the meaning of agency. Then there are those for whom intentionality is irrelevant, and what matters is the result: things change the lives of humans, and not only technological things, which is where the idea started. Now the idea is carried into every area of life, touting problematic concepts such as reinterpreting the beauty of a thing as another form of agency of the thing, as though it controlled its own aesthetic projection.[17] Other scholars write of the illusion of agency, a more palatable way to approach the issue, that focuses not on the so-called agency of the object, but on the relationship between objects and humans.[18] Still others, more tongue-in-cheek, have imagined that artworks from different cultures and periods might engage in conversation with each other when displayed together.[19] It seems preferable to stay with the old definition, but consider more rigorously moments when objects were the catalysts for change. Actor-network theory assigning agency to objects also seems to be at odds with discussions of layers of signification

15. Bruno Latour, *Reassembling the Social: An Introduction to Actor-Network-Theory* (Oxford, 2005); Carl Knappett and Lambos Malafouris, eds, *Material Agency: Towards a Non-Anthropocentric Approach* (Boston, MA, 2008); Renata Ago, 'Denaturalizing Things: A Comment', in Paula Findlen, ed., *Early Modern Things: Objects and Their Histories, 1500–1800* (London, 2013), pp. 363–68.

16. Bruno Latour, 'On Actor-Network-Theory: A Few Clarifications', *Soziale Welt*, 47.4 (1996), pp. 369–81; Alfred Gell, *Art and Agency: An Anthropological Theory* (Oxford, 1998); Marcia Anne Dobres and John E. Robb, 'Doing Agency: Introductory Remarks on Methodology', *Journal of Archaeological Method and Theory*, 12 (2005), pp. 159–66; Ian Hodder, *Entangled: An Archaeology of the Relationships between Humans and Things* (Malden, MA, 2012), pp. 25, 68, 215–16.

17. Ago, 'Denaturalizing Things', p. 367.

18. Daniel Lord Smail, *Legal Plunder: Households and Debt Collection in Late Medieval Europe* (Cambridge, MA, 2016), p. 19.

19. Wole Soyinka, *Beyond Aesthetics: Use, Abuse and Dissonance in African Art Traditions* (New Haven, CT, 2019), p. 19.

'accruing like a patina' to artworks, in that these layers of enrichment were created by a wide range of individuals and circumstances, and not by the object.[20] In addition, interpretation of perceived meaning differs according to cultural context, so crossing countries or continents, or circulating around areas that were linked, introduced all sorts of new ideas and understandings about the object itself, often unconnected to or disconnected from the meanings assigned to the objects in their places of origin by the people who created them or for whom they had been created. It is worth asking what it would have taken for usage and understanding/meaning to have remained constant with regard to particular objects. The provenance would have had to be secure, but there would also have had to have been a certain level of knowledge or understanding of the culture from which the object came. Even when the first precondition was met, the second was not. The next question is, 'Did this absence matter?' If the object were related to a belief system, it would have mattered to those who believed, but they were usually not present. Otherwise, it is unlikely in fact to have mattered, even for objects with a clear function, as change in the function of a secular item happened all the time. People make of objects what they will, repurposing them constantly; objects do not come with instructions for use that have to be followed. Analysing objects via their 'biographies', on the other hand, is straightforwardly fruitful, especially, as in the case studies that follow, if these objects have global itineraries.[21] Here Igor Kopytoff's reminder that only certain things are considered appropriate to be marked as commodities, and that this is not a permanent but an impermanent state, and that after commodification a process of singularisaton often occurs, can be helpful. Things can have eventful 'biographies', undergoing many classifications and reclassifications, leading to multiple valuations, and can move in and out of the category of commodities.[22] Here, as commodified objects from various interconnected parts of the world were brought to Europe, these successive processes and

20. Suzanne Preston Blier, 'Capricious Arts: Idols in Renaissance-Era Africa and Europe (the Case of Sapi and Kongo)', in Michael W. Cole and Rebecca Zorach, eds, *The Idol in the Age of Art: Objects, Devotions and the Early Modern World* (Farnham, 2009), pp. 11–29 at 11.

21. Anne Gerritsen and Giorgio Riello, eds, *The Global Lives of Things: The Material Culture of Connections in the Early Modern World* (London, 2016); Anne Gerritsen, 'From Long-Distance Trade to the Global Lives of Things: Writing the History of Early Modern Trade and Material Culture', *Journal of Early Modern History*, 20 (2016), pp. 526–44 at 38–41.

22. Igor Kopytoff, ,The Cultural Biography of Things: Commoditization as Process', in Arjun Appadurai, ed., *The Social Life of Things: Commodities in Cultural Perspective* (Cambridge, 1986), pp. 64–91 at 64–65, 89.

changes can often be clearly observed, adding greatly to an ability to make sense of the ebbs and flows of their allure and their meanings.

Relevance

What Renaissance Italy knew of the Portuguese voyages, and what influence Portuguese overseas expansion exerted on Renaissance Italy have become questions of some urgency in the contemporary world. They have achieved this urgency because of a new insistence upon weighing the benefits of what was gained in any process against the detriment of what was lost. This was not a way of perceiving or assessing behaviour that would have been considered in fifteenth- and sixteenth-century Europe. Nor is it straightforwardly how rulers and governments in Western democracies (let alone elsewhere) operate today, so it remains at the level of public leverage. In this new aspirational model of justice and well-being for all, certain concepts take on increased semantic weight, and the two often related concepts of provenance and possession fall into this category. In one sense, much of this book is about the Renaissance perception of these concepts in relation to extra-European objects, peoples, animals and products brought to Europe: what was understood by these concepts at the point of acquisition; when these concepts mattered, and when they did not matter; what happened to global objects when they arrived in Europe; the erasure of a pre-European past because it was deemed irrelevant.

The principal thrust of this study remains resolutely on the Renaissance. But it is interesting on occasion to rerun the fifteenth- and sixteenth-century material gathered here through a contemporary, twenty-first-century, interpretative filter. Rather than constituting a celebration of what the overseas voyages and the Italian Renaissance achieved, the material takes on a much more sinister hue. Large numbers of people were enslaved in violent circumstances; those that were sold by their fellow countrymen had already been forcibly enslaved, usually also in violent circumstances, beforehand. In a proto-colonial or imperial situation, Europeans may have believed themselves to be the legitimate owners of enslaved people whom they bought from other, mainly African, 'owners'; but people cannot be 'owned' and slavery itself was and is abhorrent—although not considered so at the time—and thus their acts of acquisition may be considered illegitimate. Many aspects of slavery in Renaissance Italy followed the tenets and ideals of Roman slavery. For example, the enslaved were employed in building projects in Tuscany and

Rome,[23] and humanists and artists, as well as patricians, prelates and the more to be expected Italian 'voyagers',[24] kept domestic slaves. The fact that the Renaissance was not a time of universal gains and freedoms has long been appreciated in other regards: as, for example, in connection with the position and treatment of women. However, the past has to be understood in period-appropriate terms, even while the terms of the present keep on shifting, allowing new interpretations to be made. What is perhaps more profitable is to realise that these considerations were of very little interest to the European acquirers of the enslaved—whose pre-European past did not matter unless a royal or princely provenance could be posited.

The Relevance of Provenance

If two core questions are posed—Why would provenance have mattered in the fifteenth and sixteenth centuries?, and, What if anything was to be gained from knowing the provenance of something?—using material from the time does not allow them to be answered satisfactorily. But perhaps hindsight can be beneficial here, and the reasons for provenance mattering today can aid analysis of why it did not matter in the same or similar ways in the fifteenth and sixteenth centuries.[25] If the same question is rerun—Why does provenance matter now?—two possible answers are clear. It matters because in the aftermath of the dislocations and thefts of World War II it can guarantee a clear right to ownership; and it matters because it can help guarantee the authenticity of an

23. See, e.g., Suzanne B. Butters, 'Le Cardinal Ferdinand de Médicis', in Philippe Morel, ed., *La Villa Médicis*, vol. 2: *Études* (Rome, 1991), pp. 170–96 at 178; and Butters, 'Ferdinand et le jardin du Pincio', in ibid., pp. 351–410 at 379.

24. Amerigo Vespucci's will of 9 April 1511, redacted in Seville, states he had five slaves, including three from the Canary Isles and one from Guinea. See Ilaria Luzzana Caraci, ed., *Amerigo Vespucci*, Nuova raccolta columbiana 21, 2 vols (Rome, 1996–99), vol. 1: *Documenti* (1996), pp. 197–208 at 202–3.

25. The realities of competitive acquisition and accumulation of ethnographic art in the eighteenth and nineteenth centuries from all over the globe are well described in Hermione Waterfield and J.C.H. King, *Provenance: Twelve Collectors of Ethnographic Art in England, 1760–1990* (London, 2009). An almost inexhaustible pool of non-European objects existed, easily and cheaply obtainable, brought back from the European overseas empires by 'explorers, missionaries, administrators, traders and military personnel' (p. 9); that is, the same sorts of people who benefited from the Portuguese trading empire in the fifteenth and sixteenth centuries to acquire objects. The collectors in the main did not collect in the field, but from these returnees. Trails relating to provenance could be either more or less complete, depending on individual whim.

object. The first reason is not helpful in a Renaissance context, where right to ownership was not in general questioned, and where possession was what mattered. In the Renaissance, possession trumped provenance. The Portuguese colonial context does however raise significant issues about the right to ownership in the twenty-first century. A question mark remains in very many cases about what would now be termed the legitimacy of acquisition of goods originating from the Portuguese trading empire. Power relations were manifestly unequal. Routes whereby goods were obtained by Portuguese and other Europeans in the fifteenth and sixteenth centuries from the Portuguese trading empire differed significantly, moving across the whole of the spectrum from legal to illegal acquisition; that is, from the exchange of diplomatic gifts,[26] and equitable trade in unforced conditions, to illicit and violent grabbing of desired goods, to punitive and immoral confiscations (as in Brazil), and to the looting of treasuries at religious sites (as in Ceylon).[27] In the absence of local, non-European records—and there are no indigenous sub-Saharan African records for the fifteenth, and few indigenous records for the first half of the sixteenth century,[28] although they do exist in India and Ceylon, for example— it is impossible to know with certainty how goods were obtained in the fifteenth and sixteenth centuries; even with records, doubts and ambiguities remain, although evidence of payment for goods in this period is clearly a suggestive pointer that the acquisition may have been legitimate. Yet ownership is now considered not only to be a financial or economic matter, but to have an ethical element. Sales do not take place in a vacuum, and the circumstances surrounding them can also indicate underlying force. While it is clear that in transacting a sale or exchange the seller values the money or goods received more than the object, the reason he or she does so is now also thought to be pertinent. Were goods being sold because of economic collapse or famine, possibly provoked by or hastened by the arrival of the Europeans? In

26. *Elfenbeine aus Ceylon: Luxusgüter für Katarina von Habsburg (1507–1578)*, ed. Annemarie Jordan Gschwend and Johannes Beltz, exh. cat., Museum Rietberg, Zurich (Zurich, 2010), pp. 37–43; Zoltán Biedermann, 'Diplomatic Ivories: Sri Lankan Caskets and the Portuguese–Asian Exchange in the Sixteenth Century', in Zoltán Biedermann, Anne Gerritsen and Giorgio Riello, eds, *Global Gifts: The Material Culture of Diplomacy in Early Modern Eurasia* (Cambridge, 2018), pp. 88–118.

27. Hugo Miguel Crespo, 'The Plundering of the Ceylonese Royal Treasure, 1551–1553: Its Character, Cost and Dispersal', in Michael Bycroft and Sven Dupré, eds, *Gems in the Early Modern World: Materials, Knowledge and Global Trade, 1450–1800* (London, 2019), pp. 35–64.

28. John K. Thornton, *A History of West Central Africa to 1850* (Cambridge, 2020), pp. 39.

moments of war or shows of violence, force interfered with usual patterns of behaviour, and sales of goods in the fifteenth and sixteenth centuries may have been the result of coercion, thus perhaps calling into question their legitimacy. These are not problems that apply only in an extra-European context: the legitimacy of many acquisitions inside Europe could similarly be questioned.

The second reason—provenance matters because it can guarantee authenticity—on the face of it seems more likely to be useful. Although views on copying were very different in the Renaissance,[29] authenticity was an issue in the sixteenth century, and the copying of desirable and popular objects, such as bezoar stones, was rampant. But in order to assure authenticity, there had to be people with expertise who understood precisely where individual items had been made and who were able to tell the difference between genuine and fake items;[30] as far as is known, that was not the case in relation to some of the more unusual pieces from the Portuguese trading empire, which could in any case have been made in more than one location. This would not have been common but, on the contrary, very rarefied knowledge. Once a certain category of object started to arrive in quantities, experts who could assess and value it would have quickly emerged too, but in the case of a few exceptional items, there was no call for this expertise and it appears not to have materialised. In order for knowledge to survive, it both has to be in someone's interests to know it, and be considered relevant: in whose interests would it have been for this very specialised knowledge to survive the move to Europe?

Documentation Adverting to Provenance

The present account does not mean to minimise the effects on historical analysis of loss of objects or of documents, both of which clearly skew attempts at understanding. If only one or two objects of value of a certain category survive now, however, it is extremely unlikely that they were originally imported into

29. Megan Holmes, 'Copying Practices and Marketing Strategies in a Fifteenth-Century Florentine Painter's Workshop', in Stephen J. Campbell and Stephen J. Milner, eds, *Artistic Exchange and Cultural Translation in the Italian Renaissance City* (Cambridge, 2004), pp. 38–54.

30. Peter Borschberg, 'The Euro-Asian Trade in Bezoar Stones (approx. 1500 to 1700)', in Michael North, ed., *Artistic and Cultural Exchanges between Europe and Asia, 1400–1900: Rethinking Markets, Workshops and Collections* (Farnham, 2010), pp. 29–43; Beate Fricke, 'Making Marvels—Faking Matter: Mediating *virtus* between the Bezoar and Goa Stones and Their Containers', in Christine Göttler and Mia Mochizuki, eds, *The Nomadic Object: The Challenge of World for Early Modern Religious Art* (Leiden, 2018), pp. 342–67, esp. 353–55.

Lisbon in their thousands or tens of thousands. Nor have basic questions about categories of objects that were being made in parts of the Portuguese trading empire, but for which there are no extant examples in Europe, yet been posed. It has always been assumed that the loss of the relevant archival documents in Lisbon means that even the most fundamental questions relating to provenance cannot be answered with assurance; but as usual with archival documentation, the situation is more complicated than that. Without the documentation, questions are legion. If one takes the case of West African goods, even which ships returned to Lisbon having put in at ports in West Africa in the late fifteenth and sixteenth centuries is not known with any certainty.[31] There are very few surviving ships' logs, so the precise routes of individual ships are unknown, but an indication of routes—and more particularly places of landfall on the African coast—can be gathered from rutters or *roteiros* (mariners' handbooks of sailing instructions) and diaries: for example, from the diary by an anonymous diarist now thought to be Álvaro Velho, who accompanied Vasco da Gama on his second voyage to India in 1497–99, first published in 1838, which has in the past been labelled a rutter.[32] And newsletters occasionally detailed routes: so a newsletter printed in Augsburg in 1504, for instance, revealed the best route to sail from Lisbon to Calicut.[33]

Similarly, the content of the cargoes on individual ships is almost entirely unknown, because nearly all the relevant documentation, such as bills of lading, invoices and cargo registers, is lost. There are details of some sort for cargoes on only a very few of the voyages on the India route—early ones dating to 1505 and 1518,[34] with later full information on that of 1587, and summaries

31. Paulo Guinote, Eduardo Frutuoso and António Lopes, *As armadas da Índia, 1497–1835* (Lisbon, 2002) is enormously useful, but does not attempt to discuss places the ships stopped en route.

32. Diogo Kopke and António da Costa Paiva, eds, *Roteiro da viagem que em descobrimento da India pelo Cabo da Boa Esperança fez Dom Vasco da Gama em 1497* (Porto, 1838); Eric Axelson, *Vasco da Gama: The Diary of His Travels through African Waters, 1497–1499* (Cape Town, 1998). See Damião Peres, *Os mais antigos roteiros da Guiné* (Lisbon, 1952) and the project on rutters entitled 'Rutter: Making the Earth Global' at https://rutter-project.org/ (accessed 6 June 2023).

33. See the newsletter by Amerigo Vespucci, *Mundus novus* (Augsburg, 1504) reproduced in facsimile and translated in *From Lisbon to Calicut*, tr. Alvin E. Prottengeier, commentary and notes by John Parker (Minneapolis, 1956).

34. Geneviève Bouchon, 'L'Inventaire de la cargaison rapportée de l'Inde en 1505', in *Mare Luso-Indicum: Études et documents sur l'histoire de l'Océan Indien et des pays riverains à l'époque de la domination portugaise*, 4 vols (Paris, 1971–80), 3, pp. 101–25; Geneviève Bouchon, *Navires et cargaisons retour de l'Inde en 1518* (Paris, 1977).

for quite a few between 1588 and 1610.[35] A stray cargo list survives from Goa in the early seventeenth century.[36] There are few bills of lading or cargo lists for cargoes taken to Lisbon from either East or West Africa for the period between the late fifteenth century and 1600.[37] This lack of documentation has until now been given as a reason why the provenance of so many goods from the Portuguese trading empire arriving in Lisbon is unknown—the evidence having been destroyed in 1755. A sole surviving Casa da Guiné treasurer's account book, from 1504–5, now in Lisbon (Fig. 1), indicates the magnitude of this loss, by revealing a whole wealth of information that would have been available if the records had survived: names of the ships; names of their crews; descriptions of their cargoes with valuations made so that taxes could be assessed.[38]

Even in this document, however, provenance of goods is not specified, so it is now apparent that the survival of these records as a series, although it would have provided a great deal to analyse, would not have provided answers to the specific questions relating to provenance posed here. Routes and places of landfall were not detailed in such records, and cargoes were bundled

35. Niels Steensgaard, 'The Return Cargoes of the Carreira da Índia in the Sixteenth and Early Seventeenth Century', in Teotónio R. de Souza, ed., *Indo-Portuguese History: Old Issues, New Questions* (New Delhi, 1985), pp. 13–31 at 16–21; see also, specifically on Chinese goods, Rui Manuel Loureiro, 'Chinese Commodities on the India Route in the Late Sixteenth and Early Seventeenth Centuries', in Annemarie Jordan Gschwend and K.J.P. Lowe, eds, *The Global City: On the Streets of Renaissance Lisbon* (London, 2015), pp. 76–93.

36. Annemarie Jordan Gschwend and K.J.P. Lowe, eds, *The Global City: On the Streets of Renaissance Lisbon* (London, 2015), appendix 7, pp. 262–66.

37. Even when fragmentary documentation exists about cargo, such as fragments of ledgers itemising daily purchases of slaves at Arguim, extant for 1508 and 1519–20, it reveals nothing about the provenance of the enslaved people: see Ivana Elbl, 'Sand and Dreams: Daily Slave Purchases at the Portuguese Coastal Outpost of Arguim (Mauretania, Saharan West Africa) (1519–1520); Full Raw Serialized Data plus Archival Analysis Annotations', *Portuguese Studies Review*, 30.1 (2022), pp. 325–54 at 329. Steensgaard, 'Return Cargoes', p. 17 mentions a report concerning the cargoes on two of the boats on the return run of 1587, where the list includes goods embarked in Mozambique.

38. Much of this account book detailing incoming cargoes from West Africa arriving in Lisbon and processed at the Casa da Guiné remains unpublished, but an edition is now being prepared by Pedro Pinto. See also A.F.C. Ryder, 'A Note on the Afro-Portuguese Ivories', *Journal of African History*, 5 (1964), pp. 363–65; Avelino Teixeira da Mota, 'Gli avori africani nella documentazione portoghese dei secoli xv–xvii', *Africa*, 30.4 (1975), pp. 580–89; Kate Lowe, 'Made in Africa: West African Luxury Goods for Lisbon's Markets', in Annemarie Jordan Gschwend and K.J.P. Lowe, eds, *The Global City: On the Streets of Renaissance Lisbon* (London, 2015), pp. 162–77 and appendix 8, p. 267.

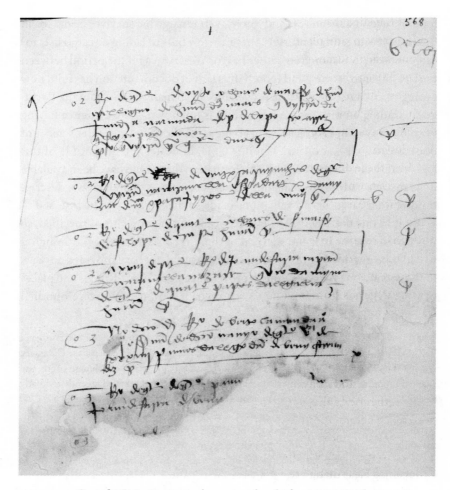

FIGURE 1. Casa da Guiné treasurer's account book, for 1504–5; Lisbon, DGLAB/TT, NA 799, 568r. Photo: Arquivo Nacional da Torre do Tombo, Lisbon—José António Silva

together from different parts of Africa and could have been uploaded piecemeal at various ports; so, although their arrival might have been recorded, unless they were correctly noted in detail in Africa upon being embarked, or noted in detail on arrival in Lisbon upon being disembarked, they would have been separated from their provenance even before they left Africa, and most certainly before they reached Europe. Cargo lists and bills of lading are not specific enough to provide cast-iron proof of provenance even in the case of cargoes of local produce, let alone for cargoes composed of goods that had already travelled from elsewhere in Africa before being loaded, or had been made partly in one place and partly in another. It appears not only that documentary sources giving clear and reliable provenance from the west coast of Africa did not exist, but also that documentation from which precise West African provenance might be able to be deduced was not required by the Portuguese crown; if occasionally one or two such records surface, offering occasional snippets of information, it is a matter of chance rather than design.

Given these documentary constraints, it appears that the primary reason for provenance mattering in the twentieth and twenty-first centuries—because it can guarantee authenticity—does not help with a consideration of provenance in the fifteenth and sixteenth centuries. Hindsight here led to the breakthrough in relation to what was considered important with respect to cargoes and goods—and it was not provenance. But that does not aid in the pressing quest to reattach provenance to objects. The centralised documentary record relating to goods from the Portuguese trading empire in the main turned a blind eye to provenance and was not concerned with it. Although it is still possible that local trading stations took a different view when they gathered goods to be transported back to Lisbon, it appears that by the time the goods reached Portugal it was usually not relevant. Much more so were questions of material, value and rarity. If provenance was not an issue, nor was the guarantee of authenticity that could have come with it. The general point has not been made before. Previously it had been assumed that confusion over provenance was a result of documentary loss, not that contemporary documents omitted to specify it, leaving the provenance of unfamiliar objects wide open and making clear that place of origin was often considered irrelevant.

Although the provenance of extra-European objects in Europe has proved in many cases to be elusive, their very presence has been interpreted as a sign of global interconnectedness,[39] and they (and all other early modern objects) have been lauded on account of their potential for reshaping the writing of early

---

39. On the concept of connected histories, see Sanjay Subrahmanyam, 'Connected Histories: Notes toward a Reconfiguration of Early Modern Eurasia', *Modern Asian Studies* 31.3 (1997), pp. 735–62; Sanjay Subrahmanyam, *Explorations in Connected History: From the Tagus to the Ganges* (New Delhi, 2005); Sanjay Subrahmanyam, 'Holding the World in Balance: The Connected Histories of the Iberian Overseas Empires, 1500–1640', *The American Historical Review*, 112.5 (2007), pp. 1359–85. The history of objects is now accepted as an important aspect of connected history.

modern history.[40] These are valid perspectives, but more thought is first required about how these objects were brought to Europe, and how they were perceived once there, before the next important steps can be taken. Their existence in Europe requires interrogation as does their labelling in accounts and registers.

The Language of Provenance

Perhaps it is useful to bear this documentary disinterest in mind when moving to examine language and terminology relating to provenance, because it now becomes clearer that contemporary European disinterest in extra-European provenance went even deeper. Not only was the documentary record constructed without any perceived need to note specific provenance (so there were no series of documents written at the time focusing on or clarifying the geographical provenance of cargoes or goods), but the language or geographically specific vocabulary necessary to allow precise provenance to be known is also absent. In the case of the west coast of Africa, for instance, while rutters and charts were full of toponyms of coastal settlements, individual trading places and landing places, the Portuguese had few words for areas or regions or provinces: even the names of African kingdoms or empires were often not known. Nor was it any better for nomenclature relating to people or peoples rather than places: the names of ethnic groups or linguistic communities were very rarely noted (an exception is the Cantino planisphere of 1502 where one of the Portuguese inscriptions refers to three separate groups in Sierra Leone: the 'Jilof', the Mandinga and the 'Cape' [i.e., Sapi]) (Plate 1),[41] and few names of African rulers were known in Europe,[42] although a handful were. Neither

40. Giorgio Riello, 'Things that Shape History: Material Culture and Historical Narratives', in Karen Harvey, ed., *History and Material Culture* (London, 2009), pp. 24–46 at 35–36, in a discussion about a Chinese Wanli porcelain wine cup in early seventeenth-century Jamestown in Virginia.

41. Ernesto Milano, *La carta del Cantino e la rappresentazione della terra nei codici e nei libri a stampa della Biblioteca estense e universitaria* (Modena, 1991), p. 148. The Wolof and the Mandinga are both ethnic groups and languages; Sapi was the name given to the peoples of coastal Sierra Leone by the Portuguese in the fifteenth and sixteenth centuries, the ancestors of the Bullom and Temne (amongst others). Nancy E. van Deusen, *Global Indios: The Indigenous Struggle for Justice in Sixteenth-Century Spain* (Durham, NC, 2015), p. 178, notes the same flattening or erasure of precision with regard to indigenous languages by the Castilian authorities in relation to peoples from the Spanish empire.

42. In the chart of the Atlas Miller containing West Africa, for example, there are no names or labels of any kind except 'Guinee'. In the charts containing India and Brazil, there are coastal place-names, but no ethnic groupings, no areas, regions or provinces, no names of rulers or

the Portuguese nor the Italian material displays sufficient, or anything like sufficient, geographical knowledge about places and peoples to pinpoint correctly the provenance of goods coming from distinct, distant locales. As a result, what is now being looked for—a proper understanding of provenance as shown in documents and terminology—is something that often did not exist at the time, and cannot now be recreated. Furthermore, twentieth- and twenty-first-century insistence on ascertaining provenance overlooks the reality that fledgling fifteenth- and sixteenth-century meanings of the term were still in formation, struggling to emerge into adulthood. In Italian, the word *provenienza* existed, but was used very rarely; the preferred word was *origine*, but this was not generally used in connection with goods or objects. The Italian *provenire* was identical to the Latin from which it derived, its etymology conferring a meaning of 'to derive/proceed from'.[43] *Provenienza* may have been the word of choice in the first instance in a contested legal or war context, when one city or country wanted to stop the import of goods from another.[44] Otherwise, 'provenance' was considered unimportant.

Examining geographical descriptors used in Portuguese and Italian relating to people and objects originating from the Portuguese trading empire, in order to help assess what Renaissance Italy knew of the Portuguese voyages, is revealing. Problems started at the top: the naming of larger categories or geographical units outside Europe presented difficulties to Europeans because of lack of relevant knowledge and languages. Zoltán Biedermann, with reference to Asia, has raised the issue of the lack of clarity surrounding the Portuguese use of the words for 'kingdom', 'empire' and 'monarchy' in the sixteenth century, and the 'blurry' meaning of the notion of a 'region',[45] complicating any possibility of stating precise provenance. Without clarity in the naming of extra-European political units or geographical regions, it is easy to understand why geographical descriptors relating to people and objects from the areas in question might also

---

kingdoms, no place-names in the interior (in Brazil, there is only 'Terra Brasilis'). See *L'Âge d'or des cartes marines: Quand l'Europe découvrait le monde*, ed. Catherine Hofmann, Hélène Richard and Emmanuelle Vagnon, exh. cat., Bibliothèque nationale de France, Paris (Paris, 2012), pp. 86–87, 90 and 93.

43. Ottorino Pianigiani, *Vocabolario etimologico della lingua italiana*, 2 vols (Rome, 1907), 2, p. 1079.

44. Battaglia, *Grande dizionario*, 14, pp. 780–81, s.v., no. 9.

45. Zoltán Biedermann, 'Imagining Asia from the Margins: Early Portuguese Mappings of the Continent's Architecture and Space', in Vimalin Rujivcharakul, H. Hazel Hahn, Ken Tadashi Oshima and Peter Christensen, eds, *Architecturalized Asia: Mapping a Continent through History* (Honolulu, 2013), pp. 35–51 at 48, 50.

be problematic. Nor did problems stop with the blurred understanding of geographical units: geography in general, and the names of discrete countries, also presented significant difficulties. Nancy van Deusen dissects court cases in sixteenth-century Castile, where the legitimacy of enslavement depended upon the origin of the enslaved person, and shows that the litigants, *índios* or indigenous people from the Spanish empire, 'relied on the murky geographical knowledge of [. . .] these territories' to steer the courts towards favourable verdicts.[46] In one particularly extreme case, Pegu (Burma) was confused with Peru.[47]

The required scholarly research on etymology and usage of many of the geographical markers necessary to make definitive statements has not been carried out, but work by Dieter Kremer on words depicting foreigners in sixteenth-century Lisbon helps to set out the parameters of the problems. Naming is a hugely complex issue, inextricably entangled with matters of provenance, yet names are often themselves local or particular, with different names used by different groups; how one ethnic entity in Brazil referred to itself and its place of habitation was not the same as the later, more random name assigned to it by the Portuguese when they arrived in the area. Nor were geographical descriptors always based on one type of information: they could be based on geographical areas, names of countries or political entities, or on linguistic or ethnic groups. Starting with people, differences in levels of information and understanding, and in Portuguese appropriation of the land, can be seen immediately in the cases of Brazil and West Africa. Indigenous people from these areas were described in a variety of ways in a variety of types of document after they had been transported to Lisbon. The Portuguese first arrived in Brazil in 1500, and Brazil was acknowledged as a country from then on in both Portuguese and Italian sources. However, indigenous people were not described as 'from Brazil' when they arrived in Portugal—this was a descriptor reserved for Europeans who had spent time there; instead, native Brazilians were described—if at all—as *índio brasil* or much more commonly just as *índio*, with actual origin sometimes being provided by context.[48] It appears that indigenous people from Brazil, at least, were rarely linked straightforwardly to their country of origin as it was known in

46. Van Deusen, *Global Indios*, p. 194.

47. Ibid., pp. 212–13.

48. Dieter Kremer, 'Ausländer im Lissabon des 16. Jahrhunderts', *Namenkundliche Informationen*, 101–2 (2012–13), pp. 97–181 at 118 and 154–55; see also Annemarie Jordan, 'Images of Empire: Slaves in the Lisbon Household and Court of Catherine of Austria', in T. F. Earle and K.J.P. Lowe, eds, *Black Africans in Renaissance Europe* (Cambridge, 2005), pp. 155–80 at 162–64, and Jorge Fonseca, *Escravos e senhores na Lisboa quinhentista* (Lisbon, 2010), pp. 215–28, where a variety of enslaved people are labelled as *índios*.

Europe, or accorded 'nationality'. Rather, like other indigenous inhabitants of the Americas and elsewhere,[49] they were labelled as *índios* or 'natives'. No place-name from Brazil, of a town or settlement, or any other form of human grouping, appears in Kremer's list in connection to a place of origin or provenance of an enslaved person, but occasionally the name of a city such as Pernambuco appears in some other context.[50] Clearly the precise provenance of enslaved peoples from Brazil, if known, was not considered to be of much interest or value.

The situation with regard to enslaved people from West Africa mentioned in Portuguese sources was not the same. For instance, the descriptor *guineu* or *guine* always refers to a sub-Saharan African—that is, to an indigenous inhabit-ant of the large, undifferentiated part of the coast of West Africa known in Europe as Guinea, rather than to a European who may have spent years living there.[51] The word Guinea had originated as a marker of ethnic and cultural difference, rather than as the name of a place, and as a geographical indicator it remained imprecise,[52] yet at least Guinea itself had not been taken over as an address only fit for Portuguese. There are a couple of instances of the word *angollas* being used in Lisbon to refer to the indigenous inhabitants of Angola—an interesting example of a more precise African term, signalling a secure prove-nance from a known African country; and one source mentions a 'natural de Congo ou de Angola',[53] but otherwise Kremer found no mention of the Kongo-lese. Known islands off Africa heavily involved in the slave trade, such as Cabo Verde and São Tomé, do not appear amongst Kremer's sample. The adjective *africano*, on the other hand, was usually reserved for Portuguese, most likely those who had lived in North Africa.[54]

These idiosyncrasies are turned on their heads when non-human goods are considered. Another random documentary survival is the log-book of the ship *Bretoa* that left Lisbon for Brazil in February 1511 and docked again in Lisbon the following October (Fig. 2). One of its outfitters and probable part-owners was the Florentine merchant resident in Lisbon, Bartolomeo Marchionni, who was deeply involved in all sorts of imperial enterprises.[55] Written by the ship's

49. See, e.g., enslaved elephant handlers from India in Portugal in 1549 and 1559 described as *índios* rather than *indianos*: Fonseca, *Escravos*, p. 219.

50. Kremer, 'Ausländer im Lissabon', p. 116.

51. Ibid., p. 148.

52. Lowe, 'Africa in the News', p. 315.

53. Kremer, 'Ausländer im Lissabon', pp. 113–14.

54. Ibid., pp. 109–10.

55. Francesco Guidi Bruscoli, *Bartolomeo Marchionni 'homem de grossa fazenda' (ca. 1450–1530): Un mercante fiorentino a Lisbona e l'impero portoghese* (Florence, 2014), pp. 109–10.

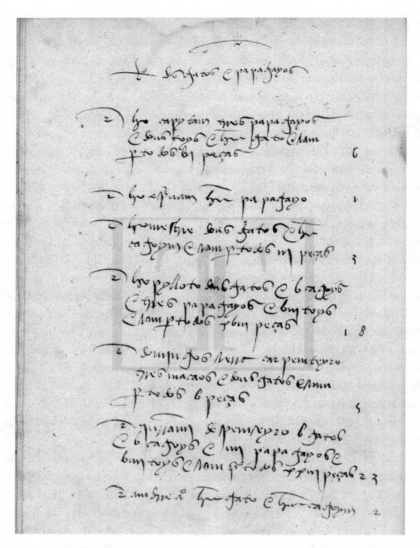

FIGURE 2. Livro da nau *Bretoa*, 1511, paper, 31.5 × 22 cm; Lisbon, DGLAB/TT, NA 759, 20v (inv. PT/TT/OVNA/759). Photo: Arquivo Nacional da Torre do Tombo, Lisbon

scribe, Duarte Fernandes, the log-book records—in addition to its principal cargo of brazil wood—seventy-two animals brought back; in the absence of Portuguese words for some of these animals, Fernandes uses their Tupi names, presumably explained to him in Brazil at the point of acquisition.[56] Tupi was the language spoken by the Tupinambá, who inhabited the area along the coastline of Brazil. One of over a hundred indigenous languages in Brazil, it was quickly given precedence by the Portuguese, as it was the first language they encountered in the new territory, and was accepted by them as the main indigenous language.[57] Very unusually, therefore, the log-book provides evidence of the process whereby new non-European words entered the Portuguese lexicon in the critical first years of cultural contact.[58]

If more log-books such as this had survived, this linguistic process could have been traced in relation to Portuguese trading posts around the world. As it is, there are two reasons why the lists in the *Bretoa*'s log-book did not have to record the provenance of the animals it carried. The first is that all of the goods were embarked in Brazil, so in the log-book their provenance was understood. (The ship made a stop at the Canaries on the way to Brazil, but took on no goods.)[59] The second is that the animals and birds were native to Brazil, and their Tupi names showed this. Without the Tupi names for parrots, they could have been confused with parrots from elsewhere, as parrots came from many parts of the world. Antonio Pigafetta included a couple of word lists gleaned from people in Brazil and Patagonia in his account of Magellan's circumnavigation of the globe in 1519–22. The one from Brazil had only a few

---

56. The text of the log-book was transcribed and published by Francisco Adolfo de Varnhagen, *Historia geral do Brazil*, 2 vols (Rio de Janeiro, 1854 and 1857), 1, pp. 427–32. On this logbook, see Annemarie Jordan Gschwend, 'Animais globais: Coleção e ostentação', in *A cidade global: Lisboa no Renascimento/The Global City: Lisbon in the Renaissance*, ed. Annemarie Jordan Gschwend and K.J.P. Lowe, exh. cat., Museu Nacional de Arte Antiga, Lisbon (Lisbon, 2017), pp. 192–201 at 193–94 and 206.

57. Aryon D. Rodrigues, 'On the Influence of Indigenous Languages on Brazilian Portuguese', *DELTA: Documentação de estudos en lingüística teórica e aplicada*, 30 (2014), available at http://www.scielo.br/scielo.php?script=sci_arttext&pid=S0102-44502014000300443&lng=en&tlng=en (accessed 16 April 2023).

58. Dante Martins Teixeira and Nelson Papavero, 'O tráfico de primatas brasileiros nos séculos XVI e XVII', in Leila Maria Pessôa, William Corrêa Tavares and Salvatore Siciliano, eds, *Mamíferos de restingas e manguezais do Brasil* (Rio de Janeiro, 2010), pp. 253–82 at 254–55; Nelson Papavero and Dante Martins Teixeira, *Zoonímia tupi nos escritos quinhentistas europeus* (São Paulo, 2014), pp. 17 and 248ff.

59. Varnhagen, *Historia geral*, 1, p. 427.

words, but the one from the Tehuelche of Patagonia was longer and fuller, and included their words for parrot and birdcage.[60]

In contradistinction to this acquisition of Brazilian nomenclature, indigenous African language or dialect words for African goods have mainly been lost or obscured, and have not passed into Portuguese. The fifteenth-century West African word list included in Eustache de la Fosse's account of his voyage to the West African coast in 1479–80, recalled and written in about 1516, contains only sixteen words, of which only three—the words for gold, cloth and brass armlet—are terms for goods that might have been exchanged.[61] P.E.H. Hair believed that the vocabulary was 'basically Akan throughout',[62] but as the three goods were recognisable using Portuguese words, these African words were redundant, and were not subsumed into Portuguese. What survives instead, captured in manuscripts and contemporary printed texts, is Afro-Portuguese pidgin or creole.[63]

It seems clear that although many permutations of descriptor existed in the documentary record of fifteenth- and sixteenth-century Lisbon, in the vast majority of cases—whether of people, animals or other goods—precise geographical provenance did not figure in common usage. If it is accepted that how the goods were acquired was of no interest to fifteenth- and sixteenth-century Europeans (possession is nine-tenths of the law), it starts to make sense that where they were acquired could seem of no consequence either. Here there seems to be a difference between Lisbon/Portugal, the city/country in Europe where the non-European goods first made landfall, and Florence/Rome, which were second and secondary European destinations. All knowledge, scientific or otherwise, is to varying extents a product of its local context.[64] Consequently,

60. Antonio Pigafetta, *Magellan's Voyage: A Narrative Account of the First Circumnavigation*, trans. and ed. R. A. Skelton, 2 vols (New Haven, CT, 1969), 1, p. 55.

61. P.E.H. Hair, 'A Note on de la Fosse's "Mina" Vocabulary of 1479–80', *Journal of West African Languages*, 3.1 (1966), pp. 55–57; David Dalby and P.E.H. Hair, 'A Further Note on the Mina Vocabulary of 1479–80', *Journal of West African Languages*, 5.2 (1968), pp. 129–31; P. E. Russell, 'Novos apontamentos sobre os problemas textuais do *Voiaige à la Guinée* de Eustáquio de la Fosse (1479–1480)', *Revista portuguesa de história*, 16 (1976), Homenagem ao Doutor Torquato de Sousa Soares, pp. 209–21.

62. Hair, 'A Note', p. 55.

63. John Lipski, *A History of Afro-Hispanic Language Contact: Five Centuries and Five Continents* (Cambridge, 2005), pp. 40, and see also 51–67.

64. David N. Livingstone, *Putting Science in Its Place: Geographies of Scientific Knowledge* (Chicago, 2003), e.g., pp. 179–86; Monica Azzolini, 'Talking of Animals: Whales, Ambergris and

locality and local conditions matter, and place can help elucidate ways in which expert knowledge contributed to an appreciation of the value of non-European objects. It is now clear that in Lisbon there were official appraisers of goods, at the very least from selected parts of the Portuguese trading empire, with the expertise to identify from its appearance not only whether a carpet came from India or Persia, but also more precisely whether it came from Cambay (Khambat) or Odiaz (Odisa).[65] Or perhaps it is more relevant to note that expert appraisers existed for some expensive categories of goods—certain luxury or prestige goods—for which it was important to distinguish carefully between items from distinct regions in order to arrive at correct valuations. These would therefore be exceptions to the rule that provenance did not matter; in such cases it clearly did. This hypothesis is backed up by evidence from the inventories of objects belonging to Catarina de Áustria, queen of Portugal, between 1525 and 1578; these inventories of extra-European luxury goods consistently recorded provenance—at least at the level of names of countries—because the provenance made the goods more valuable.[66] The method of acquisition might have been erased, but provenance, in the sense of geographical origin, was still crucial. This must have been because a sufficient number of these goods were appearing in Lisbon for expert appraisers to have a role. The state of expert knowledge in Lisbon and Florence or Rome varied according to the category of object, its quantity, its availability and its perceived desirability, so that while knowledge of porcelain was probably greater in Lisbon, for example, knowledge of coins was probably greater in Florence.

Referring to the Provenance
of Extra-European Goods in Italy

By the time Portuguese trading-empire goods had made the next leg of their journey to Italy or the Habsburg Empire, even the provenance attached to exceptional objects appears to have been shed as being no longer relevant. The

---

the Circulation of Knowledge in Seventeenth-Century Rome', *Renaissance Studies*, 31.2 (2017), pp. 297–318 at 299.

65. Hugo Miguel Crespo, 'Global Interiors on the Rua Nova in Renaissance Lisbon', in Annemarie Jordan Gschwend and K.J.P. Lowe, eds, *The Global City: On the Streets of Renaissance Lisbon* (London, 2015), pp. 120–39 at 121.

66. Annemarie Jordan, 'The Development of Catherine of Austria's Collection in the Queen's Household: Its Character and Cost', Ph.D dissertation, Brown University, 1994, p. 382 n. 5.

point is that detailed knowledge of the Portuguese trading empire was not at a premium in relation to objects in Italy, so no experts emerged with the relevant expertise. The number of goods was too small for expertise to be needed or viable. The desire to possess was more visceral and less refined or informed than that; these objects were deemed desirable, and neither how they had been acquired nor where they came from mattered to Italian buyers, agents or collectors. Returning once again to examine geographical descriptors—this time those used in Italian relating to people and objects originating from the Portuguese trading empire, in order to see what Renaissance Italy knew of the Portuguese voyages—the exercise is even more revealing than examining them in Portuguese. The word used most extensively to describe all these objects is *indiano*. This word would have caused difficulty even if it had been applicable to objects originating from either the East or the West Indies, or from India, but its usage was far wider.[67] As Jessica Keating and Lia Markey revealed in a seminal article in 2010,[68] the compilers of sixteenth-century Medici and Habsburg inventories relied heavily on the descriptor *indiano* when confronted with non-European objects that they could not place. Far from signifying a provenance in India or the New World, *indiano* positioned the essence of the object in its foreignness, but not in a specific place of origin. It masqueraded as—but was not—a geographical descriptor. It is relevant that there is no Italian equivalent of the Portuguese adjective *índio* ('native'/indigenous), that it did not enter Italian; it is as though *indiano* is used instead to signal generic indigenousness of the non-European. The extra semantic load carried by *indiano* is significant linguistically and conceptually. The word appears repeatedly in the Medici inventories of the Wardrobe or Guardroba; indeed, it is ubiquitous—not only in Medici inventories, but in all sixteenth-century inventories in Italian that included extra-European objects. The compilers used the term as recognisable shorthand, to fix 'a chaotic mix of visual and cultural information into one semantic statement', thereby acknowledging

67. Cf. Nuno Senos, 'The Empire in the Duke's Palace: Global Material Culture in Sixteenth-Century Portugal', in Anne Gerritsen and Giorgio Riello, eds, *The Global Lives of Things: The Material Culture of Connections in the Early Modern World* (London, 2015), pp. 128–44 at 132 states that in the inventory of Teodósio I, fifth duke of Bragança, China and India included a great deal: 'everything from the Cape of Good Hope to Melaka is referred to as India while China means everything east of Malacca including Japan'.

68. Jessica Keating and Lia Markey, '"Indian" Objects in Medici and Austrian-Habsburg Inventories: A Case Study of the Sixteenth-Century Term', *Journal of the History of Collections*, 23.2 (2011), pp. 283–300.

an object as non-European in origin, style or usage, but signalling that they were unable to pinpoint more specifically the provenance of one of these 'new and unusual things'.[69] In addition, it is surely relevant that one type of Medici inventory accessioned new objects according to date of entry and recorded when they left the collection, either on loan or permanently (*giornale di entrata e uscita*), another, *quaderni di ricordi o ricordanze*, was more narrative in content, and two further types categorised them either by object type (*a capi*) or by room location around the Medici residences. No inventory categorised according to place of origin or provenance, because in most cases this was not known. Following Oscar Wilde, Keating and Markey memorably write that the compilers of inventories never fell into 'careless habits of accuracy';[70] widespread employment of the waffle word *indiano* was one way in which these compilers resisted the straitjacket of accuracy. *Indiano* could be applied to people as well as to inanimate objects, leaving the person's place of origin open to speculation.[71] In this, it resembled the Portuguese or Spanish word *índio* (both an adjective and a noun) or 'indigenous person', again used as a way of signalling foreignness—a label of nearly boundless, 'geographically all-encompassing' parameters, according to Nancy van Deusen.[72]

Lia Markey's book *Imagining the Americas in Medici Florence* is extremely helpful as a point of comparison, because by the second decade of the sixteenth century, and more especially from the fourth decade onwards under Cosimo, the Medici are believed to have been engaging with information about the Americas.[73] Indeed, Markey argues that the arrival of objects from the Americas was the catalyst responsible for the projected design of the Guardaroba Nuova in the Palazzo Vecchio. At the very least, a solid case can be made for them being more on top of information about the Americas than about Africa, to take one example. It is certainly true that some objects were more recognisable than others, or made from unique materials only found in a limited area, and that Mexican featherwork, for instance, might have fallen into this category; yet there is still plenty of evidence that people in Europe

---

69. Ibid., pp. 285 and 297.

70. Jessica Keating and Lia Markey, 'Introduction: Captured Objects. Inventories of Early Modern Collections', *Journal of the History of Collections*, 23.2 (2011), pp. 209–13 at 210.

71. ASF, MdP 220, fol. 93, Cosimo I in Florence to Paolo Trenta in Pisa, 29 May 1565, Florence, Medici Archive Project, doc. ID 9408.

72. Van Deusen, *Global Indios*, p. 228.

73. Lia Markey, *Imagining the Americas in Medici Florence* (University Park, PA, 2016), pp. 1–5 and 28–45.

did not recognise featherwork as coming from Mexico. And labelling something as *indiano* and knowing that it came from Mexico are two rather different things. In the inventories under Cosimo post-1539, amongst the objects known to have come from the Americas, the only geographical descriptors used are *d'India* and *delle Indie*, which fit well with the other two, equally vague, ones used in the same section: *asiatica* and *morescha*. All that can be gleaned from this is that the compiler of the inventory thought he could discern objects in three distinct styles originating in different places. Nor is it known whether *d'India* here signified America, which is crucial to the argument.[74] In contradistinction to letters and *avvisi* arriving at the Medici court from the Spanish court, where precise provenance of events and precious metals was provided (New Spain, Peru),[75] the inventories were geographically and ethnographically silent in relation to objects from the Americas. At the other end of the scale were objects in the Medici collections, such as turtle-shell pieces, that were utterly perplexing in terms of origin, and might have come from any one of a number of places in Indonesia or around the Indian Ocean; the provenance of these was never going to be securely recognised in Europe at the time (and is still not secure even now).

It is interesting that the word *indiano* does not appear in John Florio's Italian–English dictionary *Queen Anna's New World of Words* of 1611 (or indeed his earlier and less full *A Worlde of Wordes* of 1598), perhaps revealing that it was a word used resonantly in colloquial speech and handwritten lists rather than in printed texts.[76] While the word was surely clearly recognisable in the sixteenth century for what it was—that is, a handy catch-all—it simultaneously also signalled either ignorance or laziness on the part of the inventory compiler, and a disregard for provenance. Even leaving these drawbacks aside, inventories were not uncontaminated records—no records are; all records are agenda-driven—but repositories of all sorts of social and cultural conventions and influences,[77] and geographical descriptors reflected this, so the

74. Ibid., p. 32.

75. Ibid., p. 36.

76. John Florio, *Queen Anna's New World of Words, or Dictionarie of the Italian and English Tongues* (London, 1611) does not contain adjectives derived from the names of countries (such as *cinese*) but nor does it contain geographical descriptors, such as *africano* or *indiano* that have more subtle and nuanced meanings, the sorts of words he usually did include.

77. Giorgio Riello, '"Things seen and unseen": The Material Culture of Early Modern Inventories and Their Representation of Domestic Interiors', in Paula Findlen, ed., *Early Modern Things: Objects and Their Histories, 1500–1800* (London, 2013), pp. 125–50 at 125, 127.

absence of precise provenance in inventories mirrored the greater disinterest in provenance in society at large. Some categories of object had a generally known provenance—such as China in the case of porcelain, as it was manufactured and obtainable only there at this date[78]—but it is noteworthy that geographical descriptors are more commonly attached to objects in connection with a style than with a place of origin; and the geographical descriptors attached to styles were nearly all European. So, for example, *seggiole* (chairs) were described as 'seggiole di Spagna'[79] or 'intarsiate alla portughese'.[80] Conversely some places were far less likely than others to be noted as places of origin. African objects seem to have been the least likely of all to be ascribed one. In addition, on the quite rare occasions when an extra-European provenance was attributed to these objects (when they were not described as *indiano*), either in inventories or accession records, it was often incorrect or false: an African oliphant, or ivory hunting horn, had supposedly belonged to a Japanese king, and an Aztec codex was described as coming from China.[81]

Provenance and the Guardaroba Project

These errors in attribution—or this carelessness—in relation to place of origin make it difficult to believe that objects in princely, ducal or other collections, *Wunderkammern*, *Kunstkammern* or even *studioli*,[82] could ever have been arranged or displayed thematically according to place of origin, as has sometimes been suggested. In the second edition of *Le vite de' più illustri pittori, scultori ed architettori* of 1568, Giorgio Vasari discusses in some detail how the custombuilt space of the new Medici Guardaroba in the Palazzo Vecchio in Florence would be disposed. The room was under construction, so Vasari's words were intended to give a sense of a project in progress. Nowhere in this description is there any mention of arranging the objects in the cabinets according to

---

78. On porcelain owned by the Medici, see Marco Spallanzani, *Ceramiche alla corte dei Medici nel Cinquecento* (Modena, 1994); Francesco Morena, ed., *Dalle Indie orientali alla corte di Toscana: Collezioni di arte cinese e giapponese a Palazzo Pitti* (Florence, 2005).

79. ASF, Guardaroba medicea 28, 17r, inventory of 1553.

80. ASF, Guardaroba medicea 44, 151r, inventory of 1560.

81. Daniela Bleichmar, 'Seeing the World in a Room: Looking at Exotica in Early Modern Collections', in Daniela Bleichmar and Peter Mancall, eds, *Collecting across Cultures: Material Exchanges in the Early Modern Atlantic World* (Philadelphia, 2011), pp. 15–30 at 17, 19.

82. Dora Thornton, *The Scholar in His Study: Ownership and Experience in Renaissance Italy* (New Haven, CT, 1997).

geographical clusters; there is rather a much vaguer emphasis on displaying the choicest, in terms of the most expensive and most beautiful, items.[83] However, some scholars have taken this to mean that the whole point of the Guardaroba programme was to integrate cartography, decoration and object, with the objects sorted according to place of origin: 'Cosimo's collection of feathered plumes would be placed in the cabinet behind the Mexico map, for example';[84] '[the Guardaroba Nuova] was designed specifically to store Cosimo's most precious goods from around the world within cupboards painted with detailed maps of the regions from which the objects hailed';[85] '[t]he plans for the Guardaroba [...] reorganised his objects according to provenance';[86] and '[t]he cartographic display in the Guardaroba Nuova was constructed specifically to show the provenance of the carefully catalogued objects to be housed in the cabinets behind the panels'.[87]

There is no evidence for this neat and attractive proposition. Instead, there are crippling problems connected to the assumption it involves, hinging as it does on the provenance of the objects being known, when in many (indeed most) cases it was not. Francesca Fiorani—sagely—realised this, while leaving open the possibility that 'an educated collector' might have been able to distinguish between the different provenances of ivories described as 'Moorish' in the Medici inventories (in fact from Africa) and featherwork likewise described as Moorish in the same inventories (in fact from Mexico).[88] There are at least three assumptions entangled here. Yes, educated collectors might have realised that the ivories and the featherwork did not emanate from the same culture, but it is another leap again to suggest that they might have known the ivories came from Africa, and a third leap to suppose that they knew in which part of Africa they had been carved. There were eleven maps of Africa in the Guardaroba detailing various parts of the continent.[89] In the

83. Giorgio Vasari, *Le vite de' più illustri pittori, scultori ed architettori*, ed. Gaetano Milanesi, 9 vols (Florence, 1878–85), 7, p. 634: 'le più importanti cose e di pregio e di bellezza che abbi Sua Excellenza'.

84. Mark Rosen, *The Mapping of Power in Renaissance Italy: Painted Cartographic Cycles in Social and Intellectual Context* (Cambridge, 2015), p. 87.

85. Markey, *Imagining the Americas*, p. 37.

86. Ibid., p. 38.

87. Ibid., p. 42.

88. Francesca Fiorani, *The Marvel of Maps: Art, Cartography and Politics in Renaissance Italy* (New Haven, CT, 2005), pp. 75 and 294 n. 32.

89. There were fourteen maps of Europe, fourteen of Asia, and fourteen of the West Indies: Fiorani, *Marvel of Maps*, p. 24.

sixteenth century, none of the African objects owned by the Medici was known to be from Africa, let alone ascribed to a country or region of origin. How, therefore, could they have been placed in the appropriate cabinet? [90] They could not have been, and the plan would have been impossible to execute. A smaller hitch detracting from the likelihood of the thesis is that the cabinets were closed, so objects would not have been on permanent display but rather stored: they would have had to be removed from the cabinets, that is, in order to be seen. If they could not be seen, it would make no sense to arrange them geographically, underneath maps of the places from which they originated. Perhaps unsurprisingly, the one clear example from Florence of objects being collected and displayed together with a known shared provenance relates to objects from Tuscany. In 1559 a group of objects was moved to Cosimo de' Medici's Scrittoio della Calliope in the Palazzo Vecchio: a few were extra-European, but the focus and theme of the Scrittoio was Etruscan and Tuscan art, a fitting choice for a Tuscan ruler who could understand the value of the local as well as feeling the lure of the global.[91] Most interesting here is that he chose to see Tuscany over the *longue durée*, prioritising the land and its bloodstock over any specific styles or media.

It is worth stressing that there is no evidence that global objects in general were arranged or displayed in collections, either at a personal level in *studioli* or more publicly in *Kunst-* or *Wunderkammern*, according to place of origin. It seems, however, that objects might—for obvious reasons—have been collected according to place of origin, although evidence even of this is limited. Of the many studies investigated by Dora Thornton in *The Scholar in his Study*, only one collection fell into this category: that of Carlo Helman, a gem merchant living in Venice who traded extensively with the Ottoman Empire and who amassed a collection of Turkish artefacts and dress. But while the 1606 inventory of Helman's possessions attests to his ownership of Turkish items, it does not reveal how the collected items were arranged or displayed.[92]

90. Cf. Greenfield, 'Moveable Continent', p. 206, who reaches a different conclusion: 'African objects imported into Italy during the fifteenth, sixteenth and seventeenth centuries had no fixed identities, either individually or as part of a collection, but were nevertheless likely to have been associated with sub-Saharan Africa.'

91. Andrea M. Gáldy, 'The Scrittoio della Calliope in the Palazzo Vecchio: A Tuscan Museum', in Roberta J. M. Olsen, Patricia L. Reilly and Rupert Shepherd, eds, *The Biography of the Object in Late Medieval and Renaissance Italy* (Oxford, 2006), pp. 119–29.

92. Greta Devos and Wilfrid Brulez, *Marchands flamands à Venise*, 2 vols (Rome, 1965 and 1986), 2, pp. 799–811; D. Thornton, *Scholar*, pp. 78–82.

Knowledge and Non-knowledge

Yet another node of contention is centred on the thorny issue of knowledge. Sanjay Subrahmanyam has usefully adverted to a so-called balance of ignorance in terms of (information and) knowledge between the sixteenth century and the present: people in the sixteenth century both knew and did not know things that are known in the twenty-first.[93] Some knowledge has gone forever, but when this balance of ignorance is weighted towards the present—that is, when hindsight and cumulative scholarship are admitted into the equation—it can sometimes help with the reconstruction of certain knowledge sets. When people were the conduits of knowledge, particular sets of circumstances pertained, relating to how that knowledge could be transferred. If the conduits were indigenous peoples from outside Europe, many of the trickiest circumstances involved parity of comprehension across languages. Samantha Kelly, for instance, has lucidly enumerated the ways in which the process of knowledge transfer of information obtained from the Ethiopian delegates to the Council of Ferrara-Florence, interviewed by a papal committee in 1441, and inserted by Flavio Biondo into his history of Italy *Historiarum ab inclination Romanorum imperii decades* (Venice, 1483), might have been compromised. Biondo was present at the interview. Not only did prior assumptions and understandings influence the questions asked and answers given, but multiple layers of cultural haziness and potential mistranslation (involving thought and speech in the Ethiopian vernacular Ge'ez, Arabic, Latin and Italian) lay between the information and its target audience, even before Flavio Biondo reconfigured it to suit his own viewpoint.[94] When indigenous people from outside Europe were the conduits, but the knowledge transfer was not wholly oral and also involved a practical element, the outcome could be less unstable and contingent. Animal handlers who accompanied extra-European animals, bringing with them knowledge relating to the care of those animals, first and foremost enacted the care rather than articulating it; the handing over of knowledge of that care to others occurred at a later stage of the transfer.[95] Other categories of practical

93. Subrahmanyam, *Empires*, pp. 27–28 and 54–55.

94. Samantha Kelly, 'Biondo Flavio on Ethiopia: Processes of Knowledge Production in the Renaissance', in William Caferro, ed., *The Routledge History of the Renaissance* (London, 2017), pp. 167–82 at 167–68 and 177–78.

95. Sarah Cockram, 'Interspecies Understanding: Exotic Animals and Their Handlers at the Italian Renaissance Courts', *Renaissance Studies*, 31.2 (2017), pp. 277–96.

knowledge and expertise travelled with enslaved people. It has recently been suggested, for example, that enslaved West Africans might have brought their knowledge of rice cultivation to Europe, and have been involved in the transformation of marshland along the Tagus and Sado rivers in Portugal into rice paddies.[96] By the seventeenth century, Islamic slaves and domestic servants in Livorno were being asked for information about 'Turkish' objects and herbs.[97] Retrieving this type of information requires different types of evidence from that discussed above, as well as a different mindset with respect to extra-European indigenous people.

As noted above, knowledge was often damaged or distorted or lost during long-distance travel, unless knowledge transfer itself was the goal of the journey. Very often objects appear to have travelled alone, unaccompanied by knowledge. When goods from the Portuguese trading empire arrived in Lisbon, it appears that sometimes knowledge existed about them, but more often it did not. By the time they had arrived at their next destination on the Italian peninsula, in a great many cases this knowledge too had disappeared. In this sense parts of the Italian peninsula could be designated as 'non-knowledge spaces': that is, places where non-knowledge was more pronounced despite pathways of interconnectedness being available that would have allowed knowledge to be present, ready to be activated. The question why this should be the case needs to be addressed just as much as its sibling, how. However much Florentines, for example, might present these goods as 'objects from nowhere', that did not correspond to a reality. On the contrary, the goods in question had been made by highly skilled artisans or artists, using techniques and patterns that were attractively alien to Europeans, and they very definitely came from distinctive traditions and specific places. Was it merely that knowledge of these traditions and places failed to be communicated from the

96. Miguel Carmo, Joana Sousa, Pedro Varela, Ricardo Ventura and Manuel Bivar, 'African Knowledge Transfer in Early Modern Portugal: Enslaved People and Rice Cultivation in Tagus and Sado Rivers', *Diacronie*, 44.4 (2020), pp. 45–66 at 50–52 and 57–59. Recently, pots identified as African have been found at excavations of seventeenth- and eighteenth-century sites in Lisbon. Although their place of manufacture is as yet unknown, they too might have been conduits for knowledge transfer, although of a different sort. Tânia Manuel Casimiro, José Pedro Henriques, Vanessa Filipe and Sara Simões, 'Mobility and Identities: The Case of the So-Called African Pots from Lisbon (Portugal)', *International Journal of Historical Archaeology*, 24.1 (2020), pp. 79–94.

97. Abstract of seminar paper presented to the early modern Italian history seminar at Oxford on 10 May 2022 by Federica Gigante, 'Slaves, Merchants and Scholars: Italian "Turks" and the Pursuit of Knowledge in the Seventeenth Century'.

creators and manufacturers of the goods to Europeans, that is: was it an issue of poor communication related to an absence of a common language? An argument could be made for this upon initial encounter in some cases, but not in most. Or was knowledge of indigenous objects akin to knowledge of global botany: a form of expertise that in the main was generated at the point of origin, so that knowledge production remained tacit rather than becoming explicit prior to the development of a framework of an accepted vocabulary and classificatory system?[98] In any case, the loss of knowledge highlighted here is another form of evidence that global objects in motion undergo a further process of construction, precipitated by the transition from one place to another.

In the twenty-first century, philosophers, sociologists and historians have realised that not all knowledge in the past was perceived positively under all circumstances, and that when and where it was not, an investigation of non-knowledge (the deflection or obscuring of knowledge tantamount to erasure) is in order.[99] It has always been recognised by both governments and individuals that non-knowledge had and has its uses, but the moments when suppression of knowledge, or the decision to promote or prioritise ignorance over knowledge, took place in the past have not been analysed in terms of process. William O'Reilly posits a difference between non-knowledge or knowledge-decay, understood as a 'general rejection or absence of knowledge', and ignorance, which implies 'the theoretical availability of the knowledge in question.'[100] As regards cargoes and inventories of extra-European goods, different scenarios would have required different processes. At the point when the objects were gathered, knowledge of their provenance was possible, but must have been rejected in favour of non-knowledge; by the time of their arrival in Europe, ignorance of their provenance was the only option, as although the knowledge existed, it existed in other countries and not in Europe, and so was not accessible.

If this helps to illuminate the how of the disappearance of provenance, it does not help with the why. What was served by geographical imprecision?[101] According to O'Reilly, ignorance can be exploited for a reason, for

---

98. Matthew Sargent, 'Recentering Centers of Calculation: Reconfiguring Knowledge Networks within Global Empires of Trade', in Paula Findlen, ed., *Empires of Knowledge: Scientific Networks in the Early Modern World* (London, 2018), pp. 297–316 at 301–2.

99. Peter Galison, 'Removing Knowledge', *Critical Inquiry* 31 (2004), pp. 229–43.

100. William O'Reilly, 'Non-knowledge and Decision Making: The Challenge for the Historian', in Conrad Zwierlein, ed., *The Dark Side of Knowledge: Histories of Ignorance, 1400–1800* (Leiden, 2016), pp. 397–419 at 415.

101. Bleichmar, 'Seeing the World', p. 19.

an outcome,[102] so there is planned or premeditated ignorance just as there is planned incompetence. Is it possible that rare or so-called exotic goods in Florence, by not having a fixed provenance and by being mysterious, at a time when the more remote parts of the world were being penetrated by Europeans, were valued more highly than those that came from somewhere known? If so, non-knowledge about place of origin could have been an advantage, as the object could not be pinned down and buyers and collectors were free to imagine or invent contexts and uses. Unknowability of the culture from which the object came meant that no holds were barred: any interpretation whatsoever could be inscribed upon the object. What can be surprising when considering sixteenth-century collections of extra-European material in Italy, for example, is how standardised the range of collected objects was.[103] Although heterogeneous,[104] the objects collected were limited. Thus objects without a known provenance, even if quite similar to various other objects, might have sidestepped familiarity and kept open the possibility of novelty or originality.

It is also possible that the active embracing of non-knowledge, entailing the obscuring of certain pieces of information as unimportant or even unsettling, and therefore deserving of suppression and denial, might profitably be considered as one aspect of fifteenth- and sixteenth-century early colonialism. Maybe provenance fell under the heading of 'useful non-knowledge'. This would fit with the attitudes of superiority and civilisation exhibited in varying forms, aligning itself with the conscious projection of world hierarchies that placed European countries and peoples at the top of any table, and extra-European peoples at the bottom. Removing provenance permitted the object to be seen as exotic in both a literal and a general sense: worthy of acquisition because rare, while disallowing expertise to indigenous peoples that might show up the non-expertise of Europeans. From this point of view, however, the current insistence on context collapse and context cancellation is itself another form of suppression and denial, deepening the obfuscation of the very aims that urgently need to be examined in a period-appropriate fashion in order to understand what drove them. Twenty-first-century non-knowledge is not a satisfactory response to the Renaissance attitude to provenance; instead of illuminating the problem, it intensifies it.

102. O'Reilly, 'Non-knowledge', p. 407.
103. Bleichmar, 'Seeing the World', p. 21.
104. Keating and Markey, '"Indian" Objects', p. 296.

2

The World beyond Italy

KEEPING UP-TO-DATE WITH PORTUGUESE
OVERSEAS EXPANSION: TRACKING
AND ASSIMILATING THE NEW GLOBAL
REALITIES IN FIFTEENTH- AND
SIXTEENTH-CENTURY ITALY

IN A MORE concentrated way than in chapters 3–6 that follow, this chapter is methodologically a comment on the vagaries of archival and material survival. In the absence of a self-contained set of records able to act as an anchor, such as a particular series of registers or an account journal or a collection of correspondence, all of which have internal coherence, the archival and material orphans presented here in chapter 2 are a random miscellany that have survived when many of their siblings, cousins and neighbours did not. Whatever sense can be made of them, this is a study based on 'what remains', and the academic exercise is to argue from the remains by assessing patterns and probabilities. Although survival is always an issue for archival historians, and 'what remains' is always incomplete, in this instance the gap between what there was originally and what there is now can be seen to be pronounced. The underlying principle of this book is to follow the documentation; here, however, it is also to point out the many occasions when documentation known previously to exist is no longer extant, and to attempt to make sense of the traces left behind, despite the glaring presence of absence.

Analysing in any systematic fashion the interaction of the Italian Renaissance and the Portuguese voyages around the globe, not often considered except chronologically and on a small scale in connection with each other, is far beyond the scope of the present work. Although fuelled by similar mindsets, and by a similar belief in the power of humans to effect revelatory change, the two nonetheless had fundamentally different endpoints and after-effects. Occasional areas of mutual interest or overlap, such as cartography and geography, have been more thoroughly investigated. In these fields, Portuguese fifteenth- and sixteenth-century overseas travel and exploration coincided with the importance of the classical past to Italian Renaissance humanist tradition in a fruitful, although by no means predictable or linear, manner. The limited purpose of this study is to analyse what was known at various moments to people in various circles in fifteenth- and sixteenth-century Italy about the Portuguese voyages and the Portuguese trading empire,[1] to assess what was considered important by them, and to understand what influence or impact this knowledge had; cartography and geography play their part in this. This chapter focuses on two fifteenth-century Italian ruling families, addressing in turn varieties of Italian involvement in Portuguese overseas exploration and the transmission of news of the Portuguese voyages to Italy, before turning to look more closely at what Ercole and Isabella d'Este in Ferrara and Mantua, and Lorenzo de' Medici in Florence, knew of the exploits of the Portuguese, and how they benefited from the new possibilities on offer—but in an indirect fashion, at one remove.

It is well known that people from the Italian peninsula were involved in a host of ways in the creation of the Portuguese trading empire, both actively and passively. Florentines, as well as Italians of many other stripes, provided the manpower for crucial financial, commercial, sea- and ship-related and geographical interventions at all levels, so it must have felt and seemed that their contributions were essential to the overall enterprise, starting at the top with the 'explorations' themselves.[2] How the Italians inserted themselves into the underlying structures of 'exploration' and colonisation is what is of interest. This insertion took place at all levels. The individuals most in the public eye have been those credited with captaincies of the most high-profile voyages of exploration, including iconic figures such as the Genoese Christopher Columbus, who sailed on behalf of Spain rather than Portugal, but who had spent crucial time in Lisbon, and learnt his trade on a prior trip or trips down the

---

1. Only a few authors have directly approached the question, mainly through primary documents: Radulet, *Os descobrimentos portugueses*; Carnemolla, *Fonti italiane*; Radulet, 'Coleccionar e conservar'.

2. Guido Po, 'La collaborazione italo-portoghese alle grandi esplorazioni geografiche ed alla cartografia nautica', in Luigi Federzoni, ed., *Relazioni storiche fra l'Italia e il Portogallo: Memorie e documenti* (Rome, 1940), pp. 261–322.

west coast of Africa on board Portuguese vessels.[3] Ships' captains were an international group in fifteenth- and sixteenth-century Lisbon,[4] although those on the Carreira da Índia (the 'India Run') appear to have been almost uniformly Portuguese.[5] The fact that captains recorded their exploits in their own words is critical here, as a variety of on-board diaries survived to bolster reputations—and Italians were supremely good record-keepers. Columbus kept an on-board journal of his voyages to the New World that contributed to his latter-day fame, and the same is true for the Venetian Alvise Da Mosto, known in English as Cadamosto, who kept diaries of his voyages down the west coast of Africa in 1455 and 1456.[6] However, there was often a significant time lag between the writing and publication: Da Mosto's appeared in print for the first time in 1507, approximately fifty years after his voyages.[7] Columbus's journal of his first voyage in 1492–93 has unfortunately been lost, leaving to take its place an abstract by Bartolomé de Las Casas; even this edited and abridged copy,[8] probably based on an earlier one, with many entries that lack clarity, was only published for the first time in 1825.[9] Written accounts in the first person offer a highly individualised version of what happened, a contemporary or near-contemporary rendition, projected as truth by the protagonist of the ego-document. Yet alongside and behind these high-profile Italian captains lay hundreds of other Italians in less conspicuous leadership or non-leadership nautical roles, smaller but still essential cogs in the imperial machine.

Economic historians have also tracked the Italian contributions to banking, finance and commerce that permitted the Portuguese to set up their overseas trading empire, seeing these as key to their success. The Florentine merchant

3. P.E.H. Hair, 'Columbus from Guinea to America', *History in Africa*, 17 (1990), pp. 113–29.

4. Kremer, 'Ausländer im Lissabon', e.g., pp. 135 (Flemish) and 142 (French).

5. Guinote, Frutuoso and Lopes, *As armadas*.

6. Alvise Cà da Mosto, *Le navigazioni atlantiche del veneziano Alvise Da Mosto*, ed. Tullia Gasparrini Leporace (Venice, 1966); G. R. Crone, trans. and ed., *The Voyages of Cadamosto, and Other Documents on Western Africa in the Second Half of the Fifteenth Century* (London, 1937).

7. *Paesi nuovamente retrovati et Novo Mondo da Alberico Vesputio Florentino intitulato* (Vicenza, 1507).

8. See the modern edition of Las Casas's abridgement, 'El primer viaje', in Cristóbal Colón, *Textos y documentos completos*, ed. Consuelo Varela (Madrid, 1984), pp. 15–138.

9. Las Casas's summary remained in manuscript until the library of the duke of Osuna was acquired by the Spanish state and entered the Biblioteca Nacional de España. It was first printed in 1825 in volume 1 of Martín Fernández de Navarrete, *Colección de viajes que hicieron por mar los españoles desde fines del siglo XV; con varios documentos inéditos concernientes a la historia de la marina castellana y de los establecimientos españoles en Indias*, 5 vols (Madrid, 1825–37).

Bartolommeo Marchionni can stand as an exemplar. Marchionni penetrated to the heart of the Portuguese overseas empire, securing the monopoly on slaves, being involved at multiple levels with the Carreira da Índia and financing early trading voyages to Brazil, such as that of the *Bretoa* in 1511, discussed above.[10] Yet from what is known, Columbus, Da Mosto and Marchionni were not humanistically educated Italians embodying Renaissance values, but risk-takers who grasped the opportunities in front of them, closer to the medieval merchants in Boccaccio's *Decameron* who passed in days from riches to rags to riches (and vice versa) than to those who only traced the whims of Fortune in the pages of the classical authors they were reading. Nonetheless, the Italian mercantile and maritime presence in Lisbon had important consequences, not least because individuals in these communities conveyed information about the Portuguese empire back to Italy.[11]

Italian News of Portuguese Overseas Expansion

In addition to how the Portuguese voyages were understood and assimilated in Renaissance Italy through the media of geographical writings and cartography, the more free-floating topic of the progress of the Portuguese voyages as news items reported in Renaissance Italy needs to be considered. News of the Portuguese voyages and the establishment of the worldwide Portuguese trading empire arrived first of all in Lisbon, from where it radiated out around the other commercial and political centres of Europe. The important Italian merchant community in Lisbon was a crucial conduit in this process:[12] it fed

10. Guidi Bruscoli, *Bartolomeo Marchionni*, pp. 109–10, 118–23 and 135–86.

11. See, e.g., Francesco Guidi Bruscoli, 'Da comprimarmi a protagonisti: I fiorentini in Portogallo nel Basso Medioevo (1338–1520)', *eHumanista*, 38 (2018), pp. 65–82.

12. There is an ever-growing literature on the Italians in Lisbon in this period. See for further bibliography: Prospero Peragallo, *Cenni intorno alla colonia italiana in Portogallo nei secoli XIV, XV e XVI* (2nd edn, Genoa, 1907; orig. published in *Miscellanea di storia italiana*, 3rd ser., 9, [Turin, 1904], pp. 379–462); Federigo Melis, 'Di alcune figure di operatori economici fiorentini attivi nel Portogallo, nel XV secolo', in Hermann Kellenbenz, ed., *Fremde Kaufleute auf der iberischen Halbinsel* (Cologne, 1970), pp. 56–73; Virginia Rau, 'Bartolomeo di Jacopo di Ser Vanni mercador-banqueiro florentino "estante" em Lisboa nos meados do século XV', *Do tempo e da história*, 4 (1971), pp. 97–116; Virginia Rau, 'Um florentino ao serviço da expansão ultramarina portuguesa: Francisco Corbinelli', *Memórias do Centro de Estudos de Marinha*, 4 (1974); Marco Spallanzani, *Mercanti fiorentini nell'Asia portoghese (1500–1525)* (Florence, 1997); Kate Lowe, 'Understanding Cultural Exchange between Portugal and Italy in the Renaissance', in K.J.P. Lowe, ed., *Cultural Links between Portugal and Italy in the Renaissance* (Oxford, 2000), pp. 1–16 at 6–9; Carmen M.

hungrily on the news, assessing it for new business possibilities, and passed it swiftly on via letters to friends and contacts in Italy. Examples abound for the late fifteenth and early sixteenth centuries, with a substantial number of critical letters going between Lisbon and Florence, including, for example, Amerigo Vespucci's letter to Piero Soderini of 1504 describing voyages to the Americas,[13] and those relating to Malacca and India written by Giovanni Morelli to Giansimone Buonarroti, in 1509 and 1510.[14] For a slightly later period, most of the Florentine merchant Francesco Sassetti's letters from Lisbon between 1578 and 1583 were to three correspondents: Baccio Valori, Francesco Valori and Pier Vettori, all of whom were in Florence, and news of Portugal's overseas ventures and related products constituted a significant topic of discussion.[15] Information relating to the advances and conquests made by the Portuguese around the world assuaged the desire for news to be fresh and exciting, offering—albeit with a time lag—not only something that was not known beforehand, but also something that could transform mercantile opportunities. The news itself was shaped by those who purveyed it, who misinterpreted or changed not just particulars and focus, but often overall content, and news from the other side of the world, from unknown and largely unimaginable places, was more susceptible to interference or rearrangement than most.[16] News was never something stable or fixed; it was not 'fact'. Unstable even when it came into being, it was constructed, reconstructed and repurposed in motion. Given the huge distances traversed by global news,[17] it was susceptible to additional

---

Radulet, 'La comunità italiana in Portogallo e il commercio orientale nella prima metà del Cinquecento', in Giovanna Motta, ed., *Mercanti e viaggiatori per le vie del mondo* (Milan, 2000), pp. 36–44; Luisa D'Arienzo, *La presenza degli italiani in Portogallo al tempo di Colombo* (Rome, 2004); Nunziatella Alessandrini, 'La presenza italiana a Lisbona nella prima metà del Cinquecento', *Archivio storico italiano*, 164 (2006), pp. 37–54; Nunziatella Alessandrini, 'Giovanni Dall'Olmo, un veneziano em Lisboa: Comércio e diplomacia (1541–1588)', *Ammentu*, 3 (2013), pp. 155–57; Guidi Bruscoli, *Bartolomeo Marchionni*, pp. 38–60; Guidi Bruscoli, 'Da comprimarmi'.

13. Amerigo Vespucci, *Lettera a Piero Soderini, Lisbona sett. 1504, secondo il cod. II IV 509 della Bib. Naz. di Firenze*, ed. S. G. Martini (Florence, 1957).

14. Spallanzani, *Mercanti fiorentini*, pp. 42–46.

15. Filippo Sassetti, *Lettere da vari paesi, 1570–1588*, ed. Vanni Bramanti (Milan, 1970), pp. 216–374.

16. Cf. Filippo de Vivo, 'Microhistories of Long-Distance Information: Space, Movement and Agency in the Early Modern News', *Past and Present*, 242 (2019), supplement 14, *Global History and Microhistory*, ed. John-Paul Ghobrial, pp. 179–214, for excellent examples of the transformational process involving in the retelling of 'news'.

17. See de Vivo, 'Microhistories', p. 190, on the need to ask the question of what distance did to information.

transformations during the multiple stages it took for it to go from A to B, in a process similar to the ways in which global objects took on new meanings in the course of moving from place to place as they crossed continents.

Like all other types of news, this type took many forms and travelled via many conduits along many routes. News conveyed in personal and mercantile letters carried on horseback often travelled fastest, sent by dedicated business couriers or where possible (for instance, between Seville and Genoa) utilising more communal postal services such as the *scarselle* or bags of the eponymous merchants' associations.[18] Antonio Del Vantaggio, for instance, ran a courier service between 1457 and 1480 based in Florence that extended from the Italian peninsula to most of the business centres of Western Europe, including Lisbon.[19] The most urgent communications were sent by *fanti*, who took single letters and cost more.[20] Reliability was an issue, with many couriers and postal services held up and letters stolen; in order to counteract this, copies of important communications were sent by several alternative routes in the hope that at least one letter would make it to its intended destination. The letters that went by sea usually took longer—and there were far fewer ships than couriers. Federigo Melis calculated that written communications in the period 1380 to 1500 sent by sea from Lisbon to Pisa (or by sea for the central section from Barcelona to Genoa or Pisa, and overland for the other parts) took between eighteen and a hundred and six days to arrive, but in most cases around a month.[21] Lisbon to Rome took a few days longer. Handwritten newsletters known as *avvisi*,[22] consisting of news items considered especially

18. Nikolaus Schobesberger et al., 'European Postal Services', in Joad Raymond and Noah Moxham, eds, *News Networks in Early Modern Europe* (Leiden, 2016), pp. 19–63 at 19: 'Postal communication [...] formed the essential spine to news networks.' See especially the section on Italy, pp. 26–32, and on Portugal, pp. 43–46; for the *scarsella*, see Federigo Melis, 'Intensità e regolarità della diffusione economica generale nel Mediterraneo e in Occidente alla fine del Medioevo', in Federigo Melis, *I trasporti e le communicazioni nel Medioevo*, ed. Luciana Frangiani (Florence, 1984; repr. from Wilhelm Abel et al., eds, *Mélanges en l'honneur de Fernand Braudel: Histoire économique du monde méditerranéen, 1450–1650*, 2 vols [Toulouse, 1972], 2, pp. 389–424), pp. 179–223 at 200.

19. Melis, 'Intensità e regolarità' p. 190; Francesco Guidi Bruscoli, 'I mercanti medievali e l'invio della corrispondenza: Modalità e strategie', *Archivio per la storia postale*, n.s. 8 (2016), pp. 9–31 at 16.

20. Melis, 'Intensità e regolarità', p. 191.

21. Ibid., p. 200.

22. Mario Infelise, *Prima dei giornali: Alle origini della pubblica informazione (secoli XVI e XVII)* (Rome, 2002); Zsuzsa Barbarics and Renate Pieper, 'Handwritten Newsletters as a Means of Communication in Early Modern Europe', in Francisco Bethencourt and Florike Egmond, eds, *Correspondence and Cultural Exchange in Europe, 1400–1700*, Cultural Exchange in Early

important in political terms or for merchants, put together by locals (professional writers and private individuals)[23] in each city and then circulated to other cities in part or in whole,[24] were either attached to or included in other personal, commercial or diplomatic letters in the late fifteenth century, or already stand-alone items by the beginning of the sixteenth century, whether handwritten or printed. These became more and more standardised and expected as the sixteenth century progressed. News about Portuguese progress also arrived in Italy via diplomatic personnel and correspondence. Various Italian states exchanged ambassadors with Portugal, and the Church maintained temporary or permanent official representatives, such as apostolic collectors or legates, all of whom wrote home often, dwelling on the news of the moment.

One additional, critical, but slightly different route for the transmission of news of Portuguese expansion is embodied in the example of Christopher Columbus. The imperfect nature of his surviving writings notwithstanding, one can observe in them the process whereby what is new is constantly in a state of becoming less new, of how the new evolves into just another experience from the past to be set against the immediate contemporaneity of the instantly new. News did not only travel by being passed on orally or by being written down. Those who experienced the voyages talked about them but also carried on a longer-term dialogue in their own minds, with aspects of the new information and knowledge settling into memory before being reused at a later stage for comparative purposes in discussions of the most recent geographical novelties. This is well illustrated by Columbus, who spent at least ten years in Portugal, from about 1476 onwards and, according to his own testimony scribbled in notes in the margins of two of his books, in that period sailed to Guinea and Mina. In one of his annotations he writes that he has seen the castle of São Jorge de Mina,[25] so the voyage must have been after 1482, when construction commenced. However, his

Modern Europe 3 (Cambridge, 2007), pp. 53–79; Sheila Barker, '"Secret and uncertain": A History of avvisi at the Court of the Medici Grand Dukes', in Joad Raymond and Noah Moxham, eds, News Networks in Early Modern Europe (Leiden, 2016), pp. 716–38.

23. Nikolaus Schobesberger, 'Mapping the Fuggerzeitungen: The Geographical Issues of an Information Network', in Joad Raymond and Noah Moxham, eds, News Networks in Early Modern Europe (Leiden, 2016), pp. 216–40 at 219.

24. On Italy's position, see Mario Infelise, 'News Networks between Italy and Europe', in Brendan Dooley, ed., The Dissemination of News and the Emergence of Contemporaneity in Early Modern Europe (Farnham, 2010), pp. 51–67.

25. Colón, Textos y documentos, pp. 9–10; and see P.E.H. Hair, The Founding of the Castelo de São Jorge da Mina: An Analysis of the Sources (Madison, WI, 1994).

exact position on board ship—whether nautical or mercantile, as ship's officer or commercial agent—is not known.[26] Nor is it clear—if one takes into account his further references in which he alludes, for example, to West African manatees or sea-cows (*Trichechus senegalensis*) off the Malagueta coast between Sierra Leone and the Ivory Coast (see Fig. 3)[27]—whether he went on one trip only, calling in, unusually, at both the Malagueta coast (present-day Liberia) and Mina (in present-day Ghana), or on two or more separate trips. Here one can see Columbus's mind at work digesting and ordering what had been new information from West Africa in the 1480s and using it to make sense of the even newer information from the Caribbean in the 1490s, when in January 1493 once again manatees were spotted. Even if, as Paul Hair posits, some of Columbus's references to Guinea may have been 'part of the common knowledge of those regularly employed in Guinea voyages',[28] rather than specific to Columbus himself (which is debatable), others are more securely personal. It is in this kind of comparison, of aspects of the Caribbean to aspects of Guinea, that Columbus's writings elucidate best the evolution of the new into the not-so-new, and their value still as a measure of the more recently new. One further aspect of Columbus's role in promoting, transferring and extending the newness of Africa is worthy of comment: his language. Although he was Genoese, and lived for over ten years in Portugal, none of his extant letters are in Italian or even in Portuguese;[29] yet his familiarity with the latter is clear, because his written Spanish is replete with Portuguese expressions. This reliance on Portuguese led him to transfer words the Portuguese had coined for use in Africa to flora, fauna and other indigenous novelties he encountered in the Caribbean,[30] effecting an important crossover from the Portuguese trading empire to the Spanish empire.

26. Hair, 'Columbus', pp. 117 and 125 n. 16.

27. Colón, *Textos y documentos*, pp. 111–12. The manatees were believed by the sailors to be *serenas*.

28. Hair, 'Columbus', p. 119.

29. Ibid., p. 125 n. 6. See V. I. Milani, *The Written Language of Christopher Columbus* (Buffalo, NY, 1973), p. 11 ('all the known letters of Columbus are written in Spanish'). Milani's contention is that this was because Columbus felt insecure writing official pieces in Italian because of linguistic confusion between Genoese vernacular and Tuscan/Central Italian. The two pieces by Columbus in Italian that Milani referred to showed evidence of this confusion or interchange: a sixty-word note in Italian contained at least five Spanish words, and another of twenty-six words contained 'flaws which could be equally Hispanisms or Genoesisms [*sic*]', p. 12.

30. Consuelo Varela, 'Introducción', in Cristóbal Colón, *Textos y documentos completos*, ed. Consuelo Varela (Madrid, 1984), pp. xxxvi–xl.

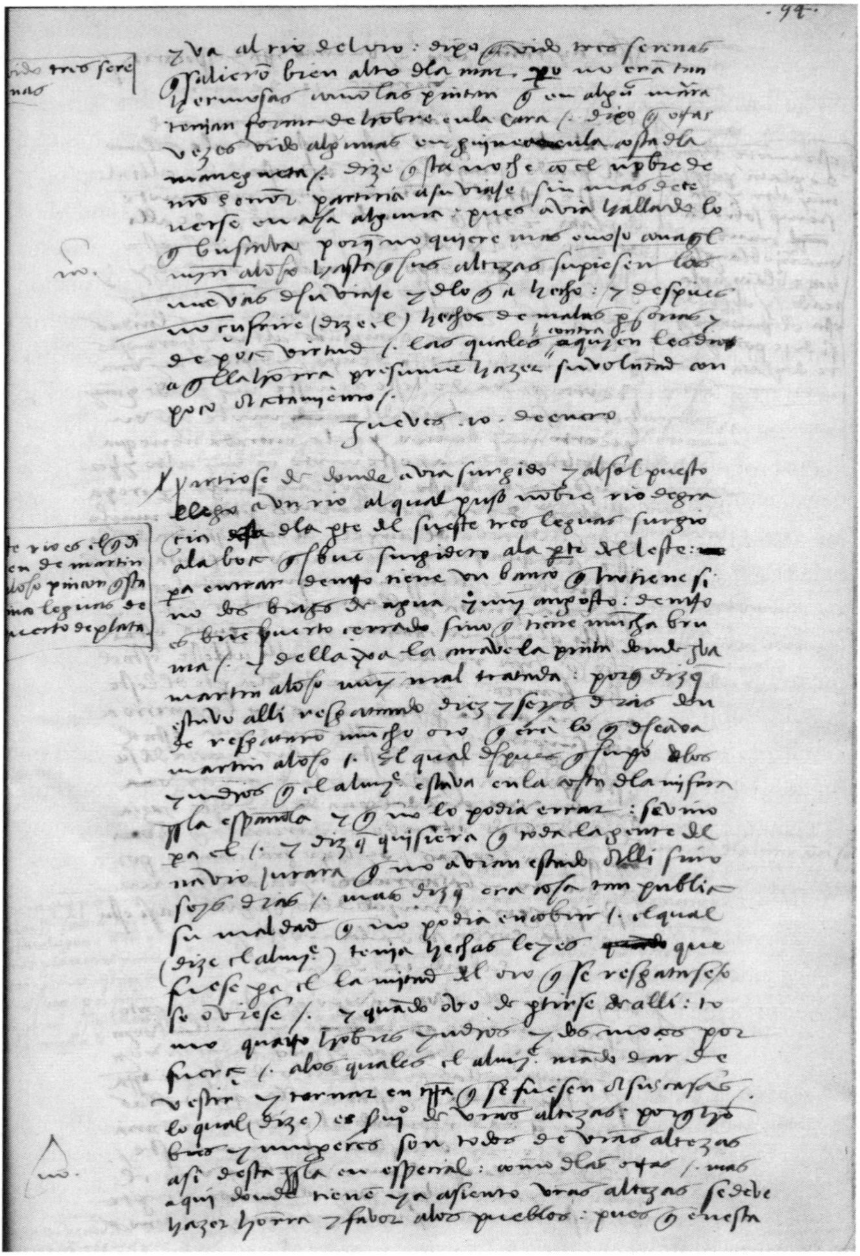

Jueves. 10. de enero

FIGURE 3. Copy by Bartolomé de las Casas (1552) of Christopher Columbus (Cristóbal Colón), 'Diario del primo viaje', 9 January 1493 (reference to West African manatees), paper, 31 × 21 cm; Madrid, Biblioteca Nacional de España, MS. Vitr. 6, 54r. Public domain

The Este and Portuguese Overseas Expansion

There is a clear break between the fifteenth and sixteenth centuries in terms of the Portuguese voyages. By 1500 the Portuguese had travelled down the length of West Africa, rounded the southern part of Africa, travelled up East Africa, and reached India; they had also travelled to the Caribbean, and made landfall in North America and Brazil. The map of the European known world had dramatically expanded, because sub-Saharan Africa and the Americas had become a part of it. As well as there being a chronological break, the various city states and republics on the peninsula expressed greater or lesser degrees of interest in these astonishing 'new' landmasses. An excellent example of the interest of three members of one late fifteenth-century Italian Renaissance ruling family in the progress of the Portuguese overseas expansion is provided by the Este of Ferrara. Why did Ercole d'Este, the ruler of an inland northern Italian court on the eastern side of the Italian peninsula (not even facing towards Portugal and Spain), expend time and money at the end of the fifteenth and beginning of the sixteenth century keeping abreast of the latest developments connected to Portuguese overseas exploration? The first and best-known piece of evidence for this interest is the so-called Cantino world chart, or planisphere as it is usually known,[31] but the Este as a family had prior form in terms of interest in geographical exploration,[32] and already owned at least one world map before they acquired the Cantino planisphere. An anonymous Catalan *mappamondo* dated to 1450–60, which, like the Cantino map, is still in the Biblioteca Estense Universitaria in Modena, arrived in the library on 11 July 1488.[33]

The Cantino chart (Plate 2)—in addition to being a spectacular piece of work—has a very particular history. Alberto Cantino was either an agent or diplomatic envoy of Ercole d'Este, or an informer or spy who travelled under cover of being a horse-dealer.[34] Whatever his precise role, Ercole appears to

31. Maria Fernanda Alegria, Suzanne Daveau, João Carlos Garcia and Francesc Relaño, 'Portuguese Cartography in the Renaissance', in David Woodward, ed., *The History of Cartography*, vol. 3: *Cartography in the European Renaissance*, in 2 parts (Chicago, 2007), part 1, pp. 975–1068 at 993–94, 1004 and 1005.

32. Milano, *La carta*, p. 88.

33. Marcel Destombes, ed., *Mappemondes AD 1200–1500: Catalogue préparé par la Commission des cartes anciennes de l'Union géographique internationale, = Imago mundi*, supplement 4 (Amsterdam, 1964), pp. 217–21 at 52; Milano, *La carta*, p. 90.

34. See, e.g., Claudio Cerreti, 'Gli ambasciatori e la cartografia', in Stefano Andretta, Lucien Bély, Alexander Koller and Gérard Poumarède, eds, *Esperienza e diplomazia: Saperi, pratiche*

have sent him to the Iberian peninsula to winkle out the most up-to-date information about the Portuguese and Spanish overseas explorations in Africa, Asia and the Americas, possibly also enjoining him to obtain a chart recording this information. At present, however, there is no evidence that the acquisition of a map was the primary purpose of his trip, which is an assumption that has been made because the Cantino map was the known outcome of it. Whether spy or an agent, he had the attributes of both. He was successful in scouting or detective work, in employing his own judgement or discernment, in making snap decisions and in operating in foreign places and liaising with various groups, even performing diplomatic or soft-power roles. The Este ruler's interest is likely, at least in part, to have been a matter of commercial espionage, even if knowledge of the establishment of trade routes and precious metals cannot have been necessary. The purpose of Cantino's mission can be deduced to some extent from its trajectory, traceable via his extant correspondence. A first letter was despatched in June 1501 from Oran or Wahran, now in Algeria, a flourishing sixteenth-century Mediterranean and African trade hub and port, and an important compulsory stop for convoys from Venice, Florence and Genoa en route to Cadiz.[35] From Oran, Cantino reported on a gold mine discovered in the Spanish Indies. Another letter was written in July 1501 from Cadiz, reporting on the triumphant return in June and July 1501, fifteen months after leaving Lisbon, of Cabral's fleet, which had made landfall in Brazil.[36] Cantino assured Ercole that he would soon tell him more precise and 'truthful' information about the 'cose riche & maravigliose' (rich and marvellous goods) that had arrived on these ships, based on the experience of having seen them with his own eyes, when they met face to face.[37] This highly significant news

---

culturali e azione diplomatica nell'Età moderna (secc. XV–XVIII)/Expérience et diplomatie: Savoirs, pratiques culturelles et action diplomatique à l'époque moderne (XVᵉ–XVIIIᵉ s.) (Rome, 2020), pp. 211–30 at 213.

35. Louis de Mas Latrie, Traités de paix et de commerce et documents divers concernant les relations des chrétiens avec des Arabes de l'Afrique septentrionale au Moyen-Âge (Paris, 1866–72), pp. 330 and 333; René Lespes, 'Oran, ville et port avant l'occupation française (1831)', Revue africaine, 75 (1934), pp. 277–335 at 292; Joshua Schreir, The Merchants of Oran: A Jewish Port at the Dawn of Empire (Stanford, CA, 2017), pp. 29–30.

36. Claudio Greppi, 'Luoghi e miti: La conoscenza delle scoperte presso la corte Ferrarese', in Marco Bertozzi, ed., Alla corte degli Estensi: Filosofia, arte e cultura a Ferrara nei secoli XV e XVI; Atti del Convegno internazionale di studi, Ferrara, 5–7 marzo 1992 (Ferrara, 1994), pp. 447–63 at 447–49.

37. ASMo, Cancelleria ducale, Estero, Ambasciatori, agenti e corrispondenti estensi fuori d'Italia, Spagna 1, Alberto Cantino to Ercole d'Este, 19 July 1501 [Cadiz].

persuaded Cantino to leave Spain and relocate to Portugal to hear more, and he wrote letters to Ercole from Lisbon in October 1501 and January 1502. The story goes that Cantino was there when news reached Lisbon on 13 September 1502 of the discovery of Ascension Island by João de Nova (on a voyage to India), and Ascension Island is included on the Cantino chart, sporting a Portuguese flag. Cantino left Lisbon for Genoa at the end of October. The timeframe for the manufacture of the chart is as circumscribed and tight as the timeframe for its subsequent acquisition by Cantino. On 19 November 1502 Cantino was in Rome, presumably on other business, from where he wrote to Ercole that the chart, costing twelve gold ducats, had been left in Genoa with Francesco Cattaneo, who then sent it to Ferrara.[38]

This narrative presents some difficulties. Information about the recent Portuguese voyages was closely guarded in Lisbon, with constantly updated master maps held under lock and key in the repository of the Casa da Índia. The assertion of earlier Portuguese scholars, such as Jaime Cortesão in the 1920s,[39] that an all-encompassing policy of secrecy (*sigilo*) more generally, in connection with the release of information in documents and chronicles, was a feature of the Avis rulers under whom the voyages were made, is contested. By the 1960s, it was being argued that the presence of the considerable number of foreign merchants in Lisbon would have made this policy unworkable.[40] Yet it seems certain that access to the latest cartographical information was restricted. The Florentine merchant Guido di Tommaso Detti wrote in August 1499 from Lisbon, after the return of Vasco da Gama's successful voyage to India, that King Manuel had ordered the collection of all the navigational charts that elucidated the route, threatening loss of life and belongings to those who disobeyed.[41] How did Cantino manage to penetrate this secret enclave and commission such an important map from an unknown Portuguese mapmaker? The chart is big,

38. Armando Cortesão and Avelino Teixeira da Mota, 'Anónimo, o planisfério "Cantino", de 1502', in *Portugaliae monumenta cartographica*, 6 vols (facsimile, Lisbon, 1987 [Lisbon, 1960]), 1, pp. 7–13 at 7–8; Milano, *La carta*, pp. 93 (reproduction of letter of 19 Nov. 1502) and 97–98. Cerreti, 'Gli ambasciatori', p. 214, suggests that while in Genoa the Cantino planisphere was itself secretly copied, and the copy, now known as the Carta Caveri, was sent to the king of France.

39. Jaime Cortesão, 'Do sigilo nacional sobre os descobrimentos: Crónicas desaparecidas, mutiladas e falseadas; Alguns dos feitos que se calaram', *Lusitania*, 1 (1924), pp. 45–81.

40. Bailey W. Diffie, 'Foreigners in Portugal and the "Policy of Silence"', *Terrae incognitae*, 1 (1969), pp. 23–34.

41. Luciano Formisano, ed., *'Iddio ci dia buon viaggio e guadagno': Firenze, Biblioteca Riccardiana, ms. 1910 (Codice Vaglienti)* (Florence, 2006), p. 145.

hand-drawn and hand-coloured, on six parchment sheets measuring overall 105 × 220 centimetres,[42] so it could hardly have been transported inconspicuously. It is rumoured that Cantino smuggled the chart out of Portugal hidden in the lining of his cloak—which would have made sense, as having obtained it illegally, he could not risk declaring it at customs when he left the kingdom. A recent hypothesis is that the planisphere was made by Pedro Reinel,[43] one of the principal mapmakers in Lisbon, working illegally;[44] certainly it was made by an expert, and this suggestion would explain its brilliance—but still does not explain how its genesis or its manufacture was possible.

In addition to information from João de Nova's trip to India in 1501–2, the Cantino map incorporated new geographical data from several other pioneering sea voyages: Columbus's first voyage to the Caribbean in 1492, Vasco da Gama's voyage to East Africa and India of 1498–99 (the very one mentioned by Detti: see above), the voyages of Pedro Álvarez Cabral and Gonzalo Coelho to Brazil in 1500–1501 and 1501–2,[45] and that of Miguel and Gaspar Corte-Real to Greenland and Newfoundland in 1501,[46] explaining the inclusion of all these areas. Except for Columbus, all of these mariners had sailed for the Portuguese crown.[47] Information about the continent of Africa, which occupied pride of place on the planisphere, appears to have come from the expeditions of Diogo

42. Joaquim Alves Gaspar, 'Blunders, Errors and Entanglements: Scrutinizing the Cantino Planisphere with a Cartometric Eye', Imago mundi, 64.2 (2012), pp. 181–200 at 182 and 196 n. 9.

43. Reinel may have been of mixed Portuguese and African ancestry: Rafael Moreira, 'Pedro e Jorge Reinel (at. 1504–60): Dois cartógrafos negros na côrte de D. Manuel de Portugal (1495–1521)', Terra Brasilis, 4 (2015), https://doi.org/10.4000/terrabrasilis.1209.

44. Alida C. Metcalf, 'Who Cares Who Made the Map? La Carta del Cantino and Its Anonymous Maker', e-Perimetron, 12.1 (2017), pp. 1–23.

45. A new piece of pergamena has been placed over part of Brazil, changing the outline of the coast and various names, in line with the new information brought by the 1501–2 expedition. See Milano, La carta, pp. 134–35.

46. According to Cantino, two ships set off on this expedition to the north, in January or February 1501. On 11 October one returned, with tales of icebergs and frozen seas, bearing fifty forcibly enslaved indigenous people (whom Cantino said he 'touched'); the second ship never returned. ASMo, Cancelleria ducale, Estero, Ambasciatori, agenti e corrispondenti estensi fuori d'Italia, Spagna 1, Alberto Cantino to Ercole d'Este, 17 October 1501, Lisbon.

47. Annemarie Jordan Gschwend and Kate Lowe, 'Princess of the Seas, Queen of Empire: Configuring the City and Port of Renaissance Lisbon', in Annemarie Jordan Gschwend and K.J.P. Lowe, eds, The Global City: On the Streets of Renaissance Lisbon (London, 2015), pp. 12–35 at 31.

Cão to Kongo in the 1480s, and from earlier voyages to Senegambia, São Jorge da Mina and Benin.[48]

More importantly, if indeed Ercole had asked for a map (which is no means certain), why would he have wanted one? One could have expected Venice to want such an object, but Ferrara is not Venice. Venice and Portugal had far more in common: both were maritime polities, and both wanted to control lucrative trading routes.[49] One of the closest parallels to what is assumed to have been Cantino's brief was that given to Lunardo Masser by the Council of Ten in Venice in 1504, which is also very close in terms of date. Masser too was a secret agent; he was sent to Lisbon, told to dress as 'an ordinary merchant' and instructed to find out as much as possible about the Portuguese voyages and the spice trade. Although he did submit a report in 1506, Lunardo did not have an easy time, and was arrested and detained in Lisbon as a spy before being allowed to return to Venice.[50] It is interesting that Venice sent a secret agent not to procure a map, but to extract information that would allow him to write a written report.

The Cantino planisphere itself may offer clues. The chart contains images of people, buildings, flora and fauna, as well as written inscriptions. Most of the written information is focused on matters of trade, which is likely to reflect the concerns of the people who had constructed the master maps in Lisbon. One of the most noticeable features is the prioritising of parrots over all other animals and birds. Three discrete types of parrot are included: West African greys (*Psittacula erithaca*) (Plate 3),[51] green parakeets in Senegambia (see Plate 1), and multicoloured Amazon parrots or macaws in Brazil (Plate 4).[52]

48. Avelino Teixeira da Mota, 'A África no planisfério português anónimo de Cantino', *Revista da Universidade de Coimbra*, 26 (1978), pp. 1–12. See p. 4 for a discussion of possible reasons for the inclusion of the gallows with the bodies of three dangling black figures at the rio dos Forcados.

49. David Chambers, 'Venetian Perceptions of Portugal c. 1500', in K.J.P. Lowe, ed., *Cultural Links between Portugal and Italy in the Renaissance* (Oxford, 2000), pp. 19–43 at 19.

50. Ibid., pp. 30–32.

51. Bruce Boehrer, *Parrot Culture: Our 2,500-Year-Long Fascination with the World's Most Talkative Bird* (Philadelphia, 2004), p. 51.

52. Ibid., p. 57. By the 1550s green parrots and green parakeets were two of the species of birds mentioned by Leonhard Thurnheysser in his work written c. 1555–56: Leonhard Thurnheysser, 'Naturbeschreibung von Portugal', in Berlin, Staatsbibliothek, MS. Germ. fol. 97, 320r. See Bernardo Herold, Thomas Horst and Henrique Leitão, A *'História Natural de Portugal' de Leonhard Thurneysser zum Thurn, ca. 1555–1556, tendo com anexo a transcrição das partes relativas a Portugal do manuscrito atribuído a Leonhard Thurneysser zum Thurn Ms. Germ. Fol. 97 da Staatsbibliothek zu Berlin* (Lisbon, 2019), pp. 106–7.

Only the African grey is referred to in writing, in the inscription for Benin and São Tomé.[53] Parrot mania raged across Europe,[54] and it is not inconceivable that it had also infected the Este court. Knowledge of and fascination for parrots was already being discussed in mid-fourteenth century Tuscany, before any of the above species were imported, when the parakeets in Europe came from India and the East. It was a topic in the Sixth Day, Tenth Tale of Boccaccio's *Decameron*. Set in Certaldo, the savagely anticlerical tale pokes fun at credulous Tuscans who believe in the possibility of a relic of a feather from the archangel Gabriel's wings, and turns on ignorance: the storyteller explains that the feather in fact comes from a parrot's tail. The *Decameron* story is set in the past, at a time when parrots were little known in Tuscany as a whole, and Certaldo is projected as a sort of backwater where the 'rough honesty' of the inhabitants ensured that most people not only had never seen a parrot, but had never even heard of one.[55] Boccaccio's disquisition on the subject is revealing, as it shows how knowledge of parrots, a certain type of exotic bird, could be used as an indicator of a community or group's engagement or lack of engagement with the new and contemporary—a gauge of whether or not they were keeping up-to-date with change.

Was Ercole's interest in the Portuguese voyages related to his aspirations for his court and his dynasty? Was he was thinking of funding voyages of exploration as a way of rivalling his neighbour Venice? Or perhaps—and this is the most likely explanation by far—he was a news addict or an armchair traveller simply swept off his feet by the expansion of the world taking place in this period, and he wanted to read about what this new world contained—and perhaps visualise it on a map. Maybe his interest was not unusual, and if one looked one could find a similar interest at many Italian courts; but his has been immortalised by the acquisition and survival of the Cantino map. One intriguing aspect of the chart is the fact that Venice rather than Ferrara is so prominently displayed—as, for example, in the vignette of the two columns of the lion and San Teodoro in the Piazzetta of San Marco (Plate 5), indicating that the artist had some knowledge of Venice. Both the choice of cities represented on maps and the city representations themselves were restricted;[56] Venice

53. Cortesão and Teixeira da Mota, 'Anónimo', p. 12.

54. Milano, *La carta*, p. 140 discusses the parrots on the Cantino and other maps, making clear Columbus's fascination with them.

55. Boccaccio, *Decameron*, 2, p. 767.

56. Biedermann, 'Imagining Asia', pp. 36–38.

would not have been an obvious choice on this Portuguese world map, and nor were the two columns in the Piazzetta routine in such representations of Venice. It is difficult to propose a plausible reason why Venice was singled out and given this degree of prominence. Could Cantino have passed himself off as a Venetian and the mapmaker included Venice as a way of currying favour? Or is it conceivable that the map was originally commissioned as a gift for Venice?[57] Or was the map made for someone else, and Cantino somehow inserted himself into the position of buyer? Many of the inscriptions are in Portuguese (so Veneça rather than Venezia),[58] with the exception of a few names in Castilian for places in South America and the islands off West Africa, and a few later additions of names in Italian,[59] and even if, as is almost certain, the mapmaker or mapmakers and the people who wrote the texts were different, it is highly unlikely that the principal mapmaker was Italian, because a foreigner would not have had access to the master maps. Without further knowledge of what precisely Cantino was commissioned to do, it remains unclear whether acquiring a map showing the most recent Iberian overseas explorations was the result of an opportunity that presented itself fortuitously in Lisbon or a central purpose of Cantino's trip.[60]

That the Este preoccupation with the Portuguese discoveries was passed on to Ercole's children is suggested by another piece of evidence—or could it have been his children's curiosity that spurred him to send Cantino to Iberia,

57. Trevor Dean reports that Ercole's relation to Venice between 1497 and 1503 was one of hostility and insecurity, but also of appeasement when dictated by circumstances, making this hypothesis quite unlikely but not altogether impossible. The political situation was complicated and alliances constantly shifted, but Ercole's ties to Venice meant that he could never ignore the city. In addition to ongoing trade disputes, Ercole's role as custodian of the *castelletto* of Pisa during the Pisan War caused friction with Venice. Venice then began to press Ercole to visit Venice as he used to: Ercole excused himself saying that as custodian of the *castelletto* he needed to maintain neutrality between Venice and Florence. Two years later, Venice was displeased at Ercole's eventual arbitral award. Ercole's animosity towards Venice was said to be 'passionate' in 1500, but in November 1503 he was reported to want to visit Venice, as things were going so badly with the French (email exchange with Trevor Dean, 13 April 2021).

58. Milano, *La carta*, p. 148.

59. Cortesão and Teixeira da Mota, 'Anónimo', p. 11.

60. The later history of the Cantino planisphere, conceived of as the biography of an object, is also intriguing. It must have been looted in the Modena riots of 1859, which were a part of the second war of Italian independence leading to the Unification of Italy, and spent some years as a screen in a *salsicceria* before being spotted in 1868 by the director of the Biblioteca Estense, who took it to the library, where it is still: Cortesão and Teixeira da Mota, 'Anónimo', p. 7.

as the evidence relating to them in fact derives from an earlier date? It is contained in a series of letters from March and April 1491 between two Este siblings: Ercole and Eleonora's son Alfonso and his sister Isabella: it was written, therefore, over ten years before Cantino's trip. At this time Alfonso would have been fourteen and Isabella, who was already in Mantua, married to Francesco II, the marquis, would have been sixteen—so this qualifies as correspondence between teenagers. Isabella was addicted to news of all sorts, as her youthful interest in the Portuguese discoveries indicates. She found Mantua far less congenial and well-informed than Ferrara and felt compelled to set up elaborate networks of correspondents and informants in order to keep abreast of news from elsewhere. Twenty years later she was still lamenting that Mantua was placed so far off the beaten track that 'one hears no news whatsoever' (non se intenda novella alcuna).[61]

On 18 March 1491 Alfonso sent his sister a copy of a letter from the humanist Zanobi Acciaiuoli,[62] in Florence, to the astrologer and medical doctor Antonio Arquata,[63] in Ferrara, based on information from Portugal, describing an unknown island off Guinea.[64] It is impossible to know where this was, as Guinea was imprecise as a geographical indicator, but it was somewhere on the west coast of Africa. The letter that must have accompanied this copy has not yet been found. On 9 April Alfonso followed this with a further letter and 'with drawings of the newly discovered environment, such as the people and their clothes, the "horses" [animals that are ridden], and the vegetation suitable for their sustenance' (in disegno le imagine de quella nova generatione retrovata, cussi de li homini col vestire loro, de' cavalli et de' arbori apti a le speciarie loro).[65] Unfortunately, these drawings of human, animal and vegetable life on the island

61. On Isabella and news, see Carolyn James, 'An Insatiable Appetite for News: Isabella d'Este and a Bolognese Correspondent', in F. W. Kent and Charles Zika, eds, *Religious Rituals, Images and Words: The Varieties of Cultural Experience in Late Medieval and Early Modern Europe* (Turnhout, 2005), pp. 375–88 at 381 and n. 18, Isabella to Francesco Gonzaga, 1 October 1503.

62. *DBI*, 1 (1960), pp. 93–94, entry by Abele L. Redigonda. Acciaiuoli was educated at the Medici court and was a friend of Marsilio Ficino and Angelo Poliziano. He was a cousin of Lorenzo di Pierfrancesco de' Medici.

63. *DBI*, 4 (1962), pp. 299–301, entry by Eugenio Garin.

64. ASMa, Archivio Gonzaga, b. 2190, published in Lowe, 'Africa in the News', pp. 327–28. See also Alessandro Luzio and Rodolfo Renier, 'La coltura e le relazioni letterarie di Isabella d'Este Gonzaga', *Giornale storico della letteratura italiana*, 33 (1899), pp. 1–62 at 38; Carlo Giglio and Elio Lodolini, *Guida delle fonti per la storia dell'Africa a Sud del Sahara esistenti in Italia*, vol. 1, Guide des sources de l'histoire de l'Afrique 5 (Zug, 1973), p. 422; Carnemolla, *Fonti italiane*, pp. 13–14.

65. Carnemolla, *Fonti italiane*, p. 11; cf. ASMa, Archivio Gonzaga, MS. E XXXI.2, b.n. 1185, Affari in Ferrara.

appear no longer to be extant, possibly destroyed in the sack of Mantua in 1633.[66] The words describing the representations of the 'new' lands or world are of interest. *Generatione* elsewhere can mean species or lineage, but here it seems clear that something more all-encompassing is intended: that is, not only a people, but in addition the natural world they inhabited. Similarly, *arbori* means not only trees, but any form of vegetation used in any way by humans, whether for food, clothing or building material. The text of the letter would suggest that the drawings were unusually holistic in their subject matter, depicting the interconnectedness of a society, not just singular aspects of it. The chain of communication between the siblings seems to have been interrupted by the non-arrival of one of Isabella's replies,[67] but in another of them she thanks Alfonso, saying that the drawing ('el designo', here in the singular) of the people and 'horses' pleased her 'as much as she could say', as had Alfonso's letter.[68] No other European drawings of fifteenth-century Africa are known of—which makes their loss all the more unfortunate, as it has to be assumed that they had been made by someone who was on the voyage (or at least were copies of drawings made by someone on the voyage). The fact that a fourteen-year-old and a sixteen-year-old were swapping this kind of information points to a highly sophisticated level of interest in the details of the Portuguese overseas expansion and the new aspects of life that exploration revealed. Their desire for currency, immediacy and novelty in relation to these news stories indicates that their curiosity was not a passing fad but an accepted part of their life at court.

One of the most famous known letters about Renaissance encounters between Portuguese and sub-Saharan Africans, written by Lorenzo di Giovanni Tornabuoni in Florence on 4 November 1486 to Benedetto Dei in Milan, described how that morning the author had been 'in piazza' with a group of 'nobili cittadini', including Zanobi del Nero, who read out a letter from a friend in Portugal recounting the conversion and baptism of a king in an unknown part of Guinea, an event whose consequences he judged 'good and important'.[69] The recipient of this letter, Benedetto Dei, was a career newspeddler, especially of

66. Carnemolla, *Fonti italiane*, p.18 n. 8.

67. *Isabella d'Este: Selected Letters*, ed. Deanna Shemek (Toronto, 2017), p. 41, ASMa, Archivio Gonzaga, b. 2904, libro 136, 85r–v.

68. *Isabella d'Este*, p. 41, ASMa, Archivio Gonzaga, b. 2904, libro 136, 85r–v: 'Ho recevuto in seme cum la lettera de V.S. el designo de li homini & cavalli de quella insula novamente scoperta in le parte Ghinea che me sono state tanto grate quanto se potesse dire.'

69. ASF, Corporazioni religiose soppresse 78 [Badia di Firenze], 317, no. 220. The letter is partially published in Armando F. Verde, *Lo studio fiorentino, 1473–1503: Ricerche e documenti*, 5 vols in 8 tomes (Pistoia, 1973–94), 3.1, p. 576. See also Lowe, 'Africa in the News', pp. 314, 317, 318, 319, 326.

foreign or global news, and his reach included Asia and sub-Saharan Africa. He proudly declared to one of his clients that 'da mme hogni sabato arete le nuove e d'Asia e d'Afriche e d'Europia senpre' (from me every Saturday you will always receive news from Asia, Africa and Europe).[70] Between the late 1480s and 1491, he is known to have regularly sent news of all sorts, including extra-European, to Ercole d'Este. Unfortunately, Dei's letters to Ercole are lost, although Ercole's replies are still extant,[71] as are Dei's letters to Francesco Gonzaga, the marquis of Mantua and Isabella d'Este's husband, to whom he offered the same news service.[72] Ercole's take-up of Dei's global newsletters lends further weight to the evidence of his interest in Portuguese overseas expansion and the novelties the 'new' landmasses promised.

Another smaller and less direct piece of evidence confirming that the Este court was a hub of news of the Portuguese voyages comes from entries by the chronicler of life in Cesena, Giuliano Fantaguzzi. Although the contemporary Ferrarese chroniclers Ugo Caleffini, Bernardino Zambotti and the writer of the *Diario ferrarese* for these years did not allude to the Portuguese overseas explorations, Fantaguzzi consistently included snippets relating to overseas expansion, and one possibility is that, although based in Cesena (some 100 km from Ferrara), he heard about these via the Este court. For example, in 1493 he reported that the king of Portugal, João II, had recently discovered islands that 'had never been seen before by anyone'.[73] The lure of discovering new places certainly lay at the heart of what made the Portuguese overseas expansion a news topic of supreme interest, linking textual, visual and cartographic representations; but why the Este in particular should have been bitten by this bug remains an open question, and why Ercole d'Este ordered the commission of the extraordinary Cantino chart—if he did, and Cantino did not just buy it on impulse when a possibility arose unexpectedly—as part of his interest, still remains to be explained.

Evidence of interest in objects from the Portuguese trading empire on the part of Eleonora d'Aragona, who married Ercole in 1473, provides additional

---

70. Letter from Dei to Francesco Gonzaga, in ASMa, Archivio Gonzaga, b. 1102, cited by Carolyn James, *The Letters of Giovanni Sabadino degli Arienti (1481–1510)* (Florence, 2002), p. 49.

71. James, *Letters of Giovanni Sabadino*, pp. 44, 48–50.

72. These letters in ASMa, Archivio Gonzaga, b. 1102, have not yet been checked for references to the Portuguese voyages.

73. Giuliano Fantaguzzi, *'Caos': Cronache cesenati del sec. xv di Giuliano Fantaguzzi*, ed. Dino Bazzocchi (Cesena, 1915), p. 45: 'mai più da homini vedute'.

clear proof that global curiosity cut across gender. An account book belonging to her, dating from 1478–85, rather than recording expenses, records the movement and circulation of her objects. In it are recorded three elephant tusks, two of which are described as small. One of these is made smaller by being cut in half, with one half being sent by Eleonora to messer Egano di Lambertini in Bologna, and the other half given on 10 January 1488 to her two children, Alfonso and Isabella d'Este, aged respectively eleven and thirteen.[74] Here the global bounty is shared out in pieces, in order to provide a sufficiency. Eleonora's educational investment in her children paid off, as Isabella picked up the bug, both for global objects and for anything else that could be described as new. For instance, Isabella instructed Gironimo Zigliolo—who kept many of Eleonora's account books and looked after the objects in her Guardaroba—to buy 'anything that is new and elegant' for her on a trip he undertook to France in 1491.[75] Both Eleonora d'Aragona and Isabella (that is, Ercole's wife and daughter) are known to have had enslaved black women and children in their households,[76] with Isabella's search to acquire the perfect young black child verging on an obsession;[77]

74. Leah R. Clark, *Collecting Art in the Italian Renaissance Court: Objects and Exchanges* (Cambridge, 2018), pp. 5–7 and 235 n. 4

75. Ibid., p. 10.

76. It is now standard, particularly in the US, to capitalise 'Black' where it refers to ethnicity/ethnic group identity, thus rendering it equivalent, above all in dignity, to terms such as 'Hispanic', 'Native American' or 'Asian' applied to people of Asian descent outside Asia. The reasoning behind this is that Black people self-identify primarily by ethnicity. The word 'black/Black' occurs with great frequency in this book, since the European reception of West Africans in the fifteenth and sixteenth centuries is a major and recurrent theme; but it is often not easy to distinguish between 'black/Black' used to refer to ethnicity, and the same word used to refer to skin colour. For the Europeans under discussion, provenance, and thereby ethnicity, was largely ignored or insignificant, whereas skin colour was a matter of fascination. The other concern with regard to capitalisation is that of anachronism: it is difficult to decide in some cases the extent to which the application of twenty-first-century and predominantly North American sensibilities to a Renaissance European context is and feels appropriate. I considered using both lower case and capitals, before deciding to standardise and stay close to the original meanings of my texts by using lower-case 'black' throughout. I should like to thank Francis Eaves for his helpful clarity with regard to this issue.

77. Kate Lowe, 'Isabella d'Este and the Acquisition of Black Slaves at the Mantuan Court', in Philippa Jackson and Guido Rebecchini, eds, *Mantova e il rinascimento italiano: Studi in onore di David S. Chambers*, (Mantua, 2011), pp. 65–76, esp. 74; Paul H. D. Kaplan, 'Isabella d'Este and Black African Women', in T. F. Earle and K.J.P. Lowe, eds, *Black Africans in Renaissance Europe* (Cambridge, 2005), pp. 125–54; Alessandro Luzio and Rodolfo Renier, 'Buffoni, nani e schiavi dei Gonzaga ai tempi d'Isabella d'Este', *Nuova antologia di scienze, lettere ed arti*, ser. 3, 34 (1891), pp. 618–50 and 35 (1891), pp. 112–46. The section on slaves is in 35 (1891), pp. 137–45.

but as yet there is no way of knowing whether she perceived or understood the link between black skin and voyages to Africa in anything but the most superficial way. Her first documented 'ownership' of a black child (*moretta*) dates from June 1491, so only a few months after her exchange of letters with Zigliolo.[78]

A final characteristic proclaims the Este as global consumers: they revelled in ownership of exotic, non-European animals, many from the Portuguese trading empire. Creating menageries in Europe was originally a royal or princely activity that simultaneously proclaimed élite status, parity with peers and dominion over nature.[79] Rulers of city states in Italy emulated the practice whenever possible, aided by the arrival of previously unknown or rare animals, predominantly but not exclusively from the Portuguese overseas territories.[80] The Este were noted for their leopards (*Panthera pardus*), available both in sub-Saharan Africa and in Asia,[81] and were known to have lions (*Panthera leo*),[82] as did most northern Italian rulers. The Este menageries extended to civets, which effectively became available in Europe only when the Portuguese started to sail down the West African coast, and to parrots, and, more unusually, Eleonora d'Aragona kept an ostrich (*Struthio camelus*), first in the palace of Belfiore and then at the Castello in Ferrara, one of whose eggs she sent to her husband in 1479.[83] Ercole was twice offered an elephant of unknown origin—maybe he was offered the same animal on two different occasions—but both

78. Lowe, 'Isabella d'Este', pp. 67–68.

79. Gustave Loisel, *Histoire des menageries de l'Antiquité à nos jours*, 3 vols (Paris, 1912), 1 (*Antiquité. Moyen Âge. Renaissance*).

80. For obvious reasons, the Portuguese monarchs in the late fifteenth and sixteenth centuries had enviable collections of these animals: Annemarie Jordan Gschwend, 'The Portuguese Quest for Exotic Animals', in *Cortejo triunfal com girafas: Animais exóticos ao serviço do poder/ Triumphal Procession with Giraffes: Exotic Animals at the Service of Power*, ed. Jessica Hallett, exh. cat., A Fundação Ricardo do Espírito Santo Silva, Lisbon (Lisbon, 2009), pp. 32–42; Almudena Pérez de Tudela and Annemarie Jordan Gschwend, 'Renaissance Menageries: Exotic Animals and Pets at the Habsburg Courts in Iberia and Central Europe', in Karl A. E. Enenkel and Paul J. Smith, eds, *Early Modern Zoology: The Construction of Animals in Science, Literature and the Visual Arts*, 2 vols (Leiden, 2007), 2, pp. 419–47 at 421–32.

81. Thomas Tuohy, *Herculean Ferrara: Ercole d'Este, 1471–1505, and the Invention of a Ducal Capital* (Cambridge, 1996), pp. 245–46.

82. Giuseppe Pardi, ed., *Diario ferrarese dall'anno 1409 sino al 1502 di autori incerti*, RIS/2, 24.7 (Bologna, 1928–33), p. 39.

83. Tuohy, *Herculean Ferrara*, pp. 60, 245, 346–47. It is not known where the ostrich at the Este court originated; it could have come from north or sub-Saharan Africa. See also Daniela Sogliani, 'Le meraviglie del mondo: Animali, fiori e altre curiosità esotiche nelle "banche dati

times circumstances intervened to impede his purchase. Suggesting that price may have fluctuated with demand, the price asked for the pachyderm varied from eight thousand to twenty thousand ducats.[84]

Continuing Interest in Mantua

Returning briefly to Mantua in the first decade of the sixteenth century, there is later proof that Isabella d'Este's interest in the Portuguese imperial world was not a passing fad, and continued beyond her teenage years. In a letter dated 2 January 1505 to Floramonte Brognolo, an apostolic protonotary and Gonzaga agent in Rome, Isabella described a pair of globes, one terrestrial and the other celestial, that stood in the *libreria* of Pope Julius II.[85] This could either have been the room used by Julius for his own personal library, before he commissioned Raphael in 1509 to paint what is now called the Stanza della segnatura (according to the humanist programme worked out by him and his advisors), or the more public library below,[86] but is more likely to have been the former. Lorenzo de' Medici's pair of globes (see below) also stood in his *libreria*, making it likely that the *libreria* was thought to be the most appropriate place for this category of object that could be seen as a visual reference tool. Title-pages and frontispieces of early sixteenth-century printed books back up this hypothesis.[87] Placing globes in a *libreria* also emphasised the Renaissance link between the textual and the visual in relation to overseas voyages. It has been proposed, however, that Isabella might have wanted the globes to place them in a room with city views, and this too would have been an apt and thoughtful pairing of

Gonzaga", in Andrea Canova and Daniela Sogliani, eds, *I Gonzaga tra Oriente e Occidente: Viaggi, scoperte geografiche e meraviglie esotiche* (Mantua, 2022), pp. 97–112 at 98.

84. Tuohy, *Herculean Ferrara*, pp. 346 and 351 n. 62.

85. Matteo Fiorini, *Sfere terrestri e celesti di autore italiano oppure fatte o conservate in Italia* (Rome, 1899), pp. 83–84; Carnemolla, *Fonti italiane*, 'Un mappamondo per Isabella d'Este e Federico Gonzaga', pp. 92–96; Molly Bourne, *Francesco II Gonzaga: The Soldier-Prince as Patron* (Rome, 2008), pp. 251, 415.

86. John Shearman, *The Vatican Stanze: Functions and Decoration* (= 'Italian Lecture', from *Proceedings of the British Academy*, 57 [1971], pp. 3–58) (London, 1972), pp. 3–58 at 14 and 16; Paul Taylor, 'Julius II and the Stanza della Segnatura', *Journal of the Warburg and Courtauld Institutes*, 72 (2009), pp. 103–41, esp. 105–8.

87. Edward Luther Stevenson, *Terrestrial and Celestial Globes: Their History and Construction, including a Consideration of Their Value as Aids in the Study of Geography and Astronomy*, 2 vols (repr., New York, 1971 [1921]), 1, pp. 60–61.

two different types of object relating to the geography and topography of travel.[88] Although from Isabella's letter it sounds as though she must have seen the globes, she did not go to Rome until 1514,[89] and so must have received comprehensive notice of them from a relative, friend or agent. In the early sixteenth century globes could be constructed in three different ways: from metal, with the map engraved on its surface; as a 'composition fashioned into a ball over a mould' on which strips of parchment or paper were pasted with hand-drawn sections of world maps; or as a ball of wood, with the map once again in manuscript on top of it.[90] The globes in the letter were *solide*, so could have been either of the last two options.

Described by Isabella as a 'cosa singolare' and on the understanding that they were very correct in their depiction, Isabella made clear she coveted Julius's globes and was firmly determined to acquire a similar pair. The correctness of their depiction must have been a reference to their incorporation of the most up-to-date information about the Portuguese voyages.[91] The globes were on feet approximately two *braccia* high,[92] and were under the safe-keeping of the superior of the library, revealing that they were considered precious. The difficulty and cost of having copies made indicates just how precious they were. Initially Brognolo told Isabella that the copies of the two globes would cost forty ducats, saying it would cost much less to make a copy on paper of another *tela* or canvas (presumably a different *mappamondo*).[93] On 20 February

88. Clifford M. Brown, 'Francesco Bonsignori: Painter to the Gonzaga Court—New Documents', *Atti e memorie della Accademia virgiliana di Mantova*, n.s. 47 (1979), pp. 81–96 at 85 and 94 n. 14.

89. Julia Cartwright, *Isabella d'Este, Marchioness of Mantua, 1474–1539: A Study of the Renaissance*, 2 vols (London, 1904), 2, p. 110. On her trip, see Alessandro Luzio, 'Isabella d'Este ne' primordi del papato di Leone X e il suo viaggio a Roma nel 1514–1515', *Archivio storico lombardo*, ser. 4, 6 (1906), pp. 99–180, 454–89; Clifford M. Brown, '"Lo insaciabile desiderio nostro de cose antique": New Documents on Isabella d'Este's Collection of Antiquities', in Cecil H. Clough, ed., *Cultural Aspects of the Italian Renaissance: Essays in Honour of Paul Oskar Kristeller* (Manchester, 1976), pp. 324–53 at 335; Carolyn James, 'Marriage by Correspondence: Politics and Domesticity in the Letters of Isabella d'Este and Francesco Gonzaga, 1490–1519', *Renaissance Quarterly*, 65.2 (2012), pp. 321–52 at 342–43.

90. Stevenson, *Terrestrial and Celestial Globes*, 1, p. 59.

91. Carnemolla, *Fonti italiane*, p. 92: 'intendimo essere iustissime'.

92. F. W. Clarke, *Weights, Measures and Money of All Nations* (New York, 1891), p. 63 calculated that a *braccio* in Rome was 30.73 inches, so two *braccia* would be 61.46 inches, or 1.56 metres.

93. Bourne, *Francesco II Gonzaga*, pp. 417–18.

Isabella stuck to her guns and agreed to the forty ducats.[94] However, six weeks later the estimate had rocketed out of control, and Isabella was being quoted two hundred ducats for copies of both globes, a price that included all the materials and the feet, or one hundred and fifty ducats for the *palle* alone, by a former pupil of the maker of the original pair called 'Ioanne Florentino'. Most interesting was Brognolo's statement that Ioanne had told him a friend of his in Florence had two globes like the ones in the *libreria*, and he thought that his friend would sell them,[95] as this points both to Florentine manufacture and the existence of multiple copies. Poor Isabella's nerve failed and she asked what the price of the terrestrial globe alone would be. On 23 May Brognolo replied that a copy on canvas of the *mappamondo* on the terrestrial globe, but without its underlying sphere, would cost twenty or twenty-five ducats; alternatively the whole terrestrial globe, as originally requested and including everything, would cost a hundred ducats.[96] The outcome of this protracted attempt at acquisition is unfortunately unclear. But it has been suggested that the celestial globe of the pair belonging to Julius has survived in the Vatican collections and can be identified as being of the hollow ball variety.[97] If this is correct, and both types of world map (globe and *mappamondo*) were hand-drawn on parchment or cloth, the disparity in price must relate to the other materials needed for the manufacture of the globe and its supporting structures.

The parrot mania that infected the Este court can be found also in a letter from Federico II Gonzaga, Isabella's son, to one of his most trusted and used agents, Jacopo Suardi, called Suardino,[98] dated 12 July 1525. He instructed him to try as hard as possible to obtain a parrot 'che sia in tutta excellentia' (that is excellent in all respects), a formulation that undoubtedly included an insistence on the ability to speak. This is confirmed by Federigo's next request, for an additional four or five parrots that in contradistinction 'non sano parlare' (don't know how to speak), at a good price, to join the other birds of various sorts in the aviary at Marmirolo.[99]

94. Ibid., p. 418.

95. Ibid., p. 419.

96. Ibid., p. 420.

97. Francesco Denza, 'Globi celesti della Specola Vaticana', in *Pubblicazioni della Specola Vaticana*, vol. 4 (Turin, 1894), pp. xvii–xxiii at xvii–xix; Fiorini, *Sfere terrestri*, pp. 85–87; Stevenson, *Terrestrial and Celestial Globes*, 1, p. 63.

98. Bourne, *Francesco II Gonzaga*, p. 52, and Sogliani, 'Meraviglie del mondo', pp. 102–3.

99. Daniela Ferrari, ed., *Giulio Romano: Repertorio di fonti documentarie*, 2 vols (Mantua, 1992), 1, pp. 90–91.

The Medici and Portuguese Overseas Expansion

There is also evidence for interest in the Portuguese overseas expansion on the part of the Medici (and others in Medicean Florence), although this has never been systematically examined. In the absence of an obvious corpus of written material or words—there are only fleeting references to maps and globes rather than comments about the latest geographical expansions—demonstrating Medici engagement at a distance, evidence has been gleaned from actions involving acquisition or possession. One way in is to examine ownership of world maps: as with the Cantino map, current ones in the late fifteenth or first decade of the sixteenth century were sought after because they were based on the newest geographical information from the Portuguese overseas voyages. The most famous *mappamondo* or world map in fifteenth-century Florence—the map that has generated the most academic discussion—is the one owned by Francesco di Matteo Castellani. In July 1459, that is, while Cosimo il vecchio de' Medici was de facto ruler of Florence, Castellani wrote a note in *Quaternuccio B*, which was a mixture of an account book and journal, that he had lent his 'big, illustrated, fully finished *mappamondo*' (el mio mappamundo grande storiato e compiuto di tucto) to maestro Paolo dal Pozzo Toscanelli, who wanted to show it to certain ambassadors from the king of Portugal. It was agreed that it would be returned a few days later, in good condition. Instead, the *mappamondo* was returned over twenty-five years later, on 2 February 1485, by the *nepote* of maestro Paolo, 'rather spoilt and worn' (alquanto guasto e stazonato).[100] It had probably spent the intervening years with the Toscanelli, but why it was suddenly returned after a twenty-five year gap is less clear. Who were these Portuguese ambassadors? Over a century ago Carlo Carnesecchi suggested that they had accompanied Gian Galeazzo Sforza or Pope Pius II, both of whom went to Florence in 1459.[101] The most likely candidate is João Fernandes de Silveira, an ambassador or emissary sent by Afonso V of Portugal to Italy between 1456 to 1460, who was with Pius II in Siena in May 1459.[102] Known to have spent time

100. Francesco di Matteo Castellani, *Ricordanze, II: Quaternuccio e Giornale B (1459–1485)*, ed. Giovanni Ciappelli (Florence, 1995), p. 33.

101. Carlo Carnesecchi, 'Paolo Toscanelli e gli ambasciatori del Re di Portogallo nel 1459', *Archivio storico italiano*, ser. 5, 21 (1898), pp. 316–18 at 317.

102. Eric Apfelstadt, 'Bishop and Pawn: New Documents for the Chapel of the Cardinal of Portugal at S. Miniato al Monte, Florence', in K.J.P. Lowe, ed., *Cultural Links between Portugal and Italy in the Renaissance* (Oxford, 2000), pp. 183–223 at 196.

in Florence,[103] he could easily have gone on there on this occasion. But he was only one ambassador, and the Castellani note specifies more than one. Also present in Florence in July 1459 was the distinguished, predominantly Portuguese, household of Cardinal Jaime of Portugal (the son of Prince Pedro, and grandson of King João I of Portugal), who died in the city on 27 August, having been attended by, amongst others, Paolo dal Pozzo Toscanelli;[104] and members of this retinue could also have been categorised as 'certain ambassadors from the king of Portugal'.[105] The ambassadors' objective in looking at the map was presumably to check and assimilate the most up-to-date cartographic information relating to the Portuguese advances in exploration and conquest along the African coast. Not only were these advances one of the most important issues of King Afonso V's reign, underpinned by papal bulls securing future territories for the Portuguese both spiritually and politically, but cosmography and cartography also offered a particularly fertile type of information exchange between Portugal and some of the Italian city states.[106] If Fernandes de Silveira was indeed one of the ambassadors, he had been in Italy since 1456. Unfortunately, there is no evidence that in this time he had seen Fra Mauro's *mappamondo* at San Michele di Murano in Venice, and the Castellani map might have been the most up-to-date approximation to it he could have found. On 24 April 1459 a copy of the Fra Mauro *mappamondo* had left Venice for Lisbon with Stefano Trevisan, and final payment for it on behalf of Afonso V was made by his ambassador or emissary, Fernandes de Silveira; but although this is an interesting piece of information, it is not proof in itself that Silveira had been in Venice.[107]

103. On Silveira's career and time spent in Italy, see Rau, 'Bartolomeo di Iacopo di Ser Vanni', p. 109 n. 36.

104. Apfelstadt, 'Bishop and Pawn', pp. 188–89; Giovanni Ciappelli, 'Carte geografiche e politica nei rapporti tra Firenze e il Portogallo nel Quattrocento', *Annali dell'Istituto storico italo-germanico in Trento/Jahrbuch des italienisch-deutschen historischen Instituts in Trient*, 32 (2006), pp. 47–70 at 65–66.

105. Ciappelli, 'Carte geografiche', pp. 56–57.

106. Angelo Cattaneo, *Fra Mauro's Mappa Mundi and Fifteenth-Century Venice* (Turnhout, 2011), pp. 49–51.

107. The precise date of the payment is unknown. The ambassador's expenses in connection with the map were repaid on 3 February 1462: João Martins da Silva Marques, ed., *Descobrimentos portugueses*, 3 vols (Lisbon, 1944–71), 3, pp. 19–21; Apfelstadt, 'Bishop and Pawn', p. 196; Cattaneo, *Fra Mauro's Mappa Mundi*, pp. 48 and 334–35, doc. 9.

It has often been claimed that the Castellani *mappamondo* is a world map previously owned by the Medici and now in the Biblioteca nazionale in Florence (Portolano 1),[108] and that it was used by Christopher Columbus.[109] These claims are now deemed unlikely. Nor does it seem probable that the note refers to a *mappamondo* painted on linen that was already owned by the Castellani in 1429,[110] for a map of that date would not have been of much interest to Portuguese ambassadors in 1459. *Carte da navigare* or sailing charts and portolans, following the opening up of sea routes, had always been part of the collections of landlubbers and were enjoyed by them from the safety of their own homes, and they and their global cousins, *mappemondo*, while not common in fifteenth-century Florence, were not exceptional in patrician or scholarly households (often with links to the Medici),[111] being owned by people such as Francesco Sassetti, the general manager of the Medici bank,[112] and the philosopher Pico della Mirandola, who was one of Lorenzo de' Medici's protégés.[113] Occasionally the routes whereby they reached Florence are known: in June 1473, for example, a *carta da navigare* was imported from Lisbon into Florence for the Portuguese Afonso Eanes (called Alfonso Iannis in Italian) via the Cambini bank.[114] As the remit of these charts and world maps

108. Nearly everything about his world map is contested: date, purpose, place of composition. See Destombes, *Mappemondes AD 1200–1500*, pp. 222–23; and Ciappelli, 'Carte geografiche', pp. 53–55.

109. The ball was set rolling by Sebastiano Crinò, 'La scoperta della carta originale di Paolo dal Pozzo Toscanelli che servì di guida a Cristoforo Colombo per il viaggio verso il Nuovo Mondo', *L'Universo*, 22 (1941), pp. 379–410. See Angelo Cattaneo, ed., *Mappa mundi 1457: Carta conservata presso la Biblioteca nazionale centrale di Firenze con la segnatura Portolano 1; Introduzione e commento* (Rome, 2008), pp. 51–56.

110. Giovanni Ciappelli, 'Introduzione', in Francesco di Matteo Castellani, *Ricordanze, II: Quaternuccio e Giornale B (1459–1485)*, ed. Giovanni Ciappelli (Florence, 1995), pp. 1–24 at 16.

111. Armando F. Verde, 'Libri tra le pareti domestiche: Una necessaria appendice a *Lo studio fiorentino, 1473–1503*', in *Tradizione medievale e innovazione umanistica a Firenze nei secoli XV–XVI (Memorie domenicane*, n.s. 18 [1987]), pp. 1–225 at 118, 176 and 197 for *carte da navigare* and *mappemondo* listed in Pupilli inventories.

112. Albinia de la Mare, 'The Library of Francesco Sassetti (1421–1490)', in C. H. Clough, ed., *Cultural Aspects of the Italian Renaissance: Essays in Honour of Paul Oscar Kristeller* (Manchester, 1976), pp. 160–201 at 173.

113. Pearl Kibre, *The Library of Pico della Mirandola* (New York, 1936), p. 187, no. 509; On Pico, see *DBI*, 83 (2015), pp. 268–75, entry by Franco Bacchelli, at 270: 'Lorenzo il Magnifico che sempre ammirò, amò e protese Pico'.

114. Florence, AOIF, 12689, fol. 170v, 25 June 1473. Eanes died in Ferrara on 22 August 1473, and a post-mortem inventory of the goods Eanes had left in the house of Francesco Cambini

increased to incorporate parts of the world brought into the European lime-
light by the activities of the Portuguese trading empire, Florentines too could
enjoy the global expansion offered by the voyages of others, simply by acquiring up-to-date examples. Unfortunately, however, there is a mismatch between the references to *mappemondo* in inventories and account books, and
extant examples now in Florence.[115]

Previously, Lorenzo de' Medici's interest has been assumed to be slight, with
the excuse given that he was almost wholly consumed by political affairs on the
Italian peninsula and did not have time or energy left to follow the unfolding
global changes. Difference in interest between Ercole d'Este and Lorenzo de'
Medici could be explained by the difference in political structure between
the two polities: Ferrara was a dukedom and Florence was a republic, and the
political priorities of dukedoms and republics differed, with dukes freer and
more able to indulge their personal enthusiasms openly. However, on closer
examination it becomes abundantly clear that Lorenzo was also making rather
strenuous efforts to follow Portuguese progress round the world. One crucial
piece of evidence for this is his almost certain commissioning of a copy of Fra
Mauro's *mappamondo* from San Michele di Murano (Plates 6 and 7).[116] If this
is correct, copies of Fra Mauro's map in Venice would have been made both
for Afonso V of Portugal in Lisbon in the 1450s and for Lorenzo de' Medici in
Florence, most probably in the 1470s. Afonso cannot have seen the original
and must have commissioned his copy on the basis of reports by others who
had seen it. Although Lorenzo went to Venice briefly at the beginning of
May 1465,[117] it is unlikely that he saw the original, but it would perhaps have
been possible for him to see a copy in Palazzo ducale, which might have

---

in Florence of that year includes a *mappa*, which is probably the Lisbon one. ASF, Monastero
dell'Arcangelo Raffaello 17 (Libro de' frati di S. Miniato), 13r: 'Item tolsi da Fruosino Calderini
1ª mappa'. See also Frederick Hartt, Gino Corti and Clarence Kennedy, *The Chapel of the Cardinal of Portugal 1434–1459 at San Miniato in Florence* (Philadelphia, 1964), p. 46 n. 25 and p. 62.

115. On extant world maps in Florence in manuscript copies of Ptolemy's 'Cosmographia',
Gregorio Dati's 'La sfera' and a world map in a manuscript copy of Henricus Martellus Germa-
nus's 'Insularium illustratum', all from the fifteenth century, see Destombes, *Mappemondes
AD 1200–1500*, pp. 247–51.

116. Cattaneo, *Fra Mauro's Mappa Mundi*, p. 59. Various factors make it almost certain that
Lorenzo was the Medici responsible for the commission. One relates to dating: a Delfino letter
of 1494 makes it clear that Delfino had carried out the Latin translations of the legends for the
map before he left Venice for Camaldoli in 1480.

117. André Rochon, *La Jeunesse de Laurent de Médicis (1449–1478)* (Paris, 1963), pp. 75–76.

whetted his appetite for ownership. Luigi Pulci wrote to him on 27 April 1465 saying how inspiring Venice would be ('Tu vedrai cose degne et varie di che suole volentieri pascersi il tuo ingegno'), and the visit was obviously considered educational in the broadest sense.[118] Lorenzo's map (if indeed it was his) was copied from the original by Florentine painters,[119] but it was a version with a significant difference, because instead of the legends appearing in the Italian vernacular, as they did in the original, they were translated into Latin by Pietro Dolfin—prior of San Michele di Murano until 1480—at some point before his departure from the post.[120] Fra Mauro's *mappamondo* included a far greater proportion of lengthy legends to coastal outlines than most maps of its time, giving the texts a particular resonance, as can be seen from its representation of the continent of Africa, still largely unknown to Europeans (Plate 7). The message seems to be clear: the full import of the map could not be understood without reading the written inserts. In May 1494 the copy with Latin legends was in Palazzo Medici on via Larga in Florence, but trying to access it to take copies of its Latin legends, as the subsequent Camaldolese prior of San Michele, Bernardino Gadolo, wanted Dolfin to do, was awkward. Florence was riven by internal faction and Piero de' Medici's expulsion lay only a few months in the future.[121] The presence of the copy of the Fra Mauro *mappamondo* in the Medici family palace can be interpreted as proof that the link between political power and representations of power through possession of territory was strong—and that Lorenzo, if he were the commissioner of the work, was indeed following Portuguese expansion, even if with a time lag and at a distance.

There is further evidence of cartographic curiosity on Lorenzo's part in connection with the Portuguese expansion down the west coast of Africa. Correspondence between Lorenzo and Niccolò Michelozzi and Giovanni Antonio d'Arezzo, two envoys of his in Rome, in December 1489 and January 1490 (that is, more than ten years before Lunardo Masser's deployment by Venice in Lisbon in 1502, and more than fifteen years before Alberto Cantino's deployment by Ercole d'Este in Lisbon in 1506) reveals Lorenzo's ownership of a number of maps of the West African coastline, and that these maps were a topic of conversation in the eternal city. This is proof that Lorenzo's interest in the Portuguese

118. ASF, MAP, XX, 150.

119. Venice, Biblioteca nazionale Marciana, MS. Lat. XI, 92 (= 3828), p. 503, cited in Cattaneo, *Fra Mauro's Mappa Mundi*, p. 58 and n. 90.

120. Cattaneo, *Fra Mauro's Mappa Mundi*, pp. 57–64.

121. Ibid., p. 58.

voyages was well known at the time, even outside Florence. According to the correspondence, the cardinal of Venice, Marco Barbo, was having painted in his palace a *mappamondo* 'di gran compasso' (large-scale) that amongst other things included 'quelli nuovi paesi di Ghinea' (the new[ly found] countries of Guinea), and Barbo thought that Lorenzo had maps with 'newer' or more up-to-date information.[122] What this *mappamondo* consisted of is open to question. An original *mappamondo* was painted between 1464 and 1469, almost certainly by Girolamo Bellavista of Venice, for Pietro Barbo (Pope Paul II),[123] who was Marco Barbo's patron, even though they were only distantly related. This *mappamondo*—according to Dengel on canvas and according to Rosen a fresco[124]—graced the walls of Pietro Barbo's palace, Palazzo Venezia, which was later inhabited by Marco Barbo—and Marco Barbo twenty years later can be observed in action gathering the most recent information about western Africa, either to update the previous map, or to include it on a further distinct, but unknown, large *mappamondo*.[125] The original map from the 1460s had disappeared by the beginning of the eighteenth century; the last reference to it dates to 1683.[126] There are no other known references to a map from 1489/90.

In 1489 Marco Barbo had given the two envoys 'un poco di disegno dell'ultimo paese trovato' (a little sketch of the most recent place reached),[127] and they in turn had sent this sketch on to Lorenzo in order to ascertain whether Lorenzo had superior, more recent information. Guinea in this context may be understood to mean anywhere on the coast of West Africa[128]— and this could be a reference to the territory 'discovered' on one of Diogo Cão's three voyages to Kongo in 1482, 1483–84 and 1485–86.[129] Lorenzo replied

122. 'il cardinale [. . .] pensa che voi habbiate qualche cosa più nuova': Lorenzo de' Medici, *Lettere*, vol. 16: *Settembre 1489–febbraio 1490*, ed. Lorenz Böninger (Florence, 2011), p. 273 and n. 14. See also Lorenz Böninger, 'Don Niccolò Germano e Arrigo Martello: Due cartografi tedeschi nella Firenze del Quattrocento', *Geostorie*, 21.1–2 (2013), pp. 9–20 at 9.

123. Ignazio F. Dengel, 'Sulla mappamundi di palazzo Venezia', *Archivio della Società romana di storia patria*, 52 (1929), pp. 501–8 at 505–6.

124. Ibid., p. 506; Rosen, *Mapping of Power*, p. 64.

125. Federico Hermanin, 'La sala del mappamondo nel palazzo di Venezia', *Dedalo*, 11 (1930–31), pp. 457–81 at 461 discusses the placement of the map within the room.

126. Dengel, 'Sulla mappamundi', p.507 and n. 3.

127. [Lorenzo de'] Medici, *Lettere*, vol. 16, , p. 273 n. 14.

128. On possible meanings of this word, see Lowe, 'Africa in the News' pp. 315–16.

129. Lowe, 'Africa in the News', p. 316; Carmen M. Radulet, 'As viagens de descobrimento de Diogo Cão: Nova proposta de interpretação', *Mare Liberum* 1 (1990), pp. 175–204. See also Anthony Disney, *A History of Portugal and the Portuguese Empire*, 2 vols (Cambridge, 2009), 2, p. 37.

to his envoys that he had set the two side by side, but that a comparison had on the contrary revealed that Barbo's sketch contained many more *luoghi* or places than his, and that his only contained four of the places that were included on Barbo's. In this letter, written on Christmas Eve 1489, Lorenzo used the word *charta* in the singular, and did not allude to any others. Spurred by this, Lorenzo promised to look for another map to try to help Barbo in his quest for the most up-to-date information about the West African coast.

In a further letter written to Michelozzi and d'Arezzo in Rome later on the same day, Lorenzo asked them to tell Barbo that he had found a new map of the recently 'discovered' places in Guinea, and that he would send it to him in Rome. An additional map he had of this area had disappeared, he continued, but he thought it would be re-found.[130] After Christmas, the exchange picked up again. On 11 January 1490 Lorenzo wrote that either that day or the next he would send the map of Guinea to Rome for Marco Barbo; he asked that after Barbo had seen it, it should be sent back to Florence. By 25 January the two envoys reported that the map had arrived, they had shown it to Barbo, and that he had been very pleased; he hoped his *mappamondo* would be a very useful cosmographical tool.[131] Rather surprisingly, perhaps, details of the African section of a painted *mappamondo* which is unfortunately no longer extant in Palazzo Venezia in Rome could, if it were still there, be traced back, at least in part, to maps of western Africa owned by Lorenzo de' Medici.

This is not the only evidence of Lorenzo's interest. Two other snippets from 1489 and 1490 confirm that he was actively using all his contacts to try to procure the most up-to-date maps of Guinea available. Maps may have appeared to offer the securest form of information about the Portuguese voyages. Contacts ranged from members of his family to foreign ambassadors and Medici bank associates or agents living abroad, as it was not obvious where the best maps might be. The first snippet dates to before Barbo's request and the previous exchange, occurring in a letter of 16 December 1489 written by Stefano de Castrocaro in Pisa to Bernardo Dovizi in Florence. Lorenzo had obviously

---

It is unlikely to be a reference to the territory surveyed by Bartolomeo Dias's rounding of the Cape of Good Hope in 1488, as there is only one known reference to Dias's voyages in Italy, on a planisphere by Francesco Rosselli, dated to 1492–93, although it is from Florence: see Ilaria Luzzana Caraci, 'Il viaggio di Bartolomeu Dias nella storia della cultura geografica italiana', in *Congresso internacional Bartolomeu Dias e a sua época: Actas*, 5 vols (Porto, 1989), 2, pp. 223–36 at 223–26.

130. [Lorenzo de'] Medici, *Lettere*, vol. 16, pp. 278–79.

131. Ibid., p. 321.

asked whether his son Cardinal Giovanni de' Medici had a *mappamondo*, to which the reply was only 'an old and very tatty one' left behind in Pisa after his departure, which was now in messer Carlo's house. Dovizi was welcome to look at it and show it to Lorenzo if that was what he wanted.[132] The second is from a few months after the exchange concerning Barbo's *mappamondo*. Philippe de Commynes wrote to Lorenzo on 21 April 1490 from Monsoreau in the Loire, saying he had spoken to Cosimo Sassetti about a map of Guinea, of which he had a 'double'.[133] Lorenzo must have been trying to acquire it. At around the same date of c. 1490 Henricus Martellus, one of the cartographers in Lorenzo's orbit, produced the maps for the codex of Ptolemy's 'Cosmographia' now in the Biblioteca nazionale in Florence (Magl. XIII, 16). The verso of the first sheet contains a description of its contents explaining that Ptolemy's 'Cosmographia' is joined with updated tables of all the harbours and coasts, to include both those known already by the ancients, which had always formed a part of the work, and those recently discovered by the king of Portugal ('a rege Portus Galli nuper repertis').[134] The ever-increasing extent of Portuguese territorial power was being closely followed in Florence by Lorenzo and his circle, and its reach was being reproduced in a variety of different textual and cartographic formats.

More evidence of Lorenzo's close monitoring of King João II's exploits is provided by the correspondence of the humanist scholar Angelo Poliziano.[135] A cluster of three related letters not only explicitly points to Lorenzo's awareness of and admiration for João II, but also reveals one of the conduits bringing information about him to Florence from Lisbon. Luís, Álvaro[136] and Tristão,[137] three sons of the chancellor of Portugal, João Teixeira, had been sent to

132. ASF, MAP, CXXIV, 283, fol. 323r–v.

133. J. Kervyn de Lettenhove, ed., *Lettres et négociations de Philippe de Commines*, 3 vols in 2 tomes (Brussels, 1868), tome 2, p. 79.

134. Cattaneo, *Fra Mauro's Mappa Mundi*, p. 61 n. 95.

135. Poliziano was one of several humanists who engaged with the Portuguese voyages, often in a glorifying fashion: Radulet, 'Coleccionar e conservar', p. 235. See also, for general background, K.J.P. Lowe, ed., *Cultural Links between Portugal and Italy in the Renaissance* (Oxford, 2000).

136. The middle brother Álvaro continued to exploit Medici connections and was later part of the *famiglia* of Cardinal Giovanni de' Medici, the future Pope Leo X: António Domingues de Sousa Costa, 'Estudos superiores e universitários em Portugal no reinado de D. João II', *Biblos*, 63 (1987), pp. 253–334 at 268.

137. Verde, *Lo studio fiorentino, 1473–1503*, 3, 1, pp. 56, 53, and 3, 2, p. 923. Luís attended classes between 1488 and 1492.

Florence to be tutored by Poliziano,[138] and all three (even though Tristão would only have been about twelve years old) probably attended Poliziano's lectures on Pliny the Elder's *Historia naturalis* during 1489–90. The evidence for this is provided by an extant copy now in the Biblioteca Nacional in Lisbon of the 1480 edition of this work published in Parma by Andrea Portilia, owned and signed by Tristão, which was probably used by all three brothers, and has notations in a number of hands. Book VIII, on land animals, starts with elephants, and includes a discussion of whether tusks are horns or teeth— 'cornua vel dentes'—which is picked up in the notations (Fig. 4).[139]

Poliziano admits that he has obtained his knowledge of the Portuguese imperial achievements in Africa from the Teixeira brothers. Given his close relationship with Lorenzo—he had entered Lorenzo's household about 1473 when he was under twenty[140]—it is very likely that Lorenzo would have met these Portuguese siblings too, and certain that he would have been party to this information. In an undated letter to João II thought to be of either 1489 or 1490,[141] which is effectively an encomium, Poliziano compares João's imperial achievements to those of Alexander and of the Romans, inserting him into a triumphant imperial genealogy. But this encomium also has an imperialising Christian twist, as Poliziano states that João is the champion of the Christian faith, converting previously unknown monarchs who eagerly received the sacrament. He ends the letter by writing that it was Lorenzo de' Medici's admiration for João that had lit his own. The two other letters in the cluster are dated: Poliziano wrote to João Teixeira on 17 August 1489, and João II wrote to Poliziano on 23 October 1491.[142]

138. Angelo Poliziano, *Opera quae quidem extitere hactenus omnia* (Basel, 1553), Book 10, pp. 138–40.

139. Vincenzo Fera, 'Studenti portoghesi alle lezioni del Poliziano su Plinio nel 1489–90: L'INC 462 della BNP', in Ana María S. Tarrío, *Leitores dos clássico: Portugal e Itália, séculos xv e xvi; Uma geografia do primeiro humanismo em Portugal* (Lisbon, 2015), pp. 13–18 at 15–16. On Andrea Portilia's publication of Pliny's *Historia naturalis*, see Roberto Lasagni, *L'arte tipografica in Parma*, 2 vols (Parma, 2013–16), 1, *Da Portilia agli Ugoleto (1471–1528)*, p. 270. There are twenty-eight known extant copies, in Italy, the UK, France, Spain, Portugal, Germany, the Vatican, Australia and the US. For the text, see Pliny the Elder, *Natural History*, with an English translation by H. Rackham, 10 vols (Cambridge, MA, 1956–63), 3, Loeb Classical Library 353, pp. 6 and 7 (Book VIII.iv.7).

140. *DBI*, 2 (1960), pp. 691–702, entry by Emilio Bigi.

141. Poliziano, *Opera omnia*, Book 10, pp. 136–38; Jean-Marc Mandosio, 'Ange Politien et les "autres mondes": L'attitude d'un humaniste florentin au xvᵉ siècle face aux explorations portugaises', *Médiévales*, 58.1 (2010), pp. 27–42 at 28.

142. Poliziano, *Opera omnia*, Book 10, pp. 138–40.

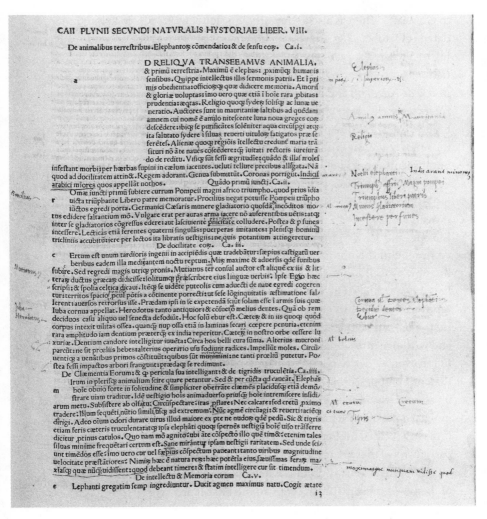

FIGURE 4. Pliny, *Historia naturalis*, Book VIII, cap. i, i3 (re elephants); Lisbon, Biblioteca Nacional de Portugal, INC 462. Public domain

The evidence for Lorenzo's intellectual engagement with the Portuguese voyages during the period 1489 to 1490, although limited, is varied and compelling. But apart from the probable commission for the copy of the Fra Mauro *mappamondo*, little to date has surfaced regarding similar interests at other points or periods in his life (but see below), although there are occasional tantalising indications that he was interested and engaged in these overseas developments. There is evidence that in the mid to late 1470s he was unhappy at Florentine and Medici bank money being used to invest in Portuguese voyages to Guinea.[143] There is also a stray surviving letter written by João II to Lorenzo, dated 15 October 1487, addressing Lorenzo as 'amico nostro carissimo', adverting to a trusted servant Afonso Leitão who had been sent to carry out negotiations with Lorenzo on João's behalf, probably in relation to the ship *Santa Maria de Nazareth* and its cargo.[144] The letter assumes familiarity and the two rulers were clearly in communication. It is possible that the momentous Portuguese advances down the west coast and around the southern tip of Africa in the 1480s fired Lorenzo's imagination in a way the previous expeditions had not, but it seems more likely that the documentation charting his interest and involvement in previous years has either not been noticed or has been lost. During the reign of João II (1481–95), the exploits of the Portuguese in Africa moved centre-stage not only in Portugal itself, but in the rest of western Europe, and Italians were agog with excitement as the Portuguese began to comprehend the outline and shape of Africa.[145] Lorenzo was fascinated by the new as well as the old, by the current as well as antiquity, and it would have been strange if he had not joined in the general wonder and curiosity at reports of 'new' lands and peoples being reached in the years before and after 1489–90. As it is, the evidence available relates mainly to a combined visual and written genre—maps—with only one example from a document or text. Often even evidence relating to maps is so pared down as to be teasing rather than full-blooded. For instance, the inventory of Lorenzo's possessions drawn up after his death in 1492 and preserved in a copy from 1512 is beyond sparing in what it divulges. Knowing that he owned four separate *mappemondo* confirms his decided interest in global affairs, but the inventory reveals no further particulars of these maps relating to origin or date or size, with each one listed merely as 'Una [carta] dipintovi el mappamondo', or a close variant.[146] One of them was presumably the copy of the Fra Mauro map.

143. See Francesco Guidi Bruscoli, '"Ànno fatto una inpresa grossa per il paese di Ghinea contro a nostra voglia": Lorenzo de' Medici and the voyage to Guinea, c. 1475–77', in Alessio Assonitis and K.J.P. Lowe, eds, *The Medici and Perceptions of Sub-Saharan Africa* (forthcoming Turnhout, 2025).

144. Guido Battelli, 'La corrispondenza del Poliziano col Re Don Giovanni II di Portogallo', *La rinascita*, 2 (1939), pp. 280–98 at 296–97. The letter is in ASF, MAP, XLVII, 2. João wrote to Piero de' Medici in May 1494 on this issue: Battelli, 'La corrispondenza', pp. 297–98.

145. Lowe, 'Africa in the News', pp. 310–28.

146. Marco Spallanzani and Giovanna Gaeta Bertelà, eds, *Libro d'inventario dei beni di Lorenzo il Magnifico* (Florence, 1992), p. 53; Ciappelli, 'Carte geografiche', p. 51; Cattaneo, *Fra Mauro's Mappa Mundi*, p. 59 and n. 92.

There is one other strand of material evidence that testifies to Lorenzo's interest in the Portuguese voyages and the way that the charting of knowledge of the world and the heavens was changing through advances in technology and updatings on globes. In 1568 Giorgio Vasari included in his *vita* of Alessio Baldovinetti the information that the *orologio dei pianeti* or planetary clock then owned by Duke Cosimo had originally been made by Lorenzo della Volpaia for Lorenzo de' Medici.[147] In August 1484 Angelo Poliziano sent Francesco della Casa a detailed written description of this clock and its functioning; at the time, Francesco was aged only twenty-three.[148] Poliziano wrote that his letter was a response to one from Francesco stating that reports of the device had been doubted, and asking for reliable information. Poliziano excused the possible obscurity of his description by alluding to the 'novelty' (*novitas*) of the object.[149]

This planetary clock has had a confused history,[150] and its relationship (if any) with two *mappemondo* or *palle* also known to have been in Lorenzo's possession is not entirely clear. One complicating factor is that the planetary clock was furnished with two globes,[151] one terrestrial and the other celestial. It may also just be coincidental that Poliziano was lent a globe that had belonged to Lorenzo, and that Lorenzo's post-mortem inventory of 1492 included a slightly obscure reference to 'due coppe dorate, entrovi dua palle tonde, dipintovi drento 2 spere' in the priest's room on the terrace, valued in conjunction with two paintings, one of them small, at the rather high sum of sixty florins.[152]

---

147. Vasari, *Le vite*, ed. Milanesi, 2, pp. 593–94.

148. *DBI*, 36 (1988), pp. 696–99, entry by Raffaella Zaccaria.

149. Angelo Poliziano, *Letters*, vol. 1: Books 1–4, ed. and trans. Shane Butler (Cambridge, MA, 2006), pp. 270–74 at 270.

150. According to the Museo Galileo in Florence, https://catalogo.museogalileo.it /multimedia/OrologioPianetiLorenzoVolpaiaBis.html (accessed 18 April 2023), Lorenzo della Volpaia made two versions of this clock, and confusion has resulted from a muddling of the two. The planetary clock mentioned by Vasari is not included in a list of extant instruments made by the Della Volpaia: Carlo Maccagni, 'The Florentine Clock- and Instrument-Makers of the Della Volpaia Family', *Der Globusfreund*, 17–20 (1969–71), pp. 92–99 at 97. The second, made in 1510, was placed in the Sala dei Gigli and later the Guardaroba Nuova in Palazzo Vecchio; it had already disappeared by the end of the sixteenth century. When Milanesi composed his edition of Vasari in the late nineteenth century, however, he claimed in the notes that the planetary clock was then in the Museo fisico fiorentino, in the room of 'macchine antiche': Vasari, *Le vite*, ed. Milanesi, 2, p. 594 n. 1.

151. https://catalogo.museogalileo.it/multimedia/OrologioPianetiLorenzoVolpaiaBis.html.

152. Spallanzani and Gaeta Bertelà, *Libro d'inventario*, p. 125.

One of the earliest registers of the Guardaroba has an entry for 27 June 1493 stating that one of the *palle* that are 'come mappamondi', usually in the *libreria* or library (in this instance), has been lent ('si prestò') to Agnolo da Montepulciano, otherwise known as Poliziano.[153] The word *palla* or sphere can here be understood to mean a globe—that is, a spherical object around which a *mappamondo* has been wrapped and attached.[154] This snippet from 1493 is proof that Poliziano's interest in the Portuguese overseas expansion and the visualisation of the world through maps continued until his death. Globes including up-to-date information from the latest Portuguese voyages and tracing the lineaments of the Portuguese trading empire across the world were concrete examples of Portugal's and João II's achievements. Francesca Fiorani discusses a pair of globes, one terrestrial (1563–68) and the other celestial, planned and partly executed by Ignazio Danti, belonging to later Medici, but does not refer to the earlier pair.[155] Yet at least one earlier pair, and maybe more, belonged to earlier Medici. An entry in Alessandro de' Medici's inventory of Palazzo Medici on via Larga from 1531 has wording quite similar to that of the 1493 Medici Guardaroba entry, and seems to echo it. It lists on 7 December 1531, as part of a job lot of objects handed over by Cresci Donati to the inventory-maker, 'II [m]apamundi in palle, uno del cielo, l'altro della tera'.[156] It is clear that there were many different types of *mappamondo*: flat ones and ones wrapped around spheres; manuscript, hand-drawn ones and printed ones; ones on vellum, on parchment and on paper.[157] However, it is almost certain that on 19

153. ASF, Guardaroba medicea 1, 20r: 'A dì 27 di giugno 1493. A messer Agnolo da Monte Pulciano si prestò una di quelle due palle che stanno in libreria che sono come mappamondi.' This volume, a 'giornale di entrata e uscita' (record of income and expenditure), includes a section running from 1483 for just over eleven years. See also Luigi Cibrario, 'Lezione storico-filologica sopra alcuni vocaboli usati nei più antichi registri della guardaroba medicea', *Archivio storico italiano*, ser. 3, 4, part 1(1867), pp. 152–65 at 157.

154. Battaglia, *Grande dizionario*, 12, p. 407, s.v. *palla*, no. 1: 'Corpo o oggetto di forma più o meno perfettamente sferica o simile a una sfera; globo, sfera'.

155. Fiorani, *Marvel of Maps*, pp. 25–26.

156. Giovanna Lazzi and Giovanna Bigalli Lulla, 'Alessandro de' Medici e il palazzo di via Larga: L'inventario del 1531', *Archivio storico italiano*, 150 (1992), pp. 1201–33 at 1227.

157. This is obvious from the inventory of 1527/8 of Alessandro Rosselli in ASF, Magistrato dei pupilli avanti il principato 190, 393r, 394v, 395r and 395v where a large variety of *mappemondo* are listed: manuscript, printed, coloured, "painted", freestanding and flat or on a globe, on cloth or paper. The inventory was published by Iodoco del Badia, 'La bottega di Alessandro di Francesco Rosselli merciaio e stampatore (1528)', in *Miscellanea fiorentina di erudizione e storia*, 2 (1887), pp. 24–30.

July 1534 these two *palle,* 'uno del ciello, l'altro della terra', were given to 'maestro Andrea Pasqualle' as a present by Alessandro de' Medici.[158] Andrea Pasquali was the personal doctor first to Alessandro and then to Cosimo I de' Medici, the latter of whom favoured him greatly.[159] The documents are specific about the two actions: in 1493 one of the globes was lent to Poliziano, and equally precise is the statement in 1534 that two globes are given to maestro Andrea Pasquali. If indeed these are the two globes that belonged to Lorenzo de' Medici, this last entry would explain why they are not to be found in later inventories of the Medici collections, as Alessandro had given them to his doctor, and they had passed for ever out of the Medici collections.

In addition to gift-giving, the changing political status of the Medici family had a significant impact on the fate of their possessions, as objects in the collections had to weather multiple moments of rupture, chaos and dispersal;[160] some survived in Medici ownership and others did not. Even if the planetary clock and globes did not survive in the collections—or did not survive beyond the end of the sixteenth century—it does seem clear from their fifteenth-century biographies that Lorenzo de' Medici should not be accused of a lack of interest in the Portuguese overseas voyages: his ownership of the clock and of the globes and maps of Africa proves otherwise. While there has been significant scholarship on the collecting practices of Lorenzo de' Medici, this aspect of his collections has previously not been mentioned, even in passing. Laurie Fusco and Gino Corti included in their book on Lorenzo as a collector a section of his '[c]riteria for selecting objects', starting with 'novelty and rarity',[161] yet they did not think to include objects related to the Portuguese

---

158. ASF, Guardaroba medicea 4, p. 11; Lazzi and Bigalli Lulla, 'Alessandro de' Medici', pp. 1214–15. On Pasquali, see Mario Battistini, 'Il medico Andrea Pasquali', in *Rivista di storia delle scienze mediche e naturali,* 8 (1926), pp. 231–33.

159. C. O. Tosi, 'Andrea Pasquali', *Illustratore fiorentino,* n.s. 12 (1915), pp. 69–70 at 70; Gaetano Pieraccini, *La stirpe de' Medici di Cafaggiolo: Saggio di ricerche sulla trasmissione ereditaria dei caratteri biologici,* 3 vols in 4 tomes (Florence, 1924–25), 2.1, e.g., pp. 34, 35, 38. In 1553, Pasquali was one of only two members of the Medici household paid the highest salary of five hundred *fiorini* (the other was the *tapezziere* Jan Rost from Brussels, known in Italian as Giovanni Rosti): ASF, Depositeria generale, parte antica 393, 1 destra and 119 destra.

160. Fiorani, *Marvel of Maps,* p. 26, says that the clock built for Lorenzo was acquired by the Parte Guelfa at the sale of Medici goods (to stop it leaving Florence) and donated to the Florentine republic.

161. Laurie Fusco and Gino Corti, *Lorenzo de' Medici: Collector and Antiquarian* (Cambridge, 2006), pp. 114–15.

voyages in whatever form. Why was there this omission? Surely everything that is known about Lorenzo would point to him engaging with every sort of current event and news item of interest. Once again, it appears that the historiographical disinclination to consider the Italian Renaissance and the Portuguese voyages around the globe in tandem worked to create a haze that obscured certain of the realities of Lorenzo's interests. Even if Lorenzo does not appear to have acquired, bar some oliphants, any sub-Saharan African goods or artefacts—although perhaps these too have simply not yet come to light—he was busily acquiring scientific instruments and maps that allowed him to understand and follow the Portuguese voyages to and around the African continent. After Lorenzo was dead, it was claimed that he had collected objects from all over the world.[162] Fusco and Corti, amongst others, label this an example of 'Renaissance hyperbole', while admitting that he did make acquisitions from outside Italy.[163] Perhaps the objects relating to the Portuguese voyages should now be acknowledged and put into this bracket.

Still further evidence that Lorenzo was involved in following and benefiting from the Portuguese explorations comes from one of the *canti carnascialeschi* entitled 'Canzona dello zibetto', said to have been written by Lorenzo himself.[164] The subject of this song with strong sexual overtones was a civet cat. It is possible that Lorenzo owned, and kept on his *fattoria* or farm at Poggio a Caiano,[165] one or more of these expensive and very desirable animals— desirable because the musky secretion from civets' scent glands were used in medicines and in the manufacture of perfume. Alvise da Mosto, who travelled down the west coast of Africa in 1455 and 1456, reported that he had been brought some of the secretions (also called civet), and skins of civet cats, but does not mention procuring a live animal.[166] The *canzona* opens with the statement that the civet 'è un animal perfetto / a molte cose' (is an animal with many uses) and that it 'vien da lungi, d'un paese strano' (comes from a strange,

162. Fusco and Corti, *Lorenzo de' Medici*, pp. 19, 342: 'ex toto orbe' (Niccolò Valori, *Vita di Lorenzo de' Medici*, trans. Filippo Valori, ed. Enrico Niccolini [Vicenza, 1991], p. 53) and 359: 'rare cose che Cosimo, Pietro e Lorenzo haveva prima radunate da varie parti del mondo' (P. Cherubino Ghirardacci, *Della historia di Bologna*, 2 vols [Bologna, 1596–1657], the first part written 1570s–1590s).

163. Fusco and Corti, *Lorenzo de' Medici*, pp. 19 and 133.

164. Lorenzo de' Medici, *Opere*, ed. Attilio Simoni, 2 vols (Bari, 1913–14), 2, pp. 245–46, no. 5 of the *canti carnascialeschi*.

165. Marco Masseti, *La fattoria di Lorenzo il Magnifico: Gli animali domestici e selvatici delle Cascine di Poggio a Caiano (Prato)* (Florence, 2015), pp. 151–57.

166. Cà da Mosto, *Le navigazioni atlantiche*, p. 100; Crone, *Voyages of Cadamosto*, p. 69.

faraway country). The place of origin of the civet is declared strange but its geo-graphical position is not mentioned. This is an early example, therefore, of a rare and expensive autochthonous sub-Saharan African commodity, in this case an animal, shedding its provenance by the time it arrives in Europe. By 1508 Leonardo Nasi, engaged in a search for a pair of civets, could write to Isabella d'Este from Florence saying that if necessary he would 'send [for them] to the island of Ghinea where they are born',[167] a fascinating mention of Guinea as the source for these animals in a letter from an agent to a would-be acquiring ruler.

Visual evidence from twenty-five years later suggests that Lorenzo also pos-sessed African parrots and monkeys on his farm. The Medici villa at Poggio a Caiano was started in 1480, but work was suspended at Lorenzo's death in 1492. His son Giovanni, elected Pope Leo X in 1513, restarted work, some of which, like the iconographic programme of the Sala di Leone X, was intended not only as a display of the mighty political reach of the Medici family but also quite concretely as a glorification of his father. The two themes coalesced in a deliber-ate merging of the classical world and the new Portuguese global empire, and a deliberate twinning of the rulers Julius Caesar and Lorenzo de' Medici. The comparison functioned by making Lorenzo a co-beneficiary of the rare and marvellous fauna that constituted one of the fruits of the Portuguese overseas voyages. Andrea del Sarto's contribution, *Tribute to Caesar* (c. 1519–21) (Plate 8), ostensibly a glorification of Roman political history, included a great number of non-native animals, some of them famously sent to Florence and probably given to Lorenzo by the Mamluk sultan of Egypt in 1487, painted as realistically as possible.[168] Among the throng are a giraffe, a lion, a turkey, a chameleon, a civet, a basketful of parrots including at least one African grey (*Psittacus erithacus*) and two monkeys. The more prominent monkey is a green or Cape Verde monkey (formerly *Cercopithecus* and latterly *Chlorocebus sabaeus*), so called because of its association with the island of Cabo Verde,[169] dressed in a hooded and boldly striped jacket, sitting on the steps to the right of the dwarf who is wearing clothing with identical stripes.[170] It is highly unlikely that the civet, parrots and

167. Cockram, 'Interspecies Understanding', p. 283.

168. Julian Kliemann, *Andrea del Sarto: 'Il Tributo a Cesare' (1519–1521)* (Poggio a Caiano, 1986), p. 12.

169. Marco Masseti and Emiliano Bruner, 'The Primates of the Western Palaearctic: A Bio-graphical, Historical and Archaeozoological Review', *Journal of Anthropological Sciences*, 87 (2009), pp. 33–91 at 54–56.

170. Masseti, *La fattoria*, p. 153; Marco Masseti, 'New World and Other Exotic Animals in the Menageries of Lorenzo il Magnifico and His Son, Pope Leo X, during the Italian Renaissance', in Arthur MacGregor, ed., *Naturalists in the Field: Collecting, Recording and Preserving the Natural*

monkeys would have been in the fresco had they not been associated with Lorenzo and formed part of his menagerie or animal collection at the farm attached to Poggio a Caiano.

The most extraordinary African animal to arrive with the Mamluk embassy in 1487 was a giraffe. Recalling the one brought back to Italy from an African campaign by Julius Caesar in 46 BC, and said to be the first to be seen in Europe since the thirteenth century,[171] this animal later was cast as a symbol of Medici reach and power,[172] appearing in a slew of Florentine depictions[173] and prefiguring later Medici interest in collecting so-called exotic animals. In fact, Sultan Qaitbay sent two giraffes to Italy in 1487: one to Ferdinando d'Aragona of Naples and the other to Lorenzo in Florence,[174] so neither the Florentine animal nor the Medici case should be seen as unique. Although sensational-seeming gifts, giraffes procured from Nubia or Ethiopia were common presents from the Mamluk sultans, used extensively in Mamluk diplomacy.[175] The animal sent to Florence has been identified as a male Nubian giraffe (*Giraffa camelopardalis camelopardalis*),[176] which came originally from sub-Saharan Africa between Sudan and Kongo;[177] now this subspecies is on the critically endangered list. Always tied to its provenance as a gift from Egypt, the giraffe was therefore known to be African, even if its precise place of origin on the African continent

---

World from the Fifteenth to the Twenty-First Century (Leiden, 2018), pp. 40–75 at 50–54 and figs. 2.6 and 2.7. There is a preparatory drawing for the animal group including the principal monkey, wearing what was at that point a jacket patterned with lozenges, in Darmstadt, Hessisches Landesmuseum, AE 1373: John Shearman, *Andrea Del Sarto*, 2 vols (Oxford, 1965), 1, plate 83 and 2, p. 325; *Andrea del Sarto: The Renaissance Workshop in Action*, ed. Julian Brooks with Denise Allen and Xavier F. Salomon, exh. cat., The J. Paul Getty Museum at the Getty Center, Los Angeles (Los Angeles, 2015), pp. 92–95, cat. no. 2.3; Masseti, 'New World', p. 50 and fig. 2.8.

171. Angelica Groom, *Exotic Animals in the Art and Culture of the Medici Court in Florence* (Leiden, 2019), p. 181.

172. Christiane L. Joost-Gaugier, 'Lorenzo the Magnificent and the Giraffe as a Symbol of Power', *Artibus et historiae*, 8.16 (1987), pp. 91–99.

173. See, e.g., *Islam e Firenze: Arte e collezionismo dai Medici al Novecento*, ed. Giovanni Curatola, exh. cat., Aula Magliabechiana, Gallerie degli Uffizi, and Museo nazionale del Bargello, Florence (Florence, 2018), p. 189, cat. no. 2; Groom, *Exotic Animals*, pp. 190–207.

174. Lorenzo Montemagno Ciseri, '*Camelopardalis*: Storia naturale e straordinaria della giraffa di Lorenzo il Magnifico', *Interpres*, 31 (2012–13), pp. 351–72 at 353.

175. Doris Behrens-Abouseif, *Practising Diplomacy in the Mamluk Sultanate: Gifts and Material Culture in the Medieval Islamic World* (London, 2014), pp. 115, 140–41.

176. Montemagno Ciseri, '*Camelopardalis*', p. 359.

177. Ibid., pp. 359, 360 and 366.

was probably not discussed. It was much commented upon in Florence at the time, but did not live long, dying in January 1489 after it caught its head on part of the roof of its stall in via della Scala.[178] A contemporary recorded that after its premature death the giraffe was flayed in an attempt to preserve its skin, and that it was universally mourned because it was considered so 'beautiful' (most likely, because it was so rare).[179] Exotic animal skins, such as those of big cats,[180] or apes, are known to have been routinely kept and displayed since classical times,[181] so the impulse here is not unusual, only the type of animal skin. Functioning as status indicators, both exotic live animals and the skins of exotic dead animals were considered suitable material for diplomatic present-giving.[182] But although live giraffes with their extraordinary height and shape made the cut, giraffe skins with their memorable patterning do not seem to have been included in this list, whereas the zebra skins with their standout stripes are known to have been thought appropriate, being given, for instance, by the ambassadors from Ethiopia to the Venetian government in 1402.[183] As will be seen in chapter 5 below, in addition to curing animal skins, proto-taxidermy was also employed to try to preserve rare birds when they died,[184] and previously unknown dead birds from around the world were also sent as high-status gifts.[185] Rarity

178. Tribaldo de' Rossi, 'Ricordanze tratte da un libro originale di Tribaldo de' Rossi', in Ildefonso di San Luigi, ed., *Delizie degli eruditi toscani*, 24 vols (Florence, 1770–89), 23, pp. 236–303 at 246–48; Giuseppe Odoardo Corazzini, ed,. *Ricordanze di Bartolomeo Masi, calderaio fiorentino dal 1478 al 1526* (Florence, 1906), p. 18; Montemagno Ciseri, '*Camelopardalis*', pp. 361–63.

179. Rossi, *Ricordanze*, p. 247.

180. See the post-mortem inventory of Francesco I de' Medici, in ASF, Guardaroba medicea 126, 47r (various animal skins including those of bears, tigers and lions) and 49r (ten lion skins).

181. According to Pliny, *Natural History*, 2, Loeb Classical Library 352, Book VI.xxxvi.200–201 (Eng. tr. p. 487), Hanno sent the skins of two wild, hairy women [female apes] he found in the Ethiopian islands back to the temple of Juno in Carthage, where they were displayed as curiosities.

182. Kate Lowe, '"Representing" Africa: Ambassadors and Princes from Christian Africa to Renaissance Italy and Portugal, 1402–1608', *Transactions of the Royal Historical Society*, 17 (2007), pp. 101–28 at 103.

183. Carlo Cipolla, 'Prete Jane e Francesco Novello da Carrara', *Archivio veneto*, 6 (1873), pp. 323–24.

184. See below, p. 181. See also P. A. Morris, *A History of Taxidermy: Art, Science and Bad Taste* (Ascot, 2010), p. 36.

185. Letter from Giovanni da Empoli in Lisbon to Lorenzo de' Medici in Rome, 19 October 1514: 'io mamdo al Sommo Pomtifice . . . uno ucello morto molto bellissimo [a bird of paradise]'. Spallanzani, *Giovanni da Empoli*, p. 213.

therefore must have been believed to consist in the size, shape, skin and patterning—all attributes that survived the transition from live animal to dead one—making the dead beast worthy of preservation once life had ebbed in addition to making the live animal attractive as a possession. Sixteenth- and seventeenth-century collections of exotic objects in Italy and elsewhere contained numerous examples of animal *naturalia*: the skeletons and carapaces of various exotic animals vied with the stuffed recreations and empty skins of others.[186] However, these gifts from the sultan, welcome and intriguing though they might have been to Lorenzo, do not constitute evidence of interest in Africa or the Portuguese trading empire per se for him; in order for that to be proven, Lorenzo would have had to ask for the animals or objects, or tried to procure them for himself: that is, he would have needed to show an active interest. On the other hand, evidence that Lorenzo's dual interest in maps charting the Portuguese overseas voyages and exotic animals were thought appropriate to those in positions of power is provided twenty years later by Paolo Cortesi's treatise *De cardinalatu*, published in 1510. In a description of the ideal decoration of the summer rooms of virtue-signalling cardinals,[187] Cortesi wrote that the learned would gain delight from painted *mappemondo*, or focused charts of recently 'discovered' places such as those around India circumnavigated by the Portuguese under King Manuel I, displayed on the walls. Similarly, accurate representations of animals, the rarer the better, were to be commended, as it revealed an admirable 'zeal for novelty'.[188] The impetus provided by Lorenzo's constant awareness of the need for legitimation of his political role, pushing him towards certain tastes and behaviours, should not be underestimated.

A further snippet indicating engagement is Lorenzo's ownership of three elephant tusks. It is unknown whether they were worked or unworked. The post-mortem inventory of Lorenzo's possessions preserved in a copy from 1512 recorded two on the *chappellinaio*, or hat-stand, in Lorenzo's room that had been overlooked by the inventory-taker, with lacunae regarding their weight and value. A third tusk, interestingly, was noted in Lorenzo's study, where he also kept his world and other maps, again recorded without description or value.[189]

186. See Bleichmar, 'Seeing the World', e.g., pp. 24 and 25.

187. It is surely not a coincidence, moreover, that Palazzo Venezia in Rome was also used as a summer residence: Dengel, 'Sulla mappamundi', p. 501.

188. Paolo Cortesi, *The Renaissance Cardinal's Ideal Palace: A Chapter from Cortesi's 'De cardinalatu'*, ed. Kathleen Weil-Garris and John F. D'Amico, trans. John F. D'Amico (Rome, 1980), pp. 94–97 and nn. 126–28.

189. Spallanzani and Gaeta Bertelà, *Libro d'inventario*, pp. 16 and 53.

Maybe the known evidence for Lorenzo's interest can even be extended slightly further by the application of common sense. One piece of the evidence for Este excitement at the Portuguese voyages examined above originated in Florence, and it is surely not too far-fetched to posit that Lorenzo had access to the same description by the humanist Zanobi Acciaiuoli, based on information from Portugal, of an unknown island of Guinea, preserved in a letter of 18 March 1491.[190] Acciaiuoli was educated at court and was a friend of Marsilio Ficino, Poliziano and Pico della Mirandola,[191] so was well placed as a conduit for current news from Portugal to be passed on to Lorenzo. It is precisely these channels of communication, between varying combinations of merchants and humanists in both Lisbon and Florence, that must have brought contemporary news stories about the Portuguese overseas voyages onto the *piazze* of Florence and into the circle of the Medici and the Florentine government. After all, as mentioned above, on 4 November 1486 Lorenzo di Giovanni Tornabuoni wrote to Benedetto Dei in Milan, describing how that morning 'in piazza' in Florence he had heard exciting news of the conversion of a king in Guinea.[192] Although exact proof is lacking, Lorenzo too must have heard this news, transmitted as so much news was by a combination of the written and the oral. The part played by orality in news transmission makes it even more difficult than usual to trace its spoken path around and across cities or communities; far easier to track is its passage in written form. One oral source of information or knowledge about West Africa readily to hand in Florence in the decades after 1460 was the enslaved sub-Saharan Africans sent to the city as domestic slaves, some of whom will be discussed in chapter 3. Yet as far as is known, Lorenzo did not make use of their knowledge, even while he negotiated to obtain maps of their homelands. For whatever reason, it is unlikely that he conceived of them as potential conduits of knowledge, although surely he must have known their provenance, and realised that they came from Guinea. This was a missed opportunity for Lorenzo in his quest to build up a picture of the Portuguese overseas exploration. Once again, the absence of enslaved black Africans in Lorenzo de' Medici's household is noteworthy; had they been in his household, he might have made the connection between their place of origin and the Portuguese voyages, and spoken to them about their African homelands.

190. See n. 64 above.

191. *DBI*, 1, pp. 93–94, entry by Abele L. Redigonda. He was also a cousin of Lorenzo di Pierfrancesco de' Medici.

192. ASF, Corporazioni religiose soppresse 78 [Badia di Firenze], 317, no. 220.

For the period of the Medici popes at the beginning of the sixteenth century, evidence also exists of interest in the Portuguese voyages and the goods that the Portuguese overseas empire could provide. When Pope Leo X made a triumphal entry into Florence, his natal city, in 1515, there was an outpouring of homage in text and in art. One notable piece representing Adam and Eve under the tree of knowledge, entitled *The Temptation of Adam* (Plate 9) was designed by the workshop of Giovanni della Robbia, and nods to new worlds seemed obvious in the representations of maize from North America (technical examinations have now revealed these were a nineteenth-century addition)[193] and a wholly green bird, most probably once again a green parakeet from Senegambia, like the ones on the Cantino map (see Plate 1), in the branches of the tree (see Plate 9).[194] These parakeets arrived in Europe early, as is shown by depictions of them for example from fourth-century BC Rome. Even now they have a wide range: in Africa, south of the Sahara from Mauretania and Senegambia eastwards to northern Uganda and Ethiopia; and in Asia, from Pakistan eastwards through India to Bangladesh and Myanmar. In the 1515 terracotta, they would definitely have been understood as originating from outside Europe.

Conclusion

What is to be made of this ragbag of traces of what once may have been a much more sustained and coordinated interest in the novelties of the Portuguese overseas expansion, both in Ferrara and in Florence? The traces indicate curiosity and covetousness with regard to certain categories of object such as maps and globes depicting the new landmasses and territories, and certain types of animal originating from the Portuguese trading empire, and give a sense of the excitement engendered by the voyages. The notion of a much enlarged world on the move piqued interest among Italian rulers, and possession was an important attribute of rulership, yet the fifteenth century struggled to arrange for much to be brought back to Portugal and then dispersed around the rest of western Europe. Exceptions were objects or goods that were already

---

193. Gregory Bailey, 'The Nineteenth-Century Reconstruction of Giovanni Della Robbia's *Adam and Eve*', *The Journal of the Walters Art Museum*, 73 (2018), pp. 70–78 at 72 and 75 n. 14.

194. Giancarlo Gentilini, *I della Robbia: La scultura invetriata nel Rinascimento*, 2 vols (Milan, 1992), 2, pp. 305 (illustration) and 332 makes no mention of the animal and vegetable life portrayed in the Garden of Eden, while Markey, *Imagining the Americas*, p. 14 believes the parrot to have come from the Americas.

known—but expensive, rare and therefore hard to acquire—that suddenly became more available, because they were immediately desirable. Imported goods of virtually all other sorts only started to be available in Europe, even to rulers in Italy, in the sixteenth century. The conjoined concepts of novelty, rarity and the non-European or exotic, already laden with allure at a theoretical level, had in general to wait for the new century to find the global goods to which they needed to attach themselves in order to exert an impossible-to-resist attraction. Precision over provenance from the outset seems to have been a minor concern, only becoming of interest where a question of quality was involved.

3

Florence's 'Black' Babies

RENAISSANCE FLORENCE MEETS
SUB-SAHARAN AFRICA: MIXED-ANCESTRY
CHILDREN AT THE OSPEDALE
DEGLI INNOCENTI

THE NEXT four chapters focus on case studies relating to three discrete time periods, to allow an impressionistic tracing of how the Portuguese trading empire had a variety of effects on Renaissance Italy, and how these shifted with changing circumstances. Each case study will have a different category of global acquisition as its primary theme; the first is people.

Lisbon and Florence

Looking in parallel at how understandings of provenance and possession were understood and managed in Florence and Lisbon helps to clarify differential experiences of empire. At first glance, the Florentine foundling hospital and orphanage, the Ospedale degli Innocenti, might appear an unlikely place to find traces of Florence's involvement in the fifteenth century with the worldwide Portuguese trading empire. It is an iconic Renaissance institution and building, and was almost immediately acknowledged as such. An early fifteenth-century foundation, financed by the Arte di Por Santa Maria (also known as the Arte della Seta, or Silk Guild), it was set up by a wealthy mercantile and patrician élite in Florence to care for babies and young children whose parents either were not able, or did not want, to look after them. In 1419 Filippo Brunelleschi was commissioned to build the *ospedale*, and started work on the loggia; later Francesco della Luca took over. It was inaugurated in 1445, and the church was consecrated in 1451. These were some of the great years of the early Florentine Renaissance, and the project of the Innocenti represented some of the highest ideals of Renaissance civic thought and aspiration: an emphasis on civic pride, reliance on patronage from groups and individuals rather than the state, a Catholic desire to help the less well-off, a belief in inclusivity and the possibility of creating some of the most beautiful buildings ever seen in the new Florentine style.

Yet while the city of Florence was honing these skills and focusing on cultural, literary, artistic and political innovations, the kingdom of Portugal in precisely the same years was sponsoring maritime and technological innovations, and authorising voyages to 'unknown' areas of the world. Looking at these dates in parallel is instructive. The first places reached by Portuguese ships were the Atlantic islands and the west coast of Africa: landfall was made at Madeira in 1419 (the year in which Brunelleschi was given the Innocenti commission) and in the 1440s the first enslaved sub-Saharan Africans were brought back to Portugal and landed at Lagos in the Algarve (the decade in which the Innocenti was inaugurated). So even if Florence was not directly involved in the Portuguese empire, how likely was it that Florence would remain untouched by all the novelties that the Portuguese were starting to import? Why would the inhabitants of a city like Florence, that set such store on being at the forefront of the new in so many areas, fail to see the attractions of Portuguese novelties? So great was the reach of Portugal's trading empire, encompassing the whole of Africa in the course of the fifteenth century, India at the end of the century, Brazil in 1500 and the Far East soon afterwards, and so quickly did its goods and peoples spread across Europe, that on the contrary, it would have been strange if Florence had not been involved in some way. This involvement may be categorised as indirect, but it took the form of new peoples and goods being quickly inserted into the culture, fabric and spaces of fifteenth-century Florence.

This case study that follows will focus on one of the novelties generated by the world on the move—the arrival of numbers of enslaved people from sub-Saharan Africa to work as domestic slaves in Renaissance Florence. This necessitates a return to Portugal. By 1500 Renaissance Lisbon had a numerically more varied mix of inhabitants than any other European city, consisting not only of indigenous Portuguese, but also of people from different countries in Europe and around the world. Even in the mid-fifteenth century, its population was mixed, and its mercantile community consisted of colonies or 'nations' of foreign merchants from northern and southern Europe,[1] drawn to

1. There is a substantial literature, both old and new on these foreign colonies. For further bibliography, see, e.g., Kellenbenz, *Fremde Kaufleute*; Spallanzani, *Mercanti fiorentini*; Lowe,

Lisbon by the exciting economic opportunities associated with the Portuguese seaborne empire. A core of these merchants was Italian—Genoese, Lucchese, Tuscan, even Florentine—and it is because of them that enslaved black men and women (but mainly women) from West Africa started to arrive in Pisa and Florence in small numbers from the 1450s. Quite literally, as soon as Africans started being shipped into Lisbon, they were shipped on to other places around Europe, especially Spain, and a few were sent to Tuscany. As a result, the great majority of sub-Saharan Africans in Tuscany and Florence during the second half of the fifteenth century can safely be assumed to have come by ship from West Africa to Portugal, and then again in another ship from Lisbon to Tuscany,[2] rather than being brought overland to North Africa from East Africa, and then brought to Sicily or Venice across the Mediterranean. These enslaved West Africans were generally young adults, who had had a life in Africa they could remember before the Portuguese arrived, and they were forcibly taken first to Portugal, and then on to Italy. It is noteworthy that these enslaved people were, as far as is known, not considered conduits of information about their homeland, unlike the Ethiopian religious who conveyed cartographic knowledge about Ethiopia to Fra Mauro in Venice for his 1459 world map.[3]

Documentation

In historical terms, it is extraordinarily fortunate that there is extant documentation relating to the presence of Africans in Florence from the fifteenth century. Florence is reputed to have the fullest fifteenth-century archives in the world, and these sometimes allow individual Africans to be tracked on their journey from the Tuscan coast to Florence, and then provide occasional

---

'Understanding Cultural Exchange', pp. 6–9; D'Arienzo, *La presenza degli italiani*; Eddy Stols, 'Lisboa: Um portal do mundo para a naçao flamenga', in Eddy Stols, Jorge Fonseca and Stijn Manhaeghe, *Lisboa em 1514: O relato de Jan Taccoen van Zillebeke* (Lisbon, 2014), pp. 7–76; Guidi Bruscoli, *Bartolomeo Marchionni*, pp. 38–60.

2. The Cambini bank books in the Innocenti archive record some of the early arrivals: AOIF, 12681, 48v includes a reference to two 'schiave nere' who arrived on a ship from Lisbon in July 1463, and 12682, 59r signals five 'schiave nere fra maschi e femine' who arrived in Livorno on a Portuguese ship in November 1464.

3. Tullia Gasparrini Leporace, *Il mappamondo di Fra Mauro* (Venice, 1956), plate 10; Piero Falchetta, *Fra Mauro's World Map, with a Commentary and Translations of the Inscriptions* (Turnhout, 2006), pp. 100–101, 200–203.

snippets of information about their lives while in the city. As well as being recorded in merchants' account books, they and their descendants can be re-corded in baptismal records, in the *catasti*, the famous series of tax records, and, last but not least, in the series of Balie e bambini (Wet-nurses and children) at the Ospedale degli Innocenti.[4] The Florentine addiction to note-taking, list-making and record-keeping exhibits an unshakeable attachment to the authority and 'immortality' of the written word. Even though there is—to some—an un-expected plethora of documentary information, the documentation could all be characterised as administrative rather than personal, 'little more than a register of [. . . an] encounter with power'.[5] What is striking is that the Africans in these Florentine encounters, and their offspring, have already been stripped of any connection to Africa by the time of their arrival on Italian soil. In the Balie e bambini registers, their places of origin are never mentioned.[6] Instead, sub-Saharan Africans can be identified in the records because their skin colour was often noted. However, the traces of these 'encounters with power' allow, and are susceptible to, marked interpretative engagement which in itself gives glimpses of the personal and emotional, and this painstaking archival and palaeographical approach is the route that offers the best results in illuminating the lives (in this case, the very short lives) of a previously ignored group or category. As the focus here is on babies, not yet at the age when they could speak, their thoughts would in any case have remained hidden from view, making them mute and vulnerable protagonists *par excellence* of 'a history of an unrecoverable past'. Another re-sponse to this situation, suggested by Saidiya Hartman, might be to consider fabulation or the writing of stories 'as a form of compensation'.[7]

4. London's Foundling Museum, for example, from September 2022 to February 2023 held an exhibition on their relevant records from the eighteenth century, entitled 'Tiny Traces: Af-rican and Asian Children at London's Foundling Hospital'.

5. Saidiya Hartman, 'Venus in Two Acts', *Small Axe*, no. 26 (vol. 12.2) (2008), pp. 1–14 at 2.

6. There are very occasional references to imprecise origins in Africa in the baptismal records of the Opera del Duomo in Florence: e.g., Florence, Opera del Duomo, Archivio storico delle fedi di battesimo di S. Giovanni, registro 226 (femmine, 1502–1513), 3 June 1503, 'Caterina et Giovanna di Ghinea'. The baptismal records of the cathedral in Naples in the later sixteenth and early seven-teenth centuries, by contrast, very often included the name of the area from which the enslaved person had come: see Giuliana Boccadamo, 'A Napoli: "Mori negri" fra Cinque e Seicento'; Boc-cadamo, '"Mori negri" a Napoli fra XVI e XVII secolo: Appendice documentaria'; and Gianfranco Salvatore, 'Analisi dei dati pertinenti del *Libro primo de' battesimi della Cattedrale di Napoli* (1583–1649)', all in Gianfranco Salvatore, ed., *Il chiaro e lo scuro: Gli africani nell'Europa del Rinascimento tra realtà e rappresentazione* (Lecce, 2021), pp. 143–56, 423–56 and 457–60 respectively.

7. Hartman, 'Venus', p. 12 (quotation), 3, 4, 11 and 12.

Very roughly, two hundred babies a year were deposited at the Innocenti from the 1450s to the 1480s, with the figures rising during that time. Between August 1461 and September 1465, 672 babies and children were deposited; between June 1472 and August 1476, 775; and between August 1476 and March 1480, 990.[8] It is worth spelling out in detail the form of the Innocenti records in Balie e bambini, the series analysed most closely here, as the contours of the records delineate the information they can provide. Unfortunately, while the names of the two women who acted as doorkeepers and guardians of the pila—the basin resembling a holy water stoup where the babies could be left—are known in 1483,[9] the names of the men who kept the written record of the arrivals between the 1450s and 1480s are as yet unknown.[10] The registers of the Balie e bambini recorded everything that the orphanage knew about the babies on their arrival,[11] and then also noted everything that happened to them while under the care of the institution subsequently. The entries followed a regular format, but there are also particularities related to who was writing the entry. At the top of the entry are written the names given to the baby. Immediately underneath is written the date and time the baby was left, who left it (if known), what this person revealed under questioning about the place the baby was born and its parentage, whether a note was attached to the baby giving information about its origin and whether it had already been baptised with certain names or should be baptised with certain names, any distinguishing marks of the baby (such as hare-lips) or special features (such as being a twin), what state the baby was in, what the baby was wrapped up in (Plate 10), and what little pieces of cloth or trinkets had been left with it. These last served to identify the child if, as happened rarely, someone came later to claim it or pick it up. A few of the descriptive comments, including those relating to skin colour, came from the experience of holding the baby and examining it: mixed ancestry would often have been visible, and so it was noted, as it was a distinguishing feature. There is no mention in these records of physiognomy or of hair, leaving skin colour as the crucial indicator of African ancestry,

8. AOIF, 489, 492 and 493.

9. AOIF, 5374, 5v–6r, 17 January 1482/3, and 45r–46r, 17 September 1483; Philip Gavitt, *Charity and Children in Renaissance Florence: The Ospedale degli Innocenti, 1410–1536* (Ann Arbor, MI, 1990), pp. 168–69.

10. A 'scrivano delle balie' is mentioned in 1556–57: Giuseppe Sparnacci, *Ordine et governo: La grande famiglia degli Innocenti nel 1556; Uno studio da scritti inediti di Vincenzo Borghini* (Florence, 2021), p. 39.

11. Gavitt, *Charity and Children*, pp. 187–89 examines the procedure on entry.

even if the terminology of colour was in a state of flux and had not yet been fixed. In the early years of the Innocenti, dark-skinned babies were a novelty, and novelties were outside the norm and commented on, even if their place of origin was not explicit and the connection to sub-Saharan Africa was not acknowledged. One of the functions of the Innocenti was to facilitate the baptism of these deposited babies (if they arrived unbaptised, as the majority did),[12] and therefore oversee their incorporation into the Christian community. But it is unlikely that those responsible for founding the Innocenti had envisaged that some of the babies would be of mixed ancestry, the children of mothers from sub-Saharan Africa, who might themselves have only been baptised—not necessarily in a formal manner[13]—in the very recent past.

Although the entries all follow the same format, they do not all contain the same information. When a baby was left in the *pila* without being observed—for example, in the middle of the night—obviously no information about its parentage or provenance could be obtained orally. Information in those cases came, if at all, from written notes. Some babies were left without a note, however, and there is no information at all about the conditions leading to the deposit of these. However, most came accompanied by stories, often transmitted by messengers, at least some of whom were paid to deposit the babies,[14] with the result that many of the attributions, even of maternity—but especially of paternity—are hearsay at best, and rumour at worst. They are the nearest one can get to the truth, but often that 'truth' leaves a lot to be desired. Those babies deposited by members of the household where the baby was born are most likely to have securely identified mothers. But the identities of mothers of babies handed to strangers in the street with instructions to take them to

12. On the issue of whether there was a fee for baptisms in fifteenth-century Florence, Karl Schlebusch believes that rather than a fixed fee there was an expectation of a contribution, but that this was not always forthcoming. The scribe noting baptisms in the records of the Opera del Duomo in mid-fifteenth-century Florence made comments that 'heavily point' to an expectation of financial recompense for the act: email from Karl Schlebusch, 11 February 2022. It is possible that people with no money whatsoever could have been deterred from baptising their babies, which might have been an additional reason for leaving them at the Innocenti, where they would automatically have been baptised.

13. See, e.g., Sergio Tognetti, 'The Trade in Black African Slaves in Fifteenth-Century Florence', in T. F. Earle and K.J.P. Lowe, eds, *Black Africans in Renaissance Europe* (Cambridge, 2005), pp. 213–24 at 217.

14. For example, AOIF, 495, 217r, 6 August 1484, a woman was paid six *quattrini* to drop off the baby.

the Innocenti may have been invented or imagined or guessed at. And the mothers of the waifs left by the Arno, or on a street or bench, or in a field, or by a shrine, or even occasionally in a lavatory,[15] had shed any link or connection to their children, and escaped into anonymity. It is also possible that maternity or paternity were in some cases ascribed maliciously, with intent to cause trouble or create a scandal, just as were many contemporary denunciations of sex crimes, for example.[16] An additional reason why the entries do not all contain precisely equivalent information is that some record-keepers were more thorough, more nit-picking than others.

One final point needs to be made. Babies were left at the Innocenti for a variety of reasons. Illegitimacy was one, although the word *bastardo* is used only once in these records, with reference to the son of a person described as a *fanciulla* (young girl), who was not identified as enslaved.[17] Having a child with a slave was another reason, although some people chose to accommodate these children within their households. And the progeny of priests, monks and nuns were sometimes left too. Women who had no husbands or partners left babies. But there were still further possibilities. Others left babies and young children because they were too poor to support them,[18] because the harvest had failed or because one of the parents had died and the family could no longer function, or because one of the parents was seriously ill, in hospital, or in prison. Still other children were left as a result of their fathers being away on business or on the galleys. Finally, genuine orphans were sometimes left, but they constitute only a very small proportion.

The great paradox at the heart of the Balie e bambini records is that the Innocenti set up a system whereby babies and young children could be left anonymously in the *pila* in the secure knowledge that they would be cared for, while at the same time developing a recording protocol whose formulae ensured that as much as possible was found out about the babies' parents and circumstances. The tension between these two objectives—assuring

15. AOIF, 494, 35v, 18 June 1480.

16. Michael Rocke, *Forbidden Friendships: Homosexuality and Male Culture in Renaissance Florence* (New York, 1996), e.g., pp. 49, 67 and 219.

17. AOIF, 492, 159v, 2 October 1474.

18. Richard C. Trexler, 'The Foundlings of Florence, 1395–1455', *History of Childhood Quarterly*, 1 (1973) (repr. in Richard C. Trexler, *Power and Dependence in Renaissance Florence*, vol. 1 (of 3): *The Children of Renaissance Florence* [Binghamton, NY, 1993], 1, pp. 7–34), pp. 259–84 at 273–75 examines the effect of failed harvests on the abandonment of children at the Ospedale di San Gallo in the 1530s.

anonymity and collecting information to assign responsibility—creates the potential for careful analysis of the entries and, over five hundred years later, allows them to be revisited and reinterpreted. An unintended consequence of the records is that blame for historical sexual abuse becomes a possibility.

A large proportion of babies left at the Innocenti were born to enslaved mothers; for example, thirty-four out of the first one hundred babies deposited there were noted as having slave mothers. In the past, slavery was an institution embedded in virtually every culture in the world: in Africa as well as Europe, in South America as well as the Far East, in ancient Rome as well as Renaissance Italy, Spain and Portugal. In the early fifteenth century, slaves in Florence were predominantly from Central Asia and the eastern Mediterranean, so tended to be Tartars, Monguls, Russians, Circassians and from the Balkans. The important point here is that there were 'white' slaves before the arrival of 'black' slaves ('black' and 'white' as descriptors of skin colour being, of course, cultural constructs, and factually incorrect ones to boot), and in Florence, there continued to be far more white slaves than black during the period. Enslaved sub-Saharan Africans were a small minority of the totality of slaves, but their skin colour made them and their children highly visible. The extent to which a negative attitude was attached to blackness in this early period is not clear, making analyses rather complicated and speculative as to whether the children of mixed African and Italian ancestry were viewed differently from those, say, of mixed Russian and Italian ancestry, and if so, in what ways. In order to gauge this, it is necessary to ask how 'whiteness' was understood. What were the parameters of 'whiteness'? Was it the case that everyone not of African ancestry was considered white? On the Italian peninsula in the fifteenth century a range of skin colours was already part of everyday reality: there were not only merchants and others from the Middle East with a darker skin colour, but also Italians from the south with darker complexions and manual labourers who spent their working lives outside and who were very tanned. Many of the people in these groups—as people with dark hair—were described as, or called, or given the nickname of *nero*/*neri*. So was it a question of degree? The novel aspect is the arrival of a small cluster of sub-Saharan Africans, who then had babies. On the continuum of skin colour from notional white to notional black, did a label of *ghezzo* or *nero* signify merely an increase in blackness, or did it include a qualitative judgement of some sort?

The enslaved African women—just like the white slaves whose babies are recorded in such numbers being left at the Innocenti—were at constant risk of sexual assault from all the men around them. For twenty-first century

Europeans, this is hugely problematic. But for women in the fifteenth century, it was a fact of life. All women who worked as part of a household in whatever capacity—and there were many different levels of service and servitude—faced this risk, as did young boys in a household. Adult males were the predators, and could effectively have sex with whomever they chose; many were restrained by religious and moral imperatives, and some by status or emotional considerations, but as the Innocenti records show, many were not. And the sexual encounters between Florentine men and sub-Saharan African women imported from West Africa as a result of the new Portuguese trading empire led to a new generation of mixed-ancestry children in Renaissance Florence.

Terminology

Fortunate though it is to have them, there are significant problems with the Innocenti documents. One is that they are mainly written records recounting oral exchanges on the cusp between the formal and the informal, with all the attendant but irretrievable interferences and losses. They are also written records documenting in the main unequal exchanges between an official at the Innocenti and someone with no authority, with the official questioning or interrogating the non-official, and that too has consequences for what was said and which parts of the oral exchange are preserved. Orality may have been the most usual medium of communication, even if increasingly in this period interwoven at various points with written text, but from this distance knowledge of oral exchanges is only available if it was written down, creating an additional layer of impediment to the understanding of its spoken reality.[19] The act of turning speech into text removes evidence of hesitation, delivery, mood, demeanour, gesture; all of which affect transmission, with the result that, in addition to whatever editing of content took place, the oral was always pared down for re-presentation in written form.

The most intractable problems, however, relate to terminology. Even if the same words are being used in the twenty-first century as were being used in the fifteenth, they often no longer have quite the same meaning. The words that are especially relevant to this discussion are *ghezzo* and *nero/negro*, as these are labels that Florentine record-takers at the Innocenti used to identify

19. For the relationship between the oral and the written in a variety of contexts, see Stefano Dall'Aglio, Brian Richardson and Massimo Rospocher, eds, *Voices and Texts in Early Modern Italian Society* (London, 2017).

African and mixed-ancestry adults and babies. The noun *ghezzo*, often understood or interpreted in the early modern period to mean a 'gypsy'—the word
used at the time in western European languages to describe a member of what
are now usually called the Roma and other groups—in these documents appears to refer instead exclusively to someone with dark skin colour and appears
not to be a reference to an individual from a defined group.[20] The use of *ghezzo*
to describe a skin colour is adjectival.[21] The word *zingaro* or *zingano*,[22] on the
other hand, does refer to a member of the ethnic group known then as 'gypsies'.
This is made clear in the 'Libro dei morti' (Register of deaths) maintained for
those who died in the Florentine hospital of Santa Maria Nuova in the later
fifteenth and early sixteenth centuries, where 'Lucia gheza' and 'Margherita
gheza' are clearly distinguished from 'Giovanni di Marco zingano'.[23] However,
the possible confusion between or conflation of dark-skinned people from
sub-Saharan Africa and dark-skinned people believed to be from Egypt but in
fact probably from north-western India—'gypsies' or Roma—does not stop
with the words employed to label them, but extends to encompass dress, behaviour, social status and occupations, all of which were markedly different
between the two groups.

20. See Florio, *Queen Anna's New World*, p. 208, where the definition of *ghezzo* includes 'ripe
and mellow; ripe and withered; differing in hew and colour from the parents; a mungrell; a
foolish fellow, a sillie gull, a shallow pate; used also for a cozening Egiptian, or Giptian' (only
the definitions from 'mungrell' onwards are nouns); Pianigiani, *Vocabolario etimologico*, 1, p. 604:
'nome del popolo che dall'Arabia meridionale in tempi remoti passò in Affrica, sulle coste sud-
ovest del Mar Rosso. Nericcio: e dicesi del colore della pelle umana, quasi simile a quella dei
mori di Barberia o degli Egiziani'; Battaglia, *Grande dizionario*, 6, p. 729: 'Nericcio, nerastro,
moresco; che ha la pelle di colore scuro; moro, negro' (only the final 'moro, negro' are nouns).

21. In 1583 Filippo Sassetti wrote from Lisbon to his friend Baccio Valori in Florence, saying
that the inhabitants of Cochin were *ghezzi*. In 1970 this was glossed by an editor of the text as
'di colore nero non molto intenso': Sassetti, *Lettere*, pp. 296 and 297 n. 2. This translation is
backed up by another passage in Sassetti's letters. Writing from Lisbon to Baccio Valori in 1578
of Muslim 'moors' in India, Sassetti explained that they were 'propriamente ghezzi, che è tra il
zingano e 'l nero': ibid., p. 220.

22. Florio, *Queen Anna's New World*, p. 615, where his definition of *zingani* includes 'counterfeit Egiptians, runnagate 'Gypsies' or Roma'; Battaglia, *Grande dizionario*, 21, p. 1080 where
zingaro as an adjective is defined as, 'Che appartiene al gruppo etnico originario dell'India
nordoccidentale e diffusosi, a partire del X sec., nel Medio Oriente, in Europa e nell'Africa
Settentrionale'; it is also a noun.

23. ASF, Ospedale di S. Maria Nuova, 730, 40v (Lucia gheza who died in 1490) and 43v
(Margherita gheza who died in 1478); ibid., 731 [Infermi e morti, 1470–1512], 116r (Giovanni di
Marco zingano who died in 1505).

Africans in general, and sub-Saharan Africans in particular, in fifteenth-century Florentine records are virtually never described as Africans, and never in the Innocenti records are they identified according to place of origin (which presumably the Florentines did not know). Nor are they identified by the generic term *etiope*, which usually signals a sub-Saharan African rather than someone from Ethiopia, that can be found in other types of document from the period. A Latin document in the Florentine notarial records, for example, dated 26 April 1474, concerns the sale for twenty-five *fiorini larghi* of 'unus puer ethiops seu ghezus' (a black or dark-skinned boy) known in his language as Hali, and later baptised as Iohannes Baptista/Giovanbattista and nicknamed Vulpinus;[24] the juxtaposition of the two adjectives *ethiops* and *ghezus* is unusual in Latin at the time. In the Innocenti records, too, Africans are distinguished not by place of origin, but by having a label attached to their skin colour. In the fifteenth-century Innocenti records, the words attached to skin colour, *ghezzo* and *nero/negro*, were used as both nouns and adjectives. Usually these words could be translated as 'light or pale black' (possibly 'dark brown') and 'black', with *ghezzo* also having a possible secondary link to 'Egyptian' (*egiziano*), already mentioned, for example in John Florio's Italian–English dictionary of 1611.[25] In other contexts, the words are predominantly used to describe colours or tones of skin, on a possible scale with *negro* being the blackest, *nero* being in-between, and *ghezzo* being the least black.

Two other entries deepen this comparative reading of *ghezzo* and *nero*, although they are not found until the 1480s, and may be the result of entries being written by a different record-taker. The first is that the formulation 'di colore ghezzo' (of *ghezzo*/black colour) is occasionally used to describe the skin colour of a baby.[26] The second is the use of the expression 'a viso gezzo' (with a g[h]ezzo/black face).[27] It used to be thought that *ghezzo* might indicate

24. ASF, NA 9700 (ser Giovanni di Piero da Stia), under date. The seller Bonaiutus Iohannis de Ponte ad Sevem was described as a 'gomitus et navigans' or 'gomitus et se exercens in navigando'. *Gomitus* is the word for a ship's boy, so the child had probably been acquired on a trading voyage. There are two versions of this sale. In the first, the boy was described as a 'puer ghezus', and in the second as a 'puer ethiops' or 'puer ghezus', and later in the second version as a 'puer ethiops', so the terms are unstable but sometimes interchangeable. It is possible that this was due to lack of knowledge of the difference between sub-Saharan Africans and 'gypsies'.

25. Florio, *Queen Anna's New World*, p. 208, but not included in the earlier edition, *A Worlde of Words* (London 1598), p. 147.

26. AOIF, 495, 302v, 6 May 1485.

27. Ibid., 304v, 11 May 1485.

a person of mixed ancestry, but now it seems certain that, in the Innocenti records at least, all three words—*ghezzo, nero* and *negro*—could be used to describe either Africans or people of mixed ancestry. But in the Innocenti records it quickly becomes clear that the first two were also being used interchangeably: that is, when someone is described in one document by one record-taker as *ghezzo*, they could elsewhere be described as *nero* by another record-taker. Not only that, but the same record-taker could also use the words interchangeably, even to describe the same person, as though there was no difference between the meanings.

What does this mean, apart from making life extremely complicated? Clearly, the terms cannot be relied upon as genuine descriptors of varieties of skin colour. One possibility is that fifteenth-century Florentines were struggling to pin down and name the new things that they saw in front of them—in this case, African parents and mixed-ancestry babies. In this respect, there is a difference between the Innocenti records and the *catasti* or tax records from the same period of the 1450s to 1480s. The tax records were financial, not at all concerned with appearance or identification, but instead concerned with prices and values. In them, an African or mixed-ancestry slave (when identified) is described simply as, for example, 'una schiava nera' (a black slave), because that was a known 'possession' that had a known value. The Innocenti records, on the other hand, served to identify the babies as much as possible, by describing their appearance and distinguishing features. Noting the colour of their skin fell into this category—even if the terms used are not precise enough to be of much help in this discussion of mixed-ancestry origin. *Ghezzo* is also more colloquial, not a basic, formal word like *nero*, meaning 'black' in general, which may be another reason for its use at the Innocenti. As a consequence, *ghezzo* virtually never appears in the *catasto*, but appears often in the Balie e bambini records.

In some instances, genuine confusion is the most likely explanation for usage. 'Gypsies' or Roma had appeared on the Italian peninsula in 1422, arriving in Bologna on 18 July, staying fifteen days, and arriving in Forlì on 7 August.[28]

---

28. Their arrival was reported in two contemporary chronicles: the anonymous *Cronica* of Bologna: Albano Sorbelli, ed., *Corpus chronicorum Bononiensium*, RIS/2, 18.1 (Città di Castello-Bologna, 1906–39), pp. 568–70, where the 'gypsies' were said to have come from Egypt; and the *Chronicon fratris Hieronymi*: Hieronymus Foroliviensis, *Chronicon fratris Hieronymi de Forolivio ab anno 1397 usque ad annum 1433*, ed. Adamo Pisani, RIS/2, 19.5 (Bologna, 1931), p. 34, where the 'gypsies' were said to have come from India and were described as 'indiani'.

Much talk accompanied them.[29] There is no record of a band of 'gypsies' passing through Florence at this date; rather there are stray records of individual 'gypsies' living and dying in Florence in the fifteenth and early sixteenth centuries.[30] In the beginning, before either group was very numerous or common, Florentines could conceivably have muddled 'gypsies' and Africans, as both had darker skin than Florentines or Tuscans, and they may have taken the lazy way out by not differentiating between the two groups. More worrying is that this confusion between sub-Saharan Africans and 'gypsies' was long-lived—it was still evident in the late sixteenth century—and may conceivably have been a deliberate choice, to bunch together two groups of outsiders. One consequence of this attitude is that 'gypsies' are often portrayed as very dark-skinned in art,[31] although they are not usually portrayed as having African physiognomies.

Example 1: A Black Baby and a Black Toddler, Probably of Mixed Ancestry, Both Born in 1451

This and the following sections will examine a number of occasions when mixed-ancestry children, identifiable as such because of their skin colour which was noted by the record-takers, were left at the Innocenti.

In the first scenario, on 17 September 1451 a baby boy was left in the *pila* with a bag of salt tied round his neck, signalling that he was unbaptised. (Salt was popularly believed to protect children from evil prior to their baptism.) A note left with the baby stated that he was the son of the female slave of Antonio d'Antonio del Papa, one or other of his parents was *ghezzo* ('nato o di ghezza o di ghezzo'), and that he was *nero*, or black.[32] What is interesting here is that because 1451 is early for black slaves to be in Florence, the automatic assumption

29. Giuliano Fantaguzzi, *Caos*, ed. Michele Andrea Pistocchi, 2 vols (Rome, 2012), 2, p. 900: 'Cingari venne in Italia del 1422 zò·ffo el duca Andrea d'Egipto remesse in la fede christiana da lo imperratore.'

30. For example, ASF, Ospedale di S. Maria Nuova, 731 [Infermi e morti, 1470–1512], 116r for Giovanni di Marco zingano, who died on 10 May 1505.

31. Paul H. D. Kaplan, 'Bartolomeo Passarotti and "Comic" Images of Black Africans in Early Modern Italian Art', in Angela Rosenthal, ed., with David Bindman and Adrian W. B. Randolph, *No Laughing Matter: Visual Humor in Ideas of Race, Nationality and Ethnicity* (Lebanon, NH, 2016), pp. 23–48 at 29 and 44, nos. 22 and 23.

32. AOIF, 486, 47v. See also A. Galeotti Flori, 'Le schiave orientali madri e nutrici allo Spedale di S. Maria degli Innocenti nel 1400', *Rivista di clinica pediatrica*, 67.4 (1961), pp. 257–64 at 263.

is not that the mother is a black slave, which it undoubtedly would have been even fifteen or twenty years later, but merely that at least one of the parents must have been black for the baby to be black. It is also clear that the Florentine record-taker believed black skin to be hereditary, and not—as in some parts of Europe, following classical authors—a condition caused by exposure to the sun. With regard to the meaning of the word *ghezzo* in this context, it has to be a skin colour descriptor. 'Gypsies' were virtually never enslaved,[33] and the mother here is specifically referred to as a slave. There were occasional sub-Saharan African slaves in Florence before 1450, but they were uncommon. Two are noted, for example, in the arbitration document relating to the legacy of Antonio, Piero and Jacopo de' Pazzi, in 1446. The references are unambiguous: to Franciscus Niger (Francesco nero) and Johannes Niger (Giovanni nero), called Giovanbiancho.[34] This last, mock-jokey nickname, the equivalent of 'John/Johnny White', can be found in most if not all the languages of western Europe at the time.

Antonio d'Antonio di Stefano di Pino del Papa, the owner of the enslaved woman, can be tracked through his tax returns in the *catasti* between 1427 (the first one) and the 1450s. In 1427 he was twelve and living only with his ten-year-old sister, Sandra, in a household without adults in the *quartiere* (quarter) of San Giovanni, and *gonfalone* (district) of Chiavi; one or both of his parents must recently have died.[35] By 1446 he had moved to Santa Croce, Ruote, and was living alone, aged thirty, with his one-year-old daughter; his wife had probably died in childbirth.[36] By 1451, the year of the Innocenti entry, he was living in the same *quartiere* in a house that used to belong to his mother, Madonna Chaterina, the wife of Filippo di Ghezo.[37] Unfortunately, the 1451 *catasto* does not contain lists of *bocche* or 'mouths'—that is, members of the household, so it is not known who was living with him. Nor are any slaves listed. It is ironic, however, that Antonio del Papa, the owner of the enslaved woman, had a mother one of whose husbands had the surname 'di Ghezo', when Antonio's female slave was the mother of the first baby to be described by the Innocenti

33. On 'gypsies', see Peter Bell and Dirk Suckow, 'Fremde in Stadt und Bild', in Peter Bell, Dirk Suckow and Gerhard Wolf, eds, *Fremde in der Stadt: Ordnungen, Repräsentationen und soziale Praktiken (13.–15. Jahrhundert)* (Frankfurt, 2010), pp. 13–32 at 26–29.

34. ASF, NA 9273 (ser Giovanni di Zanobi Gini), 156r, and Howard Saalman, *Filippo Brunelleschi: The Buildings* (University Park, PA, 1993), p. 444. Saalman misread the enslaved man's nickname as Giovanbiondo.

35. ASF, Catasto 80 (S. Giovanni, Chiavi), 220v.

36. ASF, Catasto 665 (S. Croce, Ruote), 113r.

37. ASF, Catasto 701 (S. Croce, Ruote), 95r–v.

as 'black', and which was said to be the offspring of a *ghezzo* or *ghezza*, here to be understood merely as a dark-skinned person rather than as a 'gypsy'. Can this really just be coincidence, or is there a hidden backstory? In 1457 Antonio was living in the same house on the via di Santa Maria Nuova. He was forty, his wife was twenty-five and pregnant, and they had two children, aged six and two. No slaves were declared.[38]

On 18 October 1451, a toddler of eighteen months, who already had the name Benedetto, was left at the Innocenti. The notes on his arrival are written in a hand different from that recording the entry of the black baby boy a month previously, on 17 September. Yet the October child too was categorised as *nero* or 'black' and described as the son of 'una gheza ischiava' (a 'gypsy' or black slave) called Chiara, and a *chalzolaio* or shoemaker.[39] For the reasons set out above, an enslaved gypsy is unlikely and the term *ghezza* should here also probably be understood as a skin-colour descriptor. The child was brought in by Averanza, the wife of a shoemaker who specialised in *scharpette* or small shoes for toddlers and children, who may have been the wife of the father—or just someone else in the shoemaker's circle. On 31 October the little boy was sent to the wet-nurse, where he died six weeks later, on 15 December 1451. Even though he was separated from his natal family, he was not separated from examples of their material culture, which accompanied him as he made his way through the various stages of being deposited at and incorporated into the Innocenti. Unusually, there were two pairs of *scarpette* in the short list of belongings sent with him to the wet-nurse,[40] a sign from someone in the family that the child was loved and provided for.

These two—a baby and a toddler—are the earliest children to be described as 'black' in the entry registers of the Innocenti. Following common custom there, Antonio del Papa's slave's baby was given two names, Filipo and Inocente.[41] More than sixty per cent of babies mentioned in the Florentine *ricordanze* (diaries or journals) studied by Christiane Klapisch-Zuber had a second name (while only fifteen per cent had a third name), and legitimate Catholic babies were usually allocated first names from the paternal family stock and second names that were overwhelmingly saints' names.[42] In the Innocenti, on the

38. ASF, Catasto 808 (S. Croce, Ruote), 532r–534r.

39. AOIF, 486, 50r.

40. Ibid., 50r.

41. On naming practice, see David Herlihy, 'Tuscan Names, 1200–1530', *Renaissance Quarterly*, 41.4 (1988), pp. 561–82.

42. Christiane Klapisch-Zuber, *Women, Family and Ritual in Renaissance Italy*, trans. Lydia Cochrane (Chicago, 1985), pp. 283–309 at 292.

other hand, virtually all the children deposited were given two names, and the second name often served to 'identify' the child. These descriptive names encapsulate what the Innocenti, on the basis of very little information, thought was the essence of the person: their ethnicity, their state of solvency, their skin colour, their treatment by their parents and so on. In other words, it was understood that names could allude to the circumstances of a child's birth. An instance of this occurs in Boccaccio's *Decameron*, II, 6: a baby who is born when his mother has had to flee from her natal city is named 'lo scacciato' or 'the outcast' by his mother;[43] and second names at the Innocenti can be equally startling. For example, one little girl was christened Richa, as her father was rumoured to be a very rich citizen who had said he was going to reclaim her.[44] Other children were given second names of Abbandonata (Abandoned) or—even worse—Gittata (Thrown away).[45] The distinctive second names reveal a desire on the part of the Innocenti to distinguish between foundlings and those of legitimate birth by marking the child with an inalienable name referring to their inauspicious origins. Inocente was a very common second name at the Innocenti in 1451, with eleven babies given it between 3 May and 17 September. However, under the two names at the head of the entry relating to the black baby, a different—but still a fifteenth-century—hand has written 'ghezzo' (Fig. 5).

In the notes underneath the main entry, concerned with wet-nurses and so forth, the baby is always referred to as 'Filipo et Inocente', and the word *ghezzo* is never included. Although it was possible to have three names, this therefore is not a third name but rather a descriptor, which makes its appearance here significant, as it is a comment on the baby's difference or alterity. The addition of this descriptor in a prominent position under the two given names was unnecessary, according to the internal logic of the series documentation. Within ten days, Filipo Inocente had been sent to a wet-nurse (*balia*), and he must have been a robust and healthy baby, because he managed to survive for almost two years, dying in September 1453.[46] In only one other entry does the word *ghezzo* appear: that for 'uno fanciullo maschio nero' (a black male baby)—so probably another mixed-ancestry child—born on 17 January 1484, who was

43. Boccaccio, *Decameron*, 1, p. 202 and n. 8.

44. Trexler, 'Foundlings', p. 271.

45. AOIF, 492, 181v, 14 Jan. 1474/5.

46. At least some of the babies were buried on site at the Innocenti, probably in a mass grave, where the presence of African and mixed-ancestry children make this a global graveyard: AOIF, 495, 239v, 16 October 1484.

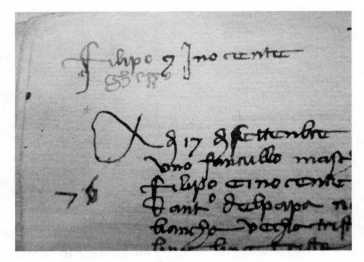

FIGURE 5. Florence, Archivio dell'Ospedale degli Innocenti 486, 47v, 'ghezzo'. Courtesy of Istituto degli Innocenti di Firenze. Photo: Kate Lowe

given the names Salimbene et Antonio, and 'ghezzo' again is added;[47] in the baptismal records, it is absent. The 17 January is the feast day of Saint Anthony, which explains the second name. There is no information available about the child's parentage.

Example 2: Ghaleotto and Lixabetta, Two Enslaved West Africans in Florence, in the 1460s and 1470s, and Their Children

The second example starts with a baby born to a black 'couple', who was left at the Innocenti on 10 December 1470. The record-taker wrote the following notes (Fig. 6): the baby was accompanied by an unrelated woman and by a slave of Bengni Strozzi called Ghaleotto.[48] By the fifteenth century, *galeotto* is the word for a man who rows on the galleys:[49] someone, that is, who has either

47. Ibid., 122v.

48. Lorenz Böninger and I are engaged in a study of Ghaleotto.

49. Already Dante was using 'galeotto' in *Purgatorio*, canto 2.27 in a sense that showed its derivation from *galea*.

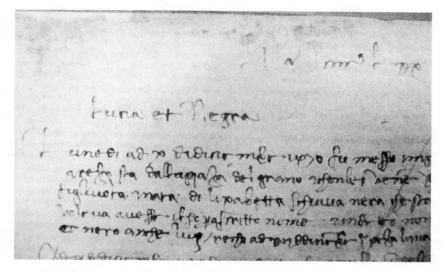

FIGURE 6. Florence, Archivio dell'Ospedale degli Innocenti 491, 339v. Courtesy of Istituto degli Innocenti di Firenze. Photo: Kate Lowe

been enslaved or has committed a crime.[50] So, once again, a person in a disadvantaged position has been inscribed with a name that alludes to an inferior status or occupation. In addition, there is the matter of the suffix. Like many suffixes, -otto is ambiguous. It is usually augmentative, carrying a suggestion of sizeableness or bigness, sometimes combined with admiration or its opposite, distaste,[51] both of which could operate in the case of a rower on the galleys. Ghaleotto said that the baby was his, that she was not baptised,[52] and that he wanted her to be named Lucia: the closest female saint's day was that of Santa Lucia, on 13 December.[53] He continued by saying that the baby's mother

50. Michael Mallett, *The Florentine Galleys in the Fifteenth Century* (Oxford, 1967), pp. 29–30 discusses the crews on galleys in the fifteenth century, when oarsmen were free rather than enslaved, and does not use the word *galeotto*. But see the definition in Pianigiani, *Vocabolario etimologico*, 1, p. 583.

51. Barbara Reynolds, *The Cambridge Italian Dictionary* (Cambridge, 1962), p. xxiv.

52. Ghaleotto and Lixabetta might not have baptised their daughter because they lacked the money to pay the priest's 'fee', not realising that many people omitted paying.

53. Lucia was the equal eighteenth female name in terms of popularity in Florence in 1470: Francesco Sestito, *I nomi di battesimo a Firenze (1450–1900): Dai registri di Santa Maria del Fiore un contributo allo studio dell'antroponimia storica italiana, Quaderni italiani de RIOn* 6 (Rome, 2013), p. 27.

was Lixabetta, a black (*nera*) slave also belonging to Bengni. The record-taker added, in a tone of surprise, that Ghaleotto himself was also black (*nero*) ('il detto Ghaleotto è nero anche lui').[54]

It must have been very surprising to a Florentine that the child had two black parents, and indeed she may be the first black child born to two sub-Saharan Africans/black parents in Florence in the Renaissance period. As slaves were not usually permitted to marry in northern or central Italy,[55] having sex while under the same roof may have been the closest these two could come to being a couple in Renaissance Florence—although one should not romanticise this, and the sex in this case too might not have been consensual. Lucia's second name, chosen presumably by the Innocenti, was Negra (Black). Negra is clearly a name, not a descriptor, but a name derived from a facet of appearance. The dividing line here between name and descriptor is that a name is for life, whereas a descriptor was valid only at the moment it was given. Nero/a is a common name in Florence but Negra is not. One baby called Nero had been born to a mother described as a 'ghezza',[56] but many others with this name were white babies, so the name Nero/a did not automatically imply that the baby was dark-skinned. Bianca[57] is also common as a girl's name, and even Bionda[58] and Mauro[59] can be found on occasion, but Negra is never otherwise used. Inscribing Lucia Negra's skin colour into her name was a particular technique of insistence.

Lucia Negra was unusual in other respects, most notably because her father accepted paternity, and tried his very best to help her. The majority of children at the Innocenti did not have fathers who acknowledged paternity. It was much more unusual for a man than for a woman to take a child to the Innocenti, and highly unusual for a father to accompany his child as it was being dropped off. Of the bearers of the first hundred children left there after its foundation in 1445, only two were fathers, and only fourteen were unrelated men, as opposed to thirty-seven unrelated women.[60] Ghaleotto not only accompanied his child

---

54. AOIF, 491, 339v and Kate Lowe, 'Black Africans' Religious and Cultural Assimilation to, or Appropriation of, Catholicism in Italy, 1470–1520', *Renaissance and Reformation/Renaissance et Réforme*, 31.2 (2008), pp. 67–86 at 70.

55. Lowe, 'Black Africans' Religious', pp. 83–84, n. 18 and below, pp. 214–15.

56. AOIF, 492, 39v, 7 January 1472/3, and 492, 238v, 11 August 1475 ('nato di una ghezza').

57. For example, AOIF, 493, 184v.

58. For example, Ibid., 319r, 23 February 1479/80.

59. For example, AOIF, 492, 283v, 22 January 1475/6.

60. Trexler, 'Foundlings', p. 265.

on 10 December when she was deposited, but he also returned two days later to drop off pieces of cloth and clothing for her, even leaving a man's shirt, 'una camicia da uomo', the equivalent of 'the shirt off his back'—an extremely rare occurrence. By then, on 11 December, Lucia had been 'lent' out to Lorenzo de' Cresci, in order to keep the milk of the wet-nurse hired by him for his expectant wife flowing whilst waiting for the baby to arrive. Lucia thus became entangled in the web of practices and conventions surrounding breastfeeding—what one historian has described as 'the market in milk'. This was not uncommon, as it allowed the orphanage to save on the costs of wet-nurses.[61] But in this case, it had tragic consequences, and Lucia died five days later, on 16 December. According to Philip Gavitt, however, and perhaps counterintuitively, the mortality rate of babies lent out in this way was lower than the rate for babies who were kept in-house at the orphanage and for those who were sent out to a wet-nurse, because of the higher standards of living of the patrician families to whom the babies were lent, and because it was in the patrician family's interests for the baby to be as healthy as possible. Of the first one hundred children left at the Innocenti, thirteen were loaned and only one died whilst on loan. Lucia's death may have been an exception.[62]

But there were precedents. Lucia's mother Lixabetta had already given birth in Florence three years earlier, on 14 September 1467, and the baby had been deposited at the Innocenti. Whoever left the baby hurried away without being seen or interrogated. The mother was described in a note attached to the baby as 'a *ghezza* called Lisabetta, the slave of Begni and Tomaxo Strozzi'; nothing was said about the father. The daughter was baptised with the names Lisabetta[63] and Mattea.[64] This baby too was lent out, and this baby too died. Lent out the first time on 16 October, she returned to the Innocenti on 11 November, but was lent out a second time on 16 November. On 14 December she died. It is legitimate to consider whether the mixed ancestry or ethnicity of these children might have contributed to higher mortality, but at present it seems that the increased likelihood of mortality was linked rather to gender than to

---

61. Lucia Sandri, 'Baliatico mercenario e abbandono dei bambini alle istituzioni assistenziali: un medesimo disagio sociale?', in Maria Giuseppina Muzzarelli, Paola Galletti and Bruno Andreolli, eds, *Donne e lavoro nell'Italia medioevale* (Turin, 1991), pp. 93–103 at 97.

62. Gavitt, *Charity and Children*, p. 206.

63. Lisabetta and its alternative forms was the tenth most popular name for girls in 1460 and the fourth in 1470: Sestito, *Nomi di battesimo*, pp. 25 and 27.

64. AOIF, 491, 58s.

ethnicity, at least in the first two decades of the hospital's existence (although the better material conditions of patrician homes should have mitigated this tendency).[65] As the examples relating to Lixabetta's two daughters date to 1467 and 1470, they fall outside the period 1452–66 that has been studied in relation to gender and mortality—and possibly with the advent of mixed-ancestry children mortality rates changed, requiring a change too in the modelling of them. The fact that no one was asked about the paternity of Lixabetta's 1467 baby means that the question of who the father was remains open. She could have been Ghaleotto's, or Bengni's or Tomaxo's (the slave owners), or have been fathered by someone outside the household.

Bengni di Jacopo di Ubertino Strozzi's tax return in the *catasto*, for Santa Maria Novella, Leon Bianco, for the year 1469, reveals that although he claimed to have virtually no money or property, he owned two slaves, one a female, valued at thirty-two florins, and the second a male, valued at twenty-five florins; neither is named.[66] Very few people who had no money or income owned two slaves, and Bengni claimed to be living alone with them,[67] creating an uncommon household unit. The difference in value was probably related to the slaves' ages: the female must have been younger, with more years of work in her. Although their skin colour is not specified—as sometimes it is in the *catasto*— these two enslaved people are almost certainly Lixabetta and Ghaleotto. Bengni was sixty-five.[68] He had two brothers, Tommaso and Giovanni,[69] and Tommaso was mentioned as part-owner of Lixabetta in 1467. The two slaves must have been acquired since 1457, as they are not mentioned in the tax return of that year: instead a slave called Lena is listed.[70] Lena was valued at forty-five florins, considerably more than the two later black slaves. Work by Marcello Berti and more recently by Joana Sequeira supplies evidence that Bengni Strozzi was living and

65. Richard C. Trexler, 'Infanticide in Florence: New Sources and First Results', *History of Childhood Quarterly*, 1 (1974), pp. 98–116 at 101; Gavitt, *Charity and Children*, pp. 212–22, esp. 212.

66. ASF, Catasto 921, 85r. Earlier tax returns for him are in Catasto 77, 215v–216r (1427); Catasto 621, 222r–224v (1442), Catasto 709, 664r–665r (1451), Catasto 818, 123r–v (1457). All relate to S. Maria Novella, Leon Bianco.

67. He was also living alone in 1427, 1451 and 1457.

68. According to his tax returns, Bengni was twenty-three in 1427, thirty-eight in 1442, fifty-four in 1457 and sixty-five in 1469.

69. ASF, Catasto 621, 222r–224v at 224v (Giovanni was forty-seven, Tommaso forty-five and Bengni thirty-eight).

70. ASF, Catasto 818, 123r–v at 123r.

working in Lisbon in 1462 and 1463,[71] thus providing an explanation for his possession of the two black slaves. He had almost certainly bought them in Lisbon, and brought them back to Florence with him when he returned, which highlights yet again the role played both by Lisbon's international merchant community and by the Portuguese trading empire in the early African diaspora in Florence. This is a neat example of the transformation in behaviour wrought on a Florentine experiencing the Portuguese trading empire in Lisbon at first hand; it additionally shows how this behaviour could be transposed to Italy.

Two further records of babies may also be part of Lixabetta, Ghaleotto and Bengni Strozzi's entangled stories. So far Lixabetta has had two babies, in 1467 and 1470, and Ghaleotto has been the father of at least one of them. On 19 September 1473, a baby girl left at the Innocenti was declared by her father to have been baptised with the names Maria and Domenicha.[72] Naming practices on the Italian peninsula and among various peoples in West Africa included naming babies according to the day of the week on which they had been born, and Domenicha as a name would fit with both these traditions. Many peoples in West Africa, such as the Akan on the Ivory Coast and in Ghana, the Fon in Benin and the Ewe in Togo, followed these naming practices, which may have originated amongst the Twi.[73] The Innocenti record-taker noted that Maria Domenicha was brought in by a 'ghezzo' called Mariotto, who said he used to live with Bengni Strozzi, and that the baby was Mariotto's daughter.[74] The use once more of the term *ghezzo* is suggestive of a less than friendly, or even neutral, record-keeper, as more black Africans were in Florence by this date, and genuine confusion over sub-Saharan Africans and 'gypsies' or Roma would

71. Marcello Berti, 'Le aziende da Colle: Una finestra sulle relazioni commerciali tra la Toscana ed il Portogallo a metà del quattrocento', in *Toscana e Portogallo: Miscellanea storica nel 650° anniversario dello Studio Generale di Pisa* (Pisa, 1994), pp. 57–106 at 86 n. 120; Joana Sequeira, 'Michele da Colle: Um mercador pisano em Lisboa no século xv', in Nunziatella Alessandrini, Susana Bastos Mateus, Mariagrazia Russo and Gaetano Sabatini, eds, *Con gran mare e fortuna: Circulação de mercadorias, pessoas e ideias entre Portugal e Itália na Época Moderna* (Lisbon, 2015), pp. 21–34 at 29.

72. Maria was the second most popular girl's name in 1470, and Domenica was the fourteenth; by 1480, Maria had slipped to sixth and Domenica to seventeenth: Sestito, *Nomi di battesimo*, pp. 27 and 29.

73. F. W. Migeod, 'Personal Names among Some West African Tribes', *Journal of the Royal African Society*, 17.65 (1917), pp. 38–45 at 30–40; John Thornton, 'Central African Names and African-American Naming Patterns', *The William and Mary Quarterly*, 50.4 (1993), pp. 727–42 at 727–28.

74. AOIF, 492, 88v.

have signalled a deeper disconnect from reality. On closer inspection, the name
Mariotto might also generate unease. It is possible to take the entry at face
value: Bengni might somehow have acquired another slave called Mariotto.
However, closer acquaintance with the lives of Bengni and Ghaleotto now make
this less likely. Much more likely is that the record-taker either misheard (a benign reading), or made a joke at Ghaleotto's expense (a less benign reading), and
that this is not Mariotto, but Ghaleotto. The name Mariotto can mean 'big fool',
from Latin *mario* (fool),[75] so it could have been a pun; but it was also a perfectly
normal and accepted name in Florence in 1470 and 1480.[76] The possibility that
this Mariotto is Ghaleotto is strengthened by two apparently repeated elements
of the man's behaviour: he brings the baby in himself, and he claims paternity,
both of which are highly unusual. It should also be noted that at this point
Mariotto/Ghaleotto is not described as a slave; instead, he is described as a
'ghezzo' and identified by the name of the person with whom he used to live.
He may have been freed, or the record-taker could have assumed that all people
with dark skin were enslaved and considered it unnecessary to underline his
legal status by declaring him to be a slave. It is also noteworthy that Mariotto/
Ghaleotto's daughter had already been baptised before she was dropped at the
Innocenti. The pieces of cloth and clothing left with her are unremarkable. Maria
Domenicha must also have been a healthy baby for she too survived nearly two
years, dying while living with a wet-nurse, on 12 August 1475.

A fourth record that relates to Ghaleotto comes from the baptismal records
in the Opera del Duomo in Florence. Born on 22 April 1479 and baptised the
following day is a baby boy, given three names, Karlo, Jacopo and Romolo,[77]
described as the son of Galeotto nero (Galeotto the black person), 'in caxa di
Nicolo Strozzi'—that is, living in the house of Niccolò Strozzi.[78] . There are
several noteworthy points about this baby. The first is that it appears this child
was born free, not enslaved and then later freed. The second is that if this really
was Ghaleotto's third or fourth child, it was his first not to be left at the Innocenti. This matters. The relevant Balie e bambini register covering this date

75. Fusco and Corti, *Lorenzo de' Medici*, pp. 20 and 220 n. 11.

76. It was twenty-fifth on the list in 1470 and had dropped to equal forty-eighth by 1480:
Sestito, *Nomi di battesimo*, pp. 26 and 28.

77. Carlo was the thirty-third most popular boy's name in 1480, Jacopo the sixth, and Romolo
equal fortieth: Sestito, *Nomi di battesimo*, p. 28.

78. Florence, Opera del Duomo, Archivio storico delle fedi di battesimo di S. Giovanni,
registro 4 (maschi e femmine, 1474–1481), 23 April 1479: 'Karlo Jacopo & Romolo di Galeotto
nero'.

(AOIF 493) records no child with these names left on or after this date, making it impossible to know if the baby survived into childhood or later life. The third point is that this was Ghaleotto's first male child. As once again there was no mention of Ghaleotto being a slave in this record, it is probable that Bengni was dead by this time, and had freed Ghaleotto in his will, or had made provision for him to go to live with his relative, Niccolò. Freedom for slaves was often partial or set at a future date, so Bengni could have freed him in his will but stipulated that before the manumission was activated, he had to work for Niccolò for a certain number of years.

Yet a new document reveals an even more complicated reality. On 21 July 1484 Niccolò Strozzi formally freed Ghaleotto 'Gholieff de Ghinea' (a Wolof from Guinea), described as of middling stature and black, but attached conditions to his freedom.[79] Ghaleotto was forbidden from leaving the house of Niccolò and Giuliano without permission; if he did so, his *liberatio* or manumission would be revoked. A second condition tied him to working in Niccolò and Giuliano's shop. Ghaleotto's life continued to be out of the ordinary for a diasporic African in Florence at this date, in terms both of life events and documentation. Even the notarial document of his manumission was unusual, as it assigned to him a place of origin (if vague) and the name of a sub-Saharan ethnic group. Ghaleotto must have provided this information himself. Most Wolofs were Muslim by the fifteenth century,[80] and by providing his ethnicity, Ghaleotto was simultaneously signalling his prior religion in Africa.

Legal Status

The legal status of babies left at the Innocenti is of relevance. All children deposited there effectively cast off or broke with their past, and were considered 'free' from the moment of their arrival; precisely how this was enacted is not known, but no baby or child at the Innocenti was enslaved. In some cases— such as that of Lixabetta and Ghaleotto—this guarantee of freedom, if appreciated, might have been a factor in their decision to leave their baby there. If Lixabetta and Ghaleotto's baby had remained in Bengni Strozzi's house with them, she would automatically have been a slave, as they were both enslaved, unless her parents' owner Bengni took the legal step of manumitting or freeing her. Looked at from the owner's point of view, a baby required care from its

79. ASF, NA 14183 (ser Giovanni Migliorelli), 246v.

80. Cà da Mosto, *Le navigazioni atlantiche*, p. 44; Crone, *Voyages of Cadamosto*, p. 31.

mother for many years, thus detracting greatly from the work that could be expected from her. Because most domestic slaves had been purchased for their potential to work, interference with that ability was unwelcome as it depreciated the outlay, with the result that owners in urban surroundings were usually unwilling to permit children born to their slaves to remain in the household. Only owners taking a longer-term view might have appreciated the advantages of gaining an additional valuable 'possession' without having to buy it. Slavery operated in different legal contexts in different jurisdictions across the Italian peninsula. According to Lombard law, children took the legal status of the parent with the lowest status, so that a child either of whose parents was enslaved would be a slave. According to Roman law, a child inherited the legal status of his/her mother, yet according to Florentine statute (a *provvisione* of 1366),[81] the legal status of a child in Florence followed that of the father.[82] This too might help to account for the number of babies of enslaved mothers deposited at the Innocenti. In the absence of an acknowledged father, if the child of an enslaved mother had kept her baby at home, that baby would have inherited her enslaved status. If the father was the head of the household, or even one of the sons, it may be that the fathers who refused to accept paternity still preferred not to allow what in fact were their children to be brought up as slaves—because in the absence of a named father, the child would have inherited the enslaved status of their mother—and so sent them to the Innocenti. In any case, all the mixed-ancestry children deposited at the Innocenti whose mothers had been born and enslaved in Africa shed their enslaved status almost immediately after birth, in the act of being deposited, and became free in addition to becoming part of the Christian community.

Example 3: Maddalena, the West African
Slave of Antonio Spinelli

A third example involves another enslaved African in Florence about whom there is a little trail of information: Maddalena, who was owned by Antonio di Lorenzo Spinelli. Antonio shared a palazzo on Borgo Santa Croce with his

81. The 1366 *provvisione* 'De sclavis & servis & eorum materia' is in *Statuta populi et communis Florentiae: Publica auctoritate collecta castigata et praeposita anno salutis MCCCCXV*, 2 vols (Friburg [1778–83]), 1, libro 3, rubrica 186, pp. 385–87 at 386.

82. Iris Origo, 'The Domestic Enemy: The Eastern Slaves in Tuscany in the Fourteenth and Fifteenth Centuries', *Speculum*, 30 (1955), pp. 321–66 at 344 and 364 n. 113.

brother Jacopo. In his *catasto* return of 1469, Antonio declared himself to be forty-six, with a pregnant wife and seven children; this, then, was Maddalena's 'family'. Her age is not given in the *catasto*, but she is valued at forty florins, fifteen more than the twenty-five florins she had cost. The only other piece of information about her in the tax record is that she is 'una schiava nera' (a black slave).[83] On 28 August 1468 a baby boy named Aghostino e Domenicho was left at the Innocenti, supposedly the son of a *fattore* (factor) of Antonio Spinelli, and Spinelli's *serva*—a word which could mean either servant or slave, but slave is clearly the meaning here—'che è ghezza' (who is *ghezza*/black).[84] This is extremely likely to be Maddalena, and Aghostino Domenicho was therefore her child, and of mixed ancestry. Finally, on 31 July 1470, a baby was brought in by one woman who said she'd been given him by a further woman, who said that the baby was the child of a slave of Antonio Spinelli who was *ghezza*. This is precisely the sort of chain of rumour attributing maternity that masquerades as truth but could be very far from it. The baby was baptised Aghostino and Francesco. No father was named—although the fact that the baby was once again named Aghostino could suggest that he had the same father as the previous baby.[85] So the second Aghostino is also likely to have been of mixed ancestry. Unfortunately, by 7 October he was dead. Little sense of Maddalena as a person permeates this tale, although it is noteworthy that at least one of her babies had a known and named father.

Example 4: A Mixed-Ancestry Cluster

A fourth cluster of entries, centred on the examination of nine further babies deposited at the Innocenti during these years who were either labelled black or *ghezzo*, or are known to have had enslaved black mothers, causes a few extra pertinent details to emerge. A baby boy left at the Innocenti on 11 August 1475 by an unnamed widow who claimed the baby had been 'nato di una ghezza' in her presence, was unbaptised on arrival, and was given the names Nero and Tiburzio by the institution.[86] The name Nero appears elsewhere,[87] even if it did not make the cut of the top fifty-two boys' names in Florence in 1470 or

83. ASF, Catasto 914, 1r, 2v, 3r.

84. AOIF, 491, 143v.

85. Ibid., 316v.

86. AOIF, 492, 238v.

87. Ibid., 39v. In this case the baby was left with a note requesting that he be given the name Nero.

1480,[88] but in this particular case it had an extra resonance, and referred to the perceived skin colour of the baby. Nero died three weeks later on 4 September 1475. On 8 May 1477 a baby named Michele and Cesare was brought to the Innocenti; his mother was said to be a black slave called Barbera belonging to Filippo di Bartolomeo Valori.[89] No father was mentioned. The woman who brought him said that they had baptised him in the house, and given him the names above, but just to make sure, the Innocenti rebaptised him on the day of his arrival with the same names. On 11 May he was lent out but returned the same day, and he too died, just over three weeks later, on 4 June. On 1 October 1477, a baby boy was left in the *pila* by an unnamed woman who said he was the child of 'una ghezza serva' of Mona Lena dagli Accieto, and he was baptised the same day with the names Arnoldo and Santi.[90] He died a few months later, on 6 January 1478.

On 2 January 1478 a baby girl born in the house of Giuliano Salviati to one of his slaves called Margherita was dropped off. The father was specifically stated to be unknown. She was given the names Buona and Salviata, thus marking her with the name of the family in whose house she was born.[91] In the Innocenti records neither the mother nor her daughter are recorded as being black, prompting the question as to why some babies were described as black whereas others were not. Maybe this mixed-ancestry baby had a lighter skin colour and appeared or could pass as 'white'. Yet two other pieces of information make it almost incontrovertible that the unseen mother was black, and so her daughter must have been of mixed ancestry. Another piece of the puzzle is provided in this case by the tax return for two groups of Salviati brothers in the same household in the *catasto* for 1469, where Margherita is listed as black: 'una schiava nera che a nome Margherita'.[92] The two sets of brothers are Giovanni and Averardo d'Alamanno, and Piero and Giuliano di Francesco d'Alamanno, who are the nephews of the first two. It is very unlikely, albeit technically possible, that in between the two dates a black enslaved Margherita had left the household and had been replaced by a white enslaved Margherita. A third piece of the puzzle is provided by the records of the Cambini bank, which divulge when Margherita arrived in Florence. She was bought

88. Sestito, *Nomi di battesimo*, pp. 26 and 28.

89. AOIF, 493, 48r.

90. Ibid., 73r.

91. Ibid., 87v.

92. ASF, Catasto 915 (S. Croce, Ruota), 422v/415v (pencil).

by Piero and Giuliano Salviati for 36.18 *fiorini di sugello* from Giovanni Guidetti, a partner and business agent of the Cambini, and transported to Florence from Lisbon on a caravel chartered by the Portuguese João Afonso that docked in Livorno in January 1465.[93] In the bank records she is listed as an item of merchandise, being described in mercantile language as 'una testa nera'.[94] Her mixed-ancestry baby fared no better or worse than many others left at the Innocenti: she was lent out on 4 January (that is, two days after her arrival), was returned on 23 January, and died four months later, on 27 May.[95]

By the 1480s the Innocenti record-takers are using the word *ghezzo* more freely. A black baby boy ('uno fanciullo maschio nero') is left at the Innocenti on 17 January 1484, and because 17 January is the feast-day of Sant'Antonio the boy was baptised Salimbene and Antonio—but 'ghezzo' appears immediately after these names, just as it had in the entry of 17 September 1451 for Filipo Inocente ghezzo. So once again, *ghezzo* is a descriptor; but written for what purpose? In this case it was certainly not a name, as it did not appear in the baptismal records,[96] affording cast-iron proof that it was being employed as a descriptor. Nothing was recorded about the baby's parents, and he died in under two months, on 14 March.[97] In the same year of 1484 a toddler of eighteen months described as 'uno fanciullo ghezzo' arrived with a note giving his name (Antonio); he too soon died, in under two months, on 19 September.[98] This formulation is repeated ('uno fanciullo gezo') for another eighteen-month-old

93. Tognetti, 'The Trade', p. 218. One of the other black enslaved females shipped by Guidetti and Bartolomeo Marchionni via the Cambini Bank in the 1470s from Lisbon to Livorno is discussed in Kate Lowe, 'A Fifteenth-Century Flesh and Blood Black Slave at Villa La Pietra: A Human Precursor to the Acton Blackamoors', in Awam Ampka and Ellyn Toscano, eds, *ReSignifications: European Blackamoors, Africana Readings* (Rome, 2016), pp. 60–67.

94. On this enslaved woman, see AOIF, 12646, 68 and 12683, 105r; Tognetti, 'The Trade', p. 218. A *testa* was a way of counting slaves using a head count. Another system viewed them as *peças*, where one *peça* was a healthy, male slave in his prime or a group of two or three who were older or feebler or female, who were equivalent to him in value: John L. Vogt, 'The Lisbon Slave House and African Trade, 1486–1521', *Proceedings of the American Philosophical Society*, 117.1 (1973), pp. 1–16 at 3 and n. 10; Peter Russell, *Prince Henry 'the Navigator': A Life* (New Haven, CT, 2000), p. 398 n. 7.

95. AOIF, 493, 87v.

96. Florence, Opera del Duomo, Archivio storico delle fedi di battesimo di S. Giovanni, registro 5 (maschi, 1482–1492), 17 January 1483/4: 'Salimbene et Antonio portato agl'Innocenti'.

97. AOIF, 495, 122v.

98. Ibid., 210v.

toddler called Donnino and Giovanni, left on 8 October 1484.[99] The usual formulation is 'uno fanciullo maschio', which is tautological as 'uno fanciullo' has already revealed the sex of the baby. 'Uno fanciullo ghezzo' breaks away from the norm, going one step further than the description 'uno fanciullo maschio nero' recorded for Salimbene Antonio above. Once again, Donnino Giovanni died in under two months, on 5 December 1484. A just-born baby girl described as 'di colore gezza' was brought to the Innocente by 'uno gezzo' on 6 May 1485 and placed in the *pila*. No information was extracted about her parentage.[100] Baptised Giovanna and Vangelista, five weeks later, on 12 June, she was dead. Finally, a ten-month-old baby was placed in the *pila* on 11 May 1485, who had with him an unusually long list of clothes, including a pair of new shoes. No note appears to have accompanied him and no information was provided about his parentage. The record-taker wrote instead that the child 'a viso gezzo' (has a black face), and, presumably as a consequence, he received as a first name Morotto (his second name was Cristofano).[101] The name Moro is yet another instance of a baby being baptised with a name carrying negative connotations, and the suffix '-otto' is once again suggestive, probably indicating that Morotto was big for his age. He died on 3 August.

What can be gleaned from these nine cases? Although the entries in the register of Balie e bambini were constructed mainly from well-worn formulae, there was sufficient flexibility for the use of terms to remain fluid in recording the arrival at the Innocenti of sub-Saharan African or mixed-ancestry babies. Whatever the word chosen to indicate it, blackness was noted. The record-takers stuck to their mission of extracting as much information as possible: from those who deposited the babies, from hearsay, from written notes, from clothing and material objects left with the children and from the babies themselves. In addition to noting the sex of the babies, and whether or not they were a twin, estimates of the age of the baby or child, a note of any peculiarities and a comment on those perceived to be 'black' or have black skin were all pieces of information that could be gleaned from an examination of the babies themselves. This last category of distinction was new, only introduced after black African enslaved women started to be shipped to Florence in the 1450s. But it was not an infallible mechanism for separating 'white' from 'black', as the case of Buona Salviata showed. Her mother was almost certainly a black African,

99. Ibid., 234v.
100. Ibid., 302v.
101. Ibid., 304v.

yet she must have been light-skinned enough not to appear black or of mixed ancestry. Even though 'Ghezzo' was never given as a name, 'blackness' or dark-ness of skin was on occasion enshrined in the names of these babies and tod-dlers, as in the cases of Nero and Morotto. In addition, the survival rate of these mixed-ancestry babies and toddlers is shockingly stark: not a single one of the nine stayed alive for longer than four months, with the shortest time being just three weeks.[102]

Example 5: the Cambini and Slaves

The encounters with the Innocenti of one final group have been extracted from the records: this time slave owners rather than enslaved people. It may sound obvious, but it is worth remembering that some slave owners were more un-principled and crueller than others. As sex often led to pregnancy in the fif-teenth century, the Innocenti records can point a finger at some of the worst offenders—such as members of the Cambini family, whose bank had a very important branch in Lisbon in the fifteenth century.[103] (It is ironic that the name Cambini could also be understood to mean 'small bankers', so that bearers of it were in effect thereby assigned a profession, but at a minor level; this reading linking the name to dealing in the market-place adds another set of connotations to their behaviour.) Many of the account books of the Cam-bini bank are now in the archive of the Innocenti. Some of the first enslaved people brought from West Africa to Florence after the Portuguese started to sail down the coast of sub-Saharan Africa were imported through the Cambini bank in Lisbon in the 1460s and 1470s.[104] When the names of the buyers of these enslaved people are checked, the level of the bank's involvement be-comes clear, as many of the slaves were sold to employees of the bank, some of whom were relatively lowly, and not awash with spare money. While not all merchants or bankers involved in the slave trade would as a matter of course have sexually exploited their slaves, it appears that at least a couple of the

102. Infant mortality rates at the Innocenti have not been worked out for the period after 1466. Nine babies is a very small sample and many babies were deposited when they were al-ready unwell, but for the period 1445 to 1466, the highest rate of infant mortality per thousand infant admissions was 627.7 for the year 1466: Gavitt, *Charity and Children*, p. 217, table 13.

103. Sergio Tognetti, *Il banco Cambini: Affari e mercati di una compagnia mercantile-bancaria nella Firenze del xv secolo* (Florence, 1999).

104. Tognetti, 'The Trade', pp. 216–24.

fifteenth-century Cambini men treated their and others' black slaves as sexual objects for their own gratification.

The sexual behaviour of one set of brothers, Francesco and Bernardo di Niccolò,[105] is exposed by the Innocenti records. Four examples of Cambini sexual involvement with slaves should suffice. In the 1469 *catasto*, Francesco's age was declared to be fifty-eight and his brother Bernardo was said to be twenty-six. The substantial household of five adults over the age of sixteen and eight children admitted to having only one slave, a black African called Giovanna.[106] On 18 May 1464 a baby boy was deposited at the Innocenti by a woman called Mona Bonvenuta, who said the parents were Bernardo di Niccolò Cambini and his slave Crestina.[107] The baby had been born that day and had already been baptised with the names Giovanni Batista and Lorenzo. The woman added that the father (that is, Bernardo Cambini) would reclaim and collect the child, but the baby died on 20 August while with a wet-nurse. This was roughly five years earlier than the 1469 tax return, so Bernardo at this point would have been about twenty-one. Crestina's skin colour or ethnicity is not mentioned. On 30 August 1467 a baby boy left at the Innocenti, with Bernardo Cambini declared to be the father and a slave belonging to Bongianni Gianfigliazzi the mother, was baptised with the names Bernardo and Chanbino, presumably in an attempt to shame the father.[108] This is an interesting entry, as it reveals that Bernardo had sex not only with his own slaves but also with slaves belonging to other people. It is unusual for both names to point a finger so blatantly at a child's father, and it may be that Bernardo's guilt was perceived as greater because he was a repeat offender—and the Innocenti did not take kindly to having to pay for a series of illegitimate children from the same person—and because impregnating another man's slave was a crime that required financial compensation to be paid to the owner, as it was akin to damaging someone

---

105. On whose business, see Luisa D'Arienzo, 'Un quaderno di lettere dell'azienda Cambini di Firenze: Circolazione di capitali in area mediterranea e Atlantica', in Cristina Mantegna and Olivier Poncet, eds, *Les Documents du commerce et des marchands entre Moyen Âge et Époque Moderne (XIIe-XVIIe siècle)* (Rome, 2018), pp. 73–94. Their *catasto* return for 1469 is in ASF, Catasto 923 (S. Giovanni, Leon d'oro), part II, 634r–636v, in which they declared 'una schiava nera' called Giovanni aged twenty-four (635r). They had a wide portfolio of interests, among which can be numbered importing 'due carte depinte' into Rome in 1453: Arnold Esch, *La Roma del primo Rinascimento vista attraverso i registri doganali* (Milan, 2012), p. 65.

106. ASF, Catasto 923 (S. Giovanni, Leon d'oro), part II, 635r.

107. AOIF, 489, 200v.

108. AOIF, 491, 54s.

else's possession.[109] The problem was not illegitimacy per se, but the altogether weightier act of tampering with what 'belonged' to someone else. Bernardo at this date would have been about twenty-five. The enslaved woman was described as 'ghezza'[110] but was presumably a sub-Saharan African, and therefore the baby would have been of mixed ancestry, but no descriptor was given to him. He survived almost seven years, until 16 May 1474.[111] On 24 January 1476/7, a baby girl was left, said to be the daughter of a *serva* (here practically certainly a slave) of Francesco Chambini. The baby was brought in by a *contadino* (peasant), and no further information was forthcoming. No father is mentioned—but the names of the child are a giveaway: Chambina et Paghola.[112] She died a month later, on 22 February. And on 26 December 1482, a baby baptised after arrival with the names Stefano and Pasquino, was deposited—but as it is the 1480s less information is forthcoming: merely that he came from the house of one of the Cambini.[113] These four references to the Cambini, two of them straightforwardly a result of Bernardo impregnating an enslaved woman, are atypical rather than unique, but do allow an impression to be formed of how enslaved women could be viewed in certain households. Some Florentine fathers who had children with enslaved women acknowledged paternity and kept their illegitimate children in their households (even if their wives insisted that the enslaved mothers were sold), as can be seen from the *catasto*,[114] but

109. Origo, 'Domestic Enemy', pp. 345–46; Steven A. Epstein, *Speaking of Slavery: Color, Ethnicity and Human Bondage in Italy* (Ithaca, NY, 2001), p. 100.

110. A slave of Bongianni Gianfigliazzi called Chaterina is recorded as the mother of a baby girl left at the Innocenti on 26 August 1468, AOIF, 491, 143s; she may have been the mother too of the earlier child. If so, the enslaved woman was black, and called Chaterina.

111. Ibid., 207s. The entry for the child spans different folios because the child lived for almost seven years, and many expenses were generated.

112. AOIF, 493, 31r.

113. AOIF, 494, 320v.

114. For example, Cosimo de' Medici acknowledged paternity of his illegitimate son Carlo, whose mother was Circassian and one of Cosimo's slaves: Dale Kent, *Cosimo de' Medici and the Florentine Renaissance* (New Haven, CT, 2000), p. 480 n. 5. In addition, Carlo was kept at home: see ASF, Catasto 468, 631r of 1437, where Carlo is included among the *bocche* in Cosimo's tax return, and Raymond de Roover, *The Rise and Decline of the Medici Bank, 1397–1494* (Cambridge, MA, 1963), p. 58. Cf. Debra Blumenthal, 'Masters, Slave Women and Their Children: A Child Custody Dispute in Fifteenth-Century Valencia', in Stefan Hanß and Juliane Schiel, eds, *Mediterranean Slavery Revisited (500–1800)/Neue Perspektiven auf mediterrane Sklaverei (500–1800)* (Zurich, 2014), pp. 229–56, esp. 252.

no children of enslaved sub-Saharan African females are known to have been kept at home in Florence in the second half of the fifteenth century.

Contrasts: Black Women, Children and Babies

It is worth contrasting the arrival of these mixed-ancestry or black babies in Florence in the 1450s to 1480s with the arrival of other known black enslaved women and children imported into Florence in the 1460s and 1470s. Before the women and children from West Africa could be sent to Florence, they had to have been forcibly removed from West Africa. In a slightly later ten-year period, from 1511 to 1522, 1,248 enslaved people were shipped from Arguin in modern-day Mauretania to Lisbon, the overwhelming majority of whom were female. Even though the record-takers at Arguin employed a category of 'babies at the breast', no figure has been computed for them. Rather, children aged two to seven years old accounted for about four per cent, girls aged eight to eighteen about ten per cent and women aged nineteen to thirty-five about fifty-four per cent.[115] These figures show that babies and young children were at a premium in Portugal, and therefore would have been correspondingly difficult to acquire in European destinations to which enslaved black Africans were shipped from Portugal, such as Florence. In addition to distinguishing between babies, children and adults, in an ideal situation pre- and post-pubescent children should also be accounted for separately wherever possible,[116] as children of different ages and stages of development were required for different reasons. The age of the onset of puberty in girls and boys is not certain for fifteenth-century Italy. Puberty was most often discussed in conjunction with capacity to contract marriage rather than as an issue about sexual maturity, although the two were then more intimately connected than now; there was a presumption of puberty at twelve for girls in Roman law, while medieval canon law judged that for girls *plena pubertas* or 'full puberty' was reached at fourteen.[117] The first three enslaved black females imported into Florence in 1461, documented in the

115. António de Almeida Mendes, 'Child Slaves in the Early North Atlantic Trade in the Fifteenth and Sixteenth Centuries', in Gwyn Campbell, Suzanne Miers and Joseph C. Miller, eds, *Children in Slavery through the Ages* (Athens, OH, 2009), pp. 20–34 at 23 (fig. 1.1) and 30.

116. Daniel Amundsen and Carol Jean Diers, 'The Age of Menarche in Medieval Europe', *Human Biology*, 45.3 (1973), pp. 363–69 at 367–68.

117. Willy Onclin, 'L'Âge requis pour le mariage dans la doctrine canonique médiévale', in *Proceedings of the Second International Congress of Medieval Canon Law*, ed. Stephen Kuttner and J. Joseph Ryan (Vatican City, 1965), pp. 237–47 at 237, 246–47.

Cambini account books, were all young women.[118] Of the next seven also imported via the Cambini bank in the 1460s, according to Sergio Tognetti, six were adults and one was a baby, who was bought with her mother.[119] Of the twenty-eight who arrived via this route in the 1470s, only two were identified as children, both estimated at ten years old, one described as 'black' and the other as 'white.'[120] Although the numbers are very small, only one black baby is to be found. This indicates that almost no black babies arrived in Florence at this time, which makes the reactions of the record-takers at the Innocenti to the mixed-ancestry babies they perceived as curious novelties more understandable.

Picking up again the theme of evidence of Este and Medici—or Ferrarese, Mantuan and Florentine—interest in the Portuguese overseas voyages, a second instructive point of comparison arises when the reception of the black babies in Florence in the 1450s to 1480s is compared to Isabella d'Este's stated desire to acquire young black children for her court in Mantua in the 1490s.[121] Here the comparison lies in an understanding of the consequences of these voyages. Were the mixed-ancestry babies at the Innocenti seen as consequences? Did Isabella appreciate black skin at some level because of its sub-Saharan African origin? Isabella certainly wanted very young children, believing that eighteen to twenty-four months was the best age at which the children could be acquired,[122] when they were at their most malleable, before they had started to pick up any habits whatsoever. However, unlike Isabella, who inherited a liking for black slaves from her mother and who led a vogue for owning black children at her own and her siblings' courts, and was prepared to pay substantial sums to acquire them,[123] the Innocenti in Florence does not seem to have viewed these black babies as valuable merchandise, or recognised them to be in demand. Had anyone in Florence realised this, the mixed-ancestry children might have found a niche occupation in Florence working for the Medici as servants rather than slaves. Difference in political formation—the gap between Lorenzo de' Medici's regime in a republic and the inherited rule of the marquis of Mantua—is partially responsible for this not happening. In general, enslaved babies in Italy who were not born in

---

118. Tognetti, 'The Trade', p. 217.

119. Ibid., p. 218.

120. Ibid., pp. 223–24.

121. Lowe, 'Isabella d'Este', pp. 65–76.

122. ASMa, Archivio Gonzaga, b. 2991, libro 1, 1v, and Luzio and Renier, 'Buffoni', 35 (1891), pp. 112–46 at 140.

123. Lowe, 'Isabella d'Este', pp. 67–68 and 70.

Italy to enslaved mothers are few and far between. Nor are there a great number of enslaved children, particularly pre-pubescent ones. It has been estimated that the median age of slaves in Genoa and Venice between 1300 and 1500, for instance, regardless of ethnicity, tended to be between fifteen and twenty-five.[124] This means that most people would not have been able to purchase enslaved children under this age, which explains why these were at such a premium: black children under the age of ten were very rare. The youngest child explicitly described as 'black' in the notarial documents tabulated by Domenico Gioffrè sold in Genoa in the fifteenth century was a girl of eight.[125] And the youngest child labelled as black ('de genere ethiopum') in the notarial documents unearthed by Charles Verlinden in fifteenth-century Venice was a boy of ten, in 1430.[126] They were the exceptions. Even more exceptional was a small black boy aged four, brought from Tripoli, who was sold in Venice in 1486 to a Milanese buyer; the four-year-old was forced to collude in his own enslavement by swearing (presumably he did not even understand or speak Italian) that he was already enslaved.[127] But while evidence is lacking that 'white' children were seen as desirable acquisitions, and their prices adjusted accordingly, it is clear that in contradistinction young 'black' children were definitely seen as desirable. Buyers did not order 'white' children in the way 'black' children were ordered. Thus, in addition to all Isabella d'Este's requests, in March 1469 two Venetian gentlemen commissioned ser Marin Zorzi to purchase two black boys aged twelve or thirteen in Seville, where there were many more enslaved children, and bring them to Venice.[128] The quite precise age specified here—just on the cusp of puberty—rings alarm bells.

124. Domenico Gioffrè, *Il mercato degli schiavi a Genova nel secolo XV* (Genoa, 1971), p. 110; Hannah Barker, 'Egyptian and Italian Merchants in the Black Sea Slave Trade, 1260–1500', Ph.D dissertation, Columbia University, 2014, p. 130; Hannah Barker, *That Most Precious Merchandise: The Mediterranean Trade in Black Sea Slaves, 1260–1500* (Philadelphia, 2019), p. 68 and figs. 2 and 3.

125. Gioffrè, *Mercato degli schiavi*, table of 'schiavi mori', under year.

126. Charles Verlinden, *L'Esclavage dans l'Europe médiévale*, 2 vols (Bruges, 1955; Ghent, 1977), 2, p. 660.

127. Ettore Verga, 'Per la storia degli schiavi orientali in Milano', *Archivio storico lombardo*, ser. 4, 32 (1905), pp. 188–99 at 196–99; Emanuel Rodocanachi, *La Femme italienne à l'époque de la Renaissance: Sa vie privée et mondaine, son influence sociale* (Paris, 1907), pp. 367–69; Kate Lowe, 'Visible Lives: Black Gondoliers and Other Black Africans in Renaissance Venice', *Renaissance Quarterly*, 66 (2013), pp. 412–52 at 420.

128. Venice, Archivio di stato di Venezia, Giudici di Petizion, Frammenti antichi, b. 13, fascicolo 'Petizion, 1468–70', 33v and 34r; Lowe, 'Visible Lives', p. 420.

Sub-Saharan Africans and 'Gypsies':
Visualising Dark-Skinned Babies

Whatever drawbacks the documentary material in Florence relating to African and mixed-ancestry babies might have, it is plentiful and therefore in quite sharp contrast to visual depictions of them. There are no known visual sources recording the African or mixed-ancestry babies at the Innocenti. The Innocenti's uniformly white and healthy babies are often presented in idealised form with blond hair. Various other visual records of idealised healthy white babies, especially putti, appear in various guises in fifteenth-century Florence. For instance, one dating from precisely the years of the Innocenti mixed-ancestry babies, 1460–70, is on a *desco da parto* or birth tray in the Horne Museum in Florence, and has the *stemme* (emblems) of the Albizzi and Soderini on the verso. Although no image of a healthy black or mixed-ancestry baby is known in Florence from this date, there is however one in Rome, from the later sixteenth century. A black or mixed-ancestry baby is depicted in the city's Ospedale di Santo Spirito in Sassia (Plate 11), one part of which functioned as an orphanage or depository for foundlings.[129] In one of the frescoes in the cycle there datable to 1575–80 and attributed to Lorenzo Sabatino and Baldassare Croce,[130] entitled 'Activities of the hospital', in the *salone* of the Palazzo del commendatore, is a group of wet-nurses with their charges. One of these holds in her arms a black or mixed-ancestry baby,[131] recognisable not only because of his darker skin colour, but because his hair is depicted differently to the hair of the white babies, in conformity with recognised Italian depictions of sub-Saharan African hair.

In general, even outside an orphanage context, there are very few paintings indeed across the fifteenth- and sixteenth-century Italian peninsula depicting

129. On S. Spirito in Sassia, see Pietro De Angelis, *L'ospedale di Santo Spirito in Saxia*, 2 vols (Rome, 1962); Eunice D. Howe, *The Hospital of Santo Spirito and Pope Sixtus IV* (New York, 1978); Carla Keyvanian, *Hospitals and Urbanism in Rome, 1200–1500* (Leiden, 2015), pp. 339–83.

130. Alessandra Rodolfo, 'Gli affreschi del palazzo del commendatore nell'ospedale di S. Spirito in Sassia', *Storia dell'arte*, 77 (1993), pp. 56–76 at 56. The fresco with the wet-nurses and babies is discussed on pp. 63–64, where is it attributed to 'Lorenzo Sabatini e scuola'; no mention is made of the black baby.

131. The fresco is discussed in Diana Bullen Presciutti, *Visual Cultures of Foundling Care in Renaissance Italy* (Farnham, 2015), pp. 210–12, and the child is described as 'of black African descent' on p. 211.

black babies or toddlers, as opposed to the greater number depicting black children. Putti may be considered to fall somewhere between these two categories.[132] It was not until the sixteenth century that the whole spectrum of varieties of skin colour seems to have been taken up in earnest in visual form, on the right-hand side of the bottom border in a 1549 folio in Graduale 814 (a gradual is a book containing the music for the mass) by Evangelista della Croce and Girolamo dei Libri in the Certosa in Pavia (Plates 12 and 13).[133] Here putti not long out of toddlerdom, of various shades of skin colour from white to black, frolic around; there are five of them, one represented as entirely black, another as entirely white and three others in gradations of skin colour in between. The young entirely black child, with tightly curled black hair, is at the centre of the line of five, of whom three dance and one plays a drum. This miniature can be traced back to a print attributed to Amico Aspertini (Plate 14), *Five Dancing Putti*, dating from the end of the second decade of the sixteenth century, copied almost immediately by Giovanni Antonio da Brescia. The five putti are in the Aspertini and da Brescia prints,[134] but one of the two head-dresses, all the anklets with little bells and the differing skin colours have been added by the miniaturists.[135] None of the five sports wings. This folio of the gradual is for Christmas Day—'Puer natus est' (A child is born)—and the Christ Child is represented in a wicker basket in a central roundel formed of laurel leaves, while an all-white group of both male and female putti appears on the left, two of whom have wings.

From Florence itself, in the last two decades of the sixteenth century, there are at least two painted representations of younger black babies, both carried in their mother's arms. A black baby is depicted by Antonio Tempesta and his workshop on the ninth vault of the *grottesche* on the ceiling of the Corridoio di Levante (East Corridor) in the Uffizi (Plate 15), in a fresco entitled *A Pagan*

132. On putti, or *spiritelli*, see Charles Dempsey, *Inventing the Renaissance Putto* (Chapel Hill, NC, 2001).

133. See the article on the recent restoration of Graduale 814: https://museilombardia .cultura.gov.it/news/un-tesoro-nascosto-i-graduali-della-certosa-di-pavia/ (accessed 19 April 2023).

134. *Amico Aspertini, 1474–1552: Artista bizzarro nell'età di Dürer e Raffaello*, ed. Andrea Emiliani and Daniela Scaglietti Kelescian, exh. cat., Pinacoteca di Bologna (Milan, 2008), pp. 315–16 and cat. nos. 132a and 132b.

135. Elizabeth Miller, *16th-Century Italian Ornament Prints in the Victoria and Albert Museum* (London, 1999), pp. 53–54. See also Elena de Laurentiis, 'Evangelista della Croce', in *Alumina. Pagine miniate*, 15, no. 59 (2017), pp. 14–23 at 18 (image) and 19 (text).

Sacrifice, the Goddess Nature and a Trophy. In this fresco described by Valentina Conticelli as 'amongst the most ambiguous of the corridor', a black woman holds a black baby in her arms. It has been convincingly argued by Conticelli that the black woman, following a long line of iconographical precedents, represents the goddess Nature, or Mother Nature.[136] Yet now it has been noticed by Lizzy Currie that the black woman wears typical 'gypsy' or Roma clothing, such as the shoulder-fastened blue and red cloak,[137] and another strong possibility is that she and her baby are depictions of 'gypsies'.[138] Given the terminology used by the record-takers at the Innocenti in the fifteenth century, this would be fascinating. As noted above, one consequence of the refusal to distinguish between 'gypsies' and sub-Saharan Africans is that 'gypsies' are often portrayed as very dark-skinned in art. That classical and historically specific explanations for the black figures can both appear simultaneously plausible emphasises the multiple ways in which black skin is perceived and yet also refuses to be easily categorised. The baby on the ceiling is portrayed face-on, with a dark skin and black wavy (but not tightly curled) hair, without an overtly African physiognomy.

The other depiction appears in the newly rediscovered painting by Bartolomeo Passerotti entitled *Homer's Riddle* (also known as *Homer and the Fishermen*), recently acquired by the Uffizi (Plate 16).[139] Painted for the Florentine Giovambattista Deti, this shows a scene on the seashore described by Pseudo-Plutarch, in which the aged blind Homer fails to crack a riddle put to him by

136. Valentina Conticelli, *Le grottesche degli Uffizi* (Florence, 2018), p. 77; Valentina Conticelli, 'Dea Natura, Diana Efesia e Diana nera: Motivi iconografici nella committenza di Francesco I de' Medici; Dallo studiolo di Palazzo Vecchio alle grottesche degli Uffizi', in Giovanni Barberi Squarotti, Annarita Colturato and Clara Goria, eds, *Il mito di Diana nella cultura delle corti: Arte, letteratura, musica* (Florence, 2018), pp. 85–101 at 91–101.

137. Written communication from Lizzy Currie, 22 August 2019.

138. On which, see Vladimyr Martelli, 'Roma tollerante? Gli zingari a Roma tra XVI e XVII secolo', *Roma moderna e contemporanea*, 3 (1995), pp. 485–509; Vladimyr Martelli, 'Tra tolleranza ed intransigenza: Vagabondi, zingari, prostitute e convertiti a Roma nel XVI–XVIII secolo', *Studi romani*, 50 (2002), pp. 250–78 at 258–67; Erwin Pokorny, 'The Gypsies and Their Impact on Fifteenth-Century Western European Iconography', in Jaynie Anderson, ed., *Crossing Cultures: Conflict, Migration and Convergence; The Proceedings of the 32nd International Congress in the History of Art* (Melbourne, 2009), pp. 597–601 at 598–99.

139. See the entry on this painting by Paul Kaplan and Kate Lowe, 'Bartolomeo Passerotti: *Homer's Riddle*', in *On Being Present*, vol. 2: https://www.uffizi.it/en/online-exhibitions/on -being-present-2#2 (accessed 18 April 2023); Marzia Faietti, ed., *Il pittore, il poeta e i pidocchi: Bartolomeo Passerotti e l'"Omero" di Giovan Battista Deti* (Livorno, 2021).

fishermen, and is so depressed by his failure that he dies.[140] Although her presence is as yet unexplained, the scene is presided over by a statuesque black woman in expensive clothes, wearing a pearl earring, holding a baby in her arms. She too wears clothes that can be read as 'gypsy' attire, with the characteristic hat and cloak clasp, but in this case the identification is additionally corroborated by a very early contemporary viewer, Raffaello Borghini, who in 1584 described the figure as a *zingana*, or 'gypsy'.[141] The baby is cradled in her arms in such a way that only the crown of the head is shown, and his/her nose and mouth; yet again, the baby's skin is dark but the hair is not tightly curled. So both of these late sixteenth-century portrayals of dark-skinned babies were probably intended to be understood as 'gypsy' or Roma rather than as sub-Saharan African babies.

Finally, a series of six extant oil paintings by Ippolito Scarsella, known as Scarsellino, part of a larger cycle commissioned around 1614 by a Ferrarese nobleman, Luigi Nigrisoli, about his legendary ancestor the African prince Nigersol of Tombut (Timbuktu),[142] also bucks the trend of non-depiction, for obvious reasons. It is useful for comparison even if it originates outside Florence. The depictions are not of a 'gypsy' baby, but of a royal African baby. Nigersol is both portrayed as a baby carried in arms in *La partenza dell'Africa* (no. 2 of the series) and as a toddler in *Il congedo da Tombut* (no. 1) and *Il comiato dell'eremità* (no. 5). Before his conversion, he wears striped clothes;[143] afterwards, he wears white.

Conclusion

Luckily, documentary material can fill some of the gaps noticeable in the visual record: the thoroughness of the Innocenti Renaissance record-takers enables the teasing out, five and a half centuries later, of some understanding

140. '(Pseudo)-Plutarch on Homer I', in Martin L. West, ed., *Homeric Hymns, Homeric Apocrypha, Lives of Homer* (Cambridge, MA, 2003), pp. 404–13 at 408–11. This text circulated in manuscript and in print in fifteenth- and sixteenth-century Italy.

141. Raffaello Borghini, *Il riposo* (Florence, 1584), p. 567.

142. Valentina Lapierre and Maria Angela Novelli, *La storia di Negro Re del lito moro: Un esempio ritrovato della narrazione pittorica dello Scarsellino* (Ferrara, 2004), pp. 14–15 and figs. 1–6. The paintings are split between private collections in Ferrara and the Museo di Capodimonte in Naples.

143. On the meaning of stripes, see Michel Pastoureau, *L'Étoffe du diable: Une histoire des rayures et des tissue rayés* ([Paris], 1991); Ruth Mellinkoff, *Outcasts: Signs of Otherness in Northern European Art of the Later Middle Ages*, 2 vols (Berkeley, CA, 1993), e.g., 1, pp. 24, 29.

of the physical and cultural encounters between Renaissance Florentines and sub-Saharan Africans. In the case of Ghaleotto and Lixabetta, the Innocenti and baptismal records allow occasional glimpses into two African lives in Renaissance Florence, by recording moments when children were born to both or either of them. If Ghaleotto had not had three or four children in this period, and Lixabetta had not had at least two, we would not even have known that they were West African, nor what their European names were. Whether people at the time picked up on the link between the Portuguese voyages to sub-Saharan Africa, and the arrival of enslaved Africans in Florence, is another matter. At no point in these records is any of these black or mixed-ancestry babies, or their mothers, described as African. Their mothers and Ghaleotto had become dissociated from their place of origin in such a way as to deny not only the relevance, but even the existence, of provenance. Enslavement for them had entailed a loss or cancellation of their past lives, with their African identity taking the greatest hit. This erasure had consequences first and foremost for them, but it also had an impact on the way they were viewed and understood by Florentines, some of whom might not have grasped that they had originally come from Africa. The mixed-ancestry babies deposited at the Innocenti inherited this severed connection; rather than being seen as African, they were however still recognised as something new: they were both Florentine and black.

Views on novelties of all kinds to be found in sub-Saharan Africa and in Portugal abounded, but diverged. For Africa, there was the adage most famously now associated with Erasmus: 'semper Africa novi aliquid apportat' (Africa is always producing something new).[144] In fact, a variant of this saying originated at some point before Aristotle's *Historia animalium*,[145] where it related exclusively to forms of animal life, and was later taken up by Pliny, from whom Erasmus took it.[146] What its verbal status was in the fifteenth century is unknown, but the saying certainly had a presence in Italy by the second half

144. Desiderius Erasmus, Adage III.vii.10, in *Collected Works of Erasmus*, vol. 35: *Adages III iv 1 to IV ii 100*, trans. and annotated by Denis L. Drysdall (Toronto, 2005), 35, pp. 220–21; Saara Leskinen, 'Two French Views of Monstrous Peoples in Sub-Saharan Africa', *Renaissance and Reformation/Renaissance et Réforme*, 31.2 (2008), pp. 29–44 at 31.

145. Aristotle, *Historia animalium*, VIII.606b.28.

146. A. V. van Stekelenburg, '*Ex Africa semper aliquid novi*: A Proverb's Pedigree', *Akroterion*, 33.4 (1988), pp. 114–20; Italo Ronca, '*Ex Africa semper aliquid novi*: The Ever-Surprising Vicissitudes of a Pre-Aristotelian Proverb', *Latomus*, 53.3 (1994), pp. 570–93.

of the fifteenth century in printed form.[147] Portugal too was becoming known at this point as a source of imported novelties, due to its overseas voyages, but in the 1460s and 1470s enslaved Africans might not have been primarily understood as falling into this category. Although the new information about mixed-ancestry babies in this chapter is fragmentary, it is important in terms of our knowledge of Florence's indirect participation in Portuguese imperialism, of the Florentine response to perceived African difference, of the early African diaspora in Italy and of Renaissance attitudes to integration and assimilation. This archival work is also part of a process of recovery: an examination of an instance where cultural presence, deliberately or not, was subsequently erased. The archival record testifies not only to the presence of sub-Saharan Africans and of mixed-ancestry babies, but to contemporary reaction to them, and is thus doubly valuable. By 1530, the political landscape had changed significantly, and the mixed-ancestry, illegitimate Alessandro de' Medici was ruler of Florence.[148]

147. Ronca, 'Ex Africa', p. 581 and n. 40, re the Aldine *editio princeps* of Pliny, *Historia naturalis* (Venice, 1469), and the printing of Polydore Vergil, *Proverbiorum libellus* (Venice, 1498).

148. John K. Brackett, 'Race and Rulership: Alessandro de' Medici, First Medici Duke of Florence, 1529–1537', in T. F. Earle and K.J.P. Lowe, eds, *Black Africans in Renaissance Europe* (Cambridge, 2005), pp. 303–25; Catherine Fletcher, *The Black Prince of Florence: The Spectacular Life and Treacherous World of Alessandro de' Medici* (Oxford, 2016). The ethnicity of Alessandro's enslaved mother is not certain.

4

Inanimate Global Goods

BUYING FOR THE MEDICI COLLECTION ON THE IBERIAN PENINSULA IN THE 1540S

THE SECOND case study focuses on goods as its primary category of global acquisition. The precise topic of this chapter—the moment of acquisition of some of the first inanimate global goods from the Portuguese and Spanish empires by Cosimo I de' Medici in 1547–48—was prompted by my discovery, in 2017, of an unpublished *filza* in the Archivio di stato in Florence: Miscellanea medicea 713. This consists of a duo of account books or account journals bound in one volume, detailing both important purchases and more minor day-to-day expenditure, resulting from a trip to the Iberian peninsula between April 1547 and March 1548 carried out by Bastiano Campana on the orders of Cosimo.[1] Greater understanding of this moment allows in-depth rumination on indirect involvement by parts of the Italian peninsula at this date in these Renaissance Iberian global empires, and the consequent benefits.

Lisbon, Florence and Livorno

Following the precedent set in the last chapter, it is helpful to look in tandem at global and local developments in Florence, Livorno and Lisbon that will aid in thinking about issues surrounding the acquisition of global goods from Lisbon for the Medici collection in the 1540s, and about chronological connections between the places. Livorno was the newcomer in this trio, but all three

---

1. The first extant letter of Campana to Cosimo in the ASF is dated 4 June 1541: Anna Bellinazzi and Claudio Lamioni, eds, *Carteggio universale da Cosimo I de' Medici: Inventario*, vol. 1: *1536–1541* (Florence, 1982), p. 263.

places had moved on greatly from their situation in 1450–80. Cosimo I de' Medici, the ruler of Florence from 1537 to 1574, had ambitious state plans for Tuscany, that called for action and changes not only in the city at the heart of his state—Florence—but also for outliers such as Livorno. Florence quickly reconfigured itself as a state capital,[2] replete with a reorganised bureaucracy and new supervisory bodies. Cosimo had gained full control of Livorno only in 1543, when he had paid the Habsburg emperor Charles V for it to be returned to him.[3] As Porto Pisano became increasingly silted with sand and unfit for purpose, Cosimo decided to shift the operations of his trading port to Livorno. Wanting to demonstrate maritime strength in order to deter the attentions of Charles V's navy, and to be seen to control the Tuscan coast, and realising that he needed a bulwark against raids by Turks, corsairs and pirates, he decided to build a Medici *fortezza* or fort at Livorno (and within it, accommodation for himself and his court).[4] The first document relating to this building campaign is dated March 1547,[5] one month before the departure of the ship described below. From the start of its sixteenth-century enlargement and repurposing, the port of Livorno was therefore conspicuously linked to global developments: via Charles V to the Spanish empire, and via the battle with the Turks over control of the Mediterranean to the Ottoman Empire. Both these links were to result in an influx of goods from the relevant imperial territories to Livorno. In the case of the Spanish empire, the goods were brought mainly from the New World, but also from the East to Seville, where they were purchased, and in the case of the Ottoman Empire, the goods were taken as booty from Turkish vessels. And it was Cosimo who reigned over this realm of goods.

2. Giorgio Spini, ed., *La nascita della Toscana: Dal Convegno di studi per il IV centenario della morte di Cosimo I de' Medici* (Florence, 1980); *Firenze e la Toscana dei Medici nell'Europa del Cinquecento: Il potere e lo spazio; La scena del principe*, ed. Franco Borsi et al., exh. cat., Fortezza del Belvedere, Florence (Florence, 1980); Sefy Hendler, 'Cosimo and the Politics of Culture: Reinventing Florence as a Cultural Capital', in *The Medici: Portraits and Politics, 1512–1570*, ed. Keith Christiansen and Carlo Falciani, exh. cat., The Metropolitan Museum, New York (New York, 2021), pp. 106–10 at 207.

3. Corey Tazzara, *The Free Port of Livorno and the Transformation of the Mediterranean World* (Oxford, 2017), ch. 1, charts the sixteenth-century changes implemented in Livorno by the Medici.

4. Lucia Frattarelli Fischer, *L'arcano del mare: Un porto nella prima età globale; Livorno* (Pisa, 2018), pp. 29 and 32.

5. Ibid., p. 29.

The sea-route between Lisbon and Livorno was well established, employed relatively regularly but not very frequently. It should be remembered that the first enslaved people from West Africa in Florence had arrived from Lisbon in Livorno in the 1460s and 1470s, seventy or eighty years earlier,[6] but at that point Livorno had been a smaller port, of little consequence. Between May 1550 and May 1551, a total of thirty-two ships docked at Livorno, four of which had *padroni* (captains) who were Portuguese and had sailed from Portugal.[7] Unfortunately, the port books detailing the cargoes being disembarked in Livorno are not extant until 1549, the year after the return of the non-European goods for Cosimo I.[8] The first ship noted in the port books that was loaded with goods in Lisbon, including goods from the Portuguese trading empire, was the *San Sebastiano* that docked in Livorno on 26 January 1560. Her main cargoes were sugar, some from São Tomé off West Africa and Santo Domingo in the Caribbean, the rest of unspecified origin, and leather 'd'India', but she also carried porcelain, quince jelly and elephant tusks, all of which items can be found in the cargo brought back by Campana from the Iberian peninsula in 1548.[9]

Lisbon in the 1540s was a significantly different place from Lisbon in 1450–80. King João III ruled from 1521 to 1557, marrying Catarina de Áustria, Charles V's sister, in 1525. The vast trading empire was still intact, but parts of it were losing money at an alarming rate; some merchants and adventurers made huge profits still, but others lost fortunes. Catarina's presence added to the mix of nationalities, and from her vantage point in Lisbon, the centre of the global empire, she was to become one of the greatest female collectors in

6. Tognetti, 'The Trade', pp. 217–19.

7. Paolo Castignoli, 'Livorno in villaggio?', *La Canaviglia*, anno 1, no. 3 (July–September 1976), pp. 97–98.

8. ASF, MdP 2079, portate di navi dal 1549 al 1611 (docking at Livorno). The records that survive are patchy, with a great deal missing, and less concerned with describing individual objects than with registering bulk items, often resorting to mentioning 'chests of goods' without recording the goods themselves. However, they do record elephant tusks, presumably because of their size, and are useful because they record the names of the people to whom individual parts of the cargoes belong. On these records, see also Fernand Braudel and Ruggiero Romano, *Navires et marchandises à l'entrée du port di Livourne (1547–1611)* (Paris, 1951); Nunziatella Alessandrini, 'I porti di Lisbona e Livorno: Mercanti, merci e "gentilezze diverse" (secolo XVI): Alcune considerazioni', in Nunziatella Alessandrini, Mariagrazia Russo and Gaetano Sabatini, eds, *'Chi fa questo camino è ben navigato': Culturas e dinâmicas nos portos de Itália e Portugal (sécs. XV–XVI)* (Lisbon, 2019), pp. 129–43.

9. ASF, MdP 2079, 13r.

sixteenth-century Europe.[10] As well as making choice purchases in Europe, she specialised in goods from the overseas empire, amassing a cornucopia of treasures, a few through the royal treasury but most as gifts or via her agents, ranging from West African ivory oliphants and raffia blankets, to bezoar stones and gold filigree baskets from Hormuz, to ivory caskets and fans, rock crystal cutlery and jewelled encrusted thimbles from Ceylon (Sri Lanka), to porcelain and lacquer from China and the Ryukyu Islands.[11] She was particularly fond of goods from Ceylon. The king of Kōṭṭe, Bhuvanekabāhu VII, sent an ambassador to Lisbon in 1542, the first ambassador from Asia to arrive in Europe, and he brought ivory caskets and other Ceylonese luxury items with him as diplomatic gifts.[12] In a summarised checklist of jewellery, silver and ivory in Catarina's collection drawn up between 1546 and 1548 are noted, for instance, two ivory caskets carved with historiated scenes, the first decorated with gold, sapphires and rubies from 'India', and the second decorated with gold and rubies from Ceylon.[13] In fact both were from Ceylon: 'India' here was a capacious, imperialising concept, whereas Ceylon really signified Ceylon. A third Ceylonese ivory casket presented to the Portuguese viceroy João de Castro, by Māyādunnē, king of Sītāvaka, in Ceylon in December 1547, was given by Castro to Queen Catarina in 1548.[14] It was not, therefore, a piece that had ever been available for purchase in Lisbon.

Raw and decorated ivory—although massively more of the former—flowed into Lisbon in these years,[15] as can be seen by the worked pieces both in Catarina's collection and among the global goods acquired for Cosimo, but their ivory pieces came originally from different continents, and represented

10. Annemarie Jordan Gschwend, 'A Forgotten *Infanta*: Catherine of Austria, Queen of Portugal (1507–1578)', in *Women: The Art of Power; Three Women from the House of Habsburg*, ed. Sabine Haag, Dagmar Eichberger and Annemarie Jordan Gschwend, exh. cat., Schloss Ambras, Innsbruck (Vienna, 2018), pp. 50–63 and catalogue entries on pp. 134–67.

11. *Women: The Art of Power* (see n. 10 above), catalogue entries, pp. 134–67.

12. *Elfenbeine aus Ceylon*, pp. 33–43; *Women: The Art of Power*, pp. 150–51, cat. no. 4.13; Biedermann, 'Diplomatic Ivories' pp. 88–98.

13. Annemarie Jordan, 'Development of Catherine of Austria's Collection', p. 272.

14. *Elfenbeine aus Ceylon*, pp. 70–1, cat. no. 18; *Women: The Art of Power*, pp. 150–1, cat. no. 4.13.

15. Karl Otto Müller, *Welthandelsbräuche (1480–1540)* (Stuttgart, 1934), p. 297 refers to a German book of tolls of 1514–15 (so thirty years earlier than Campana's trip) that discusses a list of goods available for sale in Lisbon, mentioning very beautiful and large elephant tusks from Guinea (see n. 143 below). See Christine R. Johnson, *The German Discovery of the World* (Charlottesville, VA, 2008), p. 109.

very different schools of workmanship. While the collection of the queen might have been composed of exclusive, high-end pieces—occasionally given as diplomatic gifts but more frequently acquired by agents on the ground in Ceylon or Goa—for sale in the shops and on the streets of Lisbon was merchandise of all types, but merchandise that was available to anybody to buy. In precisely these years, Cosimo instructed an underling, whose primary mission was to sell grain to Portugal,[16] to seek out on the side extra-European goods in the global emporia of Lisbon (and secondarily Cadiz and Seville), buy them and bring them back to Florence.[17] Catarina and Cosimo's status, opportunities, expertise and budgets at this point all diverged significantly, with Cosimo the unequal and lesser player under each heading, a point which becomes clearest when the particularities of Cosimo's buying trip are dissected in detail in the case study below. Or, to put it in terms of places rather than personalities, Lisbon was top dog as far as global goods were concerned, and Livorno was the new puppy on the block. Whether Cosimo perceived these goods as membership goods of the European ruling élite, or prestige goods only available to a very select few—that is, whether he was acquiring them to define himself through uniformity or through exceptionality and competition[18]—they point to an understanding that goods were signals as well as possessions. And knowledge and trumpeting of provenance had its part to play in both these processes of consumption; it was not an inconsequential factor.

It is incontrovertible that Cosimo I was a committed accumulator of a vast range of objects and things, from medals to antiquities to maps to seeds, and scholarship has gamely followed him in noting and assessing these accumulations. Yet whereas his great-grandfather Lorenzo de' Medici was what could legitimately be labelled a true 'collector', interested in forming a coherent and focused collection and involved in exercising informed choice about objects, in Cosimo early on the urge to collect in any ordered sense seems to have

16. In May 1541 there is a record of Campana being involved in grain transactions in relation to the Medici: Bellinazzi and Lamioni, *Carteggio*, p. 258.

17. Later in Cosimo's reign, and under the later Medici, buying in Lisbon—and indeed in Iberia as a whole—became much more routine. See Brian Brege, *Tuscany in the Age of Empire* (Cambridge, MA, 2021), pp. 150–53. For what was on offer in Lisbon, see *A cidade global: Lisboa no Renascimento/The Global City: Lisbon in the Renaissance*, ed. Annemarie Jordan Gschwend and K.J.P. Lowe, exh. cat., Museu Nacional de Arte Antiga, Lisbon (Lisbon, 2017).

18. Daniel Lord Smail, Mary C. Stiner and Timothy Earle, 'Goods', in Andrew Shryock and Daniel Lord Smail, eds, *Deep History: The Architecture of Past and Present* (Berkeley, CA, 2011), pp. 219–41 at 221–26.

careered out of control and become an urge to acquire, often randomly and sometimes even in bulk, whatever was available. While Lorenzo built up his own expertise and realised that the provenance of an object—at least in the sense of previous ownership—mattered greatly, choosing where possible to acquire objects given a seal of approval at the highest level as they had previously been owned by popes, cardinals and dynastic rulers,[19] Cosimo continued to believe that more was preferable to less, that quantity mattered more than quality. His focus was on possession rather than provenance or pedigree. This is a significant difference, signalling significantly different activities and leading to significantly different compilations of objects and materials. For instance, Cosimo is known for his interest in coins and medals, but it was precisely that: an interest in all coins and medals, not in any particular kind. The random nature of Cosimo's interest is multiplied because, unfortunately, both coins and medals as groups of objects were often subsumed under the term *medaglie*, and only occasionally were they distinguished between, even though different Italian terms, such as *monete* and *medaglioni*, existed for each type.[20] Cosimo wrote to Alfonso Berardi, the *bailo* (Venetian diplomatic representative) in Constantinople, in October 1546, 'Procurerete d'avere quante medaglie antiche potete d'oro, d'argento, di rame o d'altro metallo, così degli antichi romani, come de' greci, egiziachi ed altri et inviarle qua tutte a noi' (Endeavour to obtain as many coins/medals of gold, silver, copper or other metals as you can, thus ancient Roman, Greek, Egyptian and others, and send them all here to us).[21] These are the words not of a discriminating, hard-to-please buyer, but of a mass accumulator. It may be that Cosimo's less than complete education played a part in this, because the death of his father when he was seven led to interruptions and deviations. Pierfrancesco Riccio, Cosimo's tutor and later his principal secretary and *maggiordomo*, passed on to his charge a competence in Latin and a love of books—and perhaps introduced him to art[22]—but maybe did not inculcate in him a more scholarly or disciplined interest in focused collecting such as would have befitted his subsequent but unforeseen position as duke of Tuscany.

19. Fusco and Corti, *Lorenzo de' Medici*, pp. 6–10, 13–15, 211.

20. Alessandro Monti and Silvia Barbantini, eds, *Il testamento di Paolo Giovio* (Oggiono, Lecco, 1999), pp. 48 ('numismata [. . .] seu medaglias') and 72 ('le monete o i medaglioni').

21. Paola Barocchi and Giovanna Gaeta Bertelà, eds, *Collezionismo mediceo: Cosimo I, Francesco I e il Cardinale Ferdinando: Documenti, 1540–1587* (Modena, 1993), p. 3.

22. Alessio Assonitis, 'The Education of Cosimo di Giovanni de' Medici (1519–1537)', in Alessio Assonitis and Henk Th. van Veen, eds, *A Companion to Cosimo I de' Medici* (Leiden, 2021), pp. 19–44 at 30–33.

One legitimate definition of what constituted a collection in the sixteenth century emphasises systematic gathering according to established criteria and goals.[23] Certainly, the methods used by collectors to amass their collections— whether they were active or passive, whether their acquisitions were random or focused—mattered in terms of the finished product, as did their state of knowledge about what was being collected.[24] Randomness and carelessness in collecting often led to erasure of provenance. Although knowledge of provenance still suffered from the choices Cosimo made about collecting, in his case these drawbacks were mitigated to some extent by his dedicated, extensive network of agents, envoys and intermediaries or middlemen. Most fifteenth- and sixteenth-century rulers of Italian cities, states or kingdoms did not leave the safety of their own territories. Those who did so were usually propelled to this course of action by exceptional circumstances, such as war or attempts to stave off war, as when Lorenzo de' Medici went to Naples in 1479. Consequently, when they wanted to acquire objects from outside their territories, as is already well established in the scholarship, they were constrained to use intermediaries, either sending them specifically for this purpose or finding people resident in the area in question who could act on their behalf. In addition to career agents, spies and merchants, representatives of church and state were obvious candidates for this role, and nuncios, apostolic collectors, ambassadors, envoys and cardinals were all routinely used as personal shoppers by European rulers, who despatched to them their lists of desiderata. Goods desired by rulers were deemed far more mobile, and moved around far more, than rulers themselves, as the goods were possessed by them and existed to be of service. In a global context, this might be obvious, but in a European context (which is what is relevant for goods moving from the motherlands of the Iberian trading empires to Renaissance Italy) perhaps it is less so. The implications and consequences of ruler absence at the moment of acquisition require careful thought, particularly as they intersect with notions of choice and expertise. Ruler absence meant devolution of power and

23. Senos, 'Empire', p. 138, in relation to the collection of Teodósio I, fifth duke of Bragança.

24. Cf. Alison Petch, 'Chance and Certitude: Pitt Rivers and His First Collection', in *Journal of the History of Collections*, 18.2 (2006), pp. 257–66, esp. 264–65. It is noteworthy that August Henry Lane Fox Pitt Rivers (1827–1900), whose collection was donated to the University of Oxford in 1884, 'often [. . .] was content to acquire pieces for which the provenance was uncertain due to its second-hand nature' (p. 264).

agency to the intermediary or agent, who was separated from the ruler by social position, education, knowledge and a salary, although lesser educated, socially undistinguished paid agents were often more knowledgeable about the acquisitions required than better educated, socially higher, unpaid intermediaries. In the main, intermediaries were clients or friends or friends' clients, whereas agents were paid employees. However, intermediaries, lacking know-how, often had recourse to agents in their turn. On one hand, the idea of amassing a collection was firmly established as part of what was considered suitable for a ruler, as collecting defined and projected identity;[25] on the other, it is also the case that the more routine aspects of physical procurement would have been considered beneath the dignity of a ruler, and were activities best left to others, although viewing an important object before purchase, if a possibility, would not have fallen into this category.

Documentation

The new documentation in Misc. med. 713 offers new ways into considering this and other issues. Much of the information possessed hitherto about the Medici collections under Cosimo comes either from letters (in the fabulous Mediceo del Principato collection brilliantly promoted and brought into the public realm by the Medici Archive Project) or from Medici inventories, either in the form of objects listed by room or of objects listed by category or type (*a capi*),[26] in the Guardaroba. Both these types of document are immensely useful in thinking about the practices of collecting, but both also have drawbacks for historians and art historians. Letters can provide interesting and much-needed narrative and anecdote relating to objects, but it must always be remembered that, far from being agenda-free, they are rooted in power structures and are always written for a purpose. The information in them is not necessarily true. Nor is the information in inventories, which are other texts requiring, as all texts do, engagement with both language and stylistic convention in order

---

25. Paula Findlen, *Possessing Nature: Museums, Collecting and Scientific Culture in Early Modern Italy* (Berkeley, CA, 1994), pp. 293–96.

26. See, re the introduction of this system in Florence after the arrival of Eleonora and the establishment of a court, Cinzia Maria Sicca, 'Da notaio a maestro da casa: La "confezione" degli inventari a Firenze durante il principato', in Cinzia Maria Sicca, ed., *Inventari e cataloghi: Collezionismo e stili di vita negli stati italiani di antico regime* (Pisa, 2014), pp. 15–34 at 24–25.

to analyse content.[27] Italian Renaissance and grand-ducal inventories, expertly dissected by Jessica Keating and Lia Markey, Giorgio Riello, Francesco Freddolini and Cinzia Maria Sicca (amongst others),[28] often flounder in terms of descriptive power because of lack of recognition and expertise (especially in connection with unfamiliar, global objects where the compiler would have been completely at a loss), making water-tight identification of material objects in the inventories very problematic and unusual. Lists can only be as good as the list-maker's knowledge allows. Changes to the governance and political structure of Florence—that is, the introduction of a court—also had an impact on not only how the possessions of the ruler were itemised, but why, as dynastic considerations meant that tracking the movement of possessions took on added force. It should be remembered too that inventories were not compiled in order to make objects recognisable to people who could not see them, but rather were written by compilers to identify objects in front of them, and distinguish them from other objects in front of them. As Daniel Lord Smail found, in inventories from late fourteenth and early fifteenth-century Marseilles and Lucca, textual descriptions of objects in inventories are often 'thoroughly nondescript', even though he isolated twelve common and less common attributes of the objects that could be included.[29] Including information about style or place of origin was 'unusual', except for clothes and textiles, where it was merely 'relatively uncommon'. The rarest attribute of the twelve to be included was shape, followed jointly by style/place of origin and function.[30]

In the case of global goods incorporated into the Medici collections, the situation was interesting. The Medici inventories were compiled by Florentines and Tuscans who probably had never set foot outside Tuscany. The objects arrived already dissociated from original origins and contexts and

27. Riello, '"Things seen and unseen"', pp. 139–40; Francesco Freddolini and Anne Helmreich, 'Inventories, Catalogues and Art Historiography: Explaining Lists against the Grain', *Journal of Art Historiography*, 11 (2014), available at https://arthistoriography.files.wordpress.com/2014/11/freddolini_helmreich_introduction.pdf (accessed 15 April 2023).

28. Keating and Markey, '"Indian" Objects', pp. 283–300; Riello, '"Things seen and unseen"', pp. 127, 129–30; Francesco Freddolini, 'The Grand Dukes and Their Inventories: Administering Possessions and Defining Value at the Medici Court', *Journal of Art Historiography*, 11 (2014), available at https://arthistoriography.files.wordpress.com/2014/11/freddolini.pdf (accessed 15 April 2023); Freddolini and Helmreich, 'Inventories'; Sicca, 'Da notaio', pp. 15–34.

29. Smail, *Legal Plunder*, pp. 68–70.

30. Ibid., pp. 69–70.

without any oral or written explanatory paraphernalia; the compilers might never have encountered any of these global objects previously, and it is clear that once again, as in the descriptions of mixed-ancestry babies at the Innocenti, the record-takers struggled to respond to the unknown or unknowable newness of them. Place of origin, makers and function were the greatest casualties. When these inventories were re-itemised and reworked in later years, subsequent inventories virtually never included extra information about items that had appeared before. And if they did, it was not historical or geographical information, which was either forever lost or lacking, but information arising from closer visual inspection. More precisely, Medici inventories are notoriously poor at recording non-Italian provenance with any exactitude, with waffle descriptors such as *indiano* or *turco* or *moresco* often used generically to indicate foreignness. The same was true in other parts of Europe, such as German-speaking countries, where it has been appreciated for some time that information in inventories concerning the provenance of ethnographic items— or non-European objects that could then be conceived as ethnographic—in particular is usually generic or waffling,[31] but what this means or why it should be the case have been less considered.

Historical analysis is more likely to offer deeper understanding or precise identification when it involves cocktails of varying types of documentation, so working with combinations of archival sources is of paramount importance, and new types of source material are particularly welcome. The archival *fondo* Miscellanea medicea, a true miscellany, was created by chance; it consists of all sorts of documents taken by Jacopo Riguccio Galluzzi from the Mediceo del Principato collection in the later decades of the eighteenth century,[32] to be used in his *Storia del Granducato di Toscana sotto il governo di Casa Medici* (Florence, 1781), which were never returned to their original series.[33] Misc.

31. Elke Bujok, 'Ethnographica in Early Modern *Kunstkammern* and Their Perception', *Journal of the History of Collections*, 21.1 (2009), pp. 17–32 at 19–20. This is in marked contrast to German Renaissance merchants in whose interest it was to know about the precise location of desired commodities, and who therefore 'sprinkled their texts [e.g., manuals] liberally with place names'. See Johnson, *German Discovery*, p. 102.

32. On Galluzzi, see *DBI*, 51 (1998), pp. 766–69, entry by Orsola Gori Pasta.

33. For the history of the Miscellanea medicea and its relation to the Mediceo del Principato, see Silvia Baggio and Piero Marchi, 'Introduzione', in Silvia Baggio and Piero Marchi, eds, *Miscellanea medicea: Archivio di stato di Firenze*, 3 vols (Rome, 2002), 1, pp. 3–32, esp. 9–11 and 14–16. It would be fascinating to know where Misc. med. 713 had originally been archived.

med. 713 is a bound parchment volume from 1547–48,[34] containing two variously written and differently sized account books or account journals, the first
large, effectively the *registro* proper, and the second smaller, a *quaderno* in two
separate sections,[35] inserted at the end.[36] It adds a further dimension to the mix
of letters and inventories. Lisbon was the global shopping capital of Europe at
this date, containing treasures from across the globe, because Portugal's trading
empire spread from Africa to India to the Far East and on to Brazil. By comparison, Tuscany was very provincial. Work on fifteenth- and sixteenth-century
Lisbon is however hampered by the absence of some of the central archival
material, such as the records of the two great crown agencies dealing with the
overseas trading empire, the Casa da Índia and the Casa da Guinea, and their
customs documentation, and many of the records of the royal court, which
were destroyed in the great earthquake and tsunami of 1755. Material on fif-
teenth- and sixteenth-century Florence, on the other hand, exists in rich abundance, allowing the provincial to trump the global in this regard.

The account journals were meticulously kept by Bastiano Campana, who
described himself as Cosimo's *agente* or agent, and by his *servitor* or servant
Andrea di Giovanni da Doadola;[37] the handwriting of both of them occurs,
but in different sections. The accounts were kept in the first instance so that
Cosimo or his secretaries could authorise and refund money spent by

34. In the same years of 1547 and 1548 another Italian, Giovanni Ricci (1497–1574), papal
nuncio in Lisbon from 1544 to 1550, was buying goods from Portugal's trading empire. On him,
see Hubert Jedin, 'Kardinal Giovanni Ricci (1497–1574)', in *Miscellanea Pio Paschini: Studi di
storia ecclesiastica*, vol. 2 (Rome, 1949), pp. 269–358 at 312–14; Sylvie Deswarte-Rosa, 'Le Cardinal Giovanni Ricci de Montepulciano', in Philippe Morel, ed., *La Villa Médicis*, vol. 2: *Études*
(Rome, 1991), pp. 110–69; *DBI*, 87 (2016), pp. 246–49, entry by Gigliola Fragnito. Ricci sent back
the usual range of items to his home town of Montepulciano: various objects from India, parrots, three black enslaved children and porcelain: Deswarte-Rosa, 'Le Cardinal', pp. 123–24, and
Suzanne B. Butters, Elena Fumagalli and Sylvie Deswarte-Rosa, eds, with the collaboration of
Anne-Lise Desmas, *La Villa Médicis*, vol. 5: *Fonti documentarie* (Rome, 2010), pp. 13–15.

35. The paper of the *registro* measures c. 22.5 × 33 cm, and that of the *quaderno* 16 × 22 cm.

36. Beatrice Biagioli, Gabriella Cibei and Veronica Vestri, eds, *Miscellanea medicea*, vol. 3:
(451–730): Inventario (Rome, 2014), pp. 545–46.

37. ASF, Misc. med. 713, small quaderno, 1r: 'Spese fatte nel viagio di Portoghallo per mano
di Bastiano Campana agentte di sua e. ill.ma', 3r: 'Questo quadernuccio sarà tenuto per mano di
Andrea di Gio. da Doadola servitor di Bastiano Campana di Livorno'—but the handwriting
in the little *quadernuccio* is in a different hand from this. Andrea's surname presumably indicates
his family's origins in Dovodola or Doadola, in the Florentine Romagna. See Emanuele Repetti,
Dizionario geografico fisico storico della Toscana, 6 vols (Florence, 1833–46), 2, pp. 38–44.

Campana in the course of his trip, and secondarily, but more importantly, so that the Medici had a record of the purchases he made.[38] The principal account journal is in quarto and bound in parchment. It opens with a declaration that 'the *giornale* will be written by Bastiano Campana on the present voyage to Spain that I will make on the orders of the duke of Florence in connection with grain,[39] galley slaves and other goods for which I have been commissioned';[40] a couple of lines further on 'animals' are specified as part of the commission.[41] The grain was being taken from Livorno to Lisbon to be sold, whereas the other goods were being bought in Lisbon and taken back to Tuscany. In fact, the most expensive items in the return cargo were all raw materials: 'panni di stagno', blocks or squares of tin from England (used to make bronze),[42] pearls,[43] and amber.[44] On the cover of the principal account journal is written 'giornale e ricordanze' (Plate 17).[45] According to Richard Goldthwaite, by the fifteenth century the various discrete accounting books known as 'waste books'—that is, books of first entry covering a multitude of specialist accounts all of which fed into the main ledgers, the *libri di debitori e creditori*—were standardised in size (quarto) and binding (parchment) and could be bought

38. For indications of prices for goods and service in Portugal, see the database 'Prices, Wages and Rents in Portugal, 1300–1900', http://pwr-portugal.ics.ul.pt/ (accessed 22 April 2023). Campana's purchases in Lisbon were recorded in ducats and *maravedis*.

39. Selling grain in Lisbon was the principal purpose of the voyage, and Campana was involved in the transport and sale of grain on behalf of Cosimo throughout the 1550s: see, e.g., ASF, Scrittoio delle regie possessioni 4137, 173 sinistra and destra, and ASF, Scrittoio delle regie possessioni 4138, 20 sinistra. Portugal's need to acquire grain was long-standing, and was still pronounced at the end of the century: Giovanni Battista Confalonieri, *Grandezza e magnificenza della città di Lisbona: Dalle carte di Giovanni Battista Confalonieri segretario del collettore apostolico (1593–1596)*, ed. Alessandro Dell'Aria (Rovereto, 2005), p. 265: 'In Portogallo continuamente hanno mancamento de grani'.

40. ASF, Misc. med. 713, Giornale e ricordanze, 1r (but unnumbered), 'Questo giornale s^{to} A. sarà tenuto per mano di Bastiano Campana in questo presentte viagio di Spagnia farò per comandamento dello Illmo Sor Ducha di Firenze per contto di ghrani, stiavi per ghalere e altro auutone comessione'. Later in the account journal, goods are recorded as having been bought for Cosimo's wife, Eleonora.

41. ASF, Misc. med. 713, Giornale e ricordanze, 1r (but unnumbered).

42. Ibid., 6v, 72v and 76r.

43. Ibid., 6v, 75v and 78r.

44. Ibid., 78r: the amber came from 'le Indie di Portogalo' and from the Canaries.

45. D'Arienzo, 'Un quaderno di lettere', p. 75 lists a type of record in the Banco Cambini archive called 'quaderni di ricordanze'.

from a stationer with the title already written onto the parchment cover.[46] Thus the title of Campana's volume was not a reflection of his own understanding of its contents, but rather a routine label, as the writing of the title makes clear: the letters are capitals, and not in Campana's hand. The relationship between the accounts that appeared at the front of many account books and the *ricordi* or *ricordanze* that were written at the back (the combination of records that must have led to the routine label *giornale e ricordanze* in the first place) has not been unpicked.[47]

Campana's *giornale e ricordanze* contain no *ricordanze*. All the same, the *registro* appears to be eclectic, a hybrid of at least two distinct types of record melded into one. It has a dual function: recording costs, and recording extracted information that needed to be remembered. Because of this, the account journal is not easy to pigeonhole.[48] It is both personal, written by an individual, and also a record of business dealings, kept by a functionary of the Medici who was away from Tuscany on a work trip for his employer.[49] Instead of being written for later or future members of Campana's family, it was kept for the benefit of the Medici and their descendants, passing into their archive. The level of detail is very high, and nothing is too insignificant to be included: payments as small as eight *maravedis* (there were 375 *maravedis* to a gold ducat) for four eggs or three *maravedis* for porterage are recorded.[50] In one sense, therefore, the *giornale* can be seen as a superior form of expense claim, but in other notable respects it contains information about the selling and buying undertaken on the trip that is not related to exchange of money. For

46. Richard Goldthwaite, 'The Practice and Culture of Accounting in Renaissance Florence', *Enterprise and Society*, 16.3 (2015), pp. 611–47 at 617.

47. Richard Goldthwaite, 'Florentine Household Acounts, Fourteenth to Seventeenth Centuries', *Renaissance Studies*, 32.2 (2018), pp. 219–35 at 221.

48. It resembles in this respect the 'giornale o diario' of Cornelio Bianchi, physician to the Venetian consul in Damascus, from almost exactly the same period, 1542–46. Primarily an account book, it too includes occasional narrative entries that 'seemingly stretch the genre': Valentina Pugliano, 'Accountability, Autobiography and Belonging: The Working Journal of a Sixteenth-Century Diplomatic Physician between Venice and Damascus', in Annemarie Kinzelbach, J. Andrew Mendelsohn and Ruth Schilling, eds, *Civic Medicine: Physician, Polity and Pen in Early Modern Europe* (London, 2021), pp. 183–209 at 186.

49. For a checklist of Florentine private account books, see Richard Goldthwaite and Marco Spallanzani, 'Censimento di libri contabili private dei fiorentini, 1200–1600', https://www.academia.edu/40196500/CENSIMENTO_di_libri_contabili_privati_fiorentini_fino_al_1600 (accessed 22 April 2023).

50. ASF, Misc. med. 713, Giornale e ricordanze, 57v [or 58 sinistra] and 56v [or 57 sinistra].

instance—and this is where the term *ricordanze* gains in relevance[51]—some prior biographical details relating to the goods are included. Unlike the greater part of the sixteenth-century Medici inventories, the account journal offers some narrative glimpses regarding the acquisitional context, such as the intermediary's name or the seller's name, and regarding the care of the item once bought. Account books routinely include only as much detail as is necessary to confirm the financial essentials of the purchase; those in this account journal articulate interest in how and why the object was purchased, and in causation. They often explain not only how much has been spent, but why it was spent (thus, for example, a certain sum of money was spent on blankets because blankets were needed to keep the slaves warm on the voyage home). A purchase logged in the account journal was not merely one static financial transaction taking place at one given moment, but the latest in a chain of actions relating to a particular piece of merchandise that had already passed through other hands. Biography and narrative fuelled these entries, making possible a more nuanced understanding of how objects were folded into lived experience, but in a slightly oblique fashion, not in the more usual sense of learning how individual objects were used or gained in importance.[52] Even so, it is not known whether Cosimo ever saw this account journal, or whether it was viewed exclusively by Cosimo's secretaries.

Campana additionally signalled what he considered to be the thirteen main subject headings, composing a short *stratto*, or index, in his own hand by reusing part of the parchment covering wrapped around the *giornale*, which provided references to the folios of his account journal. Five headings are to people: Cosimo de' Medici, Campana's servant Andrea da Doadola, and Batista del Bizarro, Francesco di Lepe and Vettorio Giuoli, all of whom Campana had dealt with in Lisbon. Two relate to grain, and the remaining six to acquisitions: animals and birds, jams, undifferentiated but critical 'più robbe', pearls, galley slaves and black domestic slaves. All make sense and would have been expected, except for the choice of three contacts in Lisbon, who are unexpected. The prominence of jams will be explained below.

---

51. Cf. Giovanni Cherubini, 'I libri di ricordanze come fonte storica', in *Civiltà comunale: Libro, scrittura, documento; Atti del Convegno, Genova, 8–11 novembre 1988* (Genoa, 1989), pp. 567–91; Giovanni Ciappelli, *Memory, Family and Self: Tuscan Family Books and Other European Ego-documents (14th to 18th Century)* (Leiden, 2014).

52. Paula Findlen, 'Early Modern Things: Objects in Motion, 1500–1800', in Paula Findlen, ed., *Early Modern Things: Objects and Their Histories, 1500–1800* (London, 2013), pp. 3–27 at 8.

Bastiano (from Sebastiano) Campana was known to historians previously, if at all, for his involvement in the construction of two fortresses at Portoferraio on Elba, and his work on the *arsenale* in Livorno,[53] because he acted as Cosimo's agent and *provveditore della fabbrica* on these projects in the late 1540s and 1550s, the years following his return from Lisbon and Cadiz.[54] By 1559 he was *provveditore* of Livorno.[55] There is evidence that in September 1546 he had already helped facilitate the expedition of shipments of diverse objects—Spanish chairs ('chareghe di Spagna') and carpets from Alexandria—that had docked in Livorno to Cosimo's wife Eleonora di Toledo in Florence.[56] He continued to work in whatever capacity was required by his Medici master, and there are occasional glimpses of him being later involved in a chain of people acquiring goods for Cosimo: for example, in January 1561 when he was in charge of sending on 'tre barcate d'anticaglie' (three boatloads of antiquities) from Pisa to Rome.[57] He was a middle-ranking Medici functionary, one of a great army of them, undoubtedly related to the more famous Francesco Campana from Colle Val d'Elsa, one of Cosimo's secretaries,[58] but it is not known precisely how. Nor is it known how he was related to other members of the Campana family who appear in the Medici correspondence, although

53. For example, ASF, MdP 11, f. 97, MdP 638, f. 229, MdP 1174, 428r, MdP 656, 249v; Luigi Atzori and Ivo Regoli, 'Due comuni rurali del dominio fiorentino nel sec. XVI: Montopoli V.A. e Castelfranco di Sotto', in Giorgio Spini, ed., *Architettura e politica da Cosimo I a Ferdinando I* (Florence, 1976), pp. 79–164 at 148 n. 101; Lorenza De Maria and Rita Turchettti, eds, *Rotti e porti del Mediterraneo dopo la caduta dell'Impero romano d'Occidente* (Soveria Mannelli, 2004), p. 369.

54. Daniela Lamberini, *Il Sanmarino: Giovan Battista Belluzzi architetto militare e trattatista del Cinquecento*, 2 vols (Florence, 2007), 1, pp. 45, 60, 70, and 2, pp. 132–33.

55. In, e.g., ASF, Scrittoio delle regie possessioni 4138, 185 sinistra, 19 April 1559, he is described as 'provveditore di Livorno'. Cf. Andrea M. Gáldy, 'Hounds for a Cardinal', in Machtelt Israëls and Louis A. Waldman, eds, *Renaissance Studies in Honor of Joseph Connors*, 2 vols (Florence, 2013), 2, pp. 172–76 at 175.

56. ASF, MdP 1172, 350r, Bastiano Campana in Livorno to Pierfrancesco Riccio in Florence, 27 September 1546. See also Christina M. Anderson, ed., *A Cultural History of Furniture*, 6 vols (London, 2022), vol. 3: *A Cultural History of Furniture in the Age of Exploration*, ed. Christina M. Anderson and Elizabeth A. Correll, p. 90.

57. Letter of Achille Orsilago in Pisa to Cosimo de' Medici in Florence, 14 January 1560/1, ASF, MdP 487A, 669r, and Pieraccini, *Stirpe de' Medici*, 2.1, p. 28.

58. Francesco Dini, 'Francesco Campana e suoi', *Archivio storico italiano*, ser. 5, 23 (1899), pp. 289–323, and 24 (1899), pp. 13–22; *DBI*, 17 (1974), pp. 341–45, entry by M. G. Cruciani Tron Carelli; Andrea M. Gáldy, 'Lost in Antiquities: Cardinal Giovanni de' Medici (1543–1562)', in Mary Hollingsworth and Carol M. Richardson, eds, *The Possessions of a Cardinal: Politics, Piety and Art, 1450–1700* (University Park, PA, 2010), pp. 153–65 at 162 n. 27.

in the mid-1550s in several of Eleonora di Toledo's books of *debitori e creditori* he is referred to as Bastiano di Vincenzo Campana.[59]

Finding these account journals offers the hitherto unattainable pleasure of seeing precisely what was bought for Cosimo on the Iberian peninsula in 1547–48, and is doubly valuable because the journals include prices and costs, which are not usually provided in letters and inventories. Up to now, there has been rather a limited number of indications of what many objects from the Portuguese trading empire cost in Europe in the sixteenth century on the open market. In this respect, Albrecht Dürer's 1521 diary of his stay in the Netherlands is very helpful, as he was attracted by anything new and records quantities of artefacts and products from the Portuguese and Spanish overseas territories that he bought, exchanged, was given or saw during his time there. There is a direct correlation with some of the items purchased by Campana, because apart from other artists, Dürer's main (but so far unexplained)[60] contacts were the former and current Portuguese factors in Antwerp,[61] especially Francisco Pesão and João Brandão, and also Brandão's secretary, Rodrigo Fernandez d'Almada.[62]

59. ASF, Scrittoio delle regie possessioni 4137, 206 destra and 249 sinistra, and ASF, Scrittoio delle regie possessioni 4138, 42 sinistra and 188 sinistra.

60. One possible explanation may lie in Dürer's close connections to the Habsburg court because Dürer was one of Emperor Maximilian's favourite painters. Brandão might have enfolded Dürer in his circle in order to try to take advantage of these links. King Manuel of Portugal was anxious to cement close ties with the Habsburgs to elevate himself and his dynasty, and the easiest way to achieve this was through marriage. Initially, Manuel had wanted to marry his son, later João III, to Archduchess Leonor of Austria, Maximilian's granddaughter, before his own wife Maria of Castile died unexpectedly in March 1517, and he changed his plans and thought of marrying her himself. João Brandão was the envoy chosen for this mission; he arrived in 1517 in Antwerp and wrote Manuel a detailed letter about his trip and his embassy, describing his reception at the court of Margaret of Austria in Malines and Brussels. See Lisbon, DGLAB/ANTT, CC, 3.6.51, 7 February 1517. There Brandão met Leonor, who a few months later would leave the Netherlands to travel to Spain with Charles V and then on to the Lisbon court to become Manuel I's third wife in 1518.

61. On this crucial entrepôt for Portugal, with its large influx of goods from the Portuguese trading empire, see Anselmo Braamcamp Freire, *Notícia da feitoria de Flandres precedidas dos Brandões poetas do cancioneiro* ([Lisbon], 1920), and Jean-Albert Goris, *Étude sure les colonies marchandes méridionales (portugais, espagnols, italiens) à Anvers de 1488 à 1567* (Louvain, 1925).

62. Gerd Unverfehrt, *'Da sah ich viel köstliche Dinge': Albrecht Dürers Reise in die Niederlande* (Göttingen, 2007), pp. 41, 49–50; Albrecht Dürer, *Diary of His Journey to the Netherlands, 1520–21*, ed. J.-A. Goris and G. Marlier (London, 1971), e.g., pp. 58, 60 and 62. There is some uncertainty about Rodrigo Fernandez d'Almada's position.

This group of Portuguese at the cutting edge of overseeing and handling the new goods arriving in Antwerp from the Iberian empires provided Dürer with access to attractive novelties. So, for example, he acquired parrots, tortoise (or turtle) shells, porcelain, a monkey, coral, snail (or nautilus) shells and ivory salt-cellars,[63] and he saw (but did not acquire) Mexican featherwork—all items that Campana also bought twenty-five years later in Lisbon, Seville and Cadiz. Without Dürer's network of Portuguese friends and patrons, far fewer items from the Portuguese trading empire would have passed into his possession. Campana's account journal also makes clear that certain goods had been bought for Eleonora di Toledo,[64] who must therefore have specified what she wanted. A raft of recent work by Dagmar Eichberger and Annemarie Jordan,[65] amongst others, is revealing that female rulers and consorts were often more energetic and discerning buyers and collectors than their husbands; certainly different acquisitions were made on Eleonora's behalf than on Cosimo's, providing an opportunity to compare a husband and wife—a husband and wife as emotionally close as these two, moreover—in the act of acquiring global goods.

The account journal detailing important purchases included sections written chronologically, organised by date, and others that recapped virtually the same information, in which the record of expenditure was arranged according to what was purchased. Smaller, seemingly less important purchases, such as animal leads and cages, and new shoes, were also meticulously recorded: examples of the more quotidian artefacts that are also critical to an analysis of the functions and care of objects.[66] But it should not be forgotten that even if the Medici wanted to acquire exceptional pieces, not only would they probably not have recognised an exceptional piece if they had seen it, but they had to rely on their agents and middlemen and take what they could get. Later some of these pieces in the Medici collections, even if not exceptional at the time, became exceptional by dint of their survival. Following the categorisation employed in Campana's account journal, choosing one or two examples from each category of global

63. On these artefacts and animals, see the tables of prices and gifts in Unverfehrt, 'Da sah ich viel köstliche Dinge', pp. 217–220.

64. Bruce Edelstein, 'Nobildonne napoletane e committenza: Eleonora d'Aragona ed Eleonora di Toledo a confronto', Quaderni storici, n.s. 35, 104.2 (2000), pp. 295–329 discusses the patronage of the two women, focusing on paintings and raw materials necessary for the court, rather than material culture. It is noteworthy, given Campana's primary cargo from Livorno to Lisbon, that Eleonora was heavily involved in the acquisition of grain supplies: pp. 302–6.

65. See, e.g., Women: The Art of Power.

66. Findlen, 'Early Modern Things', p. 14.

goods acquired, except raw materials—thus, worked decorative pieces, animals and humans—will give a flavour of the document. The number and volume of purchases was not large. The focus here will be on the moment of acquisition, knowledge transferred at the time of acquisition, aftercare, and, where possible in a small number of cases, afterlife. Yet while an inflected understanding of all these new beginnings is easy to project and achieve, analysing a small-scale but significant buying trip in meaningful ways presents considerable challenges when trying to understand the rationale behind the purchases at the time, as opposed to their subsequent importance. Consumption is inextricably linked to choice, and yet the choices on offer are not visible in this scenario. Nor is it easy to comprehend how value or value for money was estimated.

As will be seen, Campana's inexperience of the world outside Tuscany and his lack of expertise did not preclude him from acting as a buyer of global goods for the Medici on the Iberian peninsula. His tasks of acquisition were made possible by his Italian contacts in Lisbon, probably recommended to him by the Medici. Two of the leading Italian merchants in Lisbon were Luca Giraldi[67] and Giancarlo Affaitati,[68] whose local advice and practical and financial help Campana sought on arrival, and into whose webs of contacts his requests for purchases were immediately inserted. Giraldi had direct personal experience of the Carreira da Índia as he had been captain of a ship that went there in 1540,[69] so his credentials—Florentine, a practical knowledge of India and Indian goods and years of experience as a merchant, financier and wheeler-dealer in Lisbon—were top-notch. Without these two contacts and their networks it is doubtful whether Campana would have managed to buy much of value, or collect the global goods desired by Cosimo and Eleonora.

West African Artistry: Two Kongolese Oliphants

The new information in this volume resolves one of the big debates for scholars interested in African ivory in the Renaissance: namely, how the two virtuoso Kongolese oliphants in the Pitti,[70] in the newly renamed Tesoro dei granduchi,

67. *DBI*, 56 (2001), pp. 455–57, entry by Stefano Tabacchi; Nunziatella Alessandrini, 'Contributo alla storia della famiglia Giraldi, mercanti banchieri fiorentini nella corte di Lisbona nel XVI secolo', *Storia economica*, 14.3 (2011), pp. 377–408.

68. *DBI*, 1 (1960), pp. 350–51, entry by Sergio Bertelli.

69. *DBI*, 56, p. 455.

70. On which, see Ezio Bassani, 'Antichi avori africani nelle collezioni medicee, 1', *Critica d'arte*, n.s. 21, fasc. 143 (1975), pp. 69–80 at 72–76; *Firenze e la Toscana dei Medici nell'Europa del Cinquecento: Committenza e collezionismo medicei*, ed. Paola Barocchi et al., exh. cat., Palazzo

originally arrived in Florence (Plates 18 and 19). The answer is that Campana bought them in Lisbon on 28 October 1547.[71] A third Kongolese oliphant, now in the Museo di storia naturale, antropologia e etnologia in Florence, arrived separately; it is not known by which route. The Pitti oliphants are the earliest documented and still extant Kongolese objects to be identified in Europe,[72] and therefore extremely important; their special value is multiplied many times because their date of acquisition is now known and they are still *in situ* in the collection they entered in 1548 when they were brought to Tuscany. Suzanne Preston Blier explains a process of what she terms 'metaphoric patina enhancement'—as opposed to the processes of wear and age that create physical patina—whereby an object accrues a more or less thick patina of value according to the status of its earlier owners, the length of time it has been in a collection and its list of exhibition venues:[73] on the first two counts alone, the enhanced patina of value of the two Kongolese oliphants in the Medici collection is as thick as physically possible.

The trail of these objects once in Florence is, however, initially obscured. All objects bought or otherwise acquired by the Medici should have been

---

Vecchio, Florence (Florence, 1980), p. 160, cat. no. 300 (Ezio Bassani); Ezio Bassani and William B. Fagg, *Africa and the Renaissance: Art in Ivory*, ed. Susan Vogel, with Carol Thompson, exh. cat., The Center for African Art, New York and the Museum of Fine Arts, Houston (New York, 1988), pp. 46–47, 198–201, 204, 247 and cat. nos 181 and 182; Ezio Bassani, *African Art and Artefacts in European Collections, 1400–1800*, ed. Malcolm McLeod (London, 2000), pp. 145–7 and cat. nos 483 and 484; *Il cammeo Gonzaga: Arti preziose alla corte di Mantova*, ed. Ornella Casazza, exh. cat., Le Fruttiere del Palazzo Te, Mantua (Milan, 2008), p. 297, cat. no. 70 (Francesco Morena); *Nello splendore mediceo: Papa Leone X e Firenze*, ed. Nicoletta Baldini and Monica Bietti, exh. cat., Museo delle Cappelle Medicee e Casa Buonarroti, Florence (Livorno, 2013), p. 424 (Dora Liscia Bemporad); *Diafane passioni: Avori barocchi dalle corti europee*, ed. Eike D. Schmidt and Maria Sframeli, exh. cat., Museo degli argenti, Palazzo Pitti, Florence (Livorno, 2013), pp. 74–77 (Jan-Lodewijk Grootaers); Alisa Lagamma, with contributions by Christine Giuntini, 'Out of Kongo and into the *Kunstkammer*', in *Kongo: Power and Majesty*, ed. Alisa Lagamma, exh. cat., The Metropolitan Museum of Art, New York (New York, 2015), pp. 128–59 at 138–40.

71. It is a mark of Ezio Bassani's excellence that he had correctly posited this possibility in 1980: 'Il collezionismo esotico dei Medici nel Cinquecento', in Candace J. Adelson et al., *Le arti del principato Mediceo* (Florence, 1980), pp. 55–71 at 67: 'Non si può però escludere che [...] i corni siano stati acquistati dagli agenti della signoria a Lisbona.'

72. See, most recently, Lagamma, 'Out of Kongo', p. 138.

73. Suzanne Preston Blier, 'Ways of Experiencing African Art: The Role of Its Patina', in Suzanne Preston Blier, ed., *Art of the Senses: African Masterpieces from the Teel Collection* (Boston, MA, 2004), pp. 10–23 at 22.

immediately logged in the records of the Medici Guardaroba.[74] The books
(*giornali di entrata e uscita*) detailing the entry of objects into the Guardaroba
unfortunately make no mention of them (which is why until now the route
by which they entered the collection has not been known, and nor has their
date of entry). The slightly unorthodox nature of the Campana buying trip—
an inexperienced agent, a job on the side after completion of his primary task,
possibly last-minute, few or oral instructions—is matched by the slightly
unorthodox non-registration of the objects he acquired. The system set up to
accession an object entering Medici ownership was straightforward: the date
the object entered, a short description, for light identificatory purposes, and
the name of the person who brought the object were all recorded. In the case
of the objects acquired by Campana in 1547–48, not a single one known to
have been bought on the Iberian peninsula was accessioned. Yet by 1553 the
two Kongolese oliphants, for example, were being included in Guardaroba
inventories, and from that date onwards they are always included, so they did
undoubtedly enter the Medici collections, whether immediately in 1548 or
with a bit of a delay. But if it is clear the Guardaroba entries are not complete,
the meaning the absence of an entry had when evidence exists elsewhere that
an object entered the collection is not so clear. Is it just their initial registration that is lacking? Or did these objects go elsewhere in 1548, and enter later,
still without registration, in which case the question is, Where were they
between 1548 and 1553? Recently a plausible reason for the non-registration
of these goods from the Iberian peninsula has emerged. At precisely the moment of their arrival in Livorno in March 1548, the man who oversaw the
Medici Guardaroba and who would have been responsible for accessioning
them, Pierfrancesco Riccio, effectively went on sick leave, being replaced in
this role with immediate effect by his brother—and in the ensuing confusion,
the goods may have failed to be accessioned and inventoried on their entry
into the Medici collection.[75] The double whammy, as it were, of the goods

74. On the archival *fondo*, see Maria Grazia Vaccari, *La guardaroba medicea dell'Archivio di
stato di Firenze: Inventaria* (Florence, 1997); on how it functioned, Valentina Zucchi, 'The Medici
Guardaroba in the Florentine Ducal Residences, c. 1550–1650', in Susan Bracken, Andrea M.
Gáldy and Adriana Turpin, eds, *Collecting and the Princely Apartment* (Newcastle upon Tyne,
2011), pp. 1–21; on its use in an academic study, Valentina Conticelli, '*Guardaroba di cose rare e
preziose': Lo studiolo di Francesco I de' Medici; Arte, storia e significati* (La Spezia, 2007).

75. Desirée Cappa, 'Pierfrancesco Riccio: The Rise of a Bureaucrat in the Service of the
Medici Family (1525–44)', Ph.D thesis, Warburg Institute, University of London, 2022, p. 84 and
n. 8. Information about Riccio being ordered to stop work until he was healthy again is in ASF,

failing to be registered on arrival in the collection and of Campana's account book being removed from its proper place in the Medici archives, and put instead into a miscellaneous collection, accounts for the absence until now of further information about these objects.

The two oliphants were probably carved in the coastal Kongo province of Soyo (Sonho, Sogno, Nsoyo, Sonyo).[76] Soyo had a long history as a province with a special relationship with Kongo, almost 'a land apart' in John Thornton's words, and its position near the mouth of the Kongo river also made it unusual.[77] In the *Relatione del reame di Congo*, written by Filippo Pigafetta and published in 1591 in Rome from writings and detailed conversations he had with the Portuguese merchant and explorer Duarte Lopes,[78] who had settled in Kongo before being sent in 1583 as ambassador to the pope by King Álvaro I Nimi a Lukeni lua Mvemba,[79] the province of Soyo is second of the six described.[80] In the *Relatione*, the principal province of Kongo, Bamba, receives the greatest attention, with several pages devoted to elephants. According to Pigafetta, Lopes however insisted that there were large numbers of elephants throughout the kingdom, leading to an abundance of ivory, adding that ivory was not considered valuable until after the arrival of the Portuguese.[81] The

---

MdP 638, f. 205, Cosimo I to Riccio, Livorno, 18 March 1548. See also Cappa, 'Pierfrancesco Riccio', p. 198.

76. Marc Leo Felix, 'Introduction', in Marc Leo Felix, ed., *White Gold, Black Hands: Ivory Sculpture in Congo*, 8 vols (Qiquhar, 2010–14), 1, pp. 74–87 at 77, and Marc Leo Felix, 'Trumpets and Whistles', in ibid., pp. 178–221 at 182.

77. John K. Thornton, 'Soyo and Kongo: The Undoing of the Country's Centralization', in Koen Bostoen and Inge Brinkman, eds, *The Kongo Kingdom: The Origins, Dynamics and Cosmopolitan Culture of an African Polity* (Cambridge, 2018), pp. 103–22 at 104–6; J. Thornton, *History of West Central Africa*, p. 31.

78. Filippo Pigafetta, *Relatione del reame di Congo et delle circonvicine contrade tratta dalli scritti & ragionamenti di Odoardo Lopez portoghese per Filippo Pigafetta con dißegni vari di geografia, di piante, d'habiti, d'animali & altro* (Rome, 1591).

79. Luis Martínez Ferrer, 'Álvaro II do Congo e Paulo V Borghese: Da África a Roma através do Negrita', in Luis Martínez Ferrer and Marco Nocca, eds, *'Cose dell'altro mondo': L'ambasceria di Antonio Emanuele, Principe di N'Funta, detto 'il Negrita' (1604–1608) nella Roma di Paolo V/'Coisas do outro mundo': A missão em Roma de António Manuel, Príncipe de N'Funta, conhecido por 'o Negrita' (1604–1608), na Roma de Paulo V* (Rome, 2003), pp. 23–53 at 24.

80. Anne Hilton, *The Kingdom of Kongo* (Oxford, 1985), p. 40 isolates eight major provinces of Kongo in the early sixteenth century. Most had natural resources, either as fertile, cloth-producing regions, or because of copper or shell money. Soyo was on the list because of its position: the Portuguese landed there and had to traverse it to get elsewhere.

81. F. Pigafetta, *Relatione del reame di Congo*, p. 29.

veracity of this statement is open to doubt, but certainly the arrival of foreigners anxious to buy as much ivory as possible must have caused the Kongolese to re-evaluate its worth. The description of Soyo is short, and mainly concerned with the Kingdom of Loango, which bordered it and was formerly subject to the king of Kongo. Pigafetta reported many elephants in Loango, much ivory,[82] and smaller and finer palm cloths than in the kingdom of Kongo. Ivory was abundant and iron was non-existent, so an elephant tusk would be given in exchange for an iron nail.[83] A city of Sonho near the Kongo river (also known as the Zaire river) is depicted on Lopes's map of the kingdom (Plate 20); the province was the one closest to the coast and the mouth of the river, and therefore in a good position to trade with the Portuguese. Just across the Kongo river to the north were the small but important kingdoms of Ngoyo and Kakongo.[84]

The *Relatione* includes a timely reminder that the oliphants had a function, noted there as being used to provide musical accompaniments in war to rally and encourage the warriors.[85] Not only does the outward appearance of an oliphant retain the curvature of a tusk, but the sound produced by a medium-sized oliphant is very similar to the trumpeting of an elephant, the animal from which it had been taken;[86] the oliphants can therefore refer back both visually and sonically to their prior lives as tusks on living elephants. Ivory tusks were used as hunting horns in Europe, their deep, rich utterance binding the hunters together and announcing the presence of the prey, and it is possible that oliph-ants in Africa were similarly used. This sonic function should not be forgotten in the quest to analyse the exterior artistic decoration. Several sixteenth-century sources allude to Kongolese oliphants being blown at royal or diplo-matic ceremonies.[87] For instance, they formed part of a welcome group of

82. On unworked tusks exported to Europe, see Mariza de Carvalho Soares, '"Por conto e peso": O comércio de marfim no Congo e Loango, séculos xv–xvii', *Anais do Museu Paulista: História e cultura material*, 25.1 (2017), pp. 59–86.

83. F. Pigafetta, *Relatione del reame di Congo*, p. 34.

84. See the map in Phyllis M. Martin, 'The Kingdom of Loango', in *Kongo: Power and Majesty*, ed. Alisa Lagamma, exh. cat., The Metropolitan Museum of Art, New York (New York, 2015), pp. 46–85 at 49.

85. F. Pigafetta, *Relatione del reame di Congo*, p. 20.

86. Doran H. Ross, 'Imagining Elephants: An Overview', in *Elephant: The Animal and Its Ivory in African Culture*, ed. Doran H. Ross, exh. cat., The Fowler Museum of Cultural History, UCLA (Los Angeles, 1992), pp. 1–39 at 24.

87. Robert Farris Thompson, 'Body and Voice: Kongo Figurative Musical Instruments', in Marie-Thérèse Brincard, ed., *Sounding Forms: African Musical Instruments* (New York, 1989),

musical instruments in 1491 when the Portuguese ambassador Rui de Sousa arrived in the capital to meet the Mani or Mwene Kongo.[88] Sound was the oliphant's primary *raison d'être*;[89] it was only secondarily a vehicle of artistic beauty, even if the tables appear to have been turned quite often. In Europe, the most elaborately carved oliphants lost their function as sound-producing objects and were recategorised as prestige art objects. Evidence for this lies in the absence of wear on the most extravagantly decorated oliphants that were brought to Europe and became part of the collections of royal or noble collectors—and were rarely if ever blown.[90]

The Portuguese reached the Kingdom of Kongo in the 1480s, and it was the first extra-European country officially to turn Christian in this period. However, in the following half-century, while the two countries may have traded objects and the Kongolese apparently turned Christian, the cultural gap between them remained as gaping as ever, with virtually no evidence of the meaning of culturally specific norms on either side crossing the divide. In Africa, elephants were symbols of power, held to be chiefs among animals, and their power was often harnessed by rulers to add to their own power. There was a widespread belief amongst Africans—for instance, on the Ivory Coast, in Benin and amongst the Yoruba—that the power of an elephant was enshrined in its tusks in a twofold symbolism: the animal-part (worked or unworked) stood in for or represented the whole animal, and the elephant stood in for or represented the ruler who held power.[91] Equivalence was perceived, and

---

pp. 39–45 at 41. By the seventeenth century there are missionary images of ivory trumpets being blown, in addition to textual descriptions: Cécile Fromont, *The Art of Conversion: Christian Visual Culture in the Kingdom of Kongo* (Chapel Hill, NC, 2014), pp. 40–42.

88. *MMA* 1, pp. 113 (from the chronicle of Rui de Pina: 'com muitas trombetas de marfim') and 118 (from the chronicle of Garcia de Resende, using the same words). Mwene is the Kikongo term for Mani.

89. Ezio Bassani, *Gli antichi strumenti musicali dell'Africa nera dalle antiche fonti cinquecentesche al Gabinetto Armonico del Padre Filippo Bonanni* (Padua, 1978), e.g., pp. 26–28; Marie-Thérèse Brincard, ed., *Sounding Forms: African Musical Instruments* (New York, 1989), pp. 152–23, cat. entries 102–4, by Christine Mullen Kraemer and Marie-Thérèse Brincard, re several late fifteenth- or early sixteenth-century Sapi-Portuguese oliphants.

90. A Sapi-Portuguese oliphant in a private collection in Lisbon (cat. no. 104 in Brincard, *Sounding Forms*), which I saw and handled in February 2015, does show signs of use, with rubbed parts and areas of different colour. See Bassani and Fagg, *Africa and the Renaissance*, p. 143 and cat. no. 98; Bassani, *African Art*, cat. no. 782.

91. See, e.g., Philip Ravenhill, 'Of Pachyderms and Power: Ivory and the Elephant in the Art of Central Côte d'Ivoire', in *Elephant: The Animal and Its Ivory in African Culture*, ed.

therefore existed. In some cases, representation could become transference, as it was understood that the utilisation of oliphants by humans meant that some of the attributes of the elephant were transferred to the humans: that some of the properties that lay in its different body parts could be transmitted to whoever was the new owner of those body parts.[92] Carving the tusk also meant inscribing additional meaning onto it. While Ingrid Greenfield hypothesises that African materials had a 'flexible cultural and geographic identity' at this point,[93] there is no indication that sixteenth-century Portuguese or Italians understood these flexible African identities or meanings, instead valuing ivory as a material because of its rarity in Europe, and valuing the carvings on the ivory because of the skill involved in their creation.

The first mention of the oliphants in Italy was in the Medici inventory of 1553, where they were listed as '2 corni d'avorio lavorati d'intaglio', translated by Ezio Bassani as 'two engraved ivory horns';[94] the word *lavorato* draws attention to the skill and labour behind the decoration, and 'engraved', as he suggests, can here be taken to mean 'covered with geometric decoration'.[95] The Italian word used throughout the Guardaroba records is *corni* (horns), although in many Italian inventories and other account books unworked tusks and decorated oliphants alike were correctly identified as *denti* (teeth).[96] In fact, not only were oliphants teeth rather than horns, but these oliphants were not engraved, either; rather they were carved: cut with prototypes of adzes and chiselled with knives.[97] Their colour is towards the lighter end of the ivory spectrum, which can vary in both tone and lustre, but which does not

Doran H. Ross, exh. cat., The Fowler Museum of Cultural History, UCLA (Los Angeles, 1992), pp. 115–33 at 116–17; Barbara Winston Blackmun, 'The Elephant and Its Ivory in Benin', in ibid., pp. 162–83 at 167; Henry John Drewall, 'Image and Indeterminacy: Elephants and Ivory among the Yoruba', in ibid., pp. 186–207 at 188–91, and 198: 'Elephants and rulers share the same conceptual space in Yoruba thought.'

92. Blier, 'Ways of Experiencing', p. 14.

93. Greenfield, 'Moveable Continent', p. 44.

94. Mention of the 'horns' in the 1553 inventory is in ASF, Guardaroba medicea 28, 46r: '2 corni d'avorio lavorati d'intaglio', Guardaroba medicea 30, 134r, Guardaroba medicea 31, 93r, and Guardaroba medicea 36, 134v.

95. Bassani, *African Art*, p. 146.

96. On tusks as teeth, see Jeheskel Shoshani, 'The African Elephant and Its Environment', in *Elephant: The Animal and Its Ivory in African Culture*, ed. Doran H. Ross, exh. cat., The Fowler Museum of Cultural History, UCLA (Los Angeles, 1992), pp. 42–59 at 47.

97. *African Ivories*, ed. Kate Ezra, exh. cat. The Metropolitan Museum of Art, New York (New York, 1984), p. 8.

change over time without further intervention. They are off-white rather than white. Because they have spent their life as display objects in a collection and have not been handled or used, they have not developed the yellow-brownish tinge or patina that comes when there is contact with human skin or if they are kept in the dark,[98] and it is clear that before their arrival in Europe they were not treated with any of the substances, such as palm oil and camwood powder (a red pigment frequently used cosmetically by the Kongolese),[99] that also can alter their colour.[100]

Previous plausible suggestions proposed by Ezio Bassani regarding the passage of the oliphants from Africa to Europe included their being commissioned 'for export' to be sent to the pope by the ruler of Kongo, and presented by his ambassador, or 'for local use', belonging originally to the ruler of Kongo, and then given away as gifts.[101] Alisa Lagamma, the curator of the 2015 exhibition at the Metropolitan Museum in New York entitled *Kongo: Power and Majesty* which included one of the Medici oliphants (Bg. 1879 avori, no. 2), for example, believed that this oliphant had been a presentation piece and suggested it had been given to Giovanni de' Medici, Pope Leo X, by the Portuguese embassy under Tristão da Cunha in 1514. This embassy had brought the Indian elephant known as Hanno to Rome as a gift from King Manuel I of Portugal to the pope, and Lagamma hypothesised entirely reasonably that the Kongolese oliphants had been given to the Medici pope at the same time. According to her recreation of events, the oliphants later passed to Cosimo I de' Medici and were incorporated into the Medici collections, being inventoried there from 1553.[102]

However, these hypotheses have now been supplanted by facts, and the route by which the oliphants reached Florence is now certain. But under what circumstances and how they were acquired in Africa, and from and by whom, is still to be ascertained. Given what can be deduced from a visual analysis or is already known about them, and what is known about Kongolese customs, they are most likely to have belonged to the king or one of his immediate

98. David H. Shayt, 'The Material Culture of Ivory outside Africa', in *Elephant: The Animal and Its Ivory in African Culture*, ed. Doran H. Ross, exh. cat., The Fowler Museum of Cultural History, UCLA (Los Angeles, 1992), pp. 366–81 at 367.

99. Anita Jacobson-Widding, *Red-White-Black as Mode of Thought: A Study of Triadic Classification by Colours in the Ritual Symbolism and Cognitive Thought of the Peoples of the Lower Congo* (Uppsala, 1979), pp. 163–64, 167–68.

100. *African Ivories*, p. 5.

101. Bassani and Fagg, *Africa and the Renaissance*, pp. 198–99; Bassani, *African Art*, p. 277.

102. Lagamma, 'Out of Kongo', p. 283.

family. Even compiling a trustworthy chronology of the rulers of the Kingdom of Kongo in the fifteenth and sixteenth centuries is far from easy. The most stable ruler in the first half of the sixteenth century was Afonso I Mvemba a Nzinga,[103] who ruled from 1509 to 1542, and he is the most likely donor of the oliphants. Three others who ruled in the following years up to 1547, and who are therefore possible donors, are Francisco Nkumbi a Mpudi (r. 1542), Pedro I Nkanga a Mvemba (r. 1542–45) and Diogo I Mpudi a Nzinga (r. 1545–61).[104] Yet it is worth remembering that many African sculptures were made to be one part of a more 'complex performance or ritual' and can only be properly understood with reference to their intended sphere of operation. If, as is likely, these oliphants were intended for use at a Kongolese court, they can be seen as formal statement objects, concerned with exalting and marking an existing form of authority.[105]

Regardless of the precise ownership route by which they arrived in Portugal, these oliphants are 'valuable primary sources on the culture and artistic expression of pre-colonial Kongo'.[106] Even if the first known reference to the oliphants is from 1547 in Lisbon, it is possible they could have been made before the advent of the Portuguese in the Kongo in the 1480s, in which case the oliphants would by the 1540s have already been at least sixty years old. The king of Kongo, or one of the rulers of a Kongolese province, could have chosen to give away some of his older tusks. But it is also possible that they were more recent creations, examples of a continuing strand of traditional, pre-colonial Kongolese geometric decoration that continued after the arrival of the Portuguese. Kongolese oliphant decoration, unlike that in Sierra Leone or Benin, did not change or adapt to include European motifs, but certain other attributes can indicate that the objects might have been made for European consumption. The results of assessing three basic attributes—the number of lugs, the position of the mouthpiece and the size of the oliphants (Plates 21 and 22)—are ambivalent in

103. Some of his letters exist: Louis Jadin and Mireille Dicorato, *Correspondance de Dom Afonso, roi du Congo, 1506–1543,* = *Académie royale de Belgique. Classe des sciences morales et politiques: Mémoires,* n.s. 41, no. 3 (Brussels, 1975).

104. From the 'Chronology of Kingship' in *Kongo: Power and Majesty,* ed. Alisa Lagamma, exh. cat., The Metropolitan Museum of Art, New York (New York, 2015), pp. 14–15 at 14.

105. Malcolm D. McLeod, 'Verbal Elements in West African Art', *Quaderni Poro,* 1 (1976), pp. 85–102 at 85, 99–102.

106. Alisa Lagamma, 'Kongo: Power and Majesty', in *Kongo: Power and Majesty,* ed. Alisa Lagamma, exh. cat., The Metropolitan Museum of Art, New York (New York, 2015), pp. 16–45 at 22.

terms of deciding whether these objects had been created explicitly for external consumption, as gifts to be given to foreigners. According to Marc Leo Felix, the presence of one lug on each oliphant (as opposed to the two which were standard on those destined for export), was compatible with traditional African oliphants made for Kongolese use.[107] The problem with this argument is that the larger oliphant in fact has two lugs, one near the finial and the second underneath the broad band at the hollowed end, so it would fit the specifications for an object destined for export. The lozenge or *navicella* (barque)-shaped mouthpiece is in the usual African place, on the concave side of the tusk. The two oliphants differ in size, the smaller one being 57.5 centimetres long, and the larger 83.2 centimetres; those for local consumption tend to be in the range 60–150 centimetres, while those for export tend to be between 30 and 60 centimetres, so this evidence too is inconclusive.[108] As one is considerably bigger than the other, they cannot straightforwardly be a pair that came from the same elephant, although their decoration has strong resemblances, and they exhibit the hallmarks of having been carved by the same artist or, at the very least, in the same workshop. This would not preclude them from having been made separately at different times, and indeed at the moment it is not even certain that they were acquired together in the Kongo: they could have been acquired serially.[109]

These two side-blown oliphants are believed to belong to a group of ten now in Europe (the others being in Lisbon, Paris, Toledo, Brussels, Stuttgart and Rome), seven of them from the same workshop, according to Ezio Bassani and William Fagg, and six thought by Bassani to be possibly by a single artist.[110] Trying to assign early modern African objects to artists or workshops is an activity only in its infancy; but see for example Kathryn Wysocki Gunsch's 2018 study of the Benin plaques, in which she identifies three flange pattern groups and uses these as a basis for assigning authorship to three distinct production series;[111] or the section 'Non creazione anonima ma arte di artisti' in the *Ex Africa* exhibition at the Museo civico archaeologico in Bologna in

107. Felix, 'Trumpets and Whistles', p. 184.

108. Ibid., p. 182.

109. Whether it was more usual in Kongolese culture to give a single decorated oliphant as a present, or two, has not been investigated.

110. Bassani and Fagg, *Africa and the Renaissance*, pp. 198 and 247–48; Bassani, *African Art*, p. 277, and cat. nos 280, 429, 483–84, 513, 576 and 707–10.

111. Kathryn Wysocki Gunsch, *The Benin Plaques: A Sixteenth-Century Imperial Monument* (Abingdon, 2018), pp. 74–122.

2019.[112] In no case other than that of the Medici duo can the arrival in Europe of this group of side-blown oliphants be traced to the sixteenth century, but almost certainly they must have entered then. It is possible that more of them were on sale in Lisbon when Campana made his purchases, but were bought by other people. In decorative and physical terms these two oliphants are African creations, unlike the better known Sapi-Portuguese ones, with mixed African and European compositional motifs,[113] which are known to have entered Lisbon in greater numbers (there are about forty Sapi-Portuguese oliphants still extant; none are mentioned in the one surviving Casa da Guiné treasurer's account book from 1504–5, while ivory salt-cellars and spoons both are).[114] This could be an indication that those oliphants not given as gifts from African rulers were principally bought or commissioned by members of the Portuguese royal court and the king himself, as the royal family and Portuguese court were exempt from paying the taxes recorded in the Casa da Guiné registers.[115]

The compositional banding on this odd couple of oliphants follows the same ordering of sections, even if the proportions of the sections relative to each other differ: finial, bands with lug, section with swirl, mouthpiece with different decoration, larger section of swirl, bands with or without second lug, broad band of interlace, final bands. The purely geometric decoration (Plates 23 and 24), with 'meanders, frets, swastikas and simple or interwoven lozenges' in their design combinations,[116] while classically African, appears something entirely new for Europe, because the geometric decoration represents a totality of the design, rather than only a part of it or the frame for it. The novelty of the decoration lies in the recalibration of its importance between African and European cultural norms: a peripheral detail of design

---

112. See the essay by Bernard de Grunne, 'Su alcuni maestri dell'arte africana', in *Ex Africa: Storie e identità di un'arte universale*, exh. cat., Museo civico archaeologico, Bologna (Milan, 2019), pp. 159–65, on artists and workshops (and pp. 166–79 for the illustrations of the works displayed in the exhibition).

113. The word hybrid, rather than mixed, has often been used in the past in connection with this decoration, but on problems raised by the notion of hybridity, see Carolyn Dean and Dana Leibsohn, 'Hybridity and Its Discontents: Considering Visual Culture in Colonial Spanish America', *Colonial Latin American Review*, 12.1 (2003), pp. 5–35 at 5–9.

114. Lowe, 'Made in Africa', pp. 168–70.

115. The pope and Roman court were similarly exempt from Roman customs dues: Arnold Esch, 'Roman Customs Registers: Items of Interest to Historians of Art and Material Culture', *Journal of the Warburg and Courtauld Institutes*, 58 (1995), pp. 72–87 at 72.

116. Bassani, *African Art*, p. 281.

has moved to the centre and itself become the subject matter, ousting all representational imagery. Several of these designs in isolation were ancient motifs shared by many cultures, such as the meander or fret (a type of angular spiral) which was in use already in palaeolithic times and was much in use in ancient Greece in varying patterns of interlockings.[117] The so-called complex Greek meander, later widely disseminated in visual form by Andrea Palladio in a woodcut illustration of decoration in the temple of Mars vendicatore (Mars Ultor) in Rome in his *Quattro libri dell'architettura* of 1570 (Plate 25),[118] was already visible earlier in Renaissance Italy. For example, it was widely used by Raphael: it puts in an appearance twice on the high, boxed wooden throne in his *Madonna and Child with Saint John the Baptist and Saint Nicholas of Bari* of 1505 (the '*Ansidei Madonna*') (Plate 26),[119] and in all four frescoes in the Stanza della segnatura in the Vatican of 1509–11, on the soffit of the arch that frames each composition,[120] and it is used as a framing device on the bottom edge of several of the tapestries by Pieter van Aelst and Raphael of *The Acts of the Apostles* displayed in the Sistine Chapel in 1519, including *Saint Paul Preaching at Athens* and *The Sacrifice of Lystra*.[121] Yet in all these cases the meander is one small piece of geometric decoration in a much larger whole, and not the only decoration there is. The shift in its importance gives the illusion of creating something wholly new.

117. Ibid., p. 284 n. 23; and see Calder Loth, 'The Complex Greek Meander', Institute of Classical Architecture and Art (ICAA) website, 'Classical Comments', 4 December 2016, https://www.classicist.org/articles/classical-comments-the-complex-greek-meander/ (accessed 22 April 2023). Because of the geographical reach and longevity of this decorative device, these African pieces are highly appropriate objects for study in a Warburgian sense.

118. Andrea Palladio, *Quattro libri dell'architettura*, ed. Licisco Magagnato and Paola Marini (Milan, 1980), Book 4, ch. 7, p. 274.

119. *Raphael*, ed. David Ekserdjian and Tom Henry with Matthias Wivel, exh. cat., The National Gallery, London (London, 2022), pp. 130–32, cat. no. 10, but the frets are not mentioned.

120. Loth, 'Complex Greek Meander', and *Raphael*, ed. Ekserdjian and Henry, p. 24 (fig 13), p. 25 (fig. 14), p. 44 (fig. 24) and p. 83 (fig. 54).

121. Mark Evans and Clare Browne with Arnold Nesselrath, eds, *Raphael: Cartoons and Tapestries for the Sistine Chapel* (London, 2010), pp. 113 (cat. no. 8), 115, 121 (cat. no. 10), 123; Lisa Pon, 'Raphael's *Acts of the Apostles* Tapestries for Leo X: Sight, Sound and Space in the Sistine Chapel', *The Art Bulletin*, 97.4 (2015), pp. 388–408 at 390; and Linda Wolk-Simon, 'Politics, Portraiture and the Medici Popes, 1513–34', in *The Medici: Portraits and Politics, 1512–1570*, ed. Keith Christiansen and Carlo Falciani, exh. cat., The Metropolitan Museum, New York (New York, 2021), pp. 104–119 at 106 and fig. 35; *Raphael*, ed. Ekserdjian and Henry, pp. 240–41, cat. no. 65.

Campana's accounts journal divulges two further pieces of critical information: the two oliphants—which he calls *corni*—were bought at auction, and were sold together for the price of three gold ducats and one hundred *maravedis*.[122] The information occurs twice in two different sections of the volume: the first time the precise Italian is, 'dua cornni d'avolio ghranddi comperi allo incantto in Lisbona' (two big ivory horns bought at auction in Lisbon),[123] and the second time it is, '2 cornni ghrandi d'avolio con fighure comperi al'onchanto' (two big ivory horns with shapes or forms bought at auction) (Figs. 7 and 8).[124]

The word *fighure* can be translated as 'figures', 'shapes',[125] or 'forms', the closest that the buyer could get to describing what to him were strange or unfamiliar geometric patterns. Clearly their origin was either unknown (which is most likely) or unimportant to Campana, and he did not note it (would he in any case have had any idea where the Kongo was?)—nor was the place of origin of these oliphants ever known or noted after they entered the Medici collections, until the twentieth century. The label on them in the Pitti today reads, 'Due trombe reali, Regno di San Salvador' (São Salvador was the old name of Mbanza-Kongo in Angola's north-western province). The oliphants are a perfect example of how changing countries erased the history and the cultural meaning of a global object. These objects, whilst desirable because of their material, shape, unusual decoration and rarity, and familiar because they could immediately be identified as hunting horns, were not valued because they came from the continent of Africa or more precisely from the Kingdom of Kongo. There was no added value in these affiliations—a very interesting and useful piece of information on which to ponder, which would explain why they were kept in the secret Guardaroba and were not with the maps of Africa in the Guardaroba nuova.[126] The price too indicates that these oliphants were not thought to be exceptional objects; but prices at auction are unpredictable,

122. In the text the amount paid is specified as 3¼ gold ducats, whereas in the figures it appears as 3 gold ducats and 100 *maravedis*. (Recall that there were 375 *maravedis* in a gold ducat.)

123. ASF, Misc. med. 713, Giornale e ricordanze, 4v.

124. Ibid., 78r.

125. Florio, *Queen Anna's New World*, p. 187, where the primary translation of *figura* is: 'a figure, a shape, an image, or resemblance'; Pianigiani, *Vocabolario etimologico*, 1, p. 531: 'forma esteriore delle cose diversamente plasmata e disposta, a seconda della speciale natura di esse'; Battaglia, *Grande dizionario*, 5, p. 970: 'L'aspetto esteriore di una cosa in quanto rappresentabile visivamente o descrivibile in rapporto con altre forme'.

126. Cf. Fiorani, *Marvel of Maps*, pp. 74 and 75.

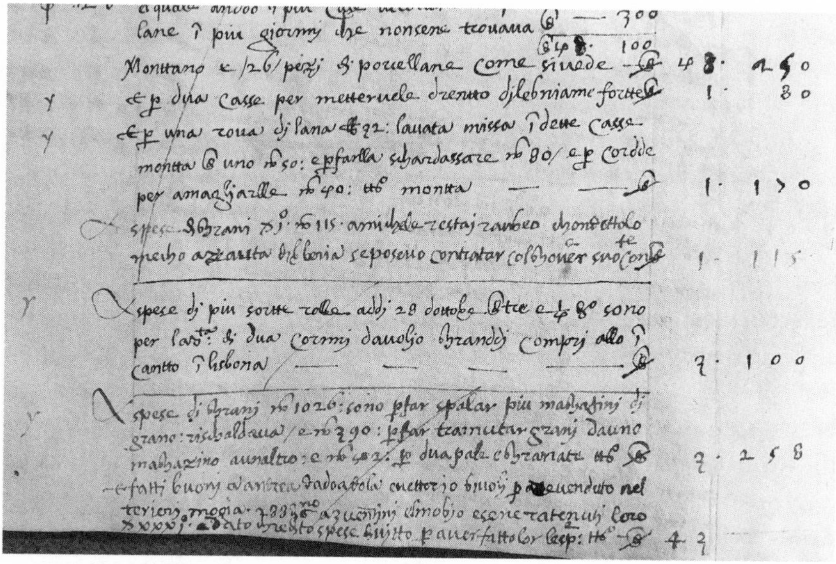

FIGURE 7. Florence, Archivio di stato, Misc. med. 713, 4v. By permission of the Italian Ministry of Culture/Archivio di stato di Firenze. Photo: Kate Lowe

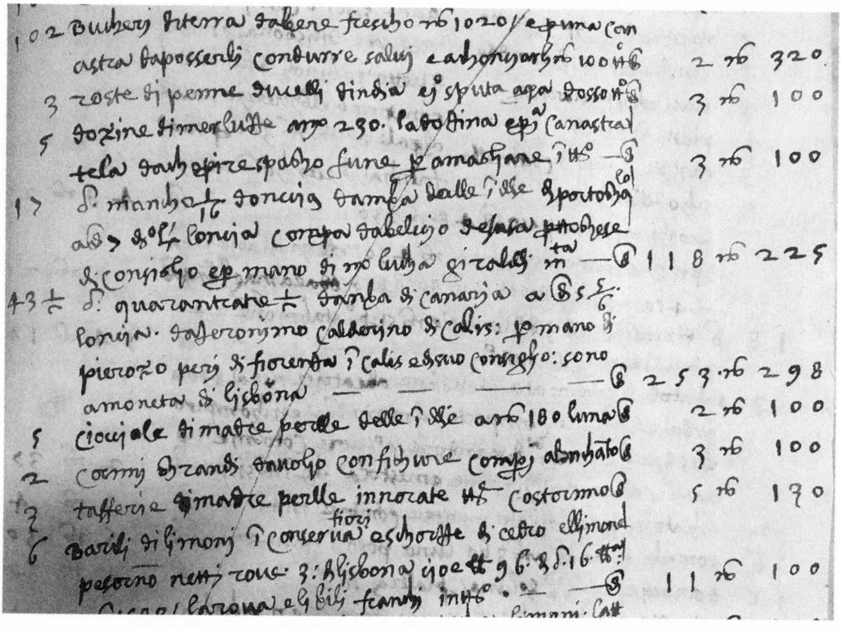

FIGURE 8. Florence, Archivio di stato, Misc. med. 713, 78r. By permission of the Italian Ministry of Culture/Archivio di stato di Firenze. Photo: Kate Lowe

as they depend upon the presence of willing buyers at a very specific moment, and unfortunately there are no other prices known for oliphants—and very few prices for other worked medium-sized or large African ivory objects— sold in Europe in this period with which to compare it. A price is known for two ivory salt-cellars ('elfenbeinerne Salzfässer') bought by Dürer in Antwerp in 1521: he paid three *gulden* for them, a not inconsiderable sum of money for him. It is worth noting that once again a pair of objects was bought. The price reflected their value as unusual objects from overseas, but did not signal their extreme rarity or preciousness. They were described in Dürer's diary as being 'kalikutische' or 'from Calicut', so their quite specific African provenance had been erased and replaced by a generic foreign place of origin.[127] In the case of the Kongolese oliphants, however, and more generally, it is important not to forget that oral information could and often did accompany or exist independently from what was written. It is therefore theoretically possible that Campana knew that the oliphants were from the Kingdom of Kongo, and informed Cosimo of this in person when he met him—but it is unlikely, because if so, or if it had been considered important, that piece of information would have become attached to the oliphants, and would have appeared somewhere in written form. However, it is known that Eleonora was in Livorno when Campana arrived back on 5 March 1548,[128] and probable that Cosimo was with her, as he is recorded as being in Livorno on 9 March 1548, when he was said to want to stay three or four further days there.[129] At this point, were Campana to have been in possession of the knowledge that the oliphants had come from the Kongo, it might still have been fresh in his mind, and he could have imparted this to Cosimo. Just as oral and written instructions and reports coexisted happily in the realm of diplomacy, it is likely that they did so too in making acquisitions for a duke.[130]

No other goods in Campana's account journal were bought at auction, and deeply satisfying though it is to know by what means the oliphants were sold in Lisbon and arrived in Florence, how they arrived in Lisbon is still unknown. The fact that they were sold at auction points to their previous owner being

127. Unverfehrt, '*Da sah ich viel köstliche Dinge*', p. 142; Dürer, *Diary*, p. 83.

128. ASF, Misc. med. 713, Giornale e ricordanze, 9r.

129. ASF, MdP 1174, 125r, Lorenzo Pagni to Pier Francesco Ricci, 5 March 1547/8.

130. Cf. Isabella Lazzarini, 'Orality and Writing in Diplomatic Interactions in Fifteenth-Century Italy', in Stefano Dall'Aglio, Brian Richardson and Massimo Rospocher, eds, *Voices and Texts in Early Modern Italian Society* (London, 2017), pp. 97–109.

someone with an African past. Unfortunately, the Lisbon archives that might have been able to supply candidates for this role (whose goods were auctioned in a relevant timeframe) were amongst those destroyed in 1755. Clearly Lisbon's sixteenth-century diary was full of auctions and markets[131]—slave auctions took place all the time, especially at the Pelourinho Velho,[132] and goods from India were sold at discounted prices on Tuesdays[133]—but 28 October 1547 was a Friday, and the most likely possibility is that the auction was either an estate sale or an auction related to children whose parents had died.[134] A good example of an estate sale in Lisbon is provided by that of Nuno da Cunha, the ninth governor of Portuguese India, from 1528 to 1538.[135] There is no list of all the objects in the sale, but it is known from a marginal note in one of Queen Catarina de Áustria's inventories that she had acquired eight Ceylonese gold bracelets from da Cunha's wife and heirs at the sale of his estate in 1545 after his death in Santarém, bought on her instructions by one of her ladies-in-waiting.[136] Post-mortem auctions, or estate sales known as *al-modenas*, were routine in Spain,[137] and if the estate were of a suitable level,

131. On mid-sixteenth-century auctions in Florence, see Ann Matchette, 'To Have and Have Not: The Disposal of Household Furnishings in Florence', *Renaissance Studies*, 20.5 (2006), pp. 702–15 at 709–10.

132. On slave auctions in Lisbon, see A. C. de C. M. Saunders, *A Social History of Black Slaves and Freedmen in Portugal, 1441–1555* (Cambridge, 1982), p. 17; Fonseca, *Escravos*, pp. 148–50; Lisbon, DGLAB/ANTT, CC, 1.51.56, re the sale of two French ships coming from Brazil. In the middle of the document are named all the places where it was customary to announce the sale.

133. Annemarie Jordan Gschwend, 'Shopping on the Rua Nova dos Mercadores', in *A cidade global: Lisboa no Renascimento/The Global City: Lisbon in the Renaissance* (Lisbon, 2017), ed. Annemarie Jordan Gschwend and K.J.P. Lowe, exh. cat., Museu Nacional de Arte Antiga, Lisbon, pp. 300–305 at 301.

134. For examples from Loulé, see Maria de Fátima Machado, *Fundo dos órfãos de Loulé: Séculos XV e XVI* (Loulé, 2016).

135. Annemarie Jordan Gschwend, 'A arte de coleccionar entre as mulheres habsburgo D. Caterina e D. Juana de Áustria e a sua busca pelo luxo/The Art of Collecting among Habsburg Women: Catherine and Juana of Austria and Their Pursuit of Luxury', in Hugo Miguel Crespo, ed., *A arte de coleccionar: Lisboa, Europa e o mundo na época moderna (1500–1800)/The Art of Collecting: Lisbon, Europe and the Early Modern World (1500–1800)* (Lisbon, 2019), pp. 34–53 at 37.

136. DGLAB/ANTT, NA 793, 1545, fol. 37v.

137. On auctions of goods, see Juan Vicente García Marsilla, 'La vida de las cosas: El mercado de objetos de segunda mano en la Valencia medieval', unpublished paper, University of Valencia.

offered another possible route to obtaining global goods.[138] They were undoubtedly also routine in Portugal, but evidence for their frequency is lacking.[139] Even such scarce documentation as is extant in relation to auctions in Florence is not available for Lisbon.[140]

There is as yet no clue at whose post-mortem auction in Lisbon in 1547 these oliphants could have been put up for sale: whether a merchant who traded in Africa or someone who had served at El Mina, or indeed someone who had been to the Kingdom of Kongo as an entrepreneur, envoy or ambassador. Kongo had only had relations with Portugal since 1488, and the number of Portuguese who had been there was relatively small. One random surviving document is the inventory of a sale that took place on São Tomé in 1507 of goods belonging to Álvaro Borges, who had died on the island. In it, an array of West African objects put in an appearance: mats, clothes, fabrics, cushions and ivories, quite a few of which are allocated a place of origin: Benin, Kongo, dos Rios (the Rivers).[141] As the sale took place in Africa, knowledge of and expertise in African matters was easy to come by, creating a stark contrast with the ignorance apparently prevalent in Florence. At the Lisbon auction, all such knowledge relating to the oliphants had probably already been erased or lost.

138. Almudena Pérez de Tudela and Annemarie Jordan Gschwend, 'Luxury Goods for Royal Collectors: Exotica, Princely Gifts and Rare Animals Exchanged between the Iberian Courts and Central Europe in the Renaissance (1560–1612)', in Helmut Trnek and Sabine Haag, eds, *Exotica: Portugals Entdeckungen im Spiegel fürstlicher Kunst- und Wunderkammern der Renaissance,* = *Jahrbuch des Kunsthistorischen Museums Wien* 3 (Mainz, 2001), pp. 1–127 at 9; Jeremy Warren, review of Almudena Pérez de Tudela Gabaldón, *Los inventarios de Doña Juana de Austria, Princesa de Portugal (1535–1573)* (Jaen, 2017), *Journal of the History of Collections,* 31.1 (2019), p. 201.

139. Arrangements made thirty-five years later in 1584 for the auction of some goods left to the Misericórdia of Porto by D. Lopo de Almeida point to probable procedures. The occasion was announced by proclamation of an employee of the judiciary, and the goods—which in this case included a coco-de-mer encased in silver—were auctioned in the courtyard of the Misericórdia to the highest bidder: Isabel dos Guimarães Sá, *O regresso dos mortos: Os doadores da Misericórdia do Porto e a expansão oceânica (séculos XVI–XVII)* (Lisbon, 2018), p. 126.

140. Lists of goods sold at auction remain rare in Florence, and no comprehensive lists exist, for example, for the auctions of Medici possessions that took place in 1495 after Piero de' Medici was forced out of Florence. Instead, there are other documents revealing the routes whereby Medici partisans were able to reacquire some of the most precious pieces before auctions took place, and notices in diaries and chronicles of three or four auctions at Or San Michele and Palazzo Medici. See Fusco and Corti, *Lorenzo de' Medici,* p. 166.

141. *Portugaliae monumenta africana,* 4 vols (1–3 and 5) (Lisbon, 2002), 5, doc. 89 (pp. 221–43).

A third possibility is that Portugal could have behaved as Venice and (probably) Florence did, and held auctions of diplomatic gifts given to Venetian ambassadors by foreign powers, as ambassadors were not allowed to keep them, presumably because of concerns about the possibility of corruption.[142] This decree sat uneasily alongside the requirements of reciprocal gift exchange demanded by diplomatic practice. As Portugal was a kingdom and not a republic, it probably did not behave in this way, as political structures dictated the particular forms that constituted circular exchange rituals.

The question of why Campana was attracted to the oliphants remains unanswered, and is at present unanswerable. They are beautiful pieces of artistry, original in a European context, so perhaps it was a combination of beauty and artistry that caught his eye. Or perhaps it was that they were the only such objects that he saw during his stay, as not many carved oliphants appear to have been imported,[143] so it was their rarity that attracted him.

Other Inanimate Acquisitions

Other intriguing objects bought for Cosimo in Lisbon on 14 August 1547 included three tortoiseshell ('testugine') fans made from the feathers of birds described as being 'dell'India', which, together with a 'sputa aqua',[144] cost three ducats and one hundred *maravedis*. The tortoiseshell—which very probably was in fact turtle-shell—would have comprised the hard backbone of the fans, including their sticks. The tortoiseshell objects were purchased from a sea captain called Diego Ferante, which is not a common name in Portugal.[145] Unfortunately, he has not yet been traced, however, and what route his ship might have been sailing is therefore unknown. Although no provenance is noted in Campana's account journal apart from 'dell'India', which merely denotes somewhere foreign outside Europe, it is rather likely that these were

---

142. Richard C. Trexler, *Public Life in Renaissance Florence* (New York, 1980), pp. 323–26, and Donald E. Queller, *Early Venetian Legislation on Ambassadors* (Geneva, 1966), pp. 42–43 and 80.

143. Unworked ivory was imported in extremely large quantities, and even when unworked, the ivory was considered beautiful. Müller, *Welthandelsbräuche*, p. 297, refers to a list of goods available for sale in Lisbon in 1514–15 from Guinea, in which ivory was described: 'zenn von olifant, die vast schon und groß sindt' (elephant tusks, that are very beautiful and big).

144. The precise wording was, 'uno sputa aqua d'osso di testugine e tre roste di simile osso', ASF, Misc. med. 731, 2v and '3 roste di penne d'ucelli d'India e i° sputa aqua d'osso', ibid., 78r.

145. Ibid., 2v. For the pilot Diogo Fernandes, see Francisco Marqués de Sousa Viterbo, *Trabalhos náuticos dos portugueses nos séculos XVI e XVII* (Lisbon, 1898), part 1, p. 98.

Mexican artefacts. If so, they arrived in Europe earlier than any previously known Mexican fans of this type, requiring a change in the received chronology relating to the making of fans. It is accepted that Mexican featherwork, whether pre-Columbian or Christian in design, generally arrived in Italy through one of two channels: via missionaries (who sent them to popes, cardinals and others) or via Spain.[146] These 1547 fans would appear to be exceptions: they reached Lisbon first and then were purchased and taken to Florence. Mexican featherwork was used by indigenous peoples either in the making of ritual objects (in which case the power of the bird was transmitted to the human user of the object)[147] or for objects of adornment. One example of a sixteenth-century feather fan made of quetzal feathers and gold, long considered to be Aztec,[148] but now thought by some to be colonial,[149] and previously in Schloss Ambras, is now in the Weltmuseum in Vienna (Plate 27); it has no tortoiseshell sticks. But a Mexican feather mosaic and hawksbill turtle-shell (*Eretmochelys imbricata*) fan, dated to the seventeenth century, that blends 'techniques and aesthetic influences used in the ancient feather arts of pre-Hispanic Mexico with European design of the Renaissance period', is extant at the Peabody Essex Museum in Salem (Plate 28), offering some possible pointers.[150] These two fans are at opposite ends of the functional spectrum, with the first probably being of ritual significance and the second being a European decorative item. As Marcy Norton has written, a number of potential processes, from cultural convergence, whereby shared elements allow the object to be valued and understood similarly in both cultures (less likely), to commodity indigenisation, whereby the receiving culture assimilates a foreign object on its own terms (more likely),

146. Corinna Tania Gallori, 'Collecting Feathers: A Journey from Mexico into Italian Collections (16th–17th Century)', in Susan Bracken, Andrea M. Gáldy and Adriana Turpin, eds, *Collecting East and West* (Newcastle upon Tyne, 2013), pp. 61–81 at 63–64.

147. Marcy Norton, 'Going to the Birds: Animals as Things and Beings in Early Modernity', in Paula Findlen, ed., *Early Modern Things: Objects and Their Histories, 1500–1800* (London, 2013), pp. 53–83 at 68–69.

148. Markey, *Imagining the Americas*, p. 175 n. 27.

149. Walter Baumgartner, 'The Aztec Feather Shield in Vienna: Problems of Conservation', *Nuevo mundo/Mundos nuevos*, 'Colloques, 2006: Feather Creations. Materials, Production and Circulation. New York Hispanic Society, Institute of Fine Arts, 17–19/06/2004', no. 1, https://doi.org.10.400/nuevomundo/1447.

150. Paula Bradstreet Richter, Mimi Leveque and Kathryn Myatt Carey, 'The Feather Fan in the Peabody Essex Museum', in Alessandra Russo, Gerhard Wolf and Diana Fane, eds, *Images Take Flight: Feather Art in Mexico and Europe, 1400–1700* (Florence, 2015), pp. 342–49 at 343, 347.

may have been at work in this cross-cultural migration of featherwork,[151] just as they were in the migration of ivory oliphants.

No trace exists in the Medici Guardaroba or in the Medici inventories relating to Campana's Lisbon fans, and it is highly unlikely that anyone—other perhaps than Diego Ferante who sold them—would have known their place of origin. Objects from the Americas were collected by the Medici, allowing them to partake in a virtual possession of the two continents. Already in 1539 Cosimo's Guardaroba included Mexican costumes and featherwork artefacts (but not featherwork fans),[152] and by 1571 Cardinal Ferdinando's inventory of that year listed a number of fans, including 'una rosta di penne di pappagallo venuta dell'India' (a fan of parrot feathers from 'India').[153] Even with this interest, no geographical knowledge remained attached to these fans ('dell'India' was not used to describe a specific place), just as Laura Laurencich-Minelli found with her newly discovered description of objects brought from the New World to Bologna by the Spaniard Domingo de Betanzos, and donated to Clement VII in 1533.[154] In this case, the requisite knowledge about the objects' provenance was undoubtedly known by Betanzos, but not passed on once he returned to Europe. Provenance, for whatever reason, was of no or limited importance in relation to these artefacts. If Mexican provenance was not a draw, however, the materials from which the fans were made might have been, if indeed Campana recognised them. Cosimo was also known to take pleasure in verbal and visual turtle imagery, adopting the motto *Festina lente*, or 'Make haste slowly', visualised for him as a turtle with a sail on its back.[155] This predilection for turtles was common knowledge at the Medici court, and the tapestry of *La Dovizia* (wealth or abundance) attributed to Angelo Bronzino (c. 1545) included both a turkey (see below) and a turtle in its idealised version of the life of plenty.[156]

The other tortoiseshell or turtle-shell object purchased with the fans from Diego Ferante was described as a 'sputa aqua', perhaps a *sputtacchiera* or

151. Norton, 'Going to the Birds', p. 70.

152. Detlef Heikamp, *Mexico and the Medici* (Florence, 1972), p. 34.

153. Ibid., pp. 16 and 36; Gallori, 'Collecting Feathers', pp. 72–74.

154. Laura Laurencich-Minelli, 'From the New World to Bologna, 1533: A Gift for Pope Clement VII and Bolognese Collections of the Sixteenth and Seventeenth Centuries', *Journal of the History of Collections*, 24.2 (2012), pp. 145–58 at 146, 154.

155. Markey, *Imagining the Americas*, pp. 17 and 129.

156. Ibid., pp. 17–18.

spittoon[157]—although what feature of the object could have led Campana to attribute this function to it is unknown. Spittoons were usually vase-shaped, without lids and with distinctive wide brims, of ancient pedigree in China, made of precious metals, stoneware, porcelain or lacquer.[158] Turtle-shell came from the carapace of one of the two species of sea turtle used in the production of decorative objects in Asia, either the green sea turtle (*Chelonia mydas*) or the hawksbill sea turtle (*Eretmochelys imbricata*),[159] and was amongst the most expensive and the most perishable of raw materials.[160] It was used in quite a range of objects, all of them luxury goods, all of them unique pieces, all of them signalling status. Objects known to be made from tortoiseshell or turtle-shell in the sixteenth century were caskets (sometimes reliquary caskets, very occasionally miniature caskets used as jewel boxes),[161] mounted *jarri* or jars, plates with or without a foot, combs and writing cabinets.[162] In addition, tortoiseshell was used in the Ottoman Empire in panels in doors and cupboards and as covers on an album of calligraphy.[163] No extant spittoon is made of tortoiseshell or turtle-shell. Many tortoiseshell and turtle-shell objects have been ascribed a provenance in India, usually in Gujarat or Goa; however, tortoiseshell was also produced and used throughout South-East Asia, so tortoiseshell objects should not automatically be labelled as Indian. The uncertainty over what category of object is being described here

157. Pianigiani, *Vocabolario etimologico*, 2, p. 1343.

158. Roberto Zaugg, 'The King's Chinese Spittoon: Global Commodities, Court Culture and Vodun in the Kingdoms of Hueda and Dahomey (Seventeenth to Nineteenth Centuries)', *Annales HSS* (English edition), 73.1 (2018), pp. 115–53 at 137 and nn. 94, 95.

159. Hugo Miguel Crespo, ed., *A arte de coleccionar: Lisboa, Europa e o mundo na época moderna (1500–1800)/The Art of Collecting: Lisbon, Europe and the Early Modern World (1500–1800)* (Lisbon, 2019), p. 244, entry no. 31 (Hugo Miguel Crespo). Ulisse Aldrovandi, *Natura picta*, ed. Alessandro Alessandrini and Alessandro Ceregato (Bologna, 2007) included illustrations of three tortoises/turtles on plates 442, 443, 452 and 453, but not of the hawksbill sea turtle (*Eretmochelys imbricata*).

160. Renato Ruotolo, 'Arredi e oggetti con la tartaruga nel Seicento', in *L'arte della tartaruga: Le opere dei musei napoletani e la donazione Sbriziolo-De Felice*, ed. Annalisa Bellerio, exh. cat., Museo Duca di Martina nella Villa Floridiana, Naples (Naples, 1995), pp. 11–21 at 11.

161. Crespo, *A arte de coleccionar*, p. 244, entry no. 31 (Hugo Miguel Crespo).

162. For examples of everything except the miniature casket or box, see *Exotica: Os descobrimentos portugueses e as câmaras de maravilhas do Renascimento*, exh. cat., Museu Calouste Gulbenkian, Lisbon (Lisbon, 2001), pp. 134–44, cat. nos 35–42.

163. *The Age of Süleyman the Magnificent*, ed. Esin Atul, exh. cat., National Gallery of Art, Washington (Washington, DC, 1987), pp. 104–5 and fig. 49a.

makes attempts to trace it in the Medici inventories and collection even more fraught than usual.[164] Clearly the description of the object in Campana's journal account is not necessarily correct, and identification of the function of an unfamiliar, extra-European object could be difficult, but Campana appears to have been able to recognise tortoiseshell or turtle-shell (or perhaps the seller informed him of the material), so the material at least should not be in doubt. Equally, the compilers of the Medici inventories did not always identify objects and functions and materials correctly, so error is possible in the inventories as well. It is more likely that Campana's tortoiseshell object either did not enter the Medici collection, or did not stay long or survive in it. Tortoiseshell does not keep well without care or intervention: it dries out, shrinks and cracks, and starts to look dull, so it is often thrown away.[165] Feathers and tortoiseshell were alike in this respect: they were fragile and needed care to survive in good condition, making their survival from the sixteenth to the twenty-first century a matter of great good fortune. Feathers could be eaten by insects, or damaged by light, acidity, temperature or humidity; when this occurred, feathers too were usually thrown away.[166]

As might have been expected, Campana acquired porcelain in Lisbon, the preeminent place in Europe for its acquisition. Even without Macau, which was settled by the Portuguese only in 1557, Portugal's other bases in South-East

164. The one extant tortoiseshell or turtle-shell bowl in the Medici collection might have been a possible match, but it has now been convincingly paired with an entry related to an object that entered the collection after 1589 but before 1634. Mario Scalini, 'Oggetti rari e curiosi nelle collezioni medicee: Esotica e naturalia', *Antichità viva*, 35.2–3 (1996), pp. 59–67 at 62; Rosangela Cuffaro, 'Fakhr Ad-Din II alla corte dei Medici (1613–1615): Collezionismo, architettura e ars topiaria tra Firenze e Beirut', *Marburger Jahrbuch für Kunstwissenschaft*, 37 (2010), pp. 209–17 at 214. Dated to the sixteenth century, the beauty of the primary material—tortoiseshell or turtle-shell—has been enhanced by what appears to be *sgraffito* decoration with a thin layer of gold. The decoration ranges from a peony on the lid to a flame frieze and strange animals or birds, 'fantastical dragons with feathers' (*Islam, specchio d'Oriente: Rarità e preziosi nelle collezioni statali fiorentine*, ed. Giovanna Damiani and Mario Scalini, exh. cat., Palazzo Pitti, Florence [Livorno, 2002], p. 95, cat. no. 75, entry by A. von Gladissi) or stylised phoenixes (conversation on 15 March 2019 with Michael Backman), on the body. This bowl has been variously attributed to India or Indonesia (*Islam, specchio d'Oriente*, p. 95, entry by A. von Gladissi), Sumatra or Tonkin (conversation on 15 March 2019 with Michael Backman), and Siam (personal communication from Hugo Crespo, 2 May 2019), with both the shape—a utilitarian cooking-pot shape—and the decoration pointing to a provenance in South-East Asia.

165. Ruotolo, 'Arredi e oggetti', p. 11; conversation on 15 March 2019 with Michael Backman.

166. Gallori, 'Collecting Feathers', pp. 78–79.

Asia facilitated access to porcelain, known as a Chinese luxury commodity produced nowhere else on earth at this date. The numbers are clear enough, although there is less clarity with relation to forms and colouring. The Medici were ahead of the crowd in appreciating the value of porcelain, but even so, the quantity of porcelain owned by them increased substantially in the period from Lorenzo de' Medici in the 1480s to Cosimo de' Medici in the 1540s. Lorenzo's father Piero had owned ten pieces of porcelain, and Lorenzo in his turn owned fifty-two pieces in addition to those given as presents by the ambassador from the sultan of Egypt in 1487.[167] They were mainly blue and white, but there were also some in celadon. In the Medici inventory of 1553, under Cosimo I, there were four hundred pieces, mainly with their colour noted, 290 of which were blue and white, 59 celadon, and the rest either white or blue.[168] Very close in date to Campana's acquisition, two important entries of porcelain into the Guardaroba are recorded, the first in February 1546, of 108 pieces, 106 of which were blue and white *tazzine* (small cups), and the second in April 1547, of 120, which entered from Livorno, possibly arriving from Egypt, that constituted a mixed bag.[169]

Campana managed, with difficulty, to acquire twenty-six pieces in Lisbon, from various sellers, by sending a middleman from house to house in a bid to find what was wanted, and as a consequence the twenty-six items were the equivalent of a job lot, a miscellaneous jumble of shapes, styles and sizes rather than a set of a single type. Not one of these pieces is recorded later as entering the Guardaroba. The vocabulary used to describe these pieces in Campana's account journal is limited. Eight shapes of porcelain are listed, including five *mescirobe* (ewers) and four *bacine* (basins), with a scattering of plates, cups, small basins and bowls. Only once is a colour mentioned, when a *bacino* is said to be 'non molto biancho' (not very white); there is no separation of blue and white from celadon, for example. Campana appears not to have known anything about porcelain, not even the most general categories, and in compiling the list, he does not seem to have known what to write, not understanding that

167. Morena, *Dalle Indie orientali*, p. 17.

168. ASF, Guardaroba medicea, 30, 34r–36r; Marco Spallanzani, *Ceramiche orientali a Firenze nel Rinascimento* (Florence, 1978), pp. 189–91; Spallanzani, *Ceramiche alla corte dei Medici*, pp. 13, 149–50; Morena, *Dalle Indie orientali*, p. 26.

169. Spallanzani, *Ceramiche alla corte dei Medici*, pp. 42, 147; Francesco Morena, 'Le collezioni di arte estremo-orientale dei granduchi medicei Cosimo I, Francesco I e Ferdinando I', in Francesco Morena, ed., *Dalle Indie orientali alla corte di Toscana: Collezioni di arte cinese e giapponese a Palazzo Pitti* (Florence, 2005), pp. 25–49, esp. 26, and cat. pp. 50–71.

the colour and decoration of the piece helped identify its date and specific provenance. Instead he concentrates on adjectives relating to size (*grande, grandetto, mezano, piccolo*), depth (*cupo* or 'deep') and fineness or delicacy (*fino*), qualities that can be assessed by examining the objects themselves, and apprehended without expertise. The most unusual adjective is applied to two ewers, one large and one small, each described as 'stiaciata' (crushed/squashed).[170] One possible explanation for this word—not one known to porcelain experts—is that it was an untutored verbal attempt to convey the visual sense that the ewers had been flattened, turned from a curved and rounded form into a thin one with square corners.[171]

The prices paid for these porcelain pieces are included in Campana's account journal, which is fortunate, as it is rare to find prices for porcelain at this date. Discussion of the prices has centred on their fall between the fifteenth and sixteenth centuries as porcelain became more accessible and available,[172] being transformed from a supremely luxurious to a more widespread, but still 'élite' product. Increased availability also led to a transformation in engagement with the functionality of the object: Cosimo and Eleonora regularly used porcelain and did not keep it firmly under lock and key as an item to be displayed. Previously it had been thought that the papal nuncio Giovanni Ricci was exaggerating when he wrote from Lisbon in May 1548 that a small piece of porcelain cost more than two ducats (he winningly described the porcelain at this price as 'transparent like jewels'),[173] and Campana's prices for a small piece suggest in October 1547 that small pieces were more likely to cost slightly less than this, probably between one and two ducats. However, Campana wrote that there was a dearth of available porcelain, and this could have worsened by 1548, pushing up the prices. And bald prices like these reveal nothing about the type or state of the porcelain, or about its attractiveness. The most striking aspect of the prices is how much the bigger and more expensive pieces were: two large basins together cost thirteen ducats, with the next most expensive object, a big *rinfreschatoio* (a metal or clay vessel for keeping liquids cool), costing four. Ensuring that these pieces of porcelain were safely packed

170. ASF, Misc. med. 713, 4v and 78v. The list on 78v is less detailed than that on 4v.

171. I am grateful to Marco Spallanzani for this suggestion.

172. Spallanzani, *Ceramiche orientali*, pp. 112–13, and 114 for a comparison of prices paid in fifteenth-century Florence with prices paid elsewhere across the Italian peninsula in the late fifteenth and early sixteenth centuries; Spallanzani, *Ceramiche alla corte dei Medici*, pp. 131–32.

173. Deswarte-Rosa, 'Le Cardinal', p. 123 and n. 53.

for transit involved still more expenditure, first of all on two strong wooden chests or cases, then on a nest of washed wool, then for the carding of the wool, and finally for cord to fasten the chests. The cost of this, two ducats and 250 *maravedis*,[174] if set alongside two ducats and 350 *maravedis* for three fine porcelain bowls, or the three ducats and one hundred *maravedis* paid for the two Kongolese oliphants, is not insignificant. The costs of packaging and shipping, clearly linked to the fragility and breakability of porcelain, is certainly a factor in keeping the prices paid for it relatively high, which is not straightforwardly related to the cost of its production.[175]

Also noted in Campana's account journal is the acquisition on 13 October 1547 of five unworked nautilus shells (from *Nautilus pompilius*), which he called 'chiociole d'India di madre perlle' (mother-of-pearl snails from 'India'); each one cost 180 *maravedis*. He bought them on the same day as he purchased nearly seventeen *oncie* (ounces) of amber for Eleonora, at a cost of 118 ducats and 225 *maravedis*, using Belico de Susa, who was Portuguese, as middleman, and paying in *contanti* (cash).[176] No provenance was given for them. Although these shells are now to be found largely in the western Pacific and coastal areas of the Indian Ocean, nautilus shells often came to Europe via China, and it is most likely that these examples did too. There is once again no record of these shells entering the Medici Guardaroba. However, the 1553 inventory contains five nautilus shells: two 'chiocciole di madreperle', full of *granati* or garnets (a type of red semi-precious stone), worked in gilt silver,[177] one used as a coarsepowder flask and the other as a finepowder flask, for an arquebus, and three other nautilus shells, described in one of the variants as 'grandi'.[178] The number is suggestive. The Medici collection also contains some spectacular worked nautilus shells from the second half of the sixteenth century, embellished in gilt silver by Flemish silversmiths,[179] and amongst the

174. ASF, Misc. med. 713, 4v.

175. Spallanzani, *Ceramiche alla corte dei Medici*, p. 131.

176. ASF, Misc. med. 713, 4r and 78r.

177. The post-mortem inventory of Alessandro de' Medici of 1537 refers to a nautilus shell worked in silver: ASF, MAP 159, 258r.

178. ASF, Guardaroba medicea 28, 34v ('2 chiocciole di madreperla, una per fiasco et l'altra per polverino da stioppi, piene di granati et fornite d'argento dorato') and 46r, and ASF, Guardaroba medicea 30, 74r.

179. Anna Maria Massinelli and Filippo Tuena, *Il tesoro dei Medici* (Milan, 1992), pp. 128–29; *Meraviglie: Precious, Rare and Curious Objects from the Medici Treasure*, ed. Marilena Mosco, exh. cat., Haags Historisch Museum, The Hague (Florence, 2003), pp. 38 and 39.

gifts sent by the Medici to the Dresden court in 1587 were four unmounted nautilus shells, two of which were unworked.[180]

As well as buying in Lisbon, Campana made purchases at Cadiz,[181] Ceres, Sanlúcar de Barrameda (which was the port for Seville, as Seville was inland), Gibraltar, Cartagena (one of the most important naval bases in sixteenth-century Spain) and Majorca, all except the last of which lay along the coastline of Spain heading from west to east; that is, on the way back from Lisbon to Livorno. All of these places presented opportunities to buy slightly different objects and goods, most originally sourced from the Spanish empire rather than the Portuguese trading empire. Many of the goods came from the New World. Once again, as in Lisbon, Campana operated in Cadiz largely in an Italian-inflected world, [182] and the names of his Italian or Italianate contacts there include Andrea and Pierozo Peri (the latter described as 'di Fiorenza in Calis'),[183] Jacopo Botti, Alessandro Chimenti and Jeronimo Calderino. He paid rent for a house in Cadiz from 9 November to 13 December 1547, but unfortunately he did not record the name of his landlord.[184]

From Cadiz, through the offices of the Botti and Peri, six chairs were purchased in April 1548 for the Medici court in Florence, whose price was reckoned as the equivalent of forty-two *scudi* and three *soldi*. Described as 'riche' or sumptuous, three were for men and three for women.[185] Both size and shape determined whether chairs were constructed for men or women. Most chairs were for men, and therefore the labelling 'da uomo' was usually redundant, and in the inventories hardly any of the chairs specified the gender of the target user—so presumably they were for men. Only the entries for women's chairs,[186] therefore, offer any possibility of being matched with the ones in

180. Barbara Marx, 'Medici Gifts to the Court of Dresden', *Studies in the Decorative Arts*, 15.1 (2007–8), pp. 46–82 at 66.

181. Some of these were of foodstuffs. Purchased in Cadiz on 12 January 1548 were six hundred smoked herrings, bought from a ship from Dieppe: ASF, Misc. med. 713, 8v.

182. Cadiz's Roman past was still much in evidence in the early sixteenth century. In 1516 the private garden of a Genoese merchant belonging to the Lomellini family included the amphitheatre: Gerard González Germain, 'Agostino Vespucci's De situ totius Hispaniae (1520): The Earliest Antiquarian Description of Spain', *Viator*, 48.1 (2017), pp. 275–95 at 286–87 and n. 79.

183. ASF, Misc. med. 713, 78r.

184. Ibid., smaller quadernuccio no. 2, 37v, under 19 December 1547.

185. Ibid., 9v and 79v.

186. A note of two sets of 'segiole da dona' re-covered in red velvet with fringes of silk and gold, totalling twenty chairs in total, appears exceptionally in the 1539 *ricordi* of the Guardaroba:

Campana's account journal.[187] A great many chairs, including types labelled for both men and for women, entered the Medici collections,[188] or appeared in Medici inventories in the second half of the sixteenth century, yet none seem thus far to have been securely linked to still existing chairs in the collection. One obvious reason for this is that the entry and inventory descriptions can be short and generic—such as 'dua seggiole intarsiate alla portoghese da ripiegarsi' (two folding chairs inlaid in the Portuguese style)[189]—but another is that chair styles and shapes were not sufficiently diverse to enable secure identification, and a third is that coverings and seats could all be replaced or changed. Other descriptors alluding to wood type ('di noce'), the 'da uomo'/'da donna' divide, or assigning a style or positing a style or presumed place of origin, such as 'alla portoghese' or 'di Spagna', are more reliable identifiers, but even the latter have severe drawbacks. The descriptions in Campana's account journal are short, with the only obvious identifier being the specification of the gender of the

---

ASF, Guardaroba medicea 13, 7v. Women's chairs were sometimes described as *bassa* (low): thus 'due seggiole basse da donna' or 'two low women's chairs' in the index to a Medici inventory of 1585: ASF, Guardaroba medicea 118, under 'S' for seggiole, in an index to the inventory. Most of the low women's chairs in the Medici collections are at the moment dated to the seventeenth century, and are of Florentine manufacture, but some prototypes may have been earlier and from Iberia. See Enrico Colle, ed., *I mobili di Palazzo Pitti: Il periodo dei Medici, 1537–1737* (Florence, 1997), p. 263, no. 97.

187. A potential match can perhaps be made with an entry in one version of the 1553 Medici inventory compiled 'a capi', that is according to category of object, that reads 'Tre seggiole di quoio da donne' (Three leather chairs for women) (ASF, Guardaroba medicea 31, 240v), as Spain was particularly noted for its use of leather in furnishings and furniture, including chairs. On X-chairs (see n. 188 below) involving leather from the Iberian peninsula, see Franklin Pereira, 'Artes do couro no medioevo peninsular, parte 4: As "sillas de cadernas" de Granada', *Al-Madan Online*, 23.2 (July 2020), available at https://issuu.com/almadan/docs/ao23-2/2?ff &showOtherPublicationsAsSuggestions=true&experiment=last-page (accessed 12 June 2023), pp. 92–106.

188. Some sixteenth-century chairs originating from the Guardaroba are now in Palazzo Davanzati in Florence. A sixteenth-century carved chair made of walnut, called 'sedia' or 'seggiola' in the inventories, often known now as an X-chair on account of its X-shaped frame, with particularly fine carvings of rosettes and leaves, is an exceptional example of a common type, often referred to as 'alla napoletana' or 'alla Spagna', with no recognisable stylistic difference known between the two. See *Firenze e la Toscana dei Medici: Committenza e collezionismo*, p. 211, cat. no. 398 (Maddalena Trionfi Honorati), and p. 213, fig. 398.

189. ASF, Guardaroba medicea 30 (this is the 1553/4 inventory arranged not according to room, as in Guardaroba medicea 28, but according to category of object), 328 destra. These chairs were essentially X-chairs (see n. 188 above) with folding rather than fixed frames.

chair's user. None of the entries in the entry books or the contemporary inventories matches these descriptions. By 1560, the number of chairs owned by the Medici had expanded exponentially, and one entry was for sixty 'seggiole da donne',[190] making any hope of identification futile.

The chairs purchased in Cadiz, and presumed to be Spanish, contrast strongly with the African chairs 'de Guiné'—from Guinea—included in the 1507 post-mortem inventory apportioning the bequests of the Infanta D. Beatriz, the mother of Manuel I. Apart from being assigned a place of origin (even if imprecise), there are two additional pieces of information about the chairs, both rather surprising: there were four of them; that is, there was the equivalent of a set of four, and they were said to be *redondas* (round).[191] The people taking the inventory had been told or themselves recognised that the chairs came from Africa (but on what basis?) but could not or did not assign their place of origin more precisely to a country or area or ethnic tradition. No other chairs described as being from Africa appear in late fifteenth- or sixteenth-century Portuguese inventories, and there are no extant chairs from Africa from this date.[192] The chairs are handed over to one of Beatriz's court ladies, Violante Rodrigues,[193] and fall from the record; they are the only overtly African objects, named as such, in Beatriz's possession. This is their first and last documentary appearance.

Cosimo's Favourites: Coins/Medals

The most significant purchase from the port of Gibraltar noted in Campana's account journal were twenty-two ancient medals or coins ('medaglie antiche'), seven of silver and fifteen of bronze. The price was low: they cost twelve *reali*, which was the equivalent of one ducat and thirty-six *maravedis*. A further note has been added to this entry: 'Sono di Lisbona' (They are from Lisbon),[194] unusually attributing a prior provenance to them. Bought in one place, they were said to come from another: the kind of information that is often desired

190. ASF, Guardaroba medicea 46, 118 sinistra.

191. Anselmo Braamcamp Freire, 'Inventário da Infanta D. Beatriz 1507', *Arquivo histórico portuguez*, 9 (1914), pp. 64–110 at 99.

192. Lowe, 'Made in Africa', p. 176.

193. See Freire, 'Inventário', pp. 98–100 and 109 for Beatriz's various bequests to Violante Rodrigues.

194. ASF, Misc. med. 713, 8r and 78v. The latter reference is a little more imprecise: '22 medaglie antiche che la metà d'argento, el resto di bronzo'.

but rarely given—and why would it be? What is the point of providing it, or attempting to provide it? Many objects for sale on the Iberian peninsula in the mid-sixteenth century would have originated from the Portuguese and Spanish empires, but by the time they went on sale on the peninsula they would have been not at their second destination, but at their third, fourth or fifth, making provenance a complicated and fraught issue. So far these coins/medals have not been identified. It is possible that 'medaglie antiche' could have been a description of ancient Roman coins or medals, as Portugal had an important Roman past,[195] which was not often a cause for comment on the Italian peninsula in the mid-sixteenth century, however, although more acknowledged at the end of the century.[196] If they were Roman coins or medals, they are the only example in Campana's haul of purchases of the acquisition of ancient or Roman objects. And if they were Roman coins or medals, not only is their provenance (in the senses both of their place of origin and their prior itinerary and history) unknown, but so too is their provenience, understood as 'the precise location where an artefact or archaeological sample was recovered archaeologically'.[197] Nor can it be said with certainty that they were coins rather than medals, although the former is much more likely. While there are considerable numbers of Portuguese Renaissance coins,[198] and a considerable

195. The inventories of D. Teódosio I of 1564–67 include a few 'medals' whose descriptions suggest that they were ancient Roman pieces: Jessica Hallett, Maria de Jesus Monge and Nuno Senos, eds, *De todas as partes do mundo: O património do 5° Duque de Bragança, D. Teodósio I/ All his Worldly Possessions: The Estate of the 5th Duke of Braganza, Teodósio*, vol. 2: *Documentos/ Documents* (Lisbon, 2018), online edition, pp. 89–90 of printed text, https://research.unl.pt/ws /portalfiles/portal/12688088/TEODOSIO_VOL_II.pdf (accessed 24 April 2023).

196. For instance, Giacomo Mendez de Vasconcellos sent to Vincenzo I Gonzaga on 12 April 1597 a copy of a book he had just finished: *De antiquitatibus Lusitaniae libri quattuor a L. Andrea Resende inchoati, a Iacobo Mendez de Vasconcellos absoluti [. . .]* (Rome, 1597; available at https://archive.org/details/bub_gb_e84Ztoyggi8C/page/n5/mode/2up?view=theater); see Barbara Furlotti, *Le collezioni Gonzaga: Il carteggio tra Roma e Mantova (1587–1612)* (Milan, 2003), p. 269, doc. 303.

197. Joyce, 'From Place to Place', pp. 48 and 54; K. Kris Hirst, 'Provenience vs. Provenance: What is the Difference?', ThoughtCo, updated 19 November 2019, https://www.thoughtco.com /provenience-vs-provenance-3971058 (accessed 24 April 2023).

198. Francisco de Holanda and his father António collaborated on the coin design for coins authorised by decree in 1544 and 1555: John Bury, *Two Notes on Francisco de Holanda* (London, 1971), p. 37, Catalogue of Francisco de Holanda's writings, drawings, paintings and architectural designs, no. 10. One, known as a São Vicente, was a gold coin worth 1,000 *reis* struck during the reigns of both João III and Sebastião; that struck under João had the national arms on the

literature on Portuguese coinage[199]—and on coinage used in the Portuguese trading empire[200]—there are no extant Portuguese Renaissance medals and no literature on Portuguese medals.

Nor, unfortunately, is there any mention of the coins/medals bought by Campana in Gibraltar in the entry books of the Guardaroba. However, in the 1553 Medici inventory there is a small collection of *medaglie* housed in the twelfth *armario* (cupboard) of the Guardaroba, consisting of six antique bronze *medaglie* circled with ebony, seventy-two other bronze *medaglie* in a little sack of yellow cloth, and eight silver ones.[201] Those circled with ebony are still in the Medici collection—but they are not Portuguese. It is possible that the Portuguese bronze examples were amalgamated with other examples, and form part of the hoard of seventy-two, and that the eight silver ones include the seven silver ones from Gibraltar: possible, but exceedingly unlikely. From the 1553 inventory arranged according to category of object (*a capi*), the supposition that these are all medals and not coins, formed because the still extant six ancient bronze medals are of Roman emperors, hardens into a fact. On 10

---

obverse, and a representation of São Vicente, the patron saint of Lisbon, and the motto 'Zelator fidei usque ad mortem' (Protector of the faith until death) on the reverse: *Desejo, desígnio e desenho/Desire, Design and Drawing: Francisco de Holanda, 1517–2017*, ed. Francisco Providência, Gabriella Casella and Margarida Cunha Belém, exh. cat., Museo do Dinheiro/Money Museum, Lisbon (Lisbon, 2017), pp. 23–25.

199. Alberto Gomes and António Miguel Trigueiros, *Moedas portuguesas na época dos descobrimentos, 1385–1580/Portuguese Coins in the Age of Discovery, 1385–1580* (Lisbon, 1992); Miquel Crusafont, Anna M. Balaguer and Philip Grierson, *Medieval European Coinage*, vol. 6: *The Iberian Peninsula* (Cambridge, 2013), pp. 419–85, 'The Kingdom of Portugal'.

200. Holanda also proposed later designs. On a foglio of Saint Jerome's *Vitas patrum* now in the Biblioteca Nacional in Lisbon, published in 1553—that is a few years after Campana's visit— he sketched some designs of new coins for the Portuguese monarch Sebastião (whose reign began in 1557), to be put into circulation both within Portugal and throughout its trading empire: Jorge Segurado, *Francisco d'Ollanda: Da sua vida e obras, arquitecto da Renascença ao serviço de D. João III, pintor, desenhador, escritor, humanista; Fac-simile da carta a Miguel Ângelo (1551) e dos seus tratados sobre Lisboa e desenho (1571)* (Lisbon, 1970); Miguel Figueira de Faria, 'Francisco de Holanda desenhador de moedas: Um novo testemunho documental', *Leituras: Revista da Bibioteca Nacional*, ser. 3, 2 (1997–98), pp. 181–88 at 181–82. Aspects of Holanda's designs were particularly adopted in coins used in Portuguese India: António Miguel Trigueiros, 'A modernidade numismática em Francisco de Holanda: Uma ciência esquecida, um ensinamento a preservar', in *Congresso internacional Francisco de Holanda, c. 1518–1584: Arte e teoria no Renascimento europeu/Art and Theory in Renaissance Europe, 22–24 Novembro/November 2018* (Lisbon, 2018), pp. 1–19 at 11–15.

201. ASF, Guardaroba medicea 28, 42r, inventoried on 7 November 1553.

July 1554 this whole group—the seventy-two *medaglie* of *metallo ordinarie* (ordinary metal) and nine (a change from the eight above) of silver, and six antique metal *medaglie* of emperors encircled with ebony—left the Guardaroba and went to the *principe*. They appeared under the heading 'Figure ritratti et altre cose di metallo' (Figures, portraits and other objects in metal).[202] Where this group originated is not known. Other silver and bronze *medaglie* are listed under a similar heading, entering the Guardaroba in 1553, but their numbers and materials do not correspond to those from Gibraltar.[203] The Portuguese coins/medals seem simply to have disappeared from sight.

Cosimo was known for his interest in coins and medals—even Campana might have been expected to know of this interest of his employer and patron, whether or not coins and medals were on a list of more focused desiderata to buy in Iberia—so it is extremely likely that the Portuguese ones bought in Gibraltar reached Florence and were amalgamated into Cosimo's collection, where they would have joined a great many other coins and medals from around the world. In the 1540s and 1550s Cosimo enriched his collection first with a haul of 407 'medaglie' discovered at Marliana, near Pistoia, in 1547, and later with another eighty-seven purchased in 1554.[204] The purchase of the twenty-two at Gibraltar falls in between these dates.

Conclusion

Campana's purchases of inanimate goods for Cosimo are heterogeneous, each nestling separately under the umbrella heading, devised by Campana himself, of 'più robbe'. The goods themselves were not limited in provenance to one or two non-European regions, but originated from across the globe: Africa, the Americas and Asia. Of those discussed here, all except the nautilus shells were worked pieces rather than unworked raw items. In all cases, however, it appears that in the first instance it was the material that was the most attractive and important factor, and that bore the most meaning for Campana: ivory, turtleshell, porcelain, rare extra-European shells and woods and feathers, precious metals. This can be deduced from the descriptions allocated by Campana to the objects, in which the materials are consistently named. Given that

202. ASF, Guardaroba medicea 30, 42 destra, and ASF, Guardaroba medicea 31, 29r.

203. Ibid., 39 destra, and ASF, Guardaroba medicea 31, 27r.

204. Eugène Müntz, *Les Collections d'antiques formées par les Médicis au XVIe siècle* (Paris, 1895), pp. 20, 45–46.

Campana was in Lisbon making the purchases, and that he probably did not know much or indeed anything about these types of material prior to this trip, it is surely relevant that he chose to itemise according to material (he must therefore in many cases have enquired orally about this when making the purchase, in order to record it) rather than according to place of origin (which at the moment of acquisition he might also have been able to ascertain). The fineness of the decoration and design, although also a prerequisite for purchase, appears to have been a secondary consideration, and design and decoration are only occasionally alluded to by Campana. Seen from this point of view, the lack of interest or the disinterest in provenance makes more sense.

5

Living Global Goods

THE ACQUISITION OF LIVING GOODS
FOR THE MEDICI FROM THE PORTUGUESE
TRADING EMPIRE: PROVENANCE AND
POSSESSION OF FLESH AND BLOOD

THIS CHAPTER is based on the same documentation as chapter 4: ASF, Miscellanea medicea 713. It consequently has the same main protagonists, Cosimo I de' Medici, Eleonora di Toledo and Bastiano Campana, and takes place against the same backdrop of Tuscany, Lisbon and Spanish places in between, such as Cadiz, Ceres, Sanlúcar de Barrameda, Gibraltar, Cartagena and Majorca. It too focuses on goods as its primary category of global acquisition, but these are goods with a difference, because they are alive, making the very notion of possession more complex. And it introduces some further, new, African and mixed-ancestry protagonists.

Leaving aside the grain that Campana was instructed to sell in Lisbon, he specifies only two goods he was commissioned to buy on the Iberian peninsula (although acknowledging there were others). Both were living, or animate, goods: the first galley slaves, and the second animals. In the sixteenth century, enslaved men, hand-picked for their physique and stamina, and rare, exotic, extra-European animals would have been seen as similarly expensive and difficult-to-procure merchandise, whose value was dependent upon their peak condition; they would therefore have been conceptualised as proximate categories of goods. The legal status of animals and enslaved persons is relevant too. Animals had no legal status in the Renaissance period. Their owners owned them; they were at liberty to treat them as they wished, to keep them alive or to kill them with impunity. Enslaved people, on the other hand, did have a legal status, but it was a diminished status in comparison to that of free people. They 'belonged' to their masters, and their masters could punish them violently, yet were legally constrained from enacting violence with an intent to kill them, although the absence of prosecutions for this crime indicates that legal systems and the societies that gave them legitimacy were usually unwilling to prosecute.[1]

The main reason for considering living goods separately from inanimate goods is that living goods necessitated markedly different treatment in order to reach their destination in good condition. It was a question not merely of packing them carefully into chests, but of actively attending to their well-being, and making sure they were warm, comfortable and well-fed—many of the animals required a special diet—during the voyage. Campana had the Renaissance equivalent of a duty of care towards them, a duty based on monetary value rather than any form of morality. Both animals and humans were expensive purchases, and Campana's remit included keeping them alive and healthy until he could deliver them to their new Medici owners in Tuscany. The entries in his account journal reveal the numerous ways in which he had to provide for both enslaved people and animals; in important ways, therefore, their roles appeared reversed. He, a Medici functionary, although free, was serving them; they, Medici 'possessions', although unfree, were being served. The galley slaves needed a mat to sleep on, and one of them required new trousers and a new shirt: Campana had to procure them.[2] When a visibly pregnant enslaved woman miscarried, Campana had to arrange not only for her to have particularly nourishing food to revive her strength but also for her dead foetus to be buried.[3] After the purchase of a monkey or parrot or civet, Campana also had to ensure that a suitable container or cage was bought for each, to make sure it could not escape and to keep it safe from harm.[4] With living goods, the acquisition itself was merely the starting point of a whole series of responsibilities for Campana, whereas with inanimate objects that was not the case.

1. Theodor Mommsen, ed., *Codex Theodosianus* (Dublin, 1970), 9.12.1 and 9.12.2; W. W. Buckland, *The Roman Law of Slavery: The Condition of the Slave in Private Law from Augustus to Justinian* (Cambridge, 1908), p. 38; Epstein, *Speaking of Slavery*, p. 63.

2. ASF, Misc. med. 713, 7v.

3. Ibid., 77r and 5r ('per soterar la chreatura'). On the vocabulary surrounding miscarriage and foetuses, see John Christopoulos, *Abortion in Early Modern Italy* (Cambridge, MA, 2021), pp. 31–42, esp. at 39–40 where usage of the word *creatura* is discussed.

4. ASF, Misc. med. 713, 77v.

Living or Animate Acquisitions: Animals

In the twenty-first century there has been a huge upsurge of scholarly interest in the treatment of animals by humans in the past. As the 1511 log-book of the *Bretoa* revealed, animals and birds from the Portuguese trading empire were eagerly acquired alongside people and objects.[5] In the fifteenth and sixteenth centuries these animals would have been looked after not for their own sake, or out of a sense that they deserved care, but because they had been expensive to buy and the money would have been wasted if they died. Because of their price tags, extra-European animals and birds captured or purchased and despatched to Europe were not wilfully mistreated, although without indigenous keepers who knew their dietary needs and how to care for them,[6] the animals would often have died because of a lack of appropriate food and shelter. Many smaller, more delicate animals and birds or ones with finicky diets must have died on the ships before they even arrived in Europe. Acquiring the knowledge necessary to keep these animals alive took time and effort. After they arrived in their new homes, some of the animals and birds that could be domesticated and live inside with their owners (such as small monkeys and parrots) would have benefited from being viewed as pets. There is plenty of evidence of ties of affection between humans and these previously wild creatures, expressed both in writing and pictorially. A portrait of Lucrezia di Niccolò Gaddi, by Santi di Tito, dated c. 1565–69, shows the little girl dressed in silk finery, in the garden courtyard behind palazzo Gaddi in Florence, accompanied by a large Brazilian macaw and a jerboa, a desert rodent with strongly developed hind legs found in Arabia, North Africa and parts of Central Asia, now known to exist in thirty-three species.[7] The girl's father was a Florentine patrician and

5. *Animais orientais: Fauna exótica no tempo dos Descobrimentos*, ed. Rui Manuel Loureiro, exh. cat., Câmara Municipal de Lagos (Lagos, 2008); *Echt tierisch! Die Menagerie des Fürsten*, ed. Sabine Haag, exh. cat., Schloss Ambras, Innsbruck (Vienna, 2015), especially the two essays therein by Annemarie Jordan Gschwend, 'Beloved Companions, Mascots and Pets: The Culture of Wild Animals in Renaissance Portugal', pp. 18–23, and '". . . underlasse auch nit mich in Portugal vnnd ander orten umb frömbde sachen zu bewerben": Hans Khevenhüller and Habsburg Menageries in Vienna and Prague', pp. 31–35.

6. Cockram, 'Interspecies Understanding', pp. 277–98.

7. Annemarie Jordan Gschwend, 'The Emperor's Exotic and New World Animals: Hans Khevenhüller and the Habsburg Menageries in Vienna and Prague', in Arthur MacGregor, ed., *Naturalists in the Field: Collecting, Recording and Preserving the Natural World from the Fifteenth to the Twenty-First Century* (Leiden, 2018), pp. 76–103 at 86–87.

friend of Francesco I de' Medici who collected antique sculpture and exotic flora and fauna which he kept in his palace gardens, known as the Paradiso dei Gaddi.[8] Most of his children died young, causing him to commission posthumous portraits of them.[9] The bird and rodent depicted with Lucrezia were probably her particular pets, but they also served as props, alluding to the collections of her father. She is not touching either the macaw or the jerboa, but she is holding cherries for the bird. This type of portrait, including usually only one animal or bird, is common amongst the élite in sixteenth-century Medicean Florence. In some ways, the build-up of affection had similar outcomes to behaviour rooted in a consideration of the best interests of the animals, yet affection for wild animals could only go so far. Many of these animals were given as playthings to children, and young children are notoriously unthinking with regard to their treatment of defenceless animals, simultaneously being attracted to them and not understanding when they fail to fall in with their human plans.

The rise of the doctrine of animal rights, a belief in treating animals as sentient beings almost on a par with humans, and an understanding that animals and their habitats have to be protected if the global environment is to survive long-term, have all combined in the twenty-first century to emphasise the importance of striking a measured balance in animal–human relations. None of this could have been foreseen in Renaissance Europe, when an ethical approach recognising the right of animals to self-existence would have been unintelligible. Animals then were treated simply as creatures that existed to be used by humans in whatever ways the latter saw fit: quarry for the hunt, slabs of meat to be eaten, beasts of burden, exhibits in a menagerie, pets for spoilt children, their body parts sources of expensive or rare materials such as ivory or turtle-shell or feathers. The animals acquired by Campana on his buying trip therefore are at the high end of the spectrum of privilege in terms of their care.

As part of the new history alluded to above, there has been an emphasis on animals being transported round the globe, especially those imported into Europe,[10] and Campana's purchases show that in terms of prestige and

8. On Niccolò Gaddi, see *DBI*, 51 (1998), pp. 160–64, entry by Vanna Arrighi.

9. *Il Cinquecento a Firenze: 'Maniera moderna' e controriforma*, ed. Carlo Falciani and Antonio Natali, exh. cat., Palazzo Strozzi, Florence (Florence, 2017), pp. 150–51.

10. For example, Annemarie Jordan Gschwend, 'Animals from Other Worlds', in *A cidade global: Lisboa no Renascimento/The Global City: Lisbon in the Renaissance*, ed. Annemarie Jordan Gschwend and K.J.P. Lowe, exh. cat., Museu Nacional de Arte Antiga, Lisbon (Lisbon, 2017), section 5, pp. 329–39, and *Echt Tierisch!*.

attractiveness as acquisitions, the exotic, non-European animals scored highly. The very first acquisition made by Campana after quantities of raw pearls was a golden lion tamarin or golden marmoset (*Leontopithecus rosalia*),[11] bought on 13 July 1547, two days after Campana's arrival in Lisbon.[12] These primates came from the Atlantic coastal forests of Brazil (only 'discovered' by Europe in 1500), and so were easily accessible to Portuguese sailors,[13] but Campana seems to have been unaware of their origin in the New World (perhaps at this point he was even unaware of Brazil): Brazil was not mentioned in the first entry in his account journal, where no place of origin was suggested. In the accounts the animal is labelled a *bugino* (*bugio* is a Portuguese word for ape),[14] so a 'little ape', but here its smallness is doubly emphasised by being mentioned

11. For specialist information on golden lion tamarins, I am very grateful to Steve Goodwin, senior keeper at London Zoo, who discussed many points about tamarins with me on 30 September 2020. Cf. Antonio Pigafetta, *Relazione del primo viaggio attorno al mondo*, ed. Andrea Canova (Padua, 1999), who writes at p. 173 of 'gati maimoni piccoli' in Brazil; Antonio Pigafetta, *The First Voyage around the World, 1519–1522: An Account of Magellan's Expedition*, ed. Theodore J. Cachey Jr (Toronto, 2007), p. 10: 'little monkeys that look like lions, only they are yellow and very beautiful'. Marco Masseti and Cecilia Veracini, 'Early European Knowledge and Trade of Neotropical Mammals: A Review of Literary Sources between 1492 and the First Two Decades of the Sixteenth Century', in Cleia Detry and Rita Dias, eds, *Proceedings of the First Zooarchaeology Conference in Portugal*, 2014, pp. 129–138 at 133, believe that the primates mentioned here are golden lion tamarins rather than 'gati maimoni'.

12. In mid-August and early September 1561, Bastiano Campana, by then *provveditore* of Livorno, dealt with the disembarkation of a different sort of foreign animal for the Medici. Two English *levrieri* or salukis arrived on a boat from England, on their way to Cosimo I de' Medici's son, Cardinal Giovanni de' Medici: Gáldy, 'Hounds for a Cardinal', 2, pp. 175–76.

13. The global transportation of animals that grew exponentially in the Renaissance was responsible for endangering some of the most desirable species, such as the golden lion tamarin; in 2010 it was calculated that in a three-year period at the beginning of the sixteenth century, about three hundred golden lion tamarins were exported from Brazil to Lisbon, a number equivalent to approximately twenty per cent of the now remaining 1,500 still surviving in their very restricted natural habitat: Teixeira and Papavero, 'O tráfico', p. 273. This number had risen to over two thousand in 2020. I am grateful to Steve Goodwin for this information in a verbal communication of 30 September 2020. He had been told of this figure in Brazil in July that year. The breed is now on the endangered list of the IUCN (International Union for Conservation of Nature), downgraded from the more serious critically endangered list in 2003: https://www .iucnredlist.org/species/11506/192327291 (accessed 24 April 2023).

14. It appears, e.g., on a Portuguese inscription near São Jorge de Mina on the Cantino map of 1502: Milano, *La carta*, pp. 137 and 148. Philippe Billé, *La Faune brésilienne dans les écrits documentaires du xvie siècle* (Paris, 2009), p. 233 traces the origin of the word to sixteenth-century Algeria but it must have been in existence before that.

twice: 'uno bugino picholo'.[15] They are one of the smallest and most striking primates in the world, belonging to the family of Callitrichidae, known in sixteenth-century Portuguese as *sagui* or *sagouin*.[16] Two marmosets are illustrated in images produced between around 1540 and 1610 respectively in the collection of Felix Platter, used as a basis for many of Conrad Gessner's illustrations for *Historiae animalium* (Zurich, 1551–58); they are both labelled with variants of these words: *sagoin* and *saguina*.[17] In a later entry in Campana's journal account, the golden lion tamarin's size was remarked upon yet again, with the claim that it was 'da tener nelle mani' ([small enough] to hold in one's hands), and it was said to be *indiano* (unhelpful in terms of origin) and to smell of musk.[18] In order for the tamarin to be held in a hand, it would have had to be a baby, as adults are usually a little too big. In Alonso Sánchez Coello's painting *Infanta Isabel Clara Eugenia and Magdalena Ruiz*, c. 1585 (Plate 29), a cotton-top tamarin sits upright on its back legs in one of Magdalena's hands and a golden lion tamarin is perched on her other arm; they touch what could be a shared nut. This type of human–animal interaction also points to a young animal, as golden lion tamarins are easily domesticated when young, whereas adults are not, and have a savage bite. In both of Campana's entries the tamarin is described as being 'del pelo de leone' (with a coat or pelt like a lion), a comment on the tactile quality of its coat.[19]

The tamarin was bought from the Frenchman Piero Fortte, using the middlemen or brokers Batista del Bizaro of Pisa (who was elsewhere described as being 'chreato di [nurtured by/part of the household of] messer Luca Giralddi')[20] and Vettorio Giuoli of Florence, for the considerable sum of nine gold ducats.[21] In all, five monkeys were acquired by Campana in Lisbon: three *babuini* or baboons (which may or may not actually have been baboons), the

15. ASF, Misc. med. 713, 1v.

16. Billé, *La Faune brésilienne*, p. 234.

17. Bernardo Urbani, 'The Seven Secluded Monkeys of Conrad Gessner', *Endeavour*, 44.1–2 (2020), https://www.sciencedirect.com/science/article/abs/pii/S0160932720300375 ?via%3Dihub (accessed 24 April 2023).

18. ASF, Misc. med. 713, 77v. All members of the Callitrichidae are known for their smells, and that of the golden lion tamarin is distinctive, rather akin to smelly hard cheese.

19. In the painting, the golden lion tamarin's hair colouration is significantly paler than its usual arresting ginger hue, indicating either that it was an older specimen or that it had been deprived of appropriate levels of ultraviolet, by being removed from Brazil to Europe.

20. ASF, Misc. med. 713, 77v.

21. Ibid., 1v.

golden lion tamarin and a *gatto mammone*[22] or green monkey (*Chlorocebus sabaeus*), with all bar the tamarin coming from sub-Saharan Africa,[23] and all bar the tamarin being commonplace in Portugal. The tamarin was also the only miniature monkey. According to Filippo Pigafetta, a great variety of monkeys, large and small, came from the province of Soyo in the Kingdom of Kongo—the same province that the oliphants are thought to have come from—some of which were very pleasing and entertaining.[24] However, even with this little boost in diverse species of animals from the Portuguese and Spanish trading empires, it remains the case that 'the Medici's collection [of animals] was modest' compared to the megafauna culled from their overseas territories and possessed by the kings of the Iberian peninsula.[25]

On 12 October 1547, almost precisely the moment Campana was buying baboons in Lisbon, Michele di Paolo Olivieri,[26] Florentine banker and financier, wrote to the most important Medicean secretary, the *maggiordomo* Pierfrancesco Riccio,[27] telling him of two baboons in his possession that he wanted to give to Eleonora di Toledo.[28] They had lost much of their fur and so he had sent them to his villa in the Mugello to recuperate, but now their fur had regrown, they were fine, and he planned to send them to Riccio so that Riccio

22. *Gatti mammoni* were already being imported into Rome in 1475, when three are noted in the customs records. Esch, *La Roma del primo Rinascimento*, pp. 44 and 62.

23. Masseti and Bruner, 'Primates of the Western Palaearctic, pp. 54 and 63.

24. F. Pigafetta, *Relatione del reame di Congo*, p. 32.

25. Groom, *Exotic Animals*, p. 70. The Medici continued to engage in exotic animal collecting and diplomacy, even if it was at quite a low level compared to Portugal and Spain: cf. Brege, *Tuscany*, pp. 183, 190–99.

26. Francesco Guidi Bruscoli, *Benvenuto Olivieri: I 'mercatores' fiorentini e la Camera Apostolica nella Roma di Paolo III Farnese (1534–49)* (Florence, 2000), pp. 34–46; Eng. trans.: Francesco Guidi Bruscoli, *Papal Banking in Renaissance Rome: Benvenuto Olivieri and Paul III, 1534–1549* (Aldershot, 2007), pp. 28–38. These baboons may have arrived via Naples, as Michele and one of his brothers were partners in a firm there. Paolo di Benvenuto Olivieri, Michele's father, had spent time in Lisbon in the 1480s and had reported back to relatives in Florence on news of Africa. See Florence, Biblioteca Riccardiana, MS. Riccardiano 1186, 3 (= 1186c), c. 84v 9 = 182v), copy of a letter written in Lisbon on 20 November 1488 by Paolo Olivieri to Sandro Pagangniotti in Florence; Zelina Zafarana, 'Per la storia religiosa di Firenze nel Quattrocento: Una raccolta privata di prediche', *Studi medievali*, ser. 3, 9.2 (1968), pp. 1017–113 at 1109–10; and Lowe, 'Africa in the News', p. 326.

27. On whom, see Cappa, 'Pierfrancesco Riccio'.

28. ASF, MdP 1173, 727r, Michele di Paolo Olivieri in the Mugello to Pierfrancesco Riccio in Florence, 12 October 1547.

could present them on his behalf to Eleonora. The letter is important, as it goes into considerable detail concerning the character, function and care of the animals. Both are male, one black, which is very tame, easy to manage and pleasing, and the other tawny, a bit wilder and more frightened, making it liable to bite. Olivieri shows he understands about the domestication of these monkeys: the first is already tame enough to be suitable as a playmate for the children of Cosimo and Eleonora—the couple already had five children by this date—while the second is just getting acclimatised to women and children. Olivieri is firm in his belief that *carezze* are necessary in the process of taming these formerly wild animals, who resemble humans in some of their actions (such as problem solving and using tools to crack open nuts), and are troublesome only in that they eat everything in the house. On their care too, he is exact in his detail. In the winter, the baboons should sleep, as they do at his house, in a barrel open on one side, lined with broken straw and stopped up on top, because otherwise they will die of cold. In the summer it does not matter how they sleep. It is telling that a banker and financier was trying to gain favour with the Medici ruler by presenting his wife with two baboons. His choice of present cannot have been fortuitous; she must have been known to have had a liking for monkeys.

Purchased by Campana in Lisbon at the same time as the golden lion tamarin was a silk cord which functioned as its lead, and 'pendenti alli orechini', or earrings, costing twenty *maravedis*.[29] Early modern miniature court pets, especially Spanish court pets, were often adorned with earrings,[30] and this little golden lion tamarin could be carried in a hand, pocket or sleeve, and put down on a lap.[31] Although there is less information about earrings for monkeys, the ears of both lap dogs and lap monkeys were pierced to take these earrings, just like those of humans, turning the animals even more firmly into accessories and playthings that could be dressed up at their owner's whim. By the seventeenth century, this was routine; this earlier reference from 1547 suggests that it was common even in the mid-sixteenth century, for monkeys as well as dogs. Fifty

29. ASF, Misc. med. 713, 77v.

30. For an example from France, see Pierre Mignard's portrait of Henriette Anne Stuart, duchesse d'Orléans, c. 1665–1670, in the National Portrait Gallery in London, where Mimy, the Bolognese spaniel, wears earrings.

31. Katharine MacDonogh, 'A Woman's Life: The Role of Pets in the Lives of Royal Women at the Courts of Europe from 1400–1800', in Mark Hengerer and Nadir Weber, eds, *Animals and Courts, c. 1200–1800* (Berlin, 2019), pp. 323–42 at 336.

years later, in 1593, Lavinia Fontana in Bologna painted a portrait of Isabella Ruini, now in the Galleria Palatina in Florence (Plate 30), in which she holds in her hands the front paws of a very small dog (a miniature spaniel?), whose back legs are on a nearby table and whose left ear is hung with a large earring of three pearl drops.[32] The dog jewellery merges seamlessly with the jewellery of the sitter. Unlike other animal fashion accessories such as dog collars and coats, monkey earrings may not have functioned to proclaim or affirm the noble status of their consumer owners, often through coats of arms,[33] as they would have been too small to be efficient purveyors of specific visual messages.

In addition to the tamarin's otic adornments, Campana noted expenses for buying butter and flour to make *bischotelli* (little biscuits) for the small *bugio*, and money paid to make these.[34] The general consensus in the sixteenth century was that care of these monkeys was troublesome;[35] by the late nineteenth and twentieth centuries, nothing had changed and the species was still considered 'delicate in captivity'.[36] Although an English source from 1570 noted that *sagouin* could be fed on food available in Europe (if primarily in southern Europe), such as apples, grapes, pears, figs and bread,[37] a major

32. *Lavinia Fontana of Bologna, 1552–1614*, ed. Vera Fortunati and Angela Ghirardi, exh. cat., Museo civico archaeologico, Bologna (Milan, 1994), pp. 90 (text) and 91 (illustration); Caroline Murphy, *Lavinia Fontana: A Painter and Her Patrons in Sixteenth-Century Bologna* (New Haven, CT, 2003), pp. 98–99 (text) and 100 (fig. 87). Murphy comments on p. 98 that the dog's earrings 'match' the owner's. Two outsize earrings resembling Christmas tree baubles hang from the ears of a small dog in a late seventeenth-century painting of the Neapolitan School, attributed to a follower of Francesco Noletti (c. 1611–1654), in which no human is portrayed.

33. John Block Friedman, 'Coats, Collars and Capes: Royal Fashions for Animals in the Early Modern Period', *Medieval Clothing and Textiles*, 12 (2006), pp. 61–94 at 63; on other monkey accessories, particularly jackets, see pp. 83–89.

34. ASF, Misc. med. 713, 57r.

35. *Echt Tierisch!*, p. 180.

36. Jonathan D. Ballou et al., 'History, Management and Conservation Role of the Captive Lion Tamarin Populations', in Devra G. Kleiman and Anthony B. Rylands, eds, *Lion Tamarins: Biology and Conservation* (Washington, DC, 2002), pp. 95–114 at 97.

37. John Caius, *De canibus britannicis, liber unus; De rariorum animalium atque stirpum historia, liber unus; De libris propriis, liber unus* (London, 1570), *De rariorum [...]* (numbering restarts for each discrete work), p. 15; see also Edward Topsell, *The History of Four-Footed Beasts and Serpents and Insects*, 3 vols (facsimile, London, 1967 [London, 1658]), 3 (*The History of Four-Footed Beasts*), 'taken principally from the *Historiae animalium* of Conrad Gessner', p. 15: 'it will eat white-bread, apples, sweet-grapes, dried in the sun, figs or pears', so slightly embellished from Caius's original.

problem in the sixteenth century lay in what to give them to eat;[38] apparently their deaths could be hastened by eating too much sugar, causing diabetic reactions. Other animals and birds also died quickly when their diets were changed or interfered with. Roger Barlow wrote in *A Brief Summe of Geographie*, which was the earliest first-hand account of the Americas in English, of the difficulties of keeping a hummingbird from islands in the Paraná river in South America alive on the voyage home in 1528: 'it lived not long for lacke of knolege to diet it or other keping'.[39] A significant proportion of any cargo involving live animals on embarkation must have incurred loss of life at sea. The hummingbird resembled the golden lion tamarin in other ways too: it was tiny (according to Barlow, 'no bigger of bodie than the toppe of a mans thombe') and both animals (at least according to Campana and Barlow) smelt of musk; after the hummingbird's death it was stuffed with moss and put in a coffer, and it even made the coffer smell 'wondrous swete'.[40] The tiny size of the golden lion tamarins made them sought-after as pets for children, and there is a marmoset (although not a golden lion one) in a 1573 portrait by Sofonisba Anguissola of Infanta Catalina Micaela, who like Isabel Clara Eugenia mentioned above was a daughter of Philip II of Spain (Plates 31 and 32). It may be relevant that the two sixteenth-century paintings of members of the Spanish royal family containing marmosets discussed here are of females; women may have been more likely to keep lap monkeys as pets, indicating that Campana's golden lion tamarin might have been destined for Eleonora di Toledo or one of her children rather than Cosimo. Golden lion tamarins must have been strikingly attractive

38. This was less true for other types of monkey. See Lauran Toorians, 'The Earliest Inventory of Mexican Objects in Munich, 1572', *Journal of the History of Collections*, 6.1 (1994), pp. 59–67, where in a 1572 list of instructions re what to feed various New World animals and birds sent from Tuscany to Duke Albrecht of Bavaria, three *bertuccie* or *Meerkhazlein* (a type of monkey) were said to be happy to eat anything but were not to be fed meat. *Bertuccie* are generally held to be Old World monkeys, like Barbary apes, but if everything else in the shipment came from the New World, it is most likely that the inventory-maker did not know the species and used a relatively generic term.

39. Roger Barlow, *A Brief Summe of Geographie*, ed. E.G.R. Taylor (London, 1932), p. 161. On Barlow's voyage and work, see Heather Dalton, *Merchants and Explorers: Roger Barlow, Sebastian Cabot, and Networks of Atlantic Exchange, 1500–1600* (Oxford, 2016).

40. ASF, Misc. med. 713, 77v, and Barlow, *Brief Summe*, p. 161. On interest in Germany in early attempts at the taxidermy of birds, see Stefan Hanß and Ulinka Rublack, 'Knowledge Production, Image Networks and the Material Significance of Feathers in Late Humanist Heidelberg', *Renaissance Quarterly*, 74.2 (2021), pp. 412–53 at 429.

acquisitions. If Campana had never seen one before, and he probably had not, it is easy to understand why he bought one as soon as he set eyes on it. It is also easy to understand why the way in which it had been acquired and where it came from did not matter to him.

Animals were acquired for a number of reasons. Small monkeys may have been placed in the category of pets, but civet cats were usually viewed as wild animals with a function: to produce the secretion used in perfumes and some medicines. Even so, there might have been more pressing status reasons for their acquisition. Civet cats in the Kongo were said by Filippo Pigafetta to have been routinely domesticated in the past by the Kongolese before the Portuguese considered domesticating them in order to extract civet.[41] Queen Catarina de Áustria, the wife of King João III, collected these animals in Lisbon, using her specially placed global agents in Africa and India to source them: they were a lifelong passion of hers.[42] It is interesting, therefore, that in addition to monkeys, Campana bought two male civet cats, most probably African (*Civettictis civetta*) rather than Asian,[43] in two different purchases. Once again, Medici desiderata tallied with those of the Portuguese monarchy, again begging the question whether the Medici wanted the animals so that they could pose as members of the European élite, or to stand out as exceptional in Italy. The first civet cat ('uno ghatto d'arghalia'), described as being 'delle Indie' (and later as 'mastio', or male), was acquired with his chain and a bone spoon for collecting the extracted *zibetto* (civet), whereas the second, aged eight months, described as 'piacevole e vero domesticho' (delightful and very tame) and later as 'mastio', needed these accoutrements to be bought separately.[44] The names of the sellers were given:

41. In the same section, Filippo Pigafetta in his *Relatione del reame di Congo*, p. 32 noted that most civet cats in Kongo came from the provinces of Pemba and Batta.

42. Almudena Pérez de Tudela and Annemarie Jordan Gschwend, 'Exotica habsburgica: La casa de Austria y las colecciones exóticas en el Renacimiento temprano', in *Oriente en palacio: Tesoros asiáticos en las colecciones reales españolas*, ed. Marina Alfonso Mola and Carlos Martínez Shaw, exh. cat., Palacio Real de Madrid (Madrid, 2003), pp. 27–44 at 31 and 37 n. 50; Pérez de Tudela and Jordan Gschwend, 'Renaissance Menageries', pp. 424–26.

43. Karl H. Dannenfeldt, 'Europe Discovers Civet Cats and Civet', *Journal of the History of Biology*, 18.3 (1985), pp. 403–31 at 408–11, discusses civet cats from India and the East. It is worthy of mention that Asian civet cats have been identified as one of the animal hosts in the global coronavirus pandemics of the twenty-first century. Jane Qiu, 'Chasing Plagues', *Scientific American*, 322.6 (June 2020), pp. 20–26 at 23: 'A Hong Kong team had reported that wildlife traders in Guangdong first caught the SARS coronavirus [in 2002] from civets.'

44. ASF, Misc. med. 713, 2r, 3v, and 77v.

Tomaso Ferera, resident in Lisbon,[45] and Arrigo Gelt, 'mercieri' in Lisbon.[46] The young civet cat could conceivably have been viewed as a pet as well as being useful. It is known, for instance, that the Florentine consul in Alexandria in the later 1540s—so coinciding precisely with Campana's trip to the Iberian peninsula—had a tame civet seen by Pierre Belon that was treated as a pet, even nuzzling people on the nose or ears (Plate 33).[47] It is interesting that in both cases the sex of the civet was specified in Campana's journal, as an ounce of civet from a female was reputed to be worth four times that of an ounce from a male.[48] Even if only the less valuable male civets were available for purchase, however, they were exceptionally expensive. The two animals cost between twenty-seven and thirty ducats, so three times what the already expensive golden lion tamarin had cost. Civet cats are recorded as being brought to Lisbon in the one extant book of accounts for the Casa da Guiné, for the financial year 1504–5: a civet cat and a parrot were together valued at six hundred *reais*, while an ivory salt-cellar and three ivory spoons were valued at seven hundred.[49] Known in Italy since the fifteenth century (as was shown by Lorenzo de' Medici's poem about them discussed in chapter 2), images of civets based on those belonging to Lorenzo's son Pope Leo X, like other 'strange' or 'bizarre' (that is, extra-European) animals and birds were, according to Vasari, included in frescoes by Giovanni da Udine in the Sala dei chiaroscuri in the Vatican palace, which no longer exist.[50] It is noteworthy how similar in terms of species the animals and birds were in Andrea del Sarto's *Tribute to Caesar* (discussed in chapter 2) and in this fresco by Giovanni da Udine. In the mid-sixteenth century civets were still rare

45. This is perhaps the 'Thomas Ferreyra janoes [i.e., genovese]' recorded in the parish of Santa Caterina in 1565: *Livro do lançamento e serviço que a cidade de Lisboa fez a el Rei Nosso Senhor no ano de 1565*, 4 vols (Lisbon, 1948), 3, p. 71. Ferreira/Ferera is an Italian name that has been given a Portuguese overlay, and the formulation in Campana's journal 'Tomaso Ferera stannte in Lisbona' indicates he was not originally from Lisbon.

46. ASF, Misc. med. 713, 2r, 3v.

47. Pierre Belon, *Les Observations de plusieurs singularitez & choses memorables trouvées en Grèce, Asie, Iudée, Egypte, Arabie & autres pays estranges* (Paris, 1554), p. 93v; discussed in Joan Barclay Lloyd, *African Animals in Renaissance Literature and Art* (Oxford, 1971), pp. 97–98.

48. Dannenfeldt, 'Europe Discovers', p. 420.

49. Jordan Gschwend and Lowe, *The Global City*, appendix 8, p. 267.

50. Giorgio Vasari, *Le vite de' più eccellenti pittori scultori e architettori*, text ed. Rosanna Bettarini, commentary ed. Paola Barocchi, 9 vols in 11 tomes (Florence, 1966–97), 4, p. 197 (life of Raphael) and 5, p. 450 (life of Giovanni da Udine).Vasari uses the words 'stranieri' and 'bizarri'. Cf. Nicole Dacos and Caterina Furlan, *Giovanni da Udine, 1487–1561* (Udine, 1987), p. 23, where one of Vasari's texts is attributed to Bellori.

and much sought after, although their numbers were to increase considerably in the second half of the century.[51]

Although the journal accounts do not say so, Campana's two civet cats were probably purchased for Eleonora di Toledo, who would have wanted their secretions in order to make perfume—and who probably also wanted to emulate Catarina de Áustria. When Lorenzo de' Medici had owned such animals in the late fifteenth century it would have been on account of their novelty and rarity, whereas Eleonora's ownership is more likely to have been linked to what they stood for and what they produced. They were classified for financial purposes in the account journal under the heading 'spese di animali'. Eleonora made strenuous efforts to obtain these cats, both from Italy and abroad, and her desire for them was well known. In December 1546 she commissioned one of the Medici secretaries, Lorenzo Pagni, to buy one for her in Venice,[52] and over ten years later, in 1557, the same Lorenzo Pagni wrote to Bartolomeo Concini about a young man who wanted a position looking after Eleonora's civet cats. It was said that he was an excellent handler and he knew how to extract the civet without having his hands bitten, unlike Eleonora's women.[53]

These animals, whether perceived primarily as wild or domesticated, had their likenesses drawn and included in the major European collections of animal illustrations of the sixteenth and early seventeenth centuries. The two albums of sixteenth-century watercolour drawings of animals rediscovered by Florike Egmond in 2010 in the University Library of Amsterdam, belonging first to Conrad Gessner and later to Felix Platter, contain a page with two rather different iterations of civets. The top one was used as the basis for the woodcut illustration of a civet in Conrad Gessner's *Historiae animalium* (Zurich, 1551–58) and is instantly recognisable as an African civet; the presence of a bowl indicates its state of captivity as does, more mystifyingly, the presence of a book under one of its paws. The bottom one, wearing a collar, is rather differently shaped, rounder, with a different, fluffier tail, and a different expression, as though it were tame; perhaps an African civet,[54] its species and place of origin are not altogether clear. It

51. Dannenfeldt, 'Europe Discovers', p. 415.

52. ASF, MdP 1172, ins. 7, 21r, Lorenzo Pagni in Pisa to Cosimo's maggiordomo (Pierfrancesco Riccio) in Florence, 17 December 1546.

53. ASF, MdP 465, fol. 203, 4 November 1557, in postscript; see Cockram, 'Interspecies Understanding', p. 294.

54. Henrietta McBurney et al., *Birds, Other Animals and Natural Curiosities*, The Paper Museum of Cassiano dal Pozzo, Series B (Natural History) 4, 2 vols (London, 2017), 2, entry on the African civet by Arthur MacGregor, no. 209, pp. 498–503 at 500.

Plate 1. Unknown Portuguese cartographer, 'Cantino planisphere' (see Plate 2), detail of three groups in Sierra Leone—Jilof, Mandinga and 'Cape'—and Senegambian green parrots; Modena, Biblioteca Estense Universitaria, inv. no. C.G.A.2. By permission of the Italian Ministry of Culture.

Photo: Gallerie Estensi, Biblioteca Estense Universitaria di Modena

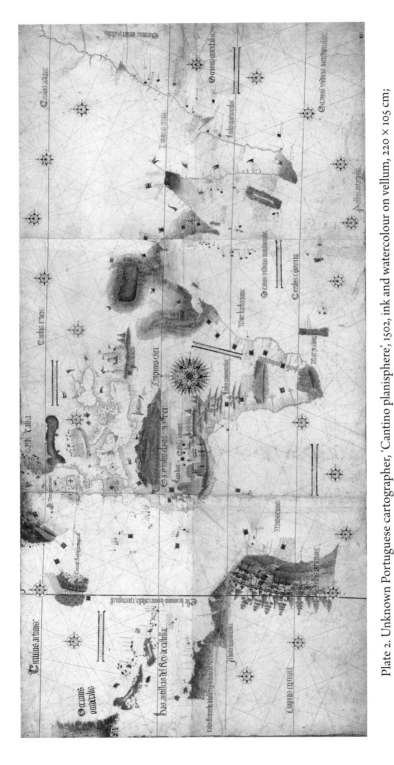

Plate 2. Unknown Portuguese cartographer, 'Cantino planisphere', 1502, ink and watercolour on vellum, 220 × 105 cm; Modena, Biblioteca Estense Universitaria, inv. no. C.G.A.2. By permission of the Italian Ministry of Culture.

Photo: Gallerie Estensi, Biblioteca Estense Universitaria di Modena

Plate 3. Unknown Portuguese cartographer, 'Cantino planisphere' (see Plate 2), detail of West African grey parrot; Modena, Biblioteca Estense Universitaria, inv. no. C.G.A.2. By permission of the Italian Ministry of Culture.

Photo: Gallerie Estensi, Biblioteca Estense Universitaria di Modena

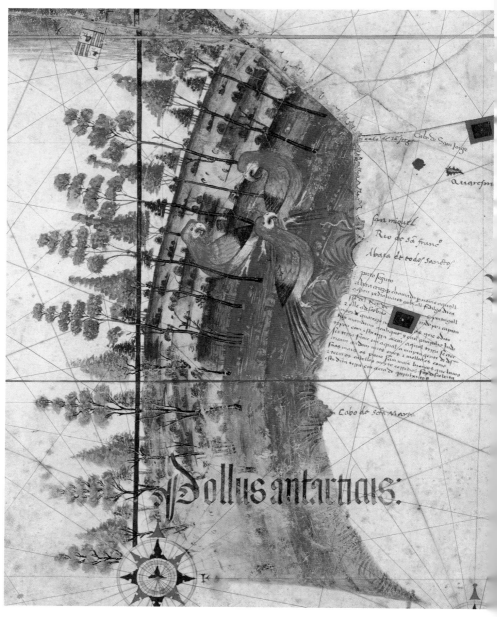

Plate 4. Unknown Portuguese cartographer, 'Cantino planisphere' (see Plate 2), detail of Brazil with multicoloured Amazon parrots or macaws; Modena, Biblioteca Estense Universitaria, inv. no. C.G.A.2. By permission of the Italian Ministry of Culture.

Photo: Gallerie Estensi, Biblioteca Estense Universitaria di Modena

Plate 5. Unknown Portuguese cartographer, 'Cantino planisphere' (see Plate 2),
detail of piazzetta of San Marco, Venice; Modena, Biblioteca Estense
Universitaria, inv. no. C.G.A.2. By permission of the Italian Ministry of Culture.

Photo: Gallerie Estensi, Biblioteca Estense Universitaria di Modena

Plate 6. Fra Mauro, *Mappamondo*, c. 1450, hand-coloured parchment glued on wooden board, c. 230 × 230 cm; Venice, Biblioteca nazionale Marciana, MS. Lat. XI, 92 (= 3828).

Plate 7. Fra Mauro, *Mappamondo* (see Plate 6), detail of 'Africa'; Venice, Biblioteca nazionale Marciana, MS. Lat. XI, 92 (= 3828).

Plate 8. Andrea del Sarto, *Tribute to Caesar*, c. 1519–21, fresco, 502 × 536 cm, detail; Villa medicea, Poggio a Caiano (Prato).

Photo: Scala, Florence

Plate 9. Giovanni della Robbia workshop, *The Temptation of Adam*, c. 1515, terracotta with glaze, 279.5 × 212 cm; Baltimore, The Walters Art Museum, acc. no. 27.219, acquired by Henry Walters, 1902.

Plate 10. Andrea della Robbia, Baby in Swaddling Clothes, 1487, glazed terracotta, diameter c. 100 cm; Florence, Ospedale degli Innocenti, external facade.

Photo: Kate Lowe

Plate 11. Lorenzo Sabatino and Baldassare Croce (attr.), *Activities of the Hospital*, 1575–80, fresco, detail of wet-nurse with mixed-ancestry baby; Rome, Ospedale di S. Spirito in Sassia, salone of the Palazzo del Commendatore.

Photo: Diana Bullen Presciutti

Plate 12. Evangelista della Croce and Girolamo dei Libri, 'Puer natus est', c. 1549, parchment; Pavia, Museo della Certosa di Pavia, Graduale 814, fol. 11r. By permission of the Italian Ministry of Culture.

Photo: Direzione regionale Musei Lombardia, Museo della Certosa di Pavia

Plate 13. Evangelista della Croce and Girolamo dei Libri, 'Puer natus est' (see Plate 12), detail of putti with differing skin colours; Pavia, Museo della Certosa di Pavia, Graduale 814, fol. 11r. By permission of the Italian Ministry of Culture.

Photo: Direzione regionale Musei Lombardia, Museo della Certosa di Pavia

Plate 14. Amico Aspertini, *Five Dancing Putti*, second decade of sixteenth century, print; New York, Metropolitan Museum of Art, gift of Mrs. Woodward Haven, 1930.

Photo: The Metropolitan Museum of Art. Public domain.

Plate 15. Antonio Tempesta and workshop, *A Pagan Sacrifice, the Goddess Nature and a Trophy*, detail of gypsy[?] mother and baby, c. 1579–81, fresco, Florence, Galleria degli Uffizi, Corridoio di Levante, *Grottesche*, vault 9. By permission of the Italian Ministry of Culture.

Photo: Gabinetto Fotografico delle Gallerie degli Uffizi—Antonio Quattrone

Plate 16. Bartolomeo Passerotti, *Homer's Riddle* (also known as *Homer and the Fishermen*), 1570–75, oil on canvas, 120 × 144 cm: Florence, Galleria degli Uffizi, inv. 1890 n. 10784. By permission of the Italian Ministry of Culture.

Photo: Gabinetto Fotografico delle Gallerie degli Uffizi—Roberto Palermo

Plate 17. Florence, Archivio di stato, Miscellanea medicea 713: external view of manuscript account journal. By permission of the Italian Ministry of Culture/Archivio di stato di Firenze.

Photo: Kate Lowe

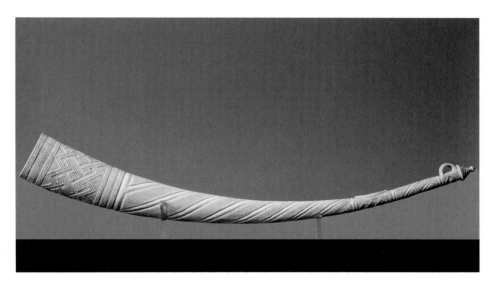

Plate 18. Oliphant, Kingdom of Kongo, first half of sixteenth century, ivory, length 57.5 cm; Florence, Palazzo Pitti, Tesoro dei granduchi, Bg 1879 Avori 3, 636318. By permission of the Italian Ministry of Culture.

Photo: Gabinetto Fotografico delle Gallerie degli Uffizi—Antonio Quattrone

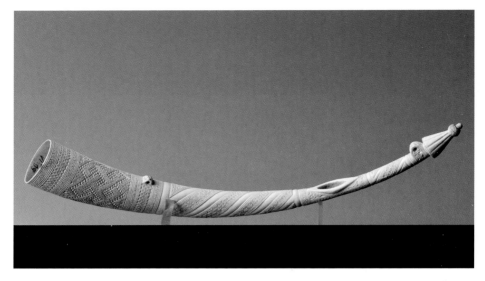

Plate 19. Oliphant, Kingdom of Kongo, first half of sixteenth century, ivory, length 83 cm; Florence, Palazzo Pitti, Tesoro dei granduchi, Bg 1879 Avori 2, 636322. By permission of the Italian Ministry of Culture.

Photo: Gabinetto Fotografico delle Gallerie degli Uffizi—Antonio Quattrone

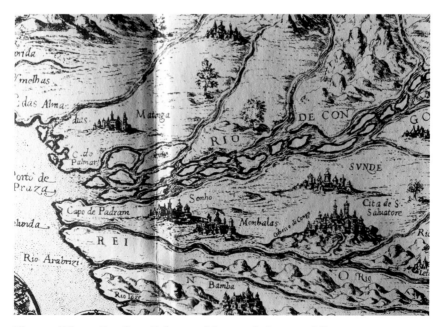

Plate 20. Filippo Pigafetta, *Relatione del reame di Congo et delle circonvicine contrade tratta dalli scritti & ragionamenti di Odoardo Lopez portoghese per Filippo Pigafetta con dißegni vari di geografia, di piante, d'habiti, d'animali & altro* (Rome, 1591), map 2, 'Tavola del Regno di Congo', 43.18 × 50.8 cm, detail.

Photo: Kate Lowe

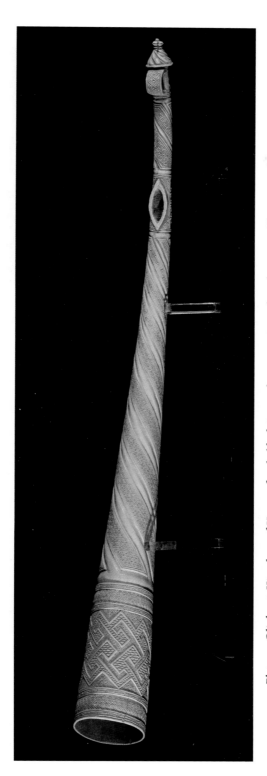

Plate 21. Oliphant, Kingdom of Kongo, first half of sixteenth century, ivory, length 57.5 cm; Florence, Palazzo Pitti, Tesoro dei granduchi, Bg 1879 Avori 3, 667608. By permission of the Italian Ministry of Culture.

Photo: Gabinetto Fotografico delle Gallerie degli Uffizi—Roberto Palermo

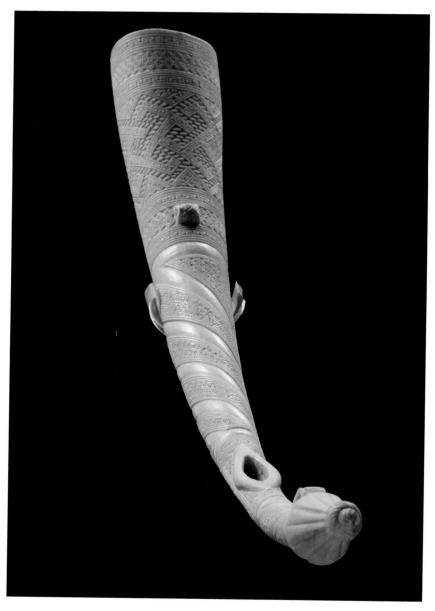

Plate 22. Oliphant, Kingdom of Kongo, first half of sixteenth century, ivory, length 83 cm; Florence, Palazzo Pitti, Tesoro dei granduchi, Bg 1879 Avori 2, 667565. By permission of the Italian Ministry of Culture.

Photo: Gabinetto Fotografico delle Gallerie degli Uffizi—Roberto Palermo

Plate 23. Kongolese oliphant shown in Plates 18 and 21, detail; Florence, Palazzo Pitti, Tesoro dei granduchi, Bg 1879 Avori 3, 636321. By permission of the Italian Ministry of Culture.

Photo: Gabinetto Fotografico delle Gallerie degli Uffizi—Antonio Quattrone

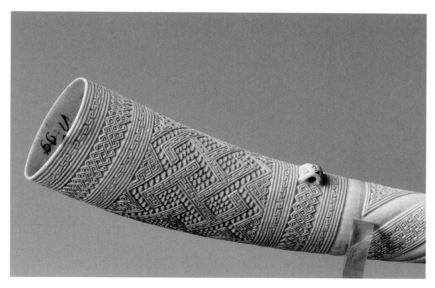

Plate 24. Kongolese oliphant shown in Plates 19 and 22, detail; Florence, Palazzo Pitti, Tesoro dei granduchi, Bg 1879 Avori 2, 636322. By permission of the Italian Ministry of Culture.

Photo: Gabinetto Fotografico delle Gallerie degli Uffizi—Antonio Quattrone

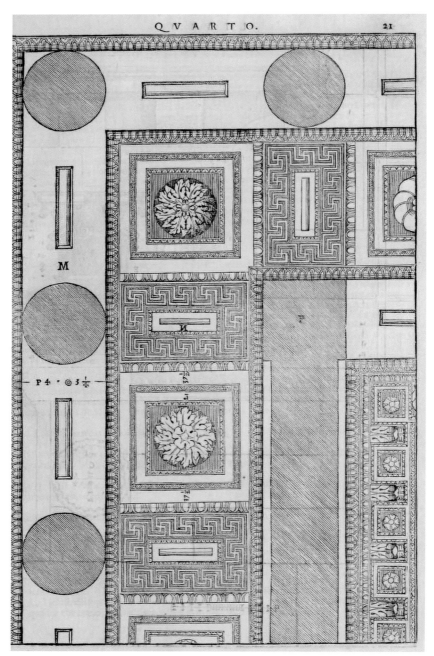

Plate 25. Andrea Palladio, *I quattro libri dell'architettura di Andrea Palladio* […]
(Venice, 1570), Bk 4, ch. 7, p. 21.

Plate 26. Raffaello Santi (Raphael), *The Virgin and Child with Saint John the Baptist and Saint Nicholas of Bari* (*The Ansidei Madonna*), 1505, oil on poplar, 216.8 × 147.6 cm; London, The National Gallery, inv. no. NG1171.

Photo: The National Gallery, London

Plate 27. Aztec feather fan, sixteenth century; Vienna, Weltmuseum, inv. no. 43381.

Photo: KHM-Museumsverband

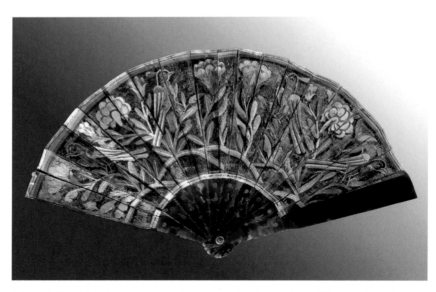

Plate 28. Fan, Mexico, seventeenth century, feather, paint, gilding and turtle-shell, 18.4 × 33.6 cm; Salem, Peabody Essex Museum, inv. no. 127310, gift of Mrs. Albert J. Beveridge. Courtesy of the Peabody Essex Museum.

Photo: Jeffrey R. Dykes

Plate 29. Alonso Sánchez Coello, *Infanta Isabel Clara Eugenia and Magdalena Ruiz*, detail of golden lion and cotton-top tamarins, c. 1585, oil on canvas; Madrid, Museo Nacional del Prado.

Plate 30. Lavinia Fontana, *Portrait of a Lady of the Ruini Family* (possibly Isabella Ruini), detail of dog with earrings, 1593, oil on canvas, 90 × 34 cm; Florence, Galleria Palatina. By permission of the Italian Ministry of Culture.

Photo: Gabinetto Fotografico delle Gallerie degli Uffizi—Claudio Giusti

Plate 31. Sofonisba Anguissola, *Infanta Catalina Micaela with a Marmoset*, 1573, oil on canvas, 56.2 × 47 cm; private collection. By permission.

Photo: Rafael Valls

Plate 32. Sofonisba Anguissola, *Infanta Catalina Micaela with a Marmoset* (see Plate 31), detail of marmoset, private collection. By permission.

Photo: Rafael Valls

Plate 33. Pierre Belon, 'Le portraict de la Civette qu'on nommoit anciennement Hyæna', in *Les Observations de plusieurs singularitez & choses memorables* (Paris, 1554), p. 93v.

Plate 34. Johannes Stradanus (known as Giovanni Stradano), *Penelope at the Loom*, 1561–62, central ceiling *tondo*; Florence, Palazzo Vecchio, Sala di Penelope.

Photo: Scala, Florence

Plate 35. Johannes Stradanus, *Penelope at the Loom* (see Plate 34), detail;
Florence, Palazzo Vecchio, Sala di Penelope.

Photo: Scala, Florence

Plate 36. Jan van der Straet (Johannes Stradanus), *Penelope at the Loom* (*Atelier de tissage ou Penelope tissant*), mid-sixteenth century, pen and brown ink preparatory drawing, diameter 23.8 cm; Paris, École des Beaux-Arts, inv. no. Mas0598_e-84245.

Photo: Beaux-Arts de Paris, Dist. RMN-Grand Palais/image Beaux-Arts de Paris

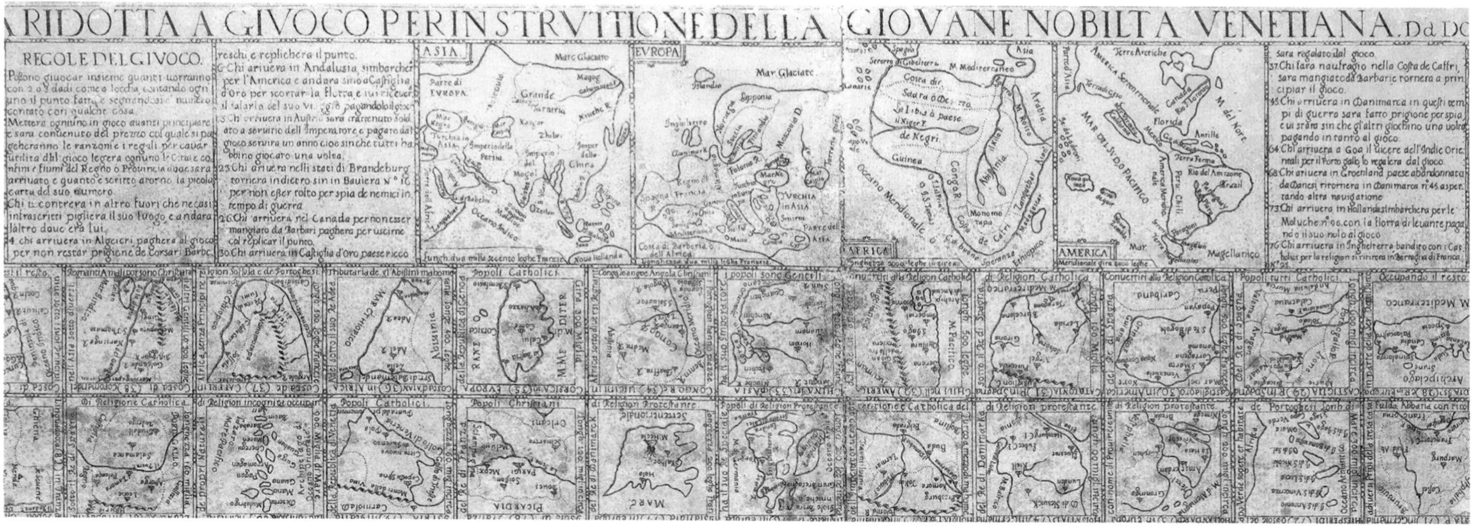

Plate 37. Anton Francesco Lucini, *Geografia ridotta a giuoco per istruttione della giovane nobilta venetiana*, mid-seventeenth century, detail including no. 37, 'Costa dei Caffri', area around Cape of Good Hope; Florence, Palazzo Pitti, inv. Castello 1911, n. 395, 635016. By permission of the Italian Ministry of Culture.

Photo: Gabinetto Fotografico delle Gallerie degli Uffizi—Claudio Giusti

Plate 38. Bezoar stone with gold filigree and ring, probably from Hormuz, late sixteenth century, height 9 cm, width 6 cm; Portugal, private collection. By permission.

Photo: Pedro Lobo

Plate 39. Bezoar stone with gold filigree and ring, late sixteenth century, height 9 cm; Vienna, Kunsthistorisches Museum, Kunstkammer 996 (at Schloss Ambras).

Photo: KHM-Museumsverband

Plate 40. Bezoar stone with inscribed gold ring, sixteenth century; Vienna, Kunsthistorisches Museum, Kunstkammer 958.

Plate 41. Ulisse Aldrovandi, *Tavole*, vol. 5.1, n.d. [later sixteenth century]: *Animali*, no. 2, civet cat; Bologna, Biblioteca Universitaria.

appears beneath the caption, 'A civet cat similar to the first one was sent by Vicentius Valensius to Gessner.'[55] The woodcut of a civet in Carolus Clusius, *Curae posteriores [...]* (Leiden and Antwerp, 1611) showed the animal wearing a collar, with short legs, a long straight tail and bristling cat-like whiskers.[56] The drawing of the African civet in Cassiano del Pozzo's paper museum, attributed to Vincenzo Leonardi (1589/90–1646), is instead positioned to emphasise the perineal area, critical for secretion from its scent gland, rather than alluding to the animal's state of domestication.[57]

Campana's Iberian trip also revealed that Cosimo and Eleonora, like most Renaissance Italian rulers, valued the possession of parrots, and were prepared to pay large sums to acquire talking ones. In Lisbon eight parrots were acquired; nothing is known of their speaking ability. Only the colour of their plumage was specified: seven were green and one was grey (presumably it was an African grey). They had been bought piecemeal from several different Portuguese vendors, along with two cages, at a cost of twenty-two ducats.[58] The account journal also revealed that a further green parrot 'che parlava' (that spoke) was bought in Livorno after the ship docked in March 1548, from the pilot's mate,[59] commissioned by Eleonora who was then in Livorno, at a cost of eighteen ducats and three hundred *maravedis*.[60] It is worth remembering that virtually all crew members working out of Lisbon would have made their own purchases of goods from the Portuguese trading empire, and one of the

55. Florike Egmond, 'A Collection within a Collection: Rediscovered Animal Drawings from the Collections of Conrad Gessner and Felix Platter', *Journal of the History of Collections*, 25.2 (2013), pp. 149–70 at 159 and 168 n. 44. The folio with the civets is Amsterdam, University Library, MS. III C 23, fol. 47, and the top image of a civet appears in Conrad Gessner, *Historiae animalium*, 4 vols (Zurich, 1551–8), 1, p. 948.

56. Carolus Clusius, *Curae posteriores seu plurimam non ante cognitarum aut descriptarum [...] aliquot animalium novae descriptiones* (Leiden and Antwerp, 1611), p. 109.

57. McBurney, et al. *Birds*, 2, entry on African civet, no. 209, pp. 498–99.

58. ASF, Misc. med. 713, 77v.

59. See Bartolomeo Crescentio, *Nautica mediterranea* (Rome, 1607), p. 85: 'il compagno del Nocchiero, quale non vi essendo piloto, egli serve in suo luogo'.

60. ASF, Misc. med. 713, 9r 'da 1° spagnuolo compagnione del nochieri della detta nave' and 77v: 'dal compagnio del nochieri della nave'. Ten years later Campana was still involved with Eleonora's parrots, paying, and being reimbursed for, a bag of *scagliuola* (canary grass: *Phalaris canariensis*) for the 'passere di Canaria' or canaries and the parrots that Eleonora kept 'in casa' (at home): ASF, Scrittoio delle regie possessioni 4138, 188 sinistra and 270 sinistra, 14 February 1559, referring to a payment in the previous year.

ways that these goods spread around the world was by being sold later in ports where the ships subsequently docked.

Spain in addition offered the chance to purchase global birds other than parrots. As the major Spanish port for the New World, Sanlúcar de Barrameda was a hub for the slave trade and a number of Italian merchants lived and worked there, engaged in the trade.[61] However, Campana did not purchase enslaved people there, but rather turkeys. On one of the few occasions where provenance is clearly stated in Misc. med. 713, a distinction is made between the eleven 'ghalline d'India di Portogallo' bought in Lisbon,[62] and the twelve 'ghalline' and seven 'ghalli delle Indie di Spagna' bought in Sanlúcar and taken to Cadiz.[63] The same words gallo or gallino dell'Indie were used for both turkeys and guinea fowl, but all turkeys at this date came from the New World. From 1511 every ship sailing from the mainland of South America and the Antilles to Seville was ordered to carry five pairs of turkeys, so Seville or Sanlúcar was where one went to buy them. The 'ghalline d'India di Portogallo',[64] probably African guinea fowl,[65] were purchased in Lisbon on 8 September 1547 for a total of three ducats and 344 maravedis (but it was acknowledged that not all the birds had been the same price): the 'ghalline' and 'ghalli delle Indie di Spagna',[66] which were turkeys, purchased in Sanlúcar, cost considerably more: twenty-four ducats and 383 maravedis. These prices are high, especially the second, which is surely astronomical for a consignment of twenty birds, indicating that these were not common, even though they had been imported into Italy since 1520.[67] The purchase of breeding pairs hints at plans to farm turkeys rather than acquisition of the birds as a form of status food. This is one of the

---

61. Antonio Moreno Ollero, *Sanlúcar de Barrameda a fines de la Edad Media* (Cadiz, 1983), pp. 167, 212.

62. ASF, Misc. med. 713, 3v and 77v.

63. Ibid., 77v.

64. Benedetto Dei had presented 'galline d'India' purchased in Alexandria to Piero de' Medici after his travels in the 1460s: Curzio Mazzi, 'Le carte di Benedetto Dei nella Medicea Laurenziana', *Rivista delle biblioteche e degli archivi*, 25 (1914), pp. 137–56, 26 (1915), pp. 148–56, 27 (1916), pp. 133–44, 28 (1917), pp. 110–20, 29 (1918), pp. 128–50; see 25 (1914), at 138.

65. Aldovrandi, *Natura picta*, plate 298 is of a '*Numida meleagris*; Faraone', which is labelled on the image 'Gallina affricana mas seu Numidisa'.

66. Ibid., plate 261 is of a 'gallo dell'Indie', from Central America, and plate 262 is of a 'gallina dell'India', also from Central America, but the species names added (*Crax rubra* and *Pauxi pauxi*) are both of curassows and not turkeys.

67. Sabine Eiche, *Presenting the Turkey: The Fabulous Story of a Flamboyant and Flavourful Bird* (Florence, 2004), p. 86; Shepard Krech III, 'On the Turkey in Rua Nova dos Mercadores',

few occasions when Campana included provenance, and the two distinct provenances from opposite sides of the globe, in conjunction with the significant difference in price, point to two different types of bird. Confusion over bird terminology in Renaissance Europe meant that the African guinea fowl and the turkey could both be referred to as a *gallo* or *gallino d'India*,[68] and confusion over geography meant that ambivalence was embedded in the tags *d'India* and *delle Indie*.[69] Only the attribution to the Portuguese and Spanish empires was unambiguous.

Purchasing and Possessing Humans: Lives of Enslavement at Court

A final type of living global goods or merchandise—enslaved people—was also acquired by Campana. The practice of slavery had not decreased in Florence, remaining as commonplace as in the fifteenth century, but Cosimo's political aspirations meant that enslaved men were increasingly acquired to row in his galleys. Here the gendered nature of the acquisitions made for the Medici becomes more pronounced: Eleonora wanted (and received) sub-Saharan African women and children for domestic service, while Cosimo needed adult men from North Africa to work in hard manual labour on the galleys. Enslaved people have always been stereotyped—as part of the dehumanisation and justification processes—but the degree of choice available to a would-be buyer in sixteenth-century Europe now generated stereotyping of a different order.[70] Filippo Sassetti laid out what he saw as the pros and cons of various enslaved people from around the world in a letter of 10 October 1578, from Lisbon, to Baccio Valori in Florence. This catalogue ranged over appearance, characteristic behaviour, skills, intelligence, aptitude for work and suitability for enslavement.[71] A letter of 12 November 1545 written to Pierfrancesco Riccio

in Annemarie Jordan Gschwend and K.J.P. Lowe, eds, *The Global City: On the Streets of Renaissance Lisbon* (London, 2015), pp. 178–85 at 182.

68. Eiche, *Presenting the Turkey*, pp. 17 and 22.

69. Scholars have struggled, often unsuccessfully, to make sense of this. See Martinho, 'Beyond Exotica', p. 191: 'the flexible—and rather convenient—use of the expression *de la India* should not be interpreted as unawareness for the place of production of goods'.

70. Kate Lowe, 'The Stereotyping of Black Africans in Renaissance Europe', in T. F. Earle and K.J.P. Lowe eds, *Black Africans in Renaissance Europe* (Cambridge, 2005), pp. 17–47.

71. Sassetti, *Lettere*, pp. 220–21.

attests to the fact that Cosimo commissioned Tommaso Cavalcanti to buy twenty slaves on his behalf, 'di buona taglia, da fatica, et più tosto bianchi che neri' (well-built, capable of heavy work, tending towards white rather than black) in Lisbon or Seville, wherever they were cheaper, and to send them on the first boats carrying sugar to Livorno, even if he had not managed to buy all of them by the time the first boats left.[72]

As far as Campana was concerned, choosing suitably strong and fit slaves to work on Cosimo's galleys appears to have been time-consuming, and for whatever reason many slaves did not make the grade. In Cadiz, Campana bought his first galley slave for Cosimo: Iusuf di Schut di Levantte,[73] described as 'turco', bought from Diego Sances by Andrea Peri of Cadiz *fiorentino* for forty ducats, variously described as complete with a length of chain. A further length and two 'anelloni' (presumably ankle cuffs) were also bought for him, in addition to a mat to sleep on, and some clothes and shoes.[74] The middleman or broker Vettorio Giuoli of Florence was despatched from Cadiz to Ceres by Campana twice at the beginning of December to appraise seven galley slaves for Cosimo.[75] He returned with only one, Francesco di Marvescho described as 'moresche', who cost thirty-four ducats and 136 *maravedis*.[76] Three further galley slaves for Cosimo were later purchased at Majorca on the return journey to Livorno. All were described as 'moro', and all came from North Africa or the old Nasrid Kingdom of Granada: Giovanni di Granata (Granada), Ascer d'Algier and Piero Giovanni di Fes. The first two cost thirty-eight ducats each, and Piero Giovanni cost thirty-four.[77] So in total five galley slaves were acquired, each costing between thirty and forty ducats, variously described as 'turco', 'moresche' and 'moro'. All can be assumed to be Muslim, and most if not all must have been enslaved in battle or raiding. Campana's purchase of slaves for Cosimo appears to fit with Cavalcanti's instructions, and the men who were bought would have been in addition to those purchased by Cavalcanti, as Cosimo's aim was to create a large pool of enslaved people to work on his galleys. The 1545 letter is

---

72. ASF, MdP 1170A, ins. 3, fol. 224, Giovanni Francesco Lottini in San Gimignano to Pierfrancesco Riccio in Florence.

73. For a discussion of the places referred to by the term 'di Levante', see Boccadamo, 'A Napoli', p. 151.

74. ASF, Misc. med. 713, 7v.

75. Ibid., 76v.

76. Ibid., 6r, 7v, 76v.

77. Ibid., 8v and 76v.

explicit in adverting to the qualities Cosimo required in his galley slaves, adding meaning and depth to Campana's narrative of acquisition two years later.

The number of enslaved people purchased by Campana was small: in addition to the five Muslim North Africans purchased for the galleys, there were five black Africans purchased for Eleonora and court life.[78] It is immediately clear that in these cases place of origin was a relevant factor and was noted: here provenance, in the sense of place of origin, mattered. The availability of enslaved sub-Saharan Africans was a direct result of Portuguese imperialism. The five sub-Saharan Africans were all bought in Lisbon: first, two boys, Simone aged eleven and Caro (or Cara) Costa aged nine, who had both just arrived in Lisbon ('venuti ora') from the Atlantic islands of Cabo Verde, a hub for slave trading, then Beatrice, aged about twenty-six, and her daughter Milizia,[79] aged four, and finally—purchased from a Portuguese friar—the twelve-year-old called Christofano. According to Campana's account journal, Christofano cost thirty-one large gold ducats, and upon arrival in Pisa he was baptised and given the name Pericho on the orders of Eleonora.[80] This precise and unusual information about naming is fortunately confirmed by the baptism records in Pisa which document that on 1 April 1548 a male was baptised with the name Perico, and a note identifies him as the slave of the duchess of Florence.[81] Perico is not an Italian name but a Spanish one, a diminutive of Pero or Pedro, and it also means 'parakeet'.[82] This is an important reference to Eleonora giving one of the enslaved children in her entourage a Spanish name. Campana's wording assigns not only the act of renaming but also the choice of the name to Eleonora, thus emphasising her attachment to Spanish cultural traditions. The name Perico appears nowhere else in the Florentine or Pisan baptism

78. At other times, Cosimo purchased or was sent black slaves: ASF, MdP 635, ins. 11, 294, Pirro Musefilo, conte della Sassetta in Naples to Cosimo in Florence, 18 December 1540. For comparative context in terms of occupation, see T. F. Earle and K.J.P. Lowe, eds, *Black Africans in Renaissance Europe* (Cambridge, 2005).

79. In Jorge Fonseca's database of over three thousand slaves in Lisbon in the sixteenth century, twenty were called Beatriz/Brita and only one was called Milícia: Fonseca, *Escravos*, p. 356.

80. ASF, Misc. med. 713, 9r: 'uno stiavo nero detto Christofano [...] el quale o batesato in Pisa e postogli nome Pericho come m'ordinò V. Ill.ma S. Duchessa'.

81. See the online database of Pisan baptisms between 1457 and 1557 at https://battesimi.sns .it/battesimi/ (accessed 8 June 2023).

82. Joan Corominas, *Diccionario crítico etimológico de la lengua castellana*, 4 vols (Berne, 1954), 3, p. 744.

records in this period. Whether Eleonora picked the name purely because she liked it or found it suitable, or also on account of its second meaning of parakeet, thereby linking the African boy to a non-European bird, is unclear, but she must have been aware of the parallels in their situations of displacement to Europe. If the three boys (aged nine, eleven and twelve) had been enslaved in the preceding few years, which is indicated by the reference to Cabo Verde, they would all have been old enough to remember their homes and families in Africa.

Eleonora, born in Spain and brought up in Naples, was the daughter of the viceroy of Naples, D. Pedro Álvarez de Toledo, marquis of Villafranca,[83] and was accustomed to having black slaves as part of her court household: her Spanish heritage,[84] and the southern Italian location of her childhood, ensured this, and it was a preference she carried with her to Florence, effecting cultural transfer. Although the Medici had always owned domestic slaves in the fifteenth century, as far as is known they were all white, female and adult;[85] Eleonora's arrival in Florence in 1539 to marry Cosimo might have been the first time that a Medici household included a black slave.[86] From that moment on, Medici letters often contained references to enslaved people, many of whom would have been black. In addition to their deployment as domestic court servants, some of them were noted for skills—such as dancing—that were valued at the Medici court. Unlike the 'retinue of black slaves' kept at the Aragonese court of Queen Maria de Luna

83. Carlos José Hernando Sánchez, 'Los Médicis y los Toledo: Familia y lenguaje del poder en la Italia de Felipe II', in Giuseppe Di Stefano, Elena Fasano Guarini and Alessandro Martinengo, eds, *Italia non spagnola e monarchia spagnola tra '500 e '600: Politica, cultura e letteratura* (Florence, 2009), pp. 55–81 at 58–59 for bibliography on Eleonora.

84. See, e.g., Núria Silleras-Fernández, '*Nigra sum sed formosa*: Black Slaves and Exotica in the Court of a Fourteenth-Century Aragonese Queen', *Medieval Encounters*, 13 (2007), pp. 546–65.

85. ASF, MAP, LXXXII, 36 (1457) and ASF, Catasto 924, prima parte, 311v. See also the unpublished paper by James Beck, 'Cosimo's Four Slaves', now available online at the ASF website, http://images.pcmac.org/SiSFiles/Schools/GA/GwinnettCounty/CentralGwinnett/Uploads/DocumentsCategories/Documents/The%20Four%20Slaves%20of%20Cosimo%20de%20Medici.pdf (accessed 25 April 2023).

86. She brought three female servants and slaves ('tres mozas de servicio entre esclavas y mozas') with her as part of her household from Naples, and they could have been black: ASF, MdP 5922A, 11, list made by Eleonora's mother María Osorio y Piementel; Chiara Franceschini, '"*Los scholares son cosa de sua excelentia, como lo es toda la Compañia*": Eleonora di Toledo and the Jesuits', in Konrad Eisenbichler, pp., *The Cultural World of Eleonora di Toledo, Duchess of Florence and Siena* (Aldershot, 2004), pp. 181–206 at 183.

at the end of the fourteenth and beginning of the fifteenth century, whose primary function was display, Eleonora's black enslaved women, whilst still ideally
visually pleasing and striking, had ceased to be considered merely as 'exotica'[87]
and were also required to be useful. In October 1540 Eleonora was pleased to
hear that the two 'mori [. . .] che ballano' ([most probably] black slaves who
dance) had arrived.[88] By December 1540 Eleonora had already requested 'doi
schiave more' (two black female slaves) from the Doria in Genoa, who apolo-
gised that they had not been able to find 'beautiful' ones as she had wanted.[89] It
seems obvious from these references that Eleonora was actively searching for
black slaves of the right sort for her household. Just as Isabella d'Este between
the 1490s and the 1520s had a very clear sense of what type of black slave she
wanted—good-looking, as dark-skinned as possible, healthy, intelligent, co-
operative and very young[90]—so it appears Eleonora was scouring Italy for
beautiful, skilful and biddable slaves, and was also on the lookout for young
children, who were impressionable and quick learners. On 10 January 1546 there
is an intriguing reference to 'due putte nere', or two little black girls, who have
not yet left Pisa because they were unwell: these too were probably already part
of, or destined to be part of, Eleonora's household.[91] It has always been slightly
surprising that Lorenzo de' Medici did not have a black slave, as the fashion for
them in Florence started during his time in power, but Eleonora's background
and the transition from a private family to a dukedom meant that customs and
expectations had changed. Eleonora's foreignness—her Spanish origin—was a
bone of contention with the Florentines, who did not take kindly to her or what
her family stood for, and they particularly objected to what they saw as her
Spanish ways of behaving, and the retention of so many Spanish people in her
entourage.[92] It is possible that her maintenance of a group or retinue of black
enslaved women might also have been perceived as un-Florentine and 'alien'.

87. Silleras-Fernández, 'Nigra sum', p. 555.

88. ASF, MdP 1169, 351v, Lorenzo Pagni in Poggio to Pierfrancesco Riccio in Florence, 8
October 1540.

89. Cosimo Conti, La prima reggia di Cosimo I de' Medici nel palazzo già della signoria di Firenze, descritta ed illustrata coll'appoggio d'un inventario inedito del 1553 etc. (Florence, 1893), p. 277,
doc. 5, Giannettino Doria to Eleonora, 4 December 1540.

90. Lowe, 'Isabella d'Este', pp. 72–73, and ch. 2 in this book.

91. ASF, MdP 1172, 25r, Vincenzo Ferrini in Lecceto to Pier Francesco Ricci in Florence.

92. Joan-Lluís Palos, '"A Spanish barbarian and an enemy of her husband's homeland": The
Duchess of Florence and Her Spanish Entourage', in Joan-Lluís Palos and Magdalena S. Sánchez,
Early Modern Dynastic Marriages and Cultural Transfer (London, 2016), pp. 165–87 at 170.

In order to make the case that southern European slavery was not a homogeneous experience in the sixteenth century, the fortunes of three of the black slaves from the 1547–48 expedition to the Iberian peninsula will be followed. Not only were their pasts probably very different, but even though they had been purchased by the same person or persons, so too their futures were wildly divergent. Caro Costa/Carocosta (Expensive/Costalot) is an extraordinary name,[93] so far as is known unique in Portugal and on the Italian peninsula; but the practice of naming slaves with puns on their attributes rather than with standard Christian names, or in addition to their Christian names, was well established (for example, Nicolas Cleynaerts's slave Carbo [Charcoal], who however also had an ordinary Christian name).[94] In this case, the reference is rather to an aspect of the boy's lived experience as understood by his purchaser. While this type of expressive name or *nome parlante*—in which the composite artefact of the surname itself signals a characteristic of the person that the author wishes to emphasise—is well known in literature,[95] its historical realities when attached to a real person have not been explored. Who gave the boy this name is unknown; it may have been his former Portuguese owner, who was a cutler, and Campana just translated it into its Italian equivalent. Or it may have been Campana, who felt that he had paid too much for him, and thought it would be amusing to inscribe this cost onto the boy. The wording in Misc. med. 713 indicates the former, as the other slave, Simone, is described by the phrase 'nominato Simone' and Caro Costa by the phrase 'detto Caro Costa'.[96] Another reading of the name is possible, but most unlikely: Caro was a saint's name, with three candidates vying for the privilege of being San Caro, although it was not

---

93. Cf. the use of the name Carapreda, a recognised name in the south of Italy whose meaning could arc between 'good acquisition' and 'precious catch/quarry/prey', in Boccaccio, *Decameron*, 2, p. 613 and nn. 5 and 6; and Giulio Herczeg, 'I cosidetti "nomi parlanti" nel *Decameron*', *Atti e memorie del VII Congresso internazionale di scienze onomastiche (Firenze-Pisa, 1961)*, 4 vols (Florence, 1962–63), 3 (1963), pp. 189–99 at 190.

94. Jorge Fonseca, 'Black Africans in Portugal during Cleynaerts's Visit (1533–1538)', in T. F. Earle and K.J.P. Lowe, eds, *Black Africans in Renaissance Europe* (Cambridge, 2005), pp. 112–21 at 119 and 121; both Christian names and nicknames are given. See also Fonseca, *Escravos*, p. 359.

95. Herczeg, 'I cosidetti "nomi parlanti"', pp. 189–90, and Michelangelo Zaccarello, 'Primi appunti tipologici sui nomi-parlanti', *Lingua e stile*, 38.1 (2003), pp. 59–84.

96. ASF, Misc. med. 713, 2r. A significant percentage of the salaried members of the Florentine ducal household in 1553 had descriptors or nicknames (ASF, Depositeria generale, parte antica 393, e.g., 33r, 43r, 44r, 45r, 47r (2), etc.), only some of which must have come into being to aid identification.

a saint's name in normal use in Portugal,[97] and Costa is a common Portuguese surname. The exact price paid for Caro Costa is unknown, but he and Simone together cost fifty gold ducats. Young boys commanded high prices, as they had a longer working life in front of them—and price was also related to attractiveness, however defined. Requests for 'beautiful young black boys'—just as requests for beautiful young boys of every other type—were commonplace. So, for example, Cardinal Ferdinando de' Medici wrote in 1580 to ask his brother to find in Seville or elsewhere four 'moretti' (young black boys) aged ten who were 'vistosi e belli' (striking and beautiful).[98] There are non-sexual reasons for wanting to possess striking ten-years-olds, who were employed as adornments, but unfortunately these are less likely to have been at play in this instance.

Regardless of the uses to which the boys' physical attractiveness might cause them to be put—and with a female owner the risks were not as great for young boys as those posed by a male owner—their material welfare was well catered for. An outlay of fifty ducats demanded that appropriate care be taken in order that the investment was not endangered.[99] So the boys had a number of new shirts, new breeches and new shoes, and had their heads shaved and washed, at a cost of one ducat and 137 maravedis. Comfortable sleep was ensured by the purchase of a hair mattress and a white cover, which cost the sum of two ducats.[100] These purchases for the two enslaved boys from Cabo Verde cost three ducats and 137 maravedis, almost exactly what the two Kongolese horns had cost (three ducats and one hundred maravedis). In mid-August further clothing ('camiciuole') costing 270 maravedis was purchased for them 'accio non patissino per el viagio' (so that they did not suffer on the voyage) to Livorno.[101] This is a telling remark, showing first that there was a concept of slave suffering, and second that every effort was being made to keep the boys in top form.

97. Bibliotheca sanctorum, 13 vols (Rome, 1961–70), 2, col. 1236 and 3, col. 875.

98. Butters, Fumagalli and Deswarte-Rosa, La Villa Médicis, vol. 5: Fonti documentarie, , p. 236.

99. Cf. Francesco Carletti, Ragionamenti del mio viaggio intorno al mondo, ed. Gianfranco Silvestro (Turin, 1958), p. 27 and Francesco Carletti, My Voyage around the World: The Chronicles of a 16th Century Florentine Merchant, trans. Herbert Weinstock (New York, 1964), p. 21 admits that they tried to 'restore' the slaves who were ill and run down from the voyage from Cabo Verde to Cartagena in 1591 'non già per carità [. . .] ma per non perdene il valore e prezzo d'essi'/'not so much out of charity [. . .] as not to lose their value and price'.

100. ASF, Misc. med. 713, 2r.

101. Ibid., 2v.

Caro Costa falls out of sight for the next few years, but he obviously was suffering, for the next mention of him, when he would have been aged thirteen, is very grim indeed. On 23 July 1551 Tommaso de' Medici *tesoriere* sends Cara Costa 'moro leghato', that is, bound, to Cosimo's principal secretary and *maggiordomo*, Pierfrancesco Riccio, on the orders of their excellencies (that is, both Cosimo and Eleonora), asking Riccio to have him fitted with irons and a chain, and an iron collar ('uno ferro con la catena et uno collare di ferro'), and to send him back as soon as possible.[102] In Italy, irons were only fitted on slaves who attempted to run away, so Caro Costa must have tried to escape. The ancient Romans had usually used slave collars for labelling and marking rather than as a form of punishment, yet most of the tags on them also contained the phrase 'Tene me ne fugiam' (Hold me, lest I flee).[103] While the two later Roman diarists Gaspare Pontani and Johannes Burchard both remarked on the iron slave collars around the necks of the one hundred *mori* or 'moors' sent by the king of Spain to the pope in 1488,[104] the letter asking Riccio to arrange for Caro Costa to be fitted with a slave collar is the earliest reference found so far to the punitive use of a slave collar in Renaissance Italy; the revival of their use on the Italian peninsula may in part be related to the Renaissance interest in the classical world, and the Roman legacy of slavery.[105] The inventory of Cardinal Ferdinando de' Medici's collection in Villa Medici in 1588 rather ominously included four lots of slave chains and four slave collars.[106] The relationship between prisoners' slave collars, made of iron with uplift at one end, and thick silver chokers, in evidence around the necks of some slaves in contemporary paintings, which were expensive pieces of jewellery, has still to be explored.

102. ASF, MdP 1176, 907r.

103. Jennifer Trimble, 'The Zoninus Collar and the Archaeology of Roman Slavery', *American Journal of Archaeology*, 120.3 (2016), pp. 447–72 at 447; *Spartaco: Schiavi e padroni a Roma*, ed. Claudio Parisi, Orietta Rossini and Lucia Spagnuolo, exh. cat., Museo dell'Ara Pacis, Rome (Rome, 2017), pp. 169–70.

104. Gaspare Pontani, *Il diario romano di Gaspare Pontani, già riferito al Notaio del Nantiporto: 30 gennaio 1481–25 luglio 1492*, ed. Diomede Toni, RIS/2, 3.2 (Città di Castello, 1907–8), p. 68; Johannes Burchard, *Johannis Burckardi Liber notarum: ab anno 1483 usque ad annum 1506*, ed. Enrico Celani, RIS/2, 32.1 (Città di Castello-Bologna, 1907–42), p. 222.

105. Paul Kaplan's 'The Slave Collar: Visible Servitude', a lecture given at the Renaissance Society of America's annual meeting in New Orleans in March 2018, included discussion of Lorenzo Pignoria's treatise *De servis et eorum apud veteres ministeriis commentarius* (Augsburg, 1613), Pignoria being the first person to write about slave collars.

106. Alessandro Cecchi and Carlo Gasparri, *La Villa Médicis*, vol. 4: *Le collezioni del cardinale Ferdinando: I dipinti e le sculture* (Rome, 2009), pp. 444 and 447.

But if Caro Costa was deeply unhappy and his life was dreadful,[107] the opposite seems to have been true of Beatrice, the adult female in the group, whose post-Portuguese life seems to have been less conflictual as she found a niche at the Medici court. Born in Pombal in Portugal around 1521,[108] she was therefore at least a second-generation immigrant and had never known a life in Africa. This Iberian heritage may have been seen as an advantage by Eleonora, because Beatrice's first language would have been Portuguese. She was purchased in October 1547 from Jorge Costa for the very high price of a hundred ducats and sixty *maravedis*, but the reason for the high price was partly dependent on her provenance: she was described as 'essere chreata' (having been 'created': brought up) by Queen Catarina.[109] As has been noted, provenance had two major elements: place of origin, and genealogy of previous owners. In a hierarchy based on previous ownership and prior possession, a former royal slave came out on top, in the same way that a royal or princely provenance added value to an object,[110] enhancing it with meta-phorical patina,[111] as Lorenzo de' Medici had understood.[112] Five days later, Beatrice's four-year old daughter Milizia was purchased from the child's father, the Portuguese Lopo d'Almeida (who was thus selling his own daughter) for twenty ducats. Campana's entry for this purchase is unequivocal: 'compra da Lupo d'Almeda portoghese sua figlia e di Beatrice sopradetta' (bought from the Portuguese Lupo d'Almeda his and the aforementioned Beatrice's daughter). [113] It seems too coincidental for the purchases of the mother and daughter not to be linked, even though different middlemen were used.

107. One possible reason why Caro Costa might have been so unhappy is that he may have been Muslim, one of the Islamicised peoples of Senegambia, as Senegambians composed the majority of enslaved people offered for sale in Cabo Verde. He could have refused to cooperate in matters relating to Christianity, attempted to run away, and been shackled as a result.

108. Because of her later history of having a child with Lopo d'Almeida, it seems plausible that Beatrice might have had a connection in Pombal with the Almeida, who were local aristocrats. See Saul António Gomes, *Pombal medieval e quinhentista: Documentos para a sua história* (Batalha Leiria, 2010), p. 58.

109. She does not appear in any list found so far of slaves in Catarina's household, but see Annemarie Jordan, 'Images of Empire'.

110. Pergam, 'Provenance as Pedigree', p. 104.

111. Cf. Blier, 'Ways of Experiencing', p. 22; Freddolini, 'Grand Dukes', p. 14.

112. Fusco and Corti, *Lorenzo de' Medici*, pp. 6–10, 13–15.

113. ASF, Misc. med. 713, 4r.

Lopo d'Almeida was a relatively common name at this date, making the man in the document rather an elusive figure, but the Lopo d'Almeida who sold his daughter must have belonged to courtly or aristocratic circles in order to have had access to Beatrice, impregnated her and kept the child. This narrows the search. The most noted person of that name was the fifth son of António de Almeida, the *contador-mor* in the Casa dos Contos do Reino, and grandson of João de Almeida, the first count of Abrantes. Investigated by the Inquisition in 1550 after spending years outside Portugal, on his death thirty-five years later he left the largest-ever bequest to the Misericórdia of Porto.[114] This man was probably not the Lopo de Almeida of Campana's buying trip, however, because he is known to have been studying in France between autumn 1544 and Easter 1550.[115] While he could conceivably have returned for visits to Portugal between those dates, it is unlikely that he was in Lisbon in October 1547 with a four-year-old daughter. The most likely candidate is another Lopo d'Almeida,[116] whose family was part of the local aristocracy in Pombal,[117] where Beatrice was born.

Considerable care and expense were expended on this enslaved mother and daughter. A mattress and a so-called Irish blanket were purchased to keep Beatrice and Milizia warm on the voyage back to Tuscany from Cadiz.[118] A further reason for Beatrice's rather high price could have been because she was pregnant, although this might also have been seen as a disadvantage, as it would clearly have interfered with her ability to work. The father of this unborn child is unknown, and the fact that Beatrice had at least two pregnancies while in the orbit of the Portuguese court points to sexual activity that was condoned or permitted. As opposed to the precariousness of being a domestic slave in an ordinary household, where sexual violence would often have been normal, being part of the retinue of a queen or the female consort of a ruler would usually have offered the highest level of safety to a female court slave, as no one would

114. Artur de Magalhães Basto, *História da Santa Casa da Misericórdia do Porto*, 2 vols (Porto, 1934, 1964), 2, p. 55; Sá, *O regresso dos mortos*, pp. 121–43.

115. Basto, *História*, 2, pp. 63–65.

116. Another person with the name Lopo de Almeida is mentioned as the master of Isabel frz. whose son, with an unknown father, was baptised in Lisbon on 17 April 1565. Isabel is described as Lopo's 'criada' (servant): Edgar Prestage and Pedro d'Azevedo, eds, *Registo da freguesia de Santa Cruz do Castello desde 1536 até 1628* (Coimbra, 1913), p. 60.

117. S. A. Gomes, *Pombal*, p. 58. See also Lisbon, Biblioteca Nacional de Portugal, Arquivo Tarouca, L. 262, morgado de Leiria, João de Barros 29, 67 and 188. The last is a dowry agreement from 1548.

118. ASF, Misc. med. 713, 5r.

have dared to interfere with or violate her without facing dire consequences. An attack on an enslaved female at court would have been viewed as an attack on the property of the queen or consort. When Beatrice miscarried late in October, her treatment belied her enslaved status. She was bought all kinds of culinary treat such as butter, almonds, eggs, honey, sweets and chicken; there is a payment for a *balia* (here indicating a midwife), and continued payments later for someone to do her laundry.[119] These last two activities—looking after pregnant women and doing laundry—were usually activities carried out by enslaved women, not ones carried out at a cost on behalf of enslaved people, emphasising how highly Beatrice was valued and how privileged her status was.

A final reason for Beatrice's high price was her highly specialised skill: she was an expert maker of quince jelly, the famous *marmelada* of Portugal, called *cotognata* or *cotognato* in Italian.[120] According to Pliny, the quince (*Cydonia oblonga*)[121] comes originally from Crete. The account journal explains that Beatrice had been purchased 'per le sue virtù' (because of her merits/talents),[122] and these lay in jam-making.[123] Slaves with special skills were much appreciated at courts across Europe. It is worth stressing again that many aspects of Roman slavery had continued in Renaissance Portugal and Italy and, as in Rome, slaves were frequently employed in positions of trust both inside and outside the household,[124] with enslaved women often being employed in what could be labelled jobs requiring particular trust, such as those involving food, or the care of children, or the preparation of medicines.[125] Queen Catarina is known to have had a sweet tooth, and in the 1520s there was a black pastry chef and confectioner in her kitchens.[126] While a roll of courtiers at the royal court in Almeirim dated 24 December 1545 listed those working in the queen's household

---

119. Ibid., 5r and 77r.

120. Campana uses the word *cotognata*. Like nearly all writers on late fifteenth- and sixteenth-century Lisbon, Giovanni Battista Confalonieri, *Grandezza e magnificenza*, pp. 190–91 and 254, praises Portuguese *cotognata*.

121. While known in Italian as 'pere cotogne', quinces are not pears even though they belong to the same subtribe Malinae that includes both apples and pears.

122. ASF, Misc. med. 713, 77r.

123. See the chapter on 'Confiseries et confitures' in Mohamed Ouerfelli, *Le Sucre: Production, commercialisation et usages dans la Méditerranée médiévale* (Leiden, 2008), pp. 581–95.

124. *Spartaco*, p. 152.

125. Jordan, 'Images of Empire', pp. 164–65.

126. Salvador Dias Arnaut, *A arte de comer em Portugal na Idade Média (Introdução a 'O livro de cozinha' da Infanta D. Maria de Portugal)* (Lisbon, 1986), pp. 54–55; Jordan, 'Images of Empire', pp. 157–58. The black pastry chef was called Domingos de Frorença.

separately, and twenty-nine are listed as cooks, there is no entry for jam-makers.[127] However, the two censuses of occupations in mid-sixteenth-century Lisbon, by Cristóvão Rodrigues de Oliveira in 1551 and João Brandão in 1552, respectively listed thirty women who made preserves,[128] and fifty women who made *marmelada*, or quince jelly[129]—which they apparently sold to people on ships going to India or Africa. Although there were occupations in Portugal that were carried out exclusively or almost exclusively by people of African descent, jam-making was not one of them, although it was gendered, being considered a female occupation. But other black jam-makers did exist in Portugal; the duke of Bragança had one, for example, aged thirty-five to forty and called Marqueza: 'Marqueza escraua preta conserueira.'[130] Portugal was renowned across Europe for its fruit and its preserves, which all visitors praised and bought.[131] Catarina is known to have prized quinces, and was regularly supplied by the friars at the Dominican convent of Nossa Senhora da Luz in Pedrógão Grande with rare and special fruit.[132] *Marmelada* was prized not only by the royal family,[133] however, but by anyone who could afford it. Certain streets in Lisbon were famous for the shops selling these preserves.

127. 'Rol da Gente Cortesã em Almeirim (1545)', transcribed by Pedro Pinto, *Fragmenta Historica—História, Paleografia e Diplomática*, 6 (2018), pp. 359–69 at 365–66.

128. Cristóvão Rodrigues de Oliveira, *Lisboa em 1551: Sumário em que brevemente se contêm algumas coisas assim eclesiásticas como seculares que há na cidade de Lisboa (1551)*, ed. José da Felicidade Alves (Lisbon, 1987), p. 99.

129. João Brandão, 'Majestade e grandezas de Lisboa em 1552', ed. Anselmo Braamcamp Freire and J. J. Gomes de Brito, *Archivo histórico portuguez*, 11 (1921), pp. 9–241 at 232.

130. Hallett, Monge and Senos, *De todas as partes*, pp. 60 and 284. Marquesa is reported as having visual impairment, p. 284.

131. For example, Niklas Lankmann, who was in Lisbon in 1451: Niklas Lankmann von Falkenstein, *Leonor de Portugal Imperatriz da Alemanha: Diário de viagem do embaixador Nicolau Lanckman de Valkenstein*, ed. Aires A. Nascimento (Lisbon, 1992), pp. 50, 51; and the Venetians Tron and Lippomano in 1581: 'Viagem a Portugal dos Cavaleiros Tron e Lippomani, 1580', in Alexandre Herculano, *Opúsculos*, vol. 6 (5th edn, Lisbon, n.d.), pp. 113–26 at 117.

132. Annemarie Jordan Gschwend, 'Rainha d'aquém e d'além-Mar: Jantar e cear à mesa de D. Catarina de Áustria na corte de Lisboa/Queen of the Seas and Overseas: Dining at Catherine of Austria's Table at the Lisbon Court', in Hugo Miguel Crespo, ed., *Á mesa do príncipe: Jantar e cear na corte de Lisboa (1500–1700); Prata, madrepérola, cristal de rocha e porcelana/At the Prince's Table: Dining at the Lisbon Court (1500–1700): Silver, Mother-of-pearl, Rock Crystal and Porcelain* (2018), pp. 10–48 at 17 and n. 16, at https://www.academia.edu/36297434/Hugo_Miguel _Crespo_ed_%C3%80_Mesa_do_Pr%C3%ADncipe_Jantar_e_Cear_na_Corte_de_Lisboa _1500_1700_At_the_Princes_Table_Dining_at_the_Lisbon_Court_1500_1700_Lisboa _AR_PAB_2018_pdf (accessed 8 June 2023).

133. See Freire, 'Inventário', p. 108 for her stores of *marmelada*.

While jam recipes might sound more like the stuff of nineteenth-century domestic fiction, when Campana purchased Beatrice he probably conceived of the project as one of commercial espionage, believing he was not just buying a slave, but buying the secret to making *marmelada*. This is made explicit in the little book of day-to-day expenses that accompanies the journal account, kept by Campana's servant Andrea da Doadola. The same day he bought her, he made a note of the money spent buying the ingredients for her to make *cotognata* (as he called it) 'per vedere quello sa fare' (to see what she can do), and the utensils that she would need in order to make it, thus making wholly transparent what her role was to be. The ingredients were recorded three times in the account journals, once in the main volume and twice in da Doadola's accounts, with slight variations, showing this was of great importance. The principal ingredients for Beatrice's recipe were the expected sugar, quince and almonds; the quantities were twelve *libre* of sugar to a hundred 'pere cotognie',[134] and one *libra* of almonds, costing respectively one ducat and eighty *maravedis*, sixty *maravedis*, and twenty *maravedis*.[135] The utensils purchased are a *calderetta*, a little cauldron or pan for cooking the *cotognata* costing one ducat and eighty *maravedis*, an iron spoon costing thirty *maravedis*,[136] and two *scatole* or flat boxes for keeping the *cotognata* once made, at a cost of forty *maravedis*.[137] In the two other variants, the purpose and materiality of the spoon were elaborated: it was to skim (*schiumare*) the *cotognata* as it cooked,[138] and it was said to be not of iron, but of copper.[139] Recipes for preserves make up twenty-four out of a total of fifty-nine in the famous *Livro de cozinha da Infanta D. Maria* from the end of the fifteenth and beginning of the sixteenth century, and included within these twenty-four are, for example, 'Marmelada de Catarina Ximenes' and 'Marmelada de D. Joana',[140] so Beatrice was in good company. The final question about Beatrice's recipe is why it might have been considered unique, as the ingredients

134. An early Italian recipe for *cotognata* is included in Quirico di Augustis, *Lumen apothecariorum cum certis expositionibus* (Venice, 1495), p. 37v. The papal chef Bartolomeo Scappi included several recipes for quinces in *Dell'arte del cuoco* (Venice, 1570), pp. 363v–364v.

135. ASF, Misc. med. 713, 8v, 57v and 62r.

136. On metal spoons in Portuguese cooking, see Paulo Dordio Gomes, 'O livro de cozinha da Infanta D. Maria', *Olaria*, 1 (1996), pp. 93–104 at 102 and 104.

137. ASF, Misc. med. 713, 57v.

138. Ibid., 62r.

139. Ibid., 8v.

140. Giacinto Manuppella, ed., *Livro de cozinha da Infanta Dona Maria, Códice Português I.E.33 da Biblioteca Nacional de Nápoles* (Lisbon, 1986), pp. 117–19 (recipe 51) and 125–27 (recipe 56); João Pedro Ferro, *Arqueologia dos hábitos alimentares* (Lisbon, 1996), pp. 88 and 93. On other jam

were the usual ones. One possibility is that Beatrice had an extra, unexpected ingredient in the *cotognata*—eggs—because in one recipe four eggs are also listed,[141] but these were perhaps used instead to make an accompaniment to the *cotognata* which would not have been eaten by itself.

Beatrice and Milizia reached Florence in 1548 and entered the service of Eleonora, and glimpses of them as they progressed through the Florentine phase of their life can be found in the Medici archives. The loss of many of the court records from Lisbon means that Beatrice comes into slightly sharper focus once she reaches Italy. Both mother and daughter are routinely included in lists of Eleonora's slaves in the Guardaroba records between 1548 and 1562, when Eleonora died. These records are immensely important not only for issues relating to dress and objects,[142] but also because they allow fine-grained analyses of the social gradations of status in quotidian use at a middle-ranking Italian court. A list drawn up on 7 January 1549 specifying Eleonora's female slaves who were to receive clothing, named Chaterina *grande*, Catherina *mora* (*grande* and *mora* are used here to distinguish between the two women), Fatima, Lucretia, Maria, Ysabella, Beatrice *mora*,[143] and Annicco.[144] Milizia was not included, perhaps because she was so young. Two of the enslaved women, including Beatrice, were described as 'mora', and as it is known that Beatrice was black, this shows that *mora* in these records could be used interchangeably with *nera*. Almost two years later, on 27 December 1550, eleven slaves are listed in a subgroup of women whose dress was provided by Eleonora. Beatrice was second on this list, and Milizia last, and it is likely that the list was arranged roughly hierarchically in terms of seniority or age (it cannot have been according to length of service, as

recipes, see João Pedro Gomes, 'Comida de rua na Lisboa moderna (sécs. XVI e XVII)', in *Diz-me o que comes: Alimentação antes e depois da cidade* (Lisbon, 2017), pp. 98–109 at 106–7.

141. ASF, Misc. med. 713, 8v.

142. Cf. Silleras-Fernández, '*Nigra sum*', pp. 551–52 and 564 for the expensive clothes ordered for slaves in the first decade of the fifteenth century at the court of Queen Maria de Luna of the crown of Aragon, and Ruth Matilda Anderson, *Hispanic Costume, 1480–1530* (New York, 1979), pp. 183, 200, 201, 211 and 244 for slaves' clothing at the Spanish court in the half century from 1480 to 1530.

143. There were two women named Beatrice in Eleonora's household: D. Beatrice Vacca, described as a 'matrona', who was one of her ladies-in-waiting, with an annual salary of seventy-two *fiorini* in 1553 (ASF, Depositeria generale, parte antica 393, 96 destra), and Beatrice from Portugal. Although there would have been no possibility of a mix up in person, in the documentary record it would have been possible, which is one reason why the enslaved Beatrice usually has 'mora' or 'nera' after her name.

144. ASF, Guardaroba medicea 15, 137r, 7 January 1548/9.

Beatrice had only been in Florence for a couple of years).[145] None of the slaves on this list is described as *nera* or *mora*, although it is known that several of them were black. All have Christian names, pointing to formal or informal baptism, apart from one who is called Fatima; another was obviously an orphan, as she has the name 'Maria dell'ospedale'. In November 1551 nine female slaves of the duchess are named. This time, Beatrice is first on the list, and Milizia is third from bottom; only Catherina *nera* is labelled as 'black'.[146] Finally, in a further, undated list, post-1551, ten slaves are named, but one has been crossed out. Once again, Beatrice heads the list, while Milizia is third from bottom. This fourth list labels Maria as 'negra' and Agia (a new slave, another one with a non-Christian name) as 'mora'.[147] In none of these lists is a place of origin specified or suggested for any slave. Africa is never mentioned. Aggregating the material from the four lists of slaves' names, it is clear that at least five were black: Beatrice, Milizia, Caterina/Caterinicca, Maria and Agia, and it is possible that all or nearly all of Eleonora's slaves were either black or of mixed ancestry. What is striking is the way that skin colour is signalled almost randomly in these records, now tagged onto one name, now another, with little consistency; and how *mora* and *nera* are used without distinction. So the question is, Why are they used at all? In the four lists, for example, Beatrice, who is known to be black, is never listed as 'Beatrice nera', but either as just 'Beatrice' or as 'Beatrice mora'. Later, however, in another Guardaroba entry from January 1556/7, she is identified by her black skin.[148] Also clear is that skin colour was fundamental to this system of labelling, and that provenance, at this point in the enslaved person's life at court, was inconsequential. Once again, however, there is no way of knowing whether a black skin was automatically and always known to have signified African ancestry in mid sixteenth-century Florence, nor whether in the Florentine mind the presence of black enslaved people in their city was realised to be a result of Portuguese imperialism.

Catching glimpses of Beatrice and Milizia as aspects of their lives at court are captured in the Guardaroba accounts permits analysis of how effectively

---

145. ASF, MdP 616, 434r. The slaves were Dianora, Beatrice, Maria, Catherina grande, Catherinicca, Anna, Ysabellicca, Fatima, Lucretia, Maria dell'ospedale and Militia.

146. ASF, Guardaroba medicea 23, 135r. The slaves were Beatrice, Maria, Chaterina grande, Catherina nera, Marticca, Fatima, Militia, Ysabellicca and Lucretia.

147. ASF, MdP 616, 436r. The slaves were Beatrice, Maria negra, Chaterina grande, Cateriniccha (crossed out), Anniccha, Isavelliccha, Lucreticcha, Militia, Fatima, Agia mora.

148. ASF, Guardaroba medicea 4, 72 (pages not folios).

these women of African ancestry who were part of the forced African diaspora in Europe—neither of whom had been born or lived in Africa—were incorporated into the fiercely hierarchical world of the Florentine court. Even though their membership of the corps of Eleonora's enslaved women proclaimed otherwise, their presence in Florence had been dissociated from Iberian imperialism, and their Portuguese past and provenance, let alone their links to Africa, were never commented on. Mother and daughter are also routinely mentioned as the intended recipients of new clothes when cloth of various sorts and colours, although mainly tan, is purchased for all of Eleonora's female slaves, documented clearly for the three years 1549, 1550 and 1551. Tan was one of the four main colours worn by Eleonora at the Medici court where, on account of the immediate political pre-history of Florence, the colour palette was usually restricted to red, grey, tan and white—unless special circumstances permitted variation.[149] This colour coding extended to the clothes considered appropriate for Eleonora's female slaves, who according to the Guardaroba account books, received a new set of work clothes at least once a year. On 7 January 1549 sixty *braccia* of 'panno di garbo tane' (tan-coloured woollen cloth)[150] were purchased to make eight *veste*, or simple one-layer dresses, for eight of her enslaved women. A different material was earmarked for a further slave, Dianora. Also purchased on the same day were ten *braccia* of tan *feltro* (felt) as interlining, twenty-six *canne* of 'pezzetta rossa' (red cloth),[151] to make eight *gammurrini* or simple long gowns, eight pairs of stockings (*calze*), a different *gammurrino* for enslaved Dianora, and thirty *braccia* of tan 'tela bottana' (cheap cloth, usually made from cotton, used here for lining) for the nine *veste* and nine *gammurrini* mentioned. [152] A *gamurra* was a simple form of long gown worn in

149. Roberta Orsi Landini, 'L'amore del lusso e la necessità della modestia: Eleonora fra sete e oro', in *Moda alla corte dei Medici: Gli abiti restaurati di Cosimo, Eleonora e don Garzia*, exh. cat., Galleria del costume di Palazzo Pitti, Florence (Florence, 1993), pp. 35–45 at 38.

150. According to Giuseppe Vittorio Parigini, *Il Tesoro del principe: Funzione pubblica e privata del patrimonio della famiglia Medici nel Cinquecento* (Florence, 1999), a *braccio* in the granducato of the sixteenth century was 0.583 metres.

151. According to Parigini, ibid., a *canna* in the granducato of the sixteenth century was 2.92 metres, making one *canna* the equivalent of five *braccia*. However, there is a difference between an architect's *canna* and a commercial or mercer's *canna*. For the latter, in Tuscany, the ratio of *canna* to *braccia* is said to be 1:4, which makes sense of the entry under discussion here, where 26 *canne* translate into 104 *braccia*. See Clarke, *Weights, Measures*, p. 76. I am grateful to Anna Teicher for help with this.

152. ASF, Guardaroba medicea 15, 137r, 7 January 1548/9.

fifteenth-century Florence that had become unfashionable by the sixteenth century,[153] and had passed into use instead by children, servants and slaves.[154] The use of the term *gammurrino*, a diminutive form of *gamurra*, for the slaves' gowns, accentuates further this process of infantilisation through dress. A few days later, on 19 January 1549, there is a payment for eighteen 'aghetti di filugello tane' or aglets of tan-coloured waste silk thread,[155] given to the same nine slaves. The material for new workaday clothes for eleven enslaved women listed on December 1550 is much the same: 108 *braccia* of 'panno tane stretto' or fine tan-coloured woollen cloth, twelve *braccia* of tan *feltro* as interlining, 'tele bottane tane' or cheap cloth for lining, and 'pezzetta rossa' for the 'gammurrini e calze'.[156] In an undated list probably from the early 1550s, the clothes assigned the ten named slaves are noted, but in their finished rather than raw state: 'una veste leonata accollata semplice' (a tawny dress with a high neck).[157] An outlier of a record from January 1557 documents the arrival of a chest from Pisa containing material to make into clothes for the enslaved women. The colours, tan and grey, remain the same, while the fabrics differ slightly: 'panno tane detti Carcassione' (tan woollen cloth known as Carcassonne) to make *sottane* or petticoats, and *fregio bigio*, a basic grey woollen cloth measured in *braccia* to make *gammurrini*, the simple long gowns.[158]

This group of entries in the *ricordanze* of the Guardaroba account books shows that Eleonora ordered the same clothes for eight out of nine of her enslaved women in order that they should be dressed identically. If not exactly livery— and livery (*livrea*) was mentioned in these account books separately[159]—this was akin to a type of uniform, and while it marked the enslaved women as one type of 'servant', the materials used for their clothes were not cheap and the garments themselves were much more sophisticated than those for slaves not

153. Carole Collier Frick, *Dressing Renaissance Florence: Families, Fortunes and Fine Clothing* (Baltimore, 2002), pp. 93, 162–63, 285 n. 37.

154. Roberta Orsi Landini, 'I singoli capi di abbigliamento', in Roberta Orsi Landini and Bruna Niccoli, *Moda a Firenze, 1540–1580: Lo stile di Eleonora di Toledo e la sua influenza* (Florence, 2005), pp. 76–169 at 95–96.

155. Luca Molà, *The Silk Industry of Renaissance Venice* (Baltimore, 2000), p. 404.

156. ASF, MdP 616, 435r.

157. Ibid., 436r. The slaves were Beatrice, Maria negra, Chaterina grande, Cateriniccha (crossed out), Anniccha, Isavelliccha, Lucreticcha, Militia, Fatima, Agia mora.

158. ASF, Guardaroba medicea 4, 70 (page not folio).

159. For example, ASF, Guardaroba medicea 23, 13v and 142v. Edelstein, 'Nobildonne napoletane', p. 302 writes of the livery of the servants of the ducal family.

working for courtly or patrician families. Slaves in artisanal homes would never have had new clothes made for them, and would have spent their days at best in cast-offs and hand-me-downs and at worst in rags. Above all, the clothes discussed here proclaimed the associated or reflected status the enslaved women received from being Eleonora's slaves and at the Medici court, and indicate the standard of living that they attained by virtue of being part of her household. Although enslaved, in some respects they can be considered fortunate within the hierarchy of enslaved people in Italy in general, because living standards at court were high and slaves were well looked after, both because they 'belonged' to Eleonora (and any perceived signs of lack of care or presentation would reflect badly on her) and because they were valuable: they were well dressed, well fed and had comfortable living conditions. The same was true of black enslaved women at Queen Catarina's court in Portugal, and Beatrice would already have been accustomed to this treatment.[160] Eleonora's female slaves as a group may have been differentiated by their clothing from other groups of women at the Medici court, such as the *cameriere* or chambermaids; these groups too, however, wore identical clothes to others in their group, such that they and their position at court could also be identified immediately by their clothing. There were a number of groupings or levels of women working for Eleonora, all wearing different 'uniforms' provided by their employer or owner. In addition to being marked by their dress throughout the day, their status difference was proclaimed by the seating plans in operation at mealtimes: the corps of enslaved women—just as the corps of chambermaids and the corps of *donzelle* or ladies-in-waiting at court—sat at their own separate table for meals.[161]

Not only that, but the status of these groups is reflected in the differences in material used, for example, for their tablecloths. At the Medici court, every single piece of cloth or clothing reflected by its quality the position of the group in the household relative to other groups. These differences could seem small, but were significant. The ladies-in-waiting were accorded Perugian-style tablecloths made from Rheims or very high quality linen 'tovaglia di rensa alla perugina'; the enslaved women were given Perugian-style tablecloths made from home-spun linen produced on the Medici's own estates: 'tovaglia nostrale alla perugina'; and the chambermaids—perhaps surprisingly—fared worst, and were given already used or second-hand home-produced cloth for theirs.[162] This

160. Saunders, *Social History*, p. 82; Jordan, 'Images of Empire', pp. 169–71.
161. ASF, Guardaroba medicea 15, 53v.
162. Ibid., 53v.

difference highlights the exalted position of the enslaved women in Eleonora's service vis-à-vis her chambermaids. The enslaved African women were rare and foreign, but more importantly they had been expensive and complicated to purchase, even if not all of them had Beatrice's particular skills. This is definitely an instance where rare meant more valuable. The chambermaids were also foreign in Eleonora's case, as they were Spanish and had accompanied her from Naples,[163] but would have been cheaper and easier to replace. Counter-intuitively, the differential legal status of the two groups produced the opposite of what might have been expected in any perception or evaluation of their worth: the free were not considered of higher status than the enslaved. But nor was the differential legal status wholly irrelevant, because the enslaved women's non-free status increased rather than diminished their value.

Status can be gauged also by a comparison of material possessions relating to levels of comfort. For instance, slaves at court slept on custom-made mattresses,[164] but rather than sleeping alone (a real luxury), they shared the mattress with various companions. Just as expensive hair mattresses had been purchased in Lisbon both for the two African boys from Cabo Verde and for Beatrice and Milizia, in order that they could sleep comfortably on the sea voyage to Italy, there is another mention once they reached Florence of the provision of an even more expensive mattress for the two relatively privileged enslaved women, in the records of the Guardaroba. Beatrice and Milizia arrived in Livorno on 5 March 1548, and on 2 June of that year the Guardaroba listed a bespoke set of sleeping accoutrements ordered by Eleonora and given to the two 'schiave more' (black slaves), consisting of a mattress of warp-cords and wool ('1° materasso di triliccio et lana'),[165] a feather pillow ('1° piumaccio') and a quilt made

163. Conti, *La prima reggia*, p. 273 and Bruce Edelstein, 'Ladies-in-Waiting in the Quartiere di Eleonora: The Iconography of Stradano's Ceiling in the Sala di Gualdrada', in Elisabetta Insabato, Rosalia Manno, Ernestina Pellegrini and Anna Scattigno, eds, *Tra archivi e storia: Scritti dedicati ad Alessandra Contini Bonacossi*, 2 vols (Florence, 2018), 1, pp. 127–55 at 128 and n. 3.

164. For precisely the same reasons of status, Robert Dudley, the earl of Leicester, had purchased a mattress for his 'blackamoor' in England in 1583: Simon Adams, ed., *Household Accounts and Disbursement Books of Robert Dudley, Earl of Leicester* (Cambridge, 1995), p. 178. On the cost and value of mattresses, cf. Paula Hohti, 'The Innkeeper's Goods: The Use and Acquisition of Household Property in Sixteenth-Century Siena', in Michelle O'Malley and Evelyn Welch, eds, *The Material Renaissance* (Manchester, 2007), pp. 242–59 at 249–50.

165. On mattresses, see Brendan Dooley, *A Mattress Maker's Daughter: The Renaissance Romance of Don Giovanni de' Medici and Livia Vernazza* (Cambridge, MA, 2014), pp. 70 and 348 n. 14: the best mattresses were made of the wool from castrated sheep.

from new cloth, either linen or cotton ('1° coltrone di tela nuova').[166] The precision of detail in the order reveals the level of engagement of Eleonora, and the quality of the items emphasises how the value and worth of Beatrice and Milizia were being turned by the duchess into an outward-facing attribute. Furthermore, on 26 February 1546/7 there is an entry for 270 *libbre* of *capecchio* (flax or hemp),[167] for stuffing mattresses (in the plural) at Poggio for the pages,[168] who numbered seventeen in July the previous year.[169] A further entry on 22 March 1546/7 recorded twenty-five *libbre* of flax or hemp for stuffing one mattress (in the singular) for the female slaves,[170] who numbered seven or eight—although it could have been an order for a replacement or an additional mattress. Most enslaved people—just like many of the urban and rural poor at this date—would have been fortunate to sleep on mattresses stuffed with straw, rather than new, expensive, custom-made ones. Enslaved people are not mentioned in a late fifteenth-century treatise, often thought to be addressed to the court of Urbino, describing the management of a *casa* or household, yet the same sorts of topics arise as with Eleonora's household: what and where members of the household should eat, what clothes they should be given, how often they should receive new ones, where they should sleep, how many people should sleep in one room, and what form their mattresses should take.[171]

A different process, that of Eleonora saving money by taking advantage of a good deal, can be discerned in an entry of 12 November 1551. On that day 70½ *braccia* of tan 'panno accordellato', or medium quality wool cloth, ribbed or corded, are bought from the *rigattiere* or second-hand dealer Agnolo Fierini, of which 54½ were used to make nine *gammurre*, or simple long gowns, for Beatrice, Maria, Catherina grande, Catherina nera, Marticca, Fatima, Militia, Isabellicca and Lucretia. The *sottane* or petticoats for the nine enslaved women

---

166. ASF, Guardaroba medicea 15, 27r. The most likely reading of this entry is that the mattress etc. were for Beatrice and Milizia, but it is possible although unlikely that they merely picked up the items on behalf of Eleonora. One strong argument against this second reading is that Miliza would only have been five, and if she had not been the recipient of the goods, she would not have been named as the courier.

167. The word used is *coperchio*, probably a version of *capechio* or *capecchio*. Cf. ASF, MdP 1177, 661r, where a 'materasso di capechio' is mentioned. See also ASF, Guardaroba medicea 4, 73 (page not folio) where a mattress 'di chappechio' is mentioned alongside one of wool.

168. ASF, Guardaroba medicea 12, 101r.

169. Ibid., 35r.

170. Ibid., 101r.

171. Sabine Eiche, ed., *Ordine et officij de casa de lo illustrissimo Signor Duca de Urbino* (Urbino, 1999), pp. 107–11.

made at the same time were instead made of new material bought in the normal way—not from a second-hand dealer—and cost more than the gowns.[172] It is known that Eleonora had habits of frugality, and was concerned both to spend and to waste as little as possible; clearly this tendency extended to buying second-hand cloth and other items. Florence had a thriving second-hand culture of exchange and resale, with over seventy used-goods shops operating in 1561,[173] but many people also acted as private brokers.[174] This cloth may have had a previous owner or owners, but it had not been made into clothes previously, because it was still all in one length. The acquisition of such a piece of cloth from a second-hand dealer by the Guardaroba for the Medici household shows that there was no negative association attached to purchases of this sort, and that Eleonora would consider purchases that were suitable to her needs wherever she found them. This untouched but previously owned cloth met the requirements for the tan material needed to fashion dresses for her enslaved women. The cost of these 54½ *braccia* of material from the second-hand dealer is not recorded, but elsewhere Eleonora paid 770 lire for 88 *braccia* and 810 lire for 108 *braccia* of material to be made into clothes for her enslaved women—and cost clearly mattered to the parsimonious duchess.[175]

Eleonora's parsimony extended to the use of gold thread, weaving and sewing, a proportion of which took place in-house. The enslaved women were conceptualised not merely as so-called exotic adornments who increased Eleonora's prestige, but were in addition workers whose labour could be usefully directed. This was a working court, heavily engaged in the feminine arts of needlework. Eleonora was interested in clothes and fashion, and the female members of her household—whatever their primary role—were all assigned secondary roles in sewing at some level, whether highly skilled or a form of manual labour. Her female entourage included seamstresses, a weaver,[176] and a cutter (whose main role was as *balia* or nurse to Eleonora's children).[177] One of her Spanish ladies-in-waiting, Ysabel de Renoso, made exquisite snoods and

---

172. ASF, Guardaroba medicea 23, 135r.

173. Ann Matchette, 'Credit and Credibility: Used Goods and Social Relations in Sixteenth-Century Florence', in Michelle O'Malley and Evelyn Welch, eds, *The Material Renaissance* (Manchester, 2007), pp. 225–41 at 230.

174. Matchette, 'To Have and Have Not', p. 709.

175. ASF, Guardaroba medicea 23, 135r, ASF, MdP 616, 434v and 435r.

176. Orsi Landini, 'L'amore del lusso', pp. 43–44.

177. Bruna Niccoli, 'Eleonora di Toledo, duchessa di Toscana, nella storia e nella leggenda', in Roberta Orsi Landini and Bruna Niccoli, *Moda a Firenze, 1540–1580: Lo stile di Eleonora di Toledo e la sua influenza* (Florence, 2005), pp. 14–21 at 19.

partlets out of gold thread for Eleonora.[178] In 1546, before the arrival of Beatrice and Milizia, Ysabel had also been occupied in making linen shirts, partlets and coifs for the seven enslaved women in the household;[179] these items included linen undergarments and accessories that were marks of civility and fashion. Yet again this signalled the unusual and contradictory situation of the enslaved women. This is an interesting example of enslaved women benefiting from what would usually be considered treatment not suited to their subjugated role, accentuated many times in this case because of the very high status of the woman carrying out the needlework from which they would then reap the rewards. The expected relationship between slave and lady-in-waiting was that the slave would work for the *donzella*, not the other way round. Being a slave at court was not in itself an occupation, but a position, and Eleonora expected the enslaved women, even those like Beatrice the jam-maker, never to be idle, but to be as busy with their needles, scissors, looms or hands as the rest of her household (and indeed she too formed part of the sewing bee).[180] So when not directed to other tasks, these women had sewing or winding/unwinding duties to perform. These could take the form of the turning of a raw material into a differently arranged finished product: they were given 'rese bianco' (perhaps yarn from a strong white linen cloth, because it is sold by weight) in order to make *pantiere* (girdles or stomach warmers), and on another occasion they were given it to turn into *ragne* (netting) for Eleonora.[181]

Beyond buying second-hand cloth and putting the female members of her household to work sewing and twisting, there is evidence of another strategy of saving employed by Eleonora in relation to her enslaved women (and the rest of her entourage, of which they were a microcosm): recycling or repurposing cloth or clothes. Recycling and repurposing were relatively common, yet this example stands out. An entry on 14 March 1551 records that the game of *trucco* (a kind of early billiards)[182] was dismantled, and the green cloth from

---

178. Orsi Landini, 'I singoli capi', pp. 119–20 and 137–38; and 'Il guardaroba di Eleonora di Toledo', in Roberta Orsi Landini and Bruna Niccoli, *Moda a Firenze, 1540–1580: Lo stile di Eleonora di Toledo e la sua influenza* (Florence, 2005), pp. 200–235 at 210 and 213.

179. ASF, Guardaroba medicea 12, 34v and 36v.

180. Roberta Orsi Landini, 'Sarti e ricamatori', in Roberta Orsi Landini and Bruna Niccoli, *Moda a Firenze, 1540–1580: Lo stile di Eleonora di Toledo e la sua influenza* (Florence, 2005), pp. 170–79 at 178.

181. ASF, Guardaroba medicea 21, 104v, 12 January 1549/50, and 107v, 23 January 1549/50.

182. Francesco Petrucci, 'Il gioco del "Trucco" nel Palazzo Chigi di Ariccia: Una rarità da Wunderkammer nella dimora barocca', *Il giornale dell'arte*, 5 June 2020, online edition,

it was made into clothes for Milizia and Grillo, described here as 'negri', or blacks.[183] It is likely that both were children. Estimated to be aged four in October 1547, Milizia must have been seven or eight in March 1551. Recycling from green cloth, probably a form of woollen baize, covering a large wooden structure like a billiard table, but bigger, similarly kitted out with ivory balls and wooden mallets, into clothes for two black children in the entourage of the duchess of Florence, is remarkable on several fronts. Repurposing of material usually took the form of recycling old clothes into newer ones, or cutting them into smaller pieces of material, but there are also more poignant examples of nuns' vestition dresses, for example, being reworked as altar cloths in convents.[184] Cloth was cloth, after all, and its former associations could be wiped by a different cultural context, so the baize's previous existence—although presumably known at court—could be irrelevant. The vibrant green colour, though, must have retained its meaning. Although green was one of the four liturgical colours, blue and green were chosen as colours for clothes at the Medici court only in 'exceptional circumstances', and green was associated above all with children and young people.[185] The commission of two sets of clothes for a girl and a boy in a matching colour is unique in these account books, and signals that in some sense the two children were conceived of as a pair, and that these clothes may have been a form of costume. Perhaps, like the black children at Isabella d'Este's court, they had been stereotyped as inherently amusing, and therefore natural entertainers, and the antics of these children in their matching clothes would have been viewed as diverting.[186] Grillo was a nickname rather than a Christian name, meaning primarily cricket or grasshopper, but it could also on occasion mean whim, caprice or fantasy,[187] so once again it could be classified as a *nome parlante* (expressive name). It could either refer to his agility in movement or ability to make big

---

https://www.ilgiornaledellarte.com/articoli/il-gioco-del-trucco-nel-palazzo-chigi-di-ariccia/133407.html (accessed 25 April 2023).

183. ASF, Guardaroba medicea 23, 77v.

184. K.J.P. Lowe, *Nuns' Chronicles and Convent Culture in Renaissance and Counter-Reformation Italy* (Cambridge, 2003), p. 234.

185. Roberta Orsi Landini, 'Lo stile di Eleonora', in Roberta Orsi Landini and Bruna Niccoli, *Moda a Firenze, 1540–1580: Lo stile di Eleonora di Toledo e la sua influenza* (Florence, 2005), pp. 22–45 at 28.

186. Luzio and Renier, 'Buffoni'; Lowe, 'Stereotyping', p. 35; Lowe, 'Isabella d'Este', pp. 65–76.

187. See the entry under *grillo* in Pianigiani, *Vocabolario etimologico*, 1, p. 646.

leaps, or to his blackness (as field crickets are black)—both of which would have emphasised his attributes—or it could inscribe the putative, belittling rationale for acquisition of the 'owner' onto the boy.

Although there is no known representation of Beatrice, it may be that in addition to documentary traces, as with various other Africans or people of mixed ancestry, there is a visual record of her daughter Milizia's presence at the Medici court, in her case fittingly in connection with sewing activities.[188] Johannes Stradanus (Jan van der Straet, known as Giovanni Stradano in Italy) painted the *tondo* in the Sala di Penelope in Eleonora's apartments on the second floor of Palazzo Vecchio (Plate 34). It was one of a series of four compositions in her apartments celebrating exemplary women from Greek mythology, the Old Testament and Roman and Florentine history.[189] The choice of Penelope,[190] and the scene in general, have long been believed to represent roles and attributes associated with Eleonora;[191] it is probable too—as with many other Florentine historical scenes—that recognisable portraits have been inserted into the group.[192] One, the young girl on the far right of the scene, next to the woman with the distaff, is represented not just with a darker skin tone than the rest of the figures, but with different dress and different hair (Plate 35). Nor is the skin colour an accident of the light or shade, because in the pen and brown ink preparatory drawing or *modello* for the *tondo*, now in the École des Beaux-Arts in Paris,[193] the body of the same girl is covered with a blue wash, extremely suggestive of an identification with Milizia (Plate 36). Milizia was of mixed ancestry—her mother was black and her father white—so the skin colour presented here would fit. None of the other women in the central part of the

188. I am indebted to Lizzy Currie for this important observation, and for discussing the drawing and *tondo* with me.

189. Andrea M. Gáldy, 'The Duke as Cultural Manager: Institutionalization and Entrepreneurship', in Alessio Assonitis and Henk Th. van Veen, eds, *A Companion to Cosimo I de' Medici* (Leiden, 2022), pp. 411–68 at 431.

190. Lizzy Currie also notes that there is a Florentine precedent for showing black figures in Penelope's entourage, in the Apollonio di Giovanni, *The Adventures of Ulysses* at the Art Institute in Chicago, where two black boys on horseback are guiding Ulysses and Penelope's mobile throne.

191. Niccoli, 'Eleonora di Toledo', p. 21 and fig. 3, with the subject of the *tondo* described as an 'ideal reflection of the life which took place in the duchess's apartments'.

192. Lowe, 'Fifteenth-Century Flesh and Blood Black Slave', pp. 62–63.

193. On the sketch, see Rick Scorza, 'A "modello" by Stradanus for the "Sala di Penelope" in the Palazzo Vecchio', *The Burlington Magazine*, 126, no. 976 (July 1984), pp. 433–37.

drawing appears with a blue wash.[194] The girl in the *tondo* is small of stature, but she could be a young, just post-pubescent teenager, as she has breasts. In 1547 Milizia was four years old, so in 1561 when Stradanus supposedly started painting these scenes, she would have been eighteen, but the artist may have changed her age and made her look younger. Finally, the girl is shown in a familiar classicising pose for Africans, with one breast bared. This accumulation of detail consistent with the representation of people of mixed ancestry, is distinctive and wide-ranging enough to make the hypothesis that this is indeed a portrait of Milizia rather plausible. A comparison of the preparatory drawing and the painted *tondo* is instructive. In the preliminary drawing many of the women are bare-breasted or are dressed in clothing accentuating their breasts, which could be interpreted as a standard sixteenth-century Italian version of the clothing of classical antiquity. Covering them up in the painted version in Eleonora's apartments adds weight to the argument that the scene is an allegory of Eleonora and her female entourage; especially if recognisable portraits were included, decorum would have demanded this. The girl on the right is the only figure who remains in draped robes in the painted version, while the others are represented with touches of sixteenth-century fashions, such as undershirts—which could be construed as yet another indicator of her ethnicity.

According to Spanish custom, Eleonora's virtue as a model of industry, busy with weaving and sewing, was regal,[195] and matched Penelope's, and if the identification of Milizia in the *tondo* is correct, Milizia's inclusion in this scene also alludes to and augments the young girl's virtue by association. The likelihood of this hypothesis being correct is additionally strengthened by the noticeable predilection at the Medici court for commissioning likenesses of both male and female members of the household: two of the Spanish women in Eleonora's entourage, Ysabel de Renoso and Juana Guevara (in Italian, Giovanna Ghevara), have been identified in portraits by Bronzino, his workshop or a follower.[196]

Turning back to Beatrice, there is, unfortunately, no record relating to her jam-making prowess after her arrival in Florence. Maybe she continued with

194. Two servants or enslaved women in the background who carry woven platters or loads on their head are similarly represented in a blue wash, and one of them is shown with an exposed breast. In the final painting, these two figures have been changed.

195. Andrea M. Gáldy, 'Tuscan Concerns and Spanish Heritage in the Decoration of Duchess Eleonora's Apartment in the Palazzo Vecchio', *Renaissance Studies*, 20.3 (2006), pp. 293–319 at 312.

196. Elizabeth Pilliod, 'Cosimo I de' Medici: Lineage, Family and Dynastic Ambitions', in *The Medici: Portraits and Politics, 1512–1570*, ed. Keith Christiansen and Carlo Falciani, exh. cat., The Metropolitan Museum, New York (New York, 2021), pp. 120–59 at 114–16, and cat. no. 27.

it, or perhaps Eleonora redirected her towards other tasks. There is one stray entry suggesting that Beatrice was allowed to carry out tasks in the innermost sanctum of Eleonora's realm, her bedchamber. In January 1557 a bedwarmer, presumably a copper or brass one, was disbursed to Beatrice 'a servici per la S.ra duchesa' (to be at the service of the duchess); that is, Beatrice was given custody of the bedwarmer, ready to put it to use when Eleonora required it.[197] The January date reflects its seasonal employment. Further evidence that Beatrice was a trusted and senior member of Eleonora's entourage—now rather an unlikely-seeming position for a slave, perhaps, but one that was very familiar in ancient Rome—comes from Eleonora's books of expenditure. Eleonora lived much of her life surrounded by groups of women who worked for her, from *donzelle* to slaves. In each group, she leant more heavily on some individuals than others, entrusting them, for instance, with the distribution of payments for services or to allocate as charity. In 1561 and 1562 she turned to Beatrice. Trust in financial matters lay at the heart of a huge variety of Renaissance Italian transactions and was a cornerstone of social relations, so it is important to find that the duchess of Florence trusted her enslaved women to carry out financial transactions, however small, enmeshing them securely in court life.[198] On 18 April 1561 three *lire*, six *soldi* and eight *denari* were disbursed to Beatrice, who gave it in cash to Pellegrino da Barga to take to the shrine of the Madonna of Montenero, a fourteenth-century miraculous Madonna outside Livorno, in order to pray for the duchess of Ferrara.[199] The duchess of Ferrara was Lucrezia, one of Cosimo and Eleonora's daughters, who had been betrothed to and later married Alfonso d'Este as a replacement bride when her older sister

197. ASF, Guardaroba medicea 4, p. 72.

198. On this, see Gene Brucker, '*Fede* and *fiducia*: The Problem of Trust in Italian History, 1300–1500', in Gene Brucker, *Living on the Edge in Leonardo's Florence: Selected Essays* (Berkeley, CA, 2005), pp. 83–103.

199. ASF, Scrittoio delle possessioni 4139, 114 sinistra: 'E a dì 18 detto [Aprile] lire tre soldi vi denari viii [. . .] pagati alla Beatrice nera portò Pellegrino da Barga contanti per portare alla Madonna di Montenero per fare oratione per la duchessa di Ferrara'. On Montenero, see D. Emiliano Lucchesi, *La Madonna di Montenero e il suo santuario nella storia, nell'arte, nella pietà cristiana* (Livorno, 1928), pp. 26–29 (for the stewardship of the gesuati), p. 197 (for devotion of the grand dukes towards Montenero—although the records of visits under the gesuati in the sixteenth century are not extant) and pp. 235–36 (for attributions to various fourteenth-century painters). On the miraculous Madonna, see Luigi Servolini, 'L'arte nel santuario di Montenero', *Liburni civitas*, 7.1 (1934), pp. 30–53 at 30–33; and Giorgio Mandalis, 'Iconografia e iconologia della Madonna di Montenero', *Erba d'Arno*, 123 (2011), pp. 42–54 (at 51–53 for the attribution to Jacopo di Michele detto il Gera).

Maria died in 1557. Three years later, on 21 April 1561, she too died, of tuberculosis;[200] payment for these prayers by her pious and despairing mother must have been in response to news of her worsening condition and impending demise. On another occasion, on 2 October 1562, Beatrice was given four *lire* to reimburse a *contadino* (peasant) who had given Eleonora *ravviggiuoli*, or soft cheeses, at Poggio.[201]

Rather than references to occupation, however, there are indications that Beatrice's marital status might have changed. Often Beatrice was labelled 'mora' or 'nera' to distinguish her from another woman named Beatrice (or Beatrice Vaccha) who was also part of Eleonora's household. On occasion, the two Beatrices are mentioned in the same sentence, making their individual identification necessary (Fig. 9); in the absence of a distinguishing surname, this was achieved by the use of the skin colour descriptor *nera* for the Portuguese Beatrice.[202]

But in addition to labels relating to skin colour, Beatrice appeared on various lists with a surname, Bottiglia, and was thus described as 'Beatrice Bottiglia mora' in one household roll of 1 February 1564 and 'Beatrice Bottiglia nera' in another of 11 June of the same year. She was included in a group of women previously in the service of Eleonora who were entitled to a pension and received a payment of one *fiorino* a month.[203] In the household roll of 1574–75 relating to Cosimo, Beatrice (described as 'Beatrice nera')—unlike some of her former co-enslaved colleagues who were then living in convents, presumably as corrodians, such as Maria nera in the Annalena and Lucia nera in San Giuseppe, and unlike Fatima, described as 'già schiava' (formerly enslaved), who was 'kept by Vaga' ([la] tiene il Vaga)—was alive but living outside an institution, and she was her own woman. The downside of that was that her pension was smaller: she received only one *scudo* a month,[204] whereas those in convents received two and a half or three.[205]

---

200. On Lucrezia, see Gabrielle Langdon, *Medici Women: Portraits of Power, Love and Betrayal from the Court of Duke Cosimo I* (Toronto, 2006), pp. 98, 99 and 137–45, and n. 28 on pp. 280–81 re Lucrezia's decline and death from tuberculosis.

201. ASF, Scrittoio delle possessioni 4139, 282 sinistra. Cosimo apparently loved these cheeses (personal communication from Alessio Assonitis, 2 November 2021).

202. ASF, Scrittoio delle possessioni 4138, 47 sinistra.

203. ASF, MdP 616, 262r and 267v. The household roll of 1553 is partially published in Conti, *La prima reggia*, pp. 271–73, but it does not include the slaves in the household.

204. In the intervening years, the *scudo* had gradually replaced the *fiorino*: see Carlo M. Cipolla, *La moneta a Firenze nel Cinquecento* (Bologna, 1987), pp. 24–26.

205. ASF, MdP 616, 357v, 20 April 1574.

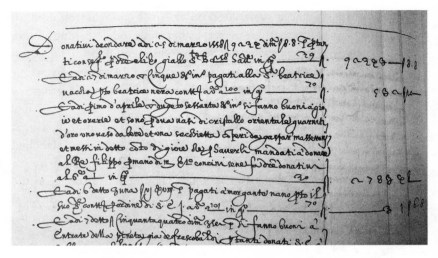

FIGURE 9. Florence, Archivio di stato, Scrittoio delle regie possessioni 4138, 47 sinistra, 'Beatrice Vaccha' and 'Beatrice nera'. By permission of the Italian Ministry of Culture/Archivio di stato di Firenze. Photo: Kate Lowe

Eleonora routinely arranged marriages and provided dowries for her ladies-in-waiting,[206] and presumably, like other rulers, for her servants; but slaves, even court slaves who in most other respects led rather privileged lives, for obvious reasons were not usually encouraged or allowed to marry. But if Beatrice had married, who was her husband? It would be highly unusual for a slave to marry a non-slave and still keep their position at court. Campana's account journal may provide an answer to this conundrum, because on 30 October 1547 there is an entry recording payment of taxes and expenses in connection with the embarkation of Beatrice, Milizia, two chests of porcelain, thirteen barrels of jams, nine 'ghaline d'India' and a civet cat, onto the caravel of Nicolo Bottiglia from Genoa,[207] which was going to take them from Lisbon to Cadiz.[208] Bottiglia is not a Tuscan name,[209] and the new account journal

206. Vincenzo Fedeli, 'Relazione di Firenze' (1561), in Eugenio Albèri, ed., *Relazioni degli ambasciatori veneti al senato*, 13 vols (Florence, 1839–63), ser. 2, vol. 1 (1839), pp. 321–83 at 352–53; Marcello Fantoni *La corte del granduca: Forme e simboli del potere mediceo fra Cinque e Seicento* (Rome, 1994), p. 111.

207. Unfortunately, no trace of Nicolo or the Bottiglia has yet been found in Genoa.

208. ASF, Misc. med. 713, 5r.

209. There is one mention in the online list of 'I blasoni delle famiglie toscane nella raccolta Ceramelli Papiani' at the Archivio di stato di Firenze website, https://www.archiviodistato.firenze.it/asfi /strumenti/i-blasoni-delle-famiglie-toscane-nella-raccolta-ceramelli-papiani (accessed 25 April 2023)

information at least provides a plausible candidate with the correct surname, and provides a cast-iron meeting place for Beatrice and Nicolo. Just as in Roman times slaves did not have the right to marry but could live in a de facto marriage (*contubernium* as opposed to *conubium*) if their owners permitted it,[210] so too Eleonora could have allowed Beatrice to 'marry' and take Bottiglia's name even though Beatrice would still have had to stay enslaved at court. But this is not very likely. Given the date of the two mentions of 'Beatrice Bottiglia' in 1564, it is more likely that she married Bottiglia after Eleonora's death and her own manumission in 1562. It was customary for domestic slaves on the Italian peninsula to be freed on the death of their owner, or at the very least to be given a roadmap and timeline towards manumission,[211] and Beatrice and Milizia were manumitted and left the court,[212] along with Eleonora's other slaves, in Eleonora's will of 16 December 1562.[213] Eleonora also left them quite substantial sums of money in order to secure their futures: Beatrice was bequeathed nine hundred *scudi*, and Milizia, described still as Beatrice's daughter, seven hundred. This too was standard practice for god-fearing owners who believed in the power of testamentary manumission to award them pious credit, thus ensuring that former members of their household would have sufficient money to live decently (or to launch themselves in a career if youngish and male) and not end up in poverty in their old age.[214] After Eleonora's death, Beatrice was paid a small additional monthly pension by the Medici for the rest of her life—and she was still alive in 1579, so she lived over thirty years in Florence, for at least seventeen of which she

---

210. Matthew J. Perry, 'Condizioni di vita e di lavoro delle schiave nell'antica Roma', in *Spartaco: Schiavi e padroni a Roma*, ed. Claudio Parisi Presicce, Orietta Rossini and Lucia Spagnuolo, exh. cat., Museo dell'Ara Pacis, Rome (Rome, 2017), pp. 62–71 at 66.

211. See Verlinden, *L'Esclavage*, 2, pp. 241–50, 540–49 and 696–704; Epstein, *Speaking of Slavery*, pp. 89–90 and 171–72.

212. Pieraccini, *Stirpe de' Medici*, 2.1, p. 59.

213. ASF, MdP 5922A, inserto 14, 132r. The will gives the additional, unusual information regarding where this money will come from: in Beatrice's case, it will come from 'tasse de comuni' and in Milizia's from 'Pisa': ibid., unnumbered folio (but perhaps 135r). The original notarial version of this will, ASF, NA 7502 (ser Filippo di Piero di Giovanni), 71r–73v, has now been published in Nicoletta Baldini, 'Il testamento di Eleonora Álvarez de Toledo duchessa di Toscana', in *Eleonora di Toledo duchessa di Toscana: I soggiorni in terra d'Arezzo*, ed. Nicoletta Baldini, exh. cat., Oratorio dei Santi Lorentino e Pergentino, Arezzo (Arezzo, 2022), pp. 92–96; the bequests to Beatrice and Milizia are at 93.

214. Lowe, 'Visible Lives', pp. 412–52 at 421–23.

received a pension.[215] After 1564 there was no further mention of Nicolo or any other Bottiglia (but neither was Beatrice mentioned in another record until 1574, so there is a ten year gap), indicating that at some point in this ten-year period Beatrice's husband must have died. Milizia, who was only nineteen in 1562, disappears from sight; she could have died, but it is more probable that she took the money and married.

Although patchy, these partial biographies show that Beatrice and Milizia were included in myriad ways in the activities of the Medici court, in terms of work environment and life beyond work. Neither their African or mixed ancestry, nor their initial slave status, put them outside the regular bounds of Florentine life. However, their relatively comfortable and full lives were almost diametrically opposed to the hellishness of Caro Costa's, who had arrived in Florence from Lisbon on the same boat as the two enslaved females, having been purchased by the same owner or owners. His experiences as a black enslaved person meant he was forced to operate in a sphere that forever excluded him from normality. These narratives of Africans, or people of African descent born in Europe, whose enslaved lives moved them from Lisbon to Florence (and in one case at least to freedom) can be traced because of the exceptional records in the Archivio di stato in Florence. Leaving aside everything else about them, they are good examples of how the forced African diaspora precipitated by the creation of the Portuguese trading empire had an impact on the Italian peninsula, even if it was indirect. But even the cases of Beatrice and Milizia cannot facilitate the unpicking, at this distance, of the question whether Tuscans at the time perceived or understood the link between Portuguese imperialism and slavery.

Conclusion: Buying and Collecting, Availability and Choice

One of the most pressing questions about Bastiano Campana's buying trip concerns his choice of goods. Apart from the specified items of galley slaves and animals, was he working to order from a list or was the choice of purchase up to him? Either is possible, as is a mixture of the two. Just as with Alberto Cantino's

---

215. ASF, MdP 616, inserto 19, 262r (1 Feb 1563/4), 267v (11 June 1564), 307r (undated, but possibly 1574, according to the information on Bia, the Medici Archive Project database, http://bia.medici.org/DocSources/), 357v (1574), 372r (1579).

mission to the Iberian peninsula examined in chapter 2, the rationale for Bastiano Campana's trip has, to a certain extent, to be reconstructed from its outcomes. Given Campana's inexperience, and the fact that he would have been a novice at gauging the value of the goods he was acquiring, it would make more sense if he had been buying to order. His declaration at the beginning of the account journal also points to this, referring to 'the present voyage to Spain that I will make on the orders of the duke of Florence in connection with grain, galley slaves and other goods for which I have been commissioned',[216] but places the emphasis on grain and slaves rather than on the rest, whereas much of the rest is what is predominantly of interest here. The other goods could have been indicated, but in a more general way. As he was leaving Lisbon for India in 1582, Filippo Sassetti was sent five hundred *scudi* by Francesco de' Medici (as well as three hundred *scudi* by Francesco on behalf of Francesco's brother, Cardinal Ferdinando), with which to buy 'qualche galanteria di cose rare et che giudicherete degne d'esser viste di qua, rimettendo tutto alla discretione et arbitrio vostro' (a delightful selection of rare things that you deem worthy of being seen here, leaving everything to your discretion and judgement).[217] But another letter reveals that Ferdinando, unlike his brother, had clearly specified at least part of what he wanted.[218] No extant letter from Cosimo or one of his secretaries to Bastiano Campana telling him what to buy has been found; unusually, there may be a known reason for this, as four hundred of Cosimo's letters to Campana were soaked ('inmolarono') or lost altogether in the 1597 flood in Florence, according to Campana's son, who donated twenty-four of those that survived back to the Medici. These twenty-four are now incorporated into the Mediceo del Principato collection in the Archivio di stato in Florence.[219] Campana's instructions, if they ever existed in written form, could have been victims of this inundation. But given that Campana's trip appears to have been a success and to have introduced goods from the Portuguese and Spanish empires unobtainable on the Italian peninsula into Florence, it would have been slightly bizarre if the Medici had not sought to replicate this success by commissioning another shopping trip to the

216. ASF, Misc. med. 713, Giornale e ricordanze, 1r (but unnumbered).

217. ASF, MdP 259, 88r, Francesco de' Medici to Filippo Sassetti, 22 December 1582. On these purchases, see Barbara Karl, '"Galanterie di cose rare . . .": Filippo Sassetti's Indian Shopping List for the Medici Grand Duke Francesco and His Brother Cardinal Ferdinando', *Itinerario*, 32.3 (2008), pp. 23–41, esp. 24.

218. Sassetti, *Lettere*, p. 451.

219. ASF, MdP 606, 1r. The job lot of twenty-four letters, a *rescritto* and a *relazione* runs from 1r to 61r.

same destination. It is therefore reassuring to find that twenty years later, on 28 August 1567, Cardinal Ferdinando de' Medici set out in a *memoriale* to Giovan Battista Uguccioni the goods he wanted Uguccioni to procure from him in 'Hispania.'[220] Hispania was the old Roman name given to the whole of the Iberian peninsula and here indicated both Spain and Portugal. There are twenty-five items on this list, including spices and aromatic ingredients such as musk, civet, ginger and pepper. Of these, five important ones are items the same as or similar to those Campana had brought to Cosimo twenty years earlier: an ivory tusk ('un dente d'avorio'), four or six of the most beautiful and biggest *chiocciole* of mother-of-pearl for making cups or saltcellars ('taze o saliera'), two *sagui* (that is, marmosets or tamarins—Ferdinando thought it necessary to explain that these were a type of small monkey), fans and a tortoiseshell *cassetta*. The balance of items favoured edible goods (such as coconuts) and raw materials over manufactured ones, although three to four thousand fish hooks from Toledo and Valladolid, and one dozen gloves from Spain and more precisely another dozen from Ocaña also appeared on the list. Most items were requested by weight, occasionally by container, in flasks (*fiaschi*) or a ceramic jar (*alberello*).

In contradistinction to the entries in Campana's account journal, these instructions show that Ferdinando was a knowledgeable shopper or collector and that provenance and authenticity were important factors for him that needed to be taken into account before purchases were made. Twelve of the twenty-five items specified provenance, even if that provenance was sometimes imprecise or vague (e.g., 'di Levante')[221]—a feather painting should come from Peru, for example, and 'acqua di fior di canella' (cinnamon fruit or berry water, perhaps a distilled botanical drink) should come from the Portuguese Indies. Even this short document contains four different variants of 'from India/Indies': 'dalle Indie di Portogallo' (the Portuguese Indies), 'd'India di Portogallo' (Portuguese India'), 'd'India' (India) and 'dalle Indie' (the Indies). Most noticeable is that not only is the provenance of the requested item noted, but that the provenances could be subdivided into three groups: from Spain or Portugal, from the Levant or Ottoman Empire and from the Portuguese and Spanish empires. In connection with items from the Iberian empires, only the Portuguese Indies, India and Peru are named, with no item assigned a provenance from Africa. Lisbon is mentioned once, but no Spanish

220. ASF, MdP 5121, 64v–65v, published in Butters, Fumagalli and Deswarte-Rosa, *La Villa Médicis*, vol. 5: *Fonti documentarie*, p. 72.

221. See above, p. 188 and n. 73 (Muslim 'di Levantte').

port is. In addition, the list included two warnings about counterfeit products: the fans must be real ones from 'the Indies' and not counterfeit ones from Spain, and the balsam 'do ponente' should not be fake but genuine ('non falsificato ma schietto'), revealing Ferdinando's anxiety about being swindled. In this case, it is clear what was intended by the use of the term 'the Indies', because the fans requested were Asian folding fans. These Japanese and Ryukyuan folding fans had only become fashionable in Spain in the late 1540s and 1550s, indicating that Spanish fakes must have appeared almost as soon as demand escalated.[222] Price and value were directly linked to authenticity, and in these cases authenticity was dependent on provenance.

Why there should be such a difference with regard to provenance between the 1547 and 1567 trips is unclear, and could relate either to Cosimo giving less detailed instructions or not knowing enough to be more precise compared to Ferdinando, who clearly knew what he wanted and was an informed buyer, or to Campana's inexperience in comparison to Uguccioni. Uguccioni was a member of the ducal household, on the payroll, on 1 March 1567,[223] and he had been in Spain before, accompanying Francesco de' Medici on his trip there in 1562–63, and even being directed to make payments, so he had pertinent first-hand experience.[224] The twenty years between 1547 and 1567 must have made many of these items more familiar in Florence, so that requesting exactly what was wanted would have been easier for Ferdinando, as precision was directly related to expertise or access to knowledge, and lack of precision signalled lack of knowledge. The instructions reveal too the guidelines underlying Medici purchases, as well as setting out the processes for sending them back to Livorno and for recording both the prices and the expenses incurred. Thus, at the foot of the *memoriale* Ferdinando did not neglect to add that over and above these items, he was leaving it to Uguccioni's discretion to send any other 'cosa rara' as long as its price was right. Nor did Ferdinando fail to emphasise that Uguccioni should procure the most 'perfect' specimens available (the first adjective chosen was 'belle' [beautiful], but this was crossed out and 'perfette'

222. Annemarie Jordan Gschwend, 'A arte de coleccionar leques asiáticos na corte de Lisboa/ The Art of Collecting Asian Folding Fans at the Lisbon Court', in Hugo Miguel Crespo, ed., *A arte de coleccionar: Lisboa, Europa e o mundo na época moderna (1500–1800)/The Art of Collecting: Lisbon, Europe and the Early Modern World (1500–1800)* (Lisbon, 2019), pp. 78–93 at 93.

223. ASF, MdP 616, inserto 19, 271r, 'Rolo della casa e provisionati della famiglia di Sua Eccellentia'. Salaries varied from one *scudo* to thirty *scudi*, and Uguccioni's sat in the middle at fifteen *scudi*; as with many others on the payroll, he had no job description.

224. ASF, MdP 5093, I, 34v and 35r.

[perfect] was inserted in its stead). The issue was clearly one of quality: Ferdinando was envisaging a situation in which choice would have to be exercised, and he wanted to ensure that only items of the finest quality were acquired. If Uguccioni did not have the requisite knowledge to judge whether something should be purchased, Ferdinando instructed him to ask for advice from someone who did. The first and third of these injunctions appear also to have been followed by Campana. If Uguccioni's instructions were simultaneously fixed and fluid, as this analysis shows, so too Campana's may have been, and many of Campana's purchases may also have been left to his discretion. Nor is it impossible that Uguccioni's *memoriale* was copied from or based on a now lost *memoriale* to Campana. Whatever the precise chronology of the process, Uguccioni's list has all the hallmarks of a repeat order.

Even if Cosimo had provided Campana with a written list of desiderata, he was not present in Portugal or Spain to oversee the purchases, so the act of choosing what to acquire was left to Campana. How much knowledge Cosimo himself possessed of the global goods on sale in Lisbon is not clear, but he is at least known to have had an interest in anything described as new. His curiosity about the new, and his desire to own or possess it, was legendary, making the word neophile—a word not in fact coined until the twentieth century and used for the first time in literature by J. D. Salinger in a short story entitled *Hapworth 16, 1924* published in the *New Yorker* in 1965[225]—an ideal one with which to describe his obsessive and relentless interest. Cosimo liked the shininess of the new, and may have been aware that it was available in many forms in Lisbon, but his only way of accessing it was by proxy. There is a glimpse of how this played out in practice in a marginal comment scribbled on a cargo list of a ship from Majorca docking at Livorno in 1560, that included '32 pezzi di canne d'India' (rattan cane). Written in what is very likely to be Cosimo's hand is, 'di queste ne vorremo vedere per non hauve mai viste' (I would like to see these because I have never seen them before) (Fig. 10).[226]

---

225. *Hapworth 16, 1924* is a thirty-thousand-word novella originally published in *The New Yorker* of 19 June 1965, and republished in the bootleg J. D. Salinger, *The Complete Uncollected Short Stories of J. D. Salinger*, 2 vols (place of publication and date of publication unknown, but in the US and c. 1967), 2, pp. 71–107. The term neophile was used on p. 81 in a derogatory sense to describe Mr. Nelson: 'a born neophile and enthusiastic talebearer and gossip'.

226. ASF, MdP 2079, 15r, dated 17 August 1560. The ship was the *Santa Maria del Biscione*. See also Braudel and Romano, *Navires et marchandises*, pp. 35–36. Alessio Assonitis (personal communication of 25 February 2019) agrees that there is a strong possibility that the hand is Cosimo's.

FIGURE 10. Florence, Archivio di stato, Mediceo del Principato 2079, 15r,
17 August 1560, annotation in Cosimo de' Medici's hand. By permission of the
Italian Ministry of Culture/Archivio di stato di Firenze. Photo: Kate Lowe

What, if anything, can be gained or deduced by analysing types of goods not
purchased by Campana on his Iberian trip? Given Campana's almost complete
lack of experience and ignorance of the world outside Europe, perhaps the first
thing to note is that he bought objects from all four continents. He did not, for
example, concentrate on one continent to the exclusion of others, a style of
operating that would have necessitated much greater knowledge of provenance
than he possessed. Nor did he buy only old objects, or antiquities (if he had
known what they were). And nor did he buy only one or two categories of
object—ivories, say, but from various different countries. Instead, he seems to
have adopted a policy of object-by-object acquisition. He was not engaged in
purchasing from particular cultural traditions or milieux or countries. So although he bought porcelain, universally known only to be manufactured in
China, he did not buy any Chinese manuscripts, books or paintings, which
were also probably available, although fewer in number and less talked about.
Queen Catarina owned two Chinese printed books, which the Spaniard Bernardino de Escalante claimed to have held in his hands around 1570 in Catarina's
library in Lisbon; Escalante's own book on China, *Discurso de la navegacion que
los portugueses hazen à los reinos y provincias del Oriente y de la noticia que se tiene*

de las grandezas del reino de la China, was published in Seville in 1577.[227] Catarina may have been attracted to these because they were so far outside her normal
conception of a book, and the Chinese characters were suitably and appealingly
foreign. Her possession of them indicates that collectors were happy to acquire
objects that they could not understand, even at the most elementary level—but
for whatever reason, Campana did not buy any such pieces for either Cosimo
or Eleonora. If he really cared as little about provenance as these investigations
suggest, he was probably unaware that porcelain and Chinese printed books,
scrolls and paintings came from the same empire.

Whether by design or accident, Campana also failed to acquire any non-
European objects connected to indigenous religious or belief systems. So-called
idols—the word used at the time across Western European languages—from
Mexico and parts of West Africa are known to have reached Italy, and even
England, and it is therefore probable that some were available in the first port
of European call—Lisbon—for purchase, even if references to material 'idols'
in Portugal are very rare (an account of 1631 mentions 'idols' or fetishes in the
form of statues being sent by a Jesuit missionary in the field from the Kongo to
the Jesuit provincial in Portugal, for example).[228] But either Campana was not
tempted by these because he thought that their material form was not sumptuous enough and they would therefore not have had a high monetary value, or he
was put off because their rawness indicated a form of power that he could somehow recognise and found worrying.[229] What information there is indicates that
such 'idols' were understood in Europe from the fifteenth century to be part of
the fabric of much of the world outside Europe, and in particular that of non-
literate societies. More than this is usually not clear. What 'idols' were, or what
role they played in society, or how their power was believed to operate were
topics outside the reach of most Europeans until after the middle of the sixteenth century. In 1542—so only five years before Campana's trip—Paolo
Giovio wrote to a go-between instructing him to ask Hernando Cortés for 'una

227. Rui Manuel Loureiro, 'Ecos portugueses nos impressos hispalenses de Bernardino de
Escalante', in Fernando Quiles, Manuel Fernández Chaves and Antónia Fialho Conde, eds, *La
Sevilla lusa: La presencia portuguesa en el Reino de Sevilla durante el Barrocco/A presença portu-
guesa no Reino de Sevilha no período barroco* (Seville, 2018), pp. 236–51 at 241, 246.

228. Louis Jadin, 'Un grand missionnaire du Congo, le père jésuite Pedro Tavares, 1629–34',
Révue du clergé africain, 11.2 (1956), pp. 137–42 at 141, cited in Lagamma, 'Kongo: Power and
Majesty', in *Kongo: Power and Majesty*, ed. Alisa Lagamma, p. 268, n. 12. But references to 'idols'
in Portugal are few and far between.

229. Blier, 'Capricious Arts', p. 15.

qualche cosa bizarre de idolo di Temistitan' (a bizarre idol of some kind from Temistitan) for his museum.[230] In 1572 Francesco de' Medici sent chest-loads of New World objects and animals to Duke Albrecht V of Bavaria, and recorded in the inventory of their contents was 'an idol in human shape composed of different chosen seeds made in Mexico where people not only worship it but also sacrifice human beings to its unclean spirit'.[231] Three separate travellers to Cabo Verde between 1479 and 1595—Eustache de la Fosse, Duarte Pacheco Pereira and André Alvares d'Almada—mentioned islands in the Kingdom of the Sapi called the islands of the Ídolos because of the wooden 'idols' found by the Portuguese when they first went there.[232] No wooden 'idols' from West Africa are known to have made their way to Italy before those forcibly seized by the Capuchin friar Andrea da Pavia, who had returned from a stay between 1688–91 in the province of Soyo (Sonho, Nsoyo, Sonyo) in the Kingdom of Kongo—the province from which the two oliphants discussed in chapter 4 above had come—with a trunk full of 'idols', which were confiscated by the secretary of the Congregazione De propaganda fide in 1692.[233] But smaller and humbler charms could easily have done so. Thomas Platter the Younger, a Swiss physician, for example, visited the collection of exotica of a Mr Cope in London in 1599, and saw 'an African charm made of teeth' (Einer Segen auß Affrica von Zeenen).[234] Suzanne Preston Blier has argued that the negativity associated with African 'idols' may also have adversely affected the European reception of secular and religious African artworks which were similarly deemed capable of channelling harm towards the unsuspecting viewer, but evidence for this view remains hard to find.[235] Translocation to Europe was usually sufficient for an object to

230. Markey, *Imagining the Americas*, pp. 38 and 172 n. 41.

231. Toorians, 'Earliest Inventory', pp. 63–64 for the Italian and German versions of the inventory. The Italian word used was *idolo*, and the German *Abgott*. See also Markey, *Imagining the Americas*, p. 50.

232. Eustache de la Fosse, 'Voyage à la côte occidentale d'Afrique en Portugal et en Espagne (1479–1480)', ed. R. Foulché-Delbosc, *Revue hispanique*, 4 (1897), pp. 174–201 at 180; Duarte Pacheco Pereira, *Esmeraldo de situ orbis*, trans. and ed. George H. T. Kimble (London, 1937), pp. 94–95; Duarte Pacheco Pereira, *Esmeraldo de situ orbis*, ed. Joaquim Barradas de Carvalho (Lisbon, 1991), pp. 283–84; André Alvares d'Almada, *Tratado breve dos rios de Guiné do Cabo Verde*, ed. António Luís Ferronha (Lagos, 2006), p. 96; Lowe, 'Made in Africa', pp. 165–66.

233. Bassani, *African Art*, p. 161; Blier, 'Capricious Arts', pp. 20–21.

234. Thomas Platter, *Thomas Platters des Jüngeren Englandfahrt im Jahre 1599* (Halle-Saale, 1929), p. 43; Thomas Platter, *Thomas Platter's Travels in England, 1599*, trans. and intro. by Clare Williams (London, 1937), p. 171; Lowe, 'Made in Africa', p. 165.

235. Blier, 'Capricious Arts', p. 15.

shed its contextual wraparound in such a way that it became dissociated permanently from its former nexus of power and lost its potential to cause harm. In any case, the sharpness of the line between objects now thought of and labelled ethnographic and those now thought of and labelled as works of art must always have depended upon the level of education, strength of religious belief and cultural prejudices of the person dividing objects between the two categories.

It is doubtful that Campana had ever left Tuscany before April 1547; Cosimo's previous use of him had involved grain and the organisation of its shipment. Nor is he known to have had any experience of or interest in decorative art, or in any of the other purchases he made on the trip. Thus it seems clear that he had no relevant expertise. So how did he set about his duties of acquisition? Two elements may have operated in his favour. The first was the standing and local know-how of the leading Italian merchants in Lisbon, Luca Giraldi and Giancarlo Affaitati, who were his primary contacts. The same scenario of insertion was repeated with Jacopo Botti in Cadiz and Seville and Andrea and Pierozzo Peri in Cadiz.[236] These Italian networks in Lisbon and Cadiz/Seville, operating in this instance through companies, facilitated all encounters and put experienced and trusted middlemen, Italian and Portuguese, who were able to operate in Portuguese and Spanish, at the disposal of Campana. The ability to tap into these networks was a necessary precondition for the success of his mission.[237] Recent studies have stressed that it was versatility that characterised the best so-called cultural agents: their ability to supply whatever was needed[238]—and they achieved this through the quality of their contacts.[239]

236. Angela Orlandi, 'Al soffio degli Alisei: Mercanti fiorentini tra Siviglia e il Nuovo Mondo', *Archivio storico italiano*, 169 (2011), pp. 477–505, esp. 480 for bibliography on Tuscans/Florentines in Seville; Angela Orlandi, 'Tuscan Merchants in Andalusia: A Historiographical Debate', in Catia Brilli and Manuel Herrero Sánchez, eds, *Italian Merchants in the Early-Modern Spanish Monarchy: Business Relations, Identities and Political Resources* (London, 2017), pp. 13–32.

237. All the Lisbon sellers and middlemen used by Campana were male. Even though one of the commissioners, Eleonora di Toledo, was female, the world of these acquisitions in Lisbon was exclusively male.

238. Marika Keblusek, '*Mercator sapiens*: Merchants as Cultural Entrepreneurs', in Marika Keblusek and Badeloch Vera Noldus, eds, *Double Agents: Cultural and Political Brokerage in Early Modern Europe* (Leiden, 2011), pp. 95–109 at 100.

239. Marika Keblusek, 'Introduction: Profiling the Early Modern Agent', in Hans Cools, Marika Keblusek and Badeloch Noldua, eds, *Your Humble Servant: Agents in Early Modern Europe* (Hilversum, 2006), pp. 9–15 at 13, and Marika Keblusek, 'Introduction: Double agents in Early Modern Europe', in Marika Keblusek and Badeloch Vera Noldus, eds, *Double Agents: Cultural and Political Brokerage in Early Modern Europe* (Leiden, 2011), pp. 1–9 at 4.

Expertise in these circumstances could be recast from the more specialised knowledge that enabled someone to know which objects were worth purchasing into a form of proxy knowledge, at one remove, that enabled someone to know whom to contact to make the purchases required. While Campana generally stayed firmly inside Florentine and Tuscan networks in his mercantile dealings on the Iberian peninsula, he did occasionally stray into the arms of Ligurians or Genoese, or even merchants from Lombardy; the Affaitati, whose services he used in Lisbon, were originally from Cremona, for example. One might have imagined that Campana would have contacted merchants who had traded in São Tomé and Cabo Verde and were now living in Lisbon in order to acquire African objects, and merchants who had traded in India to acquire Indian objects,[240] but there is no sign that he did this, although the middlemen employed may have done so.

The second element operating in Campana's favour was that choice may not have been much of an issue. A small comment in Misc. med. 713 in relation to porcelain indicates this, as a Portuguese *sensale* or middleman called Ghuercio (a nickname meaning 'one-eyed') was paid three hundred *maravedis* in October 1547 for going round from house to house over a number of days trying to rustle up pieces of Chinese porcelain for Cosimo 'che non sene trovava' (because they were not to be found).[241] Giovanni Ricci, the papal nuncio in Lisbon between 1544 and 1550, does not appear in Campana's account journal, but he and Campana could have been competing for some items, such as porcelain, which both bought. Six ships arrived back from Goa and Cochin in January 1547,[242] so Ricci, being on the spot, may have been more fortunate than Campana, who only arrived later in the year, as the ships must have carried porcelain in their cargoes.[243] By October 1547 Campana may not have been required to make an informed or aesthetic selection from the Chinese porcelain available to him, but merely to purchase it piece by piece until he had a sufficient quantity.

240. For examples of these, see the *Livro do lançamento*, e.g., 1, p. 338 ('Antonio Nunnez mercador que he no Cabo Verde') and 2, p. 187 ('Francisco Jorge mercador que veo de San Tomee').

241. ASF, Misc. med. 713, 4v.

242. Guinote, Frutuoso and Lopes, *As armadas*, p. 116.

243. Annemarie Jordan Gschwend, '*Olisipo, emporium nobilissimum*: Global Consumption in Renaissance Lisbon', in Annemarie Jordan Gschwend and K.J.P. Lowe, eds, *The Global City: On the Streets of Renaissance Lisbon* (London, 2015), pp. 140–61 at 146 and 160 n. 24. Manuel I of Portugal had already decreed in 1522 that a third of the cargo on Portuguese ships going from China to Goa must be porcelain and damasks, thus hastening the importation of greater quantities of porcelain into Europe. On Ricci, see above p. 133 n. 34.

Campana's comment on the difficulty of finding porcelain in Lisbon leads directly to a third point about acquisition: that it involved not just Cosimo, who was at the end of the chain, and Campana, who might have been thought to be at the beginning, but often several other people before him. If three or four people lay between Cosimo and his purchases, and he had no hand in exercising choice over which individual objects should be chosen, does it make sense to regard his involvement at this point as truly a matter of collecting? Surely this must affect the way in which the Medici collections are conceptualised. It is of course a form of shorthand to describe the ultimate owner or possessor as the collector, but it seems incorrect in relation to the acquisition of at least some of these Portuguese and Spanish imperial goods, except on a purely financial level. Collecting can be seen as a process with various stages or phases, from the initial idea or desire in the mind of the buyer to own a particular category of thing or living being, to setting its acquisition in motion through commissioning and despatching people to find and buy those things or beings, to the act of acquisition often performed by intermediaries or agents, their transport back to the buyer, and their subsequent arrangement and display with similar things, as part of a group wherein the multiple variants of the type impress and fascinate more than a single object would do.[244] An alternative point of view might therefore rely on the argument that even though this type of collecting did not involve discernment, the exercise of taste or aesthetic judgement, or indeed the selection of individual objects by Cosimo, it could still be described as collecting on his part, because he had set the purchasing in train. In this scenario, money, rather than aesthetic or informed choice, is the paramount characteristic of a collector—but later display of the collection could also play a role, maybe reinforcing the legitimacy of the label. In the case of the 1547–48 buying trip, the situation is even murkier, because it is not known whether Cosimo specifically requested, for example, a tusk or oliphant—or even whether he specified ivory as a category of material. He might merely have requested that Campana purchase anything rare or interesting or novel that he saw on the Iberian peninsula. If Cosimo did not specify ivory or a tusk, could

244. Federico Botana, 'Tammaro de Marinis, Vittorio Forti, and the Acquisition of Islamic Manuscripts for J. P. Morgan in Constantinople in 1913', *Manuscript Studies*, 7.2 (2022), pp. 237–69 at 240, comments that most 'attention has been given to the beginning and the end of this process', rather than the middle, carried out by intermediaries such as Campana in this case, and Forti in his own. Botana is also very clear-sighted on the serendipitous nature of many collections (p. 269).

the purchase of the Kongolese oliphants, for example, correctly be described, in its inception at least, as collecting by Cosimo? Accepting Cosimo as a collector in this case would mean accepting an interpretation and understanding of a collector at its most basic and unvarnished: a collector is someone who collects, who amasses a collection, regardless of how he or she does it. And what of the enslaved people bought for the Medici? How do they fit into this analysis? Cosimo's galley slaves cannot be considered a collection. They were the necessary engine that powered his fleet of ships and the workforce that enabled his vast imperial project to fortify Tuscany from Elba to Arezzo and beyond; they did not form part of his court entourage. But Eleonora's sub-Saharan African women and girls could be seen as a type of collection, designed for display at court in order to make a statement.

Although documents are lacking, a final point about how Cosimo himself judged Campana's Iberian mission may be deduced from the latter's subsequent career in the former's employment. Cosimo must have been pleased with his Portuguese and Spanish purchases, because Campana was quickly promoted to further positions of trust and placed in charge of overseeing Cosimo's building projects in Elba, meaning that he was responsible for the disbursement of considerable sums of money.[245] The Iberian venture, on which Campana had proved his worth, was a stepping-stone to greater things.

Centuries after the afterlives of the objects and people have settled, hindsight edges in, with its starkly unsettling perspectives. With hindsight, what would have been the best goods to buy? What was the Portuguese trading empire offering for sale in Lisbon (and the Spanish empire offering for sale in Cadiz) that Renaissance Italy should have bought? Did Cosimo only want the most unusual, the most current, the temporarily glittering? Did he have a notion of the longer term in relation to individual objects, as opposed to building a collection and leaving a legacy? Did he set the rules, or like surprises? Some of the variables affecting what would make goods valuable or abhorrent in the twenty-first century are far beyond the comprehension of those in the sixteenth—a classic example of the imbalance of ignorance—but pondering which goods would have been the best options is a game; so why not play it? Ignoring the attractions of rarity and the appeal of the exotic and non-European at the time, it is intriguing to consider which purchases provided

245. In August 1549 Pierfrancesco Riccio was given 2,800 *scudi d'oro in oro* to send to Campana in Elba, and in July 1551 he was sent 1,866⅔ *scudi d'oro in oro*: ASF, Guardaroba medicea 13, pp. 82 and 84.

long-lasting value, noting or deducing their provenance where possible. The most expensive items were enslaved humans: the most expensive Muslim man, described as originating in the area between Cairo and Constantinople, purchased to work on one of Cosimo's galleys, cost forty ducats, and the most expensive of Eleonora's sub-Saharan Africans, a woman, purchased to work in her entourage at court, cost a staggering one hundred ducats and sixty *maravedis*. Humans were time-limited, so were not purchased for posterity. Whole live animals also cost more than dead animal body parts, however enhanced. The two civet cats, probably African, cost twenty-seven and a half and thirty ducats respectively, and with luck, provided civet for several years. The tamarin from Brazil cost nine gold ducats; it might have lasted a few years at best, but probably did not survive the winter. The two Kongolese oliphants, on the other hand, together cost three gold ducats and one hundred *maravedis*, and are amongst the earliest still extant African artefacts to have entered and stayed in the same European collection from the sixteenth century onwards. Their value is inestimable today. The provenance of the oliphants was not mentioned, and Beatrice's place of origin was noted as Pombal, so in neither case was the African link made explicit, which omission simultaneously erased the part played by the Portuguese trading empire in their histories. They were left as possessions originating from elsewhere.

6

Global Sensibilities

POSSESSING CONSCIOUSNESS OF THE
GLOBAL WORLD IN RENAISSANCE ITALY:
A PAPAL OFFICIAL'S EXPERIENCE
IN 1590S LISBON

THE THIRD case study will focus, as its category of global acquisition, on the more intangible, yet crucial, aspects of the acquisition and possession, in Renaissance Italy, of consciousness of the global world, via the Portuguese trading empire. This will involve looking at sets of correspondence written from Lisbon by an Italian papal official in the 1590s; that is, after the kingdom of Portugal had itself been incorporated into the greater kingdom of Spain, under Philip II, in 1580. Once again, fifty years after the moment that was analysed in the preceding chapters, the principal cities and milieux under scrutiny have changed, leading to different inflexions of interaction, varied concerns with provenance and different understandings of worldwide acquisition and possession. The papacy was by nature and definition more global than the Florentine state, and the administrative and religious structures of the church straddled Catholic countries around the world. Yet the concerns of some of the personnel of the curia were similar to those of the personnel of the Medicean state. In the 1590s, the papacy was developing new policies and extending its reach, especially under Ippolito Aldobrandini, who was elected Clement VIII at the beginning of 1592, and remained in post until 1605. Portugal's loss of independence had many practical as well as existential adverse aspects for the Portuguese, one of which was that it led the English (who were at war with Spain) to justify attacking Portuguese shipping. As a consequence, far fewer of the ships on the Carreira da Índia made it back to Lisbon with their cargoes from the East intact, resulting in a dearth of global goods. The centre of global operations moved from Lisbon to Seville;[1] Lisbon was downgraded, diplomatic representation in Portugal suffered, and Italian officials reported in detail how this change affected their treatment. However, the aspects that remained constant are perhaps just as apparent from the correspondence under analysis.

The Italian in question was Fabio Biondi (1533–1618), a native of Montalto in the Marche, from a family related to the Peretti. He studied law, served as secretary to various cardinals and started to be promoted late in life after his patron Felice Peretti was elected pope in 1585 and took the name Sixtus V. Sixtus appointed Biondi patriarch of Jerusalem in 1588. Nominated apostolic collector in Portugal by Clement VIII at the end of September 1592,[2] in August 1593 he was additionally appointed vice-legate in Portugal.[3] He resided in Lisbon for four years, from 11 March 1593 to 27 March 1597.[4] In his position as collector, he was responsible for ensuring the collection of revenues due to the Church both from within Portugal and across the overseas Portuguese empire, so the position entailed a close scrutiny of all kinds of financial and mercantile activity.[5] Diplomatic powers were achieved by the addition of the further post of vice-legate.[6] These two positions held in tandem can be usefully compared with the more important and high-profile post of nuncio (*nunzio*), in particular with that of nuncio to Madrid, used to reward those who had not been promoted to the cardinalate; although of lesser status, Biondi's posts in Lisbon meant that he was the foremost papal representative in that city,[7] and they too combined political and religious matters with a recognised role at court.[8] And

1. The markets followed the seat of power, and in 1595, for example, Biondi wrote that Madrid was at that date a better place than Lisbon to buy jewels: ASV, Fondo Confalonieri 28, 363v.

2. Henry Biaudet, *Les Nonciatures apostoliques permanentes jusqu'en 1648* (Helsinki, 1910), col. 163 and p. 255. Bearing a date of 26 October 1592, Biondi's instructions from Clement VIII for this position are in ASV, Fondo Confalonieri 34, 5r–7r.

3. *DBI*, 10 (1968), pp. 526–27 (anon.). For the instructions re this position, dated 9 August 1593, formulated by the legate, Cardinal Archduke Albrecht of Austria, see ASV, Fondo Confalonieri 31, 37r–41r.

4. ASV, Fondo Confalonieri 11, 82r and 120r.

5. Before the Great Schism of 1378–1417, the position of apostolic collector had sometimes been simultaneously diplomatic and financial, but afterwards the financial elements were uppermost.

6. Peter Partner, *The Pope's Men: The Papal Civil Service in the Renaissance* (Oxford, 1990), p. 66.

7. See Sergio Filippi, *I rappresentanti diplomatici della Santa Sede in Portogallo e la chiesa di Nostra Signora di Loreto in Lisbona* (Vatican City, 2022).

8. Maria Antonietta Visceglia, *Roma papale e Spagna: Diplomatici, nobili e religiosi tra due corti* (Rome, 2010), pp. 52, 55, 64–65.

like the nuncios in Madrid and many other high-ranking prelates, Biondi had studied law.[9] Clement VIII's patronage continued after Biondi's return to Rome: in 1602, Clement appointed him *maggiordomo* and prefect of the Vatican Palace, positions which he held until his death in 1618.[10] Registers of Biondi's official and personal correspondence from Lisbon are held in the Vatican archives: the former in Segretaria di stato, Portogallo, the main repository of papal correspondence relating to diplomacy and politics, and the latter in Fondo Confalonieri.[11]

Biondi must have acquired a level of familiarity with the Portuguese language during his residence in Lisbon in order to have been able to operate. However, he admitted in a letter of 27 January 1596, that is, after he had spent just under three years in Lisbon, that he 'did not possess Portuguese' (non possedo la lingua portughese), by which he appears to have meant not that he did not speak or understand Portuguese, but that his command of the language did not allow him to express himself as he would wish.[12] His use of the word 'possess' is fitting in this context, suggesting a broad and capacious, rather than a one-dimensional, understanding of what possession of a language—as of a consciousness of the global—might involve.

9. Ibid., pp. 53–54.

10. Filippo Maria Renazzi, *Notizie storiche degli antichi vicedomini del Patriarchio Lateranense e de' moderni prefetti del sagro palazzo apostolico ovvero maggiordomi pontefizi* (Rome, 1784), pp. 109–10 at 110 discusses Biondi's epitaph in S. Silvestro al Quirinale, carved while Biondi was still alive, and mentions his chapel in the same church.

11. Although parts of Biondi's correspondence in the Vatican archives have been analysed previously by scholars, the focus of the research has not been on Biondi himself, but on two of the Portuguese prelates with whom he corresponded: Frei Aleixo de Meneses, the archbishop of Goa, and D. Afonso de Castelo Branco, the bishop of Coimbra. See Carlos Alonso O.S.A, 'Documentacíon inédita para una biografía de Fr. Alejo de Meneses, O.S.A., arzobispo de Goa (1595–1612)', *Analecta Augustiniana*, 27 (1964), pp. 263–333; Carlos Alonso O.S.A, 'Eleccion y consagración de Alejo de Meneses, O.S.A, como arzobispo de Goa (1594–1595)', *Analecta Augustiniana*, 49 (1986), pp. 91–135; José Pedro Paiva, 'A Diocese de Coimbra antes e depois do Concílio de Trento: D. Jorge de Almeida e D. Afonso Castelo Branco', in *Sé Velha de Coimbra: Culto e cultura* (Coimbra, 2005), pp. 225–53; Cátia Teles e Marques, 'Cultura material e diplomacia eclesiástica: As relações e a troca de presentes entre o bispo-conde de Coimbra D. Afonso de Castelo Branco e a Corte Papal (1590–1615)', *Revista de história da sociedade e da cultura* 14 (2014), pp. 183–207.

12. ASV, Fondo Confalonieri 28, 423r, Biondi to Bishop Cappella maggiore, 27 January 1596: 'scrivo in italiano perchè sicome non possedo la lingua portughese, così non havrei potuto esprimere il mio concetto a gusto mio'.

One of the more interesting questions to consider is whether the ways in which Biondi's role in the acquisition of global goods and global points of view differed from those of Bastiano Campana, discussed in the previous case study, and if so, whether it led to a different outcome or conclusion. Campana was a secular employee of Cosimo de' Medici, uneducated and without prior knowledge of foreign culture and experience of foreign travel, instructed by Cosimo to make acquisitions on his behalf. He acted as Cosimo's agent, and was able to utilise his employer's contacts and work within his networks, but the Iberian trip was his initiation into this role as a cultural broker, and he had no track record of competence. He made acquisitions for only two people: Cosimo and Eleonora. However, after selling his grain, buying goods was the sole reason for his presence in Lisbon, whereas for Biondi, buying was a sideline. Biondi was, in his own words a 'ministro del papa',[13] sent by him to Lisbon with a financial brief: to ensure the collection of monies owing to the papacy. He was not an agent, yet a foreign posting was understood to carry with it an opportunity for small-scale trading,[14] which Biondi's network, and Biondi himself, exploited. As far as is known, he purchased nothing for the pope, although he did buy objects for a range of cardinals and others in Rome, and for various patrons who had aided him in his career, across the Italian peninsula, as well as buying for himself and his family. Whether his patrons found him a satisfactory pseudo-agent or intermediary is an intriguing question; it is possible that by blurring the distinction, and treating their client as though he were an agent, they avoided paying for an agent but in return had to accept inferior service, from a less than dedicated man in the middle. Yet although in many ways Campana's and Biondi's functions were different, their roles and behaviours mirrored each other. Both received requests for goods that in the main they attempted to fulfil, with more or less success; in the process, their understandings of the Portuguese overseas trading empire—whether measured in terms of its ships, or its reach, or its enslaved peoples, or its gold and jewels—increased substantially, but only within certain rather circumscribed limits.

13. Ibid., 746v, Biondi to the collettore, 15 March 1597.

14. Pugliano, 'Accountability', p. 187 makes this point in relation to Cornelio Bianchi taking the position of physician to the Venetian consul in Damascus in the 1540s. In addition to being a medical doctor, Bianchi acted as an entrepreneur and made the most of being in Syria. He transformed imported goods from Venice and Cyprus into more desirable objects by having them decorated by expert metalworkers in Damascus, and then shipped them back to Venice and sold them at a profit.

There is no evidence that either Campana or Biondi ever considered the morality of any aspect of an overseas trading empire, or worried about possible harm caused by the tremendous translocation of peoples, products, flora and fauna that was set in motion. Neither questioned the legitimacy of what they saw and bought. Both accepted instead that global Lisbon offered singular advantages. Both acquired slaves but, like nearly all Italians in the sixteenth century, they did not concern themselves with how the non-Christians had become enslaved, nor with whether or not slavery should exist.

Biondi's secretary in Lisbon was Giovanni Battista Confalonieri (1561–1648), who was born in Rome to a family of Milanese origin, and who attended the Collegio romano of the Jesuits, learning Hebrew and Greek in addition to Latin. He was secretary to Cardinal Alfonso Gesualdo before being employed by Biondi. While in Lisbon, he wrote a penetrating analysis of the city entitled *Grandezza e magnificenza della città di Lisbona*, based on the template of Giovanni Botero's *Delle cause della grandezza delle città libri III* of 1588.[15] In later life, Confalonieri exercised the office of prefect of the archive of Castel Sant'Angelo—hence the existence there of his own private papers, the Fondo Confalonieri, in no less than eighty-nine volumes.[16] His authorship and the survival of his archive have made him more noted than his former boss.

Documentation

As in the previous case studies, the category of record under analysis here requires careful consideration. Letters have always been a recognised and accepted source for historians,[17] even if with caveats,[18] but their inclusion in

15. Kate Lowe, 'Foreign Descriptions of the Global City: Renaissance Lisbon from the Outside', in Annemarie Jordan Gschwend and K.J.P. Lowe, eds, *The Global City: On the Streets of Renaissance Lisbon* (London, 2015), pp. 36–55 at 37.

16. *DBI*, 27 (1982), pp. 778–82, entry by Anna Foa.

17. There is a vast secondary literature on fifteenth- and sixteenth-century letters written in Italian, although not many general methodological or theoretical concerns relevant to a range of different types of letter are addressed. But see Maria Luisa Doglio, *L'arte delle lettere: Idea e pratica della scrittura epistolare tra Quattro e Seicento* (Bologna, 2000); Gabriella Del Lungo Camiciotti, 'Letters and Letter Writing in Early Modern Culture: An Introduction', *Journal of Early Modern Studies*, 3.3 (2014), pp. 17–35.

18. Giles Constable, *Letters and Letter Collections* (Turnhout, 1976), pp. 11–12 stressed that their value as historical sources always had to be 'evaluated in the light of their literary character', but he also stated that they were the preeminent source for medieval history (p. 66).

the matrix of historical records worthy of study has been incremental, by type, as fashions have changed emphases on historical subjects and on their admissibility: originally mainly royal, diplomatic and bureaucratic, then mercantile and missionary, and last of all private and domestic[19]—with a sharp focus on women's letters—were thought worthy of analysis.[20] Letters are the opposite of a new type of source only now being mined for new types of material, as would be the case of inventories, for example. They are an old type of source, always valued, but one in which the status of exemplars that had been previously ignored or little studied is constantly being adjusted as additional authors and topics come to be deemed historically important. In evolutionary terms, there is scholarly consensus that Italian chancery letters were the models for all other types of letter sent on the Italian peninsula from an identifiable sender to a named recipient.[21] At least a hundred years before Biondi's many-faceted, vernacular correspondence, in the mid- to late fifteenth century, a more interesting and flexible version of the chancery letter had evolved alongside its formulaic ancestor: composed in Italian, and multipurpose, a fitting vehicle for official business such as politics, diplomacy and news, but also for familial and kinship communication.[22] Perhaps on account of this consensus, there has been surprisingly little recent scholarly interest in the subject of how letters as a category of record can or should be used as historical sources. Merchants' letters, for example, have been analysed for what can be learnt from them of the speed of the postal service, or letters from women have been analysed for what they can reveal about 'women's issues' such as motherhood. But virtually nothing has been written about the letter and historical information[23]—although Filippo de Vivo's article on how the news of a minor skirmish between the Spanish and the Venetians in the southern Adriatic in 1617 was variously reported raises many questions pertinent to this issue.[24]

19. For example, John Najemy, *Between Friends: Discourses of Power and Desire in the Machiavelli–Vettori Letters of 1513–1515* (Princeton, NJ, 1993).

20. For example, Meredith Ray, *Writing Gender in Women's Letter Collections of the Italian Renaissance* (Toronto, 2009).

21. Francesco Senatore, 'Ai confini del "mundo de carta": Origine e diffusione della lettera cancelleresca italiana (XIII—XVI secolo)', *Reti medievali*, 10 (2009), pp. 239–91.

22. Senatore, 'Ai confini', pp. 243–51; James, 'Marriage by Correspondence', p. 325.

23. Writing about the scholarly information compiled into reference works in the same period, Ann Blair defined information (in contradistinction to data and knowledge) as decontextualised small 'items', ripe when taken up to be 'rearticulated'. Ann M. Blair, *Too Much to Know: Managing Scholarly Information before the Modern Age* (New Haven, CT, 2010), p. 2.

24. De Vivo, 'Microhistories', pp. 192–97, 202–5.

In addition, rather than viewing a letter as an historical artefact and acknowledging that the writing of it was just as deserving of cultural analysis as was reported conversation or a speech, historians in the past often took its contents at face value, simply extracting the historical information from it, and thus separating it yet further from its context, in yet another example of context collapse, this time *avant la lettre*. Yet as any sociolinguistic study would show, the language and content of an historical letter—as a contemporary communication—are entirely dependent on the symmetry or asymmetry of the sender and the recipient,[25] and therefore the choice of content, and the way in which it is presented, need to be reconsidered in the light of this. As Trevor Dean (following Habermas) clearly laid out in relation to letters from the Rangoni, a leading noble family in Modena, to the duke of Ferrara in the late fifteenth and early sixteenth centuries, all letters are 'always "strategic", "power-laden and goal-directed", never merely communicative.'[26] In addition to motive, the bias of the sender always requires consideration, just as what is left out is as revealing as what is included. Nor is there always a single sender or *mittente*, although that is how it was recorded in Italian archival collections in the past. Instead, many letters are examples of mediated writing, whereby there is collaboration between the author, the secretary, the scribe and perhaps others—and this is true for the correspondence, both professional and personal, of Fabio Biondi. In a similar vein, although in general there is only one addressee, a number of people beyond the addressee probably had access to the text of the letter, especially if the letter was sent in a professional capacity, as many of Biondi's were, to an important administrative unit of the curial bureaucracy.[27] A final point concerns interaction and comprehension, for a letter is written in the hope or with the expectation that its meaning will be

25. Per Linnell and Thomas Luckmann, 'Asymmetries in Dialogue: Some Conceptual Preliminaries', in Ivana Marková and Klaus Foppa, eds, *Asymmetries in Dialogue* (Hemel Hempstead, 1991), pp. 1–20, esp. 6–8.

26. Trevor Dean, 'The Dukes of Ferrara and Their Nobility: Notes on Language and Power', in Marco Gentile and Pierre Savy, eds, *Noblesse et États princiers en Italie et en France au XVᵉ siècle* (Rome, 2009), pp. 365–74 at 368. See also Paul D. McLean, *The Art of the Network: Strategic Interaction and Patronage in Renaissance Florence* (Durham, NC, 2007), p. 37: 'Quotidian letter writing was [. . .] a formalized, routinized, strategic interactional behavior.'

27. James Daybell and Andrew Gordon, 'New Directions in the Study of Early Modern Correspondence', *Lives and Letters*, 4.1 (2012), pp. 1–7 at 3; Marina Dossena, 'The Study of Correspondence: Theoretical and Methodological Issues', in Marina Dossena and Gabriella Del Lungo Camiciotti, eds, *Letter Writing in Late Modern Europe* (Amsterdam, 2012), pp. 13–29 at 18.

clear to the intended recipient; that it will be decipherable by the addressee.[28] Non-comprehension would void the message and negate interaction.

The official correspondence in Segretaria di stato, Portogallo, is composed of original letters dictated by Biondi and written down predominantly, but not exclusively, in Confalonieri's hand. The personal correspondence of Fabio Biondi in the manuscript registers of outgoing correspondence in the Fondo Confalonieri are secretarial drafts of letters despatched,[29] also written in the hand of Confalonieri, who therefore had to write each letter out twice. These drafts contain corrections, indicating that Biondi sometimes had to make several attempts before he captured precisely what he wanted to say. Much of Biondi's large correspondence is deceptively bland, in comparison, for example, to that of Filippo Sassetti, penned in his own hand in Lisbon in the 1570s and 1580s, which is far more lively, more learned, and more varied,[30] yet there is a great deal to be gleaned even from relatively bland letters. Many letter writers, especially Italian letter writers of the late fifteenth and sixteenth centuries, are chatty and interested in detail. Biondi dictated letters in which he did not linger over or expand on subjects, however, sticking to the point as though the letters were written out of a sense of duty—which his official ones certainly were[31]—and were constantly being composed under constraints of time. His letters also make clear that he was risk-averse and miserly or, at the very least, careful with money. Yet his dry comments are precious for the worldview they reveal in passing or as background to his main narratives. He is useful precisely because he is a kind of witness who may generally be passed over, as he does not trumpet global news or novelties: a representative of the many who were not particularly in thrall to the lure of the new and so-called exotic. His contribution is to personify a certain undemanding level of global consciousness. He was undeniably in the right place at the right time; the letters allow one to

28. Dossena, 'Study', p. 28.

29. In commenting on the difference between official and private letter writing in Renaissance Italy, Paul McLean, *Art of the Network*, p. 44, has characterised private letter writing as 'far more idiomatic, far less polished, far more often hasty in its composition', but in Biondi's case haste seems to have crossed the divide. McLean noted that personal correspondence was 'fraught with the presentation of complex motives through elaborate codes and conventions', but, again, the official and private letters of Biondi shared this trait.

30. Sassetti, *Lettere*.

31. 'Il debito dello scrivere' was a powerful motivation for those who worked overseas for ecclesiastical and secular bureaucracies or governments as well as for those keeping in touch with their families. Cf. James, 'Marriage by Correspondence', p. 326.

glean some sense of what global information was circulating in Lisbon, absorbed by a papal official whose mind in the main was on other matters, and to observe this information being passed on to correspondents back in Italy. The focus in this chapter is on information relating to the Portuguese trading empire, but it will also be helpful to analyse some other global and sensationalist local stories as points of comparison, showing what sort of item was on his radar. It is instructive, and slightly unusual, to have letters from Lisbon at this date to a such a wide variety of Italian correspondents in Biondi's public world and private circles: the papal secretary of state (usually a cardinal), other cardinals, his secular patrons, fellow curial officials in Rome, nuncios in Spain, those in charge of his affairs in Italy, his siblings and their families. These correspondents ranged from social equals to superiors to those lower down the social scale, encompassing ecclesiastical, secular and familial contacts, and the correspondence varied in frequency from a single letter to a regular series of them. It is also pertinent—and slightly ironic, because Biondi stopped writing in his own hand when he became important enough not to do so—that in the years prior to Biondi's posting to Lisbon, which merited the acquisition of his own full-time secretary, he, Biondi, had been the full-time secretary of Cardinal Alessandro Montalto, the cardinal nephew of Felice Peretti, Pope Sixtus V. Included in the Fondo Confalonieri in the Vatican are not only Biondi's letters, when Confalonieri was his secretary, but six volumes of Montalto's letters from 1586 to 1592, when Biondi was Montalto's secretary,[32] illustrating clearly the stepped, hierarchical stages of a career dependent upon papal patronage, with its stage-appropriate scribal activities.

The News according to Biondi

News has enjoyed a surge in popularity as an academic topic in the last twenty years, and in particular in the last decade.[33] The first section of this case study will examine news of the world incorporated in Biondi's correspondence,[34]

---

32. ASV, Fondo Confalonieri 48–53.

33. For example, Infelise, *Prima dei giornali*; Brendan Dooley, ed., *The Dissemination of News and the Emergence of Contemporaneity in Early Modern Europe* (Farnham, 2010); Andrew Pettegree, *The Invention of News: How the World Came to Know about Itself* (New Haven, CT, 2014); Joad Raymond and Noah Moxham, eds, *News Networks in Early Modern Europe* (Leiden, 2016) and de Vivo, 'Microhistories', pp. 179–214.

34. Cf. James, *Letters of Giovanni Sabadino*, esp. chs 3 and 4, re news, information and news gathering.

investigating information and assumptions about global affairs in late sixteenth-century Lisbon, as relayed back to Italy by a papal official.[35] It is not sufficient or satisfactory merely to assess which items of global news Biondi includes in his correspondence; one has also to ask why these items were chosen. In addition to understanding that the choice of the written form, and the relationship between sender and recipient, greatly influence content, it has to be remembered that the person composing the letter, Biondi, was not a blank slate, but a man with personal and professional interests, and likely to prioritise or linger longer over topics that intersected with these. It is well known that one of the most important conduits of information and news is people: ambassadors, agents, merchants, government officials, missionaries and ecclesiastical officials, whether cardinals, bishops or legates, at the top end, or sailors and travelling artisans and workers at a less exalted level.

In my study of news of Africa arriving from Portugal and circulating in northern and central Italy in the 1480s and 1490s, it became apparent that many aspects of what was happening were only obliquely observed or altogether misunderstood by the letter-writers, originating as the news did in faulty or incomplete prior information, before being passed along a chain of people in various oral or written forms.[36] One hundred years later, in what ways was news of the world construed differently and comprehended before reaching its destination city of Rome? As discussed in chapter 2, news—always unstable—was constructed and changed as it travelled, and global news—emanating from farthest away—had the greatest potential for construction and change of any sort of news. Biondi's letters allow a glimpse of the kind of news about world affairs available to Lisbon residents, the greater part of which arrived by sea on ships from the Carreira da Índia or from Africa; he also had news from the so-called New World of the Americas, and news from Madrid, incorporating news from across the Spanish empire. Much will have come by word of mouth, spoken by members of the ships' crews from the cabin boy to the captain, but some would also have arrived in written form from, for example, merchants, government officials and missionaries who needed to keep their superiors informed of foreign conditions. Biondi's letters also show what sort of news was sent on to the Italian peninsula, allowing calculations to be made about possession of

35. In an article in 2007 I examined the kinds of information and cultural assumptions that travelled with ambassadors from sub-Saharan Africa to Renaissance Portugal and Italy: Lowe, '"Representing" Africa'.

36. Lowe, 'Africa in the News', p. 310.

consciousness of the global world in the context of the papal curia. Working in a cardinal's household in Rome, Biondi had been at the heart of a worldwide system of ecclesiastical news, but in Lisbon, he was at the epicentre of much more varied and up-to-date global news networks, powered by the Portuguese trading empire; news of various sorts buzzed around the world: real news, false news, altered news, wishful news, fearful news, rumours (malicious or otherwise). Often truthiness can be seen more clearly than reality, however defined. Even without an intention to deceive, however, news was often just wrong, in precisely the same way that news of Africa a hundred years earlier had been wrong, because it was based on faulty information or incorrect understanding. In May 1598, by which time Confalonieri was in Madrid, where he had been lent as secretary to the Italian nuncio,[37] news arrived at the Spanish court that Biondi was dead, and Confalonieri could not stop crying. But this was incorrect news, as the 'balorda et idiota corriere' (stupid and idiotic courier) had muddled the patriarchs of Jerusalem and Constantinople, and it was the latter who had died.[38] This kind of confusion and inaccuracy must have been very common, especially when couriers carried oral rather than written messages, which had the potential to become akin to Chinese whispers.

In terms of global news, what constituted newsworthiness for Biondi, and to which sorts of news story, of whatever degree of accuracy, did he pay attention? The kind of information relating to world news that Biondi passed on to the Segretaria di stato at the papal curia differed from that sent to patrons and clients, although there could be some overlap. Most revealing are the one- or two-page handwritten *avvisi* (newsletters) included in each of his official communications to the Segretaria di stato. By this date *avvisi* were in use across much of Europe; they had evolved out of merchants' letters and ambassadorial letters, combining elements of both to form their own, independent genre of news communication.[39] The *avvisi* included in Biondi's correspondence are shorn of the standard paraphernalia of a letter, as they have no author and no addressee, but rely instead only on the title 'Avviso', a place of origin ('di

---

37. *DBI*, 27, p. 780.

38. ASV, Fondo Confalonieri 32, 458v, Bartolomeo Rota to Biondi, Madrid, 18 May 1598. The Patriarch of Constantinople who died on 17 December 1597 was Prosper Rebiba: Konrad Eubel, *Hierarchia catholica medii aevi*, 4 vols (Münster, 1901–10), 4, p. 162.

39. Infelise, *Prima dei giornali*, pp. 3–5; Mario Infelise, 'From Merchants' Letters to Handwritten Political *avvisi*; Notes on the Origins of Public Information', in Francisco Bethencourt and Florike Egmond, eds, *Correspondence and Cultural Exchange in Europe, 1400–1700*, Cultural Exchange in Early Modern Europe 3 (Cambridge, 2007), pp. 33–52, esp. 33–35.

Lisbona') and a date.[40] The Lisbon compilers of these precious documents are unknown. It is possible to speculate that someone in Biondi's household may have played a role in deciding their content during the period he resided in Lisbon, as both the letter of 22 October 1594 from Biondi to the secretary of state and papal nephew, Cardinal Pietro Aldobrandini, for example, and an *avviso* of the same date, are in the same hand. Or maybe the letter-writer merely translated the *avviso* from Portuguese into Italian. In terms of content, the letter and *avviso* both report the funeral of Francesco Giraldi,[41] the son of Luca Giraldi, who had facilitated some of Campana's purchases for Cosimo in 1547. Biondi says in his letter that with Giraldi's death he has lost 'un buon aiuto' (a helpful contact) with the governors of Portugal, but the writer of the *avviso* goes further, singling out Biondi's presence as a mourner at the rain-dowsed ceremony (both accounts refer to the unrelenting rain).[42] Many of the Lisbon *avvisi* from this date sent to Rome and the copies of Biondi's letters to Cardinal Aldobrandini are written in the same hand. The choices made by the compilers of these newsletters as to what to include—like the decisions made by agents such as Bastiano Campana in the second case study above—could have far-reaching consequences; in this case, decisions about diplomacy, war and trade could all depend on the contents of the *avvisi*. Nor it is known how many people might have been privy to their contents, or indeed read them, once they reached Rome (perhaps they were read aloud in meetings or, if the news was especially important, at a congregation of cardinals), but multiple personnel in the Segretaria di stato would have been aware of their semi-regular arrival and would have had access to them if need be.

Biondi, like many others, characterised Lisbon as the greatest port in the world.[43] From the time of his arrival there, he sent shipping news back to the papacy, and in Lisbon shipping news dominated the news agenda. In a letter of 3 April 1593 to his boss, the secretary of state Pietro Aldobrandini,[44]

40. See, on these *avvisi*, Barbarics and Pieper, 'Handwritten Newsletters', pp. 53–79, and on these standardisations, pp. 60–61.

41. Francesco was ambassador to France and England, and governor of Bahia: *DBI*, 56 (2001), pp. 455–57, entry by Stefano Tabacchi, at 456.

42. ASV, Segretaria di stato, Portogallo 9, 376r–v, and 377r.

43. Ibid., 159v, 20 November 1593.

44. Pietro Aldobrandini was made secretary of state in September 1592, aged only twenty-one, but was not elevated to the cardinalate until his uncle Clement's first promotion in September 1593, so at this point he was secretary of state but not yet a cardinal. See *DBI*, 2 (1960), pp. 107–12, entry by Elena Fasano Guarini.

Biondi wrote, 'Qui non habbiamo cosa di momento nè si parla d'altro che delle navi che partono o che si aspettano dall'Indie' (Here there is nothing of moment and the only talk is of ships leaving and ships awaited from 'the Indies'),[45] and the *avviso* of 5 April 1593 listed the five ships going to 'le Indie', the forty ships going to Brazil, São Tomé and other parts of the Guinea coast,[46] and caravels going to the Azores and Madeira.[47] Two years later, a letter of 15 April 1595 from Biondi to Cardinal Pietro Aldobrandini reported that three days earlier the ships on the Carreira da Índia had left, along with about thirty-five vessels leaving for other parts of the world, such as the Azores, Brazil, São Tomé, Mina and Italy.[48] Two months later, in May 1595, all the talk was of the fifty-four ships that made up the incoming *flotta* from Peru.[49] This information should have been correct, as it was easily certifiable in Lisbon. Yet according to Raffael Fantoni, who wrote his *relazione* on the Kingdom of Portugal in 1600, the schedule of shipping departures was more complex, with different destinations necessitating different departure dates, and some convoys much smaller than others. The Florentine concurred that the fleet for India left in March, but stated that a fifteen- to twenty-ship fleet for São Tomé left Lisbon between 2 December and 2 January, and returned in August or September, carrying its cargo of slaves and sugar, and twenty or twenty-five smaller ships left each year for Brazil, a few at a time.[50] Global shipping news not only considered the place of origin or place of destination of the voyages, but, often more importantly, it lingered over details of the cargo, most often the inbound cargo; information about these cargoes therefore could spread knowledge of the provenance of goods. But even this was complicated, as often the inbound fleets put in at more than one country and usually the goods were not differentiated

45. ASV, Segretaria di stato, Portogallo 9, 13r.

46. Andrea Massing, 'Mapping the Malagueta Coast: A History of the Lower Guinea Coast, 1460–1510 through Portuguese Maps and Accounts', *History in Africa*, 36 (2009), pp. 331–65 at 335 n. 9, writing of the 1460s declares that the usual departure date for ships leaving from Iberia to go to the Guinea coast was October. They would arrive at Cabo Verde in November, and return by mid-February. By the 1590s this had changed, and the shipping news in Biondi's correspondence does not accord with this timetable.

47. ASV, Segretaria di stato, Portogallo 9, 16r.

48. ASV, Segretaria di stato, Portogallo 10, 73r–v.

49. Ibid., 89r.

50. Louis Demoulin, 'Le Portugal, son économie et son traffic d'outre-mer vers 1600, vus par le florentin Raffael Fantoni', in *Bulletin de L'Institut historique belge de Rome*, 44 (1974), Miscellanea Charles Verlinden, pp. 157–73 at 169, 171 and 172.

according to where they were picked up, let alone the place or places (many were composite objects, with different parts made in different areas or countries by artisans with the necessary skills) where they might have been made. Biondi included an unusually detailed account of the money, gold, silver, stones and pearls carried by the royal fleet from New Spain, anchored in Havana in Cuba in 1594, describing these as 'robbe registrate che fuori di queste ne vengano molto nascoste' (registered goods, but in addition there were many concealed goods).[51] This account was quantitative, gauging numbers and values, separating what belonged to the Spanish monarch from what belonged to other, unnamed individuals; separating too money and gold emanating from Peru, New Spain, Cuba and Honduras; listing raw materials like cochineal, indigo, musk and silk; and chests and cases of gold, pearls, emeralds and silver. It is uncommon to find even this level of engagement with provenance, but it did not extend to the raw materials or jewellery.

The constant to-and-fro of ships to all parts of the Portuguese trading empire meant that channels of communication—even with a long delay—existed along which world news could travel. War (and changes in possession of countries) loomed large within these, not only because war affected trade, which was the basis of the empire, but because the rise and fall of foreign powers has always been newsworthy. The Lisbon *avviso* of 6 August 1594 reported that the 'king' of Japan had conquered a large kingdom called Coray that bordered on China, commenting too that the king of Japan intended to conquer China.[52] In fact, the invasion of Korea by Japan had started in May 1592 and continued until 1598, so this news was a very partial reading of the situation. But it was this reading that was despatched to Rome as the basis of truth on the back of information from Portuguese-controlled areas in South Asia and the Far East. In another wild global news story, from May 1596, Biondi passed on the 'information' that the great Portuguese ship *Madre de Deus*[53] had sunk off the African coast near Melinde (now in Kenya) with only fifty-five or sixty men saved, half of whom were then eaten by 'Caffirs', while the other half made their way with great difficulty to Hormuz.[54] The *Madre de Deus* in reality was attacked in 1592 by English privateers off the Azores in one of the encounters of the episodic Anglo–Spanish War, captured and taken back to Dartmouth, where a great deal of her precious

51. ASV, Segretaria di stato, Portogallo 10, 309r.
52. ASV, Fondo Confalonieri 15, 336r.
53. There is a model of her in the Museu da Marinha in Lisbon.
54. ASV, Fondo Confalonieri 15, 347v.

cargo from Goa was looted and dispersed around England.[55] Rumours about cannibalistic 'Caffirs' were not confined to news stories in *avvisi* and letters, but even found their place in a mid-seventeenth-century board game. In Anton Francesco Lucini's engraving *Geografia ridotta a giuoco per istrutione della giovane nobiltà venetiana*, a game played with dice like a precursor of Monopoly, the world was divided into 153 little squares around a plan of Venice, and the player progressed around the board/world.[56] The worst that could happen was to land on square no. 37, the area around the Cape of Good Hope (Plate 37). In the small insert of instructions at the top of the game were set out the forfeits; no. 37 reads, 'Whoever is shipwrecked on the "costa dei Caffri" will be eaten by barbarians, and [in terms of the game] will have to return to the beginning [i.e., square no. 1]'. This is the equivalent of the instructions in Monopoly, 'Go directly to Jail. Do not pass Go'.

The place of women in the Portuguese imperial project was touched on very briefly in these newsletters. An *avviso* from Lisbon dated 2 April 1594 lingered over two rather different categories of women who met the same fate of being sent overseas to countries with significant Portuguese trading links—and therefore with men born in Portugal, known as *reinóis*—in order to be married there.[57] Six *donzelle* were sent on the India run to be married 'in quelle parti' (in those parts); they were said to be impoverished gentlewomen of noble birth who had been collected in a convent set up for this purpose in Lisbon. The ships bound for Angola, on the other hand, contained twelve *convertite*, or former prostitutes, travelling at the king's expense, sent to the governor of Angola with instructions to arrange their marriages.[58] It is not clear how far, if at all, the social status and past activity of the women was related to the choice made for them of their destination and future lives, but the divide in destination seems rather fixed. All female orphans in the royal orphanage, the Recolhimento

55. On which, see Guinote, Frutuoso and Lopes, *As armadas*, p. 142, and Elsje van Kessel, 'The Inventories of the *Madre de Deus*: Tracing Asian Material Culture in Early Modern England', *Journal of the History of Collections*, 32.2 (2020), pp. 207–23.

56. This boardgame was on show in the exhibition in Florence *Dai depositi 1: Ritratti di paesi, mari e città*, curated by Matteo Ceriana, Anna Bisceglia, Fausta Navarro and Daniele Rapino, Palazzo Pitti, Galleria Palatina, 15 October 2014–1 February 2015 (inv. Castello 1911, no. 395; no catalogue available).

57. On the phenomenon, see Timothy J. Coates, *Convicts and Orphans: Forced and State-Sponsored Colonizers in the Portuguese Empire, 1550–1755* (Stanford, CA, 2001), pp. 141–77.

58. ASV, Fondo Confalonieri 15, 326r.

do Castelo (de São Jorge) were sent either to India or Brazil.[59] All reformed prostitutes in the last decade of the sixteenth and throughout the seventeenth century were sent to Angola or Mozambique, with the exception of one group who were sent to Maranhão in Brazil.[60]

The compilers of the Lisbon *avvisi* included few news stories from Portugal that did not concern diplomacy, war and trade, but when they did, these tended to be sensationalist, scandalous or both. The *avviso* of 2 September 1595 told the tale of a man accused of having sex with his *àsino* (donkey), who was burnt, along with his donkey (as though the donkey had agency in choosing to have sex performed on it),[61] on Tuesday, which was market day, in the main market square of Rossio. The man accused of bestiality had been denounced by two men and two women, but almost immediately after his execution it was decided that it was a false accusation, and they in their turn were condemned to suffer the same fate.[62] This story matters here because it shows that the notion of the false or untrue was an accepted fact of life, with false accusations taking their place alongside false news. The story is also relevant because it is rooted in Lisbon's imperial haunts: the Tuesday market in Lisbon included a large number of goods, some of them second-hand, from across the Portuguese trading empire, but especially from India. But the story of 1595 is more complicated still, as an almost exact equivalent can be found in the writings of a Neapolitan chronicler under the year 1604. In this case Andrea, the owner of the donkey, was denounced to the criminal authorities in Naples by some of his enemies after a quarrel; the authorities tortured him until he confessed he had had sex with his donkey, causing him to be hanged, and then burnt along with the donkey. This account of the punishment is corroborated by evidence

---

59. Coates, *Convicts and Orphans*, pp. 142–8.

60. Ibid., pp. 139–40.

61. Although an animal did not possess reason, and could not sin, whenever it had been used for sexual purposes it had to be burnt because it was the instrument through which the sin was committed, and it could not be allowed to survive as a 'memory' of it. See James A. Brundage, *Law, Sex and Christian Society in Medieval Europe* (Chicago, 1987), pp. 212–14, 313–14, 398–400, 472–74 and 533–36; James Brundage, 'Sex and Canon Law', in Vern L. Bullough and James A. Brundage, eds, *Handbook of Medieval Sexuality* (New York, 1996), pp. 33–50 at 43; Susanne Hehenberger, 'Dehumanised Sinners and Their Instruments of Sin: Men and Animals in Early Modern Bestiality Cases, Austria, 1500–1800', in Karl A. E. Enenkel and Paul J. Smith, eds, *Early Modern Zoology: The Construction of Animals in Science, Literature and the Visual Arts*, 2 vols (Leiden, 2007), 2, pp. 381–417 at 388–93.

62. ASV, Segretaria di stato, Portogallo 10, 198r–v, and Fondo Confalonieri 15, 343r.

from the archives of the Bianchi della giustizia, who name the unfortunate man as Andrea del Colle. According to the chronicler, one of the denouncers was tortured shortly afterwards on account of another crime, and confessed to having falsely accused Andrea, thus bringing about his own hanging.[63] This could be dismissed as an urban myth were it not for the archival evidence. How is it possible that these two 'events' took place within a ten-year period, in both Lisbon and Naples? Did the Lisbon case become a *cause celèbre* and act as a precedent, ushering in a whole series of copycat denunciations? For that to be plausible, the Lisbon *avvisi* (or the news therefrom) must have been sent also to Naples, and the story of the man accused of having sex with his donkey must have circulated amongst the population there; but at present the reach or degree of proto-syndication of *avviso* news items is not known. Is the explanation perhaps simply that bestiality was a surefire way of persuading criminal or ecclesiastical authorities to act against enemies, as it was considered the most serious of the so-called unnatural sins?

All the while, alongside these news stories, Biondi also reported back to Rome on the fulfilment of his other tasks. Thus on 25 November 1595 he wrote to Cardinal Pietro Aldobrandini about a *processo* (trial) against the Capuchin friar Michele di Coimbra nominated to the bishopric of San Salvatore in Kongo—and included what he called 'the usual sheet of news'.[64] The separation between religious affairs and other news, relayed by different media, was here acknowledged, but religious news occasionally made it into the *avvisi* and much non-religious news was relevant to the workings of the Catholic church, so the separation did not always hold.

Cosas peregrinas, or 'Wandering Objects'

Shifting the focus from global news to global objects or products mentioned in Biondi's correspondence, it is clear that Lisbon functioned as an epicentre or entrepôt for such objects. Yet what is known of Biondi's own material concerns during his time in Lisbon suggests that his relocation to the hub of the Portuguese trading empire did not make a great impact on his already formed Roman tastes. The historical artefacts of classical antiquity in Rome lured him in a way that global goods in Lisbon failed to do. Even so, as will be seen below, he did buy a smattering of global goods that he sent or took with him back to

63. Carlo D'Addosio, *Bestie delinquenti* (Naples, 1992 [1892]), p. 88.
64. ASV, Segretaria di stato, Portogallo 10, 279v.

Italy. He also had a soft spot for global animals such as monkeys and parrots that he considered amusing playthings (again, see below), as did many others in Rome who kept exotic animals and birds as pets and set up menageries and aviaries. Overall, however, with few exceptions, Biondi was conservative in his tastes, valuing the historical offerings from Italy above the contemporary offerings from round the world that his appointment to a posting in Lisbon put within easy reach. Instead of taking advantage of Lisbon's world of goods, he stayed aligned with Roman cultural norms. Wanting to keep, and enhance, antiquities found on one's own property, with all their associations, was standard cultural practice in sixteenth-century Rome. Biondi's correspondence shows that foremost in his thoughts were his Roman house and its garden on the slopes of Montecavallo on the Quirinal Hill, to which he returned in his mind as often as he could. He had been given this house by the Marchesa Claudia Ferrero Fieschi in 1585 as a reward for services to her family,[65] and he was firmly attached to it, writing that whatever pleasurable recreation he had in the world emanated from 'quel povero luogo' (that decrepit place).[66] Left to his own devices, he would not have gone abroad, and he constantly bewailed being in Lisbon and longed to be back in Rome. One reason for his attachment was that excavation in the garden of the house was yielding results—and Biondi was a small-time collector of ancient sculpture. In January 1594 he wrote to his brother Domenico that Don Cesare (Piazza?) had written a few months before to say that digging in the garden they had found 'una bella testa', presumably an ancient Roman head.[67] In June 1596, after it became known that a torso thought to be of Cupid—but in reality likely to have been of Apollo—had been excavated in his garden,[68] he became embroiled in a series of epistolary and other manoeuvres to hold onto it and not be forced to hand it over either to his patron, Cardinal Alessandro Montalto, or his patron's best friend, Cardinal Francesco Maria Del Monte, a particularly knowledgeable but rather sharp collector

65. Yvan Loskoutoff, 'The "Cupid Affair" (1596): Cardinal Francesco Maria Del Monte as a Collector of Antiquities', *Journal of the History of Collections*, 25.1 (2013), pp. 19–27 at 21 and n. 37.

66. ASV, Fondo Confalonieri 28, 469v, Biondi to Ruggero Tritonio, abbot of S. Maria di Pinerolo, who was Cardinal Montalto's secretary, 8 May [mistake for June?] 1596. On Tritonio, see https://www.dizionariobiograficodeifriulani.it/tritonio-ruggero/ (accessed 27 April 2023).

67. ASV, Fondo Confalonieri 27, 423v.

68. The sculptor Flaminio Vacca recorded the find in his memoirs, but appears to have muddled the dates of two separate finds of 1594 and 1596. See Rodolfo Lanciani, *Storia degli scavi di Roma e notizie intorno le collezioni romane di antichità*, 4 vols (Rome, 1902–12), 4, p. 99.

of ancient sculpture.[69] Another long-running lament of Biondi is his lack of money, even though he apparently returned to Rome with a substantial sum, and at his death left a sizeable estate.[70] In July 1596, for instance, he writes to his brother Domenico that he does not care about having plates made of silver, that for him eating off maiolica is sufficient—although this kind of comment between family members is always suspect.[71]

Even at the time, it was recognised that there was a category of things known as *cosas peregrinas*. This could mean both 'rare or strange objects' or 'wandering objects'—there was some crossover between the two meanings, as rarity was usually the consequence of removal from familiar territory—and was a suggestive and evocative phrase indicating foreignness and rarity as well as mobility and restlessness, with some objects more suitable than others to join their ranks, and with different gradations of success.[72] The word *peregrinas* encapsulates a feeling of movement. Now the phrase would be translated without hesitation as 'global objects', but keeping a sense of both the intricacies and levels of meaning seems important. Why certain types of object, such as bezoar stones, became desirable across the globe, acquiring this label, has not been satisfactorily explained, and like many fashions, may not be entirely susceptible to rational analysis.

While interest in 'wandering objects' as a category soared in the sixteenth century, it is still unusual to find it encapsulated in a document revealing a familiarity with a great many locations across the globe. Included in the Confalonieri *fondo* is an undated list in Spanish of a slight variant, *mercaderias peregrinas*, or 'rare or strange merchandise'/'wandering merchandise'—in fact, foreign or wandering raw materials—accompanied by the names of the places from which the goods could be obtained,[73] which could date from Confalonieri's period in Spain as secretary to the nuncio Camillo Caetani from 1597 to 1600.[74] Whoever compiled this document possessed a sophisticated knowledge not only of the world's political geography, but also of its natural resources; precision of provenance of products provided the rationale for its existence. Gold

69. ASV, Fondo Confalonieri 28, 469v, Biondi to Abbate Tritonio, Cardinal Montalto's secretary, 8 May [mistake for June?] 1596; Loskoutoff, '"Cupid Affair"', pp. 19 and 21 and n. 34. The manoeuvres were successful, and the Cupid/Apollo, renamed the Genio Borghese, is now in the Louvre.

70. Loskoutoff, '"Cupid Affair"', p. 19.

71. ASV, Fondo Confalonieri 28, 657v, Biondi to Domenico Biondi, 3 July 1596.

72. ASV, Fondo Confalonieri 45, 58r–60v.

73. ASV, Fondo Confalonieri 45, 61r–63v.

74. *DBI*, 27, p. 780.

is the first item, listed as available under the headings 'Asia' (with three places of origin named), 'Islas de Asia' (eight places), 'America' (eight places), 'Islas d'ella' (three places) and 'Africa' (six places). Highly unusual in its degree of specificity, this list signals that around the world were twenty-eight countries or areas known to produce gold or have access to it. Gold was followed by silver, diamonds, pearls, rubies, turquoises and amethysts before there was a change to animal products, starting with ivory and including civet and musk, before another change to all sorts of spices, and a number of less easily pigeon-holed products such as sugar and cotton. Sixteen places in Asia and the East Indies could supply ginger, a commodity with one of the most numerous points of acquisition.[75] The majority of these raw materials, although available in a number of places, were not available in both Asia and in Africa (although silver, pearls and sugar were) or in both Asia and America (although pearls, for instance, were). When the political situation or war interfered with trade routes, it was easier if there were several sources, especially if one was to the west and another to the east. Given the multiple local and global criss-crossing trade routes along which these 'foreign or wandering raw products' (*mercade-rias peregrinas*) travelled, it is hardly surprising to find that 'foreign or wandering objects' (*cosas peregrinas*) travelled similar distances to be acquired by willing buyers on the other side of the globe. What is perhaps more remarkable is to note which objects were the most desired.

Even though gold and silver topped the list of global wandering raw products, and some gold and gold objects from around the globe (in the case of West Africa, a bracelet, a basket, beakers and a cup)[76] are known to have reached Lisbon, Biondi's correspondence does not reveal any requests from Italy for either of these metals, or for any objects made from them. This absence is very nearly replicated in the archival records from this date still extant in Lisbon relating more generally to precious metals in and from Africa.[77] In addition to the six places in Africa on the list reported as producing gold, two

---

75. ASV, Fondo Confalonieri 45, 62r–v.

76. *Portugaliae monumenta africana*, 2, pp. 408–10; Annemarie Jordan Gschwend and Kate Lowe, 'Renaissance Lisbon's Global Sites', in *A cidade global: Lisboa no Renascimento/The Global City: Lisbon in the Renaissance*, ed. Annemarie Jordan Gschwend and K.J.P. Lowe, exh. cat., Museu Nacional de Arte Antiga, Lisbon (Lisbon, 2017), pp. 243–55 at 248.

77. One exception is provided by a letter of 17 February 1580 from the interim 'ruler' of Portugal, the viceroy Duarte de Castelo-Branco, to Philip II of Spain, before Philip arrived in Portugal in December 1580 to take over the Portuguese crown. In it, Castelo-Branco writes of the ambassador from Angola who was at the Lisbon court in 1580 and had brought with him samples of the

places in mainland Africa were reported as producing silver, Ethiopia and Bagamidri (or Bēgamedr; one of the kingdoms of Ethiopia),[78] and the island of Madagascar.[79] Given that Europeans knew about and were keenly interested in gold and silver as materials for decorative objects of the highest quality, it is unclear why more gold and silver objects from Africa are not recorded as arriving in Lisbon (the 1755 destruction notwithstanding), and why no references have yet been found to gold or silver objects from Africa—with the possible exception of Ethiopian crosses—reaching the Italian peninsula in the Renaissance period. Unworked gold from the Portuguese trading empire arriving in Portugal could be commandeered by the Portuguese,[80] either to be used in the Portuguese mint or to be made into works of art by Portuguese goldsmiths. In the first few decades of the sixteenth century unworked gold was minted into a large gold coin, the *português*, of very high quality, which circulated widely,[81] often featuring in Portuguese and other shipwrecks from the period.[82] Other

---

excellent silver available in Angola. Lisbon, Biblioteca da Ajuda, MS. 49-X-4, fols 360r–361r. Angolan silver was not known to the list-maker of the foreign or wandering raw materials.

78. The kingdom of Bēgamedr is mentioned by Francisco Álvares in his book on the Portuguese embassy to Ethiopia in 1520; in it, Álvares wrote of Bēgamedr's reputation for having seams of silver: Francisco Álvares, *Verdadeira informação sobre a Terra do Preste João das Índias (II)*, ed. Luís de Albuquerque (Lisbon, 1989), p. 105; Francisco Álvares, *The Prester John of the Indies: A True Relation of the Lands of the Prester John, Being the Narrative of the Portuguese Embassy to Ethiopia in 1520*, ed. C. F. Beckingham and G.W.B. Huntingford, 2 vols (Cambridge, 1961), 2, p. 460.

79. ASV, Fondo Confalonieri 45, 61v.

80. This seems not to have been the case with gold from the Spanish empire, some of which appears to have trickled into Italy. For example, Isabella and Ferdinando are reputed to have sent some of the first gold from the New World to Alexander VI, who used it on the ceiling of S. Maria Maggiore in Rome. The story in printed form can be dated to 1621: Philip J. Jacks, 'Alexander VI's Ceiling for Santa Maria Maggiore in Rome', *Römisches Jahrbuch für Kunstsgeschichte*, 22 (1985), pp. 63–82 at 65.

81. Hugo Miguel Crespo, ed., *Comprar o mundo: Consumo e comércio na Lisboa do Renascimento/Shopping for Global Goods: Consumption and Trade in Renaissance Lisbon* (Lisbon, 2020), pp. 34–36.

82. See, e.g., the wreck of the *Bom Jesus* near to Oranjemund in Namibia, where c. 8% of 2,100 coins recovered were *portugueses* from the reign of João III: Bruno Werz, 'Saved from the Sea: The Shipwreck of the *Bom Jesus* (1533) and Its Material Culture', in Annemarie Jordan Gschwend and K.J.P. Lowe eds, *The Global City: On the Streets of Renaissance Lisbon* (London, 2015), pp. 88–93 at 91–92. Müller, *Welthandelsbräuche*, p. 297 refers to a German book of tolls of 1514–15 that discusses a list of goods available for sale in Lisbon, mentioning 'gold da man die crusadi ausmacht' (gold from which they make the *cruzados*), from Guinea. See Johnson, *German Discovery*, p. 110.

unworked gold, brought from Kilwa in East Africa by Vasco da Gama on his voyage of 1504–5, was famously used by the goldsmith and playwright Gil Vicente to create the monstrance of Belém in 1506, now in the Museu Nacional de Arte Antiga in Lisbon; information about how it came into being was recorded in an inscription on the monstrance itself.[83] By the end of the sixteenth century, there is still a dearth of material relating to gold or gold objects from the Portuguese trading empire known to have been in Lisbon, and requested in Italy. Biondi's secretary Giovanni Battista Confalonieri, in his *Grandezza e magnificenza della città di Lisbona*, distinguished between imports of materials and products from outside Portugal that were kept in Lisbon and those that were exported; he wrote of gold from Mina being kept in the city and adverted to the excellent work of goldsmiths in Lisbon (although without reference to the source of the gold they used).[84] Elsewhere, he alluded to foreign materials exported through Lisbon, mentioning gold *patacconi*—Brazilian gold coins, sent to 'the Indies'— and gold itself, sent to Constantinople and Turkey, stating that the returns made on these two exports were forty per cent and fifty per cent respectively.[85] So maybe the high returns made on gold meant that it was often re-exported rather than being kept in Lisbon.

Global Goods

It is worth recapping the outlets in Lisbon where goods from the Portuguese trading empire were on sale. These six types of site clearly indicate that there were mechanisms and prices to allow a multiplicity of buying experiences, and to cater to a variety of purchasers, not merely the only one mentioned by Biondi: that of buying from newly arrived boats. In itself, this in turn may show that Biondi was not the best person to ask to make a purchase, because although he was keenly aware of the power relations attendant on obligations and reciprocity, he appears to have lacked the behavioural flexibility to adapt

83. *A Custódia de Belém: 500 Anos*, ed. Leonor D'Orey and Luísa Penalva, exh. cat., Museu Nacional de Arte Antiga, Lisbon (Lisbon, 2010), pp. 20 and 111. Other objects reputed to have been made in Lisbon from the first gold brought from India include a gold cross decorated with precious stones offered by Manuel I to the Convento de Cristo in Tomar: Celina Bastos and Anísio Franco, 'A Custódia de Belém e o ouro de Quíloa: A lenda das Índias', in *A Custódia de Belém*, ed. Leonor D'Orey and Luísa Penalva, exh. cat., Museu Nacional de Arte Antiga, Lisbon (Lisbon, 2010), pp. 126–39 at 133.

84. Confalonieri, *Grandezza e magnificenza*, pp. 179 and 253–54.

85. Ibid., p. 180.

when circumstances required it. How many of these outlets were actually used by Biondi is not clear, but he certainly had a variety of options in terms of where he could source his goods, if he had chosen to exercise them. The first was for goods to be bought directly from incoming ships arriving from the East. Biondi's correspondence makes it clear that this was his preferred or default option, but in the mid to late 1590s, very few ships managed to escape the predations of the English or the unpredictability of the weather on the route home, and so very few arrived back in Lisbon with their cargoes, creating a temporary dearth of certain goods.[86] On account of this, during Biondi's period in residence, alternative options such as buying from specialist shops and from private individuals, small-time collectors and agents, who were already in possession of goods acquired at an earlier date when cargoes were still arriving, might have been preferred. The diarist for the Venetian ambassadors Vincenzo Tron and Girolamo Lippomano, who visited Lisbon in 1581, recorded the delights of the Rua Nova in Lisbon with its infinity of shops, including four or six selling goods brought 'dall'Indie' (from 'the Indies'), such as porcelain, nautilus shells, coco de mer seeds and caskets inlaid with mother-of-pearl (which they recognised were very expensive at that date).[87] Yet Biondi scarcely acknowledges the existence of these objects, let alone the shops selling them, seeming to focus only on anticipating the cornucopia of new goods when the ships eventually arrived. Auctions and markets offered further alternative routes to purchase, but Biondi does not refer to these options either, although Campana fifty years earlier had scored a fabulous success when he bought at auction.

It has recently become clear that there was yet another site where these overseas goods were available to buy, but maybe only for a select few: the Casa da Mina (or Guiné) and the Casa da Índia, the Africa and India warehouses, royal repositories for the products of global trade. Biondi makes no mention of this possibility and it may be that he was not entitled to take advantage of buying from there. Who precisely would have been eligible to buy directly

86. See Confalonieri's account of this in ibid., p. 269.

87. Lisbon, Biblioteca da Ajuda, Rerum Lusitanicarum, V (46-IX-5): 'Commentarii per Italia, Francia, Spagna e Portogallo overo relazione del viaggio de Signori Cavalieri Tron e Lippomani eletti ambasciatori dalla Republica Veneta al Re Cattolico per complimentare Sua Maestà per la conquista di Portogallo l'anno MDLXXXI', 263r. Parts of this diary were translated into Portuguese: 'Viagem a Portugal dos Cavaleiros Tron e Lippomani, 1580', in Herculano, Opúsculos, 6, pp. 113–26. Another copy of this manuscript is in BAV, Fondo Reginense latino 949.

from the Casa da Índia is not known, nor whether or not this practice continued after Spain took control of Portugal in 1580. An early, humanistically educated tourist, travelling for pleasure, the German medical doctor Hieronymus
Münzer, embarked on a trip to France and the Iberian peninsula in 1494–95,
spending 26 November to 11 December 1494 in Portugal. On the eve of the
feast of Santo André on 30 November, King João II gave the order to conduct
him and his companions to the Casa da Mina, where they were shown not only
the goods waiting to be sent by the king to sub-Saharan Africa but also those
belonging to the king that had originated there.[88] In this case, provenance—at
least continental provenance—was secure. Münzer enumerated grains of paradise (a type of cardamom), branches and bunches of pepper, elephant tusks
and gold, all of which had come from West Africa. This passage is well known,
yet it is now apparent that a visit to one of these global warehouses, far from
being a privilege granted only to Münzer, was or became a recognised route
for would-be buyers to find the purchases they desired. Unfortunately, Münzer
does not reveal whether he bought anything, and if so what. New information
from an account book of 1560–68 recording the purchases of jewellery and
gemstones by three Augsburg merchants and agents in the Fugger office in
Lisbon shows that they bought directly from the Casa da Índia,[89] probably
continuing a well-established practice.

It is surely always worthwhile rehearsing the arguments as to why choices
in consumption mattered, and what they could indicate. Consumption is as
much a political act as a material one, and the goods obtained should be seen
as a social investment. Biondi's correspondence reveals a stream of requests
addressed to him in Lisbon from contacts of every sort in Italy asking for his
help in obtaining specific extra-European goods. Biondi understood these requests for what they were: political and social favours were being called in for
favours done for him in the past, and he was storing up credit for others by
providing favours that he in his turn could redeem in the future. He was en-
meshed in a series of familial, secular and ecclesiastical patronage systems

88. Jérôme Münzer, *Voyage en Espagne et au Portugal (1494–1495)*, ed. Michel Tarayre (Paris,
2006), pp. 132–33.

89. Annemarie Jordan Gschwend, 'Comprar gemas de todo o mundo em Lisboa: Em busca
de diamantes indianos, gemas asiáticos, pérolas de Ormuz e esmeraldas peruanas/Shopping
for Global Gems in Lisbon: The Quest for Indian Diamonds, Asian Gemstones, Pearls from
Hormuz and Peruvian Emeralds', in Hugo Miguel Crespo, ed., *Comprar o mundo: Consumo e
comércio na Lisboa do Renascimento/Shopping for Global Goods: Consumption and Trade in
Renaissance Lisbon* (Lisbon, 2020), pp. 20–31 at 21, 25.

whose myriad participants saw his posting to Lisbon as an opportunity to acquire and possess objects that were much more expensive and difficult to acquire in Italy. However tedious this might have been at a day-to-day level, Biondi too must have rejoiced at the possibilities for networking advancement offered by Lisbon's markets of goods that provided ready access to coveted presents, if presents were needed, or to particular types of specific object, if precise objects were ordered, either by patrons or by friends.

One noticeable change in the fifty-year period from the acquisition of the rarest possible objects for Cosimo in the 1540s to requests to Biondi from Italian patrons and clients in the 1590s is for global objects with a specific function. The objects were still rare in Europe, and could not be obtained at home, but they were useful as opposed to decorative. In this sense, indiscriminate neophilia had been replaced by a more focused, less exciting consumerism. People knew what they wanted to possess. Yet again, the precise place of origin of the object appears to have been irrelevant; the only thing that mattered was possession of it. It is clear that precision itself in relation to knowledge of objects was not valued by Biondi's correspondents except in a small number of cases. Paradoxically, although by the 1590s knowledge of the global had had fifty more years to be internalised in Europe, in this Italian correspondence knowledge of global products and goods seems to have shrunk rather than expanded. Biondi's letters reveal that his patrons and friends had a small number of desiderata that were thought to be available in Lisbon from the overseas empire, with the same things being requested time and time again. No one in this correspondence in the 1590s ever asked for anything new or thought that something that had never been seen before would appear on the market, or told Biondi just to buy indiscriminately; that moment had passed. For example, it is noticeable that there were no requests for some of the certainly arresting and unusual objects already obtained by cardinals in Rome by mid-century, which might have been thought to be available in Lisbon, such as the petrified elephant's jaw in the collection of Cardinal Gaddi,[90] noted by Ulisse Aldrovandi

---

90. This could be either Niccolò (d. 1552) or Taddeo (cardinal 155761), but is more likely to be the latter. On Niccolò, see Eubel, *Hierarchia catholica*, 3, p. 35; *DBI*, 51 (1998), pp. 161–64, entry by Vanna Arrighi; on Taddeo, see Eubel, *Hierarchia catholica*, 3, p. 35; *DBI*, 51 (1998), pp. 173–74, entry by Vanna Arrighi—but in neither entry is there mention of any cultural or collecting activities. The most noted collector in the family was another Niccolò (1537–91), mentioned in chapter 30, a friend of Francesco I de' Medici, who is known to have had a small collection of natural history specimens: *DBI*, 51 (1998), entry by Vanna Arrighi, pp. 164–65 at 165.

in 1558.[91] In the intervening fifty years, most of the goods requested from Biondi had moved from being quite extraordinarily exclusive to being material signs of a certain social or political status, but one that enveloped a far greater range of people.

The move towards more routine purchases might be a contributory factor in explaining why not a single one of the objects mentioned in Biondi's correspondence has yet been tracked down and identified. But it is not the sole or even the main reason, which is that none of Biondi's correspondents—unlike the Medici—left a collection that survived. If any of these objects are still extant, they have been separated not only from their original place or places of provenance around the world, but also from their point of entry into Italy, and from any connection to the Italian families who sent to Lisbon for their acquisition. They are adrift, having lost the histories of their subsequent owners and provenances in addition to losing their maker's name and place of origin.

If requests had been more adventurous, moreover, Biondi would have been unlikely to be able to fulfil them. As noted above, fewer ships from the Carreira da Índia managed to return to Lisbon for a period in the 1590s, mainly because they were intercepted by the English. In June 1594 Biondi wrote that there had been 'two or three years' in which no ships arrived from India, and that last year one had arrived but with most of its cargo gone, and the rest 'putrid'.[92] On 1 April 1595 Biondi wrote to Monsignor Ratta that in the time he had been in Lisbon (that is, the two years from 11 March 1593 to 1 April 1595), only two ships from the India run had limped into Lisbon, one in the worst possible condition.[93] Some years were still good. An *avviso* of 10 August 1596 recorded the arrival of the *San Pantaleone*, one of the ships on the India run, saying that four out of five ships had now arrived, with only the *San Simone* missing.[94] But, unfortunately for his friends, Biondi's residence in Lisbon coincided with a period of great uncertainty and loss in terms of ships bringing back goods from the Persian Gulf, South and South-East Asia, the Far East, and the New World, and most of the time he was unable to help them with their requests. However,

91. Ulisse Aldrovandi, *Delle statue antiche, che per tutta Roma in diversi luoghi & case si veggono*, included in Lucio Mauro, *Le antichità delle città di Roma, breuissimamente raccolte da chiunque ne ha scritto ò antico ò moderno [...]* (Venice, 1558), p. 190: 'meravigliosa cosa è un mascella, ch'egli ha di elefante petrificata, ma con i suoi denti'. Eleonora di Toledo too had an elephant's jawbone in her room in Florence by 1574: Groom, *Exotic Animals*, p. 209.

92. ASV, Fondo Confalonieri 28, 9v, Biondi to Martio Colonna, 25 June 1594.

93. Ibid., 130r, Biondi to Mons. Ratta, 1 April 1595.

94. Ibid., 360r.

in the process of explaining why he could not oblige, more information about global affairs percolated back into Italy, attached, as it were, to the histories of material objects. For instance, in May 1595 Biondi had been sent six hundred *scudi d'oro* and commissioned by Alfonso II d'Este, the duke of Ferrara, to acquire a string of pearls for his third wife, Margarita Gonzaga.[95] A year later, in May 1596, he reported on the rather slow progress of this commission to collect the necessary hundred pearls 'di cinque o sei grani' (of five or six grains)[96] to construct the string.[97] He explained that there had never been such a dearth ('penuria') of jewels in Lisbon, and most particularly of pearls from the East Indies (as shipping from the East was being harried by English corsairs), of which there were very few and these extremely expensive. Most people instead bought pearls from the West Indies which went to Seville and Madrid—on fleets which were still managing to arrive from the Americas— and Biondi recommended that this course of action might be a better bet. He reported that he had spent three years putting together a string of fifty or sixty mediocre pearls in part-fulfilment of his commission.[98] In July 1595 he heard that Alfonso had indeed found suitable pearls in Madrid.[99] This tale of a commission for a string of pearls that was difficult to fulfil gives more hard information about the non-arrival of the *naus* from the East than might have been expected, showing that biographies of objects as presented in letters can also be fertile territory for studies of levels of global consciousness.

In April 1596 Biondi did manage to send a part-load of chests, containing various global and Portuguese goods, on board the ship *Stella* from Lisbon to Livorno. Although the destinations and destinatees of the seven chests are known—one was to be sent to Turin to the Contessa Zana Langosca de La Motta, the wife of Conte Alfonso Langosco de La Motta, one of the *maggior-domi* at the Savoy court and a frequent ambassador to Madrid,[100] one to Turin to Biondi's vicar Cesare Piazza, three to his brother Domenico Biondi at Montegiordano in Rome, one to the protonotary Pietro Giorgio Camagna[101] in Rome, and the last to Gian Paolo Tetrarossi in Rome—only the contents of

95. Ibid., 322v, Biondi to Antonio Fermo, 20 May 1595.

96. A grain is a quarter of a carat in weight, i.e., 50 mg.

97. ASV, Fondo Confalonieri 28, 620r, Biondi to Antonio Fermo, 11 May 1596.

98. Ibid., 620r.

99. Ibid., 354r.

100. *DBI*, 63 (2004), pp. 237–38, entry by Andrea Merlotti.

101. Biondi described him as 'mio auditore' in a letter of 11 December 1593: ASV, Segreteria di stato, Portogallo 9, 184r.

the first were recorded: fifty or sixty pieces of porcelain and some Portuguese terracotta vases known as *buccheri*.[102] Porcelain was a perennial favourite, always in demand in Rome and across the Italian peninsula, yet not once is its Chinese origin mentioned. The reason for the lack of provenance might be thought to differ in this case from that regarding other categories of object: it was common knowledge in Europe that porcelain came from China and was available from nowhere else, so it was an object with an inbuilt provenance: a provenance was inherent in the material. However, even this origin could be interfered with or rendered generically by authors in moments of laziness or imprecision. Giovanni Battista Confalonieri wrote that in Lisbon there was an abundance of Indian porcelain ('porcellana d'India', so Indian in the widest possible sense, meaning eastern), which was available at a good price when the ships arrived (from the East).[103] When in 1562 the archbishop of Braga, Bartolomeu dos Mártires, suggested to Pius IV a switch at table from silver to porcelain, he explained that the new tableware 'vêm da India, fazem-se na China' (comes from India, is made in China).[104] Coming 'from India' here effectively meant coming on the ships on the Carreira da Índia—but it was used as a sort of shorthand, that could obscure the real provenance unless it were already understood. In this rendition of provenance, it could be two-tiered, referring both to the place of manufacture and the place from which the object was despatched. This has important implications for other moments when the formulation 'd'India' is used, as in these instances too India may have been the place of despatch rather than the place of origin or manufacture.

Unfortunately, there is little information about where in Lisbon or how Biondi collected these particular pieces of porcelain. In letters to his patrons, he often lamented the difficulties of finding porcelain in Lisbon at a reasonable price, yet in letters to family members, or his household, he is able to report that he has sent chests containing it to Italy. For example, in April 1595 he told Monsignore Ratta, who had asked for porcelain, that rather than pay exorbitant prices he should wait until the arrival of next year's ships carrying goods

102. ASV, Fondo Confalonieri 28, 451r, 452r–v, Biondi to Giovan Girolamo Albano, 26 April 1596.

103. Confalonieri, *Grandezza*, p. 256.

104. *Vida de Dom Frei Bertolameu dos Martyres do Ordem dos Pregadores arcebispo e senhor de Braga primas das Espanhas [. . .]*, arranged by Luis de Cacegas (Viana, 1619), p. 91; Frei Luís de Sousa, *A Vida de Dom Frei Bertolameu dos Mártires*, ed. Aníbal Pinto do Castro (2nd edn, Lisbon, 2015 [1984]), p. 256; Spallanzani, *Ceramiche alla corte dei Medici*, p. 123 (and n. 5 for further bibliography); Morena, *Dalle Indie orientali*, p. 42; Marques, 'Cultura material', p. 195.

from China.[105] However, just six weeks later, on 13 May, he wrote to his sister-in-law, Settimia Biondi,[106] that he had just sent her a chestful of porcelain. [107] In December 1595, Biondi was again telling a Monsignor Canobio that porcelain was not to be found in Lisbon, but offered to share some of his own trove of it when he returned to Italy.[108] It is clear from his letters that he collected porcelain piecemeal, presumably because that was his best or only option. For example, he wrote to Conte Alfonso Langosco de La Motta in March 1596 that he had bought a dozen porcelain *scudelle* (bowls), and would get other forms of porcelain elsewhere.[109] In April 1596 he told Motta, at that point ambassador to Spain, that he was sending two dozen pieces of porcelain to Italy on the ship *Stella* leaving for Livorno. The second dozen pieces were *piaderelle* (little dishes), which he complained had been very expensive.[110] It is unclear how what were two dozen pieces on 20 April had grown by 26 April to become the fifty or sixty pieces sent to Countess Zana Langosca de la Motta.[111] The ship did not sail until some time between 30 May and 2 June.[112]

In the same letter of 13 May 1595 to Settimia, Biondi reported he had also sent her 'uno tavolino di legno santo'.[113] This *tavolino* was a small wooden tray, a *tavoleiro* or *tabuleiro* in Portuguese, and *legno santo* is the contemporary Italian translation of the Portuguese word *pau-santo*, similar to the French *palissandre*. It is a generic word, but at this date it is known to refer to rosewood of the *Dalbergia* species. The mention of this small tray in a letter is a good example of the mystery and the limitations of archival material. In contradistinction to working from an object, when a great deal can be deduced by minute examination and analysis, working from an archival record of an object means that a great deal can never be securely known without further records, or without retrieving the object itself or depictions of it. However, subjecting the archival record to detailed examination and analysis can lead to contextual

105. ASV, Fondo Confalonieri 28, 130r–v, Biondi to Mons. Ratta, 1 April 1595.

106. In ibid., 10r, Settimia is addressed as Biondi's *cognata* and at 267v she is addressed as 'Signora Settimia Condopoli de Biondi'.

107. Ibid., 149r, Biondi to Settimia Biondi, 13 May 1595.

108. Ibid., 416r, Biondi to Monsignor Giovan Battista Canobio, 23 December 1595.

109. Ibid., 441v, Biondi to Conte Alfonso Langosco della Motta, 30 March 1596.

110. Ibid., 449v, Biondi to signore ambasciadore Motta, 20 April 1596.

111. It may be relevant that the higher number appears in a letter to Giovan Girolamo Albano, ibid., 451r.

112. Ibid., 468v and 635v.

113. Ibid., 149r, Biondi to Settimia Biondi, 13 May 1595.

enlightenment. Different species of trees from different parts of the world produce wood that has traditionally been referred to as *pau-santo* or rosewood. In the sixteenth century, Brazil was not producing furniture or worked wooden pieces, so it is much more probable that what Biondi bought was an object made from East Indian rosewood (*Dalbergia latifolia*) rather than Brazilian rosewood (*Dalbergia nigra*).[114] At the end of the sixteenth century Taná or Thane (in present-day Mumbai) in India would have been the most likely centre of production for a rosewood tray,[115] which could either be inlaid with other exotic woods or lacquered.[116] It is a measure of the immensity of Lisbon's status as a global entrepôt that there are two possible interpretations of this archival item, with widely divergent provenances, one from India, and the other from tropical America. Working across multiple languages increases the likelihood of misidentification of objects and materials, and the wood specified in this example shows the pitfalls of greeting false friends. It might have been thought that another possibility was that this wood was the *pau santo* or holy wood known as *lignum vitae* (*Guaiacum sanctum* or *Guaiacum officinale*), as *lignum vitae* is a type of *palo santo*, a hard wood from the Caribbean and the northern coast of South America, now on the endangered list in many countries. There are many types of *palo santo*, some used as incense in the Americas and others used for medicinal purposes. But *palo santo* is neither the Portuguese/Brazilian *pau-santo* (*Dalbergia nigra*) nor the Indian variety (*Dalbergia latifolia*): *pau-santo* is rosewood.

Portuguese goods, such as *buccheri* (terracotta vases) from the town of Estramoz, were also in demand in Italy at this date, although they became much more desirable and fashionable items at European courts in the seventeenth century.[117] As well as porcelain, Campana fifty years earlier in 1547 had also

---

114. The tray may have been made in Portugal, however, or anywhere else from any type of rosewood available on the market. If Biondi had been writing a century later its place of manufacture would be more difficult to identify, as in the seventeenth century and eighteenth centuries much furniture made from rosewood or *jacarandá* also came from Brazil.

115. Hugo Miguel Crespo, ed., *Choices* (Lisbon, 2016), pp. 148–52 discusses the luxury furniture production at Thane.

116. For an example of a tray made of Indian wood that was then lacquered, see Ulrike Körber, 'The "Three Brothers": Sixteenth-Century Lacquered Indo-Muslim Shields or Commodities for Display?', in Annemarie Jordan Gschwend and K.J.P. Lowe, eds, *The Global City: On the Streets of Renaissance Lisbon* (London, 2015), pp. 212–25 at 218–19, 222–23, and fig. 212.

117. Brandão, 'Majestade e grandezas', p. 35 and n. 80; Cristina Marchisio, 'Siguiendo la senda de los búcaros: Cosme III de Toscana en España y Portugal (1668–1669)', in *El viaje a*

purchased *buccheri*, probably for Eleonora rather than Cosimo, and clearly they had not lost their appeal.[118] Nor had Portugal's famed fruit preserves, which were still greatly valued in Italy, with *cotognato* sent back to Italy by Biondi whenever possible.[119] Another long-established Portuguese speciality available in Lisbon was the navigational chart, however distantly related to the Cantino planisphere analysed above in chapter 2. Although a Portuguese product, it was grounded in global knowledge. When Monsignor Curzio Frangipani asked Biondi to acquire one on his behalf, Biondi replied that a good manuscript one cost sixty or seventy *scudi*, and was only useful for navigational purposes, whereas a very beautiful one printed in Flanders (and available in Venice), giving the same information, cost only five *scudi*.[120] Printing clearly signalled a decrease in price and an increase in number and availability.

The Desirability of Bezoars

The most requested item in Biondi's correspondence was the bezoar stone, the global object *par excellence* of this period. The second half of the sixteenth century and the first decades of the seventeenth saw an exponential rise in the demand for these stones believed by many to counteract poison and to have other curative, magical or semi-magical properties. Their appeal cut across the division between popular and élite culture, inflamed both by the study of *materia medica* by humanists on one hand, and by a desperation-fuelled wish to try anything to stay alive when confronted by plague or poison on the other. At first sight, they are unlikely *naturalia* or natural products to take off as objects of desire because they are the opposite of glamorous: they are stone-like masses, composed of gallstones and hair, found in the gastro-intestinal systems of certain ruminants. Yet on further consideration they embody many Renaissance

---

Compostela de Cosme III de Médicis, ed. José Manuel García Iglesias, Xosé A. Neira Cruz and Cristina Acidini Luchinat, exh. cat., Museo Diocesano, Santiago de Compostela (Santiago de Compostela, 2004), pp. 287–307 at 301. They were also desired objects from Mexico at this date.

   118. ASF, Misc. med. 73, 2v.

   119. ASV, Fondo Confalonieri 28, 14r, Biondi to Signora Dorotea Ferrera Bobba, the sister of Biondi's old employers, Cardinals Pier Francesco (cardinal 1560–66) and Guido (cardinal 1565–85) Ferreri, and a very long-standing patron of Biondi, 1 July 1594; ibid., 14v, Biondi to Silvio Alberighi, 2 July 1594 (on a ship leaving for Genoa he sent a chest containing thirty-eight *scatole* of *cotognato*, with instructions to whom they should be given); ibid., 468v, Biondi to Domenico Biondi, 8 June 1596.

   120. Ibid., 181r, Biondi to Mons. Curzio Frangipani, 11 June 1594.

virtues. They are small and portable; they are rare, expensive and foreign (European ruminants do not have them); they have a wide range of applications and uses, medicinal as well as talismanic; they can be dressed up with expensive gold filigree workmanship, and turned into *artificialia* or man-made objects. Their nondescript nature allows projection. They were viewed by consumers as having a strict hierarchy in terms of desirability. Oriental ones were more desired than occidental. Oriental bezoars came from goats (especially *Capra aegagrus*, since 1996 an endangered species on the IUCN red list) and deer (*Antilope cervicapra*, or blackbuck) in Turkey, Persia and parts of the Indian subcontinent, with particularly prized ones coming from Khorāsān or Khurasan; the occidental variety came from alpacas and llamas in Peru.[121] The word bezoar appears to be of Persian origin, meaning help against poison, and this was one of its main uses in the sixteenth century. In their favour was the fact that they were reputed to be simultaneously preventative and curative.[122] Discussion of bezoars also straddled the intellectual divide that set the authority of texts against direct experience in the mid-sixteenth century: both printed texts and anecdotal evidence sang their praises, accepting their paramountcy. After mid-century, Garcia de Orta's *Colóquios dos simples e drogas he cousas medicinais da Índia*, published in Goa in 1563, tipped the balance irrevocably away from ancient texts in favour of direct experience,[123] but bezoars continued to be objects of desire. Bezoar stones as talismanic objects coming from elsewhere additionally provide an excellent example of a belief system going in reverse: that is, not Christianity going to indigenous peoples, but belief systems from indigenous peoples coming to Christians.

In the 1560s the Portuguese factor in Antwerp, Ruy Mendes, asked Queen Catarina de Áustria's help in acquiring six large bezoars for her brother, Ferdinand I. She found them in Lisbon. Mendes wrote a short report on the stones, praising oriental bezoars (as opposed to occidental ones, from Peru), saying

121. Jorge M. dos Santos Alves, 'A pedra-bezoar—realidade e mito em torno de un antídoto (séculos XVI e XVII), in Jorge M. Dos Santos Alves, Claude Guillot and Roderich Ptak, eds, *Mirabilia asiatica: Produtos raros no comércio marítimo/Produits rares dans le commerce maritime/ Seltene Waren im Seehandel* (Wiesbaden, 2003), pp. 121–34 at 122–23, 126.

122. Fricke, 'Making Marvels', p. 348.

123. See, e.g., colloquy 45 of Garcia de Orta, *Colóquios dos simples e drogas he cousas medicinais da Índia* (Goa, 1563) which was on bezoar stones; and António Manuel Lopes Andrade, 'Garcia de Orta and Amato Lusitano's Views on *materia medica*: A Comparative Perspective', in Palmira Fontes da Costa, ed., *Medicine, Trade and Empire: Garcia de Orta's 'Colloquies on the Simples and Drugs of India' (1563) in Context* (London, 2016), pp. 147–66 at 159.

the best ones of all come from Persia, followed by those from an island near Ceylon, and the Malay peninsula.[124] In 1580 Filippo Sassetti in Lisbon found a bezoar for a friend Baccio Valori in Florence, who perhaps wanted protection against plague. Sassetti recommended encircling the bezoar with gold, and wearing it around the neck, as might have been the intention with two extant sixteenth-century mounted specimens topped with rings, in a private collection in Portugal and the Kunsthistorisches Museum in Vienna (Plates 38 and 39).[125] Bezoars that were wearable were clearly talismanic rather than curative, and were not intended to be ingested. In January 1586, when he was in Cochin in India, Sassetti wrote at length about bezoars and their efficacy against illnesses in a letter to another friend in Florence, Lorenzo Canigiani, saying that those extracted from half-alive (or not quite dead) animals were the best.[126] He reserved his greatest praise for a *porcospino*, a stone extracted from a range of porcupines found across the Malay peninsula,[127] which he valued so highly that he told his correspondent never to lend it to anyone.

Biondi's correspondence indicates that the desire to possess these stones had not abated in Italy in the 1590s,[128] and it did not abate in the seventeenth century either.[129] In June 1595 Biondi told Duke Alfonso II d'Este, who had asked him for several bezoars, that none were to be found, and that if they were, they would be very expensive, so he would have to wait for the arrival of ships with new items. Already Biondi was distinguishing between oriental and occidental bezoars, saying that only the oriental ones were worthwhile,[130] although no further differentiation between provenance appears in the correspondence. Biondi let slip that he had bought some big ones the previous year for six or seven ducats per *ottava* but had not bought the smaller ones costing four or five ducats per *ottava*.[131] Marzio Colonna, who requested bezoars in

124. *Echt Tierisch!*, pp. 276–77.

125. Sassetti, *Lettere*, pp. 246–47; Lowe, 'Foreign Descriptions', p. 49.

126. Sassetti, *Lettere*, pp. 505–7.

127. Ibid., pp. 505–6; Borschberg, 'Euro-Asian Trade', p. 30; Fricke, 'Making Marvels', p. 353. See also Carletti's account of porcupine stones in Malacca in 1600: Carletti, *Ragionamenti*, p. 207; Carletti, *My Voyage*, p. 195.

128. It continued for decades more: Marques, 'Cultura material', pp. 191–94.

129. See the section on bezoars by Caterina Napoleone and Ian Rolfe in McBurney et al., *Birds*, 2, pp. 674–77, 679 and figs. 273–75.

130. ASV, Fondo Confalonieri 28, 340v–341r. See also Confalonieri, *Grandezza*, pp. 270–71.

131. ASV, Fondo Confalonieri 28, 341r.

June 1594, was given the answer that ships from India had not arrived for the past two or three years—although Biondi immediately contradicted this by saying that one had arrived the previous year but with all its most precious treasures already disembarked before it reached Lisbon.[132] To Giovan Francesco Ranzo in July 1594 he said the same.[133] Yet by 9 July Biondi was writing to Martio Colonna that he had not been able to find any small, perfect bezoars, but he had found some larger ones, weighing seven or eight *ottave*—a sixteenth-century bezoar in the Kunstkammer of the Kunsthistorisches Museum in Vienna with a gold ring inscribed in Spanish with its weight: PIEDRA . BESOHAR . FINISSIMA . PESA . OCHO . ONCAS (Plate 40) makes a good comparison—and he indicated the price.[134] In 1596 he was still getting requests for bezoars. He found one for the ambassador from Savoy, explaining it was small but good, and that those that were broken ('rotte') were more securely authentic than whole ones that could easily be falsified, indicating that fakes were in circulation and methods of assessing authenticity needed to be devised.[135] The possibility that bezoars might be fake would have inhibited Biondi and made him think twice before paying up front, because if he did so he might not have been able to recoup his outlay.

Given that whatever talismanic and curative powers bezoar stones might have been thought to possess, they were not Christian powers, this trafficking in bezoars to Italy by the apostolic collector and legate in Portugal, directly from ships returning from the Portuguese overseas empire, could be considered bizarre. Of course, lines between formal religions and other belief systems were fluid, but emphasising the talismanic powers of bezoars is more problematic for the Church than believing they had curative physical powers. It is one thing to turn a blind eye to the use of coral in a domestic setting by parents hoping thereby to provide a modicum of protection for children,[136] but quite another to permit prelates to wear bezoars as talismans. Believing that possession of these stones could ward off an almost unlimited range of

132. Ibid., 9v.

133. Ibid., 13r.

134. ASV, Fondo Confalonieri 28, 20r.

135. Ibid., 432v.

136. Jacqueline Marie Musacchio, 'Lambs, Coral, Teeth and the Intimate Intersection of Religion and Magic in Renaissance Tuscany', *Medieval and Renaissance Texts and Studies*, 296 (2005), pp. 139–56 at 151–53.

illnesses is effectively tantamount to believing in 'magic', however defined, denying the decision-making prowess or grace of God. On the other hand, the idea that certain gems, stones and other natural products were curative was still prevalent in the sixteenth century, and bezoars are discussed in the medical rather than the theological literature.[137] Problems may have been avoided in terms of their curative properties because they were believed to have been physically rather than spiritually efficacious against poison. Biondi was far from being alone in the ecclesiastical hierarchy in engaging in the great bezoar hunt, either for himself or others. The stones were omnipresent among the college of cardinals, for example, not to speak of dynastic regimes on the Italian peninsula. Cardinal Francesco Gonzaga had one in the 1480s;[138] Cardinal Carlo Borromeo was sent one by his aunt Margherita Trivulzi in June 1572 (she had been given it by Cosimo I de' Medici);[139] and even Cardinal Baronio, a well-known Catholic hard-liner who embraced poverty and died with very few possessions, had a bezoar stone listed in his post-mortem inventory of 1607–12.[140] The laity in Italy collected on a grander scale: the 1588 post-mortem inventory of the Portuguese merchant banker in Rome António da Fonseca listed at least twenty-one bezoar stones, half *orientali* and half from Peru,[141] and Ferdinando Gonzaga of Mantua had a cabinet full of bezoars in 1617.[142]

137. See, e.g., Andrea Bacci, *De venenis et antidotis* (Rome, 1586), published in the year he was appointed doctor to Sixtus V.

138. D. S. Chambers, *A Renaissance Cardinal and His Worldly Goods: The Will and Inventory of Francesco Gonzaga (1444–1483)* (London, 1992), pp. 80 and 163.

139. Paola Venturelli, 'Splendore e ornamento: Oggetti e materiali preziosi tra Carlo e Federico Borromeo', in *Carlo e Federico: La luce dei Borromeo nella Milano spagnola*, ed. Paolo Biscottini, exh. cat., Museo diocesano, Milan (Milan, 2005), pp. 122–33 at 129.

140. Maria Antonietta Visceglia, 'La Biblioteca tra Urbano VII (15–27 settembre 1590) e Urbano VIII (1623–1644): Cardinali, bibliotecari, custodi, *scriptores*', in *La Vaticana nel Seicento (1590–1700): Una biblioteca di biblioteche* (Vatican City, 2014), pp. 77–121 at 84.

141. James W. Nelson Novoa, 'Saperi e gusti di un banchiere portoghese a Roma nel Rinascimento: L'inventario di António da Fonseca', *Giornale di storia*, 10 (2012), pp. 1–19 at 16; James Nelson Novoa, 'Unicorns and Bezoars in a Portuguese House in Rome. António da Fonseca's Portuguese Inventories', *Ágora: Estudos clássicos em debate*, 14.1 (2012), pp. 91–111 at 97; James W. Nelson Novoa, *Being the Nação in the Eternal City: New Christian Lives in Sixteenth-Century Rome* (Peterborough, Ontario, 2014), p. 198.

142. Marnie P. Stark, 'Mounted Bezoar Stones, Seychelles Nuts, and Rhinoceros Horns: Decorative Objects as Antidotes in Early Modern Europe', *Studies in the Decorative Arts*, Fall/Winter 2003–4, pp. 69–94 at 69 and 74.

The importance and suitability of bezoars as global gifts sent by those outside Europe is also apparent in Biondi's correspondence, but in this case he is the recipient, not the giver. One of his correspondents was Frei Aleixo de Meneses,[143] prior of Nossa Senhora de Graça, the monastery of Augustinian hermits in Lisbon,[144] whose appointment as archbishop of Goa had been supported and facilitated by Biondi in 1595. It is slightly ironic that Biondi felt Meneses was an excellent candidate precisely because the position required a God-fearing man rather than someone interested in merchandise or goods ('mercantie'),[145] as from then on Meneses sent a stream of Indian merchandise, most of it with a medicinal function, some on the cusp between the talismanic and the medicinal, to his patron. Biondi had consecrated him archbishop in Lisbon at Easter 1595 before he set sail for India.[146] As a result, and in the hope of continued preference and advancement, Meneses felt beholden to Biondi, and repeatedly sent him presents from his new place of residence. Biondi left Lisbon in March 1597 to return to Rome, and gifts from Meneses were sent on to Rome via Lisbon. All the bezoars Meneses sent to Biondi were supposedly sent for medicinal rather than talismanic or collecting purposes. In this instance, the Portuguese trading empire offered Meneses the opportunity to acquire medicinal items not freely available in Europe. Each of the three sets of gifts included bezoar stones intended for ingestion, described by Carla Alferes Pinto as 'an edible gift [. . .] destined to disappear from the start' by being ground down and used as medicine.[147] These stones should therefore be differentiated in terms of function from the two types destined for preservation, often augmented with gold or silver mounts: the first sent like Filippo Sassetti's to ward off illness, and the second sent as pieces for show in *Wunder-* or *Kunstkammern*. The fate of individual bezoar stones must have depended upon the character and personality of the patron to whom they were sent, or for whom they were acquired.

143. Carla Alferes Pinto, 'The Diplomatic Agency of Art between Goa and Persia: Archbishop Friar Aleixo Meneses and Shah ʿAbbās I in the Early Seventeenth Century', in Zoltán Biedermann, Anne Gerritsen and Giorgio Riello, eds, *Global Gifts: The Material Culture of Diplomacy in Early Modern Eurasia* (Cambridge, 2018), pp. 150–70 at 150. On Meneses's artistic patronage, see Carla Alferes Pinto, '"Traz à memória a excelência de suas obras e virtudes": D. Frei Aleixo de Meneses (1559–1617), mecenas e patrono', *Anais de história de além-mar*, 12 (2011), pp. 153–80.

144. ASV, Segretaria di stato 9, 461r; Pinto, '"Traz à memória"', pp. 164–65.

145. Ibid., 461r, Biondi to Pietro Aldobrandini, 17 December 1594.

146. ASV, Fondo Confalonieri 28, 302r, and Alonso, 'Eleccion y consagración', p. 132.

147. Pinto, 'Diplomatic Agency', pp. 167–68.

While in Goa, Meneses always sent Biondi a Christmas letter, and on 21 December 1595 he wrote to say he was sending a (rarefied type of) bezoar stone from a porcupine, a *porcospino*,[148] a very fine ordinary bezoar, a stone ring ('anello di pietra') to staunch blood, and a cross made of rock crystal.[149] Just as Sassetti in Cochin had been able to source *porcospini* that he could send to his friends in Florence, so too Meneses in Goa had privileged access to, and was able to acquire, *porcospini* to send to his patron Biondi. Porcupine bezoars were amongst the more expensive substances of animal origin, and have been estimated to cost as much per carat (a unit of weight) as diamonds.[150] When questioned by Meneses in 1597 as to the arrival of these first presents, Biondi replied that he had not received them.[151] In his Christmas letter of 22 December 1599, Meneses outlined all three of his gift-giving attempts. The first gifts, sent in 1596 with an Augustinian, did not arrive. The second set—more bezoar stones and another *porcospino*—were entrusted to a Franciscan who was robbed and murdered en route, so they too failed to reach Lisbon. The third time the courier was a Jesuit, and the presents were more elaborate and diversified: as well as bezoars and a *porcospino*, Meneses sent a large coconut husk or shell ('cosca', for *casca*)—in fact from a coco de mer (*Lodoicea maldivica*) seed—from the Maldives, mounted by a silver eagle with eyes of rubies, that contained within itself part of the coconut's kernel, another 'edible gift destined to disappear', because it was a noted antidote to poison when ground with wine. He also sent two rhinoceros horn cups and several pieces of 'pau de Malaca', deemed very efficacious in the treatment of fever.[152] The coco de mer, as was true for a number of these huge seeds from the Maldives,[153] was

148. Peter Borschberg, 'The Trade, Use and Forgery of Porcupine Bezoars in the Early Modern Period (ca. 1500–1750)', *Oriente*, 14 (2006), pp. 60–78.

149. ASV, Fondo Confalonieri 31, 387v, and Alonso, 'Documentacíon inédita', p. 283.

150. Borschberg, 'Trade, Use and Forgery', pp. 62 and 70.

151. ASV, Fondo Confalonieri 28, 732v, and Alonso, 'Eleccion y consagración', p. 134.

152. ASV, Fondo Confalonieri 31, 385r–v, and Alonso, 'Documentacíon inédita', pp. 299–300.

153. Luís Manuel Mendonça de Carvalho and Francisca Maria Fernandes, '*Exotica naturalia*: O enigma do coco-do-mar', *Artis: Revista do Instituto de História da Arte da Faculdade de Letras da Universidade de Lisboa*, 9–10 (2020–11), pp. 153–62; João Paulo S. Cabral, 'O extraordinário coco das Maldivas (Seychelles): Lendas, mitos e realidades de história natural nos séculos XVI–XVIII/The Extraordinary Maldives' (Seychelles) Coconut: Legends, Myths and Realities of Natural History in the Sixteenth to Eighteenth Centuries', in Celeste Gomes, Ana Rola, Isabel Abrantes, eds, *História das ciências para o ensino: Atas de Colóquio II*, (ebook, 2014), pp. 5–29, https://dokumen.tips/documents/historia-das-ciencias-para-o-ensino-atas-do-coloquio-ii.html?page=5 (accessed 27 April 2023).

mounted with silver in Goa before being shipped to Lisbon,[154] and the ones mentioned for sale in shops on the Rua Nova in Lisbon in 1581 were probably similarly mounted.[155] The rhinoceros horn cups too were thought to possess supernatural powers and function as antidotes to poison;[156] originating in East Africa (where the rhinoceroses had larger horns than the Asian ones, for example from Sumatra) and sent to southern China to be carved, they were also often given gold filigree mounts and decoration in Goa before they were shipped to Portugal.[157] It would be difficult to think of an object that could have wandered more than this. Meneses's gifts in 1599 showed him to be engaging more widely with some of the smaller-scale goods on offer in Goa, but all of them remained medicinal, even if the coco de mer mounted by the silver eagle (that opened and could be used to store valuables) and the rhinoceros horn cups would have remained as functional material artefacts after the bezoar stones had been ground up and consumed. In the final list, therefore, the medicinal and the decorative mingled and merged, indicating the enormous consumer potential of accessing the Portuguese trading empire. It is known that the Jesuit and the presents he carried reached Lisbon, but by then Biondi had returned to Rome. Half of the presents were sent on by sea, whereas the other half the Jesuit took with him by land.[158] The final destination for these expensive and rare hybrid objects, simultaneously natural and man-made, originally from the Maldives and East Africa but finessed in southern China and Goa, was not Lisbon, but Italy; their biography is clearly trans-global, indicative of multiple connectivities and contexts, European as well as Asian.

In the previous case study, Campana's inexperience and lack of expertise were examined, and in this one it is important to remember that Biondi too was in no way an expert with specialist knowledge of objects and prices, although his letters from Lisbon betray that he did acquire a little local know-how.

154. Jordan Gschwend, 'Olisipo', p. 158 and fig. 150.

155. Lisbon, Biblioteca da Ajuda, Rerum Lusitanicarum, V (46-IX-5): 'Commentarii per Italia, Francia, Spagna e Portogallo overo relazione del viaggio de Signori Cavalieri Tron e Lippomani eletti ambasciatori dalla Republica Veneta al Re Cattolico per complimentare Sua Maestà per la conquista di Portogallo l'anno MDLXXXI', 263r.

156. Stark, 'Mounted Bezoar Horns', pp. 69, 85–87. Bruno A. Martinho, 'Rhino Horns and Scraps of Unicorn: The Sense of Touch and the Consumption of Rhino Horns in Early Modern Iberia', Luxury, 8.1 (2021), pp. 77–103 argues that consumption of rhino horns was fuelled by a perception that touch could effect transformation.

157. Jordan Gschwend, 'Olisipo, p. 158 and fig. 148.

158. Alonso, 'Documentacíon inédita', pp. 303–4.

Presumably, like Campana, he used contacts and middlemen to jostle his way to the front of the queue of buyers, but unlike Campana he stayed in Lisbon for years, giving him more opportunity to learn about values and market prices. He was well aware that others in Lisbon had the expertise he lacked (which would have included knowledge of provenance), and that being involved in a patron–client relationship with these men could be advantageous. On 15 August 1595 he wrote to the papal nuncio in Spain asking for his help.[159] In the Casa da Índia in Lisbon where all the goods coming from India were assessed for taxes due to the king, there was a particular functionary called a *valeadore* whose job it was to value jewels. The present incumbent was old and ill, and had obtained permission to nominate his successor; he had nominated Simon Rodrighez, one of the principal lapidaries of the city.[160] Now the governors had put this nomination out for consultation. Biondi was very desirous of Rodrighez getting the job, and asked the nuncio in Madrid to recommend him too. Biondi's interest in this jewel expert suggests that he knew and trusted him and was intending to use his services again in the future. Having a 'friend' in such a job was a way both of ensuring access to expertise and of eliciting favours and first refusal on some incoming jewels.

What Biondi Bought

The outstanding question begging to be addressed is why Biondi was not asked for a greater range of consumer products from Portugal's overseas empire. Can it really be the case that his patrons and friends in Italy did not know what was on offer in Lisbon, when the glorious diversity of goods coming into the city from Portugal's overseas empire was already the talk of Europe more than one hundred years earlier? Or was it only very discerning buyers who now looked for rare and expensive pieces, with many Italians already accustomed to mid-range Asian, Brazilian and Far Eastern goods—and the very discerning would not have used Biondi as their agent? One way of assessing this is to examine more closely what Biondi was buying for himself. His letters, including appraisals of his possessions, reveal him to be a relatively low-level, cost-conscious and conservative buyer or collector, but a buyer and collector nonetheless. Apart from reports regarding the fulfilling of commissions for

159. ASV, Fondo Confalonieri 28, 529r–v.

160. In mid-sixteenth-century Lisbon there had been thirty-two lapidaries: Oliveira, *Lisboa em 1551*, p. 94.

friends and patrons, his correspondence includes a semi-continuous stream of information about the acquisitions—purchases or gifts—he made in Lisbon that he is sending back to Italy to await his return. Although he does not articulate it directly, the posting to Lisbon offered him the chance to acquire possessions that he would not normally have been able to obtain easily, if at all, in Rome. The purchases are a mixed bag, with provenances in a range of European and extra-European countries and regions; usually not expensive or rare, they include the most obvious items alongside some less likely pieces, and gifts in addition to bought objects for his own household and ecclesiastical use. As well as Chinese porcelain and the little East Indian table made of 'holy wood' and the Portuguese *cotognato* mentioned above, Biondi referred to a clock (*orologio*) he had been given that he characterised as 'molto nobile' (very superior). The donor was Cardinal Archduke Albrecht of Austria, Philip II's nephew and Maximilian II's son, who was Philip II's viceroy or legate in Portugal.[161] The clock was conceptualised as a parting gift from the legate of Portugal before he left Lisbon in 1595 to his vice-legate, Biondi: an example of a present being given by a superior to an inferior.[162] Even if considered a reward for merit,[163] meaning that Albrecht had found Biondi to be an excellent vice-legate, this gift is exceptional, in terms of category of object and rarity.

While the majority of pieces and items mentioned by Biondi are not assigned a place of origin or provenance, one subset is consistently described as 'della China/Cina'. This designation could be capacious, and probably indicated the Far East in a general rather than a precise way, but it was not as infinitely elastic as 'dell'India' which had effectively become dissociated from any geographic

161. ASV, Fondo Confalonieri 28, 209r, Biondi to Domenico Biondi, 3 September 1594. On Albrecht, see Francisco Caeiro, *O archiduque Alberto de Austria: Vice-rei e inquisidor-mor de Portugal, cardeal legado do papa, governador e depois soberano dos Paises Baixos; História e arte* (Lisbon, 1961); Annemarie Jordan Gschwend, 'In the Shadow of Philip II, *El Rey Lusitano*: Archduke Albert of Austria as Viceroy of Portugal (1583–1593)', in Werner Thomas and Luc Duerloo, eds, *Albert & Isabella, 1598–1621: Essays* (Turnhout, 1998), pp. 39–46.

162. ASV, Fondo Confalonieri 14, 351r–355v, in particular 353r, 'Facciata d'avanti dell'oriuolo donato dal Rev.mo Card.le Alberto d'Austria legato di Portogallo al Patriarca di Gerusalemme suo vicelegato', and 353v, 'Facciata di dietro dell'oreuolo'. From these descriptions, this was an extraordinary clock. Transporting it from Lisbon to Rome proved tricky and expensive: ASV, Fondo Confalonieri 34, 126r, where Pietro Giorgio Camagna sets out the list of expenses for the trip.

163. Cf. Natalie Zemon Davis, *The Gift in Sixteenth-Century France* (Madison, WI, 2000), pp. 96–97.

place. The objects given this epithet by Biondi can generally be classified as in-deed Chinese, even if they might have been made by overseas Chinese living outside China in parts of South-East Asia. In January 1595 Biondi wrote that he had sent his Chinese writing box or writing cabinet, here described as a 'studiolo della China' (in Portuguese 'escritório/escrivaninha da China'), in a caravel leav-ing for Livorno, presumably to Rome to await his return.[164] These fall-front writ-ing boxes or writing cabinets (the distinction between writing boxes and writing cabinets was one of size)[165] were made in southern China and nearby countries that had Chinese populations, such as Vietnam, for the European export market; modelled on contemporary European prototypes and often made in ebonised, gilded and/or lacquered wood with metal locks, hinges and handles. The extant examples of these boxes or cabinets are dated to c. 1580–c. 1620,[166] so are pre-cisely coterminous with Biondi's residence in Lisbon. Chinese writing boxes and cabinets are not included in the list of objects purchased for Cosimo I in the 1547 buying trip to Lisbon as they did not exist in that form at that time, only appear-ing on the market in the later sixteenth century. The references in letters and lists in the Mediceo del Principato *fondo* in Florence to *scrittoini* and *scrittori* from the 1580s could be to Chinese objects, even though Chinese provenance is never specified.[167] One correspondent in Setubal, Luigi Dovara, a diplomatic envoy of Francesco de' Medici to Spain between 1579 and 1584,[168] writing to Antonio Serguidi in Florence on 21 April 1582, strikingly proposes a very differ-ent place of origin: 'uno scrittoino di quelli che si fanno qua in Portogallo che non sono mali' (a fall-front writing cabinet of those made here in Portugal which are not bad).[169] Lisbon was an important centre for furniture production that

164. ASV, Fondo Confalonieri 28, 266v, Biondi to Camagna, 21 January 1595.

165. On fall-front cabinets, see Martinho, 'Beyond Exotica', pp. 212–52.

166. *Jóias da Carreira da Índia*, ed. Hugo Miguel Crespo, exh. cat., Museu do Oriente, Lisbon (Lisbon, 2014), pp. 44 and 105, cat. no. 22; Crespo, 'Global Interiors', p. 137, cat. no. 12, figs. 123–25; Crespo, *Choices*, pp. 288–303, cat. no. 25; Hugo Miguel Crespo, 'A casa de Simão de Melo', in *A cidade global: Lisboa no Renascimento/The Global City: Lisbon in the Renaissance*, ed. Annemarie Jordan Gschwend and K.J.P. Lowe, exh. cat., Museu Nacional de Arte Antiga, Lisbon (Lisbon, 2017), pp. 210–27 at 222–23, cat. no. 213, and 226–27, cat. no. 249.

167. ASF, MdP 1212, inserto 3, fol. 470, Luigi Dovara in Setubal to Antonio Serguidi in Flor-ence, 21 April 1582: 'scrittoino'; MdP 5113, inserto 2, fol. 577, Giulio Battaglini from Monzon to Pietro di Francisco Usimbardi in Rome, 12 September 1585: 'scrittorio'.

168. *DBI*, 41 (1992), pp. 573–76, entry by Diana Toccafondi Fantappiè.

169. ASF, MdP 1212, inserto 3, fol. 470, Luigi Dovara in Setubal to Antonio Serguidi in Flor-ence, 21 April 1582. It is possible that the label 'di Portugal' used elsewhere might refer not only to Portugal but to Portuguese Asia.

predominantly made pieces for home consumption, unlike Augsburg, for example, which produced fine marquetry works also for the export market. There were many cabinet makers in Lisbon at the time, who produced less luxurious pieces than those made in Germany or Italy, so a cabinet of Portuguese production is not an outlandish suggestion.[170] However, a few years later the Italian word used for boxes and cabinets changes from *scrittoini* or *scrittori* to *studioli*. Like Biondi in 1595,[171] Giovanni Battista Confalonieri in *Grandezza e magnificenza della città di Lisbona* in the mid-1590s uses *studioli*,[172] making it more certain that the objects referred to in Biondi's correspondence are the fall-front writing boxes or cabinets from southern China.

A further fall-front writing box or cabinet ascribed a provenance in China was given to Biondi by D. Afonso Castelo Branco, the bishop of Coimbra, in January 1597, as a farewell gift to cement their relationship. It was the major item in a list of gifts itemised by Castelo Branco in a letter written to Confalonieri as Biondi's secretary, and it was labelled in Portuguese as an 'escritorio da China'.[173] The other objects were six pairs of fine leather gloves smeared with ambergris perfume or fragrant oil, a 'penteador [comb] da India', the still much-valued *marmelada* and three nautilus shells, described here as 'busios da China' (seashells from China).[174] Rather interestingly, Castelo Branco

---

170. If the fall-front writing cabinet referred to by Dovara was Portuguese, it could have also been manufactured in the Azores, where such objects were made for export from large juniper trees native to the islands (*Juniperus brevifolia*). I am grateful to Hugo Crespo for this suggestion, and for discussing these cabinets with me. Francisco Ernesto de Oliveira Martins, 'Mobiliário açoriano: Do cedro ao jacarandá com cedro, séculos XV ao XVIII', in José Olivio Rocha and Mariana Mesquita, eds, *Angra, a Terceira e os Açores nas rotas da Índia e das Américas: A propósito dos 500 anos da passagem de Vasco da Gama por Angra em 1499* (Angra do Heroísmo, 1999), pp. 73–91; Pedro Dias, 'O fabrico de mobiliário na ilha Terceira, no século XVI', in Pedro Dias, Dalila Rodrigues and Fernando Grilo, eds, *Manuelino: À descoberta da arte do tempo de D. Manuel I* (Lisbon, 2002), circuito 14; Pedro Pascoal F. de Melo, 'Um pouco conhecido mobiliário açoriano dos séculos XVI e XVII', *Açoriano oriental* (30 December 2012), p. 19.

171. ASV, Fondo Confalonieri 28, 266v, Biondi to Camagna, 21 January 1595.

172. Confalonieri, *Grandezza e magnificenza*, p. 180. The references in the Mediceo dopo il Principato volumes in 1618 are to *studioli*: ASF, MdP 2951, unfoliated, Alessandro Senesi in Mantua to an unnamed correspondent, probably Andrea Cioli in Tuscany, 2 June 1618: 'studiolo'; and MdP 2951, unfoliated, Alessandro Senesi in Mantua to Curzio Picchena in Tuscany, 7 June 1618: 'studiuolo'.

173. ASV, Fondo Confalonieri 39, 44r and 53v, D. Afonso Castelo Branco in Coimbra to Confalonieri, the 'secretary' of Biondi, in Lisbon, 6 January 1597, and Marques, 'Cultura material', p. 200.

174. The word *búzio* is only used for the shells of sea snails.

appears to have been more willing than Biondi to attribute provenance to the non-European presents he wanted to give to his friend in order to place him in a position of obligation. Even if the place of origin attached might have been vague or incorrect, of the five items on his list of gifts, two were ascribed a provenance in China, and one in India. Castelo Branco sent his servant to visit Biondi on his behalf with the presents, and then also instructed him to accompany Biondi to Rome.

When Biondi left Lisbon in 1597, his possessions of any value had to be given the equivalent of an object passport ('il pasaporto delle robbe')[175] in order for them to be able to leave Portugal and Spain without being subject to a tax or duty. Licences had to be obtained for all luxury and extra-European goods crossing the border from Portugal into Castile, even though exemptions from paying duties should have been given automatically to foreign diplomats or other foreigners carrying out duties on behalf of their rulers. Applications were made to the Câmara de Castilla that controlled the borders, and if approved, exit papers were issued for the objects, to be shown at customs and border crossings.[176] Biondi should have been in the category of foreigners who were exempt from paying duty, but his application did not go smoothly. Negotiations continued for months, from November 1596 to his departure in March 1597, with Biondi outraged at the thought that the tax might be applied to used or second-hand objects, especially any with an ecclesiastical function. In the course of the correspondence connected to the luxury and extra-European goods, Biondi claimed that he had owned the *scrittorio*—there was no reference to it being Chinese here—for two years, and valued it at fifteen or twenty ducats.[177] Claiming an object had been owned for some time and thus had dropped in value was a familiar ploy—but this cannot have been the writing cabinet or box given by Castelo Branco in January 1597, and may have been one he had indeed owned for two years. In the same letter of 14 December 1596 to Bartolomeo Rota in Madrid, the *famigliare* of Camillo Caetani who was the papal nuncio to Spain and who was trying to help him expedite the passport for these possessions, Biondi described two further objects as 'della China', both of which were expensive textiles. The first was described by

175. ASV, Fondo Confalonieri 32, 462r, Bartolomeo Rota in Madrid to Biondi in Rome, 18 May 1598. The letter also contains a discussion of a *porcospino* stone in a box given as a present to Biondi by someone in Lisbon.

176. Pérez de Tudela and Jordan Gschwend, 'Luxury Goods', pp. 1–4.

177. ASV, Fondo Confalonieri 28, 717r, Biondi to Rota, 14 December 1596.

Biondi as a 'coperto della China', a bedcover.[178] He claimed this was a used object, that could not be worth more than fifty or sixty ducats (a not inconsiderable sum, nevertheless). The second object, a chasuble ('pianeta della China'), he had bought some time ago at a cost, if he remembered correctly, of sixty ducats; it was blessed and he used it to celebrate mass.[179] That is, he was making a case for it being an ecclesiastical vestment with a function, even if it was a rare and ornate piece.[180]

A few, miscellaneous final possessions presumably purchased by Biondi in Lisbon were included for safe transit in the more secure packaging of the first writing box or cabinet of January 1595, which must therefore have been rather large: three books (including a 'Teatro del mundo spagnolo'[181] and a 'Teatro di Terra santa'[182]), a pair of terrestrial and celestial globes packed into two barrels, and the carapace of a turtle ('una coccia o sia coperta di tartaruga d'acqua').[183] The books and globes incorporating maps and representations of other territories are more normal fare for educated Italians with an interest in visualising the wider world, recognised embodiments and conveyors of global knowledge. So too is the navigational chart, mentioned earlier, that Monsignor Curzio Frangipani asked Biondi to acquire on his behalf, in which transaction Biondi showed himself to be somewhat knowledgeable, certainly in relation to cost and options.[184] As has been seen, Lorenzo de' Medici and Alfonso and Isabella d'Este were already buying globes and charts in the late fifteenth and

178. This was perhaps similar to one from China or Macau dated 1680–1720, measuring 292 × 207 cm: Guus Röell and Dickie Zebregs, *Uit verre streken/From Distant Shores: Luxury Goods from Dutch Trading Ports in the West Indies, East Indies, China, Japan and Africa, 17th to 19th Centuries* (Maastricht, June 2017), no. 51, bed cover.

179. ASV, Fondo Confalonieri 28, 717r, Biondi to Rota, 14 December 1596.

180. A late seventeenth-century embroidered silk chasuble now in a private collection, probably made for the Dominicans in Macau, measuring 110 × 74 cm, may give some idea of what Biondi's looked like: Crespo, 'Global Interiors', pp. 128 and 129, and fig. 113.

181. Probably the Spanish edition of Abraham Ortelius, *Theatrum orbis terrarum* or *Theatro de la tierra universal* (Antwerp, 1588). A copy of *Theatrum mundi* with some letters of Paolo Beni is listed elsewhere in Biondi's belongings (AS, Fondo Confalonieri 34, 239r), and Paolo Beni, still at that point a Jesuit, was in Madrid in May and June 1595, from where he wrote to Biondi (ASV, Fondo Confalonieri 33, 444r and 446r–v).

182. Probably Cristiano Adricomio (or Christian Kruik van Adrichem), *Teatro di terra santa* of 1570, a work in three parts. See Sigismondo da Venezia, *Bibliografia universale sacra e profana* (Venice, 1842), p. 243.

183. ASV, Fondo Confalonieri 28, 266v, Biondi to Camagna, 21 January 1595.

184. Ibid., 181r, Biondi to Mons. Curzio Frangipani, 11 June 1594.

early sixteenth centuries, and Biondi was carrying on the tradition at the end of the sixteenth. The reference to globes either originating in Lisbon or being traded through the city is interesting. Virtually no research has been carried out on globes made in Lisbon, but while no extant globes manufactured in Portugal have so far been identified, there are a few known archival references to them.[185] It makes sense that globes (*esferas*)[186] were manufactured in Lisbon, because of the number of cartographers who lived in the city, working for the crown in the Casa da Índia and the Casa da Mina. Indeed, in January 1514 Manuel I ordered a certain *mestre* Dieguo to make a *poma* or globe by using information taken from the most secure nautical charts and by working with the best cartographers.[187] The turtle's carapace, on the other hand, offered an alternative entry into the word of global raw materials, a *cosa peregrina* representing the allure of the extra-European. The turtle could have been one of two species, the green sea turtle (*Chelonia mydas*) or the hawksbill sea turtle (*Eretmochelys imbricata*), but it is more likely to be the latter, as it is much more beautiful and is the raw material from which Gujarati caskets were made. Biondi's financial position probably dictated that he bought a carapace rather than paying substantially more to acquire a finished luxury object. Whereas it is possible that he possessed books relating to the Spanish empire before his sojourn in Portugal, it is most unlikely that he would have possessed a turtle carapace, which could stand as a tangible physical example of the global products that late sixteenth-century Lisbon offered to would-be consumers.

However, whether or not Biondi himself was a particularly adventurous acquirer of global goods, and whether or not he was especially interested in material culture (or preferred instead to think about the garden at his house in Rome), should not have influenced requests from his correspondents. By the 1590s all educated and worldly people would have known about Lisbon's emporium of goods. That they did not know very much about individual goods should not be a surprise, as knowledge of objects has always been possessed by a small élite, and possession of objects or even the desire to possess objects

185. Thomas Horst and Luís Tirapicos are working on Portuguese globes. For a reference to a Portuguese globe, see Metcalf, 'Who Cares Who Made the Map?', p. 17 and n. 11. For Spanish globes, see Agustín Hernando, 'Die Herstellung von Erd- und Himmelsgloben in Spanien', in *Der Globusfreund*, 59/60 (2014), pp. 162–201, esp. 167 (for reference to Magellan and Portugal).

186. Anthony Vieyra, *A Dictionary of the Portuguese and English Languages in Two Parts, Portuguese and English: and English and Portuguese*, 2 vols (London, 1773), 1, p. 235, where one of the definitions of *esfera* is 'a globe representing the earth or sky'.

187. Viterbo, *Trabalhos náuticos*, part 1, p. 87.

does not signify knowledge of the objects of desire. Returning to Sanjay Subrahmanyam's notion of the balance of ignorance between centuries, referred to in chapter 1 above ('Knowledge and Non-knowledge'), this is a clear-cut case of people in the twenty-first century, who were not present, knowing so much more—however pock-marked by questions, and however faulty and erroneous—than people in the sixteenth century who were there at the moment of acquisition.

Living Animals and Birds

Other objects and items repeatedly requested by Biondi's Italian correspondents were pearls, civet cats (Plate 41), monkeys and parrots, all of which had been on everybody's lists since they first became available from Portuguese overseas trading posts in the fifteenth century (in the case of the civets, monkeys and parrots) and early sixteenth (in the case of pearls).[188] There was nothing new about them. As seen in chapter 2, Lorenzo de' Medici had been interested in civets, monkeys and parrots,[189] and as shown in chapter 5, examples of all of these animals—and pearls—had been purchased for Cosimo de' Medici and Eleonora di Toledo on the 1547 Lisbon and Cadiz trip. Bezoars, on the other hand, had not been on these lists. Individuals possessing civets, monkeys and parrots on the Italian peninsula in the 1590s were therefore adding nothing of substance to consciousness of the Portuguese trading empire. Campana in 1547 had bought two civet cats, which were among his most expensive purchases.[190] In Lisbon, civet cats belonging to the nobility or attached to the court, like two belonging to Beatriz, duchess of Beja, already at the beginning of the sixteenth century had accessories—in this case collars—studded with gold and precious stones.[191] In this respect, even though they were essentially wild animals and not pets, they resembled small children, being animate but dependent creatures upon which or whom the wealth of their owners or parents could be displayed and inscribed. As noted in chapter 4, some of these

188. Their availability in Lisbon already in 1514–1515 was noted in the German book of tolls discussed by Müller, *Welthandelsbrauche*, pp. 297–99. At this date, parrots, monkeys and civets were listed from Sub-Saharan Africa, monkeys and parrots from Brazil, and civets and parrots from India.

189. Masseti, *La fattoria*, pp. 151–57 (civets).

190. ASF, Misc. med. 713, 2r and 3v.

191. Freire, 'Inventário', p. 83; Isabel dos Guimarães Sá, 'The Uses of Luxury: Some Examples from the Portuguese Courts from 1480 to 1580', *Análise social*, 44.192 (2009), pp. 589–604 at 594.

cats, if obtained as kittens, were domesticated in the sixteenth century. The possibility of domestication was a bonus, part of the civet's attraction, transforming a wild animal into a tame, but still exotic, almost-pet. In 1585 Cardinal Ferdinando de' Medici wrote from Rome to Francesco I de' Medici in Florence, including a sentence about a civet cat he was sending to him, saying it was 'piacevolissimo' (most delightful), if one liked civets.[192]

Yet again, fifty years on from Campana's trip, for Biondi, availability was an issue. Asked for a *gattino dell'India* or male civet kitten (*maschetto* is specified) in the summer of 1595 for the marchese d'Este, Biondi replied in a letter of 12 August to Conte Alfonso Langosco de La Motta, that he had possessed three or four of these *animaletti* but that all had died of cold the previous winter.[193] Now he had another, but it was a poor specimen. Even if he were able to find a decent specimen in Lisbon, he would not know how to send it back to Italy, as sending it 'a posta' (by post)[194] was not worth the expense. On precisely the same day, Biondi wrote much the same to the marchese d'Este, saying that civet kittens were not available in Lisbon at that time (and if they were, they would belong to one of the principal *signori* and by implication therefore would not be for sale). He advised instead that the marchese should wait: three or four ships were expected shortly in Lisbon from São Tomé, which would be bringing civet cats, and to circumvent the difficulties of transport Biondi offered to bring a civet back with him when he returned to Italy.[195]

In addition to civets, Biondi was also the fond owner of *gatti mammoni*, so-called green monkeys (*Chlorocebus sabaeus*). In August 1594 he told Marzio Colonna that he was waiting for the arrival of the next ships that would bring 'gattini mamoni' (young green monkeys) from Mina, or more correctly from the Portuguese Castelo de São Jorge da Mina.[196] In this case, it was obvious that Biondi did know the place of origin of the wildlife he wanted—or at least, the origin of the fleets carrying his favoured species, which could have been transported from further afield to the ships, or been picked up from Cabo Verde. He revealed to Colonna that he had had many of these small monkeys but they

192. Butters, Fumagalli and Deswarte-Rosa, *La Villa Médicis*, vol. 5: *Fonti documentarie*, p. 295.

193. Civets may also have died from lack of a proper diet. Carletti, *Ragionamenti*, p. 12; Carletti, *My Voyage*, p. 8, reveals that in the Cabo Verde Islands, civet were fed very cheaply on cooked fish, which may not have been the case in Portugal and Italy.

194. ASV, Fondo Confalonieri 28, 527v, Biondi to Conte Langosco della Motta, 12 August 1595.

195. Ibid., 367v, Biondi to the marquis d'Este, Alfonso II, 12 August 1595.

196. This is Elmina in what is now coastal Ghana.

had died, as they did not endure the cold well.[197] This comment referring to monkeys in the plural, and containing the word 'many', suggests that Biondi liked monkeys, and had bought young ones in order to keep them as domestic pets. By March 1597 his attachment to his 'scimie' had deepened, and he admitted to Monsignor Castris in March 1597 that he had had a whole army ('essercito') of them in his house, but they had all died, and that he would not be able to replace them until ships returned from São Tomé.[198] In the intervening period in Lisbon, Biondi had learnt that African green monkeys came on the boats from São Tomé as well as from Mina: in the case of animals that were only available to purchase straight off the ships, awareness of the place of origin became overlaid with that of the place of embarkation. Regardless of ties of affection, the difficulties of keeping alive and properly fed animals that had been transported out of their natural habitats and away from their natural food supplies meant that they usually survived only a short time in Lisbon, and had to be constantly replaced by the latest arrivals. These comments highlight the economic perils of shopping or collecting on someone else's behalf. In the same way that Biondi feared buying fake bezoars because it might leave him unable to recoup his investment, he feared buying vulnerable animals because they might die before they reached their new owners, and in this case too he would be left out of pocket.

Parrots, parakeets and macaws (often lumped together under the umbrella term 'parrot') were just as scarce as civets and green monkeys in Lisbon during the years Biondi lived there.[199] He was obviously keen on them as pets too, and kept parrots as well as green monkeys in his house. The Cantino map of 1502 had shown three types of parrot: African greys and ring-necked or rose-ringed green parakeets in West Africa, and multicoloured Amazon parrots or macaws in Brazil.[200] Yet categorisation of these desirable acquisitions was not made according to place of origin (Africa or the New World), or colour, but according to those parrots that talked and those that did not. The power of intelligent speech has always been a hallmark of humans, and the knowledge that parrots could talk was deeply troubling as well as deeply exciting. Were

197. ASV, Fondo Confalonieri 28, 204v, Biondi to Marzio Colonna, 20 August 1594.

198. Ibid., 745v–746r, Biondi to Mons. Castris, 15 March 1597.

199. Cardinal Ferdinand de' Medici wrote in 1580 to his brother D. Piero asking him to buy some 'rare and beautiful' parrots in Seville or wherever else he chose: Butters, Fumagalli and Deswarte-Rosa, *La Villa Médicis*, vol. 5: *Fonti documentarie*, p. 236.

200. Boehrer, *Parrot Culture*, pp. 51 and 57.

they examples of the marvels of nature? Was their speech a sign of almost-human intelligence? Or was it just a question of mindless repetition? The notion of animals that spoke did not seem particularly far-fetched in the context of the opening up of vast tracts of territories across the world, as myriad previous seeming impossibilities became plausible.[201] Talking parrots were not in fact a Renaissance novelty, but had been part of the classical world: Alexandrine parakeets (*Psittacula eupatria*) from India, that could mimic basic speech, reached Europe and were known about.[202] What the Portuguese joining up of the world changed was the availability and number of talking parrots introduced into Renaissance Italy, and with the arrival of the African grey came a parrot with a real gift for mimicry and speech. These were infinitely desirable,[203] and are acknowledged even now as the best talkers.[204] Another reason for the proliferation of parrots in the sixteenth century is that they were hardier than many of the other animals and birds being transported around the world, and did not suffer the catastrophic casualties that dislocation and travel inflicted on some of the wild cats or monkeys, although they too died if not properly cared for.[205] The extant documentation shows that the greater number of parrots arriving in Europe led to a democratisation of their ownership, as they evolved from being items for rulers into domestic pets for a much wider range of people.[206]

Alvise da Mosto returned from his trips to Senegambia in the 1450s with more than 150 'parrots', at least some of which must have been talkers.[207] The most basic speech probably extended to a few non-consecutive words, although even these could be found charming. Madonna Cleofe Buzi from Bologna had a parrot that called her by name, a piece of information rated interesting enough to be included in a chronicle of the late fifteenth and early sixteenth centuries.[208] The ability to speak well—to be *ben parlante*—was praised, whether

---

201. Brian Cummings, 'Pliny's Literate Elephant and the Idea of Animal Language in Renaissance Thought', in Erica Fudge, ed., *Renaissance Beasts: Of Animals, Humans and Other Wonderful Creatures* (Urbana, IL, 2003), pp. 164–85.

202. Boehrer, *Parrot Culture*, pp. 1–21.

203. On Cassiano del Pozzo's African grey, see McBurney et al., *Birds*, 1, pp. 410–11.

204. Irene Maxine Pepperberg, *The Alex Studies: Cognitive and Communicative Abilities of Grey Parrots* (Cambridge, MA, 1999).

205. Jordan Gschwend, 'Emperor's exotic and New World Animals', p. 98.

206. Norton, 'Going to the Birds', pp. 71–74.

207. Cà da Mosto, *Le navigazioni atlantiche*, p. 66; Crone, *Voyages of Cadamosto*, p. 48.

208. Fantaguzzi, *Caos*, ed. Pistocchi, 1, p. 501.

it was attributed to men and women in Boccaccio's *Decameron*,[209] or to African greys. Even though Campana on his Iberian trip had bought nine parrots, probably all for Eleonora di Toledo,[210] the duchess always wanted more. In 1551 she was sent a 'pappagallino' or little parrot by Balduino del Monte, Pope Julius III's brother, which pleased her greatly, even though its prowess in speaking was not mentioned.[211] The demand for talking parrots, especially those that told jokes or stories, remained sky-high throughout the sixteenth century. Many birds after arrival in Europe were sent to Italy, and parrots seem to be one of the few items popularly known to have arrived in Europe from overseas Portuguese territories, especially West Africa and Brazil, but also from parts of the East such as the Moluccas. Antonio Pigafetta's account of Fernão de Magalhães's (Ferdinand Magellan's) first voyage round the world in 1519–22 included local words for different kinds of parrot in the Moluccas and an assessment of their speaking ability.[212]

However, which language these transnational parrots spoke or mimicked in Europe is another matter altogether. Young ones may have picked up vocabulary or set pieces from two or three languages. Seven parrots were included in the shipment of gifts including some from the New World sent by Francesco de' Medici to Duke Albrecht V of Bavaria in May 1572: three were described in the Italian inventory as 'small' (that is, young), and able to learn any language. Three of the four 'big' or fully grown ones received individual assessments of their speaking ability: the green one spoke 'eccellentemente', the red one 'assai bene' (well enough), and one of the two grey ones spoke 'indiano'.[213] Describing a foreign-seeming object as *indiano* is one thing; describing the language spoken by a parrot as *indiano* is another—but it may just be that the inventory-maker found the words spoken by the parrot unintelligible, and used a lazy word to describe them.[214] The parrot speaking an unintelligible foreign language is

---

209. For example, Boccaccio, *Decameron*, 1, p. 110 and 2, pp. 718, 1063.

210. ASF, Misc. med. 713, 77v.

211. ASF, MdP 1176, 972r, Tommaso di Iacopo de' Medici at Poggio a Caiano to Pier Francesco Riccio, 14 September 1551.

212. A. Pigafetta, *Relazione del primo viaggio*, p. 306; A. Pigafetta, *The First Voyage around the World*, p. 102.

213. Toorians, 'Earliest Inventory', pp. 63 and 64; Markey, *Imagining the Americas*, p. 50.

214. Cf. Paula Findlen, 'Afterword: How (Early Modern) Things Travel', in Anne Gerritsen and Giorgio Riello, eds, *The Global Lives of Things: The Material Culture of Connections in the Early Modern World* (London, 2015), pp. 241–46 at 241–44 on Jean de Léry's Brazilian parrot in 1558 that mimicked Tupinambá and French.

described as 'bigio' (grey), making it likely this was an African grey, which presumably spoke in one of the indigenous languages of West Africa. But do the assessments of the other two fully grown parrots indicate that they spoke Italian?

Some parrots could recite set pieces of Latin or Italian. Cardinal Ascanio Sforza (d. 1505) is reputed to have paid the enormous sum of a hundred ducats for a parrot that could recite the 'Credo' without making a mistake.[215] One *dito*, or story centred on a witticism, concerns a parrot from Mina in West Africa—very probably an African grey—sent by King Manuel of Portugal to Pope Leo X sometime between 1513 and 1521.[216] One day the pope asked the parrot in Latin what it was thinking; it replied in Latin, 'I am thinking about the past, the present and what is to come.' As a result, the pope had the bird killed. The unfortunate fate of this parrot is related to the notion that curiosity is the devil's work, and that the parrot was dabbling in dangerous knowledge. In a nice twist, the pope—according to the *dito*—was exhibiting fear of knowledge. 'What is to come' meant not just the future in a vague sense, but referred to the Last Judgement proclaimed by Christian doctrine.

Requests directed to Biondi for parrots seem prosaic, by contrast: merely specifying a required number, with no mention of place of origin, type or colour, let alone prowess in chatting, knowledge of religion or a sense of humour.[217] It is interesting, however, that he seems to have been aware of who owned parrots in Lisbon and which ones might be available to buy, as though parrot collectors had memorised a mental map of the city showing availability of the birds by house or street. In July 1594 Biondi told Marzio Colonna that he knew of a merchant who owned an 'excellent' parrot and would see if he could buy it. He warned however that its transport to Italy might be problematic without a dedicated handler, as no one wanted the job of carrying parrots.[218] By August 1594 he was telling Colonna that he was waiting for ships bringing 'papagalli' from the Spanish Indies.[219] In March 1597 he told another sad tale to Monsignor Castris, this time about losing pet parrots, both from

215. Gerolamo d'Adda, *Indagini storiche, artistiche e bibliografiche sulla libreria Visconteo-Sforzesca del Castello di Pavia: Appendice alla prima parte* (Milan, 1879), p. 52; Francesco Malaguzzi Valeri, *La corte di Lodovico il moro: La vita privata e l'arte a Milano nella seconda metà del Quattrocento* (Milan, 1913), p. 742; Cockram, 'Interspecies Understanding', p. 295.

216. *Echt Tierisch!*, p. 288.

217. For example, ASV, Fondo Confalonieri 28, 9v.

218. Ibid., 20r, Biondi to Marzio Colonna, 9 July 1594.

219. Ibid., 204v, Biondi to Marzio Colonna, 20 August 1594.

death and more surprisingly from theft, complaining that a few days before a parrot had been stolen from his house that he described as 'la meglior cosa del mondo' (the best thing in the world).[220] This is high praise from the usually unemotional Biondi, and might suggest that the stolen parrot could speak. However, he went on to acknowledge that if ships did not arrive from Brazil, he would not be able to replenish his stock of parrots before his return to Italy,[221] so the stolen parrot is unlikely to have been a talented African grey mimic, and was more likely to have been a fabulously colourful parrot from the Amazon.

Importing Attitudes and Behaviours

Inanimate goods and living animals and birds were two distinct categories of import, a discussion of which allows calibration of one sort of consciousness of the global. A third category, classifiable as intangible, could be social and cultural behaviours and attitudes from the Portuguese empire, imported first of all into Renaissance Lisbon, and from there dispersed around Renaissance Italy. Lisbon's status as the premier global city in Europe in the sixteenth century made it a place where many new behaviours and attitudes were formed and fomented. Not only did consciousness of the global world arrive in Lisbon before spreading out round Europe, but the global itself arrived in Lisbon in many guises, making new responses to it necessary. Lisbon had a very mixed population in the sixteenth century, reflecting the diversity of its worldwide trading empire and Iberian religious policies, making interaction between different parts of this global population inevitable.[222] Roberto Fontana, a previous apostolic collector in Portugal in the late 1570s and early 1580s, wrote of Lisbon, 'nelle città et porti [. . .] concorrono genti d'ogni legge et natione' (in the cities and ports people of every religion and region converge).[223] Biondi's experiences in Lisbon caused him to develop new attitudes. He can be observed struggling to find the best words to describe an encounter with this diversity, which in his case was a diversity of origin of a community of Dominicans. In a letter to Cardinal Archduke Albrecht of Austria's secretary Mattias

220. Ibid., 745v–746r, Biondi to Mons. Castris, 15 March 1597.

221. Ibid.

222. Kate Lowe, 'The Global Population of Renaissance Lisbon: Diversity and Its Entanglements', in Annemarie Jordan Gschwend and K.J.P. Lowe, eds, *The Global City: On the Streets of Renaissance Lisbon* (London, 2015), pp. 56–75.

223. ASV, Fondo Confalonieri 34, 43r–v.

Otthen of 25 February 1595, Biondi dictated to Confalonieri a description of eating the Sunday before in the refectory of the monastery of Santo Domingo in Lisbon with a hundred or so friars. Biondi dictated, and Confalonieri wrote down in the copybook, three formulations, each time deleting the previous ones, before Biondi was satisfied with what he was saying. His first attempt to characterise the hundred friars was 'd'ogni razza' (of every people),[224] but this was crossed out. His next attempt was 'de tutti i colori che' (of all the [skin] colours that), but this was replaced with 'de quanti colori' (of as many [skin] colours as) and the 'che' was removed, the sentence ending 'sono in Lisbona' (there are in Lisbon). So his final phrasing was, 'of as many skin colours as there are in Lisbon'.[225] The change from an emphasis on peoples to an emphasis on skin colour is typical of fifteenth- and sixteenth-century Italians, and ties in neatly with the case study in chapter 3 on attempts to describe the skin colour of mixed-ancestry babies at the Innocenti in the mid-fifteenth century. It seems that Biondi did not consider describing the friars by their place of origin or provenance, which he would not have known; alluding to their diversity of skin colour was an easier and more satisfactory solution. Being able to follow his authorial changes makes his hesitation and desire to express himself correctly doubly unusual and precious. The changes also suggest that letters dictated by Biondi to Confalonieri were first of all written down in the copybook of letters—which explains the presence of corrections—and afterwards a fair copy was written out to be despatched to the chosen recipient, in which case the letters in the copybook must have been the originals, and the stand-alone letters the copies.

In Lisbon, probably unlike in his previous life in Italy, Biondi encountered an array of different sub-Saharan Africans, and analysing his response to them may elucidate cultural attitudes and behaviours. Like everyone else in Europe at this date, for Biondi status was an issue of paramount importance. His response to two Africans in markedly different social positions (from opposite ends of the social scale) clearly illustrates this, showing that for Biondi black skin alone was not a reason for inferior status or inferior treatment. On his

224. Cf. Lowe, 'Isabella d'Este', pp. 70–71. Florio, *Queen Anna's New World*, p. 424 translated *razza* as 'a race, a kind, a broode, a stocke, a descent, a linage [*sic*], a pedigree'—but meanings of 'race' at this point in English were different from meanings now. Scholarly research into the use of the word *razza* in fifteenth- and sixteenth-century Italy has not yet been undertaken. See usefully, on related terminology, Epstein, *Speaking of Slavery*, pp. 21–24.

225. ASV, Fondo Confalonieri 28, 285v, Biondi to Cardinal Archduke Albrecht's secretary Mattias Otthen, 25 February 1595.

arrival in Lisbon in March 1593, he immediately became embroiled in the case of an apostate, previously an Augustinian friar originally from Lisbon, who had recently died in 'le Indie'.[226] Apostates were one of the few categories of people whose goods reverted to the papacy at death, so Biondi moved in on the man's possessions, which included a black slave. Biondi gave thought about what to do with this enslaved man, and his solution and its explanation were ingenious. He had taken the slave into his house, he said, because the man needed to eat, but he hoped that when the case was wrapped up, he would be able to buy the slave for fifty *scudi*. He explained that more money would not be obtained for him, because, although young, he was 'basso di statura e di brutto aspetto' (short and ugly), the complete opposite of what the Medici were requesting; they wanted black slaves who were 'striking and beautiful'. The clincher for Biondi was not the supposed unattractiveness of the slave, but the wish to avoid reputational damage to the papacy, and his next piece of pseudo-justification takes one's breath away: as the enslaved man was a Christian it would not be appropriate for the Camera Apostolica to be seen to sell him at a public auction, as lay people did in Lisbon with slaves they no longer wanted. It is fascinating that Biondi also had to have four goes at dictating this sentence to Confalonieri, with much crossing out, before he settled on a form of words. The first change was minor, relating to the inventory of 'mobili' (here, moveable possessions) that included the slave. The second attempted to rebuff the as yet unspoken criticism that as the enslaved man was a Christian it was not 'proper' that he should be auctioned (crossed out is 'et perche è christiano non mi par che si convenga che si metti all'i[word left unfinished]'). The third crossed out 'alla Camera apostolica di metterlo in vendita all'incanto' (a repeat of the sentiment that the sight of the Camera Apostolica putting a slave up for auction was not fitting); the fourth substituted 'public auction' for 'auction'.[227] In this case, all these corrections made very little difference to the final iteration, but they are an acknowledgement that Biondi could not dictate this passage without stumbling over the formulations. He undoubtedly realised that what he was writing and doing was morally dishonest, that possessing an enslaved man who was a Christian, in whatever form, even if legal, was morally dubious; but this knowledge did not stop him trying to buy the slave at a knock-down price. There is no reason to suppose that Biondi had a black slave in Italy before he went to

226. ASV, Fondo Confalonieri 27, 92r–v, Biondi to the tesoriere generale, Lisbon, 2 October 1593.
227. Ibid.

Lisbon—or indeed any slave—so this was probably his first encounter at a personal level with the institution of slavery. But given that he could see that it was inadvisable for the Camera Apostolica, the central financial body of the Catholic church, to sell a Christian slave at public auction, he cannot have been unaware of the moral issues underpinning his own purchase. Certainly it is instructive to compare the cleric Biondi's words on the situation surrounding this enslaved man with the words of his exact but secular contemporary, the Florentine merchant Francesco Carletti, writing around the 1590s. Carletti articulates at length his great moral unease at participating in the slave trade in Cabo Verde, which he describes as 'un traffico inumano et indegno della professione et pietà cristiana' (an inhuman traffic unworthy of a professed and pious Christian), declaring it even more shameful if the enslaved people had been baptised.[228] However, the end result was the same in both cases, moral doubt notwithstanding: Carletti too chose to profit from joining the ranks of slave traders and slave owners, rather than foregoing profit and publicly condemning the practice. Morality was no match for greed.

This example from the bottom of the social scale indicates that Biondi, while not questioning the institution of slavery, did not equate blackness with it, but just accepted the black man's enslaved status. When confronted with a Kongolese ambassador at the top of the social scale, he similarly accepted the man's ambassadorial status without hesitation, and the two forged a friendly relationship. The language in which the friendship was conducted is not known. The exact position of Kongo might not have been entirely clear to Biondi. In his correspondence, he positioned the Kingdom of Kongo both as 'verso la costa di Guinea' (towards the Guinea coast) and 'nell'Ethiopia' (in 'Ethiopia').[229] It could be argued that the opportunity to meet high-ranking sub-Saharan Africans on an equal footing occurred because of Lisbon's position as hub of the empire. In the rest of Europe before this date the possibility of friendship between a high-status sub-Saharan African and a papal official, for example, would have been virtually unimaginable,[230] yet a concrete example of precisely that in the Lisbon of the 1590s provides rather tangible

228. Carletti, *Ragionamenti*, p. 18; Carletti, *My Voyage*, p. 13.

229. *MMA* 3, pp. 496, 517. This is 'Ethiopia' in the sense of sub-Saharan Africa.

230. In the next decade, it became a possibility too in Rome: Lowe, '"Representing" Africa', and Kate Lowe, 'Visual Representations of an Élite: African Ambassadors and Rulers in Renaissance Europe', in *Revealing the African Presence in Renaissance Europe*, ed. Joaneath Spicer, exh. cat., The Walters Art Museum, Baltimore (Baltimore, 2012), pp. 98–115.

evidence of acceptance of equivalence between 'black' and 'white'. António Vieira, the resident Kongolese ambassador in Lisbon, was sent by his close relative King Álvaro II (Mpanzu a Nimi (r. 1587–1614)), the eighth Christian king of Kongo,[231] to negotiate the creation of a separate bishopric for his realm.[232] When Vieira set off for the Spanish court in November 1595, Biondi wrote two personal recommendations on his behalf. In the first, to the archbishop of Évora, he declared Vieira to be worthy of the prelate's benevolence and grace—that is, worthy of the archbishop's attention—on account of all his good qualities, most especially the strength of his religion.[233] The archbishop, D. Teutonico de Braganza,[234] and the ambassador, Vieira, shared one further characteristic: they both had royal blood. In the second recommendation, to the nuncio in Spain, Biondi described Vieira as 'molto buon christiano' (a very good Christian) and 'modestissimo' (very humble).[235] Biondi's positive assessment of Vieira was echoed by Rudolf II's ambassador to Spain, Hans Khevenhüller, writing from Madrid on 30 December 1595. In a classic example of the 'black but . . .' formulation that set 'blackness' and good qualities in a linguistically antagonistic relationship,[236] Khevenhüller characterised Vieira as 'coal black [colschwartzer] but shy and [. . .] very modest'.[237] Biondi went even further in his pen portrait of Vieira in another letter of August 1596, to the humanist, curial administrator and author of a treatise on education Silvio Antoniano,[238] who, like Biondi, was part of Clement VIII's patronage network: Vieira has good religious habits and

231. BAV, Urb. lat. 1076, part I, 21v.

232. Richard Grey, 'A Kongo Princess, the Kongo Ambassadors and the Papacy', in David Maxwell, ed., with Ingrid Lawrie, Christianity and the African Imagination: Essays in Honour of Adrian Hastings (Leiden, 2002), pp. 25–40 at 31.

233. ASV, Fondo Confalonieri 28, 401r, Biondi to the Archbishop of Évora, 27 Nov. 1595. See also Grey, 'Kongo Princess', p. 31.

234. Eubel, Hierarchia catholica, 3, p. 191.

235. ASV, Fondo Confalonieri 28, 566v, Biondi to the nuncio in Spain, 27 Nov. 1595. See also Grey, 'Kongo Princess', p. 31.

236. Kate Lowe, 'The Global Consequences of Mistranslation: The Adoption of the "black but . . ." Formulation in Europe, 1440–1650', Religions, 3 (2012), pp. 544–55.

237. Linz, Oberösterreichisches Landesarchiv, Khevenhüller-Briefbücher 5, 271r–272v.

238. On whom, see DBI, 3 (1961), pp. 511–15, entry by Paolo Prodi; Elisabetta Patrizi, Silvio Antoniano: Un umanista ed educatore nell'età del Rinnovamento cattolico (1540–1603), 3 vols (Macerata, 2010). Unfortunately, the corpus of 166 known letters from Antoniano published by Patrizi, 2, pp. 573–887 does not include any to Biondi. Antoniano was secretary of the college of cardinals from 1568 to 1592 and was then appointed secretary of briefs by Clement VIII before being given a red hat by the same pope in 1599.

is 'so well instructed in Christian doctrine and ecclesiastical histories that it is certainly a marvel.'[239] What Biondi made abundantly clear was that he considered it quite extraordinary that someone from somewhere so far away from Christian Europe could be like this; he was amazed, as he put it, that 'vi siano christiani di questa qualità' (there are [in Kongo] Christians of this quality). But his amazement appears to arise out of the 'remoteness' of Kongo from Europe,[240] rather than from any belief in the inherent inability of sub-Saharan Africans to understand or adapt to the Christian religion. The quality of Vieira's religious fervour was not the only reason for Biondi's championing of the ambassador from Kongo; there were in addition political factors influencing his behaviour, as his letters made clear. It was important that Vieira returned to Africa with a good impression of the Church's high-ranking personnel in order that the pope's plans for a new bishopric in Kongo could be realised.

The Biondi–Vieira relationship reveals another aspect of how the Portuguese trading empire could facilitate global consciousness in Renaissance Italy, specifically via papal channels, by bringing people with privileged extra-European knowledge into Europe and providing occasions when that knowledge could be passed on. Finding evidence of this is quite unusual—even when it took place, few traces of it remain. In 1595 in Lisbon, Biondi carried out an official interrogation of Vieira in Latin, asking him thirteen questions, religious and non-religious, to ascertain the state of Catholicism in the Kingdom of Kongo.[241] How this interrogation played out in practice is unclear. There is no evidence that Vieira spoke Italian, but perhaps he spoke in Portuguese (which he knew) and it was translated by an interpreter. In either case, the scribe described in the document as Thomas de Cruce (da Cruz), the notary to the legation, then wrote down the official Latin version, using canon law terminology gleaned from the ecclesiastical courts, such as describing Vieira as a *testis*, or witness: someone who gives evidence in court. The first part of the first question is startlingly basic: 'In which region of the world is the Kingdom of Kongo?' (Or, more simply, 'Where is Kongo?'). The last part of the first question asked, 'How do you know this?' (Quae sit causa scientiae?) Vieira was able to reply that he was Kongolese, and was a *vicinus*,[242] or inhabitant (in modern parlance,

239. ASV, Fondo Confalonieri 34, 678v.

240. The word 'remoto'/'remoti' was a refrain in Biondi's recommendatory letters.

241. ASV, Fondo Borghese II, 23–24, 173r–174r, and *MMA* 3, pp. 500–504.

242. See, e.g., Albert Blaise, *Lexicon latinitatis medii aevi praesertim ad res ecclesiasticas investigandas pertinens* (Turnhout, 1975), p. 956.

a 'citizen', a man involved in social and political life) of the capital city, M'banza-Kongo, known in Italian as San Salvatore and Portuguese as São Salvador, and that he possessed 'veram notitiam' of Kongo.[243] In legal terms, *notitia* is associated with a report that is known to be truthful or with a legal and binding document, so *vera notitia* is a showy but unnecessary double emphasis on truth. The source was cast-iron. This particular question, requiring explicit disclosure of how Vieira obtained his information, shows that first-hand empirical knowledge of the Kongo was at a premium, and that it was understood that misinformation and disinformation were common. Vieira's full and interesting replies fed into later *relazioni* about the Kongo, and provide an important early example of information on West Africa from an African informant. He also went into detail about Kongolese religious practices ('idol' worshippers were severely punished, and could even be burnt), religious institutions such as confraternities and seminaries, and about holdings there of religious paraphernalia such as relics.[244]

Possession of this knowledge directly from a valued and trusted African source contributed to a change in papal policy towards Kongo. Biondi adopted Vieira's cause. He agitated on Vieira's and Kongo's behalf, supporting the erection of a cathedral and the creation of a new bishopric, separate from that of São Tomé, lobbying the secretary of state, Cardinal Aldobrandini, to achieve the desired result. And although Vieira died before he could proceed to Rome, as Biondi suggested he should, Antonio Emanuele, marquis of Funda, known in Rome as Ne-Vunda,[245] was appointed his successor and finally made it to Rome in January 1608 after a journey via Brazil that had taken over three years.[246] On arrival, Antonio Emanuele was taken to the suite of rooms in the Vatican that Cardinal Bellarmine had previously occupied (an instance of

243. ASV, Fondo Borghese II, 23–24, 173r and v, and *MMA* 3, pp. 500–501.

244. ASV, Fondo Borghese II, 23–24, 173v–174r, and *MMA* 3, pp. 502–4.

245. François Baziota, *Ne-Kongo en Afrique Centrale*, xve–xviiie siècles (Rome, 1971), p. 13. 'Ne' is a prefix that signified respect or honour, and some scholars posit that the Ne Vunda family, consisting of high-ranking and close relatives of the king, was from the province to the south of the River Kongo called Sundi. John Thornton, however, in a personal communication of 20 February 2021, contends that Funta was a district in Soyo, and that Antonio Emanuele was involved in the administration of the church there.

246. Lowe, '"Representing" Africa', pp. 120–23, and Paul H. D. Kaplan, 'Italy, 1490–1700', in *The Image of the Black in Western Art*, vol. 3.1: *From the 'Age of Discovery' to the Age of Abolition: Artists of the Renaissance and Baroque*, ed. David Bindman and Henry Louis Gates Jr (Cambridge, MA, 2010), pp. 93–190 at 160–67.

status by association), known colloquially, because of their position and quality, as 'Paradise'.[247] This measure of high respect was arranged by none other
than Fabio Biondi, now back in Rome and the *maestro di palazzo* of Paul V.[248]
Clearly, the after-effects of the global friendship forged between Biondi and
Vieira in Lisbon were transported back to Rome, causing Biondi to acknowledge publicly by his behaviour towards Antonio Emanuele how important this
embassy was, setting in train a similar papal response that was crucial for future
papal–Kongolese relations.

Conclusion

Examining the official and private correspondence of a mid-ranking,
conservative-minded Italian papal official posted to Lisbon in the 1590s helps
define the arc of attitudes towards what was offered by the Portuguese trading
empire. Sent serendipitously to Portugal to collect revenues for the church,
with no known prior interest in the global, Biondi found himself asked by
Italian religious and secular acquaintances alike to procure a stream of global
goods, including global animals, available in Lisbon but not available in Italy.
He dutifully replied to their requests, although without much show of enthu-
siasm, often explaining why the purchases were not possible or advisable, but
at other times sending what he could. These acquaintances were using Biondi
as their de facto agent, because it was convenient for them—but he lacked the
flexibility, initiative and contacts that were the hallmarks of valued and fully
functioning agents. Instead, he was part of an ecclesiastical patronage system
tying the papacy and curia to provincial Italy. The client of some of his correspondents, he owed them a social and political debt, but they did not pay him.
Even those towards whom he exhibited clientage ties of affection might have
been more successful in attaining what they wanted if they had paid instead of
calling on an old friend in their patronage network. Just being in Lisbon did
not make Biondi the best man for the job, albeit ties of patronage dictated that
he had to respond to requests. Alongside these requests, meanwhile, in letters
to his family and intimates, Biondi revealed that he was engaged in collecting
a limited selection of global goods, on the side, as it were, of his day job—but
he displayed pleasure only in relation to monkeys and parrots, which he obviously enjoyed. Snarled up in political and nationalistic bureaucracy when he

247. ASV, Fondo Borghese I, 721, 190v.
248. *DBI*, 10, p. 527.

was finally given permission to leave Portugal, he fought a battle not to pay for an exit permit for the global objects he was taking with him back to Italy, labelling some of them, such as a Chinese chasuble, 'second-hand' and 'ecclesiastical'. Throughout Biondi exhibited no excitement at the opportunities for acquisition that had landed in his lap, or wonder at the objects themselves. He bought a restricted range of global objects, both for his friends and acquaintances and for himself. Had he been or become someone with interest or expertise, his purchases would have been different. He accepted what he found in Portugal—goods from all over the Portuguese trading empire—as though they were all goods from Portugal, thereby in effect reducing the global to the local. Their provenance was in the main not something he considered or dwelt on, but something irrelevant. It was their availability that was important: the fact that he could buy them.

His attention to global news was similarly pared down. Whilst he dutifully included a *foglio* of *avvisi* whenever possible in his letters to the secretary of state, his boss in Rome, he was interested primarily in Portuguese overseas news when he thought it might affect his job as apostolic collector.

If one asks whether there is any evidence to support the proposition that Biondi was changed by his stay in Lisbon—whether his acquisition of a global consciousness through his encounter with the myriad offerings of the Portuguese trading empire left any lasting impression—there is only one crystal clear example that it did. Biondi's meeting and friendship with António Vieira in Lisbon affected him to the extent that he ever afterwards championed the cause of Kongolese Christianity. The place of origin of Vieira mattered. Consciousness of the global world during Biondi's stay in Lisbon in this case broke through the barrier of limited interest by being attached to an individual. There is, however, one last irony connected to Biondi's stay in Lisbon and his encounter with the global, a matter of unintended consequences. Once back in Rome, he did not shed his association with Lisbon and the global; rather, he and Confalonieri became the conduits of choice for the bishop of Coimbra, D. Afonso de Castelo Branco, who had known both of them in Portugal, to channel presents from the Portuguese overseas territories to the pope and cardinals in order to curry favour. Biondi's apprenticeship in Lisbon in terms of acquiring global goods led to an afterlife as an intermediary in global goods at the highest levels of the papal court. In January 1597 Castelo Branco set up a supply chain via his servant who was to accompany Biondi back to Rome. Using it, he sent bezoar stones to three cardinals, pairs of gloves smeared with ambergris perfume or fragrant oil to three other cardinals, and beads made from *calambuco* (agarwood), a fragrant, dark, resinous wood, to a further two, including Cardinal Baronio.[249] The curial prelate Biondi was needed in order to facilitate the final leg of the journeys of these expensive presents made of non-European materials, by ensuring the objects reached their chosen recipients. In December 1596 Castelo Branco had already arranged for Biondi to take a bezoar stone to Rome for Clement VIII, declaring it one of the best in terms of quality that had arrived that year from 'India'.[250] Biondi was no longer required to find the objects; his new role consisted in passing the sourced presents to the pope and cardinals to whom he had daily access, meaning that his contribution to the great game of placing global acquisitions had moved to a different stage of its trajectory. There is no evidence that Biondi's acquisition of global consciousness increased his knowledge of provenance in ways that translated into any more meaningful changes in direction or behaviour. For inanimate goods, animals and people from the Portuguese trading empire in late sixteenth-century Italy, it remained the case that what mattered was not where they had come from, but who now possessed them.

249. ASV, Fondo Confalonieri 39, 44r. See also Paiva, 'Diocese de Coimbra', p. 236 (where the letter is dated October 1597 instead of January). The presents were 'luvas d'ambar' and 'contas de calambuco'.

250. ASV, Segretaria di stato, Portogallo 6, 265r and 270v; Marques, 'Cultura material', p. 192.

Parting Thoughts

KNOWLEDGE, IGNORANCE
AND NON-KNOWLEDGE

KNOWLEDGE, IGNORANCE, non-knowledge and knowledge decay all coexisted in the Renaissance. Much scholarly work has concentrated on the upsurge in knowledge produced by Europe's increasing awareness of the wider world in the same period; what has not been considered is that the existence of the wider world for Europe also increased dramatically and with immediate effect the possibilities for ignorance and non-knowledge, which in turn allowed imprecision, ambiguity and confusion to gain the upper hand in many encounters and exchanges. The documents analysed here clearly indicate that in many spheres of social interaction, knowledge of provenance was not central enough to the transaction to be recorded, and therefore can be said not to have been valued. Perhaps the main point to be made is that forced migration of people and objects from a greatly enlarged global area led, predictably, to an enlargement of diasporic terrain, but did not automatically lead to an increase in diasporic knowledge relating to provenance. A subsidiary question of interest is whether the erasure of provenance was an unintended and unforeseen by-product of enlarging the field of operation, or intentional.

The prevalence of imprecision as a mode of dealing with a surfeit of unknown knowledge is apparent in the terminology employed to signal foreignness (in particular, non-Europeanness) of both people and inanimate objects. Imprecision was useful. It could also be subtly misleading, as in the ambiguous formulation 'comes from India, is made in China', especially when the first part of the formulation, 'comes from India', became a kind of shorthand. This phrase prioritised the place of embarkation—India—over the place of origin—China, and lulled the unwary or careless into believing that India was the place of origin. It is also the case that the 'enlargement' of their world meant that Europeans were initially ill-equipped to be knowledgeable about goods or peoples from the other side of the globe that were part of complex supply chains crossing multiple areas, obscuring a series of places of origin en route.

Analysing the place of possession in the mindset of fifteenth- and sixteenth-century Italy, on the other hand, reveals its primacy; in theory circumscribed by law, in practice it was rarely troubled by moral and ethical concerns. Provenance, by contrast, appears often to have been deemed unimportant; but the issue could gain traction under certain circumstances, especially when monetary value was at stake; it was never an ethical matter. It is possible that on occasion knowledge of provenance might also have been considered disadvantageous, because limiting.

While it is relatively easy to engage with theories about the transnational and the transcultural, and to emphasise the connectedness of parts of the world, it emerges that it is much more difficult to find concrete evidence of knowledge or understanding of the Portuguese empire in Renaissance Florence and Rome, except in little pockets of interest. This is not what might have been expected—but it could help explain why the Italian Renaissance and the Portuguese expansion have so infrequently been looked at in tandem. Enslaved people from sub-Saharan Africa were shipped to Lisbon, and then on to Florence, where they worked as domestic slaves, but their pasts had been erased, and the Portuguese role in their diaspora had been erased along with them. Unusual objects from around the world were transported back to Lisbon and Cadiz and shipped to Tuscany, in virtually all cases with their place or origin erased and their Portuguese or Spanish provenance lost. Global news of varying sorts made its way from Lisbon to Rome, but much of it was incorrect or partial. Occasionally cultural attitudes travelled from Lisbon to Italy, but almost certainly without being recognised as originating in the Portuguese empire. Why was there this erasure, or lack of interest in, or indifference to, precision at ground level in relation to the provenance of many objects and people (as opposed to the more rarefied level of embassies, printed geographical texts and travel literature, maps, and various visual representations, some of which genuinely reflected new knowledge, but all of which could also suffer from indifference to precision)? Was there just very suddenly far too much that was unknown and unknowable? Or was it the consequence of moving across double or multiple sites of possession? Or, as in the contemporary world, was it a question of information overload, and global fatigue? People and goods circulated, and ended up in various parts of Italy; once there, did it really matter how they had arrived or where they had come from? Perhaps Florentines and Romans were operating on an early need-to-know basis. From the evidence presented here, it would seem that there was an upsurge in ignorance and non-knowledge at the very time that the possibilities of new knowledge were increasing exponentially. These novel and suggestive findings are at odds with current scholarship on cartography, diplomacy and travel literature, indicating that prior beliefs about provenance and possession need to be reconceptualised.

BIBLIOGRAPHY

Archive Sources

Amsterdam, University Library

MS III C 23

Berlin, Staatsbibliothek

MS. Germ. Fol. 97

Florence, Archivio dell'Ospedale degli Innocenti [AOIF]

486, 489, 491, 492, 493, 494, 495, 5374, 12646, 12681, 12682, 12683 and 12689

Florence, Archivio di stato di Firenze

Catasti 77, 80, 621, 665, 701, 709, 808, 818, 915, 921, 923 and 924
Corporazioni religiose soppresse 78 [Badia di Firenze], 317, no. 220
Depositeria generale, parte antica 393
Guardaroba medicea 1, 4, 12, 13, 15, 21, 23, 28, 30, 31, 36, 44, 46, 72, 118 and 126
Magistrato dei pupilli avanti il principato 190
Mediceo avanti il Principato [MAP], XX, 150; XLVII, 2; LXXXII, 36; CLIX; CXXIV, 283
Mediceo del Principato [MdP] 11, 13, 220, 259, 465, 487A, 606, 616, 635, 638, 656, 1169, 1170A, 1172,
    1173, 1174, 1176, 1177, 1212, 2079, 2951, 5093, 5113, 5121 and 5922A
Miscellanea medicea [Misc. med.] 713
Monastero dell'Arcangelo Raffaello 17
Notarile antecosimiano [NA] 7502, 9273, 9700, and 14183
Ospedale di S. Maria Nuova 730 and 731
Scrittoio delle regie possessioni 4137, 4138 and 4139

Florence, Biblioteca Riccardiana

MS Riccardiano 1186

293

Florence, Opera del Duomo

Archivio storico delle fedi di battesimo di S. Giovanni, registri 4, 5 and 226

Linz, Oberösterreichisches Landesarchiv

Khevenhüller-Briefbücher 5

Lisbon, Biblioteca da Ajuda

MS. 49-X-4
Rerum Lusitanicarum, V (46-IX-5)

Lisbon, Biblioteca Nacional de Portugal

Arquivo Tarouca, L. 262
INC 462

Lisbon, Direccão-Geral do Livro, dos Arquivos e das Bibliotecas, Arquivo Nacional Torre do Tombo [DGLAB/ANTT]

Corpo Cronológico [CC], 1.51.56 and 3.6.51
Núcleo Antigo [NA] 793, 759 and 799

Madrid, Biblioteca Nacional de España

MS. Vitr. 6

Mantua, Archivio di stato di Mantova [ASMa]

Archivio Gonzaga, b. 1102, 2190, 2904 and 2911
Archivio Gonzaga, MS. E XXXI.2, b.n. 1185, Affari in Ferrara

Modena, Archivio di stato di Modena [ASMo]

Cancelleria ducale, Estero, Ambasciatori, agenti e corrispondenti estensi fuori d'Italia, Spagna 1

Modena, Biblioteca Universitaria Estense

C.G.A.2

Vatican City, Archivio Segreto Vaticano [ASV] (now renamed the Archivio Apostolico Vaticano)

Fondo Borghese I, 721
Fondo Borghese II, 23–24

Fondo Confalonieri 11, 14, 15, 27, 28, 31, 32, 33, 34, 39, 45, 48–53
Segretaria di stato, Portogallo 6, 9, 10

Vatican City, Biblioteca Apostolica Vaticana [BAV]

Fondo Reginense latino 949
Urb. lat. 1076, part I

Venice, Archivio di stato di Venezia

Giudici di Petizion, Frammenti antichi, b. 13

Venice, Biblioteca nazionale Marciana

Ms. Lat. XI, 92 (= 3828)

Published Primary Sources*

Adams, Simon, ed., *Household Accounts and Disbursement Books of Robert Dudley, Earl of Leicester* (Cambridge, 1995)

Aldrovandi, Ulisse, *Delle statue antiche, che per tutta Roma in diversi luoghi & case si veggono*, included in Lucio Mauro, *Le antichità delle città di Roma, breuissimamente raccolte da chiunque ne ha scritto ò antico ò moderno [...]* (Venice, 1558)

Aldrovandi, Ulisse, *Natura picta*, ed. Alessandro Alessandrini and Alessandro Ceregato (Bologna, 2007)

Álvares, Francisco, *The Prester John of the Indies: A True Relation of the Lands of the Prester John, Being the Narrative of the Portuguese Embassy to Ethiopia in 1520*, ed. C. F. Beckingham and G.W.B. Huntingford, 2 vols (Cambridge, 1961)

Álvares, Francisco, *Verdadeira informação sobre a Terra do Preste João das Índias (II)*, ed. Luís de Albuquerque (Lisbon, 1989)

Alvares d'Almada, André, *Tratado breve dos rios de Guiné do Cabo Verde*, ed. António Luís Ferronha (Lagos, 2006)

Augustis, Quirico de, *Lumen apothecariorum cum certis expositionibus* (Venice, 1495)

Axelson, Eric, *Vasco da Gama: The Diary of his Travels through African Waters, 1497–1499* (Cape Town, 1998)

Bacci, Andrea, *De venenis et antidotis* (Rome, 1586)

Badia, Iodoco del, 'La bottega di Alessandro di Francesco Rosselli merciaio e stampatore (1528)', in *Miscellanea fiorentina di erudizione e storia*, 2 (1887), pp. 24–30

* Note that in the sections of the Bibliography that follow, Portuguese and Spanish surnames are by default listed alphabetically by the assumed patronymic: in the Portuguese case, this is the last surname given; in the Spanish case, it is the first. Italian double surnames meanwhile are in general listed by the first of these names (and, for contemporary surnames, under 'D'/De/Del', etc. if the name includes it); and listing of English double surnames reflects author preference insofar as this can be ascertained.

Baldini, Nicoletta, 'Il testamento di Eleonora Álvarez de Toledo duchessa di Toscana', in *Eleonora di Toledo duchessa di Toscana: I soggiorni in terra d'Arezzo*, ed. Nicoletta Baldini, exh. cat., Oratorio dei Santi Lorentino e Pergentino, Arezzo (Arezzo, 2022), pp. 92–96

Barlow, Roger, *A Brief Summe of Geographie*, ed. E.G.R. Taylor (London, 1932)

Barocchi, Paola, and Giovanna Gaeta Bertelà, eds, *Collezionismo mediceo: Cosimo I, Francesco I e il Cardinale Ferdinando; Documenti, 1540–1587* (Modena, 1993)

Belon, Pierre, *Les Observations de plusieurs singularitez & choses memorables trouvées en Grèce, Asie, Iudée, Egypte, Arabie & autres pays estranges* (Paris, 1554)

Boccaccio, Giovanni, *Decameron*, ed. Vittore Branca, 2 vols (Bologna, 2004)

Boccadamo, Giuliana, '"Mori negri" a Napoli fra XVI e XVII secolo: Appendice documentaria', in Gianfranco Salvatore, ed., *Il chiaro e lo scuro: Gli africani nell'Europa del Rinascimento tra realtà e rappresentazione* (Lecce, 2021), pp. 423–56

Borghini, Raffaello, *Il riposo* (Florence, 1584)

Brandão, João, 'Majestade e grandezas de Lisboa em 1552', ed. Anselmo Braamcamp Freire and J. J. Gomes de Brito, *Archivo histórico portuguez*, 11 (1921), pp. 9–241

Brásio, António, ed., *Monumenta missionaria africana: África ocidental (1471–1531)* (Lisbon, 1952) [*MMA* 1]

Brásio, António, ed., *Monumenta missionaria africana: África ocidental (1570–1599)* (Lisbon, 1953) [*MMA* 3]

Burchard, Johannes, *Johannis Burckardi Liber notarum: ab anno 1483 usque ad annum 1506*, ed. Enrico Celani, RIS/2, 32.1 (Città di Castello-Bologna, 1907–42)

Butters, Suzanne B., Elena Fumagalli and Sylvie Deswarte-Rosa, with the collaboration of Anne-Lise Desmas, *La Villa Médicis*, vol. 5: *Fonti documentarie* (Rome, 2010)

Cà da Mosto, Alvise, *Le navigazioni atlantiche del veneziano Alvise Da Mosto*, ed. Tullia Gasparrini Leporace (Venice, 1966)

Caius, John, *De canibus britannicis, liber unus; De rariorum animalium atque stirpum historia, liber unus; De libris propriis, liber unus* (London, 1570)

Carletti, Francesco, *My Voyage around the World: The Chronicles of a 16th Century Florentine Merchant*, trans. Herbert Weinstock (New York, 1964)

Carletti, Francesco, *Ragionamenti del mio viaggio intorno al mondo*, ed. Gianfranco Silvestro (Turin, 1958)

Carnemolla, Stefania Elena, *Fonti italiane dei secoli XV–XVII sull'espansione portoghese* (Pisa, 2000)

Castellani, Francesco di Matteo, *Ricordanze, II: Quaternuccio e Giornale B (1459–1485)*, ed. Giovanni Ciappelli (Florence, 1995)

Clusius, Carolus, *Curae posteriores seu plurimam non ante cognitarum aut descriptarum [...] aliquot animalium novae descriptiones* (Leiden and Antwerp, 1611)

Colón, Cristóbal, *Textos y documentos completos*, ed. Consuelo Varela (Madrid, 1984)

Colonna, Francesco, *Hypnerotomachia Poliphili* (Venice, 1499)

Confalonieri, Giovanni Battista, *Grandezza e magnificenza della città di Lisbona: Dalle carte di Giovanni Battista Confalonieri segretario del collettore apostolico (1593–1596)*, ed. Alessandro Dell'Aria (Rovereto, 2005)

Corazzini, Giuseppe Odoardo, ed., *Ricordanze di Bartolomeo Masi, calderaio fiorentino dal 1478 al 1526* (Florence, 1906)

Cortesi, Paolo, *The Renaissance Cardinal's Ideal Palace: A Chapter from Cortesi's 'De cardinalatu'*, ed. Kathleen Weil-Garris and John F. D'Amico, trans. John F. D'Amico (Rome, 1980)

Crescentio, Bartolomeo, *Nautica mediterranea* (Rome, 1607)

Crone, G. R., trans. and ed., *The Voyages of Cadamosto, and Other Documents on Western Africa in the Second Half of the Fifteenth Century* (London, 1937)

Dürer, Albrecht, *Diary of His Journey to the Netherlands, 1520–21*, ed. J.-A. Goris and G. Marlier (London, 1971)

Eiche, Sabine, ed., *Ordine et officij de casa de lo illustrissimo Signor Duca de Urbino* (Urbino, 1999)

Erasmus, Desiderius, *Collected Works of Erasmus*, vol. 35: *Adages III iv 1 to IV ii 100*, trans. and annotated by Denis L. Drysdall (Toronto, 2005)

Isabella d'Este: Selected Letters, ed. Deanna Shemek (Toronto, 2017)

Fantaguzzi, Giuliano, *Caos*, ed. Michele Andrea Pistocchi, 2 vols (Rome, 2012)

Fantaguzzi, Giuliano, 'Caos': *Cronache cesenati del sec. XV di Giuliano Fantaguzzi*, ed. Dino Bazzocchi (Cesena, 1915)

Fedeli, Vincenzo, 'Relazione di Firenze' (1561), in Eugenio Albèri, ed., *Relazioni degli ambasciatori veneti al senato*, 13 vols (Florence, 1839–63), ser. 2, vol. 1 (1839), pp. 321–83

Fernández de Navarrete, Martín, *Colección de viajes y descubrimientos que hicieron por mar los españoles desde fines del siglo XV; con varios documentos concernientes a la historia de la marina castellana y de los establecimientos españoles en Indias*, 5 vols (Madrid, 1825–37)

Ferrari, Daniela, ed., *Giulio Romano: Repertorio di fonti documentarie*, 2 vols (Mantua, 1992)

Florio, John, *Queen Anna's New World of Words, or Dictionarie of the Italian and English Tongues* (London, 1611)

Florio, John, *A Worlde of Words* (London 1598)

Formisano, Luciano, ed. 'Iddio ci dia buon viaggio e guadagno': *Firenze, Biblioteca Riccardiana, ms. 1910 (Codice Vaglienti)* (Florence, 2006)

Foroliviensis, Hieronymus, *Chronicon fratris Hieronymi de Forolivio ab anno 1397 usque ad annum 1433*, ed. Adamo Pisani, RIS/2, 19.5 (Bologna, 1931)

Fosse, Eustache de la, 'Voyage à la côte occidentale d'Afrique en Portugal et en Espagne (1479–1480)', ed. R. Foulché-Delbosc, *Revue hispanique*, 4 (1897), pp. 174–201

From Lisbon to Calicut, tr. Alvin E. Prottengeier, commentary and notes by John Parker (Minneapolis, 1956)

Gessner, Conrad, *Historiae animalium*, 4 vols (Zurich, 1551–58)

Ghirardacci, P. Cherubino, *Della historia di Bologna*, 2 vols (Bologna, 1596–1657)

Giambullari, Pierfrancesco, *Lezioni di messer Pierfrancesco Giambullari, aggiuntovi L'origine della lingua fiorentina, altrimenti Il gello* (Milan, 1827)

Herold, Bernardo, Thomas Horst and Henrique Leitão, *A 'História Natural de Portugal' de Leonhard Thurneysser zum Thurn, ca. 1555–1556, tendo com anexo a transcrição das partes relativas a Portugal do manuscrito atribuído a Leonhard Thurneysser zum Thurn Ms. Germ. Fol. 97 da Staatsbibliothek zu Berlin* (Lisbon, 2019)

Jadin, Louis, and Mireille Dicorato, *Correspondance de Dom Afonso, roi du Congo, 1506–1543*, = *Académie royale de Belgique. Classe des sciences morales et politiques: Mémoires*, n.s. 41, no. 3 (Brussels, 1975)

James, Carolyn, *The Letters of Giovanni Sabadino degli Arienti (1481–1510)* (Florence, 2002)

Kopke, Diogo, and António da Costa Paiva, eds, *Roteiro da viagem que em descobrimento da India pelo Cabo da Boa Esperança fez Dom Vasco da Gama em 1497* (Porto, 1838)

Lankmann von Falkenstein, Niklas, *Leonor de Portugal Imperatriz da Alemanha: Diário de viagem do embaixador Nicolau Lanckman de Valkenstein*, ed. Aires A. Nascimento (Lisbon, 1992)

Lettenhove, J. Kervyn de, ed., *Lettres et négociations de Philippe de Commines*, 3 vols in 2 tomes (Brussels, 1868)

Livro do lançamento e serviço que a cidade de Lisboa fez a El Rei Nosso Senhor no ano de 1565, 4 vols (Lisbon, 1948)

Luzzana Caraci, Ilaria, ed., *Amerigo Vespucci*, vol. 1: *Documenti*, Nuova raccolta columbiana 21, 2 vols (Rome, 1996 and 1999)

Manuppella, Giacinto, ed., *Livro de cozinha da Infanta Dona Maria, Códice Português I.E.33 da Bibioteca Nacional de Nápoles* (Lisbon, 1986)

Medici, Lorenzo de', *Lettere*, vol. 16: *Settembre 1489–febbraio 1490*, ed. Lorenz Böninger (Florence, 2011)

Medici, Lorenzo de', *Opere*, ed. Attilio Simoni, 2 vols (Bari, 1913–14)

Mommsen, Theodor, ed., *Codex Theodosianus* (Dublin, 1970)

Münzer, Jérôme, *Voyage en Espagne et au Portugal (1494–1495)*, ed. Michel Tarayre (Paris, 2006)

Oliveira, Cristóvão Rodrigues de, *Lisboa em 1551: Sumário em que brevemente se contêm algumas coisas assim eclesiásticas como seculares que há na cidade de Lisboa (1551)*, ed. José da Felicidade Alves (Lisbon, 1987)

Orta, Garcia de, *Colóquios dos simples e drogas he cousas medicinais da Índia* (Goa, 1563)

Ortelius, Abraham, *Theatrum orbis terrarum* or *Theatro de la tierra universal* (Antwerp, 1588)

Paesi nuovamente retrovati et Novo Mondo da Alberico Vesputio Florentino intitulato (Vicenza, 1507)

Palladio, Andrea, *I quattro libri dell'architettura*, ed. Licisco Magagnato and Paola Marini (Milan, 1980)

Pardi, Giuseppe, ed., *Diario ferrarese dall'anno 1409 sino al 1502 di autori incerti*, RIS/2, 24.7 (Bologna, 1928–33)

Pereira, Duarte Pacheco, *Esmeraldo de situ orbis*, trans. and ed. George H. T. Kimble (London, 1937)

Pereira, Duarte Pacheco, *Esmeraldo de situ orbis*, ed. Joaquim Barradas de Carvalho (Lisbon, 1991)

Peres, Damião, *Os mais antigos roteiros da Guiné* (Lisbon, 1952)

Pigafetta, Antonio, *The First Voyage around the World, 1519–1522: An Account of Magellan's Expedition*, ed. Theodore J. Cachey Jr (Toronto, 2007)

Pigafetta, Antonio, *Magellan's Voyage: A Narrative Account of the First Circumnavigation*, trans. and ed. R. A. Skelton, 2 vols (New Haven, CT, 1969)

Pigafetta, Antonio, *Relazione del primo viaggio attorno al mondo*, ed. Andrea Canova (Padua, 1999)

Pigafetta, Filippo, *Relatione del reame di Congo et delle circonvicine contrade tratta dalli scritti & ragionamenti di Odoardo Lopez portoghese per Filippo Pigafetta con dißegni vari di geografia, di piante, d'habiti, d'animali & altro* (Rome, 1591)

Pignoria, Lorenzo, *De servis et eorum apud veteres ministeriis commentarius* (Augsburg, 1613)

Platter, Thomas, *Thomas Platters des Jüngeren Englandfahrt im Jahre 1599* (Halle-Saale, 1929)

Platter, Thomas, *Thomas Platter's Travels in England, 1599*, trans. and intro. by Clare Williams (London, 1937)

Pliny the Elder, *Historia naturalis* (Venice, 1469)

Pliny the Elder, *Natural History*, with an English translation by H. Rackham, 10 vols (Cambridge, MA, 1956–63)

Poliziano, Angelo, *Letters*, vol. 1: Books 1–4, ed. and trans. Shane Butler (Cambridge, MA, 2006)

Poliziano, Angelo, *Opera quae quidem extitere hactenus omnia* (Basel, 1553)

Pontani, Gaspare, *Il diario romano di Gaspare Pontani, già riferito al Notaio del Nantiporto: 30 gennaio 1481–25 luglio 1492*, ed. Diomede Toni, RIS/2, 3.2 (Città di Castello, 1907–8)

Portugaliae monumenta africana, 4 vols (1–3 and 5) (Lisbon, 1993–2002)

Prestage, Edgar, and Pedro d'Azevedo, eds, *Registo da freguesia de Santa Cruz do Castello desde 1536 até 1628* (Coimbra, 1913)

'Rol da Gente Cortesã em Almeirim (1545)', transcribed by Pedro Pinto, *Fragmenta Historica— História, Paleografia e Diplomática*, 6 (2018), pp. 359–69

Rossi, Tribaldo de', 'Ricordanze tratte da un libro originale di Tribaldo de' Rossi', in Ildefonso di San Luigi, ed., *Delizie degli eruditi toscani*, 24 vols (Florence, 1770–89), 23, pp. 236–303

Salinger, J. D., *The Complete Uncollected Short Stories of J. D. Salinger*, 2 vols (n.p., n.d. [c. 1967])

Salinger, J. D., 'Hapworth 16, 1924', *The New Yorker*, 19 June 1965

Salvatore, Gianfranco, 'Analisi dei dati pertinenti del *Libro primo de' battesimi della Cattedrale di Napoli* (1583–1649)', in Gianfranco Salvatore, ed., *Il chiaro e lo scuro: Gli africani nell'Europa del Rinascimento tra realtà e rappresentazione* (Lecce, 2021), pp. 457–460

Sassetti, Filippo, *Lettere da vari paesi, 1570–1588*, ed. Vanni Bramanti (Milan, 1970)

Scappi, Bartolomeo, *Dell'arte del cuoco* (Venice, 1570)

Soderini, Giovanvettorio, *Il trattato degli animali domestici*, ed. Alberto Bacchi Della Lega (Bologna, 1903)

Sorbelli, Albano, ed., *Corpus chronicorum Bononiensium*, RIS/2, 18.1 (Città di Castello-Bologna, 1906–39)

Sousa, Frei Luís de, *A Vida de Dom Frei Bertolameu dos Mártires*, ed. Aníbal Pinto do Castro (2nd edn, Lisbon, 2015 [1984])

Spallanzani, Marco, *Giovanni da Empoli, un mercante fiorentino nell'Asia portoghese* (Florence, 1999)

Spallanzani, Marco, *Mercanti fiorentini nell'Asia portoghese (1500–1525)* (Florence, 1997)

Spallanzani, Marco, and Giovanna Gaeta Bertelà, eds, *Libro d'inventario dei beni di Lorenzo il Magnifico* (Florence, 1992)

Statuta populi et communis Florentiae: Publica auctoritate collecta castigata et praeposita anno salutis MCCCCXV, 2 vols (Friburg [1778–83])

Topsell, Edward, *The History of Four-Footed Beasts and Serpents and Insects*, 3 vols (facsimile, London, 1967 [London, 1658])

Unverfehrt, Gerd, *'Da sah ich viel köstliche Dinge': Albrecht Dürers Reise in die Niederlande* (Göttingen, 2007)

Valori, Niccolò, *Vita di Lorenzo de' Medici*, trans. Filippo Valori, ed. Enrico Niccolini (Vicenza, 1991)

Vasari, Giorgio, *Le vite de' più eccellenti pittori scultori e architettori*, text ed. Rosanna Bettarini, commentary ed. Paola Barocchi, 9 vols in 11 tomes (Florence, 1966–97)

Vasari, Giorgio, *Le vite de' più illustri pittori, scultori ed architettori*, ed. Gaetano Milanesi, 9 vols (Florence, 1878–85)

Vergil, Polydore, *Proverbiorum libellus* (Venice, 1498)

Vespucci, Amerigo, *Lettera a Piero Soderini, Lisbona sett. 1504, secondo il cod. II IV 509 della Bib. Naz. di Firenze*, ed. S. G. Martini (Florence, 1957)

Vespucci, Amerigo, *Mundus novus* (Augsburg, 1504)

'Viagem a Portugal dos Cavaleiros Tron e Lippomani, 1580', in Alexandre Herculano, *Opúsculos*, vol. 6 (5th edn, Lisbon, n.d.), pp. 113–26

Vida de Dom Frei Bertolameu dos Martyres do Ordem dos Pregadores arcebispo e senhor de Braga primas das Espanhas [. . .], arranged by Luis de Cacegas (Viana, 1619)

West, Martin L., ed., *Homeric Hymns, Homeric Apocrypha, Lives of Homer* (Cambridge, MA, 2003)

Secondary Sources

African Ivories, ed. Kate Ezra, exh. cat., The Metropolitan Museum of Art, New York (New York, 1984)

L'Âge d'or des cartes marines: Quand l'Europe découvrait le monde, ed. Catherine Hofmann, Hélène Richard and Emmanuelle Vagnon, exh. cat., Bibliothèque nationale de France, Paris (Paris, 2012)

The Age of Süleyman the Magnificent, ed. Esin Atul, exh. cat., National Gallery of Art, Washington (Washington, DC, 1987)

Ago, Renata, 'Denaturalizing Things: A Comment', in Paula Findlen, ed., *Early Modern Things: Objects and Their Histories, 1500–1800* (London, 2013), pp. 363–68

Alegria, Maria Fernanda, Suzanne Daveau, João Carlos Garcia and Francesc Relaño, 'Portuguese Cartography in the Renaissance', in David Woodward, ed., *The History of Cartography*, vol. 3: *Cartography in the European Renaissance*, in 2 parts (Chicago, 2007), part 1, pp. 975–1068

Alessandrini, Nunziatella, 'Contributo alla storia della famiglia Giraldi, mercanti banchieri fiorentini nella corte di Lisbona nel XVI secolo', *Storia economica*, 14.3 (2011), pp. 377–408

Alessandrini, Nunziatella, 'Giovanni Dall'Olmo, un veneziano em Lisboa: Comércio e diplomacia (1541–1588)', *Ammentu*, 3 (2013), pp. 155–57

Alessandrini, Nunziatella, 'I porti di Lisbona e Livorno: Mercanti, merci e "gentilezze diverse" (secolo XVI): Alcune considerazioni', in Nunziatella Alessandrini, Mariagrazia Russo and Gaetano Sabatini, eds, *'Chi fa questo camino è ben navigato': Culturas e dinâmicas nos portos de Itália e Portugal (sécs. XV–XVI)* (Lisbon, 2019), pp. 129–43

Alessandrini, Nunziatella, 'La presenza italiana a Lisbona nella prima metà del Cinquecento', *Archivio storico italiano* 164 (2006), pp. 37–54

Alonso, Carlos, O.S.A, 'Documentacíon inédita para una biografía de Fr. Alejo de Meneses, O.S.A., arzobispo de Goa (1595–1612)', *Analecta Augustiniana*, 27 (1964), pp. 263–333

Alonso, Carlos, O.S.A, 'Eleccion y consagración de Alejo de Meneses, O.S.A, como arzobispo de Goa (1594–1595)', *Analecta Augustiniana*, 49 (1986), pp. 91–135

Alves, Jorge M. dos Santos, 'A pedra-bezoar—realidade e mito em torno de un antídoto (séculos XVI e XVII)', in Jorge M. Dos Santos Alves, Claude Guillot and Roderich Ptak, eds, *Mirabilia asiatica: Produtos raros no comércio marítimo/Produits rares dans le commerce maritime/Seltene Waren im Seehandel* (Wiesbaden, 2003), pp. 121–34

Amico Aspertini, 1474–1552: Artista bizzarro nell'età di Dürer e Raffaello, ed. Andrea Emiliani and Daniela Scaglietti Kelescian, exh. cat., Pinacoteca nazionale di Bologna (Milan, 2008)

Amundsen, Daniel, and Carol Jean Diers, 'The Age of Menarche in Medieval Europe', *Human Biology*, 45.3 (1973), pp. 363–69

Anderson, Christina M., ed., *A Cultural History of Furniture*, 6 vols (London, 2022), vol. 3: *A Cultural History of Furniture in the Age of Exploration*, ed. Christina M. Anderson and Elizabeth A. Correll

Anderson, Ruth Matilda, *Hispanic Costume, 1480–1530* (New York, 1979)

Andrade, António Manuel Lopes, 'Garcia de Orta and Amato Lusitano's Views on *materia medica*: A Comparative Perspective', in Palmira Fontes da Costa, ed., *Medicine, Trade and Empire: Garcia de Orta's 'Colloquies on the Simples and Drugs of India' (1563) in Context* (London, 2016), pp. 147–66

Andrea del Sarto: The Renaissance Workshop in Action, ed. Julian Brooks with Denise Allen and Xavier F. Salomon, exh. cat., The J. Paul Getty Museum at the Getty Center, Los Angeles (Los Angeles, 2015)

Animais orientais: Fauna exótica no tempo dos Descobrimentos, ed. Rui Manuel Loureiro, exh. cat., Câmara Municipal de Lagos (Lagos, 2008)

Apfelstadt, Eric, 'Bishop and Pawn: New Documents for the Chapel of the Cardinal of Portugal at S. Miniato al Monte, Florence', in K.J.P. Lowe ed., *Cultural Links between Portugal and Italy in the Renaissance* (Oxford, 2000), pp. 183–223

Arnaut, Salvador Dias, *A arte de comer em Portugal na Idade Média (Introdução a 'O livro de cozinha' da Infanta D. Maria de Portugal)* (Lisbon, 1986)

Assonitis, Alessio, 'The Education of Cosimo di Giovanni de' Medici (1519–1537)', in Alessio Assonitis and Henk Th. van Veen, eds, *A Companion to Cosimo I de' Medici* (Leiden, 2021), pp. 19–44

Atzori, Luigi, and Ivo Regoli, 'Due comuni rurali del dominio fiorentino nel sec. XVI: Montopoli V.A. e Castelfranco di Sotto', in Giorgio Spini, ed., *Architettura e politica da Cosimo I a Ferdinando I* (Florence, 1976), pp. 79–164

Azzolini, Monica, 'Talking of Animals: Whales, Ambergris and the Circulation of Knowledge in Seventeenth-Century Rome', *Renaissance Studies*, 31.2 (2017), pp. 297–318

Baggio, Silvia, and Piero Marchi, 'Introduzione', in Silvia Baggio and Piero Marchi, eds, *Miscellanea medicea: Archivio di stato di Firenze*, 3 vols (Rome, 2002), 1, pp. 3–32

Bailey, Gregory, 'The Nineteenth-Century Reconstruction of Giovanni Della Robbia's *Adam and Eve*', *The Journal of the Walters Art Museum*, 73 (2018), pp. 70–8

Ballou, Jonathan D., Devra Kleiman, Jeremy Mallinson, Anthony B. Rylands, Claudio Padua and Kristin Leus, 'History, Management and Conservation Role of the Captive Lion Tamarin Populations', in Devra G. Kleiman and Anthony B. Rylands, ed., *Lion Tamarins: Biology and Conservation* (Washington, DC, 2002)

Barbarics, Zsuzsa, and Renate Pieper, 'Handwritten Newsletters as a Means of Communication in Europe, 1400–1700', Cultural Exchange in Early Modern Europe 3 (Cambridge, 2007), pp. 53–79

Barclay Lloyd, Joan, *African Animals in Renaissance Literature and Art* (Oxford, 1971)

Barker, Hannah, *That Most Precious Merchandise: The Mediterranean Trade in Black Sea Slaves, 1260–1500* (Philadelphia, 2019)

Barker, Sheila, '"Secret and uncertain": A History of *avvisi* at the Court of the Medici Grand Dukes', in Joad Raymond and Noah Moxham, eds, *News Networks in Early Modern Europe* (Leiden, 2016), pp. 716–38

Bassani, Ezio, *African Art and Artefacts in European Collections, 1400–1800*, ed. Malcolm McLeod (London, 2000)

Bassani, Ezio, 'Antichi avori africani nelle collezioni medicee, 1', *Critica d'arte*, n.s. 21, fasc. 143 (1975), pp. 69–80

Bassani, Ezio, *Gli antichi strumenti musicali dell'Africa nera dalle antiche fonti cinquecentesche al Gabinetto Armonico del Padre Filippo Bonanni* (Padua, 1978)

Bassani, Ezio, 'Il collezionismo esotico dei Medici nel Cinquecento', in Candace J. Adelson et al., *Le arti del principato Mediceo* (Florence, 1980), pp. 55–71

Bassani, Ezio, and William B. Fagg, *Africa and the Renaissance: Art in Ivory*, ed. Susan Vogel, with Carol Thompson, exh. cat., The Center for African Art, New York and the Museum of Fine Arts, Houston (New York, 1988)

Basto, Artur de Magalhães, *História da Santa Casa da Misericórdia do Porto*, 2 vols (Porto, 1934, 1964)

Bastos, Celina, and Anísio Franco, 'A Custódia de Belém e o ouro de Quíloa: A lenda das Índias', in *A Custódia de Belém: 500 Anos*, ed. Leonor D'Orey and Luísa Penalva, exh. cat., Museu Nacional de Arte Antiga, Lisbon (Lisbon, 2010), pp. 126–39

Battaglia, Salvatore, *Grande dizionario della lingua italiana*, 25 vols (Turin, 1961–2009)

Battelli, Guido, 'La corrispondenza del Poliziano col Re Don Giovanni II di Portogallo', *La rinascita*, 2 (1939), pp. 280–98

Battistini, Mario, 'Il medico Andrea Pasquali', in *Rivista di storia delle scienze mediche e naturali*, 8 (1926), pp. 231–33

Baziota, François, *Ne-Kongo en Afrique Centrale, xve–xviiie siècles* (Rome, 1971)

Behrens-Abouseif, Doris, *Practising Diplomacy in the Mamluk Sultanate: Gifts and Material Culture in the Medieval Islamic World* (London, 2014)

Bell, Peter, and Dirk Suckow, 'Fremde in Stadt und Bild', in Peter Bell, Dirk Suckow and Gerhard Wolf, eds, *Fremde in der Stadt: Ordnungen, Repräsentationen und soziale Praktiken (13.–15. Jahrhundert)* (Frankfurt, 2010), pp. 13–32

Bellinazzi, Anna, and Claudio Lamioni, eds, *Carteggio universale da Cosimo I de' Medici: Inventario*, vol. 1: *1536–1541* (Florence, 1982)

Berti, Marcello, 'Le aziende da Colle: Una finestra sulle relazioni commerciali tra la Toscana ed il Portogallo a metà del quattrocento', in *Toscana e Portogallo: Miscellanea storica nel 650° anniversario dello Studio Generale di Pisa* (Pisa, 1994), pp. 57–106

Biagioli, Beatrice, Gabriella Cibei and Veronica Vestri, eds, *Miscellanea medicea*, vol. 3:(451–730): *Inventario* (Rome, 2014)

Biaudet, Henry, *Les Nonciatures apostoliques permanentes jusqu'en 1648* (Helsinki, 1910)

Bibliotheca sanctorum, 13 vols (Rome, 1961–70)

Biedermann, Zoltán, 'Diplomatic Ivories: Sri Lankan Caskets and the Portuguese–Asian Exchange in the Sixteenth Century', in Zoltán Biedermann, Anne Gerritsen and Giorgio Riello, eds, *Global Gifts: The Material Culture of Diplomacy in Early Modern Eurasia* (Cambridge, 2018), pp. 88–118

Biedermann, Zoltán, 'Imagining Asia from the Margins: Early Portuguese Mappings of the Continent's Architecture and Space', in Vimalin Rujivcharakul, H. Hazel Hahn, Ken Tadashi Oshima and Peter Christensen, eds, *Architecturalized Asia: Mapping a Continent through History* (Honolulu, 2013), pp. 35–51

Billé, Philippe, *La Faune brésilienne dans les écrits documentaires du XVIᵉ siècle* (Paris, 2009)

Blackmun, Barbara Winston, 'The Elephant and Its Ivory in Benin', in *Elephant: The Animal and Its Ivory in African Culture*, ed. Doran H. Ross, exh. cat., The Fowler Museum of Cultural History, UCLA (Los Angeles, 1992), pp. 162–83

Blair, Ann M., *Too Much to Know: Managing Scholarly Information before the Modern Age* (New Haven, CT, 2010)

Blaise, Albert, *Lexicon latinitatis medii aevi praesertim ad res ecclesiasticas investigandas pertinens* (Turnhout, 1975)

Bleichmar, Daniela, 'Seeing the World in a Room: Looking at Exotica in Early Modern Collections', in Daniela Bleichmar and Peter Mancall eds, *Collecting across Cultures: Material Exchanges in the Early Modern Atlantic World* (Philadelphia, 2011), pp. 15–30

Blier, Suzanne Preston, 'Capricious Arts: Idols in Renaissance-Era Africa and Europe (the Case of Sapi and Kongo)', in Michael W. Cole and Rebecca Zorach, eds, *The Idol in the Age of Art: Objects, Devotions and the Early Modern World* (Farnham, 2009), pp. 11–29

Blier, Suzanne Preston, 'Ways of Experiencing African Art: The Role of Its Patina' in Suzanne Preston Blier, ed., *Art of the Senses: African Masterpieces from the Teel Collection* (Boston, MA, 2004), pp. 10–23

Blumenthal, Debra, 'Masters, Slave Women and Their Children: A Child Custody Dispute in Fifteenth-Century Valencia', in Stefan Hanß and Juliane Schiel, *Mediterranean Slavery Revisited (500–1800)/Neue Perspektiven auf mediterrane Sklaverei (500–1800)* (Zurich, 2014), pp. 229–56

Boccadamo, Giuliana, 'A Napoli: "Mori negri" fra Cinque e Seicento', in Gianfranco Salvatore, ed., *Il chiaro e lo scuro: Gli africani nell'Europa del Rinascimento tra realtà e rappresentazione* (Lecce, 2021), pp. 143–56

Boehrer, Bruce, *Parrot Culture: Our 2,500-Year-Long Fascination with the World's Most Talkative Bird* (Philadelphia, 2004)

Böninger, Lorenz, 'Don Niccolò Germano e Arrigo Martello: Due cartografi tedeschi nella Firenze del Quattrocento', *Geostorie*, 21.1–2 (2013), pp. 9–20

Borschberg, Peter, 'The Euro-Asian Trade in Bezoar Stones (approx. 1500 to 1700)', in Michael North, ed., *Artistic and Cultural Exchanges between Europe and Asia, 1400–1900: Rethinking Markets, Workshops and Collections* (Farnham, 2010), pp. 29–43

Borschberg, Peter, 'The Trade, Use and Forgery of Porcupine Bezoars in the Early Modern Period (ca. 1500–1750)', *Oriente*, 14 (2006), pp. 60–78

Botana, Federico, 'Tammaro de Marinis, Vittorio Forti, and the Acquisition of Islamic Manuscripts for J. P. Morgan in Constantinople in 1913', *Manuscript Studies*, 7.2 (2022), pp. 237–69

Bouchon, Geneviève, 'L'Inventaire de la cargaison rapportée de l'Inde en 1505', in *Mare Luso-Indicum: Études et documents sur l'histoire de l'Océan Indien et des pays riverains à l'époque de la domination portugaise*, 4 vols (Paris, 1971–80), 3, pp. 101–25

Bouchon, Geneviève, *Navires et cargaisons retour de l'Inde en 1518* (Paris, 1977)

Bourne, Molly, *Francesco II Gonzaga: The Soldier-Prince as Patron* (Rome, 2008)

Brackett, John K., 'Race and Rulership: Alessandro de' Medici, First Medici Duke of Florence, 1529–1537', in T. F. Earle and K.J.P. Lowe, eds, *Black Africans in Renaissance Europe* (Cambridge, 2005), pp. 303–25

Braudel, Fernand, and Ruggiero Romano, *Navires et marchandises à l'entrée du port di Livourne (1547–1611)* (Paris, 1951)

Brege, Brian, *Tuscany in the Age of Empire* (Cambridge, MA, 2021)

Brincard, Marie-Thérèse, ed., *Sounding Forms: African Musical Instruments* (New York, 1989)

Brown, Clifford M., 'Francesco Bonsignori: Painter to the Gonzaga Court—New Documents', *Atti e memorie della Accademia virgiliana di Mantova*, n.s. 47 (1979), pp. 81–96

Brown, Clifford M., '"Lo insaciabile desiderio nostro de cose antique": New Documents on Isabella d'Este's Collection of Antiquities', in Cecil H. Clough, ed., *Cultural Aspects of the Italian Renaissance: Essays in Honour of Paul Oskar Kristeller* (Manchester, 1976), pp. 324–53

Brucker, Gene, '*Fede* and *fiducia*: The Problem of Trust in Italian History, 1300–1500', in Gene Brucker, *Living on the Edge in Leonardo's Florence: Selected Essays* (Berkeley, CA, 2005), pp. 83–103

Brundage, James A., *Law, Sex and Christian Society in Medieval Europe* (Chicago, 1987)

Brundage, James A., 'Sex and Canon Law', in Vern L. Bullough and James A. Brundage eds, *Handbook of Medieval Sexuality* (New York, 1996), pp. 33–50

Buckland, W. W., *The Roman Law of Slavery: The Condition of the Slave in Private Law from Augustus to Justinian* (Cambridge, 1908)

Bujok, Elke, 'Ethnographica in Early Modern *Kunstkammern* and Their Perception', *Journal of the History of Collections*, 21.1 (2009), pp. 17–32

Bury, John, *Two Notes on Francisco de Holanda* (London, 1971)

Butters, Suzanne B., 'Le Cardinal Ferdinand de Médicis', in Philippe Morel, ed., *La Villa Médicis*, vol. 2: *Études* (Rome, 1991), pp. 170–96

Butters, Suzanne B., 'Ferdinand et le jardin du Pincio', in Philippe Morel, ed. *La Villa Médicis*, vol. 2: *Études* (Rome, 1991), pp. 351–410

Caeiro, Francisco, *O archduque Alberto de Austria: Vice-rei e inquisidor-mor de Portugal, cardeal legado do papa, governador e depois soberano dos Paises Baixos; História e arte* (Lisbon, 1961)

Il cammeo Gonzaga: Arti preziose alla corte di Mantova, ed. Ornella Casazza, exh. cat., Le Fruttiere del Palazzo Te, Mantua (Milan, 2008)

Carmo, Miguel, Joana Sousa, Pedro Varela, Ricardo Ventura and Manuel Bivar, 'African Knowledge Transfer in Early Modern Portugal: Enslaved People and Rice Cultivation in Tagus and Sado Rivers', *Diacronie*, 44.4 (2020), pp. 45–66

Carnesecchi, Carlo, 'Paolo Toscanelli e gli ambasciatori del Re di Portogallo nel 1459', *Archivio storico italiano*, ser. 5, 21 (1898), pp. 316–18

Cartwright, Julia, *Isabella d'Este, Marchioness of Mantua, 1474–1539: A Study of the Renaissance*, 2 vols (London, 1904)

Carvalho, Luís Manuel Mendonça de, and Francisca Maria Fernandes, '*Exotica naturalia*: O enigma do coco-do-mar', *Artis: Revista do Instituto de História da Arte da Faculdade de Letras da Universidade de Lisboa*, 9–10 (2020–11), pp. 153–62

Casimiro, Tânia Manuel, José Pedro Henriques, Vanessa Filipe and Sara Simões, 'Mobility and Identities: The Case of the So-Called African Pots from Lisbon (Portugal)', *International Journal of Historical Archaeology*, 24.1 (2020), pp. 79–94

Castignoli, Paolo, 'Livorno in villaggio?', *La Canaviglia*, anno 1, no. 3 (July–September 1976), pp. 97–98

Cattaneo, Angelo, *Fra Mauro's Mappa Mundi and Fifteenth-Century Venice* (Turnhout, 2011)

Cattaneo, Angelo, ed., *Mappa mundi 1457: Carta conservata presso la Biblioteca nazionale centrale di Firenze con la segnatura Portolano 1; Introduzione e commento* (Rome, 2008)

Cecchi, Alessandro, and Carlo Gasparri, *La Villa Médicis*, vol. 4: *Le collezioni del cardinale Ferdinando: I dipinti e le sculture* (Rome, 2009)

Cerreti, Claudio, 'Gli ambasciatori e la cartografia', in Stefano Andretta, Lucien Bély, Alexander Koller and Gérard Poumarède, eds, *Esperienza e diplomazia: Saperi, pratiche culturali e azione diplomatica nell'Età moderna (secc. XV–XVIII)/Expérience et diplomatie: Savoirs, pratiques culturelles et action diplomatique à l'époque moderne (XVᵉ–XVIIIᵉ s.)* (Rome, 2020), pp. 211–30

Chambers, David, 'Venetian Perceptions of Portugal c. 1500', in K.J.P. Lowe, ed., *Cultural Links between Portugal and Italy in the Renaissance* (Oxford, 2000), pp. 19–43

Chambers, D. S., *A Renaissance Cardinal and His Worldly Goods: The Will and Inventory of Francesco Gonzaga (1444–1483)* (London, 1992)

Cherubini, Giovanni, 'I libri di ricordanze come fonte storica', in *Civiltà comunale: Libro, scrittura, documento; Atti del Convegno, Genova, 8–11 novembre 1988* (Genoa, 1989), pp. 567–91

Christopoulos, John, *Abortion in Early Modern Italy* (Cambridge, MA, 2021)

Ciappelli, Giovanni, 'Carte geografiche e politica nei rapporti tra Firenze e il Portogallo nel Quattrocento', *Annali dell'Istituto storico italo-germanico in Trento/Jahrbuch des italienisch-deutschen historischen Instituts in Trient*, 32 (2006), pp. 47–70

Ciappelli, Giovanni, 'Introduzione', in Francesco di Matteo Castellani, *Ricordanze, II: Quaternuccio e Giornale B (1459–1485)*, ed. Giovanni Ciappelli (Florence, 1995), pp. 1–24

Ciappelli, Giovanni, *Memory, Family and Self: Tuscan Family Books and Other European Egodocuments (14th to 18th Century)* (Leiden, 2014)

Cibrario, Luigi, 'Lezione storico-filologica sopra alcuni vocaboli usati nei più antichi registri della guardaroba medicea', *Archivio storico italiano*, ser. 3, 4, part 1 (1867), pp. 152–65

A cidade global: Lisboa no Renascimento/The Global City: Lisbon in the Renaissance, ed. Annemarie Jordan Gschwend and K.J.P. Lowe, exh. cat., Museu Nacional de Arte Antiga, Lisbon (Lisbon, 2017)

Il Cinquecento a Firenze: 'Maniera moderna' e controriforma, ed. Carlo Falciani and Antonio Natali, exh. cat., Palazzo Strozzi, Florence (Florence, 2017)

Cipolla, Carlo M., *La moneta a Firenze nel Cinquecento* (Bologna, 1987)

Cipolla, Carlo, 'Prete Jane e Francesco Novello da Carrara', *Archivio veneto*, 6 (1873), pp. 323–24

Clark, Leah R., *Collecting Art in the Italian Renaissance Court: Objects and Exchanges* (Cambridge, 2018)

Clarke, F. W., *Weights, Measures and Money of All Nations* (New York, 1891)

Coates, Timothy J., *Convicts and Orphans: Forced and State-sponsored Colonizers in the Portuguese Empire, 1550–1755* (Stanford, CA, 2001), pp. 141–77

Cockram, Sarah, 'Interspecies Understanding: Exotic Animals and Their Handlers at the Italian Renaissance Courts', *Renaissance Studies*, 31.2 (2017), pp. 277–96

Colle, Enrico, ed., *I mobili di Palazzo Pitti: Il periodo dei Medici, 1537–1737* (Florence, 1997)

Constable, Giles, *Letters and Letter Collections* (Turnhout, 1976)

Conti, Cosimo, *La prima reggia di Cosimo I de' Medici nel palazzo già della signoria di Firenze, descritta ed illustrata coll'appoggio d'un inventario inedito del 1553 etc.* (Florence, 1893)

Conticelli, Valentina, 'Dea Natura, Diana Efesia e Diana nera: Motivi iconografici nella com-
mittenza di Francesco I de' Medici; Dallo studiolo di Palazzo Vecchio alle grottesche degli
Uffizi', in Giovanni Barberi Squarotti, Annarita Colturato and Clara Goria, eds, *Il mito di
Diana nella cultura delle corti: Arte, letteratura, musica* (Florence, 2018), pp. 85–101

Conticelli, Valentina, *Le grottesche degli Uffizi* (Florence, 2018)

Conticelli, Valentina, *'Guardaroba di cose rare e preziose': Lo studiolo di Francesco I de' Medici;
Arte, storia e significati* (La Spezia, 2007)

Corominas, Joan, *Diccionario crítico etimológico de la lengua castellana*, 4 vols (Berne, 1954)

Cortesão, Armando, and Avelino Teixeira da Mota, 'Anónimo, o planisfério "Cantino", de 1502',
in *Portugaliae monumenta cartographica*, 6 vols (facsimile, Lisbon, 1987 [Lisbon, 1960]), 1,
pp. 7–13

Cortesão, Jaime, 'Do sigilo nacional sobre os descobrimentos: Crónicas desaparecidas, mutiladas e falseadas; Alguns dos feitos que se calaram', *Lusitania*, 1 (1924), pp. 45–81

Costa, António Domingues de Sousa, 'Estudos superiores e universitários em Portugal no reinado de D. João II', *Biblos*, 63 (1987), pp. 253–334

Crespo, Hugo Miguel, ed., *A arte de coleccionar: Lisboa, Europa e o Mundo na época moderna
(1500–1800)/The Art of Collecting: Lisbon, Europe and the Early Modern World (1500–1800)*
(Lisbon, 2019)

Crespo, Hugo Miguel, 'A casa de Simão de Melo', in *A cidade global: Lisboa no Renascimento/
The Global City: Lisbon in the Renaissance*, ed. Annemarie Jordan Gschwend and K.J.P. Lowe,
exh. cat., Museu Nacional de Arte Antiga, Lisbon (Lisbon, 2017), pp. 210–27

Crespo, Hugo Miguel, ed., *Choices* (Lisbon, 2016)

Crespo Hugo Miguel, ed., *Comprar o mundo: Consumo e comércio na Lisboa do Renascimento/
Shopping for Global Goods: Consumption and Trade in Renaissance Lisbon* (Lisbon, 2020)

Crespo, Hugo Miguel, 'Global Interiors on the Rua Nova in Renaissance Lisbon', in Annemarie
Jordan Gschwend and K.J.P. Lowe, eds, *The Global City: On the Streets of Renaissance Lisbon*
(London, 2015), pp. 120–39

Crespo, Hugo Miguel, 'The Plundering of the Ceylonese Royal Treasure, 1551–1553: Its Character, Cost and Dispersal', in Michael Bycroft and Sven Dupré, eds, *Gems in the Early Modern
World: Materials, Knowledge and Global Trade* (London, 2019), pp. 35–64

Crinò, Sebastiano, 'La scoperta della carta originale di Paolo dal Pozzo Toscanelli che servì di guida
a Cristoforo Colombo per il viaggio verso il Nuovo Mondo', *L'Universo*, 22 (1941),
pp. 379–410

Cropper, Elizabeth, 'Vernacular Identities: The Accademia fiorentina and the Poetics of Portraiture', in *The Medici: Portraits and Politics, 1512–1570*, ed. Keith Christiansen and Carlo
Falciani, exh. cat., The Metropolitan Museum, New York (New York, 2021), pp. 48–78

Crusafont, Miquel, Anna M. Balaguer and Philip Grierson, *Medieval European Coinage*, vol. 6:
The Iberian Peninsula (Cambridge, 2013)

Cuffaro, Rosangela, 'Fakhr Ad-Din II alla corte dei Medici (1613–1615): Collezionismo, architettura e ars topiaria tra Firenze e Beirut', *Marburger Jahrbuch für Kunstwissenschaft*, 37 (2010),
pp. 209–17

Cummings, Brian, 'Pliny's Literate Elephant and the Idea of Animal Language in Renaissance
Thought', in Erica Fudge, ed., *Renaissance Beasts: Of Animals, Humans and Other Wonderful
Creatures* (Urbana, IL, 2003), pp. 164–85

A Custódia de Belém: 500 Anos, ed. Leonor D'Orey and Luísa Penalva, exh. cat., Museu Nacional de Arte Antiga, Lisbon (Lisbon, 2010)

Dacos, Nicole, and Caterina Furlan, *Giovanni da Udine, 1487–1561* (Udine, 1987)

D'Adda, Gerolamo, *Indagini storiche, artistiche e bibliografiche sulla libreria Visconteo-Sforzesca del Castello di Pavia: Appendice alla prima parte* (Milan, 1879)

D'Addosio, Carlo, *Bestie delinquenti* (Naples, 1992 [1892])

Dalby, David, and P.E.H. Hair, 'A Further Note on the Mina Vocabulary of 1479–80', *Journal of West African Languages*, 5.2 (1968), pp. 129–31

Dall'Aglio, Stefano, Brian Richardson and Massimo Rospocher, eds, *Voices and Texts in Early Modern Italian Society* (London, 2017)

Dalton, Heather, *Merchants and Explorers: Roger Barlow, Sebastian Cabot, and Networks of Atlantic Exchange, 1500–1600* (Oxford, 2016)

Dannenfeldt, Karl H., 'Europe Discovers Civet Cats and Civet', *Journal of the History of Biology*, 18.3 (1985), pp. 403–31

D'Arienzo, Luisa, *La presenza degli italiani in Portogallo al tempo di Colombo* (Rome, 2004)

D'Arienzo, Luisa, 'Un quaderno di lettere dell'azienda Cambini di Firenze: Circolazione di capitali in area mediterranea e Atlantica', in Cristina Mantegna and Olivier Poncet, eds, *Les Documents du commerce et des marchands entre Moyen Âge et Époque Moderne (XIIe–XVIIe siècle)* (Rome, 2018), pp. 73–94

Davis, Natalie Zemon, *The Gift in Sixteenth-Century France* (Madison, WI, 2000)

Daybell, James, and Andrew Gordon, 'New Directions in the Study of Early Modern Correspondence', *Lives and Letters*, 4.1 (2012), pp. 1–7

Dean, Carolyn, and Dana Leibsohn, 'Hybridity and Its Discontents: Considering Visual Culture in Colonial Spanish America', *Colonial Latin American Review*, 12.1 (2003), pp. 5–35

Dean, Trevor, 'The Dukes of Ferrara and Their Nobility: Notes on Language and Power', in Marco Gentile and Pierre Savy, eds, *Noblesse et États princiers en Italie et en France au XVe siècle* (Rome, 2009), pp. 365–74

De Angelis, Pietro, *L'ospedale di Santo Spirito in Saxia*, 2 vols (Rome, 1962)

De la Mare, Albinia, 'The Library of Francesco Sassetti (1421–1490)', in C. H. Clough, ed., *Cultural Aspects of the Italian Renaissance: Essays in Honour of Paul Oscar Kristeller* (Manchester, 1976), pp. 160–201

De Laurentiis, Elena, 'Evangelista della Croce', in *Alumina. Pagine miniate*, 15, no. 59 (2017), pp. 14–23

Del Lungo Camiciotti, Gabriella, 'Letters and Letter Writing in Early Modern Culture: An Introduction', *Journal of Early Modern Studies*, 3.3 (2014), pp. 17–35

De Maria, Lorenza, and Rita Turchettti, eds, *Rotti e porti del Mediterraneo dopo la caduta dell'Impero romano d'Occidente* (Soveria Mannelli, 2004)

Demoulin, Louis, 'Le Portugal, son économie et son traffic d'outre-mer vers 1600, vus par le florentin Raffael Fantoni', in *Bulletin de L'Institut historique belge de Rome*, 44 (1974), Miscellanea Charles Verlinden, pp. 157–73

Dempsey, Charles, *Inventing the Renaissance Putto* (Chapel Hill, NC, 2001)

Dengel, Ignazio F., 'Sulla mappamundi di palazzo Venezia', *Archivio della Società romana di storia patria*, 52 (1929), pp. 501–8

Denza, Francesco, 'Globi celesti della Specola Vaticana', in *Pubblicazioni della Specola Vaticana*, vol. 4 (Turin, 1894), pp. xvii–xxiii

Desejo, desígnio e desenho/Desire, Design and Drawing: Francisco de Holanda, 1517–2017, ed. Francisco Providência, Gabriella Casella and Margarida Cunha Belém, exh. cat., Museo do Dinheiro/Money Museum, Lisbon (Lisbon, 2017)

Destombes, Marcel, ed., *Mappemondes AD 1200–1500: Catalogue préparé par la Commission des cartes anciennes de l'Union géographique internationale*, = *Imago mundi*, supplement 4 (Amsterdam, 1964), pp. 217–21

Deswarte-Rosa, Sylvie, 'Le Cardinal Giovanni Ricci de Montepulciano', in *La Villa Médicis*, vol. 2: *Études* (Rome, 1991), pp. 110–69

De Vivo, Filippo, 'Microhistories of Long-Distance Information: Space, Movement and Agency in the Early Modern News', *Past and Present*, 242 (2019), supplement 14, *Global History and Microhistory*, ed. John-Paul Ghobrial, pp. 179–214

Devos, Greta, and Wilfrid Brulez, *Marchands flamands à Venise*, 2 vols (Rome, 1965 and 1986)

Diafane passioni: Avori barocchi dalle corti europee, ed. Eike D. Schmidt and Maria Sframeli, exh. cat., Museo degli argenti, Palazzo Pitti, Florence (Livorno, 2013)

Dias, Pedro, 'O fabrico de mobiliário na ilha Terceira, no século XVI', in Pedro Dias, Dalila Rodrigues and Fernando Grilo, eds, *Manuelino: À descoberta da arte do tempo de D. Manuel I* (Lisbon, 2002)

Diffie, Bailey W., 'Foreigners in Portugal and the "Policy of Silence"', *Terrae incognitae*, 1 (1969), pp. 23–34

Dini, Francesco, 'Francesco Campana e suoi', *Archivio storico italiano*, ser. 5, 23 (1899), pp. 289–323, and 24 (1899), pp. 13–22

Disney, Anthony, *A History of Portugal and the Portuguese Empire*, 2 vols (Cambridge, 2009)

Dobres, Marcia Anne, and John E. Robb, 'Doing Agency: Introductory Remarks on Methodology', *Journal of Archaeological Method and Theory*, 12 (2005), pp. 159–66

Doglio, Maria Luisa, *L'arte delle lettere: Idea e pratica della scrittura epistolare tra Quattro e Seicento* (Bologna, 2000)

Dooley, Brendan, ed., *The Dissemination of News and the Emergence of Contemporaneity in Early Modern Europe* (Farnham, 2010)

Dooley, Brendan, *A Mattress Maker's Daughter: The Renaissance Romance of Don Giovanni de' Medici and Livia Vernazza* (Cambridge, MA, 2014)

Dossena, Marina, 'The Study of Correspondence: Theoretical and Methodological Issues', in Marina Dossena and Gabriella Del Lungo Camiciotti, eds, *Letter Writing in Late Modern Europe* (Amsterdam, 2012), pp. 13–29

Drewall, Henry John, 'Image and Indeterminacy: Elephants and Ivory among the Yoruba', in *Elephant: The Animal and Its Ivory in African Culture*, ed. Doran H. Ross, exh. cat., The Fowler Museum of Cultural History, UCLA (Los Angeles, 1992), pp. 186–207

Earle, T. F. and K.J.P. Lowe, eds, *Black Africans in Renaissance Europe* (Cambridge, 2005)

Echt tierisch! Die Menagerie des Fürsten, ed. Sabine Haag, exh. cat., Schloss Ambras, Innsbruck (Vienna, 2015)

Edelstein, Bruce, 'Ladies-in-Waiting in the Quartiere di Eleonora: The Iconography of Stradano's Ceiling in the Sala di Gualdrada', in Elisabetta Insabato, Rosalia Manno, Ernestina Pellegrini and Anna Scattigno, eds, *Tra archivi e storia: Scritti dedicati ad Alessandra Contini Bonacossi*, 2 vols (Florence, 2018), 1, pp. 127–55

Edelstein, Bruce, 'Nobildonne napoletane e committenza: Eleonora d'Aragona ed Eleonora di Toledo a confronto', *Quaderni storici*, n.s. 35, 104. 2 (2000), pp. 295–329

Egmond, Florike, 'A Collection within a Collection: Rediscovered Animal Drawings from the Collections of Conrad Gessner and Felix Platter', *Journal of the History of Collections*, 25.2 (2013), pp. 149–70

Eiche, Sabine, *Presenting the Turkey: The Fabulous Story of a Flamboyant and Flavourful Bird* (Florence, 2004)

Elbl, Ivana, 'Sand and Dreams: Daily Slave Purchases at the Portuguese Coastal Outpost of Arguim (Mauretania, Saharan West Africa) (1519–1520); Full Raw Serialized Data plus Archival Analysis Annotations', *Portuguese Studies Review*, 30.1 (2022), pp. 325–54

Elfenbeine aus Ceylon: Luxusgüter für Katharina von Habsburg (1507–1578), ed. Annemarie Jordan Gschwend and Johannes Beltz, exh. cat., Museum Rietberg, Zurich (Zurich, 2010)

Epstein, Steven A., *Speaking of Slavery: Color, Ethnicity and Human Bondage in Italy* (Ithaca, NY, 2001)

Esch, Arnold, *La Roma del primo rinascimento vista attraverso i registri doganali* (Milan, 2012)

Esch, Arnold, 'Roman Customs Registers: Items of Interest to Historians of Art and Material Culture', *Journal of the Warburg and Courtauld Institutes*, 58 (1995), pp. 72–87

Eubel, Konrad, *Hierarchia catholica medii aevi*, 4 vols (Münster, 1901–10)

Evans, Mark, and Clare Browne with Arnold Nesselrath, eds, *Raphael: Cartoons and Tapestries for the Sistine Chapel* (London, 2010)

Exotica: Os descobrimentos portugueses e as câmaras de maravilhas do Renascimento, exh. cat., Museu Calouste Gulbenkian, Lisbon (Lisbon, 2001)

Faietti, Marzia, ed., *Il pittore, il poeta e i pidocchi: Bartolomeo Passerotti e l''Omero' di Giovan Battista Deti* (Livorno, 2021)

Falchetta, Piero, *Fra Mauro's World Map, with a Commentary and Translations of the Inscriptions* (Turnhout, 2006)

Fantoni, Marcello, *La corte del granduca: Forme e simboli del potere mediceo fra Cinque e Seicento* (Rome, 1994)

Faria, Miguel Figueira de, 'Francisco de Holanda desenhador de moedas: Um novo testemunho documental', *Leituras: Revista da Bibioteca Nacional*, ser. 3, 2 (1997–98), pp. 181–88

Feigenbaum, Gail, 'Manifest Provenance', in Gail Feigenbaum and Inge Reist, eds, *Provenance: An Alternate History of Art* (Los Angeles, 2012), pp. 6–28

Felix, Marc Leo, 'Introduction', in Marc Leo Felix, ed., *White Gold, Black Hands: Ivory Sculpture in Congo*, 8 vols (Qiquhar, 2010–14), 1, pp. 74–87

Felix, Marc Leo, 'Trumpets and Whistles', in Marc Leo Felix, ed., *White Gold, Black Hands: Ivory Sculpture in Congo*, 8 vols (Qiquhar, 2010–14), 1, pp. 178–221

Fera, Vincenzo, 'Studenti portoghesi alle lezioni del Poliziano su Plinio nel 1489–90: L'INC 462 della BNP', in Ana María S. Tarrío, *Leitores dos clássicos: Portugal e Itália, séculos XV e XVI: Uma geografia do primeiro humanismo em Portugal* (Lisbon, 2015), pp. 13–18

Ferro, João Pedro, *Arqueologia dos hábitos alimentares* (Lisbon, 1996)

Filippi, Sergio, *I rappresentanti diplomatici della Santa Sede in Portogallo e la chiesa di Nostra Signora di Loreto in Lisbona* (Vatican City, 2022)

Findlen, Paula, 'Afterword: How (Early Modern) Things Travel', in Anne Gerritsen and Giorgio Riello, eds, *The Global Lives of Things: The Material Culture of Connections in the Early Modern World* (London, 2015), pp. 241–46

Findlen, Paula, 'Early Modern Things: Objects in Motion, 1500–1800', in Paula Findlen, ed., *Early Modern Things: Objects and Their Histories, 1500–1800* (London, 2013), pp. 3–27

Findlen, Paula, *Possessing Nature: Museums, Collecting and Scientific Culture in Early Modern Italy* (Berkeley, CA, 1994)

Fiorani, Francesca, *The Marvel of Maps: Art, Cartography and Politics in Renaissance Italy* (New Haven, CT, 2005)

Fiorini, Matteo, *Sfere terrestri e celesti di autore italiano oppure fatte o conservate in Italia* (Rome, 1899)

Firenze e la Toscana dei Medici nell'Europa del Cinquecento: Committenza e collezionismo medicei, ed. Paola Barocchi et al., exh. cat., Palazzo Vecchio, Florence (Florence, 1980)

Firenze e la Toscana dei Medici nell'Europa del Cinquecento: Il potere e lo spazio; La scena del principe, ed. Franco Borsi et al., exh. cat., Fortezza del Belvedere, Florence (Florence, 1980)

Fletcher, Catherine, *The Black Prince of Florence: The Spectacular Life and Treacherous World of Alessandro de' Medici* (Oxford, 2016)

Fonseca, Jorge, 'Black Africans in Portugal during Cleynaerts's Visit (1533–1538)', in T. F. Earle and K.J.P. Lowe, eds, *Black Africans in Renaissance Europe* (Cambridge, 2005), pp. 112–21

Fonseca, Jorge, *Escravos e senhores na Lisboa quinhentista* (Lisbon, 2010)

Franceschini, Chiara, '"*Los scholares son cosa de sua excelentia, como lo es toda la Compañia*": Eleonora di Toledo and the Jesuits', in Konrad Eisenbichler, ed., *The Cultural World of Eleonora di Toledo, Duchess of Florence and Siena* (Aldershot, 2004), pp. 181–206

Frattarelli Fischer, Lucia, *L'arcano del mar: Un porto nella prima età globale; Livorno* (Pisa, 2018)

Freire, Anselmo Braamcamp, 'Inventário da Infanta D. Beatriz 1507', *Arquivo histórico portuguez*, 9 (1914), pp. 64–110

Freire, Anselmo Braamcamp, *Notícia da feitoria de Flandres precedidas dos Brandões poetas do cancioneiro* ([Lisbon], 1920)

Frick, Carole Collier, *Dressing Renaissance Florence: Families, Fortunes and Fine Clothing* (Baltimore, 2002)

Fricke, Beate, 'Making Marvels—Faking Matter: Mediating *virtus* between the Bezoar and Goa Stones and Their Containers', in Christine Göttler and Mia Mochizuki, eds, *The Nomadic Object: The Challenge of World for Early Modern Religious Art* (Leiden, 2018), pp. 342–67

Friedman, John Block, 'Coats, Collars and Capes: Royal Fashions for Animals in the Early Modern Period', *Medieval Clothing and Textiles*, 12 (2006), pp. 61–94

Fromont, Cécile, *The Art of Conversion: Christian Visual Culture in the Kingdom of Kongo* (Chapel Hill, NC, 2014)

Furlotti, Barbara, *Le collezioni Gonzaga: Il carteggio tra Roma e Mantova (1587–1612)* (Milan, 2003)

Fusco, Laurie, and Gino Corti, *Lorenzo de' Medici: Collector and Antiquarian* (Cambridge, 2006)

Gáldy, Andrea M., 'The Duke as Cultural Manager: Institutionalization and Entrepreneurship', in Alessio Assonitis and Henk Th. van Veen, eds, *A Companion to Cosimo I de' Medici* (Leiden, 2022), pp. 411–68

Gáldy, Andrea M., 'Hounds for a Cardinal', in Machtelt Israëls and Louis A. Waldman, eds, *Renaissance Studies in Honor of Joseph Connors*, 2 vols (Florence, 2013), 2, pp. 172–76

Gáldy, Andrea M., 'Lost in Antiquities: Cardinal Giovanni de' Medici (1543–1562)', in Mary Hollingsworth and Carol M. Richardson, eds, *The Possessions of a Cardinal: Politics, Piety and Art, 1450–1700* (University Park, PA, 2010), pp. 153–65

Gáldy, Andrea M., 'The Scrittoio della Calliope in the Palazzo Vecchio: A Tuscan Museum', in Roberta J. M. Olsen, Patricia L. Reilly and Rupert Shepherd, eds, *The Biography of the Object in Late Medieval and Renaissance Italy* (Oxford, 2006), pp. 119–29

Gáldy, Andrea M., 'Tuscan Concerns and Spanish Heritage in the Decoration of Duchess Eleonora's Apartment in the Palazzo Vecchio', *Renaissance Studies*, 20.3 (2006), pp. 293–319

Galeotti Flori, A., 'Le schiave orientali madri e nutrici allo Spedale di S. Maria degli Innocenti nel 1400', *Rivista di clinica pediatrica*, 67.4 (1961), pp. 257–56

Galison, Peter, 'Removing Knowledge', *Critical Inquiry* 31 (2004), pp. 229–43

Gallori, Corinna Tania, 'Collecting Feathers: A Journey from Mexico into Italian Collections (16th–17th Century)', in Susan Bracken, Andrea M. Gáldy and Adriana Turpin, eds, *Collecting East and West* (Newcastle upon Tyne, 2013), pp. 61–81

Gaspar, Joaquim Alves, 'Blunders, Errors and Entanglements: Scrutinizing the Cantino Planisphere with a Cartometric Eye', *Imago mundi*, 64.2 (2012), pp. 181–200

Gasparrini Leporace, Tullia, *Il mappamondo di Fra Mauro* (Venice, 1956)

Gavitt, Philip, *Charity and Children in Renaissance Florence: The Ospedale degli Innocenti, 1410–1536* (Ann Arbor, 1990)

Gell, Alfred, *Art and Agency: An Anthropological Theory* (Oxford, 1998)

Gentilini, Giancarlo, *I della Robbia: La scultura invetriata nel Rinascimento*, 2 vols (Milan, 1992)

Gerritsen, Anne, 'From Long-Distance Trade to the Global Lives of Things: Writing the History of Early Modern Trade and Material Culture', *Journal of Early Modern History*, 20 (2016), pp. 526–44

Gerritsen, Anne, and Giorgio Riello, eds, *The Global Lives of Things: The Material Culture of Connections in the Early Modern World* (London, 2016)

Giglio, Carlo and Elio Lodolini, *Guida delle fonti per la storia dell'Africa a sud del Sahara esistenti in Italia*, vol. 1, Guide des sources de l'histoire de l'Afrique 5 (Zug, 1973)

Gioffrè, Domenico, *Il mercato degli schiavi a Genova nel secolo XV* (Genoa, 1971)

Goldthwaite, Richard, 'Florentine Household Accounts, Fourteenth to Seventeenth Centuries', *Renaissance Studies*, 32.2 (2018), pp. 219–35

Goldthwaite, Richard, 'The Practice and Culture of Accounting in Renaissance Florence', *Enterprise and Society*, 16.3 (2015), pp. 611–47

Gomes, Alberto, and António Miguel Trigueiros, *Moedas portuguesas na época dos descobrimentos, 1385–1580/Portuguese Coins in the Age of Discovery, 1385–1580* (Lisbon, 1992)

Gomes, João Pedro, 'Comida de rua na Lisboa moderna (sécs. XVI e XVII)', in *Diz-me o que comes: Alimentação antes e depois da cidade* (Lisbon, 2017), pp. 98–109

Gomes, Paulo Dordio, 'O livro de cozinha da Infanta D. Maria', *Olaria*, 1 (1996), pp. 93–104

Gomes, Saul António, *Pombal medieval e quinhentista: Documentos para a sua história* (Batalha Leiria, 2010)

González Germain, Gerard, 'Agostino Vespucci's *De situ totius Hispaniae* (1520): The Earliest Antiquarian Description of Spain', *Viator*, 48.1 (2017), pp. 275–95

Goris, Jean-Albert, *Étude sure les colonies marchandes méridionales (portugais, espagnols, italiens) à Anvers de 1488 à 1567* (Louvain, 1925)

Greppi, Claudio, 'Luoghi e miti: La conoscenza delle scoperte presso la corte Ferrarese', in Marco Bertozzi, ed., *Alla corte degli Estensi: Filosofia, arte e cultura a Ferrara nei secoli XV e XVI; Atti del Convegno internazionale di studi, Ferrara, 5–7 marzo 1992* (Ferrara, 1994), pp. 447–63

Grey, Richard, 'A Kongo Princess, the Kongo Ambassadors and the Papacy', in David Maxwell, ed., with Ingrid Lawrie, *Christianity and the African Imagination: Essays in Honour of Adrian Hastings* (Leiden, 2002), pp. 25–40

Groom, Angelica, *Exotic Animals in the Art and Culture of the Medici Court in Florence* (Leiden, 2019)

Grunne, Bernard de, 'Su alcuni maestri dell'arte africana', in *Ex Africa: Storie e identità di un'arte universale*, exh. cat., Museo civico archaeologico, Bologna (Milan, 2019), pp. 159–65

Guidi Bruscoli, Francesco, *Bartolomeo Marchionni 'homem de grossa fazenda' (ca. 1450–1530): Un mercante fiorentino a Lisbona e l'impero portoghese* (Florence, 2014)

Guidi Bruscoli, Francesco, *Benvenuto Olivieri: I 'mercatores' fiorentini e la Camera Apostolica nella Roma di Paolo III Farnese (1534–49)* (Florence, 2000)

Guidi Bruscoli, Francesco, 'Da comprimarmi a protagonisti: I fiorentini in Portogallo nel Basso Medioevo (1338–1520)', *eHumanista*, 38 (2018), pp. 65–82

Guidi Bruscoli, Francesco, 'I mercanti medievali e l'invio della corrispondenza: Modalità e strategie', *Archivio per la storia postale*, n.s. 8 (2016), pp. 9–31

Guidi Bruscoli, Francesco, '"Ànno fatto una inpresa grossa per il paese di Ghinea contro a nostra voglia": Lorenzo de' Medici and the voyage to Guinea, c. 1475–77', in Alessio Assonitis and K.J.P. Lowe, eds, *The Medici and Perceptions of Sub-Saharan Africa* (forthcoming Turnhout, 2025)

Guidi Bruscoli, Francesco, *Papal Banking in Renaissance Rome: Benvenuto Olivieri and Paul III, 1534–1549* (Aldershot, 2007)

Guinote, Paulo, Eduardo Frutuoso and António Lopes, *As armadas da Índia, 1497–1835* (Lisbon, 2002)

Hair, P.E.H., 'Columbus from Guinea to America', *History in Africa*, 17 (1990), pp. 113–29

Hair, P.E.H., *The Founding of the Castelo de São Jorge da Mina: An Analysis of the Sources* (Madison, WI, 1994)

Hair, P.E.H., 'A Note on de la Fosse's "Mina" Vocabulary of 1479–80', *Journal of West African Languages*, 3.1 (1966), pp. 55–57

Hanß, Stefan, and Ulinka Rublack, 'Knowledge Production, Image Networks and the Material Significance of Feathers in Late Humanist Heidelberg', *Renaissance Quarterly*, 74.2 (2021), pp. 412–53

Hartman, Saidiya, 'Venus in Two Acts', *Small Axe*, no. 26 (vol. 12.2) (2008), pp. 1–14

Hartt, Frederick, Gino Corti and Clarence Kennedy, *The Chapel of the Cardinal of Portugal 1434–1459 at San Miniato in Florence* (Philadelphia, 1964)

Hehenberger, Susanne, 'Dehumanised Sinners and Their Instruments of Sin: Men and Animals in Early Modern Bestiality Cases, Austria, 1500–1800', in Karl A. E. Enenkel and Paul J. Smith, eds, *Early Modern Zoology: The Construction of Animals in Science, Literature and the Visual Arts*, 2 vols (Leiden, 2007), 2, pp. 381–417

Heikamp, Detlef, *Mexico and the Medici* (Florence, 1972)

Hendler, Sefy, 'Cosimo and the Politics of Culture: Reinventing Florence as a Cultural Capital', in *The Medici: Portraits and Politics, 1512–1570*, ed. Keith Christiansen and Carlo Falciani, exh. cat., The Metropolitan Museum, New York (New York, 2021), pp. 106–10

Herczeg, Giulio, 'I cosidetti "nomi parlanti" nel *Decameron*', *Atti e memorie del VII Congresso internazionale di scienze onomastiche (Firenze-Pisa, 1961)*, 4 vols (Florence, 1962–63), 3 (1963), pp. 189–99

Herlihy, David, 'Tuscan Names, 1200–1530', *Renaissance Quarterly*, 41.4 (1988), pp. 561–82

Hermanin, Federico, 'La sala del mappamondo nel palazzo di Venezia', *Dedalo*, 11 (1930–31), pp. 457–81

Hernando, Agustín, 'Die Herstellung von Erd- und Himmelsgloben in Spanien', in *Der Globusfreund*, 59/60 (2014), pp. 162–201

Hernando Sánchez, Carlos José, 'Los Médicis y los Toledo: Familia y lenguaje del poder en la Italia de Felipe II', in Giuseppe Di Stefano, Elena Fasano Guarini and Alessandro Martinengo, eds, *Italia non spagnola e monarchia spagnola tra '500 e '600: Politica, cultura e letteratura* (Florence, 2009), pp. 55–81

Hilton, Anne, *The Kingdom of Kongo* (Oxford, 1985)

Hodder, Ian, *Entangled: An Archaeology of the Relationships between Humans and Things* (Malden, MA, 2012)

Hohti, Paula, 'The Innkeeper's Goods: The Use and Acquisition of Household Property in Sixteenth-Century Siena', in Michelle O'Malley and Evelyn Welch eds, *The Material Renaissance* (Manchester, 2007), pp. 242–59

Holmes, Megan, 'Copying Practices and Marketing Strategies in a Fifteenth-Century Florentine Painter's Workshop', in Stephen J. Campbell and Stephen J. Milner, eds, *Artistic Exchange and Cultural Translation in the Italian Renaissance City* (Cambridge, 2004), pp. 38–54

Horodowich, Elizabeth, *The Venetian Discovery of America: Geographic Imagination and Print Culture in the Age of Encounters* (Cambridge, 2018)

Howe, Eunice D., *The Hospital of Santo Spirito and Pope Sixtus IV* (New York, 1978)

Infelise, Mario, 'From Merchants' Letters to Handwritten Political *avvisi*; Notes on the Origins of Public Information', in Francisco Bethencourt and Florike Egmond, eds, *Correspondence and Cultural Exchange in Europe, 1400–1700*, Cultural Exchange in Early Modern Europe 3 (Cambridge, 2007), pp. 33–52

Infelise, Mario, 'News Networks between Italy and Europe', in Brendan Dooley, ed., *The Dissemination of News and the Emergence of Contemporaneity in Early Modern Europe* (Farnham, 2010), pp. 51–67

Infelise, Mario, *Prima dei giornali: Alle origini della pubblica informazione (secoli XVI e XVII)* (Rome, 2002)

Islam e Firenze: Arte e collezionismo dai Medici al Novecento, ed. Giovanni Curatola, exh. cat., Aula Magliabechiana, Gallerie degli Uffizi, and Museo nazionale del Bargello, Florence (Florence, 2018)

Islam, specchio d'Oriente: Rarità e preziosi nelle collezioni statali fiorentine, ed. Giovanna Damiani and Mario Scalini, exh. cat., Palazzo Pitti, Florence (Livorno, 2002)

Jacks, Philip J., 'Alexander VI's Ceiling for Santa Maria Maggiore in Rome', *Römisches Jahrbuch für Kunstgeschichte*, 22 (1985), pp. 63–82

Jacobson-Widding, Anita, *Red-White-Black as Mode of Thought: A Study of Triadic Classification by Colours in the Ritual Symbolism and Cognitive Thought of the Peoples of the Lower Congo* (Uppsala, 1979)

Jadin, Louis, 'Un grand missionnaire du Congo, le père jésuite Pedro Tavares, 1629–34', *Révue du clergé africain*, 11.2 (1956), pp. 137–42

James, Carolyn, 'An Insatiable Appetite for News: Isabella d'Este and a Bolognese Correspondent', in F. W. Kent and Charles Zika, eds, *Religious Rituals, Images and Words: The Varieties of Cultural Experience in Late Medieval and Early Modern Europe* (Turnhout, 2005), pp. 375–88

James, Carolyn, 'Marriage by Correspondence: Politics and Domesticity in the Letters of Isabella d'Este and Francesco Gonzaga, 1490–1519', *Renaissance Quarterly*, 65.2 (2012), pp. 321–52

Jedin, Hubert, 'Kardinal Giovanni Ricci (1497–1574)', in *Miscellanea Pio Paschini: Studi di storia ecclesiastica*, vol. 2 (Rome, 1949), pp. 269–358

Johnson, Christine R., *The German Discovery of the World* (Charlottesville, VA, 2008)

Jóias da Carreira da Índia, ed. Hugo Miguel Crespo, exh. cat., Museu do Oriente, Lisbon (Lisbon, 2014)

Joost-Gaugier, Christiane L., 'Lorenzo the Magnificent and the Giraffe as a Symbol of Power', *Artibus et historiae*, 8.16 (1987), pp. 91–99

Jordan, Annemarie, 'Images of Empire: Slaves in the Lisbon Household and Court of Catherine of Austria', in T. F. Earle and K.J.P. Lowe, eds., *Black Africans in Renaissance Europe* (Cambridge, 2005), pp. 155–80

Jordan Gschwend, Annemarie, 'Animais globais: Coleção e ostentação', in *A cidade global: Lisboa no Renascimento/The Global City: Lisbon in the Renaissance*, ed. Annemarie Jordan Gschwend and KJ.P. Lowe, exh. cat., Museu Nacional de Arte Antiga, Lisbon (Lisbon, 2017), pp. 192–201

Jordan Gshwend, Annemarie, 'Animals from Other Worlds', in *A cidade global: Lisboa no Renascimento/The Global City: Lisbon in the Renaissance*, ed. Annemarie Jordan Gschwend and K.J.P. Lowe, exh. cat., Museu Nacional de Arte Antiga, Lisbon (Lisbon, 2017) section 5, pp. 329–39

Jordan Gschwend, Annemarie, 'A arte de coleccionar entre as mulheres habsburgo D. Caterina e D. Juana de Áustria e a sua busca pelo luxo/The Art of Collecting among Habsburg Women: Catherine and Juana of Austria and Their Pursuit of Luxury', in Hugo Miguel Crespo, ed., *A arte de coleccionar: Lisboa, Europa e o mundo na época moderna (1500–1800)/The Art of Collecting: Lisbon, Europe and the Early Modern World (1500–1800)* (Lisbon, 2019), pp. 34–53

Jordan Gschwend, Annemarie, 'A arte de coleccionar leques asiáticos na corte de Lisboa/The Art of Collecting Asian Folding Fans at the Lisbon Court', in Hugo Miguel Crespo, ed., *A arte de coleccionar: Lisboa, Europa e o mundo na época moderna (1500–1800)/The Art of Collecting: Lisbon, Europe and the Early Modern World (1500–1800)* (Lisbon, 2019), pp. 78–93

Jordan Gschwend, Annemarie, 'Beloved Companions, Mascots and Pets: The Culture of Wild Animals in Renaissance Portugal', in *Echt tierisch! Die Menagerie des Fürsten*, ed. Sabine Haag, exh. cat., Schloss Ambras, Innsbruck (Vienna, 2015), pp. 18–23

Jordan Gshwend, Annemarie, 'Comprar gemas de todo o mundo em Lisboa: Em busca de diamantes indianos, gemas asiáticos, pérolas de Ormuz e esmeraldas peruanas/Shopping for Global Gems in Lisbon: The Quest for Indian Diamonds, Asian Gemstones, Pearls from Hormuz and Peruvian Emeralds', in Hugo Miguel Crespo, ed., *Comprar o mundo: Consumo e comércio na Lisboa do Renascimento/Shopping for Global Goods: Consumption and Trade in Renaissance Lisbon* (Lisbon, 2020), pp. 20–31

Jordan Gschwend, Annemarie, 'The Emperor's Exotic and New World Animals: Hans Khevenhüller and the Habsburg Menageries in Vienna and Prague', in Arthur MacGregor, ed., *Naturalists in the Field: Collecting, Recording and Preserving the Natural World from the Fifteenth to the Twenty-First Century* (Leiden, 2018), pp. 76–103

Jordan Gschwend, Annemarie, 'A Forgotten *Infanta*: Catherine of Austria, Queen of Portugal (1507–1578)', in *Women: The Art of Power. Three Women from the House of Habsburg*, ed.

Sabine Haag, Dagmar Eichberger and Annemarie Jordan Gschwend, exh. cat., Schloss Ambras, Innsbruck (Vienna, 2018), pp. 50–63

Jordan Gschwend Annemarie, 'In the Shadow of Philip II, *El Rey Lusitano*: Archduke Albert of Austria as Viceroy of Portugal (1583–1593)', in Werner Thomas and Luc Duerloo eds, *Albert & Isabella, 1598–1621: Essays* (Turnhout, 1998), pp. 39–46

Jordan Gschwend, Annemarie, '*Olisipo, emporium nobilissimum*: Global Consumption in Renaissance Lisbon', in Annemarie Jordan Gschwend and K.J.P. Lowe, eds, *The Global City: On the Streets of Renaissance Lisbon* (London, 2015), pp. 140–61

Jordan Gschwend, Annemarie, 'The Portuguese Quest for Exotic Animals', in *Cortejo triunfal com girafas: Animais exóticos ao serviço do poder/Triumphal Procession with Giraffes: Exotic Animals at the Service of Power*, ed. Jessica Hallett, exh. cat., A Fundação Ricardo do Espírito Santo Silva, Lisbon (Lisbon, 2009), pp. 32–42

Jordan Gschwend, Annemarie, 'Shopping on the Rua Nova dos Mercadores', in *A cidade global: Lisboa no Renascimento/The Global City: Lisbon in the Renaissance*, ed. Annemarie Jordan Gschwend and K.J.P. Lowe, exh. cat., Museu Nacional de Arte Antiga, Lisbon (Lisbon, 2017), pp. 300–305

Jordan Gschwend, Annemarie, '". . . underlasse auch nit mich in Portugal vnnd ander orten umb frömbde sachen zu bewerben": Hans Khevenhüller and Habsburg Menageries in Vienna and Prague', in *Echt tierisch! Die Menagerie des Fürsten*, ed. Sabine Haag, exh. cat., Schloss Ambras, Innsbruck (Vienna, 2015), pp. 31–35

Jordan Gschwend, Annemarie, and K.J.P. Lowe, eds, *The Global City: On the Streets of Renaissance Lisbon* (London, 2015)

Jordan Gschwend, Annemarie, and Kate Lowe, 'Princess of the Seas, Queen of Empire: Configuring the City and Port of Renaissance Lisbon', in Annemarie Jordan Gschwend and K.J.P. Lowe, eds, *The Global City: On the Streets of Renaissance Lisbon* (London, 2015), pp. 12–35

Jordan Gshwend, Annemarie, and Kate Lowe, 'Renaissance Lisbon's Global Sites', in *A cidade global: Lisboa no Renascimento/The Global City: Lisbon in the Renaissance*, ed. Annemarie Jordan Gschwend and K.J.P. Lowe, exh. cat., Museu Nacional de Arte Antiga, Lisbon (Lisbon, 2017), pp. 243–55

Joyce, Rosemary A., 'From Place to Place: Provenience, Provenance and Archaeology', in Gail Feigenbaum and Inge Reist, eds, *Provenance: An Alternate History of Art* (Los Angeles, 2012), pp. 48–60

Kaplan, Paul H. D., 'Bartolomeo Passarotti and "Comic" Images of Black Africans in Early Modern Italian Art', in Angela Rosenthal, ed., with David Bindman and Adrian W. B. Randolph, *No Laughing Matter: Visual Humor in Ideas of Race, Nationality and Ethnicity* (Lebanon, NH, 2016), pp. 23–48

Kaplan, Paul H. D., 'Isabella d'Este and Black African Women', in T. F. Earle and K.J.P. Lowe, eds., *Black Africans in Renaissance Europe* (Cambridge, 2005), pp. 125–54

Kaplan, Paul H. D., 'Italy, 1490–1700', in *The Image of the Black in Western Art*, vol. 3.1: *From the 'Age of Discovery' to the Age of Abolition: Artists of the Renaissance and Baroque*, ed. David Bindman and Henry Louis Gates Jr (Cambridge, MA, 2010), pp. 93–190

Karl, Barbara, '"Galanterie di cose rare . . .": Filippo Sassetti's Indian Shopping List for the Medici Grand Duke Francesco and His Brother Cardinal Ferdinando', *Itinerario*, 32.3 (2008), pp. 23–41

Keating, Jessica, and Lia Markey, '"Indian" Objects in Medici and Austrian-Habsburg Inventories: A Case Study of the Sixteenth-Century Term', *Journal of the History of Collections*, 23.2 (2011), pp. 283–300

Keating, Jessica, and Lia Markey, 'Introduction: Captured Objects. Inventories of Early Modern Collections', *Journal of the History of Collections*, 23.2 (2011), pp. 209–13

Keblusek, Marika, 'Introduction: Double Agents in Early Modern Europe', in Marika Keblusek and Badeloch Vera Noldus, eds, *Double Agents: Cultural and Political Brokerage in Early Modern Europe* (Leiden, 2011), pp. 1–9

Keblusek, Marika, 'Introduction: Profiling the Early Modern Agent', in Hans Cools, Marika Keblusek and Badeloch Noldua, eds, *Your Humble Servant: Agents in Early Modern* Europe (Hilversum, 2006), pp. 9–15

Keblusek, Marika, '*Mercator sapiens*: Merchants as Cultural Entrepreneurs', in Marika Keblusek and Badeloch Vera Noldus, eds, *Double Agents: Cultural and Political Brokerage in Early Modern Europe* (Leiden, 2011), pp. 95–109

Kellenbenz, Hermann, ed., *Fremde Kaufleute auf der iberischen Halbinsel* (Cologne, 1970)

Kelly, Samantha, 'Biondo Flavio on Ethiopia: Processes of Knowledge Production in the Renaissance', in William Caferro, ed., *The Routledge History of the Renaissance* (London, 2017), pp. 167–82

Kent, Dale, *Cosimo de' Medici and the Florentine Renaissance* (New Haven, CT, 2000)

Kessel, Elsje van, 'The Inventories of the *Madre de Deus*: Tracing Asian Material Culture in Early Modern England', *Journal of the History of Collections*, 32.2 (2020), pp. 207–23

Keyvanian, Carla, *Hospitals and Urbanism in Rome, 1200–1500* (Leiden, 2015)

Kibre, Pearl, *The Library of Pico della Mirandola* (New York, 1936)

Klapisch-Zuber, Christiane, *Women, Family and Ritual in Renaissance Italy*, trans. Lydia Cochrane (Chicago, 1985)

Kliemann, Julian, *Andrea del Sarto: 'Il Tributo a Cesare' (1519–1521)* (Poggio a Caiano, 1986)

Knappett, Carl, and Lambos Malafouris, eds, *Material Agency: Towards a Non-Anthropocentric Approach* (Boston, MA, 2008)

Kopytoff, Igor, 'The Cultural Biography of Things: Commoditization as Process', in Arjun Appadurai, ed., *The Social Life of Things: Commodities in Cultural Perspective* (Cambridge, 1986), pp. 64–91

Körber, Ulrike, 'The "Three Brothers": Sixteenth-Century Lacquered Indo-Muslim Shields or Commodities for Display?', in Annemarie Jordan Gschwend and K.J.P. Lowe, eds, *The Global City: On the Streets of Renaissance Lisbon* (London, 2015), pp. 212–25

Krech, Shepard, III, 'On the Turkey in Rua Nova dos Mercadores', in Annemarie Jordan Gschwend and K.J.P. Lowe, eds, *The Global City: On the Streets of Renaissance Lisbon* (London, 2015), pp. 178–85

Kremer, Dieter, 'Ausländer im Lissabon des 16. Jahrhunderts', *Namenkundliche Informationen*, 101–2 (2012–13), pp. 97–181

Lagamma, Alisa, 'Kongo: Power and Majesty', in *Kongo: Power and Majesty*, ed. Alisa Lagamma, exh. cat., The Metropolitan Museum of Art, New York (New York, 2015), pp. 16–45

Lagamma, Alisa, with contributions by Christine Giuntini, 'Out of Kongo and into the *Kunstkammer*', in *Kongo: Power and Majesty*, ed. Alisa Lagamma, exh. cat., The Metropolitan Museum of Art, New York (New York, 2015), pp. 128–59

Lamberini, Daniela, *Il Sanmarino: Giovan Battista Belluzzi architetto militare e trattatista del Cinquecento*, 2 vols (Florence, 2007)

Lanciani, Rodolfo, *Storia degli scavi di Roma e notizie intorno le collezioni romane di antichità*, 4 vols (Rome, 1902–12)

Langdon, Gabrielle, *Medici Women: Portraits of Power, Love and Betrayal from the Court of Duke Cosimo I* (Toronto, 2006)

Lapierre, Valentina, and Maria Angela Novelli, *La storia di Negro Re del lito moro: Un esempio ritrovato della narrazione pittorica dello Scarsellino* (Ferrara, 2004)

Lasagni, Roberto, *L'arte tipografica in Parma*, 2 vols in 3 parts (Parma, 2013–16)

Latour, Bruno, 'On Actor-Network-Theory: A Few Clarifications', *Soziale Welt*, 47.4 (1996), pp. 369–81

Latour, Bruno, *Reassembling the Social: An Introduction to Actor-Network-Theory* (Oxford, 2005)

Laurencich-Minelli, Laura, 'From the New World to Bologna, 1533: A Gift for Pope Clement VII and Bolognese Collections of the Sixteenth and Seventeenth Centuries', *Journal of the History of Collections*, 24.2 (2012), pp. 145–58

Lavinia Fontana, 1552–1614, ed. Vera Fortunati and Angela Ghirardi, exh. cat., Museo civico archaelogico, Bologna (Milan, 1994)

Lazzarini, Isabella, 'Orality and Writing in Diplomatic Interactions in Fifteenth-Century Italy', in Stefano Dall'Aglio, Brian Richardson and Massimo Rospocher, eds, *Voices and Texts in Early Modern Italian Society* (London, 2017), pp. 97–109

Lazzi, Giovanna, and Giovanna Bigalli Lulla, 'Alessandro de' Medici e il palazzo di via Larga: L'inventario del 1531', in *Archivio storico italiano*, 150 (1992), pp. 1201–33

Leskinen, Saara, 'Two French Views of Monstrous Peoples in Sub-Saharan Africa', *Renaissance and Reformation/Renaissance et Réforme*, 31.2 (2008), pp. 29–44

Lespes, René, 'Oran, ville et port avant l'occupation française (1831)', *Revue africaine*, 75 (1934), pp. 277–335

Linnell, Per, and Thomas Luckmann, 'Asymmetries in Dialogue: Some Conceptual Preliminaries', in Ivana Marková and Klaus Foppa, eds, *Asymmetries in Dialogue* (Hemel Hempstead, 1991), pp. 1–20

Lipski, John, *A History of Afro-Hispanic Language Contact: Five Centuries and Five Continents* (Cambridge, 2005)

Livingstone, David N., *Putting Science in its Place: Geographies of Scientific Knowledge* (Chicago, 2003)

Loisel, Gustave, *Histoire des menageries de l'Antiquité à nos jours*, 3 vols (Paris, 1912), vol. 1: *Antiquité. Moyen Âge. Renaissance*

Loskoutoff, Yvan, 'The "Cupid Affair" (1596): Cardinal Francesco Maria Del Monte as a Collector of Antiquities', *Journal of the History of Collections*, 25.1 (2013), pp. 19–27

Loureiro, Rui Manuel, 'Chinese Commodities on the India Route in the Late Sixteenth and Early Seventeenth Centuries', in Annemarie Jordan Gschwend and K.J.P. Lowe, eds, *The Global City: On the Streets of Renaissance Lisbon* (London, 2015), pp. 76–93

Loureiro, Rui Manuel, 'Ecos portugueses nos impressos hispalenses de Bernardino de Escalante', in Fernando Quiles, Manuel Fernández Chaves and Antónia Fialho Conde, eds, *La Sevilla lusa: La presencia portuguesa en el Reino de Sevilla durante el Barroco/A presença portuguesa no Reino de Sevilha no período barroco* (Seville, 2018), pp. 236–51

Lowe, Kate, 'Africa in the News in Renaissance Italy: News Extracts from Portugal about Western Africa Circulating in Northern and Central Italy in the 1480s and 1490s', *Italian Studies*, 65.3 (2010), pp. 310–28

Lowe, Kate, 'Black Africans' Religious and Cultural Assimilation to, or Appropriation of, Catholicism in Italy, 1470–1520', *Renaissance and Reformation/Renaissance et Réforme*, 31.2 (2008), pp. 67–86

Lowe, Kate, 'A Fifteenth-Century Flesh and Blood Black Slave at Villa La Pietra: A Human Precursor to the Acton Blackamoors', in Awam Ampka and Ellyn Toscano, eds, *ReSignifications: European Blackamoors, Africana Readings* (Rome, 2016), pp. 60–67

Lowe, Kate, 'Foreign Descriptions of the Global City: Renaissance Lisbon from the Outside', in Annemarie Jordan Gschwend and K.J.P. Lowe, eds, *The Global City: On the Streets of Renaissance Lisbon* (London, 2015), pp. 36–55

Lowe, Kate, 'The Global Consequences of Mistranslation: The Adoption of the "black but . . ." Formulation in Europe, 1440–1650', *Religions*, 3 (2012), pp. 544–55

Lowe, Kate, 'The Global Population of Renaissance Lisbon: Diversity and Its Entanglements', in Annemarie Jordan Gschwend and K.J.P. Lowe, eds, *The Global City: On the Streets of Renaissance Lisbon* (London, 2015), pp. 56–75

Lowe, Kate, 'Isabella d'Este and the Acquisition of Black Slaves at the Mantuan Court', in Philippa Jackson and Guido Rebecchini, eds, *Mantova e il rinascimento italiano: Studi in onore di David S. Chambers* (Mantua, 2011), pp. 65–76

Lowe, Kate, 'Made in Africa: West African Luxury Goods for Lisbon's Markets', in Annemarie Jordan Gschwend and K.J.P. Lowe, eds, *The Global City: On the Streets of Renaissance Lisbon* (London, 2015), pp. 162–77

Lowe, Kate, '"Representing" Africa: Ambassadors and Princes from Christian Africa to Renaissance Italy and Portugal, 1402–1608', *Transactions of the Royal Historical Society*, 17 (2007), pp. 101–28

Lowe, Kate, 'The Stereotyping of Black Africans in Renaissance Europe', in T. F. Earle and K.J.P. Lowe, eds, *Black Africans in Renaissance Europe* (Cambridge, 2005), pp. 17–47

Lowe, Kate, 'Understanding Cultural Exchange between Portugal and Italy in the Renaissance', in K.J.P. Lowe, ed., *Cultural Links between Portugal and Italy in the Renaissance* (Oxford, 2000), pp. 1–16

Lowe, Kate, 'Visible Lives: Black Gondoliers and Other Black Africans in Renaissance Venice', *Renaissance Quarterly*, 66 (2013), pp. 412–52

Lowe, Kate, 'Visual Representations of an Élite: African Ambassadors and Rulers in Renaissance Europe', in *Revealing the African Presence in Renaissance Europe*, ed. Joaneath Spicer, exh. cat. The Walters Art Museum, Baltimore (Baltimore, 2012), pp. 98–115

Lowe, K.J.P., ed., *Cultural Links between Portugal and Italy in the Renaissance* (Oxford, 2000)

Lowe, K.J.P., *Nuns' Chronicles and Convent Culture in Renaissance and Counter-Reformation Italy* (Cambridge, 2003)

Lucchesi, D. Emiliano, *La Madonna di Montenero e il suo santuario nella storia, nell'arte, nella pietà cristiana* (Livorno, 1928)

Luzio, Alessandro, 'Isabella d'Este ne' primordi del papato di Leone X e il suo viaggio a Roma nel 1514–1515', *Archivio storico lombardo*, ser. 4, 6 (1906), pp. 99–180, 454–89

Luzio Alessandro, and Rodolfo Renier, 'Buffoni, nani e schiavi dei Gonzaga ai tempi d'Isabella d'Este', *Nuova antologia di scienze, lettere ed arti*, ser. 3, 34 (1891), pp. 618–50 and 35 (1891), pp. 112–46

Luzio, Alessandro, and Rodolfo Renier, 'La coltura e le relazioni letterarie di Isabella d'Este Gonzaga', *Giornale storico della letteratura italiana*, 33 (1899), pp. 1–62

Luzzana Caraci, Ilaria, 'Il viaggio di Bartolomeu Dias nella storia della cultura geografica italiana', in *Congresso Internacional Bartolomeu Dias e a sua época: Actas*, 5 vols (Porto, 1989), 2, pp. 223–36

Maccagni, Carlo, 'The Florentine Clock- and Instrument-Makers of the Della Volpaia Family', *Der Globusfreund*, 17–20 (1969–71), pp. 92–99

MacDonogh, Katharine, 'A Woman's Life: The Role of Pets in the Lives of Royal Women at the Courts of Europe from 1400–1800', in Mark Hengerer and Nadir Weber, eds, *Animals and Courts, c. 1200–1800* (Berlin, 2019), pp. 323–42

Machado, Maria de Fátima, *Fundo dos órfãos de Loulé: Séculos XV e XVI* (Loulé, 2016)

Malaguzzi Valeri, Francesco, *La corte di Lodovico il moro: La vita privata e l'arte a Milano nella seconda metà del Quattrocento* (Milan, 1913)

Mallett, Michael, *The Florentine Galleys in the Fifteenth Century* (Oxford, 1967)

Mandalis, Giorgio, 'Iconografia e iconologia della Madonna di Montenero', *Erba d'Arno*, 123 (2011), pp. 42–54

Mandosio, Jean-Marc, 'Ange Politien et les "autres mondes": L'attitude d'un humaniste florentin au XVᵉ siècle face aux explorations portugaises', *Médiévales*, 58.1 (2010), pp. 27–42

Marchisio, Cristina, 'Siguiendo la senda de los búcaros: Cosme III de Toscana en España y Portugal (1668–1669)', in *El viaje a Compostela de Cosme III de Médicis*, ed. José Manuel García Iglesias, Xosé A. Neira Cruz and Cristina Acidini Luchinat, exh. cat., Museo Diocesano, Santiago de Compostela (Santiago de Compostela, 2004), pp. 287–307

Markey, Lia, *Imagining the Americas in Medici Florence* (University Park, PA, 2016)

Marques, João Martins da Silva, ed., *Descobrimentos portugueses*, 3 vols (Lisbon, 1944–71)

Marques, Cátia Teles e, 'Cultura material e diplomacia eclesiástica: As relações e a troca de presentes entre o Bispo-conde de Coimbra D. Afonso de Castelo Branco e a Corte Papal (1590–1615)', *Revista de história da sociedade e da cultura* 14 (2014), pp. 183–207

Martelli, Vladimyr, 'Roma tollerante? Gli zingari a Roma tra XVI e XVII secolo', *Roma moderna e contemporanea*, 3 (1995), pp. 485–509

Martelli, Vladimyr, 'Tra tolleranza ed intransigenza: Vagabondi, zingari, prostitute e convertiti a Roma nel XVI–XVIII secolo', *Studi romani*, 50 (2002), pp. 250–78

Martin, Phyllis M., 'The Kingdom of Loango', in *Kongo: Power and Majesty*, ed. Alisa Lagamma, exh. cat., The Metropolitan Museum of Art, New York (New York, 2015), pp. 46–85

Martínez Ferrer, Luis, 'Álvaro II do Congo e Paulo V Borghese: Da África a Roma através do Negrita', in Luis Martínez Ferrer and Marco Nocca, eds, *'Cose dell'altro mondo': L'ambasceria di Antonio Emanuele, Principe di N'Funta, detto 'il Negrita' (1604–1608) nella Roma di Paolo V/'Coisas do outro mundo': A missão em Roma de António Manuel, Príncipe de N'Funta, conhecido por 'o Negrita'; (1604–1608), na Roma de Paulo V* (Rome, 2003), pp. 23–53

Martinho, Bruno A., 'Rhino Horns and Scraps of Unicorn: The Sense of Touch and the Consumption of Rhino Horns in Early Modern Iberia', *Luxury*, 8.1 (2021), pp. 77–103

Martins, Francisco Ernesto de Oliveira, 'Mobiliário açoriano: Do cedro ao jacarandá com cedro, séculos XV ao XVIII', in José Olivio Rocha and Mariana Mesquita, eds, *Angra, a Terceira e os Açores nas rotas da Índia e das Américas: A propósito dos 500 anos da passagem de Vasco da Gama por Angra em 1499* (Angra do Heroísmo, 1999), pp. 73–91

Marx, Barbara, 'Medici Gifts to the Court of Dresden', *Studies in the Decorative Arts*, 15.1 (2007–8), pp. 46–82

Mas Latrie, Louis de, *Traités de paix et de commerce et documents divers concernant les relations des chrétiens avec des Arabes de l'Afrique septentrionale au Moyen-Âge* (Paris, 1866–72)

Masseti, Marco, *La fattoria di Lorenzo il Magnifico: Gli animali domestici e selvatici delle Cascine di Poggio a Caiano (Prato)* (Florence, 2015)

Masseti, Marco, 'New World and Other Exotic Animals in the Menageries of Lorenzo il Magnifico and His Son, Pope Leo X, during the Italian Renaissance', in Arthur MacGregor, ed., *Naturalists in the Field: Collecting, Recording and Preserving the Natural World from the Fifteenth to the Twenty-First Century* (Leiden, 2018), pp. 40–75

Masseti, Marco, and Emiliano Bruner, 'The Primates of the Western Palaearctic: A Biographical, Historical and Archaeozoological Review', *Journal of Anthropological Sciences*, 87 (2009), pp. 33–91

Masseti, Marco, and Cecilia Veracini, 'Early European Knowledge and Trade of Neotropical Mammals: A Review of Literary Sources between 1492 and the First Two Decades of the Sixteenth Century', in Cleia Detry and Rita Dias, eds, *Proceedings of the First Zooarchaeology Conference in Portugal*, 2014, pp. 129–38

Massinelli, Anna Maria, and Filippo Tuena, *Il tesoro dei Medici* (Milan, 1992)

Massing, Andrea, 'Mapping the Malagueta Coast: A History of the Lower Guinea Coast, 1460–1510 through Portuguese Maps and Accounts', *History in Africa*, 36 (2009), pp. 331–65

Matchette, Ann, 'Credit and Credibility: Used Goods and Social Relations in Sixteenth-Century Florence', in Michelle O'Malley and Evelyn Welch, eds, *The Material Renaissance* (Manchester, 2007), pp. 225–41

Matchette, Ann, 'To Have and Have Not: The Disposal of Household Furnishings in Florence', *Renaissance Studies*, 20.5 (2006), pp. 702–15

Mazzi, Curzio, 'Le carte di Benedetto Dei nella Medicea Laurenziana', *Rivista delle biblioteche e degli archivi*, 25 (1914), pp. 137–56, 26 (1915), pp. 148–56, 27 (1916), pp. 133–44, 28 (1917), pp. 110–20, 29 (1918), pp. 128–50

McBurney, Henrietta, Paula Findlen, Caterina Napoleone, Ian Rolfe, Arthur MacGregor, Arturo Morales-Muñiz, Eufrasia Roselló-Izquierdo, Kathie Way and Onno Wijnands, *Birds, Other Animals and Natural Curiosities*, The Paper Museum of Cassiano dal Pozzo, Series B (Natural History) 4, 2 vols (London, 2017)

McLean, Paul D., *The Art of the Network: Strategic Interaction and Patronage in Renaissance Florence* (Durham, NC, 2007)

McLeod, Malcolm D., 'Verbal Elements in West African Art', *Quaderni Poro*, 1 (1976), pp. 85–102

Melis, Federigo, 'Di alcune figure di operatori economici fiorentini attivi nel Portogallo, nel XV secolo', in Hermann Kellenbenz, ed., *Fremde Kaufleute auf der iberischen Halbinsel* (Cologne, 1970), pp. 56–73

Melis, Federigo, 'Intensità e regolarità della diffusione economica generale nel Mediterraneo e in Occidente alla fine del Medioevo', in Federigo Melis, *I trasporti e le communicazioni nel*

Medioevo, ed. Luciana Frangiani (Florence, 1984), pp. 179–223; repr. from Wilhelm Abel et al., eds, *Mélanges en l'honneur de Fernand Braudel: Histoire économique du monde méditerranéen, 1450–1650*, 2 vols (Toulouse, 1972), 2, pp. 389–424

Mellinkoff, Ruth, *Outcasts: Signs of Otherness in Northern European Art of the Later Middle Ages*, 2 vols (Berkeley, CA, 1993)

Melo, Pedro Pascoal F. de, 'Um pouco conhecido mobiliário açoriano dos séculos XVI e XVII', *Açoriano oriental* (30 December 2012)

Mendes, António de Almeida, 'Child Slaves in the Early North Atlantic Trade in the Fifteenth and Sixteenth Centuries', in Gwyn Campbell, Suzanne Miers and Joseph C. Miller, eds, *Children in Slavery through the Ages* (Athens, OH, 2009), pp. 20–34

Meraviglie: Precious, Rare and Curious Objects from the Medici Treasure, ed. Marilena Mosco, exh. cat., Haags Historisch Museum, The Hague (Florence, 2003)

Metcalf, Alida C., 'Who Cares Who Made the Map? *La Carta del Cantino* and Its Anonymous Maker', *e-Perimetron*, 12.1 (2017), pp. 1–23

Migeod, F. W., 'Personal Names among Some West African Tribes', *Journal of the Royal African Society*, 17.65 (1917), pp. 38–45

Milani, V. I., *The Written Language of Christopher Columbus* (Buffalo, NY, 1973)

Milano, Ernesto, *La carta del Cantino e la rappresentazione della terra nei codici e nei libri a stampa della Biblioteca estense e universitaria* (Modena, 1991)

Miller, Elizabeth, *16th-Century Italian Ornament Prints in the Victoria and Albert Museum* (London, 1999)

Molà, Luca, *The Silk Industry of Renaissance Venice* (Baltimore, 2000)

Montemagno Ciseri, Lorenzo, '*Camelopardalis*: Storia naturale e straordinaria della giraffa di Lorenzo il Magnifico', *Interpres*, 31 (2012–13), pp. 351–72

Monti, Alessandro, and Silvia Barbantini, eds, *Il testamento di Paolo Giovio* (Oggiono, Lecco, 1999)

Morena, Francesco, 'Le collezioni di arte estremo-orientale dei granduchi medicei Cosimo I, Francesco I e Ferdinando I', in Francesco Morena, *Dalle Indie orientali alla corte di Toscana: Collezioni di arte cinese e giapponese a Palazzo Pitti* (Florence, 2005), pp. 25–49

Morena, Francesco, *Dalle Indie orientali alla corte di Toscana: Collezioni di arte cinese e giapponese a Palazzo Pitti* (Florence, 2005)

Moreno Ollero, Antonio, *Sanlúcar de Barrameda a fines de la Edad Media* (Cadiz, 1983)

Morris, P. A., *A History of Taxidermy: Art, Science and Bad Taste* (Ascot, 2010)

Mota, Avelino Teixeira da, 'A África no planisfério português anónimo de Cantino', *Revista da Universidade de Coimbra*, 26 (1978), pp. 1–12

Mota, Avelino Teixeira da, 'Gli avori africani nella documentazione portoghese dei secoli XV–XVII', *Africa*, 30.4 (1975), pp. 580–89

Müller, Karl Otto, *Welthandelsbräuche (1480–1540)* (Stuttgart, 1934)

Müntz, Eugène, *Les Collections d'antiques formées par les Médicis au XVIᵉ siècle* (Paris, 1895)

Murphy, Caroline, *Lavinia Fontana: A Painter and Her Patrons in Sixteenth-Century Bologna* (New Haven, CT, 2003)

Musacchio, Jacqueline Marie, 'Lambs, Coral, Teeth and the Intimate Intersection of Religion and Magic in Renaissance Tuscany', *Medieval and Renaissance Texts and Studies*, 296 (2005), pp. 139–56

Najemy, John, *Between Friends: Discourses of Power and Desire in the Machiavelli–Vettori Letters of 1513–1515* (Princeton, NJ, 1993)

Nello splendore mediceo: Papa Leone X e Firenze, ed. Nicoletta Baldini and Monica Bietti, exh. cat., Museo delle Cappelle Medicee e Casa Buonarroti, Florence (Livorno, 2013)

Nelson Novoa, James W., *Being the Nação in the Eternal City: New Christian Lives in Sixteenth-Century Rome* (Peterborough, Ontario, 2014)

Nelson Novoa, James W., 'Saperi e gusti di un banchiere portoghese a Roma nel Rinascimento: L'inventario di António da Fonseca', *Giornale di storia*, 10 (2012), pp. 1–19

Nelson Novoa, James, 'Unicorns and Bezoars in a Portuguese House in Rome: António da Fonseca's Portuguese Inventories', *Ágora: Estudos clássicos em debate*, 14.1 (2012), pp. 91–111

Niccoli, Bruna, 'Eleonora di Toledo, duchessa di Toscana, nella storia e nella leggenda', in Roberta Orsi Landini and Bruna Niccoli, *Moda a Firenze, 1540–1580: Lo stile di Eleonora di Toledo e la sua influenza* (Florence, 2005), pp. 14–21

Norton, Marcy, 'Going to the Birds: Animals as Things and Beings in Early Modernity', in Paula Findlen, ed., *Early Modern Things: Objects and their Histories, 1500–1800* (London, 2013), pp. 53–83

Norton, Marcy, *Sacred Gifts, Profane Pleasures: A History of Tobacco and Chocolate in the Atlantic World* (Ithaca, NY, 2008)

Onclin, Willy, 'L'Âge requis pour le mariage dans la doctrine canonique médiévale', in *Proceedings of the Second International Congress of Medieval Canon Law*, ed. Stephen Kuttner and J. Joseph Ryan (Città del Vaticano, 1965), pp. 237–47

O'Reilly, William, 'Non-knowledge and Decision Making: The Challenge for the Historian', in Conrad Zwierlein, ed., *The Dark Side of Knowledge: Histories of Ignorance, 1400–1800* (Leiden, 2016), pp. 397–419

Origo, Iris, 'The Domestic Enemy: The Eastern Slaves in Tuscany in the Fourteenth and Fifteenth Centuries', *Speculum*, 30 (1955), pp. 321–66

Orlandi, Angela, 'Al soffio degli Alisei: Mercanti fiorentini tra Siviglia e il Nuovo Mondo', *Archivio storico italiano*, 169 (2011), pp. 477–505

Orlandi, Angela, 'Tuscan Merchants in Andalusia: A Historiographical Debate', in Catia Brilli and Manuel Herrero Sánchez, eds, *Italian Merchants in the Early-Modern Spanish Monarchy: Business Relations, Identities and Political Resources* (London, 2017), pp. 13–32

Orsi Landini, Roberta, 'L'amore del lusso e la necessità della modestia: Eleonora fra sete e oro', in *Moda alla corte dei Medici: Gli abiti restaurati di Cosimo, Eleonora e don Garzia*, exh. cat., Galleria del costume di Palazzo Pitti, Florence (Florence, 1993), pp. 35–45

Orsi Landini, Roberta, 'Il guardaroba di Eleonora di Toledo', in Roberta Orsi Landini and Bruna Niccoli, *Moda a Firenze, 1540–1580: Lo stile di Eleonora di Toledo e la sua influenza* (Florence, 2005), pp. 200–235

Orsi Landini, Roberta, 'Sarti e ricamatori', in Roberta Orsi Landini and Bruna Niccoli, *Moda a Firenze, 1540–1580: Lo stile di Eleonora di Toledo e la sua influenza* (Florence, 2005), pp. 170–79

Orsi Landini, Roberta, 'I singoli capi di abbigliamento', in Roberta Orsi Landini and Bruna Niccoli, *Moda a Firenze, 1540–1580: Lo stile di Eleonora di Toledo e la sua influenza* (Florence, 2005), pp. 76–169

Orsi Landini, Roberta, 'Lo stile di Eleonora', in Roberta Orsi Landini and Bruna Niccoli, *Moda a Firenze, 1540–1580: Lo stile di Eleonora di Toledo e la sua influenza* (Florence, 2005), pp. 22–45

Ouerfelli, Mohamed, *Le Sucre: Production, commercialisation et usages dans la Méditerranée médiévale* (Leiden, 2008)

Paiva, José Pedro, 'A Diocese de Coimbra antes e depois do Concílio de Trento: D. Jorge de Almeida e D. Afonso Castelo Branco', in *Sé Velha de Coimbra: Culto e cultura* (Coimbra, 2005), pp. 225–53

Palos, Joan-Lluís, '"A Spanish barbarian and an enemy of her husband's homeland": The Duchess of Florence and Her Spanish Entourage', in Joan-Lluís Palos and Magdalena S. Sánchez, *Early Modern Dynastic Marriages and Cultural Transfer* (London, 2016), pp. 165–87

Papavero, Nelson, and Dante Martins Teixeira, *Zoonímia tupi nos escritos quinhentistas europeus* (São Paulo, 2014)

Parigini, Giuseppe Vittorio, *Il Tesoro del principe: Funzione pubblica e privata del patrimonio della famiglia Medici nel Cinquecento* (Florence, 1999)

Partner, Peter, *The Pope's Men: The Papal Civil Service in the Renaissance* (Oxford, 1990)

Pastoureau, Michel, *L'Étoffe du diable: Une histoire des rayures et des tissue rayés* (Paris, 1991)

Patrizi, Elisabetta, *Silvio Antoniano: Un umanista ed educatore nell'età del Rinnovamento cattolico (1540–1603)*, 3 vols (Macerata, 2010)

Pepperberg, Irene Maxine, *The Alex Studies: Cognitive and Communicative Abilities of Grey Parrots* (Cambridge, MA, 1999)

Peragallo, Prospero, *Cenni intorno alla colonia italiana in Portogallo nei secoli XIV, XV e XVI* (2nd edn, Genoa, 1907; orig. published in *Miscellanea di storia italiana*, 3rd ser., 9, [Turin, 1904], pp. 379–462)

Pérez de Tudela, Almudena, and Annemarie Jordan Gschwend, 'Exotica habsburgica: La casa de Austria y las colecciones exóticas en el Renacimiento temprano', in *Oriente en palacio: Tesoros asiáticos en las colecciones reales españolas*, ed. Marina Alfonso Mola and Carlos Martínez Shaw, exh. cat., Palacio Real de Madrid (Madrid, 2003), pp. 27–44

Pérez de Tudela, Almudena, and Annemarie Jordan Gschwend, 'Luxury Goods for Royal Collectors: Exotica, Princely Gifts and Rare Animals Exchanged between the Iberian Courts and Central Europe in the Renaissance (1560–1612)', in Helmut Trnek and Sabine Haag, eds, *Exotica: Portugals Entdeckungen im Spiegel fürstlicher Kunst- und Wunderkammern der Renaissance, = Jahrbuch des Kunsthistorischen Museums Wien 3*, ed. Helmut Trnek and Sabine Haag (Mainz, 2001), pp. 1–127

Pérez de Tudela, Almudena, and Annemarie Jordan Gschwend, 'Renaissance Menageries: Exotic Animals and Pets at the Habsburg Courts in Iberia and Central Europe', in Karl A. E. Enenkel and Paul J. Smith, eds, *Early Modern Zoology: The Construction of Animals in Science, Literature and the Visual Arts*, 2 vols (Leiden, 2007), 2, pp. 419–47

Pergam, Elizabeth A., 'Provenance as Pedigree: The Marketing of British Portraits in Gilded Age America', in Gail Feigenbaum and Inge Reist, eds, *Provenance: An Alternate History of Art* (Los Angeles, 2012), pp. 104–22

Perry, Matthew J., 'Condizioni di vita e di lavoro delle schiave nell'antica Roma', in *Spartaco: Schiavi e padroni a Roma*, ed. Claudio Parisi Presicce, Orietta Rossini and Lucia Spagnuolo, exh. cat., Museo dell'Ara Pacis, Rome (Rome, 2017), pp. 62–71

Petch, Alison, 'Chance and Certitude: Pitt Rivers and His First Collection', in *Journal of the History of Collections*, 18.2 (2006), pp. 257–66

Pettegree, Andrew, *The Invention of News: How the World Came to Know about Itself* (New Haven, CT, 2014)

Pianigiani, Ottorino, *Vocabolario etimologico della lingua italiana*, 2 vols (Rome, 1907)

Pieraccini, Gaetano, *La stirpe de' Medici di Cafaggiolo: Saggio di ricerche sulla trasmissione ereditaria dei caratteri biologici*, 3 vols in 4 tomes (Florence, 1924–25)

Pilliod, Elizabeth, 'Cosimo I de' Medici: Lineage, Family and Dynastic Ambitions', in *The Medici: Portraits and Politics, 1512–1570*, ed. Keith Christiansen and Carlo Falciani, exh. cat., The Metropolitan Museum, New York (New York, 2021), pp. 120–59

Pinto, Carla Alferes, 'The Diplomatic Agency of Art between Goa and Persia: Archbishop Friar Aleixo Meneses and Shah ʿAbbās I in the Early Seventeenth Century', in Zoltán Biedermann, Anne Gerritsen and Giorgio Riello, eds, *Global Gifts: The Material Culture of Diplomacy in Early Modern Eurasia* (Cambridge, 2018), pp. 150–70

Pinto, Carla Alferes, '"Traz à memória a excelência de suas obras e virtudes": D. Frei Aleixo de Meneses (1559–1617), mecenas e patrono', *Anais de história de além-mar*, 12 (2011), pp. 153–80

Plaisance, Michel, 'Une première affirmation de la politique culturelle de Côme Ier: La transformation de l'Académie des "Humidi" en Académie Florentine (1540–1542)', in André Rochon, ed., *Les Écrivains et le pouvoir en Italie à l'époque de la Renaissance* (Paris, 1973), ser. 1, pp. 361–438

Po, Guido, 'La collaborazione italo-portoghese alle grandi esplorazioni geografiche ed alla cartografia nautica', in Luigi Federzoni, ed., *Relazioni storiche fra l'Italia e il Portogallo: Memorie e documenti* (Rome, 1940), pp. 261–322

Pokorny, Erwin, 'The Gypsies and Their Impact on Ffteenth-Century Western European Iconography', in Jaynie Anderson, ed., *Crossing Cultures: Conflict, Migration and Convergence; The Proceedings of the 32nd International Congress in the History of Art* (Melbourne, 2009), pp. 597–601

Pon, Lisa, 'Raphael's *Acts of the Apostles* Tapestries for Leo X: Sight, Sound and Space in the Sistine Chapel', *The Art Bulletin*, 97.4 (2015), pp. 388–408

Presciutti, Diana Bullen, *Visual Cultures of Foundling Care in Renaissance Italy* (Farnham, 2015)

Pugliano, Valentina, 'Accountability, Autobiography and Belonging: The Working Journal of a Sixteenth-Century Diplomatic Physician between Venice and Damascus', in Annemarie Kinzelbach, J. Andrew Mendelsohn and Ruth Schilling, eds, *Civic Medicine: Physician, Polity and Pen in Early Modern Europe* (London, 2021), pp. 183–209

Qiu, Jane, 'Chasing Plagues', *Scientific American*, 322.6 (June 2020), pp. 20–26

Queller, Donald E., *Early Venetian Legislation on Ambassadors* (Geneva, 1966)

Radulet, Carmen M., 'Coleccionar e conservar, produzir e divulgar em Itália documentação sobre *Os descobrimentos portugueses* (sécs. xv–xvii)', in *As novidades do mundo: Conhecimento e representação na época moderna; Actas das VIII Jornadas de história ibero-americana e XI Reunião internacional de história da náutica e da hidrografica* (Lisbon, 2003), pp. 225–40

Radulet, Carmen M., 'La comunità italiana in Portogallo e il commercio orientale nella prima metà del Cinquecento', in Giovanna Motta, ed., *Mercanti e viaggiatori per le vie del mondo* (Milan, 2000), pp. 36–44

Radulet, Carmen M., *Os descobrimentos portugueses e a Itália: Ensaios fililógico-literários e historiográficos* (Lisbon, 1991)

Radulet, Carmen M., 'As viagens de descobrimento de Diogo Cão: Nova proposta de interpretação', *Mare Liberum* 1 (1990), pp. 175–204

Raphael, ed. David Ekserdjian and Tom Henry with Matthias Wivel, exh. cat., The National Gallery, London (London, 2022)

Rau, Virginia, 'Bartolomeo di Jacopo di Ser Vanni mercador-banqueiro florentino "estante" em Lisboa nos meados do século XV', *Do tempo e da história*, 4 (1971), pp. 97–116

Rau, Virginia, 'Um florentino ao serviço da expansão ultramarina portuguesa: Francisco Corbinelli', *Memórias do Centro de Estudos de Marinha*, 4 (1974)

Ravenhill, Philip, 'Of Pachyderms and Power: Ivory and the Elephant in the Art of Central Côte d'Ivoire', in *Elephant: The Animal and Its Ivory in African Culture*, ed. Doran H. Ross, exh. cat., The Fowler Museum of Cultural History, UCLA (Los Angeles, 1992), pp. 115–33

Ray, Meredith, *Writing Gender in Women's Letter Collections of the Italian Renaissance* (Toronto, 2009)

Raymond, Joad, and Noah Moxham, eds, *News Networks in Early Modern Europe* (Leiden, 2016)

Renazzi, Filippo Maria, *Notizie storiche degli antichi vicedomini del Patriarchio Lateranense e de' moderni prefetti del sagro palazzo apostolico ovvero maggiordomi pontefizi* (Rome, 1784), pp. 109–10

Repetti, Emanuele, *Dizionario geografico fisico storico della Toscana*, 6 vols (Florence, 1833–46)

Reynolds, Barbara, *The Cambridge Italian Dictionary* (Cambridge, 1962)

Richter, Paula Bradstreet, Mimi Leveque and Kathryn Myatt Carey, 'The Feather Fan in the Peabody Essex Museum', in Alessandra Russo, Gerhard Wolf and Diana Fane, eds, *Images Take Flight: Feather Art in Mexico and Europe, 1400–1700* (Florence, 2015), pp. 342–49

Riello, Giorgio, '"Things seen and unseen": The Material Culture of Early Modern Inventories and Their Representation of Domestic Interiors", in Paula Findlen, ed., *Early Modern Things: Objects and Their Histories, 1500–1800* (London, 2013), pp. 125–50

Riello, Giorgio, 'Things that Shape History: Material Culture and Historical Narratives', in Karen Harvey, ed., *History and Material Culture* (London, 2009), pp. 24–46

Rochon, André, *La Jeunesse de Laurent de Médicis (1449–1478)* (Paris, 1963)

Rocke, Michael, *Forbidden Friendships: Homosexuality and Male Culture in Renaissance Florence* (New York, 1996)

Rodocanachi, Emanuel, *La Femme italienne à l'époque de la Renaissance: Sa vie privée et mondaine, son influence sociale* (Paris, 1907)

Rodolfo, Alessandra, 'Gli affreschi del palazzo del commendatore nell'ospedale di S. Spirito in Sassia', *Storia dell'arte*, 77 (1993), pp. 56–76

Röell, Guus, and Dickie Zebregs, *Uit verre streken/From Distant Shores: Luxury Goods from Dutch Trading Ports in the West Indies, East Indies, China, Japan and Africa, 17th to 19th Centuries* (Maastricht, June 2017)

Ronca, Italo, '*Ex Africa semper aliquid novi*: The Ever-Surprising Vicissitudes of a Pre-Aristotelian proverb', *Latomus*, 53.3 (1994), pp. 570–93

Roover, Raymond de, *The Rise and Decline of the Medici Bank, 1397–1494* (Cambridge, MA, 1963)

Rosen, Mark, *The Mapping of Power in Renaissance Italy: Painted Cartographic Cycles in Social and Intellectual Context* (Cambridge, 2015)

Ross, Doran H., 'Imagining Elephants: An Overview', in *Elephant: The Animal and Its Ivory in African Culture*, ed. Doran H. Ross, exh. cat., The Fowler Museum of Cultural History, UCLA (Los Angeles, 1992), pp. 1–39

Ruotolo, Renato, 'Arredi e oggetti con la tartaruga nel Seicento', in *L'arte della tartaruga: Le opere dei musei napoletani e la donazione Sbriziolo-De Felice*, ed. Annalisa Bellerio, exh. cat., Museo Duca di Martina nella Villa Floridiana, Naples (Naples, 1995), pp. 11–21

Russell, P. E., 'Novos apontamentos sobre os problemas textuais do *Voiaige à la Guinée* de Eustáquio de la Fosse (1479–1480)', *Revista portuguesa de história*, 16 (1976), pp. 209–21

Russell, Peter, *Prince Henry 'the Navigator': A Life* (New Haven, CT, 2000)

Ryder, A.F.C., 'A Note on the Afro-Portuguese Ivories', *Journal of African History*, 5 (1964), pp. 363–65

Sá, Isabel dos Guimarães, *O regresso dos mortos: Os doadores da Misericórdia do Porto e a expansão oceânica (séculos XVI–XVII)* (Lisbon, 2018)

Sá, Isabel dos Guimarães, 'The Uses of Luxury: Some Examples from the Portuguese Courts from 1480 to 1580', *Análise Social*, 44.192 (2009), pp. 589–604

Saalman, Howard, *Filippo Brunelleschi: The Buildings* (University Park, PA, 1993)

Sandri, Lucia, 'Baliatico mercenario e abbandono dei bambini alle istituzioni assistenziali: un medesimo disagio sociale?', in Maria Giuseppina Muzzarelli, Paola Galletti and Bruno Andreolli, eds, *Donne e lavoro nell'Italia medioevale* (Turin, 1991), pp. 93–103

Sargent, Matthew, 'Recentering Centers of Calculation: Reconfiguring Knowledge Networks within Global Empires of Trade', in Paula Findlen, ed., *Empires of Knowledge: Scientific Networks in the Early Modern World* (London, 2018), pp. 297–316

Saunders, A. C. de C. M., *A Social History of Black Slaves and Freedmen in Portugal, 1441–1555* (Cambridge, 1982)

Scalini, Mario, 'Oggetti rari e curiosi nelle collezioni medicee: Esotica e naturalia', *Antichità viva*, 35.2–3 (1996), pp. 59–67

Schobesberger, Nikolaus, 'Mapping the *Fuggerzeitungen*: The Geographical Issues of an Information Network', in Joad Raymond and Noah Moxham, eds, *News Networks in Early Modern Europe* (Leiden, 2016), pp. 216–40

Schobesberger, Nikolaus, Paul Arblaster, Mario Infelise, André Belo, Noah Moxham, Carmen Espejo and Joad Raymond, 'European Postal Networks', in Joad Raymond and Noah Moxham, eds, *News Networks in Early Modern Europe* (Leiden, 2016), pp. 19–63

Schreir, Joshua, *The Merchants of Oran: A Jewish Port at the Dawn of Empire* (Stanford, CA, 2017)

Scorza, Rick, 'A "modello" by Stradanus for the "Sala di Penelope" in the Palazzo Vecchio', *The Burlington Magazine*, 126, no. 976 (July 1984), pp. 433–37

Segurado, Jorge, *Francisco d'Ollanda: Da sua vida e obras, arquitecto da Renascença aos serviço de D. João III, pintor, desenhador, escritor, humanista; Fac-simile da carta a Miguel Ângelo (1551) e dos seus tratados sobre Lisboa e desenho (1571)* (Lisbon, 1970)

Senatore, Francesco, 'Ai confini del "mundo de carta": Origine e diffusione della lettera cancelleresca italiana (XIII–XVI secolo)', *Reti medievali*, 10 (2009), pp. 239–91

Senos, Nuno, 'The Empire in the Duke's Palace: Global Material Culture in Sixteenth-Century Portugal', in Anne Gerritsen and Giorgio Riello, eds, *The Global Lives of Things: The Material Culture of Connections in the Early Modern World* (London, 2015), pp. 128–44

Sequeira, Joana, 'Michele da Colle: Um mercador pisano em Lisboa no século XV', in Nunziatella Alessandrini, Susana Bastos Mateus, Mariagrazia Russo and Gaetano Sabatini, eds, *Con gran mare e fortuna: Circulação de mercadorias, pessoas e ideias entre Portugal e Itália na Época Moderna* (Lisbon, 2015), pp. 21–34

Servolini, Luigi, 'L'arte nel santuario di Montenero', *Liburni civitas*, 7.1 (1934), pp. 30–53

Sestito, Francesco, *I nomi di battesimo a Firenze (1450–1900): Dai registri di Santa Maria del Fiore un contributo allo studio dell'antroponimia storica italiana*, = Quaderni italiani de RIOn 6 (Rome, 2013)

Shayt, David H., 'The Material Culture of Ivory outside Africa', in *Elephant: The Animal and Its Ivory in African Culture*, ed. Doran H. Ross, exh. cat., The Fowler Museum of Cultural History, UCLA (Los Angeles, 1992), pp. 366–81

Shearman, John, *Andrea Del Sarto*, 2 vols (Oxford, 1965)

Shearman, John, *The Vatican Stanze: Functions and Decoration* (= 'Italian Lecture', from *Proceedings of the British Academy*, 57 [1971], pp. 3–58) (London, 1972)

Shoshani, Jeheskel, 'The African Elephant and Its Environment', in *Elephant: The Animal and Its Ivory in African Culture*, ed. Doran H. Ross, exh. cat., The Fowler Museum of Cultural History, UCLA (Los Angeles, 1992), pp. 42–59

Sicca, Cinzia Maria, 'Da notaio a maestro da casa: La "confezione" degli inventari a Firenze durante il principato', in Cinzia Maria Sicca, ed., *Inventari e cataloghi: Collezionismo e stili di vita negli stati italiani di antico regime* (Pisa, 2014), pp. 15–34

Sigismondo da Venezia, *Bibliografia universale sacra e profana* (Venice, 1842)

Silleras-Fernández, Núria, '*Nigra sum sed formosa*: Black Slaves and Exotica in the Court of a Fourteenth-Century Aragonese Queen', *Medieval Encounters*, 13 (2007), pp. 546–65

Simões, Catarina Santana, 'The Symbolic Importance of the "Exotic" in the Portuguese Court in the late Middle Ages', *Anales de Historia del Arte*, 24 (2014), pp. 517–25

Smail, Daniel Lord, *Legal Plunder: Households and Debt Collection in Late Medieval Europe* (Cambridge, MA, 2016)

Smail, Daniel Lord, Mary C. Stiner and Timothy Earle, 'Goods', in Andrew Shryock and Daniel Lord Smail, eds, *Deep History: The Architecture of Past and Present* (Berkeley, CA, 2011), pp. 219–41

Soares, Mariza de Carvalho, '"Por conto e peso": O comércio de marfim no Congo e Loango, séculos XV–XVII', *Anais do Museu Paulista: História e cultura material*, 25.1 (2017), pp. 59–86

Sogliani, Daniela, 'Le meraviglie del mondo: Animali, fiori e altre curiosità esotiche nelle "banche dati Gonzaga"', in Andrea Canova and Daniela Sogliani eds, *I Gonzaga tra Oriente e Occidente: Viaggi, scoperte geografiche e meraviglie esotiche* (Mantua, 2022), pp. 97–112

Soyinka, Wole, *Beyond Aesthetics: Use, Abuse and Dissonance in African Art Traditions* (New Haven, CT, 2019)

Spallanzani, Marco, *Ceramiche alla corte dei Medici nel Cinquecento* (Modena, 1994)

Spallanzani, Marco, *Ceramiche orientali a Firenze nel Rinascimento* (Florence, 1978)

Sparnacci, Giuseppe, *Ordine et governo: La grande famiglia degli Innocenti nel 1556; Uno studio da scritti inediti di Vincenzo Borghini* (Florence, 2021)

Spartaco: Schiavi e padroni a Roma, ed. Claudio Parisi Presicce, Orietta Rossini and Lucia Spagnuolo, exh. cat. Museo dell'Ara Pacis, Rome (Rome, 2017)

Spini, Giorgio, ed., *La nascita della Toscana: Dal Convegno di studi per il IV centenario della morte di Cosimo I de' Medici* (Florence, 1980)

Stark, Marnie P. 'Mounted Bezoar Stones, Seychelles Nuts, and Rhinoceros Horns: Decorative Objects as Antidotes in Early Modern Europe', *Studies in the Decorative Arts*, Fall/Winter 2003–4, pp. 69–94

Steensgaard, Niels, 'The Return Cargoes of the Carreira da Índia in the Sixteenth and Early Seventeenth Century', in Teotónio R. de Souza, ed., *Indo-Portuguese History: Old Issues, New Questions* (New Delhi, 1985), pp. 13–31

Stevenson, Edward Luther, *Terrestrial and Celestial Globes: Their History and Construction, including a Consideration of Their Value as Aids in the Study of Geography and Astronomy*, 2 vols (repr., New York, 1971 [1921])

Stols, Eddy, 'Lisboa: Um portal do mundo para a naçao flamenga', in Eddy Stols, Jorge Fonseca and Stijn Manhaeghe, *Lisboa em 1514: O relato de Jan Taccoen van Zillebeke* (Lisbon, 2014), pp. 7–76

Subrahmanyam, Sanjay, 'Connected Histories: Notes toward a Reconfiguration of Early Modern Eurasia', *Modern Asian Studies* 31.3 (1997), pp. 735–62

Subrahmanyam, Sanjay, *Empires between Islam and Christianity, 1500–1800* (Albany, NY, 2019 [Delhi, 2018])

Subrahmanyam, Sanjay, *Explorations in Connected History: From the Tagus to the Ganges* (New Delhi, 2005)

Subrahmanyam, Sanjay, 'Holding the World in Balance: The Connected Histories of the Iberian Overseas Empires, 1500–1640', *The American Historical Review*, 112.5 (2007), pp. 1359–85

Taylor, Paul, 'Julius II and the Stanza della Segnatura', *Journal of the Warburg and Courtauld Institutes*, 72 (2009), pp. 103–41

Tazzara, Corey, *The Free Port of Livorno and the Transformation of the Mediterranean World* (Oxford, 2017)

Teixeira, Dante Martins, and Nelson Papavero, 'O tráfico de primatas brasileiros nos séculos XVI e XVII', in Leila Maria Pessôa, William Corrêa Tavares and Salvatore Siciliano, eds, *Mamíferos de restingas e manguezais do Brasil* (Rio de Janeiro, 2010), pp. 253–82

Thompson, Robert Farris, 'Body and Voice: Kongo Figurative Musical Instruments', in Marie-Thérèse Brincard, ed., *Sounding Forms: African Musical Instruments* (New York, 1989), pp. 39–45

Thornton, Dora, *The Scholar in his Study: Ownership and Experience in Renaissance Italy* (New Haven, CT, 1998)

Thornton, John, 'Central African Names and African-American Naming Patterns', *The William and Mary Quarterly*, 50.4 (1993), pp. 727–42

Thornton, John K., *A History of West Central Africa to 1850* (Cambridge, 2020)

Thornton, John K., 'Soyo and Kongo: The Undoing of the Country's Centralization', in Koen Bostoen and Inge Brinkman, eds, *The Kongo Kingdom: The Origins, Dynamics and Cosmopolitan Culture of an African Polity* (Cambridge, 2018), pp. 103–22

Tognetti, Sergio, *Il banco Cambini: Affari e mercati di una compagnia mercantile-bancaria nella Firenze del XV secolo* (Florence, 1999)

Tognetti, Sergio, 'The Trade in Black African Slaves in Fifteenth-Century Florence', in T. F. Earle and K.J.P. Lowe, eds, *Black Africans in Renaissance Europe* (Cambridge, 2005), pp. 213–24

Toorians, Lauran, 'The Earliest Inventory of Mexican Objects in Munich, 1572', *Journal of the History of Collections*, 6.1 (1994), pp. 59–67

Tosi, C. O., 'Andrea Pasquali', *Illustratore fiorentino*, n.s. 12 (1915), pp. 69–70

Trexler, Richard C., 'The Foundlings of Florence, 1395–1455', *History of Childhood Quarterly*, 1 (1973) (repr. in Richard C. Trexler, *Power and Dependence in Renaissance Florence*, vol. 1 (of 3): *The Children of Renaissance Florence*, [Binghamton, NY, 1993], pp. 7–34), pp. 259–84

Trexler, Richard C., 'Infanticide in Florence: New Sources and First Results', *History of Childhood Quarterly*, 1 (1974), pp. 98–116

Trexler, Richard C., *Public Life in Renaissance Florence* (New York, 1980)

Trigueiros, António Miguel, 'A modernidade numismática em Francisco de Holanda: Uma ciência esquecida, um ensinamento a preservar', in *Congresso internacional Francisco de Holanda, c. 1518–1584: Arte e teoria no Renascimento europeu/Art and Theory in Renaissance Europe, 22–24 Novembro/November 2018* (Lisbon, 2018), pp. 1–19

Trimble, Jennifer, 'The Zoninus Collar and the Archaeology of Roman Slavery', *American Journal of Archaeology*, 120.3 (2016), pp. 447–72

Tuohy, Thomas, *Herculean Ferrara: Ercole d'Este, 1471–1505, and the Invention of a Ducal Capital* (Cambridge, 1996)

Vaccari, Maria Grazia, *La guardaroba medicea dell'Archivio di stato di Firenze: Inventoria* (Florence, 1997)

Van Deusen, Nancy E., *Global Indios: The Indigenous Struggle for Justice in Sixteenth-Century Spain* (Durham, NC, 2015)

Van Stekelenburg, A. V., '*Ex Africa semper aliquid novi*: A Proverb's Pedigree', *Akroterion*, 33.4 (1988), pp. 114–20

Varela, Consuelo, 'Introducción', in Cristóbal Colón, *Textos y documentos completos*, ed. Consuelo Varela (Madrid, 1984)

Varnhagen, Francisco Adolpho de, *Historia geral do Brazil*, 2 vols (Rio de Janeiro, 1854 and 1857)

Venturelli, Paola, 'Splendore e ornamento: Oggetti e materiali preziosi tra Carlo e Federico Borromeo', in *Carlo e Federico: La luce dei Borromeo nella Milano spagnola*, ed. Paolo Biscottini, exh. cat., Museo diocesano, Milan (Milan, 2005), pp. 122–33

Verde, Armando F., 'Libri tra le pareti domestiche: Una necessaria appendice a *Lo studio fiorentino, 1473–1503*', in *Tradizione medievale e innovazione umanistica a Firenze nei secoli XV–XVI*, =*Memorie domenicane*, n.s., 18 (1987), pp. 1–225

Verde, Armando F., *Lo studio fiorentino, 1473–1503: Ricerche e documenti*, 5 vols in 8 tomes (Pistoia, 1973–94)

Verga, Ettore, 'Per la storia degli schiavi orientali in Milano', *Archivio storico lombardo*, ser. 4, 32 (1905), pp. 188–99

Verlinden, Charles, *L'Esclavage dans l'Europe médiévale*, 2 vols (Bruges, 1955; Ghent, 1977)

Vieyra, Anthony, *A Dictionary of the Portuguese and English Languages in Two Parts, Portuguese and English, and English and Portuguese*, 2 vols. (London, 1773)

Visceglia, Maria Antonietta, 'La Biblioteca tra Urbano VII (15–27 settembre 1590) e Urbano VIII (1623–1644): Cardinali, bibliotecari, custodi, *scriptores*', in *La Vaticana nel Seicento (1590–1700): Una biblioteca di biblioteche* (Vatican City, 2014), pp. 77–121

Visceglia, Maria Antonietta, *Roma papale e Spagna: Diplomatici, nobili e religiosi tra due corti* (Rome, 2010)

Viterbo, Francisco Marqués de Sousa, *Trabalhos náuticos dos portugueses nos séculos XVI e XVII* (Lisbon, 1898)

Vogt, John L., 'The Lisbon Slave House and African Trade, 1486–1521', *Proceedings of the American Philosophical Society*, 117.1 (1973), pp. 1–16

Warren, Jeremy, review of Almudena Pérez de Tudela Gabaldón, *Los inventarios de Doña Juana de Austria, Princesa de Portugal (1535–1573)* (Jaen, 2017), *Journal of the History of Collections*, 31.1 (2019), p. 201

Waterfield, Hermione, and J.C.H. King, *Provenance: Twelve Collectors of Ethnographic Art in England, 1760–1990* (London, 2009)

Werner, Michael, and Bénédicte Zimmermann, 'Beyond Comparison: *Histoire croisée* and the Challenge of Reflexivity', *History and Theory*, 45.1 (2006), pp. 30–50

Werz, Bruno, 'Saved from the Sea: The Shipwreck of the *Bom Jesus* (1533) and Its Material Culture', in Annemarie Jordan Gschwend and K.J.P. Lowe, eds, *The Global City: On the Streets of Renaissance Lisbon* (London, 2015), pp. 88–93

Wolk-Simon, Linda, 'Politics, Portraiture and the Medici Popes, 1513–34', in *The Medici: Portraits and Politics, 1512–1570*, ed. Keith Christiansen and Carlo Falciani, exh. cat., The Metropolitan Museum, New York (New York, 2021), pp. 104–19

Women: The Art of Power; Three Women from the House of Habsburg, ed. Sabine Haag, Dagmar Eichberger and Annemarie Jordan Gschwend, exh. cat., Schloss Ambras, Innsbruck (Vienna, 2018)

Wysocki Gunsch, Kathryn, *The Benin Plaques: A Sixteenth-century Imperial Monument* (Abingdon, 2018)

Zaccarello, Michelangelo, 'Primi appunti tipologici sui nomi-parlanti', *Lingua e stile*, 38.1 (2003), pp. 59–84

Zafarana, Zelina, 'Per la storia religiosa di Firenze nel Quattrocento: Una raccolta privata di prediche', *Studi medievali*, ser. 3, 9.2 (1968), pp. 1017–113

Zaugg, Roberto, 'The King's Chinese Spittoon: Global Commodities, Court Culture and Vodun in the Kingdoms of Hueda and Dahomey (Seventeenth to Nineteenth Centuries)', *Annales HSS* (English edition), 73.1 (2018), pp. 115–53

Zucchi, Valentina, 'The Medici *Guardaroba* in the Florentine Ducal Residences, c. 1550–1650', in Susan Bracken, Andrea M. Gáldy and Adriana Turpin, eds, *Collecting and the Princely Apartment* (Newcastle upon Tyne, 2011), pp. 1–21

Doctoral Theses/Dissertations

Barker, Hannah, 'Egyptian and Italian Merchants in the Black Sea Slave Trade, 1260–1500', Ph.D dissertation, Columbia University, 2014

Cappa, Desirée, 'Pierfrancesco Riccio: The Rise of a Bureaucrat in the Service of the Medici Family (1525–44)', Ph.D thesis, Warburg Institute, University of London, 2022

Greenfield, Ingrid, 'A Moveable Continent: Collecting Africa in Renaissance Italy', Ph.D dissertation, University of Chicago, 2016

Jordan, Annemarie, 'The Development of Catherine of Austria's Collection in the Queen's Household: Its Character and Cost', Ph.D dissertation, Brown University, 1994

Martinho, Bruno A., 'Beyond Exotica: The Consumption of Non-European Things through the Case of Juan de Borja (1569–1626)', Ph.D thesis, European University Institute, 2018

Online Sources

https://battesimi.sns.it/battesimi/

http://bia.medici.org/DocSources/

https://catalogo.museogalileo.it/multimedia/OrologioPianetiLorenzoVolpaiaBis.html

https://www.dizionariobiograficodeifriulani.it/tritonio-ruggero/

https://www.iucnredlist.org/species/11506/192327291

https://museilombardia.cultura.gov.it/news/un-tesoro-nascosto-i-graduali-della-certosa-di
-pavia/

http://pwr-portugal.ics.ul.pt/

https://www.uffizi.it/en/online-exhibitions/on-being-present-2#2

Baumgartner, Walter, 'The Aztec Feather Shield in Vienna: Problems of Conservation', *Nuevo
mundo/Mundos nuevos*, 'Colloques, 2006, Feather Creations. Materials, Production and
Circulation. New York Hispanic Society, Institute of Fine Arts, 17–19/06/2004', no. 1,
https://doi.org.10.400/nuevomundo/1447

Beck, James, 'Cosimo's Four Slaves', http://images.pcmac.org/SiSFiles/Schools/GA
/GwinnettCounty/CentralGwinnett/Uploads/DocumentsCategories/Documents
/The%20Four%20Slaves%20of%20Cosimo%20de%20Medici.pdf

'I blasoni delle famiglie toscane nella raccolta Ceramelli Papiani', https://www.archiviodistato
.firenze.it/asfi/strumenti/i-blasoni-delle-famiglie-toscane-nella-raccolta-ceramelli-papiani

Cabral, João Paulo S., 'O extraordinário coco das Maldivas (Seychelles): Lendas, mitos e reali-
dades de história natural nos séculos XVI–XVIII/The Extraordinary Maldives' (Seychelles)
Coconut: Legends, Myths and Realities of Natural History in the Sixteenth to Eighteenth
Centuries', in *História das ciências para o ensino: Atas de Colóquio II*, ed. Celeste Gomes, Ana
Rola and Isabel Abrantes (ebook, 2014), pp. 5–29, https://dokumen.tips/documents
/historia-das-ciencias-para-o-ensino-atas-do-coloquio-ii.html?page=5

*De antiquitatibus Lusitaniae libri quattuor a L. Andrea Resende inchoati, a Iacobo Mendez de Vas-
concellos absoluti* [...] (Rome, 1597), available at https://archive.org/details/bub_gb
_e84Ztoyggi8C/page/n5/mode/2up?view=theater

Freddolini, Francesco, 'The Grand Dukes and Their Inventories: Administering Possessions and
Defining Value at the Medici Court', *Journal of Art Historiography*, 11 (2014), available at
https://arthistoriography.files.wordpress.com/2014/11/freddolini.pdf

Freddolini, Francesco, and Anne Helmreich, 'Inventories, Catalogues and Art Historiography:
Explaining Lists against the Grain', *Journal of Art Historiography*, 11 (2014), available at
https://arthistoriography.files.wordpress.com/2014/11/freddolini_helmreich
_introduction.pdf

Goldthwaite, Richard, and Marco Spallanzani, 'Censimento di libri contabili private dei fiorentini, 1200–1600', https://www.academia.edu/40196500/CENSIMENTO_di_libri
_contabili_privati_fiorentini_fino_al_1600

Hallett, Jessica, Maria de Jesus Monge and Nuno Senos, eds, *De todas as partes do mundo: O
património do 5° Duque de Bragança, D. Teodósio I/All his Worldly Possessions: The Estate of
the 5th Duke of Braganza, Teodósio*, vol. 2: *Documentos/Documents* (Lisbon, 2018), online
edition, pp. 89–90 of printed text, https://research.unl.pt/ws/portalfiles/portal/12688088
/TEODOSIO_VOL_II.pdf

Hirst, K. Kris, 'Provenience vs. Provenance: What is the Difference?', ThoughtCo, updated 19
November 2019, https://www.thoughtco.com/provenience-vs-provenance-3971058

Jordan Gschwend, Annemarie, 'Rainha d'aquém e d'além-mar: Jantar e cear à mesa de D. Catarina de Áustria na corte de Lisboa/Queen of the Seas and Overseas: Dining at Catherine of
Austria's Table at the Lisbon Court', in Hugo Crespo, ed., *Á mesa do príncipe: Jantar e cear*

na corte de Lisboa (1500–1700);: prata, madrepérola, cristal de rocha e porcelana/At the Prince's Table: Dining at the Lisbon Court (1500–1700); Silver, Mother-of-pearl, Rock Crystal and Porcelain (2018), pp. 10–48, available at https://www.academia.edu/36297434/Hugo_Miguel_Crespo _ed_%C3%80_Mesa_do_Pr%C3%ADncipe_Jantar_e_Cear_na_Corte_de_Lisboa_1500 _1700_At_the_Princes_Table_Dining_at_the_Lisbon_Court_1500_1700_Lisboa_AR _PAB_2018_pdf

Kaplan, Paul, and Kate Lowe, 'Bartolomeo Passerotti: *Homer's Riddle*', in *On Being Present*, vol. 2: https://www.uffizi.it/en/online-exhibitions/on-being-present-2#2

Loth, Calder, 'The Complex Greek Meander', The Institute of Classical Architecture and Art (ICAA) website, 'Classical Comments', 4 December 2016, https://www.classicist.org /articles/classical-comments-the-complex-greek-meander/

García Marsilla, Juan Vicente, 'La vida de las cosas: El mercado de objetos de segunda mano en la Valencia medieval', unpublished paper, University of Valencia

Moreira, Rafael, 'Pedro e Jorge Reinel (at. 1504–60): Dois cartógrafos negros na côrte de D. Manuel de Portugal (1495–1521)', *Terra Brasilis*, 4 (2015), https://doi.org/10.4000/terrabrasilis .1209

Palladio, Andrea *I quattro libri dell'architettura di Andrea Palladio [. . .]* (Venice, 1570), available at https://openlibrary.org/works/OL3299016W/Quattro_libri_dell%27architettura

Pereira, Franklin, 'Artes do couro no medioevo peninsular, parte 4: As "sillas de cadernas" de Granada', *Al-Madan Online*, 23.2 (July 2020), available at https://issuu.com/almadan/docs /ao23-2/2?ff&showOtherPublicationsAsSuggestions=true&experiment=last-page, pp. 92–106

Petrucci, Francesco, 'Il gioco del "Trucco" nel Palazzo Chigi di Ariccia: Una rarità da Wunderkammer nella dimora barocca', *Il giornale dell'arte*, 5 June 2020, online edition, https:// www.ilgiornaledellarte.com/articoli/il-gioco-del-trucco-nel-palazzo-chigi-di-ariccia /133407.html

Rodrigues, Aryon D. 'On the Influence of Indigenous Languages on Brazilian Portuguese', *DELTA: Documentação de estudos en lingüística teórica e aplicada*, 30 (2014), http://www.scielo .br/scielo.php?script=sci_arttext&pid=S0102-44502014000300443&lng=en&tlng=en

'Rutter: Making the Earth Global', https://rutter-project.org/

Urbani, Bernardo, 'The Seven Secluded Monkeys of Conrad Gessner', *Endeavour*, 44.1–2 (2020), https://www.sciencedirect.com/science/article/abs/pii/S0160932720300375?via%3 Dihub

NAME INDEX

Page numbers in *italics* refer to figures

Enslaved People

Page numbers in *italics* refer to figures.

A NOTE ON THE TYPE

This book has been composed in Arno, an Old-style serif typeface in the classic Venetian tradition, designed by Robert Slimbach at Adobe.